THE SCOTS GUARDS
1919–1955

**HER MAJESTY
QUEEN ELIZABETH II**
Colonel-in-Chief
SCOTS GUARDS

From a photograph taken outside Buckingham Palace on the 5th June 1952 after the first Birthday Parade of her reign. In her hat the Queen is wearing the silver star presented to her by the members of the Third Guards Club. Her horse, Winston, is carrying the state saddlery of the Regiment

THE SCOTS GUARDS
1919-1955

Compiled by
DAVID ERSKINE

PUBLISHED BY
THE NAVAL AND MILITARY PRESS

This History
is dedicated,
by Gracious Permission,
to
Her Majesty
QUEEN ELIZABETH II
Colonel-in-Chief
Scots Guards.

Foreword

As Colonel of Her Majesty's Scots Guards I am glad to introduce this volume which carries our Regimental history on from 1919 to the present time. These were eventful years but naturally the account of the part played by the Regiment in the Second World War occupies much of the book.

All Scots Guardsmen, reading this account, will feel renewed pride in the achievements described here. It is clear that the great traditions of the Regiment were, and still are, in safe keeping.

In particular, everyone will be struck by the success with which the Scots Guards adapted themselves to modern warfare: battalions and individuals distinguished themselves in almost every known role in addition to traditional infantry.

On behalf of the Third Guards I should like to express my thanks to the author, Captain the Hon. D. H. Erskine, for the excellent work he has done in producing this most readable history.

YORK HOUSE,
   ST. JAMES'S PALACE.

28th June, 1956

Henry
Colonel.

Contents

DEDICATION	v
FOREWORD BY FIELD MARSHAL H.R.H. THE DUKE OF GLOUCESTER, K.G., P.C., K.T., K.P. etc., COLONEL OF THE REGIMENT	vii
LIST OF ILLUSTRATIONS	xiii
LIST OF MAPS	xv
PREFACE	xvii

PART I

BETWEEN THE WARS: 1919–1939	3

* * *

The Second World War: 1939–1945

PART II

SCANDINAVIA: 1940	19
I. *The Fifth Battalion*	21
II. *Norway—The First Battalion*	26
(a) Narvik	
(b) Expedition to Mö	
(c) Retreat to Bodö	
(d) Evacuation	

PART III

THE REGIMENT AT HOME: 1939–1945	53
I. *The First Battalion*	53
II. *Regimental Headquarters*	56
III. *The Training Battalion*	60
IV. *The Holding Battalion*	65

PART IV

AFRICA: 1939–1943	73
I. *The Second Battalion*	75
(a) Eighteen Months' Wait	
(b) Summer in the Desert	
(c) *Crusader*	
(d) Retreat to the Gazala Line	

CONTENTS

   (e) Rigel Ridge
   (f) The Alamein Position
   (g) "Maidan Serenade"
   (h) Syria and the Great Trek
   (i) Revenge at Medenine
   (j) Through the Mareth Line
  II. *The First Battalion* 131
   (a) Journey to North Africa
   (b) The Medjez Salient
   (c) The Final Offensive
        (i) Preparation
        (ii) The Break-in
        (iii) The Bou
 III. *The Second Battalion* 152
       The End at Hammamet
  IV. *Celebration and Preparation* 155

PART V

ITALY: 1943–1947 165

   I. *The Second Battalion* 167
   (a) Salerno
   (b) Across the Volturno
   (c) Camino—"First time up"
   (d) Camino—"Second time up"
   (e) Across the Garigliano
  II. *The First Battalion—Anzio* 196
   (a) Preparing for a Landing
   (b) A Quiet Landing
   (c) The Advance
   (d) The Night Attack
   (e) Defence
   (f) Carroceto Station
   (g) In Reserve
 III. *Prelude to the Summer Advance* 227
   (a) Re-organisation
   (b) Castel di Sangro
   (c) Cassino
  IV. *The Advance to the Arno* 234
   (a) The Road to Rome
   (b) The Road to Florence
        (i) Over the Hills to Florence: 1st Battalion
        (ii) Up the Tiber and down the Arno: S Company

CONTENTS

V. *The Apennines* 262
   (a) The Autumn Advance
   (b) The Winter Months

VI. *To the Po and Victory* 296
   (a) A Final Reorganisation
   (b) The Spit
   (c) The Argenta Gap
   (d) The Chase to the Po

VII. *Tito and Trieste* 316

PART VI

NORTH-WEST EUROPE: 1944–1946 323

I. *The Years of Preparation* 324
   (a) The Third Battalion
   (b) The Fourth Battalion

II. *Normandy* 337
   (a) *Goodwood*
   (b) The Churchills cross to France
   (c) The Battle of Caumont
   (d) Infantry in the Bocage
   (e) The Tanks at Estry
   (f) The Tanks at Chênedollé
   (g) Sourdevalle
   (h) Refit and Refresh

III. *The Low Countries* 367
   (a) Brussels Liberated
   (b) Hechtel
   (c) The Attempt to Reach Arnhem
   (d) The Churchills Come Up
   (e) Tilburg
   (f) Through the Peel to the Maas
   (g) The Pause and Alarms of the Winter
   (h) The Second Battalion Re-enters the Field

IV. *Into Germany:* Veritable 399
   (a) Through the Siegfried Line
   (b) The Advance South-eastwards
   (c) Winnekendonk Stormed
   (d) Holding the Ring
   (e) Bonninghardt
   (f) X Company Disbanded

V. *From the Rhine to the Baltic* 421
   (a) The Bridgehead
   (b) To Münster

(c) The Celtic Group across the Rhine
(d) The Churchills Fight from Celle to Uelzen
(e) To the Baltic
(f) The Second Battalion's Fierce finale

VI. *The Occupation* 460

* * * *

PART VII

POST WAR: 1945–1954 469
        Including Malaya 1948–1951

APPENDICES

Appendix A	Roll of Honour	503
	Including Statistics of Casualties	526
Appendix B	Honours and Awards	528
Appendix C	Officers and Warrant Officers who held the principal appointments	538
Appendix D	Orders of Battle	542
Appendix E	Officers' Services	559
Appendix F	The Dress of the Regiment, by Major J. Swinton	589
INDEX		599

List of Illustrations

Frontispiece Her Majesty QUEEN ELIZABETH II

1.	H.R.H. The Duke of York, 24th Colonel	*facing*	64
2.	Norway: the snows		65
3.	Norway: the retreat		65
4.	Desert ruffians		80
5.	The White Sands of Mersa Matruh		80
6.	Desert Order Group		81
7.	Anti-tank guns arrive		81
8.	Medenine: the battle		144
9.	Medenine: the booty		144
10.	The Bou from the plain		145
11.	From the top of the Bou		145
12.	Parade in Salerno Stadium		160
13.	G Company in San Clemente		160
14.	Monte Camino: the terraces		161
15.	Monte Camino		161
16.	Rocchetta e Croce		208
17.	Minturno		208
18.	Embarking for Anzio: Left Flank		209
19.	Embarking for Anzio: the *Derbyshire*		209
20.	The Battlefield of Carroceto		224
21.	Castel di Sangro		225
22.	Patrol in the sun		225
23.	Monte Sole		320
24.	Comacchio floods		320
25.	Normandy: tanks at Chênedollé		321
26.	Normandy: briefing before battle		321
27.	Third Battalion weapons: an assortment		336
28.	Third Battalion weapons: Honey Tank		336
29.	Third Battalion weapons: Scout Car		336

LIST OF ILLUSTRATIONS

30.	With the 15th Scottish Division: on the road to Tilburg	337
31.	With the 15th Scottish Division: attacking the Siegfried Line	337
32.	With the American parachutists: Munster	448
33.	Through the woods to Uelzen	448
34.	On the way to Cuxhaven	449
35.	Landing on Heligoland	449
36.	H.R.H. The Duke of Gloucester, 25th Colonel	464
37.	The Second Battalion at Potsdam	464
38.	General Eisenhower with the Third Battalion	465
39.	General Alexander inspects a Guard of Honour	465
40.	Malaya: mortars in action	480
41.	Malaya: Left Flank's tiger	480
42.	Holyroodhouse, 28th June 1951	481
43.	Captain The Lord Lyell, V.C.	496
44.	Orders of Dress, 1956	497

List of Maps

I	Scandinavia	20
II	Narvik	30
III	The Dalsklubben Position	36
IV	Dalsklubben to Bodö	*facing* 48
V	The Scots Guards in the Mediterranean, *inset*, the Nile Delta	*facing* 73
VI	The Egyptian Frontier	*facing* 84
VII	*Crusader* and the Retreat to the Gazala Line	*facing* 96
VIII	The Gazala Position	*facing* 106
IX	Rigel Ridge	
X	The Alamein Position	110
XI	Southern Tunisia	*facing* 128
XII	The Battle of Medenine	
XIII	Medjez-el-Bab and The Bou	*facing* 150
XIV	Northern Tunisia	*facing* 160
XV	The Battipaglia Area	168
XVI	The Advance to Rocchetta	176
XVII	Monte Camino	180
XVIII	The Minturno Sector	190
XIX	The Anzio Beach-head	200
XX	The Carroceto Sector	*facing* 224
XXI	Southern Italy	*facing* 234
XXII	Monte Piccolo	236
XXIII	Monte San Michele	250
XXIV	The Advance through Central Italy	*facing* 262
XXV	The Battle of Monte Catarelto	270
XXVI	The Monte Sole Sector	278
XXVII	Monte Penzola	292
XXVIII	North from Florence	*facing* 294
XXIX	The Fossa Marina	304

LIST OF MAPS

XXXA	The Comacchio Flank	*facing* 320
XXX	From Normandy to the Rhine	*facing* 337
XXXI	Caumont	344
XXXII	Estry	354
XXXIII	Chênedollé	360
XXXIV	Normandy	*facing* 368
XXXV	Beeringen and Hechtel	370
XXXVI	Tilburg	380
XXXVII	Meijel to the Maas	386
XXXVIII	The Maastricht Appendix	392
XXXIX	Winnekendonk	408
XL	Crossing the Romer	418
XLI	*Veritable* and the Rhine Crossing	*facing* 424
XLII	Celle to Uelzen	440
XLIII	Visselhövede	450
XLIV	From the Rhine to the Baltic, *inset* Münster	*facing* 462
XLV	Malaya	474

Preface

THIS book is designed to be a continuation of, and complementary to, the previous historical works on the Scots Guards. It carries on the story of the Regiment from the close of *The Scots Guards in the Great War: 1914–1918*, and the Appendices are designed to bring up to date those contained in Sir Frederick Maurice's *The Scots Guards: 1642–1914*. The first and last parts of the present volume deal respectively with the periods of peace after 1918 and after 1945, but it is the account of the Regiment's activities in the Second World War of 1939–1945 which occupies the bulk of the book.

At the outset a word must be said about the authorship of this volume. Originally Captain Michael Trappes-Lomax undertook the task, but after completing the history of the Second Battalion and part of that of the First Battalion he was unable to continue owing to the demands of his other work at the College of Heralds. Major John Swinton then took up the pen and completed the stories of the First, Third, Fourth, Fifth and Holding Battalions and of the two independent Companies; this he did despite the fact that for part of the time he was in Australia on the staff of the Governor-General. Early in 1954 I was given the task of completing it.

The main rearrangement I have made has been to tell the story of the Regiment chronologically by campaigns, instead of adopting the scheme of the two previous authors, which was to tell it by Battalions. I feel that the final arrangement enables the reader to see more clearly the Regiment's part in the grand strategy of a world-wide conflict, and also does something to draw together into one Regimental tradition the very diverse activities and characteristics of its component battalions. This rearrangement has involved a liberal, and sometimes drastic, use of scissors and paste, with much compression and amendment besides. Compression has, perhaps, been the main task, for in its original state the text covering the war years was about one third as long again as the version here printed. In many instances passages from the work of Captain Trappes-Lomax and Major Swinton have been adopted in their entirety, but I wish to emphasise that responsibility for accuracy, style and content is mine, and mine alone. More especially is this the case where I have had the temerity to allow expressions of opinion to creep in. I am most grateful to my two predecessors for the extensive researches they carried out, the benefits of which have accrued to me.

The stage on which the drama of the war was played out was enormous. It is remarkable that, whereas in the Kaiser's War neither of the Battalions was at any time more than two hundred and fifty miles from Wellington Barracks, in Hitler's War they penetrated beyond the Arctic Circle, fought in the North African deserts, marched the length of Italy and advanced from the Channel to the Baltic. Not only did the Regiment continue in its traditional role of infantry but it adapted itself to the mysteries of mechanised and armoured warfare, and even made an attempt at a ski battalion. New weapons, new equipment, new climates and new tactics were all successfully mastered.

This is, consequently, a long book, especially since in these days of the typewriter and printing press it is not any lack of material, but rather an *embarras de richesse*, which hinders the historian. The framework is, of course, constructed from the various official War Diaries which were written up daily throughout the war by either the Adjutant or Intelligence Officer of each Battalion. These are at best dry stuff, and to enliven the story recourse has been made to many excellent official and unofficial narratives, diaries, letters and reminiscences, both from within the Regiment and from without. The bibliography of the late war is already enormous, and no attempt has been made to mention all the relevant printed books. An exception should, however, be made in the case of the histories of the other four Regiments of the Brigade of Guards, and another exception should be made in the case of Mr. Patrick Forbes's *6th Guards Tank Brigade*. The study of the past copies of *The Household Brigade Magazine* will be found very rewarding to those seeking detailed accounts of the Regiment's activities, particularly in peace-time. For war-time activities I have found particularly useful the narrative accounts compiled by battalions and brigades immediately after the various phases of the campaigns. Outstanding among these are Major D. Traill's account of Anzio, Captain A. R. A. Hobson's account of the advance to Florence and Captain H. W. Llewellyn Smith's account of the Third Battalion's battles. The post-war production *Operations of the 24th Guards Brigade: August 1944–May 1945*, containing as it does a lavish supply of specially printed coloured maps, might well serve as a model for this type of work. In addition to the printed and typed word, many individuals have been consulted, both orally and by post.

But however many documents are read, however many indexes are searched, and however many memories are jogged, it is impossible, even in a book as long as this, to mention all the incidents worthy of note and all the deserving persons. It is natural and proper to wish to see one's name and exploits recorded in print, but, in that desire, I fear that the majority of today's readers will have to be disappointed. It should be remembered that on every day in every battalion there are something like eight or nine hundred separate experiences, in which each individual sees a different facet of the battle. Therefore when, as is inevitable, anyone finds that his most exciting, most triumphant, most frightening or most boring moment has been described in, to him, inappropriate terms, or, more likely, that it has not been described at all, I would ask him to take his disappointment philosophically. While final responsibility for any omission or inaccuracy rests with me, I would say in my defence that, as far as is now possible, every part of the narrative has been read by some person who was present at the actions described.

I am conscious that one large and important group of soldiers has been somewhat neglected in these pages. It is rarely possible to describe a battle in greater detail than a bare outline of the doings of the rifle companies and tank squadrons. In consequence there is little about the part played by the men of the Headquarter and Support Companies and by the men of the echelons. The services of these men were vital to the victories and well-being of their comrades farther forward, and it is intended as no denigration of their work that they are so rarely mentioned. Moreover, many of the older soldiers and "characters" of a battalion were to be found among their ranks. Often, when the rifle companies were being subjected to a steady drain of casualties, it was these men who gave continuity to the life of the battalion and who were the sure guardians of its traditions.

Some may think that I have devoted overmuch space to the two independent companies, S and·X. I make no apology on this score. In telling their stories I have tried to illustrate what went on *inside* a company in battle; in this context I would draw particular attention to the long account of X Company's fight at Hechtel in September 1944. None will deny that S and X Companies were units of the highest quality and that both were admirable advertisements to the army at large of the military virtues of the Scots Guards. Their histories, I think, reassert the inestimable value of the British Regimental system and, in particular, emphasise the value of the principle that men should always be commanded by officers of their own regiment. The Brigade of Guards was indeed fortunate to be able to observe this rule throughout the war, an advantage denied to the Regiments of the Line.

The photographs have been selected to illustrate what Scots Guardsmen looked like, the equipment they used and the country they fought in.

On behalf of the Regiment I wish humbly to thank Her Majesty Queen Elizabeth The Queen Mother for her gracious kindness in providing the photograph of the late King as Colonel of the Regiment.

Others to whom thanks are due are Lady Lyell for providing the photograph of the late Lord Lyell, V.C., and Mrs. M. N. Romer for the use of photographs belonging to the late Lieutenant-Colonel G. A. D. Taylor (Nos. 2, 3, 8 and 12). Officers of the Regiment who have lent photographs from their collections are Major R. A. Abercromby (14, 15, 16, 17 and 20); Major M. D. D. Crichton-Stuart (4 and 5); Captain D. L. Bankes (25, 26 and 38); Major J. Swinton (40); and Captain J. H. B. Acland (41). Save for Nos. 10, 11, 42 and 44, the remainder have been provided by the Imperial War Museum and are Crown Copyright.

The maps have been drawn by Mr. Frank Thompson and Mr. William Conroy of the Polish section of the Royal Engineers Survey Production Centre, Park Royal. They deserve the reader's thanks for their patience and skill in the face of many orders and counter-orders, as does Major I. E. Sleep, R.E., who has been most helpful in providing material and information.

In the main the compilation and accuracy of the Appendices has been the responsibility of Regimental Headquarters, and much hard work has been done on them by the Orderly Room and Records Office staffs. I have made myself responsible for the statistical table of casualties in Appendix A; for the arrangement of the Honours and Awards in Appendix B; and, in Appendix D, for the compilation of the Orders of Battle. The Nominal Roll of Officers, Appendix E, has been prepared by Regimental Headquarters on the same principles as the corresponding Roll in Volume II of *The Scots Guards: 1642–1914*. It is much regretted that reasons of space have precluded the use of a far more detailed Roll, to the compilation of which Major V. F. Erskine Crum devoted much time and trouble.

Gratefully I acknowledge the relief afforded me by Major Swinton, who wrote Appendix F describing the changes in dress since 1914. The fact that at least twenty-one different forms of head-dress can be identified in the illustrations gives some idea of the complexity of his task.

I would like to put on record my gratitude to all those members of the Regiment, both past and present, who, at considerable inconvenience to themselves, have answered my enquiries and corrected my misapprehensions, particularly to the five senior officers who read the proofs and advised me on their general content. They were Major-General Sir John Marriott, Brigadiers H. L. Graham and C. I. H. Dunbar, Colonel H. N. Clowes and Lieutenant-Colonel T. F. R. Bulkeley. Again I wish to emphasise that the ultimate responsibility for the text is not theirs, but mine.

Finally I feel it would not be invidious if I were to single out the holders of two appointments for special praise. During the whole course of writing the Regimental Adjutants and Superintending Clerks at Birdcage Walk have given uncomplaining assistance. The book would never have appeared without their help.

PART I

Between the Wars: 1919–1939

IN March 1919 both battalions of the Scots Guards, the First under the command of Lieutenant-Colonel Sir Victor Mackenzie, Bt., D.S.O., M.C., and the Second under Lieutenant-Colonel J. A. Stirling, D.S.O., M.C., returned to London from Cologne. They had both been abroad over four and a half years, and in those years the bloodiest battles in the Regiment's history had been fought—and won. With their comrades of the Guards Division they took part in that formation's special victory march through the capital,[1] and also in the general Victory Marches in London, Paris, Edinburgh and Glasgow.

The men who marched in the ranks of the Regiment's contingents were no longer called Privates, for on the 22nd November 1918 King George V had ordered that they were to bear the title of Guardsmen "as a mark of His Majesty's appreciation and pride of the splendid services rendered by the Brigade of Guards during the war". The grant of this honour was contained in a letter from the King's Private Secretary to the Major General Commanding the Brigade of Guards, and at the time the Director of Personal Services at the War Office advised that there was no need for any further official confirmatory action. But, several years later, the Judge-Advocate's Department threw doubt on the propriety of using the title in legal proceedings. The lawyers were placated by Army Order 222 of 1923.

Demobilisation was soon in full spate. Recruiting in the immediate post-war days was slow, in the inevitable reaction against all things military. The battalions dwindled away from their peace establishment of 714 all ranks, and the height standard for recruits was lowered to five feet seven inches. So weak were battalions that frequently they were forced to borrow men from each other to enable them to carry out important duties.

By 1920 the pattern of peace-time routine had appeared. The Brigade of Guards was expected to have two of its ten regular battalions available for service overseas. The stations to which these

---

[1] Bella and Bertha, the two Flanders cows acquired by the Second Battalion in 1914, had their place in this march. Later they were retired to the meadows at Blythswood, near Glasgow, where they ended their days. They are commemorated by two models in silver which now adorn the Officers' Mess of the Battalion.

battalions were sent were not usually "East of Suez", though, as will be seen, exceptions did occur. The eight battalions at home were divided between Aldershot, where the embryo Expeditionary Force was stationed, Windsor, and the barracks in London; the most unpopular station was Warley in Essex.

At home a battalion carried out individual training during the winter months, and musketry at Pirbright during the spring. In April and May the refining fire of "Spring Drills" preceded the high season for ceremonial in London and at Windsor. After playing Romans and Early Britons, Redcoats and Fuzzy-Wuzzies, or Crusaders and Saracens, or executing impeccable displays of arms-drill for the benefit of the taxpayer (and Service Charities) at the Aldershot Tattoo, the battalions went on manœuvres in August and September. In October the general post of Change of Quarters ended the military year before leave and the revels of Hogmanay heralded the New.

In July 1920 both battalions found a Guard of Honour for the State visit of Their Majesties King George V and Queen Mary to Edinburgh. On this occasion for the first time since 1914 bearskin caps and scarlet tunics appeared. They were seen in London for the first time at the Opening of Parliament in February 1921, on which occasion the King's Guard was found by the First Battalion. In April the Castle Guard at Windsor found by the Second Battalion appeared in the same order; and in October 1922 the same battalion, then stationed in the Hyde Park Cavalry Barracks, mounted its first King's Guard in home service clothing since before the war. At the same time troops stationed in the West End were ordered to "walk out" during the weekends in tunic and forage cap; for Church Parade bearskins were to be worn. It should be noted that few men "walked out" in plain clothes during this period, permission to do so being a highly valued privilege awarded only to Non-Commissioned Officers and Guardsmen of good character, and one which was automatically withdrawn after any breach of good conduct.

The return of a more colourful uniform was no doubt largely responsible for the improvement in recruiting from the autumn of 1921 onwards. In January 1922 no less than eighty-seven volunteers joined K Company at the Depot. The height standard was raised by two stages to five feet ten inches, though the somewhat invidiously described "*bona-fide* Scotsman" was allowed to be one inch shorter. In 1923 recruiting figures went from strength to strength, and the raising of the height standard to six foot in 1925 had the effect of reducing the monthly intake from fifty-five to three; in consequence squads composed of recruits for all the regiments of the Brigade had to be formed at the Depot. Thereafter the height standard fluctuated as the need for replacements varied. Throughout the inter-war period the Regiment rarely lacked recruits; it was usually in the enviable position of being able to pick and choose from those who presented themselves. The attractions of good comradeship, sport and education which the Army of this date offered, were powerful draws; three years with the Colours and a "very good" character on discharge to the Reserve was the surest way to qualifying for any Police Force in the United Kingdom; by 1939 it was estimated that some five hundred Reservists were serving in the Police.

Another, and far less pleasing, cause of the improved enlistment figures was undoubtedly the growing number of the unemployed and the resulting industrial strife. In April 1921 during the Coal Strike the First Battalion was moved in motor transport, an unusual event in itself, in the middle of the night after only two hours' notice to the Supply Reserve Depot at Deptford. So serious a view was taken of the situation that Reservists were re-called to bring both battalions to full strength; but after a tense fortnight, during which the First Battalion remained at Deptford and the Second Battalion at Windsor as a mobile reserve, the strikers went back to work and the Reservists were allowed to go home—this time by march route. Again, in the spring of 1926, when both battalions were at Pirbright firing their annual courses, the General Strike was called. The First Battalion went once again to the Supply Depot at Deptford; the Second went first to the H.A.C. Headquarters at Armoury House and the London Rifle Brigade Headquarters in Bunhill Row, later moving to the Tower, with outlying detachments throughout the East End. This unpleasant task lasted a fortnight until the Strike was broken, and the battalions returned to Pirbright. In 1931 the First Battalion stood by for fear of trouble from the "Hunger Marchers" who were converging on London, but fortunately there was none.

From 1907 Field Marshal Lord Methuen had been Colonel of the Regiment; he took the keenest interest in the Regiment's welfare and activities, and it was with the greatest regret that all Scots Guardsmen, retired and serving, heard of his death on 30th October 1932. A very short while before his death he wrote a farewell message to the Regiment which read "Scots Guards Comrades Goodbye Methuen Colonel", the original of which was later presented to the Regiment by Lady Methuen and a facsimile copy given to every officer and man serving in the Regiment at the time. He was borne to his grave by Warrant Officers of the Regiment and by Warders of the Tower of London, of which he was Constable.

Lord Methuen was succeeded, as 24th Colonel, by Major-General His Royal Highness the Duke of York, who followed Lord Methuen's example in the interest and trouble he took to see to all the Regiment's affairs. When, in 1936, on the abdication of his brother King Edward VIII, the Duke of York ascended the Throne as King George VI, he appointed as 25th Colonel his younger brother, Major-General His

Royal Highness the Duke of Gloucester, who retains the appointment to this day. Annually the Colonel inspected both battalions and also K Company at the Depot. As is customary, all three Sovereigns who reigned during the period honoured the Regiment by assuming the Colonelcy-in-Chief.

The names of those who held the other important appointments in the Regiment will be found in Appendix C.

On the 23rd November 1932, the Regiment suffered another severe loss when Major-General A. B. E. Cator, C.B., D.S.O., at that time Major-General Commanding the Brigade of Guards and General Officer Commanding the London District, died after a heart attack in the hunting field. He had commanded the Regiment from 1920 to 1923.

Other distressing deaths which took place among serving officers were those of Major Sir Frederick Fitz-Wygram, Bt., M.C., who died in the 'flu epidemic of 1920; Second-Lieutenant H. F. D. Coghill of the Second Battalion, killed in a motor-car accident in 1927; Major C. H. Seymour, M.C., of the First Battalion, formerly Regimental Adjutant and Commandant of the Guards Depot, who was killed in a riding accident in 1931; and Lieutenant the Hon. T. S. Fermor-Hesketh, Adjutant of the Second Battalion, and Second-Lieutenant B. A. Ludford-Astley, of the same battalion, both of whom were killed when an aircraft piloted by the former crashed in France in June 1937.

The organisation of the Regiment was unchanged during the period. In 1924 Regimental Headquarters moved from what is now the site of the Officers' Mess at Wellington Barracks to the first floor of the former Grenadier Reservists Stores at the east end of the square. In the same year the Lieutenant-Colonel Commanding the Regiment (then Colonel G. C. B. Paynter, C.M.G., D.S.O.) resumed the additional command of one of the London Territorial Brigades; this system continued until 1939, four of the Lieutenant-Colonels Commanding in the Brigade of Guards having Territorial Brigades, while the fifth was nominated to command the 4th Guards Brigade of the 2nd Division on mobilisation.

The Standing Orders of the Regiment had not been revised since 1882, and it was during the term of command of Colonel F. G. Alston, C.M.G., D.S.O., that a new edition was published in 1931. Since Colonel Alston was familiarly known to his friends and brother officers as "Cook" it was not surprising that this volume soon became known throughout the Regiment as the "cookery book", a light-hearted title which in no way detracted from its authority.

Regular Officers were recruited both through Sandhurst and from the Universities. In 1924 the Supplementary Reserve was formed, and, after a slow start, this source provided a valuable fund of trained junior officers. Candidates were required to do training with one of the battalions on appointment, and thereafter annually for a short period.

If the Regiment underwent no drastic change in organisation, the battalions did. In 1919 they each had four rifle companies, each of four platoons, each with four sections. There was a large Battalion Headquarters, and the transport was horsed. In 1921 Headquarter Wing was formed: this included the signals, transport, administrative sections and the medical personnel. There was also a Medium Machine Gun Platoon.

In 1925 "The Wing" again changed its organisation. It was divided into four groups: (i) Signallers, and the Regimental Sergeant-Major and his minions; (ii) the Medium Machine Guns, four in all; (iii) the Quartermaster and the transport; and (iv) the Drums, trained as stretcher bearers.

In 1928 a radical change was made. In the Wing an anti-tank platoon of four weapons replaced the machine-guns; the rifle companies were reduced to three, the fourth being turned into a machine-gun company, with twelve guns on the peace establishment and sixteen in war. In the First Battalion there was now B(MG) Company and in the Second F(MG) Company.

In 1938 machine-guns disappeared from the Infantry Battalion's establishment, and B and F Companies reverted once again to an infantry role. The rifle companies were now organised into three platoons of three sections, and the two-inch mortar and Boys' Anti-tank Rifle began to appear; the reliable Bren displaced the rather cumbersome Lewis as the light automatic weapon. Additional boys aged fifteen were allowed to be recruited to provide for the host of specialists an Infantry Battalion now required, and Mr. Hore-Belisha's reforms (which promoted by time instead of by vacancy) gave higher rank to ten officers overnight.

The new rank of Warrant Officer, Class III was introduced; this was the Platoon Sergeant-Major (PSM), who was junior to the Company Sergeant-Major, but senior to the Company Quartermaster Sergeant. There were to be two in each rifle company, commanding platoons, and six in Headquarter Company commanding specialist platoons. It was an emergency measure due to the lack of junior officers, and was abandoned after the early campaigns of 1940. For the time being the establishment of Officers was reduced by four to twenty-four. The establishment of the battalion was raised by sixty-three Other Ranks. Finally, to suit the new tactical organisation, the new drill was introduced: the Thin Red Line became three deep.

* * *

The battalions went abroad four times during the Peace.

China

1927

On the 2nd April 1927 the Second Battalion, commanded by Lieutenant-Colonel Sir Victor Mackenzie, was warned for service in China; it was to be part of the 1st Infantry Brigade commanded by Colonel B. N. Sergison-Brooke. The chronic state of civil war which is China's lot had recently endangered the foreign concessions at Hang-Kow and Shanghai; a considerable force of British troops, including the 2nd Battalion Coldstream Guards, had already been despatched, but more were needed. The Battalion was at once made up to the Colonial establishment of twenty-eight Officers and 860 Other Ranks at the expense of the First Battalion; the latter was left with little more than two companies, and, until the Second's return, was much below strength, as the War Office would not permit the recruiting of more than sixty men above the combined peace establishments of the two battalions.

The Second Battalion embarked at Southampton in the *City of Marseilles* on the 11th April, being seen off by a large contingent of the First Battalion and a host of relatives and friends. After an uneventful passage, with calls at Port Said, Colombo and Singapore, the Battalion disembarked at Kowloon, the mainland port of Hong Kong, on the 17th May.

The Battalion's first billet was the great pile of the Peninsular Hotel which dominates the Kowloon water-front and commands a magnificent view across the harbour to Hong Kong Island beyond. They shared this smart accommodation with the Welch Regiment until late September, when they moved to the more popular hutted camp at Sham-shui-Po, three miles away on the other side of the Kowloon peninsula. Their first duty had been a familiar one, though in an unfamiliar climate and surrounding; in intense heat, wearing khaki drill and sun helmets, they took part in the King's Birthday Parade on the Happy Valley Race Course on Hong Kong Island.

Liaison with the Royal Navy, and especially with the cruiser *Delhi*, was a prominent feature of their life, until, in November, they moved inland into the heart of the New Territories to Lo-Wu, a camp site below the frontier hills not far from the small town of Fanling. Here they pitched a tented camp, and training was the order of the day. Those who experienced this camp tell lurid stories of typhoons and floods, pythons and cobras, hornets and wasps, and even of a wolf; the twenty-five mile march back to Sham-shui-Po in November brought a welcome change of station. Before they left Lo-Wu the Battalion constructed on the hillside above the camp a large white Scots Guards star which, surrounded by the words "Second Battalion Scots Guards", to this day is evidence to confound the scoffer who asserts that "the Guards never go East of Suez".

Shortly after Christmas a detachment of F Company under Captain C. A. A. Robertson was sent by sea to take over the guard duties at Shameen, the British concession at Canton, some eighty miles up the pirate-infested Pearl River. In the New Year the Battalion was further split by the departure of Right Flank to take over the Government House and Headquarters guards from the King's Own Scottish Borderers on Hong Kong Island. After a month the Shameen detachment was relieved by another from G Company under Captain H. L. Graham, M.C., and it was during their spell of duty that a *rapprochement* was made between Canton and Hong Kong. They found themselves in close liaison with Chinese troops for the first time in the Regiment's history, mounting a Guard of Honour at the official meeting of the British Minister, Sir Miles Lampson, and the Chinese Governor, Marshal Lai-Chai-Sum. In March they rejoined the Battalion.

1928

In May Sir Victor Mackenzie completed his tenure of command of the Second Battalion and sailed for home via America in the liner *Empress of Russia*. The whole Battalion went to Kowloon Docks to see him off; he was accompanied as far as Shanghai by a picquet of the Battalion, the first of many such parties which sailed up and down the China coast as an anti-piracy precaution in the months to come.

Lieutenant-Colonel E. T. C. Warner, D.S.O., M.C., succeeded to the command. Under him an ambitious combined operation was carried out with Naval Air Support, and Left Flank was landed from seven destroyers on the difficult coast of the New Territories.

At the end of June, after thirteen months in Hong Kong, the Battalion received orders to move to Shanghai, an extremely small cargo boat, the *Yuang Sang*, being hurriedly converted for the purpose; the voyage took four days. At Shanghai the greater part of the Battalion was billeted in the New World Building in the centre of the city, with one company at Tongshan on the outskirts. Here they remained six months, which were militarily uneventful. Many good friends were made, particularly among the Scottish Company of the Shanghai Volunteer Corps, the 4th Regiment of the United States Marines, and among the local St. Andrew's Society; the Battalion engaged in every kind of sport and competition, and were successful in many.

On the 21st January 1929 the Battalion embarked once again in the *City of Marseilles*, this time for home, having on the previous day carried out a march through Shanghai in pouring rain during which they had been accorded two Guards of Honour, one Russian and the other Scottish, both found from the troops of the Shanghai Volunteer Corps. They arrived at Southampton in bitter weather on the 28th February, went by train to Warley, and soon moved to Chelsea. Here on the 28th May both battalions were inspected by Field Marshal Lord Methuen, who was accompanied by his predecessor, Field

1929

Marshal H.R.H. the Duke of Connaught, then Colonel of the Grenadier Guards; in his experience, said the Colonel, he had never seen a finer turn-out.

That summer a weird apparition was sighted in home waters. The Press reported "Ascot Sunday Thrill" and "Fearsome Monster on the Thames"; it was the Second Battalion's Dragon Boat which they had brought home with them. It was launched at the Guards Boat Club at Maidenhead with appropriate Chinese explosions and later progressed as far upstream as Boulter's Lock. According to one account, "Weird Chinese oaths escaped the fifteen paddlers while a diminutive individual heavily and hotly disguised in Chinese costume [Captain Robertson] kept on beating a gong." The Chinese oaths were at their fiercest when a firework exploded in the boat.

Egypt

The second tour of foreign service was that of the First Battalion in Egypt from November 1935 to December 1936.

The occasion of their being sent to Egypt was the crisis provoked by Italy's designs on Abyssinia; on the 1st November the Battalion, commanded by Lieutenant-Colonel A. H. C. Swinton, M.C., sailed in the transport *Somersetshire* with full mobilisation equipment, and without the families; they disembarked at Alexandria on the 13th. They were stationed under canvas at Sidi Bishr Camp, nine miles to the east of the town, where they were placed under command of Brigadier J. H. T. Priestman, commanding 13th Infantry Brigade. During December Left Flank and one Platoon of B (Machine Gun) Company under Major H. L. Graham, M.C., moved up to Mersa Matruh by road to reinforce the garrison of this small port on the Western Desert coast some hundred and forty miles back from the Libyan frontier. In January 1936 the Battalion moved up from the Delta to join them. The journey had been made by sea in a filthy little vessel, the *Zafaran*, which had just disembarked a cargo of goats, but had failed to land their fleas. Colonel Swinton refused to allow the Battalion to embark until the ship had been disinfected.

Two months were spent in the Western Desert under canvas in Montrose Camp; most of this time was occupied in digging defensive positions in blinding duststorms which filled in the trenches as soon as they had been dug. By the end of March the tense situation had abated; the Battalion was withdrawn to Cairo where they took over Kasr-el-Nil Barracks from the 3rd Battalion Grenadier Guards.

An unforeseen problem now arose. Before embarking for Egypt the Battalion had been converted from horsed to motor transport, the first battalion in the Brigade of Guards to be so transformed; but since no officers or men were trained to the necessary trades a composite Motor Transport Section made up of motor-trained Non-Commissioned

Officers and Guardsmen from all Regiments of the Foot Guards, under command of Lieutenant H. M. Sainthill, Coldstream Guards, had been formed for the beginning of the Battalion's Egyptian tour, until sufficient Scots Guards drivers could be trained and sent out. On arrival at Alexandria no vehicles were forthcoming and so the Battalion had hired a taxi which was their sole transport for several weeks. Eventually vehicles were provided, and these went with the Battalion to Mersa Matruh; but by the time they came to leave for Cairo, they were all completely worn out and had to be left behind. Thus the Battalion arrived at Kasr-el-Nil without vehicles, and their consternation at finding the entire horsed transport of the 3rd Grenadiers drawn up, waiting to be taken over, can well be imagined. Motor transport was not seen again until the Battalion returned to England.

In Cairo ceremonial once again predominated. The funeral of King Fuad and the arrival of King Farouk were followed by the new King's first visit to the British High Commissioner, Sir Miles Lampson; on this occasion the Battalion mounted a Guard of Honour. In June they trooped their Regimental Colour at Gezira to mark King Edward's birthday. Otherwise their sojourn in Cairo was uneventful, until the Battalion embarked in the *Laurentic* at Port Said and disembarked at Southampton on the 7th December 1936.

Palestine

In the absence of the First, the Second Battalion had also made a brief visit to the East. On 20th September 1936 under the command of Lieutenant-Colonel W. P. A. Bradshaw, D.S.O., they sailed from Southampton in the motor-vessel *Vandyck*, disembarking at Haifa on the 30th. In Palestine the Arab revolt had been raging, but almost immediately after the Battalion's arrival affairs improved, and the worst was over. They went up by train (*quarante hommes ou huit chevaux*) to Jerusalem, where they were quartered in Balaclava Camp. Apart from their march through Jerusalem, which inspired Pipe-Major J. B. Robertson to write the well-known tune, their stay was taken up with a few pacification patrols, some guard duties in sangars on the hills, and a great deal of sight-seeing. On her next round voyage to the Mediterranean the *Laurentic* brought home the Battalion and the 3rd Coldstream, and they landed at Southampton on the 29th December. All ranks received the General Service medal with the clasp "PALESTINE".

Egypt

On the 19th November 1938 the Second Battalion, commanded by Lieutenant-Colonel J. C. O. Marriott, C.V.O., D.S.O., M.C., embarked again, this time over seven hundred strong, in the transport *Dorsetshire* for what was planned to be a routine tour of two years in Egypt.

They landed at Alexandria on the 3rd December, where G Company was left as garrison, and went on to the familiar Kasr-el-Nil Barracks, where they relieved the 1st Battalion Irish Guards. In January, with G Company, they went to Helwan Camp for training, and then on in February to Mersa Matruh where they found the sands as white and the dust as irritating as the First Battalion had said. In April they returned to Kasr-el-Nil, where in August the routine nature of their tour was ended by the threat of war with Germany; they did not arrive home until April 1944, after the adventures to be described later in this book. A brief period of alarm had sent the advance party hurrying to Palestine, but it was recalled, and all eyes were from then on directed westward.

*   *   *

There remains but to chronicle several diverse matters which complete the story of the Regiment between the Great Wars.

Both battalions had their full share of ceremonial. It would be tedious to give a list of all the important events in which they took part, but special note should be made of a few.

In October 1926 eight hundred ex-Scots Guardsmen paraded on the Horse Guards Parade with large detachments from each battalion and from the rest of the Brigade of Guards for the unveiling of the Guards Divisional Memorial by the Duke of Connaught, during which the massed Pipes of the Regiment played the "Flowers of the Forest", and a miniature division clad in battle order marched past.

In the following year a Colour Party from the First Battalion attended the opening of the Scottish National War Memorial in Edinburgh Castle.

Royal occasions of special note were the funerals of Queen Alexandra in 1925, for which both battalions were on parade; the lying-in-state and funeral of King George V in 1936, when sixteen officers took part in the vigil in Westminster Hall, and a detachment of the Second Battalion and their Pipers marched in the procession at Windsor; and, finally, the Coronation of King George VI and Queen Elizabeth in 1937, for which both battalions were on parade. The detachment which marched in the procession on this occasion boasted an average height of six feet and four inches.

Standards of drill from one age to another are a frequent source of vehement argument; few would disagree that in the 'thirties the standard of the Regiment's drill was of the highest. For confirmation we can rely on the remark made by General Weygand in 1933 at the unveiling of Marshal Foch's statue opposite Victoria Station. A Guard of Honour was mounted by the Second Battalion, and at the conclusion of the ceremony, the General was heard to remark to his aide-de-camp: "It is only in England that military ceremonial is carried out to perfection."

The final big parade in which the Regiment took part before the war broke out was in Paris. To emphasise the solidity of the Entente a detachment of all regiments of the Brigade, including ninety of the First Battalion, under the command of Colonel W. P. A. Bradshaw, D.S.O., then commanding the Regiment, marched down the Champs Elysées in the Bastille Day Parade on the 14th July 1939. Their reception was thunderous; it was said the band could not be heard for the cheers, and a Paris paper wrote "La France uset tout son cœur dans cette acclamation."

The Colours of the two battalions, which had been presented to them in 1905 and 1912, were replaced in July 1921 when King George V presented new sets on the Horse Guards Parade to all eight battalions of the three senior regiments of the Foot Guards; the company badges borne on the Regimental Colours were those of the 21st and 22nd Companies. These Colours when presented did not carry the Great War Battle Honours; these, thirty in number, were awarded in 1924. On the 25th March of that year both battalions paraded at Chelsea Barracks to receive the Colours from Lord Methuen; the ten Honours which were allowed to be borne on the Colours had been newly embroidered on them.

The Second Battalion received new Colours from King Edward VIII on 16th July 1936; the parade, in which six battalions of the Foot Guards took part, was held in Hyde Park. It was on this occasion, while he was riding back to Buckingham Palace down Constitution Hill, that a disgruntled Irishman called McMahon threw a pistol at His Majesty, fortunately causing him no harm. The old set of colours was laid up in the Chapel of the Guards Depot.

The First Battalion received a new set of colours from King George VI in the gardens of Buckingham Palace on the 23rd June 1937; it was the first set His Majesty had presented since his accession. The old set was laid up in the Chapel of Chelsea Barracks.

The sets presented in 1936 and 1937 were those in use at the outbreak of war in 1939, when those of the First Battalion went into safekeeping at Buckingham Palace, and those of the Second went into a bank in Cairo. The Regimental Colours displayed the badges of No. 23 and No. 24 Companies.

The Depot Company (K) remained at Caterham throughout this period, save for an excursion to Warley and Canterbury from November 1927 to September 1929, due to the persistent outbreaks of diphtheria in Caterham Barracks.

The Regimental Band continued to provide its high standard of music. In 1922, and again in 1933, it visited Canada; in 1939 it went to Holland, and was to visit South Africa in 1940 had war not broken out. In 1930 the pitch of all instruments was ordered by the War Office to be changed from high to low, and this entailed considerable expense.

Changes in dress have been dealt with in a separate Appendix. One important event should however be recorded here. In February 1926 King George V ordered the introduction of the feather bonnet in place of the Glengarry cap as the full-dress headdress of the pipers. The hackles were to be of the Royal Colours of red and blue. In March the pipers of the First Battalion made their first appearance in the new bonnets at the State Banquet at Buckingham Palace given in honour of the King and Queen of Afghanistan. They were not taken into wear by the Second Battalion until it returned from China in 1929.

Another event worthy of note in the story of the Pipers was that on 18th April 1923 the Bank Picquet was accompanied by one of their number for the first time; this practice has continued ever since.

Finally, in 1938 the officers of the Regiment provided fifteen new pipe banners for each Battalion; these were first carried in November of that year at the State Banquet given at Buckingham Palace for King Carol of Rumania.

Two historical works on the Regiment were published, long-awaited, as is their wont. In 1925 Major-General Sir Cecil Lowther completed the story of the Regiment in the Great War; two previous authors, Mr. F. Loraine Petre and Mr. Wilfred Ewart had died during the course of writing the work, the latter having had the misfortune to be shot at a New Year Party in Mexico City.

In 1934 Major-General Sir Frederick Maurice completed the History of the Regiment from its raising in 1642 until the outbreak of the Great War; this work had previously been entrusted to General Sir V. Aylmer Haldane, who had, however, been unable to complete it. In December of the same year a Scots Guards Exhibition was held at 39 Grosvenor Square; a host of articles, uniforms, prints, paintings and relics were assembled, which gave a unique and unprecedented view of the Regiment throughout its existence.

In 1934, as part of the movement to link the armies of the Dominions more firmly with that of the Home Country, the alliance was approved between the Scots Guards and the Winnipeg Grenadiers. Ever since, any member of this Canadian Regiment has always been welcomed by the Regiment, and they in their turn have extended the warmest hospitality to any Scots Guardsman in Canada.

Sport and Musketry were fields in which all ranks of the Regiment won many honours during the Peace. To set them all out would take far too long, for their victories in Bayonet Fencing, Swimming, Athletics, Boxing and at Bisley were legion. One exceptional performance was that of Lieutenant G. F. Johnson in 1929, then Adjutant of the First Battalion and now Major-General Commanding the Household Brigade, who, with an aggregate score of 171, became the first commissioned officer ever to win the King's Medal for the Champion Shot of the Regular and Territorial Armies; in the previous year he had won the Army Hundred Cup. And in 1920 Major G. H. Loder won the Derby with "Spion Kop", a success which made his every word oracular at the annual Hogmanay Dinner when he commanded the First Battalion from 1925 to 1929.

*   *   *

But the joys of sport were gradually dimmed by the deepening war clouds which gathered towards the middle 'thirties. Economy[1] gave way to rearmament; at the Munich Crisis of 1938 the Second Battalion had spent a period at Pirbright packed and labelled for Czechoslovakia, where it was thought it might form part of an international force to supervise a plebiscite; but the Germans ordered otherwise. In the summer of 1939 the Reservists were recalled in six groups for ten days' training with the First Battalion; on 3rd September the Regiment was at war again.

[1] In 1931 all ranks of the Second Battalion had volunteered to save public money by foregoing their train journey to Windsor when Change of Quarters came round, and to march instead. This patriotic gesture fired the imagination of Fleet Street to such an extent that a mere nineteen-mile march received an extraordinary amount of publicity—which was not confined to Great Britain; the *Bangkok Times* published a large photograph of the Battalion marching through Frimley Green above the caption "as a gesture of economy Boy Scouts in England march fifteen miles".

PART II

Scandinavia : 1940

THE outbreak of war with Germany in September 1939 found the First Battalion, commanded by Lieutenant-Colonel T. B. Trappes-Lomax, in Chelsea Barracks, and the Second Battalion, commanded by Lieutenant-Colonel J. C. O. Marriott, at Matruh in the Western Desert of Egypt. In the east there were no hostilities, for Italy found the moment inopportune to enter the conflict. In the west Lord Gort took the Expeditionary Force to France, where for eight months quiet reigned in the "phoney war".

It was expected that the First Battalion would join the B.E.F. in the early summer of 1940; the training which the Battalion underwent was directed to this end. Mobilisation Orders had been received on the evening of 1st September, and the Battalion was promptly made up to full strength. Training was pushed on vigorously, and parties went to Woking, Pirbright and Rainham on various exercises and courses, including one in that even then barely adequate weapon, the anti-tank rifle. On 17th October the Battalion moved for further training to Martinique Barracks at Bordon, where the only sign of enemy activity was an air raid warning "Yellow" on 10th November. On 3rd December it returned to London, the Battalion Headquarters, C Company, and Left Flank going to Regent's Park Barracks, and Right Flank and B Company to the Duke of York's Headquarters, Chelsea. Public duties were mounted, and training and recreation continued, the latter taking the forms of football matches and visits to theatres. On the 8th a practice alarm in the small hours showed that the duty Company could be ready to move off in twenty minutes, and on the 13th the Battalion had its first close contact with the enemy, providing the escort for a party of German prisoners from the Tower to their destination in Hertfordshire. Lieutenant and Quartermaster J. Turner died on the 20th and Lieutenant and Quartermaster A. Ross took over on the 27th. Christmas and Hogmanay were celebrated in the customary manner, and the intensive training that followed brought increasing rumours of the Battalion's destination.

All this was very different from the sudden clash and slaughter of 1914.

While Lord Gort's army was slowly built up in France, another part of Europe attracted the attentions of Allied strategists. This was Scandinavia. In these northern lands, rarely before visited by British

MAP

troops, and never before by the Regiment, two separate problems worried the statesmen.

The first, and militarily the most important, was the German iron-ore traffic from the Swedish mines at the head of the Baltic Sea. During the summer the Germans could with impunity carry these essential supplies by sea from Luleå to the German ports. The Allies could not get at them. But in winter the Baltic is ice-bound, and for many years it had been the practice to send the ore by rail into Norway to the port

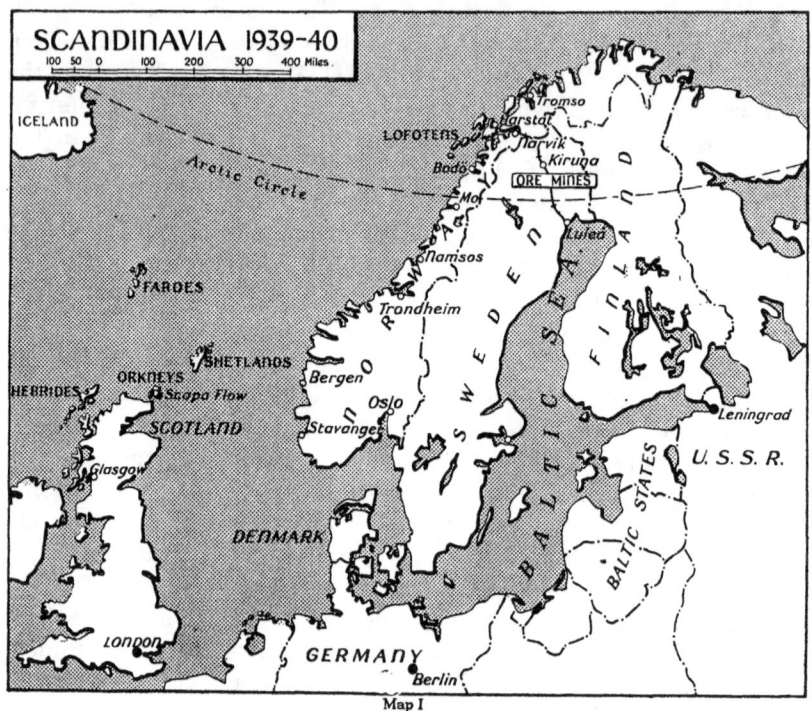

Map I

of Narvik, where it was loaded into ships and taken down the long, exposed coast to Germany. Here indeed there seemed a chance for the Allies to exert their overwhelming superiority on the surface of the sea. There was, however, an added complication. Off the Norwegian coast are some thousands of islands, large and small, and between these islands and the mainland run deep channels, known as the Leads, through which laden ships can sail without venturing on the high seas. Safe under the protection of Norwegian neutrality a steady flow of ore was assured to Germany. The object of the Admiralty was to force these ships out of Norwegian territorial waters, and to this end plans for laying minefields in Norwegian waters or for the seizure of Narvik were under constant discussion.

The second Scandinavian problem was that of Finland. In August 1939, to the utter discomfiture of Britain and France, Soviet Russia had signed her unholy alliance with Nazi Germany. Such a *mariage de convenance* did nothing to make either partner less suspicious of the other, and, on her part, Russia set about strengthening her defences against her new ally, particularly around her main naval arsenal of Leningrad. Demands were successfully made on the smaller Baltic States, but Finland refused to comply. Russia attacked her in December 1939, entirely miscalculating the military force required, and underestimating the stubbornness of the Finns. Their gallant defence excited the admiration of the free world, and several idealistic and impractical schemes for volunteer armies were bandied about in the sincere though ineffective desire to help Finland in her struggle.

I. THE FIFTH BATTALION

Any expeditionary force sent from the west in winter would have to traverse Norway and Sweden. The French, who had their celebrated Chasseurs Alpins to call upon, were the prime movers in this venture, but a British contingent of two divisions was earmarked to accompany them. It was deemed essential that there should be a small British unit trained in ski and winter warfare to supplement our contribution. This unit was the Fifth (Special Reserve) Battalion, Scots Guards. The whole affair was rushed and improvised and the history of this remarkable and unique formation (inevitably nicknamed "The Snowballers") must be read with the atmosphere of hurry and bustle constantly in mind.

Instead of teaching a trained and disciplined body of soldiers to ski, the War Office chose to recruit its new battalion from already experienced skiers, and with this object in view volunteers had already been called for during January 1940. On February 3rd telegrams were dispatched all over the world directing the volunteers to report to Quebec Barracks at Bordon on the 6th, an order which must have caused some amusement to those who received their telegrams in such places as India and Hong Kong. Meanwhile, an advance party and skeleton staff, found from all Regiments of the Brigade and including a strong section from Regimental Headquarters, were moved to Bordon to prepare for the arrival of the unknown snowmen. Lieutenant-Colonel J. S. Coats, M.C., Coldstream Guards, a distinguished winter-sports expert, was selected to command the Battalion, and, for his Adjutant, Captain W. D. M. Raeburn, Scots Guards, also a well-known skier, was flown home specially from the Second Battalion in Egypt. Major B. Mayfield, also from the Regiment, became Second-in-Command.

Feb. 3

Colonel Coats was told to have his battalion ready and equipped for service overseas by 1st March. Thus, from the outset, no more than twenty-three days were available for the assembly, organisation, military training, equipment, inoculation and general preparation of a force of men collected at the shortest notice not only from all ranks and branches of the Army throughout the world, but from civil life as well.

Feb. 6

One thousand volunteers had responded to the appeal sent out in January, and when they arrived at Bordon on February 6th or in small parties during the following three weeks, each was interviewed by Colonel Coats or by one of his senior officers and closely cross-examined as to his qualifications. During these interviews several were found to have only the unwanted experience of lumbering, or of snow-shoe work, or of mountaineering, and therefore could not be accepted; many more had only negligible experience of skiing, and these, with a few undesirables, had also to be rejected. From the remainder the Battalion had now to be formed, and the choosing of the officers proved to be the most difficult problem.

Six hundred commissioned officers had come forward as volunteers from all arms of the Service, including many Majors and Captains, some of whom had been commanding companies in the B.E.F., and from all of these only four Company Commanders, an Assistant Adjutant and fifteen Subalterns were required. Once the final choice had been made, those who had not been selected were asked to relinquish their commissions and to remain with the Battalion in the ranks. The process was to be known as "de-gazetting", and those who agreed to the proposal were to continue to receive their existing pay as officers and to be eligible for time promotion in the normal way, although absent from commissioned rank; at the end of their period of special service they would be free to resume their commissions. There were many who declined to accept these terms, but one hundred and sixty-seven officers including three from the Regiment,[1] agreed to serve in the ranks as non-commissioned officers or Guardsmen; a further seventy-two Officer Cadets transferred from their various Training Units under similar arrangements to become Guardsmen.

The majority of the non-commissioned officers were drawn from this commissioned source and, in the main, de-gazetted officers carried out their new duties as Sergeants and Corporals with success. The same applied to the Company Sergeant-Majors and Company Quartermaster Sergeants of the Ski Companies, although the latter, who were assisted throughout the first weeks at Bordon by regular non-commissioned officers, later proved to be one of the Battalion's weaknesses.

Of the remainder, one hundred and eighty came direct from civil life; the Battalion roll contained the names of men from all parts of

[1] Second Lieutenants A. H. C. Maxwell, A. D. Stirling and C. O'M. Farrell.

the Empire, Regulars, Territorials, veterans of the Spanish War, soldiers of fortune, undergraduates; in fact any man who could ski with a modicum of competence—provided he was aged more than twenty, and less than forty.

Amongst this strange assortment were several whose pre-war experience on Arctic or Himalayan expeditions was to prove invaluable. Four of these, all of whom had been members of Greenland expeditions led by Gino Watkins (whose brother also served in the Battalion), were given charge of the special Arctic equipment as Instructors. Captain M. Lindsay, Royal Scots Fusiliers, commanded this section and was appointed Assistant Adjutant; under him F. Spencer Chapman[1] (who had helped to design much of the equipment at the War Office earlier in the year), J. M. Scott and Q. T. P. M. Riley, all served as non-commissioned officers. The Medical Officer, Lieutenant E. H. L. Wigram, R.A.M.C., had also been a member of the 1936 Everest Expedition; frost-bite and snow blindness were not new to him.[2]

The volunteers were organised into four Ski Companies; Right Flank, W, X and Left Flank; there was a small Battalion Headquarters, the meagre equipment of which lacked even a wireless. Soon the Battalion was increased to five companies by the arrival from the Training Battalion at Pirbright of a company of trained Scots Guardsmen; these became Y Company, commanded by Captain R. D. M. Gurowski; none of them had even seen a ski before. The loan of a company from the First Battalion to do the fatigues about the camp enabled the new Battalion to concentrate on its worries, undistracted by the cares of housekeeping. Equally valuable to Colonel Coats was the loan of Captain C. Rooker, R.A.P.C., to help solve the pay puzzles of this bizarre Battalion; not surprisingly, there was a multitude of such problems.

Life at Bordon during the second half of February was hectic. Volunteers were continually arriving and requiring to be interviewed and kitted out, while the rest of the Battalion spent its time in suitable Physical Training, watching demonstrations and listening to a comprehensive course of lectures on such subjects as sledge loading, snow-camping and the avoidance of frost-bite. It was not until the last days of the month that their sole armament, the new Number 4 Lee-Enfield rifle, arrived, and it was then that the alarming fact emerged that many of the rank and file had never before handled, let alone fired, a service rifle. There were no Brens.

---

[1] Previously known to the public as the hero of the ascent of Chomolhari (24,000 feet) in 1937 and subsequently as the author of *The Jungle is Neutral*, a book which all officers joining the Second Battalion in Malaya from 1948 to 1951 were ordered to read.

[2] For Order of Battle, see p. 557.

SCANDINAVIA: 1940

Feb. 29   On the 29th February Lieutenant-General Sir Bertram Sergison-Brooke, Major-General Commanding the Brigade of Guards, and Colonel E. W. S. Balfour, Lieutenant-Colonel Commanding the Regiment, visited Bordon. In his address to the Battalion the Major-General bade them "God-speed and a victorious return".

Mar. 2 On the 2nd March in deepest secrecy, their destination known to the Commanding Officer alone, the Battalion embarked at Southampton and landed in

Mar. 3 France the next day, somewhat to the confusion of those who had predicted a voyage to Scandinavia or even to the North Pole, though to the satisfaction of those who favoured the Caucasus. The riddle was

Mar. 4 solved, after a non-stop train journey across France, by the sight of Mont Blanc as the train arrived at Chamonix, an event which was immediately broadcast by "Lord Haw-Haw" of the German wireless, reported in the French Press the next day, and even quoted in the London *Daily Telegraph*. But, as usual, the troops themselves were expressly forbidden to mention their whereabouts in their letters home; one Guardsman was taken before his Company Commander for writing "I must not tell you where we are for fear of endangering the Fleet".

The companies were billeted in great comfort on the many hotels; the heavy baggage meandered across France for two days in a goods

Mar. 5 train, and it was not until the third day after their arrival that ski equipment could be issued. This short period of inactivity revealed an unforeseen defect. Cooks, trained or natural, are rarely to be found among parties of volunteer skiers; it turned out that hardly a man had ever been inside a kitchen for a useful purpose in his life. In consequence the first meals prepared in billets were mostly uneatable. To the joy of the local *patrons*, the majority of the Battalion forsook their cooks and fed in the nearby restaurants and cafés.

The advanced season of the year made for many difficulties in ski training. Not the least of these was the fact that the Commanding Officer of the 199th Battalion of Chasseurs Alpins (a reserve and not particularly energetic unit stationed in Chamonix) to whom Colonel Coats looked for guidance, had forbidden his men to leave the valley for fear of avalanches. This seemed over-cautious, as the local civilians had no such qualms and were still enjoying their winter sports. As a result the only demonstration which the Battalion were able to see during their stay was one of a small and exceedingly simple attack by two French platoons against a third, carried out on the flat at the bottom of the valley. In other ways, however, the Chasseurs were most hospitable. They lent ski instructors, which enabled the Battalion to organise its own training programme, which was blessed by glorious weather. They also lent cooks.

In the Ski Companies all sections were organised both as ski and sledge troops, an unsatisfactory arrangement which necessitated every man being trained both as a scout and as a member of a sledge-hauling team, for on patrol both jobs would be expected of him. This was asking a lot, especially of the men of Y Company, none of whom had ever before been on skis. However, under the able instruction of two well-known amateur skiers, Sergeant W. R. Bracken and Corporal E. W. A. Richardson, they picked up the technique so rapidly that some French officer who saw them after four days' training found it hard to believe that these young Regular soldiers were beginners. The more proficient companies went off on cross-country treks with full equipment, or were instructed in the difficult arts of sledge loading and the use of man-hauling harness.

On the 9th March, as they were about to embark on their more advanced training in tactics and movement, a telephone message was received by Major A. F. Purvis, Scots Guards, the Battalion's Liaison Officer, asking him to find someone who could speak Hindustani, as orders would be passed in that language later in the evening. The Battalion had no difficulty in finding such an interpreter, but this ruse must have put the Germans to some inconvenience to get a Hindustani monitor on to the line with such speed. On the following day the news went out from Berlin that "the Fifth Battalion Scots Guards will leave Chamonix by train at seven o'clock on the morning of Monday, March 11th". The prediction was only ten minutes out; that was the fault of the French train. This hurried departure was the result of the desperate military situation of the Finns. The Red Army had planned its spring attack with overwhelming force, and their troops were now making decisive headway. On 2nd March the French had decided to send a force of fifty thousand "volunteers"; the British were to land on the Norwegian coast to assist them in their passage. The first landing was to be on the 20th.

Throughout the long train journey across France rumours improved; they were off to Greenland, to Murmansk, to Bordon for disbandment. No-one really knew. The gloom of this period of uncertainty was deepened by lengthy waits of many hours' duration in drafty warehouses at each end of the Channel crossing. Once in England, hope was renewed. Those who had failed to come up to standard in France were sent back to their units and the remainder entrained for the north. Thursday, March 14th found them crossing the border; on the same day they embarked on a Polish liner at Glasgow Docks. Here they found themselves no longer Britain's only Arctic troops, for all around them was a complete division, said to be suitably equipped for winter warfare. But the Russians forestalled the expedition. In the train on the journey north, the Adjutant had heard over the wireless the news that the Finnish Prime Minister had gone to Moscow to seek terms. While loading was still in progress at Glasgow, the order cancelling the venture was received. An armistice had been concluded; the Fifth Battalion was no longer required. They returned to Bordon, and, in less than a week, had been dispersed in all directions.

The history of this Battalion is an example of the amateurish improvisations to which British Governments are forced to resort at the outbreak of our wars. It was truly a unique battalion, the value of which was never tested in battle in a terrain and climate for which it was intended. It is perhaps ironical to observe that when, later in the war, the 52nd (Lowland) Division was thoroughly trained for mountain and winter warfare, that formation first entered the line in—Holland! And it cannot be judged wise to have concentrated in one poorly equipped and untrained unit so many leaders and potential leaders. It was indeed fortunate that these men were not flung away in an altruistic and ill-prepared side-show, but were saved to go forward to many and varied exploits in decisive theatres of war.

II. NORWAY – THE FIRST BATTALION

(a) *Narvik*

The Finnish problem in Scandinavia had been solved—by the Russians; Norway, the iron-ore trade and the blockade remained. After seven months' hesitation the Government finally resolved on the 3rd April that the minefields should be laid on the 8th, and that the 24th Guards Brigade, commanded by Brigadier the Hon. W. Fraser, D.S.O., M.C., together with a French regiment, should be landed at Narvik with orders to advance to the Swedish frontier. Other landings were to be made elsewhere on the Norwegian coast to forestall the expected German counter-moves. It was unknown in London that on 16th March Hitler had made *his* decision to attack Norway on 9th April. The mêlée which resulted from these two intentions developed into the Norwegian campaign, in which the First Battalion were the first British troops ashore. It is most important to bear in mind that until the 9th April, all our preparations—and there were preparations —had been directed towards an *unopposed* landing in a passive, if not friendly, country. This was a sad miscalculation.

The Battalion had had its share of the alarms of the previous month. From the 11th to the 15th March all preparations had been made to follow in the wake of the Fifth. The cry of "Wolf!" raised too often must have suggested itself to many minds when preparations were again put in hand on All Fool's Day. Sceptics were silenced by a visit from His Majesty the King on the 3rd, accompanied by the Major-General and Colonel Balfour. All officers were presented to him, and His Majesty was loudly cheered by all ranks on leaving. On the evening of the 6th, after two more cancellations, the Battalion moved off through the quiet streets to Euston where the Major-General, the Lieutenant-Colonel and many other officers of the Regiment had come to wish them good fortune in what might lie ahead. By half-past ten, the two crowded trains had drawn out into the darkness, and next morning, after a close-packed but cheerful journey, arrived in pouring rain at Glasgow Docks. It was the first occasion since 1712 that a regular battalion of the Regiment had been in Scotland, but the need for security gave no opportunity to mark the occasion, and by noon it had left the shelter of a convenient Customs shed and embarked on the 13,000-ton Polish motor ship *Batory*.[1] *April 7*

At 1245 the *Batory* moved out into the Clyde and dropped down to the Tail of the Bank off Greenock to await the completion of the convoy. Moored nearby were a number of other merchant vessels and H.M. ships *Warspite* and *Aurora* and seven destroyers. Arctic clothing was issued. It included quilted sleeping bags, capok greatcoats, sheepskin jackets, snowboots and white fur caps, and any doubts that may have remained about the Battalion's destination were dispelled. During the evening the congestion (there were a number of "details" on board as well as the Battalion) was somewhat eased by the dubious process of separating B Company from its kits, ammunition and baggage which, with one platoon under Lieutenant the Lord John Hope, were transferred to the *Aurora*.

April 8th dawned dank and cloudy, but with less rain than the previous day. P.T. was started on the crowded decks and arrangements made for a route march on the 9th, and, perhaps for reasons which might have seemed obvious the day before, B Company's platoon and baggage were restored to the *Batory*. That day the news came of the German invasion of Norway, and the *Warspite* and some of the destroyers sailed to take part in operations off the Norwegian coast. Most of the night was spent by fatigue parties in the laborious but necessary process of restoring all the stores and baggage in one of the holds in order that those things needed first should be accessible. The next day, for reasons of security, the route march was cancelled and, as the ships lay grey and still below the entrance to the Gareloch, men looked out across the ruffled water to land that for many held memories of home. *April 8* *April 9* *April 10*

At about one in the morning of the 10th (Narvik had fallen to the Germans the previous afternoon) the *Batory* moved off down the Clyde, and by four o'clock she was off the Mull of Kintyre experiencing a heavy swell. In company with her was another Polish liner, the *Chobry*, with the Hallamshire Territorial Battalion on board, and an escort of destroyers. "The sea was blue and the sun shone brightly as we sailed up the coast of Scotland between the mainland and the Hebrides. After the usual ship's inspection and P.T. parades, everyone

[1] For Order of Battle, see p. 543.

sunbathed all over the decks and it was all much more like a Mediterranean cruise than a military expedition setting off to war."

April 11 At 0600 on the 11th the little convoy arrived at Scapa Flow which it found "bristling with warships, dummy and otherwise. Not too cold but windy." P.T. and ski exercises followed, and about midday a force consisting of Right Flank (Captain A. D. Crabbe), B Company (Major J. H. Elwes), and a Headquarter Company detachment, the whole under the command of Major H. L. Graham, M.C., the Second in Command of the Battalion, was transferred to the cruiser *Southampton* with the object of carrying out a landing north of Narvik and of supporting the Norwegians in an endeavour to recapture that town.

April 12 At 1230 on the 12th the *Batory* and *Chobry* once more got under way with their escort and made for a rendezvous twenty miles north of Cape Wrath, where they were joined by the *Empress of Australia*, the *Monarch of Bermuda* and the *Reina del Pacifico*, with a further escort of warships. The *Southampton* sailed independently an hour later. On board the liners were, besides some Territorial Battalions, the 1st Irish Guards and the 2nd South Wales Borderers, which with the Battalion made up the 24th Guards Brigade; no one in the two Guards Battalions had ever met his opposite number in the Borderers before,

April 13 let alone trained with them. On the 13th the convoy ran into heavy weather, and at least one officer found that "it really became magnificent" to see the way the warships with decks awash thrust through the great seas. But others were in no state to take an interest. At 1000

April 14 on the 14th, still in heavy weather, the *Batory* crossed the Arctic Circle. That night part of the convoy with the Territorial Battalions broke away and formed the expeditions which operated in Central Norway in the Namsos area. It had become cold, "but not desperately so", and as wild rumours circulated as to possible destinations, further interest was added to the day by the thud of depth charges and the gyrations of the destroyers, and the sight of what was credibly reported

April 15 to be an enemy submarine. By the morning of the 15th the waste of waters of the North Sea had been left behind and the convoy was steaming up Hadsel Fiord at the northern end of the Lofoten Islands. "The scenery was magnificent, and the weather was equally perfect. A brilliant sun shone down out of a bright blue sky on to a mountain landscape covered with a mantle of snow down to the water's edge." Peaceful fishing villages dotted the shore, and it seemed hard to believe that this land was about to become a theatre of war. It also, perhaps, seemed hard to believe that the Battalion's carriers, which were believed to be following in another transport, would find snow a suitable surface on which to manœuvre, or that, in the circumstances, the Battalion's bicycles would be a really effective means of intercommunication.

About noon the convoy arrived off Harstad, at the north-eastern end of the island of Hinnoy, and three hours later the Battalion disembarked; the Commanding Officer was the first ashore, carrying a Polish lance from which fluttered a pennant of the Brigade Colours; it had been presented to the Battalion by the Captain of the *Batory*. The Navy in the meantime dealt successfully with the German submarine U 49, which was found lurking in the bay about a quarter of a mile away. The Norwegians, happily, were gratified by the arrival, and, to their cheers, added welcome help in moving baggage and supplies: co-operation rendered doubly useful by the fact that the Battalion had been sent to the defence of Norway with no transport whatsoever beyond pedal cycles: excellent machines, but of little use in moving three-inch mortars. The two-inch mortars, which could easily be carried, were unprovided with high-explosive bombs; only smoke had been supplied. The keynote of the expedition had been resonantly struck.

Harstad, which held Force Headquarters, then under the command of Admiral of the Fleet the Earl of Cork and Orrery, provided reasonably comfortable billets, and by evening everyone was settled in and slit trenches dug in the snow, and news received that Major Graham's force from the *Southampton* was at Salangen on the mainland between thirty and forty miles north by east of Narvik.[1] Communication with this force was hardly of a satisfactory nature, for no wireless sets had been provided and the probability of the public telephone being tapped by enemy agents reduced conversation to an uninformative and platitudinous level, while the alternative methods of communicating by boat, motor car and sledge were likely to result in messages being merely of historical interest by the time of receipt.

The Commanding Officer's conference next afternoon was repeatedly interrupted by air raids, and, though no one in the Battalion was injured, a Military Policeman was killed, and it became clear that the billets assigned to the Battalion were much too congested. Other billets in small wooden houses on the outskirts of the town were quickly found, and next day the baggage was once more manhandled through the snow, which was made no less unpleasant by the incipient

MAP II

April 16

---

[1] On the 14th, immediately after the Second Battle of Narvik in which H.M.S. *Warspite* and her attendant destroyers had annihilated the German flotilla, Lord Cork had made strenuous efforts to divert the *Southampton* carrying Major Graham's detachment for an immediate landing, together with seamen and marines from other warships, *in the harbour* of Narvik. The message, together with other contradictory orders, was eventually received in the *Southampton* while the Scots Guards were in the act of disembarking at Salangen: General Mackesy, the force commander, decided to adhere to the original plan.

In the light of what is now known of the demoralized state of the German troops and sailors after the *Warspite's* victory, it is hard to resist the conclusion that a swift, bold landing on the 14th or 15th would have had a good chance of achieving a decisive success.

thaw. Air raids, mostly from a great height, were thenceforward a daily occurrence, but no bombs fell in the Battalion area. Though damage and loss occurred in other parts of the town, no casualties were suffered by the Battalion.

The first few days passed pleasantly enough, and the clear sunny days made up for the cold nights when about ten degrees of frost were normal. There were about four feet of snow on the level, and healthy exercise if not success was achieved with the narrow Norwegian skis which proved a difficulty even to the few accustomed to Switzerland. But a blizzard gradually worked up to full intensity, and when it was

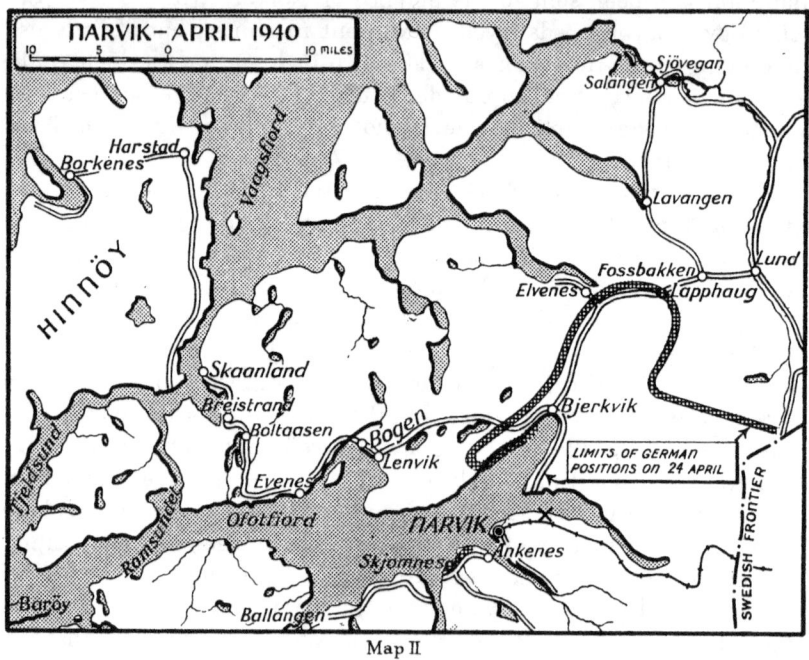

Map II

over another two feet had been added to the snow. Movement became impossible off the roads and, so far as attacking the Germans in and around Narvik was concerned, "we might just as well have been back in London". However, there was hope of achieving some degree of mobility, for, after arriving late and disembarkation being further delayed by a snowstorm, the Transport and Carrier Officers (Lieutenants R. D. Cardiff and A. D. Murray) arrived in Harstad on the afternoon of the 21st. Even so, the hope came to nothing, for the transport and carriers had been placed in another ship which, it later appeared, had been diverted to Tromsö, about ninety miles further north, and were not seen again for three weeks. However, useful employment was found for the drivers in unloading ships—the pioneers who came in the same vessel with this object in view had been

April 21

sent straight back to England, apparently on the grounds that their arrival was unexpected—and the carrier crews, armed with Bren guns, acted as anti-aircraft protection to the local motor fishing boats, "puffers", which were used as transports in the fiords. Those less actively employed found interest in the activities of alleged Nazi agents, whose use of signalling lamps verged upon the blatant. One such episode near one of the anti-aircraft posts—small snow forts with a Bren gun in the middle—led to the temporary arrest of the Mayor of Harstad and a number of his callers.

On 30th April the South Wales Borderers landed on the west side of the Ankenes peninsula, the next peninsula west of Narvik. Brigadier Fraser, who accompanied them, was wounded by a mortar bomb while reconnoitring the approaches to Narvik, and Lieutenant-Colonel Trappes-Lomax took over command of the Brigade. *April 30*

On 1st May Major Graham returned with his force, which had been relieved by a demi-brigade of Chasseurs Alpins, and assumed command of the Battalion. His force had failed to capture Narvik by an immediate assault, as Lord Cork had hoped, and indeed had been employed on no more arduous a task than acting as long-stop to the Norwegians in the Salangen and Fossbakken areas north of the railway linking Narvik and Sweden. It was perhaps as well that nothing more was asked of them, for the snow was six feet deep and, while four hundred pairs of skis were awaiting them on arrival, only three men in the force were able to ski. However, the first dead Germans were seen and on the whole the time had passed pleasantly and usefully enough. The most uncomfortable episode was the great blizzard, when the men were without food for twenty-four hours before supplies could be got through by sledge. For the rest, those who could ski had ample opportunity for pleasurable activity; and those who could not, for the less pleasurable effort of learning. But the expedition was no idle holiday, and on 2nd May, two officers recorded that they had been able to get undressed for the first time for over a week. *May 1*

During the evening of 1st May the Battalion (less B Company which had remained to guard Harstad, and C Company (Captain P. Steuart-Fothringham), which on the 29th April had been sent to Bodö in the destroyer *Ardent* to defend the airfield against a possible attack by parachute troops), embarked in the net-layer *Protector* in preparation for an attack on Narvik from the sea. A short run down the Tjeldsund brought Left Flank (Major the Viscount Garnock) and part of Headquarter Company (Captain F. H. H. B. Harris) to Evenskjaer (Skaanland) where they disembarked with the help of "puffers", Headquarters being established at Breistrand four miles to the south, and Left Flank at Boltaasen another three miles further on. "Unloaded into small boats, unloaded on to quay, unloaded on to only four trucks (seven journeys), unloaded at Breistrand again. Altogether six and a half loads of about 35 tons each in 36 hours and no sleep, all manhandled." Right Flank remained on board and was taken down the narrow Ramsundet to Evenes on the northern shore of the Ofotfiord where the normal landing difficulties were enhanced by the shallowness of the water, and where it found a platoon of the Irish Guards who were occupying positions further to the east. Everything was ready for the assault on Narvik—except the means of getting there and any preliminary training in combined operations.

May 4
On the 4th the Brigade Commander received orders to assault Narvik on the 8th. A reconnaissance was accordingly carried out in the *Aurora* (Captain L. H. K. Hamilton, R.N.) and a plan made, based on landing on the only available sloping beach. Before the plan was given out, however, it was discovered that there were only four landing craft in Norway. In consequence, a further reconnaissance was

May 5
carried out on the 5th with the purpose of finding suitable places where comparatively deep draught vessels, such as puffers, could approach the rocks. On this occasion the Brigade Commander was accompanied by Major Graham and the Commanding Officer of the Irish Guards (Lieutenant-Colonel W. D. Faulkner, M.C.) and other officers of the two Battalions, who all wore Naval caps in order to give the affair a purely nautical appearance. The *Aurora* had some successful practice shoots, but it was found that the only possible landing places, each giving only a platoon frontage, were on the eastern side of Narvik Peninsula (marked X on map) and would have entailed a long observed approach—there is no darkness in northern Norway in May—and a forming-up place within machine-gun and mortar range of the Germans on the other side of the inlet. Fortunately, Colonel Trappes-Lomax was able, though with some difficulty, to get due attention paid to these as well as to various other factors that had hitherto been overlooked; they included the complete absence of air cover and the facts that the flat trajectory of the naval guns made adequate support at essential points impossible, and that there were not sufficient deep-draught vessels anyway. The attempt was postponed. The Brigade was saved from an immolation that would have gained nothing but an expenditure of enemy ammunition. Instead, the Battalion practised landings in the Tjeldsund from any available local boats and pushed on with the preparation of an airfield near Skaanland.

(b) *Expedition to Mo*

With every day that passed, the need for air cover had become more urgent. On the night of 2nd/3rd May the British forces had been evacuated from southern Norway. Thence-forward the German aircraft were able to concentrate with ever increasing force upon the Navy in the Narvik area; they did not bother, normally, about the land forces; the land forces could wait. On the 4th the Polish destroyer *Grom* was sunk by a bomb, another Polish destroyer had the narrowest of escapes next day, and the *Aurora* received a direct hit on a turret and suffered several casualties. On the 6th, the Battalion saw its first British aircraft, six Skuas from the *Ark Royal*, and enemy air activity immediately lessened. But the Germans soon discovered that the carrier-based Skua was a very different thing from a land-based Hurricane or Spitfire, and renewed their attacks with undiminished vigour: H.M.S. *Enterprise* had a hundred and fifty bombs aimed at her in one afternoon and lost her Commander and was riddled with bomb splinters. It was urgent that the Germans advancing from the south should not be able to use Bodö, where the aerodrome was now rapidly clearing of snow, for fighters to engage the British fighters when they should arrive at Skaanland and Bardufoss further to the north; still more so that, with the additional air support that Bodö would make possible, they should not press on and relieve their now closely beleaguered garrison of Narvik. It was decided that the only British troops available, the 24th Guards Brigade, should be given the task of holding up the enemy advance on Bodö, and that the Poles and the French should press on with clearing the Narvik area from the north. The Irish Guards were withdrawn from their positions on Bogen Bay and one company from the ruins of Skjomnes where it had gone to support the South Wales Borderers and the French engaged in clearing the Ankenes peninsula. The South Wales Borderers, who, with the aid of the *Aurora's* six-inch guns, had recently repulsed a counter-attack with heavy loss to the enemy, were withdrawn from their investment of Ankenes, their place being taken by the Polish Carpathian Brigade. The successful assault on Narvik was to be made by others.

May 6

Early in the morning of the 11th (Holland and Belgium had been attacked on the previous day), the Battalion, to which Colonel Trappes-Lomax had returned, had embarked at Skaanland, their destination Mo, a small town about a hundred and thirty miles south of Bodö. It had been a difficult task to reassemble the Battalion, for the only transport available was a few Norwegian trucks and the thaw had made the road almost unusable. However, it was achieved, and in the face of the usual difficulties—"embarked on puffers, transferred from puffers to the cruiser *Enterprise*. Usual luggage trouble—far too bloody much"—the embarkation was carried out; at seven the little convoy set off for Mo. It had been arranged at the time of embarkation that either the Irish Guards or the South Wales Borderers should follow in the next few days. An urgent request for the immediate despatch of C Company from Bodö was refused.

May 11

MAP IV

The choice of Mo as the position where the German Army was to be delayed had perhaps been dictated by the fact that there the fiords approach within seventeen miles of the Swedish frontier. But

3—S.G.H.

appreciation of the situation during the voyage brought to light serious disadvantages. First among them was the narrowness of the entrance through the Ran Fiord, which gave insufficient room for ships to manœuvre in the event of air attack; and indeed the Navy was soon forced to confirm that, far from being able to stay in the fiord, it could not undertake to return with supplies. The second, a corollary of the first, was that all supplies would have to be despatched from Harstad by sea to Rognan at the head of the Saltdalsfiord, and thence over land by the eighty miles of road through the hills to Mo; and as this road, except for occasional passing places, was fit only for single-line traffic for about twenty-three miles where it passed through a snow-cap, the chances of adequate supplies coming through were unknown. Nor was it known if the snow had in fact cleared. Finally there was the disadvantage inherent in all hill positions when held by an inadequate force; there is always another hill beyond. Against Alpine troops there was no possibility of holding these seventeen miles and preventing the position from being turned. And, apart from that, in the absence of the Navy, there was nothing to prevent the Germans crossing the fiord to the west, cutting the road from Rognan, and taking the position from the rear.

In addition to the *Enterprise*, the convoy that sailed for Mo consisted of the destroyer *Hesperus*, the sloop *Fleetwood*, and the *Margot*, a small merchantman, and divided among the ships were the Battalion (less C Company), a troop of four 25-pounder guns, three Bofors anti-aircraft guns, and a party of Royal Engineers. It was in all conscience a small enough force to stop the advance of the fresh German 2nd Mountain Division, even with the help of some exhausted Independent Companies (remnants of the Territorial Force in central Norway and under the command of Colonel C. McV. Gubbins, M.C.[1]) driven north from the Namsos area, and two weak, ill-equipped and untrained Norwegian battalions of doubtful keenness. The Battalion's orders were to hold Mo "at all costs". It had supplies for fourteen days.

The speed of the convoy was limited to eight knots by the *Margot* but, though German aircraft were seen, no bombing attacks developed. On the other hand it was rough and seasickness claimed the majority. The officers and men in the *Hesperus* and *Enterprise* were looked after with true Naval hospitality, but the same could not be said for those on board s.s. *Margot*.

During the afternoon an urgent appeal for help was received from Hemnes, a peninsula joined by a narrow neck of land to the mainland about fifteen miles south-west of Mo. It appeared that about three hundred Germans had been landed there, that the Navy had sunk

[1] Later Major-General Sir Colin Gubbins, K.C.M.G., D.S.O., M.C., Commander Special Forces and Special Operations Executive.

their transport, but only after they had all landed, that they were being reinforced from sea-planes, and that there was only one weary Independent Company, No. 3, and a company of Norwegians (Captain T. Ellinger)[1] between them and a further advance towards Mo. The *Enterprise*, with Battalion Headquarters and Left Flank on board, immediately increased speed to twenty-five knots. At about 0500 on the 12th, after shelling the Germans at Hemnes on the way, the *Enterprise* arrived off Mo.

May 12

The bombing fortunately only began when all the men were on shore, though the baggage was still on the quay, and the only losses were one empty puffer sunk by a bomb, a number of rifles swept off the quay, and half the quay destroyed when the *Margot* rammed it in the excitement of a raid. Had the bombing begun earlier, the results might have been disastrous, for the *Enterprise* could not get alongside and the men had to be packed into puffers and then disembarked in single file up a twelve-foot ladder. As it was, the *Margot* wished to leave with the 25-pounders and their vehicles still on board, on the grounds that she could not wait for three hours while they were unloaded. But the Gunner Battery Sergeant-Major bet her Captain a bottle of whisky that they could do it in an hour, and he agreed to wait. They did it in thirty-five minutes—and got two bottles.

That evening, after an exhausting rushed march with full equipment and carrying all weapons, the Battalion was in position at Dalsklubben, seven miles along the road to Hemnes.

The position was not only the best available, but was one of considerable natural strength. The right flank rested on the fiord, and the Dals river in spate across the front was virtually uncrossable except by two bridges both of which were covered by fire and could easily be destroyed. Its weakness lay on the left where the ground rose steeply and the trees, though not yet in leaf, made it impossible to get an adequate field of fire. To have made that flank secure probably another battalion would have been needed to the south-east. But the Irish Guards had not yet embarked. And in the meantime the need for dealing with a possible attack from the hills to the south and southeast had to be subordinated to the immediate task of guarding against a German advance along the road from Hemnes. This was likely to occur at any time, for the tired Independent Company on the isthmus at Finneid was in danger of being overrun.

MAP III

The right forward position covering the main road bridge was given to Right Flank (Captain Crabbe), the left, covering the second bridge and the left flank, to Left Flank (Lord Garnock). Every eventuality

---

[1] Captain Ellinger, a Dane serving in the Norwegian Army, later attached himself with his machine-guns to the Battalion, and did invaluable service throughout the subsequent fighting.

had been foreseen, including a descent by parachutists to the southeast. Against that there was no counter. It occurred.

It would, of course, have been desirable to post some troops on the heights above the positions, but this was quite out of the question in view of the weakness of the force, and the fact that the British were unable to move over the deep snow with which the hills were covered.

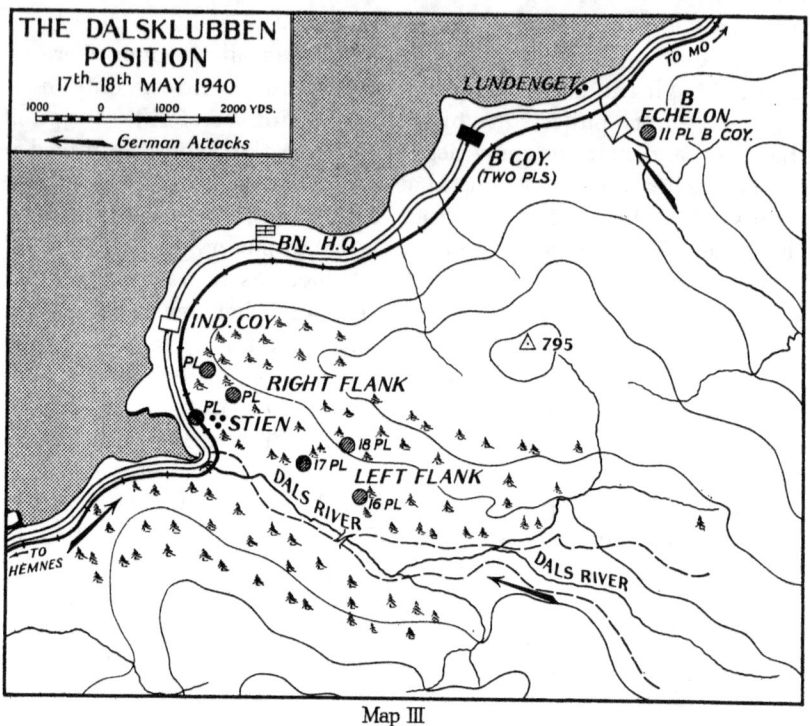

Map III

It was hoped that three small Norwegian ski detachments would watch this danger, but they did little.

The night of the 12th/13th was undisturbed, but was one of the most miserable spent in Norway. The men were exhausted from the bucketing they had received on the voyage, from their forced march, and from the labour of digging, or of building log defences where the rock made digging impossible. They had neither sleeping bags nor blankets nor hot food. Fires were impossible owing to the risk of giving away the positions, and to the bitter cold of the Arctic night was added a steady fall of snow that melted as it fell. But the spring had come, and thereafter it was fine.

May 13   Consolidation of the position was continued on the 13th, but the Battalion was still further weakened by withdrawing B Company (Major Elwes) to Ytteren, north of Mo, to guard against an attack on

Mo from the rear in the event of the Germans choosing to advance on the western side of the Ran Fiord.

Captain G. A. D. Taylor, the Intelligence Officer, who went up to the position of the 3rd Independent Company on the isthmus, found the situation "very interesting. . . . Micks are due tomorrow, which will help". But the Irish Guards did not embark until the evening of the 14th, and shortly after midnight, their transport, the *Chobry*, was sunk by a bomb which killed Lieutenant-Colonel Faulkner and five other senior officers. After scenes of disciplined heroism for which parallel must be found in the loss of the *Birkenhead*, they were taken back to Harstad in the escorting destroyers. The only hope of support then lay in the South Wales Borderers. But the cruiser *Effingham* in which they were travelling ran on an uncharted rock and became a total loss, and they too were taken back to Harstad by their escort. Instead of a brigade being in position when the attack developed at Dalsklubben, there was only one exhausted Independent Company and one Battalion less two companies; "which undoubtedly made a very big difference". Whether in the circumstances a Brigade could have held Mo for more than a few days is a matter that can never be decided.

In the meantime, Colonel Trappes-Lomax, who had again handed over command of the Battalion to Major Graham, had formed an improvised Headquarters and was organising the immediate defence of Mo. Instead of a Guards Brigade, the force available consisted of B Company, about two miscellaneous platoons of British troops, and one hopelessly ill-equipped Norwegian battalion; a second Norwegian battalion was at Korgen on the main road about nine miles south of Finneid. In the face of the rapid advance of between three and four thousand Germans its position was plainly untenable, and during the night of the 13th/14th it too withdrew to Mo. "Never slept a wink! Norwegian lorries withdrawing through us all night." When morning came, the left flank was even more exposed.

On the 14th, Colonel Trappes-Lomax, Major Graham, Major Elwes and Colonel Roscher Nielsen, commanding the Norwegians, made a reconnaissance of the position at Ytteren in order that B Company might be relieved and enabled to return to the Battalion, and the withdrawal of the hopelessly outnumbered Independent Company from Finneid was ordered for the 15th. German aeroplanes were over all day, and at about 1700 the attack along the isthmus began. After about four hours it became clear that that position could not be held, and the Independent Company was ordered to withdraw into B Company's old reserve position behind the Battalion. This it did successfully, covered by the artillery and Captain Ellinger's machine-guns and a platoon under Lieutenant H. L. St. V. Rose, who were in action for about three hours and finally had to withdraw when dive-bombing

May 14

in the clear bright night was added to mortars and machine-guns. But considerable casualties had been inflicted on the enemy, and one of our destroyers which put in a fortunate appearance had had a successful shoot on Hemnes and had blown up a dump which burned all night.

May 15   The 15th brought bad news—"Damn it. The Dutch have surrendered! A nasty blow"—and continuous enemy air activity, both reconnaissance and ground-strafing. One machine was brought down by Bofors and the pilot and gunner captured with valuable information. But this success could do nothing to offset the general position, which, the War Diary grimly records, was "anything but satisfactory".

May 16   About midday next day, the Dalsklubben bridge was blown with a thousand pounds of gelignite: "Tremendous bang and blast and very effectively done". Later in the afternoon, the Bofors had another success and brought down a flying-boat on the far side of the fiord where the Norwegians, after an ineffective engagement with each other, killed one of the occupants and captured four. That night the wooden bridge in front of Left Flank was also demolished, a somewhat perilous proceeding as it had to be done by hand, and anyone who had slipped would almost inevitably have been drowned in the torrent. However, "a good time was had by all, as there is nothing more fun than a nice bit of destruction".

May 17   At 1400 on the 17th, Germans, whose strength opposite the Battalion is now known to have been about 1,750 men, were seen advancing in large numbers up the coast road, and half an hour later, the firing began. "We evacuate H.Q. and move to quarry," Captain Taylor wrote, "I evacuate O.P. for a less conspicuous one. Both places plastered by German gun 20 minutes later!" Heavy firing continued throughout the afternoon and evening, lessening to mortar only and machine-guns, but the only supply route remained under constant machine-gun fire, and the Germans working round to the left flank were out of range of machine-guns and "unget-at-able" to the artillery who, owing to the patchy snow giving perfect camouflage, were unable to spot the German fire positions. However, Right Flank had one successful shoot when the enemy tried to lay planks across the girders of the blown bridge; a fair number were shot down and carried away into the fiord. The front remained intact, but on the left the situation was deteriorating rapidly.

At about 1800 Left Flank received its last message from Battalion Headquarters before the wires were cut by shellfire. It was to the effect that Norwegian patrols had reported that about a hundred and fifty German parachutists had landed about seven miles to the south-east on the frozen lake that was the source of the Dals. About an hour later this was confirmed by an exhausted Norwegian boy, aged about twelve, who said that his father had told him to run as fast as he could and say that a large German force, alleged to be in Norwegian uniform, was advancing down the valley and was already near at hand. In the meantime, the Germans beyond the Dals, advancing out of range, had brought machine-guns into the woods across the river ready to give covering fire when the enveloping parachute force should be in a position to attack.

The attack on the left began about 2130 and the fighting quickly became confused in the twilight of the Norwegian night. All the advantages lay with the enemy, whose automatics were superior to rifles in close fighting among trees, and who could vary their positions of attack at will, causing the defenders to leave their positions to meet each new threat. It was fighting in which the utmost skill and initiative were necessary qualities which were displayed in the highest degree by No. 16 Platoon (Lieutenant A. H. R. M. Ramsay)[1] which bore the brunt of the attack, and in particular by Guardsman J. H. Bryson who inflicted heavy casualties on the enemy and was an inspiration to all.[2] Although this defence by movement was successful in keeping the enemy at bay, it was clear that with the coming of full daylight, the situation would be completely changed, for then the defenders would be in view of the machine-gunners across the Dals. Only one thing could restore the situation: a counter-attack round the rear of the position to take each part of the enemy in flank in turn. It was clear that the exhausted Independent Company in reserve could not undertake this. There remained only Right Flank. Lord Garnock set off to arrange for this in person. He had already reached their nearest section when he was wounded by a German firing at about twenty-five yards. Captain J. A. Milburne now arrived on a similar errand, and Captain Crabbe lent him one platoon under PSM Day to reinforce the left-hand sector.

By midnight, the situation was critical, for Left Flank was virtually surrounded and the loss of its area would leave the whole flank of the Battalion position exposed. In addition, another party of parachutists was attacking B Echelon in the Lundenget Valley, about four miles to the rear, and the only supply route to the Battalion was in danger of being cut. Forward communication by telephone had long since ceased in spite of all efforts, in particular those of Guardsman Howard, to maintain it. The line to Force Headquarters, however, remained, and B Company was hurriedly ordered forward to a covering position west of Lundenget, where it found that B Echelon had temporarily driven off the attackers; and at 0200 on the 18th, the Battalion was ordered to withdraw. It had suffered between seventy and eighty

May 18

---

[1] Lieutenant Ramsay, who was wounded, died on Active Service in South Africa in August 1943.

[2] Guardsman Bryson, who also on two occasions rescued wounded men under heavy fire, was awarded the D.C.M. He died of wounds in Italy on 26th February, 1944, while serving in the Second Battalion. See page 195.

casualties of whom three were killed or mortally wounded. The relatively small number of killed, which included CSM F. Higham of Right Flank, was probably due to the fact that the German tommy-gunners appeared to rely on volume rather than accuracy, and that the German four-inch mortar bombs exploding in the snow seemed to have a charge disproportionate to their cases, and had blast rather than fragmentation value.

Part of Left Flank and Right Flank moved first, covered by the Independent Company, which in turn was covered by Battalion Headquarters. The remainder of these two companies never received the order; but Captain Crabbe realised the situation when he found Battalion Headquarters abandoned, and withdrew with the remainder of Right Flank and No. 16 Platoon of Left Flank. By about 0430 the Battalion had passed through B Company after having the pleasure of seeing the Germans, who had a weakness for Verey Lights, mortared by their own mortars. All kits had been lost, for there was not transport to move them. B Echelon also was safely withdrawn, but as it only had five locally acquired broken-down lorries, everything but rations, small arms ammunition and the wounded had to be abandoned. "There is little doubt," the War Diary records, "that enemy troops had been collecting in the valleys leading to the position for several days before, so that the attack, which was admirably timed, should take place from all directions simultaneously." Some of these troops were landed by parachute "but although the continual arrival of sea planes had been reported daily, no action either of an offensive or reconnaissance nature had been possible, owing to the complete absence of any air support whatsoever."

A defensive position was quickly taken up on the ridge north-east of Lundenget and orders sent to B Company to withdraw once more into reserve. But the Germans had already penetrated behind Major Elwes's position, and of the four runners, two were lost in trying to get through, and the Company continued to struggle up a precipitous, snow-covered hill to get into a better covering position. It succeeded, but two men fainted in the process and crashed two hundred feet, fortunately into more snow at the bottom. Two more men were sent down to help them back to the Battalion and all four were cut off by the Germans. They managed to remain hidden, and eventually made their way to Sweden.

By 0900 it was clear that the Lundenget position was untenable and a withdrawal to the north of Mo was ordered. Headquarter Company once more acted as rearguard, and the most successful withdrawal was largely due to the inspiring example and gallant stand made by the rearmost party under PSM W. H. Washington. By 1500 the rear of the column had passed through Mo, dumps of petrol and ammunition had been destroyed, and the two bridges over the Rana

River, a mile and a half north-east of the town, had been blown on Major Graham's orders. A few minutes later the Germans entered Mo, where, the day before, the flags had been flying in celebration of the Norwegian national holiday.

The Battalion had one day's rations left. Of B Company there was no sign.[1]

During the previous night Colonel Gubbins had arrived in Mo, having been appointed by General Auchinleck to command the area, and he ordered the withdrawal. His arrival enabled Lieutenant-Colonel Trappes-Lomax to return to the Battalion and relieved him of the difficult decision whether the orders to hold Mo "at all costs" meant that the whole force had to be sacrificed on the chance that a few days might be gained. That evening the retreat to Bodö began.

(c) *Retreat to Bodö*

May 18

Like nearly all retreats, the withdrawal to Bodö was entered upon by men outnumbered and already weary. "Long dreary road, back to Sandheien. . . . Harassed by aircraft. Arrived dead beat, welcome rum ration and slept on hard floor quite well. Total 15-hour battle and 18–20-mile route march." On the way they had passed through C Company which had, at last, been hurried down from Bodö by road and was holding a covering position at Rosvoll. Bodö was a hundred and thirty-five miles away. The only link was one inferior road crossing and recrossing a river in narrow valleys. On either side were mountains deep in snow. The often-promised air cover did not come, and each movement of the long column was known to the enemy almost as soon as it began. Of B Company there was still no sign.

May 19

At 0930 on the 19th, the Battalion set off once more, marching in perfect order "down a lovely gorge, but very vulnerable from S.E. flank across river". But the only enemy activity was a little machine-gunning from the air, and one aeroplane was brought down by Bofors. By about 1500 the Battalion had reached Strandjorden, where it had a meal and rested until nearly midnight, before pressing on to Storvolden, about twenty miles away from Sandheien. In the meantime, at about 1600, a telephone message reached Force Headquarters at Krokstranden, saying that B Company had succeeded in reaching the road a few miles north of Mo. The message might well have been a trap, but the chance had to be taken, and Lieutenant-Colonel Trappes-Lomax immediately ordered Captain Harris and the Battalion transport (now three Norwegian lorries, salvaged by the genius of Lieutenant R. C. Petre) back down the road to meet them.

[1] In *The Campaign in Norway* by T. K. Derry (H.M.S.O.) at page 186 it is stated that Colonel Trappes-Lomax told the Norwegians that the Scots Guards had lost two companies. This is not accurate. In fact the Commanding Officer said that B Company was missing, and that C Company was still at Bodö.

May 20

The rearmost covering position, held by C Company at Neavernes, was passed through, and at Storfosshei, about three miles down the road, the transport party found B Company settling down to a long overdue meal. By 0600 on the 20th B Company was back at Krokstranden and the Battalion was complete, though still without carriers and transport, for the first time since the campaign began. B Company's experience had been physically exhausting. Only four men had been lost, and "everybody was frightfully pleased and feeling much better for this really magnificent feat". They had crossed two mountain ranges in deep snow and a large and turbulent river—"about the size of the Thames at Putney, only much more rapid"—in three rowing boats that took three men at a time. The going was such that one man fainted from exhaustion a few hours after starting. Only the finding of two boxes of food hidden under a fir tree prevented complete exhaustion. But for the judgment and determination of Major Elwes, supported in particular by Captain Count Erik Lewenhaupt,[1] a Swedish officer attached to the Battalion at Dalsklubben, and PSM D. H. Tolmie, to whom the preservation of his platoon was due, it could never have been achieved.

Early in the morning of the 20th orders were received from General Auchinleck at Harstad to fight a defensive action in the Krokstranden area. "You have now reached a good position for defence. Essential to stand and fight denying enemy opportunities for outflanking in less difficult country further north. I rely on Scots Guards to stop enemy." As, among other factors, there was a single-track road cut through six feet of snow behind the position; as the Norwegian Battalions and the Independent Company, less one platoon, had already crossed this covered by the Battalion; as all supplies would have to come back down this road under constant air attack; and as the inevitable flanking movements could only be countered by placing men on mountains where it was impossible to supply them, the position was plainly less satisfactory than it may have appeared on a map over two hundred miles away. In consequence of a telephone conversation with Harstad that evening these orders were amended to a fighting withdrawal. In the meantime, Lieutenant-Colonel Trappes-Lomax had received written orders from Colonel Gubbins, the Force Commander: "You will only withdraw from any position you hold if in your opinion there is serious danger to the safety of your force." Taking into consideration the topographical and supply position, and the fact that a force amounting to a Mountain Division was advancing along the road from the south, that danger might have been deemed already to exist. However, by midnight three alternative positions had been chosen, the companies had been placed in the first position, and C Company had been in contact with enemy cyclists.

[1] It is with regret that the death of Count Lewenhaupt in 1954 is recorded.

FIRST BATTALION

The 21st was mainly notable for enemy reconnaissance and machine-gunning from the air, and there was no sign of the British fighters whose help had been promised daily. Major Graham was sent to reconnoitre what was said by those at Harstad to be a good defensive position in the neighbourhood of Viskiskoia north of the snow-belt, and was machine-gunned by low-flying aeroplanes. In the afternoon C Company and Right Flank were attacked on Position A at Raufjellet, three miles north-west of Krokstranden, and retired to Position C north of Randalsvolden, a little to the south of the edge of the snow-belt, passing through B Company and Left Flank in Position B at Andfjellneset, nearly three miles south-east of Krokstranden, on the way.

May 21

At dawn on the 22nd Position B was attacked and, in spite of the courageous efforts of Captain Ellinger with his three machine-guns, the enemy managed to penetrate a considerable distance past the position on its left flank, and in the course of the afternoon the companies successfully withdrew to Position C. "I ventured to remind the Commanding Officer," Captain Ellinger wrote soon after, "that the C Position was risky because it obviously was impossible to fight greatly superior forces with our backs to a twenty-mile-wide snow-belt. Through this barrier there was but one narrow road kept open by snow-ploughs and lined by high, perpendicular snow walls. Only at certain points was it possible for two cars to pass one another. One well-aimed bomb would completely stop all motor-transport. To pass the snow-belt with a battalion would require both skill and luck in avoiding observation by the enemy. To try to cross the snow-belt while an action was actually going on would surely spell disaster."

May 22

But Colonel Trappes-Lomax had foreseen all this and more. Transport was essential if the snow-belt was to be crossed in the hours of twilight. When the Norwegian battalions crossed on the night of the 19th/20th, each of their lorries carried a Scots Guardsman: to ensure that they came back. Also essential was a secure embussing area, and it was to provide this that Position C had been chosen.

Providentially, the Germans had slackened their advance after their losses at Position B and were no longer maintaining contact. It remained to ensure that any German who approached Position C should not return with the information that it was no longer a defensive position but a forming-up place for a move. Aircraft had been over intermittently all day, troubling the tired men with machine-gun and cannon fire. Evening was approaching, and preparations for the move being made when a reconnaissance machine flew up and down the valley, presumably taking photographs. Orders at the time forbade firing at hostile aircraft, for fear of giving away position and also to conserve ammunition. When a Bren gun opened up, the usual cries arose: "Take that man's name!" When the aircraft faltered the cries turned to "I think you've got him". It crashed, and the Battalion's intention was not revealed.¹ "Shortly afterwards," Captain Ellinger recorded, "a German patrol of twelve bicyclists appeared on the road. Corporal Nass succeeded in shooting eight of them, but four managed to take cover in a ditch. They were all taken care of by a carrier." This carrier, which had been salvaged from the wreck of the *Effingham*, was one of the two in the platoon from the 3rd Independent Company attached to the Battalion, and, under Second-Lieutenant Anderson, played an important part as rear party to the Battalion throughout the retreat. This officer's courage and ability undoubtedly helped to secure the safe withdrawal of the Battalion by engaging cyclist patrols. He was continuously in action for about seventy hours, and his conduct was worthy of the highest praise. That night the treeless snow-belt was crossed in buses in perfect order and without the loss of a man.

Why the Germans failed to press on and, by maintaining contact, make the crossing of the snow-belt impossible, can only be a matter for surmise. It would seem likely that the loss of the reconnaissance aircraft and of the twelve cyclists had convinced them that on Position C the Battalion was going to await the end. In the circumstances, therefore, no purpose would be served by further losses. The Battalion was trapped. There was time for leisurely deployment, a pincer-movement over the silent wastes of snow, the cutting of the supply line. The rest could be left to starvation and a steady pounding from the air. (During the previous two days every car crossing the snow-belt had been chased and machine-gunned from the air.) Whatever the exact details of the reasoning on which their inaction was based, one thing is clear: they had underrated their opponents and had fallen into the error of over-confidence. Had they sent more aircraft, or one more patrol, everything might have been different. It was an error for which they were to pay dearly in the years to come.

May 23   By midnight the Battalion were back in the positions reconnoitred by Major Graham at Viskiskoia. Here again things were far from satisfactory. In the first place, as the War Diary frankly records, "the men were utterly exhausted and a certain demoralisation had set in, in consequence of fatigue, loss of kit, a succession of rearguard actions, and continuous menace from the air, which invariably disclosed every position to the enemy and enabled him, without interference, to harass the Battalion and base his plans on certain knowledge." In the second place, the old difficulty of the flanks still remained. On the right, it was clear that the 2nd Independent Company (which had come back to the line) could not be expected to maintain themselves without means of supply among mountains which gave a succession of false crests. To the left rear, the Junkerdalen gave a perfect covered

---

[1] Unfortunately for the historian, the man's name was not taken; after much investigation it transpires that the insubordinate, but accurate, Bren gunner was Lance-Corporal S. Moorhouse. He was later killed in action in Tunisia; see p. 142.

approach to the position assigned to the 3rd Independent Company at Storjord. Compared with the general tactical position, the absence of ammunition for the two-inch mortars, and the loss of all artillery signalling appliances, whereby the field guns could only be used in directly observed fire—for which the position was unsuited—seemed trivial matters. In spite of these things, orders were received from Colonel Gubbins to hold the position until the 27th, and the tired men settled down to get what rest they could during the few remaining hours of twilight.

At about 1500 the German attack on the Viskiskoia position began, and a little later the Commanding Officer, who had gone back to reconnoitre the next rearguard position at Storjord, returned and announced that he had been ordered to report back at Harstad on the ground that, in crossing the snow-belt, he had not carried out Colonel Gubbins' orders. "This crushing blow," the War Diary records, "took place in the middle of an enemy attack, and it is hardly to be wondered at that the morale of both officers and men was still further shaken by the loss of a Commanding Officer for whose personality and ability everyone had the highest respect and in whom everyone had the greatest confidence." One of the officers, in some notes for a private diary, did not feel bound to that studied moderation in language customary in an official document: "C.O. comes back and says he had been sacked! for saving his Battalion presumably? Anyway someone is nearly lynched. This is quite monstrous. Battle develops. . . ." In the circumstances there was a certain irony in the fact that Colonel Gubbins, on coming in the afternoon to see the position that he had ordered to be held until the 27th, should find it advisable to order its evacuation at once.

The battle developed as had been foreseen. The Germans were soon in occupation of the high ground on the right and the whole position was enfiladed. The Battalion's one remaining three-inch mortar had a successful shoot, but despite all efforts could not neutralise the concentrated fire of the German mortars; and the two-inch mortars had no ammunition. To machine-gun and cannon fire from the air, too, there was no adequate reply. For the promised air support did not come, and one of the Bofors had been hopelessly ditched the second day back from Mo. At 1800 the withdrawal was ordered. At 2000 it began. By midnight the Battalion, now again under the command of Major Graham, was back in position at Storjord. Through the untiring efforts of Lieutenant Petre and Lieutenant W. M. Burgess, R.A.M.C., all casualties had been safely evacuated in inadequate transport in a succession of journeys along a road under enemy fire.

May 24

The Storjord position was plainly no more satisfactory than that at Viskiskoia, and as the half light of night merged into day the enemy began the normal uninterrupted reconnaissance from the air interspersed with machine-gun and cannon fire whenever suitable targets were found. In the course of it the Commanding Officer's and Intelligence Officer's obscurely acquired cars were attacked from about fifty feet while they were sleeping inside: "A bullet each through the cars and a cannon between. We were so sleepy we scarcely moved, but just watched rather interestedly. However we heard him coming back and scuttled off to the woods to finish sleep." Later in the morning orders were received to hold the position at least until 1800 in order to give the Irish Guards time to get into position at Pothus about thirteen miles further north, where the road crossed again to the west side of the river about nine miles south of Rognan at the head of the Saltdals Fiord. In spite of the enemy starting their attack just as the withdrawal was beginning, the operation was once more carried out in perfect order, and the rear positions were successfully occupied and abandoned without any interference except from the air. Shortly after midnight

May 24/25 that night the Battalion passed through the Irish Guards in and about the Pothus woods. Normally on such occasions considerable banter of a traditional kind is exchanged between the "Jocks" and the "Micks". There was no banter that night. The men were utterly exhausted. They had marched nearly a hundred miles in a week, fighting rearguard actions, outflanked and outnumbered, and continually attacked from the air. They had lost everything but their personal weapons, and what they stood up in.

On the same day the Cabinet in London made the final decision to abandon Northern Norway.

After the standard delays transport arrived to take the Battalion back to Rognan where it had breakfast. Further confusion and delay followed—normal enough, but irksome to weary men—but eventually the chaotic transport was reduced to order and by evening companies were billeted over a wide area in and around Hopen with Battalion Headquarters at Godones and B Company in scenery of astonishing beauty overlooking the Straumen Maelstrom.

May 26 The 26th was passed in much needed rest—one officer preceded "a good night's sleep" with fifteen hours out of the previous twenty-four—but already signs of further activity were apparent. For the news came through that the Irish Guards under Captain H. C. McGildowny were being attacked at Pothus, and a reconnaissance had to be made at Bodö where the Battalion was to take over from the South Wales Borderers. In fact, the Irish Guards had already been outflanked and forced to withdraw from Pothus and the Germans were pressing them hard as they fought a magnificent rearguard action back to Rognan.

May 27 The rest was all too short. On the 27th orders to take over at Bodö were received. As there was not transport and Bodö was ten miles west of Hopen and the position had to be occupied by 1830 a considerable rush was necessary. The Commanding Officer immediately hurried to

Bodö to make final arrangements. Almost immediately, out of the clear blue sky of the perfect spring day, the German bombers set about the methodical destruction of the little town. Probably not more than a dozen bombers were used—their leisurely unloading and return led some to believe that there were eighty—and about two hundred heavy bombs were dropped. At once flames gripped the houses, almost all of which were built of wood, and the civilian population, escaping into the streets, was machine-gunned from the air. The hospital, a large building, clearly marked, on a rise of ground on the outskirts of the town, came in for particular attention. In it were the majority of the Battalion's eighty-four casualties as well as the sick, including Captain H. N. Clowes, the Adjutant, who had been there with jaundice since the 19th.[1] Fortunately the hospital was strongly built and stood up to the attack long enough to enable all to be evacuated except those buried under fallen masonry. The ubiquitous Captain Ellinger was quickly on the scene. "Some of my Scots Guards friends had arrived and gave splendid help at the hospital. It was amazing that among all that misery and suffering around me I do not remember having heard a single cry. Everybody did his very best; discipline and morale were perfect. The Norwegian nurses were—as always—splendid: we soldiers owe them a big debt of gratitude."

The main radio building in Bodö had been destroyed, together with four-fifths of the houses in the little town. But in the wrecked transmitting house outside the machinery was still workable. That night it spoke for the last time. Over and over again from the blackened and smoking ruins of that township of the dead went out a recording of the great death hymn of Björnson and Edvard Grieg: "The mighty host of saints we see as a thousand mountains clad in snow."

The next day passed in comparative quiet—"only reconnaissance planes and machine-gunning from the air,"—and Right Flank, the only company to move to Bodö the previous day, was brought out again and rejoined the other companies in preparation for the possible occupation of positions between the Soloi Lake and the Saltdals Fiord between Bodö and Hopen. That day news was received that the Irish Guards were in action at Fauske on the north side of the fiord. During the early morning of the 29th orders were issued for the evacuation of Bodö. The Battalion with the South Wales Borderers on its left was to hold the Soloi Line and be the last to leave, and by midnight it was in position with Battalion Headquarters near the coast at Hunstad and B Company under Captain J. Godman as outpost at Hopen. It was "the first really good defensive position which the Battalion has occupied and on which the Germans could have been held." Only one enemy seaplane was over that day, and that night the

May 28

May 29

[1] Lieutenant D. S. Wedderburn had taken over the appointment.

Independent Companies and a few others were safely got away in two destroyers.

May 30   The 30th proved a perfect day for a withdrawal, with Scotch mist and rain until late in the evening, and partly by road and partly by sea the Irish Guards moved back to Bodö, whence by midnight they were evacuated in three destroyers. But the enemy was following closely and by 1830 they had made contact with B Company, and the Hopen bridge had been blown. During the evening a considerable engagement developed, and heavy mortar and machine-gun fire was put down by the Germans who were seen to suffer a number of casualties, particularly where they came under artillery fire to the east of

May 31   the blown bridge. But by 0200 next morning it was clear that the left flank of the position was being turned and it became necessary to withdraw, covered by one of the Borderers' carriers. Two hours later the Company was back in Battalion Reserve. Unaccountably, the enemy failed to press on and regain contact. The day passed very slowly. It was clear and sunny and any movement could have been seen for miles. It may be that the enemy again yielded to over-confidence, or that the affair at Hopen bridge had taught him caution. At 1900 six aircraft made a reconnaissance of the Battalion area, and more bombs were dropped on Bodö, where an empty puffer was sunk. At 1915 the withdrawal began. Left Flank and C Company led, followed an hour later by Right Flank covered by B Company, which in turn withdrew at 2120 to hold a last position in front of Bodö in conjunction with a company of South Wales Borderers. Right Flank sighted a cyclist patrol just before starting, but, perhaps warned by the fate of its predecessor south of the snow-belt, it took no action and the withdrawal was completed without interference. The remaining kit and transport was destroyed, and by midnight the last man had passed through the ruins of Bodö and the Battalion had embarked in the destroyers *Echo* and *Delight*. It had suffered ninety-seven casualties, of whom thirteen were killed and thirty-six were taken prisoner. Its only stores were six thousand rounds of ammunition.

(d) *Evacuation*

June 1   At 1300 on 1st June the Battalion arrived at Borkenes, ten miles
MAP II   west of Harstad, and moved to a billeting area where it was discovered not only that no preparations had been made but that the Mess drink supply had disappeared from Harstad. However, the first was quickly settled by local action, and in the course of that and the two following
June 2   days the second was put right largely through the generous help of the Irish Guards. Next day Lieutenant-General Auchinleck, who had succeeded Lord Cork in supreme command, visited the Battalion; he was the first General Officer to do so.

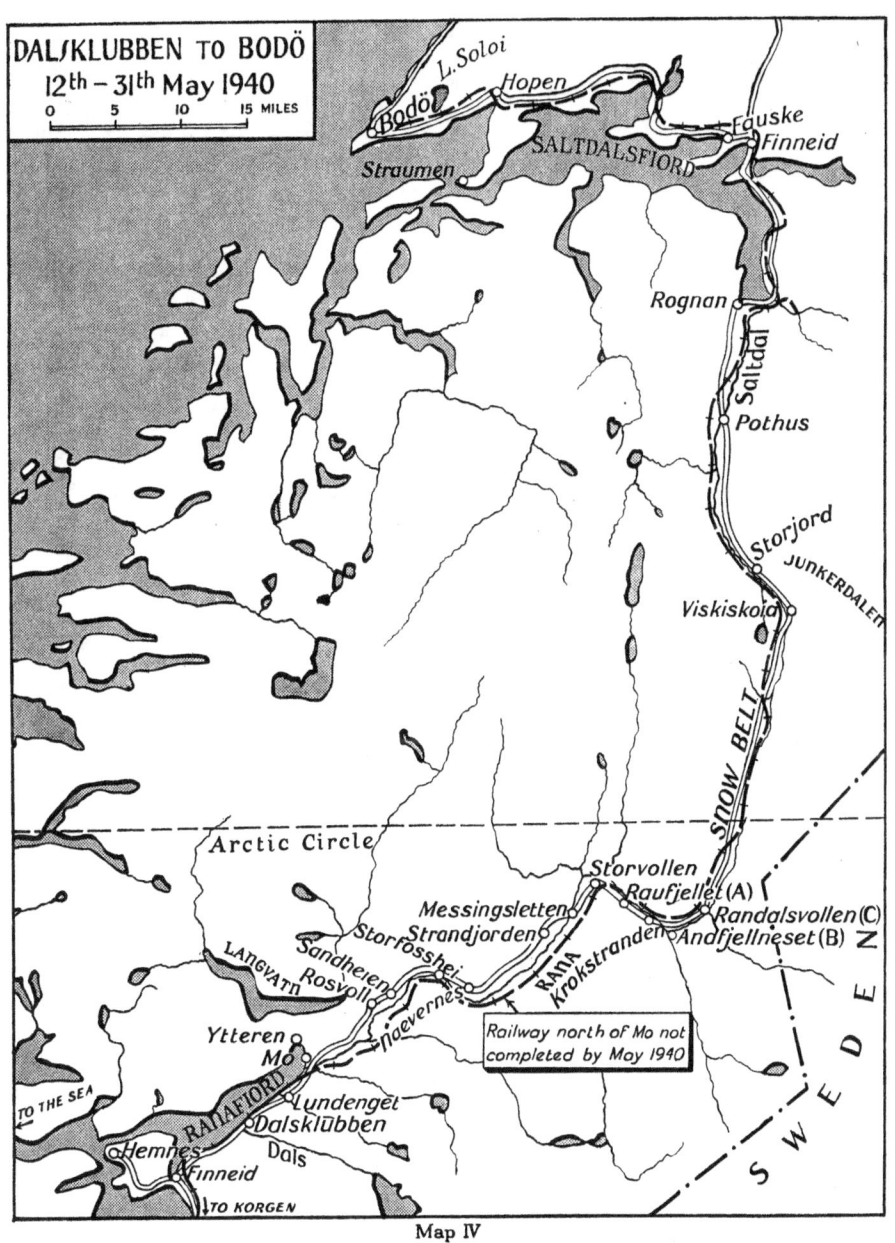

Map IV

FIRST BATTALION

On the 3rd the Irish Guards passed through once more, and the 4th was spent in preparing for a move next day: "probably is home, but the authorities still say Tromsö".

But it was soon clear that it was not to be Tromsö, for when the Transport Officer asked that the order for the destruction of his brand-new trucks be rescinded, on the ground that he could easily get them back to Tromsö by road after one short sea-crossing to the mainland, his petition was refused.

At 2120 on the 5th the Battalion, less Left Flank, embarked once more in H.M.S. *Delight*. In the early hours of the 6th the Battalion, rather disappointed at finding itself almost back at its starting point owing to bad weather, transhipped to the H.T. *Franconia*, where it was joined about midday by Left Flank. The next day it was blowing a little and overcast and the escort for the six great liners was found to be only the training cruiser *Vindictive* and one destroyer. However, no bombers appeared, and the day and night passed quietly. At 0100 next day the appearance of a German reconnaissance machine caused some disquiet, but a thick mist came down and hid the convoy for the rest of the day, and the arrival of four more destroyers and the battleship *Valiant* the previous day gave an added sense of security. Others were less fortunate; the German battle-cruisers *Scharnhorst* and *Gneisenau* fell upon the aircraft-carrier *Glorious*, the destroyers *Ardent* and *Acasta* and the empty transport *Orama*, and sank them. An increase in warmth was felt in the air that day, and at night it was almost dark. The 9th was a lovely day, hot and very calm, and the Outer Hebrides were passed, friendly and welcoming across the quiet water. At about 0700 on the 10th, the day that Italy declared war, the convoy reached Gourock once more.

On the 11th the Battalion moved into billets at Coatbridge; there they were rejoined by a detachment, consisting mainly of the sick, under Captain Clowes, which had been taken in the *Vindictive* direct from Bodö to the Orkneys; they had been held there *incomunicado* until the evacuation was complete. On the 16th the completed Battalion travelled to London when it was met by Colonel Balfour. It went into the billets which was to be its home for many months to come at Elder Road, West Norwood.

It had been a disappointing episode. But even the bitterest reverses at the beginning of a war may be of value when the lessons from them are learned. There was much to be learned from Norway. In the first place, since the expedition was not allowed to start until too late, it was doomed to failure. For the delay enabled the Germans to occupy every airfield in the country, and a force that might have held Norway, if the wildest hopes had been fulfilled, could not possibly have reconquered it without aerial support. The air is the only defence against the air; aircraft carriers, unless in such numbers as to give constant air superiority, were at that stage of the war so vulnerable to air attack as to be a liability rather than an asset. But even apart from the question of the air, the expedition, ill-planned and ill-equipped, was totally inadequate for the situation which developed. Against an invading force of seven German divisions, two of which were Mountain Divisions, were sent one division, mostly of half-trained Territorials, one brigade of Chasseurs Alpins, one brigade of the Foreign Legion and one brigade of Poles. In the circumstances such trifles as the lack of two-inch mortar ammunition could only make a difference of days.

The result was inevitable; we were beaten. But in such circumstances, for the participants, survival itself was a triumph. So far as the Battalion was concerned, it had played its part. The 24th Guards Brigade had been given a task that might well have required a division. And when the moment came only the Battalion, less one company, was able to reach the Brigade area. Perhaps it was best that the remainder of the Brigade should not arrive. To extricate a battalion was one of those feats in which skill and judgment would have been of no avail without a degree of good fortune. To have disengaged a brigade through the snowcap under the concentrated air attack that must have developed might have been impossible.

PART III

The Regiment at Home: 1939–1945

I. THE FIRST BATTALION

THE First Battalion returned to a country which was now beleaguered. The history of its activities in the next three years is typical of that of many battalions of the Army. It was a period first of improvised defence; secondly of intense preparation for the next battles; and thirdly of re-equipment and reorganisation. In those years the whole Army grew in confidence and reputation; now that the financial stringencies of peacetime had passed, it was possible to put into effect many improvements which had long been desired. When the Battalion sailed for North Africa early in 1943 it had the advantages of more realistic training, better weapons, and fitter men than it had been able to take to Norway in 1940.

1940

On 17th June, the day after its arrival at West Norwood, the defence commitments of the Battalion were outlined as follows: one Duty Company to be at half an hour's notice; five per cent of the rest of the Battalion and one officer of each company to remain in barracks; and one company at Beckenham (Left Flank) to man five road blocks in the line of the river Cray. Three days later sufficient transport arrived to lift the Battalion at war strength less reinforcements. Training started at once and included the use of the Molotov Cocktail, a primitive firebomb consisting of a bottle of oil and petrol and a simple igniting device, with which it was hoped to set invading tanks on fire, and the Battalion began to take part in the preparation of defensive positions in and around London. On 15th July His Majesty visited the Battalion and, after seeing the companies at work, stayed to tea and met all the officers who were able to attend.

On 16th August enemy air activity over London developed and road blocks were manned. Two days later came gunfire and the sound of bombs and dogfights were seen in the summer sky. In the evening of the 6th September, to the accompaniment of heavy anti-aircraft fire and the glow of great fires in the Surrey Dock area, the code word for "Invasion Imminent" was received. The Duty Company was immediately put at fifteen minutes' notice to move and all officers were recalled. Four days later a party of fifty-five men under Lieutenant F. G. Mann was sent to help the fire-fighters in the Surrey Docks, and on the 14th B Company, at Mount Mascal, was attacked but suffered no casualties though its billets had to be evacuated temporarily.

1941

The winter of 1940–41 was spent in constant training, punctuated by sporting events, and visits of distinguished personages, among whom was the then Secretary of State for War, Mr. Anthony Eden. Promotion came to many on the formation of the Third Battalion in October, when the Battalion found five Company Commanders, the Quartermaster and many senior warrant officers and non-commissioned officers for the new Battalion.

In January an exercise was held in the Titsey Park area. As this involved a day march of seventeen miles, a night attack and a march home of fourteen miles on ice-bound roads, it was described in the War Diary as "a fairly severe test". It also reminded many of the snow and weariness in Norway less than a year before. A similar march was done on the night of 4th/5th February after a Brigade exercise at Holmbury Hill, twenty-one miles being covered in ten and a half hours, fourteen miles again being over ice-bound roads. The 21st was also a notable day, and brought older memories of the inadequacies of the days of peace, for it was only then, after two previous attempts had failed owing to the breakdown of the engine that pulled the targets, that the anti-tank rifle party was able to conclude its practice shoot. Further suggestions of peacetime came early the following month, when it was found that both in demonstration and in exercise tanks were still represented by carriers. Although the man with the red flag was now disappearing, a vivid imagination, it seemed, was still the first requisite in training.

On 18th March Lieutenant-Colonel H. L. Graham, M.C., relinquished command of the Battalion. He had been with it throughout the campaign in Norway, and knew its capabilities. "I know that the Battalion will carry out successfully any task it is asked to undertake," he wrote in a farewell message, "and that it will cover itself in glory." That prophecy was to be fulfilled. Lieutenant-Colonel M. D. Erskine, who had been second-in-command since the previous July, succeeded Lieutenant-Colonel Graham in command.

On the 26th the Battalion started its new role of Reconnaissance Battalion for the Brigade Group. Four days later it took part as such in a London District Exercise, and further experience was gained on 8th April in a Battalion exercise held in the Titsey Park–Limpsfield–Crockham Hill area. On 24th and 25th April, in particularly bitter weather, the Battalion took part in an inter-Brigade exercise with the 29th Independent Brigade Group in the Newhaven area. Three days later Spring Drills began and on 3rd May a Battalion Parade was held at Dulwich College. This was the first such parade since the outbreak of war, and the display was highly satisfactory.

On 14th May the Brigade Commander, Brigadier F. A. M. Browning, carried out an inspection of the Battalion in training, and on the 17th the Battalion won the Inter-Battalion competition in the Regimental Sports at Pirbright. Three days later it left West Norwood and moved into camp at Buckhurst Park, Sussex, where it remained until 13th June in almost continuous rain, and the operations on the South Downs and in Ashdown Forest were carried out in seas of mud. In the evening of the 15th, after one night in billets in Brighton followed by two days in a South-Eastern Command exercise, the Battalion returned to Elder Road. Lovely summer weather immediately set in and fortunately continued throughout an exercise in the Eastern Command that lasted from the 21st to the 25th. On the 30th the Battalion left Elder Road once more and moved into billets in Kenley where it entered upon new duties in support of the aerodrome. These entailed much hard preparation and several exercises were held during July, that on the 21st seeing the first appearance of the Brigade Reconnaissance Company.

From 4th to 8th August the Battalion took part in a Corps exercise in the Tenterden area, afterwards moving into billets in Tenterden and carrying out firing in very unfavourable weather at Hythe and Lydd and other ranges. On the 17th the Battalion returned to Kenley and on 17th September it moved to billets at Chislehurst where it was to remain for the next seven months, taking part in various exercises as well as putting in much hard work on the more detailed aspects of training. From 15th to 20th December three officers and two hundred other ranks attended daily at Mount Pleasant Post Office, Paddington, to help with the Christmas mail. Christmas and Hogmanay were celebrated in the usual way, and the New Year was seen in at a dance held by the Sergeant's Mess in the Village Hall, which was attended by a number of guests including the new Brigade Commander, Brigadier W. P. A. Bradshaw.

January 1942 was cold and snowy, and on the 6th, 7th and 8th the Battalion took part in a Brigade exercise against part of the 3rd Division, making a long night move in transport over ice-bound roads on the last night. On the 15th Colonel Balfour visited the Battalion to watch the courses in the novel Battle Drill which had begun two days before. Further snow fell during February, which was very cold throughout, and the Battalion added one more to its many activities, sending the Pipe Band and platoons to take part in marches in support of various Warship Weeks.

On 18th March a Battalion Parade was held to celebrate the Tercentenary of the raising of the Regiment, and on the 19th Pipe-Major A. MacDonald took part in a Tercentenary broadcast for the B.B.C.[1]

---

[1] The "official" date for the raising of the Regiment is 1st May 1662, but the Regiment has much justification for looking upon this occasion as but a reassembling of that regiment which Archibald, Marquess of Argyll, received Letters Patent to command dated 18th March 1641, that date being the equivalent of what, since the reform of the calendar, would now be given as 18th March 1642. As the Marquess of Argyll had raised his regiment about two years before he was commissioned to command it, it is possible that the celebration of the Tercentenary was unduly delayed.

Training in May was diversified by Hardening Training in the Worthing area, sniping and street fighting courses and instructive and exhausting visits by two composite platoons to the Commando School at Achnacarry.

On 9th June Lieutenant-Colonel Erskine relinquished command of the Battalion and was succeeded by Lieutenant-Colonel the Viscount Dalrymple, M.B.E. On the 22nd the Battalion moved to a training area at Blandford St. Giles in Dorset whence it took part almost continuously in various exercises until the 8th July, when it moved to Rainscombe House, Pewsey, and took part in further exercises in the Marlborough training area until its return to Chislehurst on the 20th. On 16th August the Battalion moved to the Royal Schools at Wanstead, and training thenceforward was chiefly under company arrangements and included Field Firing on the Singleton ranges. On 7th October various aspects of life in the Battalion were photographed for distribution in America, and on two occasions, in the following month, aerial photographs were taken of it taking part in convoy moves.

The foregoing catalogue of exercises, courses, visits, marches and moves gives some idea of the steps which were taken to produce a revived British Field Army, skilled at arms and of a high morale. To this end also had been directed many sporting, athletic and social occasions. By the end of October 1942, with the Eighth Army now striking its decisive blow at El Alamein, the call was about to come for several divisions in Britain to take part in the descent in French North Africa. On the 1st November the order came for the First Battalion to mobilise; within a week it was on its way to Scotland, and on the first stage of its journey back into the line.

Before the deeds of the Scots Guards in Africa are recounted, a brief account must be given of how the Regiment was administered and maintained at home.[1]

II. REGIMENTAL HEADQUARTERS

At the outbreak of war Colonel E. W. S. Balfour, D.S.O., O.B.E., M.C., returned from retirement to take command of the Regiment in place of Colonel W. P. A. Bradshaw, D.S.O., who assumed command of the 4th Infantry Brigade on mobilisation. At the same time Captain the Hon. P. C. Kinnaird, M.C. relieved Captain A. V. C. Douglas as Regimental Adjutant.

The reign of Colonel Balfour lasted for more than four years, during which he steered the Regiment through the greatest expansion in its long history. In all, some 597 officers and 13,150 men wore the

[1] The history of the First Battalion continues on p. 131. For the home service of the Second see p. 395; for the Third p. 324; and for the Fourth p. 333.

uniform of the Scots Guards between the years 1939 and 1945.[1] This number was composed of Regulars serving at the outbreak of war, of Reservists recalled to the Colours, of volunteers, and of those called up under the National Service Acts; by far the greater number of them joined during the period of Colonel Balfour's command.

To the Lieutenant-Colonel Commanding the Regiment fell innumerable tasks. He had to raise the Training, Holding, Fifth, Third and Fourth Battalions; he had to see that an adequate number of suitably trained men were available for draft to battalions abroad; he welcomed or wished God's speed to battalions and drafts as they came and went to and from the Kingdom; he was responsible for selecting suitable candidates for commissions in the Regiment (and few will forget their first interview with Colonel "Bill"!); he fought the battles for the preservation of the Regiment's identity and integrity, the value of which harassed planners and subversive theorists were liable to discount in the interests of a tidy, mathematical allocation of the nation's limited manpower; he preserved that contact between the families of officers and men without which a Regiment would indeed be a soulless conception; and, as if the foregoing duties were insufficient, he was charged with the command of the North-East London Sub-District, and with the mothering of many cadet units in the Metropolis. In all this he was assisted by the Regimental Adjutant; and in addition an Assistant Regimental Adjutant was appointed. All these officers would have had an impossible task but for the help of Superintending-Clerk H. Smith, who presided in the office throughout the war.

As with the Army in general manpower was always the most pressing problem. From the Regiment there was a constant efflux of excellent warrant officers and non-commissioned officers, as they went to bolster up the discipline and standards of the ever-expanding Army; there were few Commands which did not covet these valuable men. In addition 760 men left the ranks of the Regiment to take commissions elsewhere in the Army. Many others were transferred to other corps in which their special qualifications were needed, especially to the Military Police, the Army Physical Training Corps, the Airborne Troops, the Commandos, the Indian Army and to African Regiments. The Regiment also provided a large share of the Railway Transport Officers' Staff at the great London termini. In the face of all these calls the Lieutenant-Colonel had to ensure that there was always an adequate supply of men for despatch to the service Battalions.

Especially was it difficult to maintain the strength of the Battalions in the Mediterranean Theatre. In the Middle East, and later in the Central Mediterranean, a huge military empire had grown up, which swallowed up in a multitude of "jobs" and exotic side-shows many of

[1] For the years 1914–18, the figures were 447 and 12,648.

the reinforcements intended for the Battalions. The records of Regimental Headquarters might show a total of Scots Guards officers and men far exceeding the establishments of the Battalions in the theatre, yet Commanding Officers were constantly in need of suitable men once action had been joined.

The success of the Lieutenant-Colonels throughout the war in surmounting these problems is evidenced by the fact that when in April 1945 the First, Second and Third Battalions all entered the final month's fighting, they did so at full strength. The narrowness of the margin by which this was achieved can be seen by the fact that in Italy the fit reinforcements for the First Battalion amounted to but a score, and in Germany the Second Battalion had to disband one company after four weeks' fighting. At the beginning of May when the war came to an end there was not one fit and fully trained Subaltern officer, infantry or armoured, available at home as a reinforcement.

In December 1943 Colonel Balfour was succeeded in command of the Regiment by Colonel E. D. Mackenzie, C.M.G., D.S.O.; three months previously Major Kinnaird had been succeeded as Regimental Adjutant by Major A. D. B. Pearson. The whole Regiment realised the value of the services which Colonel Balfour and Major Kinnaird had given.[1] Colonel Mackenzie's term of office did not last long, as on the death of his brother, Lieutenant-Colonel Sir Victor Mackenzie he had to resign his appointment for personal reasons. He was succeeded on the 30th May 1944 by Colonel W. H. Wynne Finch, M.C.

By 1944 communications with the Armies overseas had much improved, and the Lieutenant-Colonels managed (for it cannot be said that much assistance was given them from on high) to visit the Battalions in the Mediterranean Theatre. Both Colonel Mackenzie and Colonel Wynne Finch went to Italy, the former going up to the Anzio beach-head to see the First Battalion and to Minturno to see the Second, having previously been to Egypt in order to hunt down "fit men in another army in another continent" who were badly needed in the Battalions.

It was during Colonel Wynne Finch's term of command that Regimental Headquarters suffered its greatest blow. At a quarter past eleven on the morning of Sunday 18th June 1944 a jet-propelled flying bomb (the German V.1) dived onto the Guards' Chapel when it was full of worshippers. By great good fortune the congregation on that Sunday was the smallest it had been for many months, but nevertheless the Regiment suffered sad losses. Lieutenant-Colonel J. M. Cobbold, Lieutenant H. W. Dods, Second-Lieutenant J. A. G. Duberly and two other ranks were among those killed. The Orderly Room and offices

---

[1] The death of Major Kinnaird in 1948, and that of Colonel Balfour in 1955 are recorded with deep regret.

of the Headquarters in Birdcage Walk were wrecked by the blast, but fortunately the valuable collection of medals and relics preserved there was intact. Regimental Headquarters had to be moved to the Records Office in Egginton House, 25 Buckingham Gate, where it remained until it could be moved back to Birdcage Walk after the war. Hardly was the Headquarters established in Egginton House than further damage was sustained on the 23rd June when the next-door house received a direct hit. Despite the destruction of every window, no further move was made.

Thereafter Colonel Wynne Finch commanded the Regiment until the conclusion of hostilities, presiding over the early stages of demobilisation until succeeded on 1st August 1945 by Colonel G. F. Johnson, D.S.O.; and on the 10th July Major Pearson was succeeded as Regimental Adjutant by Major A. D. Murray.

The Band

Throughout the war the Regimental Band was administered from Regimental Headquarters. Under Captain S. Rhodes, the Director of Music, it gave concerts the length and breadth of the United Kingdom, not only to the Regiment, but to a multitude of others as well; it gave frequent broadcasts, and did its share of duty mounting and dismounting the King's Guard, which took place at Buckingham Palace almost without interruption on alternate days throughout the war. In the winter of 1944–45, the Band visited the 21st Army Group in Holland and Belgium, giving many concerts to the troops behind the lines. For this tour all members of the Band received the France and Germany Star. At the conclusion of hostilities the Band was flown to Germany, where it visited Berlin and Hamburg, and took part in the "Farewell to Armour" parade of the Guards Division at Rotenburg. On its way home the Band went to Brussels for the Guards Division's parade commemorating the liberation of that city. Finally, in December 1945 the Band went to Trieste and Pola on the Adriatic, intending to participate in the ceremony at which the First Battalion was to receive its Colours from Home; bad weather prevented the parade, but the entertainment the Band provided was, as always, greatly appreciated.

The Depot

In October 1939 the Recruit Company, K, moved from Caterham to London to join the Chelsea Wing of the Guards Depot which was being formed for the Grenadier and Scots Guards under Major R. A. Abercromby, M.C., of the Regiment. Here it was joined by a new company, L, and in June 1940 by another, J. These early months were a period of hectic activity for the staff, during which the normal recruits' course was at times reduced to eight weeks. In the first fifteen months of the war no less than 2,103 volunteers and 1,021 conscripts were passed through the companies, at an average rate of seven or eight squads a month. By early 1941 the great rush of volunteers had subsided, and the companies moved back to Caterham.

At Caterham K Company proved able to cope with the steady intake of conscripts, but whenever abnormally large numbers were allocated to the Regiment, L Company was temporarily reformed. The recruits' courses in drill and elementary weapon training were punctuated by air-raids and flying bombs; during the attacks of the latter in the summer of 1944 scenes recalling Waterloo were re-enacted, as, on the blast of a whistle, squads lay down in their ranks on the square whenever a diving bomb seemed to threaten their safety. The recruits' period at the Depot was normally sixteen weeks (though later in the war this was reduced to twelve), after which the squads passed out for their advanced weapon training and tactics to the Training Battalion at Pirbright.

III. THE TRAINING BATTALION

The Training Battalion was formed at Pirbright Camp on the 1st September 1939 by Lieutenant-Colonel A. H. C. Swinton, M.C. His Adjutant was Captain I. K. Matheson[1] and his Quartermaster Lieutenant A. Ross; within a few weeks both these had left for other appointments in the Field Force, and were succeeded by Captain A. D. B. Pearson and Lieutenant H. Morley respectively. The Regimental Sergeant-Major was L. C. Archer, M.M., whose name and fame were to spread far beyond the confines of the Regiment, and for the next five years, first as Sergeant-Major and later as Quartermaster, he remained a sure custodian of the traditions and standards of the Scots Guards.

Especially in the early months of the war the strength and organisation of the Battalion were in constant flux. Headquarter and Specialist Company remained throughout the war, but the other companies were frequently changing. At first they were lettered from N to R, N and R being Right and Left Flank respectively, but often companies were in abeyance, or new ones were formed; there was, at one stage, even a Z 2 Company!

From the day of the Battalion's formation the Reservists flooded in, but it must be admitted that when His Majesty the King visited Pirbright on the 12th September he found the arrangements and equipment for their training inadequate. So poorly prepared was the country that for the use of a battalion of 1,200 men there were but five Bren guns and insufficient rifles; for transport there were two staff cars and two commandeered civilian vans. It was with one of

[1] He was killed in action while attached to G.H.Q., B.E.F., on 23rd May 1940.

these, a G.W.R. delivery van, that Captain A. S. H. Drummond-Moray performed a noble service. Sent to the Ordnance Depot at Weedon with authority to draw 2 Bren Guns, by some mysterious stroke of fortune he arrived with authority for the issue of 12 guns, and returned in triumph with his prize. Thus were difficulties solved, as the Army moved out of the era of dummy weapons and of men with flags representing tanks.

In the spring of 1940 the Battalion, which in November had welcomed some three hundred Police reservists, shrank in size and moved to more comfortable quarters. At the end of April nearly half the strength left for the Tower of London to form the Holding Battalion; simultaneously the Training Battalion moved from the antiquated A and B Lines to the new D Lines. The Guardsmen lived in "Spider" huts, which had been intended to house the Militiamen called up under the pre-war conscription measure of 1939. A "Spider" consisted of a central section containing wash-rooms, shower-baths, lavatories, a drying-room and boiler-room (known as "the Ablutions" and forming, as it were, the "body" of the insect), and, radiating from the body and connected to it by covered passages, six barrack rooms disposed in groups of three, each containing about thirty men; in addition there were small cubicles to serve as NCOs' bunks. The Battalion retained this excellent accommodation until its disbandment.

The training of recruits fresh from their grounding in drill and small arms at the Depot was the major task of the Battalion throughout the war. At first there was a grave lack of instructors who could teach the recruits and reservists what modern tactics were about. To this period belongs the celebrated trench system on Tunnel Hill. Here, under the veteran eyes of Captains P. D. S. Waters and R. N. Macdonald-Buchanan, an elaborate layout of defences was dug in the very best style of 1918. Outmoded though these field-works were shortly to be proved, they provided an excellent training ground for day and night exercises, and, above all, in digging. They were much used by the first Canadian Divisions which arrived at Aldershot in the winter of 1939–40; the Canadians seemed to delight in the use of live ammunition in their night exercises. It was a magnificent trench system, but it was not of this war.

The lack of up-to-date battle experience among the instructors was, of course, common throughout the Army, both at home and in the B.E.F. But what they lacked in experience, the instructors made up for in imagination and keenness. New drills and tactics were devised for new problems; tank-hunting, street fighting and camouflage were only three of the special subjects to which new thought was successfully directed. Without a doubt the early training at Pirbright produced highly creditable results, but nevertheless, until the end of the African Campaign in the early summer of 1943, when several wounded officers and NCOs from both Battalions came home, it was very much a case of the blind leading the blind. In the meanwhile, late in 1942, an invaluable institution had been created in the North of England. This was the School of Infantry at Barnard Castle, which started life as the G.H.Q. Battle School. The battle-school movement had its origins in the Divisions which returned from Dunkirk. After the elimination of a few cases of artificial bloodthirstyness, which had attracted unfavourable criticism in Parliament and in the Press, the movement rapidly caught on throughout the Field Army at home; and with the creation of the School at Barnard Castle a common doctrine of infantry tactics could be disseminated throughout the training establishments which were not part of the Field Army. To the School of Infantry went many young officers and NCOs; these returned imbued with the energetic and intensely practical tactics taught there. The new instructors quickly imparted their enthusiasm to the recruits, and there can be little argument that, for young soldiers, no better system of field training could have been devised.

The doctrines of Barnard Castle had their heyday at Pirbright after the disbandment of the Fourth Battalion. For in the autumn of 1943, shortly after Lieutenant-Colonel Swinton had handed over command to Lieutenant-Colonel A. V. C. Douglas, there arrived a body of officers and NCOs who had attended a special course at the School. At the same time the Battalion acquired its own battle-camp at Warren Camp, Llandwrog, near Caernarvon. From there it was possible to motor daily into the mountains of the Snowdon range, and there to carry out most realistic field training with live ammunition for all weapons, which had previously been restricted to the confined field-firing ranges of the South of England. No-one who attended this camp of Nissen huts among the sand-dunes will forget its exhilarating atmosphere. The initial enthusiasm which, as long as hostilities lasted, was never lost, owed much to Major J. S. Sanderson and Captains the Hon. W. H. Vestey and A. S. Neilson. Those who attended it came away with a new confidence in themselves and a new familiarity with their weapons—and they came away fitter physically than they had ever been before.

Besides producing men for the rifle companies of the Battalions, there were also specialists to be trained at Pirbright. Anti-tank gunners, three-inch mortar men, wireless operators, pioneers, carrier and vehicle drivers were all turned out in the quantities estimated to be required in the service battalions. Also, from 1941 onwards, a few men each month had to be sent to the Guards Armoured Training Wing, which, with the Training Battalion of the Coldstream, occupied the older part of the camp. In this Wing they were initiated into the mysteries of the tank before joining the Third Battalion. The men sent for armoured training had to be of the highest quality, and it was with reluctance that the infantry side of the Regiment parted with the best two or three men from each squad.

Endless chores and fatigues burdened the Training Battalion, a chronological catalogue of which would be tedious in the extreme. Over six years a helping hand was given to all who demanded it; activities and recreations were varied and innumerable.

Drill squads from all over the Army; drill courses at Aldershot for Canadians, who were alleged to wear tartan ties and gloves and to have lead weights in their trousers to give a better shape to the over-hang —an energetic period of "marking time" ensuring the removal of the weights before the next parade! The initiation into the military mysteries and jollifications of the crew of H.M.S. *Wallace*, including Sub-Lieutenant Prince Philip of Greece, R.N. (now Admiral of the Fleet H.R.H. the Duke of Edinburgh, K.G., K.T.); the "matelots" when going out of camp reporting to the Sergeant of the Guard as "a few chaps going ashore". Recruiting marches in Scotland; marches in "War Weapons" and "Warships" Weeks' processions. Training the American Squadron of the Home Guard. The attachment of all sorts of people; the First Battalion's friend of the Norwegian campaign, Captain Ellinger; the Regiment's Chinese Officer, Second-Lieutenant Kung. The assault course, the ranges, the forced marches, the night exercises. Pine trees, sand, heath fires. 180-a-side company football on the square; bicycle polo on the square; the Regimental Games in 1941 between the First, Third, Training and Holding Battalions, with the Old Soldiers' race including a Chelsea Pensioner who had taken part in the Egyptian Campaign of 1882; in 1942 shooting for the Quaich presented by Colonel Swinton, with the Scots Guards Association, five battalions and the Depot Company competing. In the same year the pageant presented in the camp theatre to commemorate the Tercentenary of the Raising of the Regiment; film-making for "The Way Ahead", and "standing in" as "extras" for expensive stars in the dangerous parts. The return early in 1944 of three officers and 141 men from the Second Battalion—the "Five Year Men"; the return of the released Prisoners of War at the end of hostilities; the return of thousands of Scots Guardsmen before leaving the Regiment on demobilisation. An Officers' Mess shared with the Coldstream and Armoured Training Wing, full of hordes of newly-joined ensigns and a few gnarled "dugouts", whose stamina was maintained by the catering miracles of Sergeant Callow, Coldstream Guards. The noise of pipes, drums and fifes being played simultaneously under resonant corrugated-iron roofs. The packed trains to and from Brookwood station, and the long walk back to camp in the evening. Hogmanay parties of happy memory. This list gives but a glimpse of the many facets of the Battalion's life.

Two activities must be noted in greater detail.

In the summer of 1942 Right Flank was transformed into the Brigade of Guards Pre-O.C.T.U. Company. Here potential officers for all regiments of the Foot Guards were sent after completing their recruit training at the Depot, and before going on to the Officer Cadet Training Units at Sandhurst and Aldershot. The greater number of the candidates were for the infantry battalions, but there was always a small squad destined for the armoured units, which was administered by Right Flank, but did most of its work in the Armoured Training Wing. The success of the training in Right Flank, which was commanded for most of the time by Major E. R. M. Alston, M.B.E., is evidenced by the fact that, in the first fifteen months of the Pre-O.C.T.U.'s existence, of the 363 candidates who took the tests for entry to the O.C.T.U.s only nine were rejected.

Finally, the Training Battalion played a "cloak and dagger" part in the saga of the war's most notable prisoner. On 10th May 1941 Rudolf Hess, Hitler's Deputy, took it upon himself to descend by parachute in the Borders in a vain and crazy attempt to persuade Britain to make peace with Germany, and thus allow the latter a "free hand" in Europe, particularly against Russia, who was to be attacked six weeks later.

On the 17th Hess had arrived at the Tower and was in the custody of the Holding Battalion; the same day Colonel Sir Geoffrey Cox and Lieutenant-Colonel T. E. G. Nugent (respectively A.A. and Q.M.G., London District, and Brigade Major, Brigade of Guards) came to Pirbright, where they held a conference with Lieutenant-Colonels Swinton and Lord Stratheden, who commanded the Coldstream Training Battalion. To avoid eavesdroppers this took place in the middle of the Officers' Mess croquet lawn. The upshot was that Colonel Swinton was to arrange for the transfer of Hess from the Tower to Mychett Place, a substantial Victorian house near Aldershot. Here a stout entanglement of barbed wire was to be erected, and within it Hess was to be detained under a guard found by the Pirbright Battalions; to deepen the mystery, Mychett was designated "Camp Z". For the next two days three hundred Pioneers laboured at the fence. It was, to quote from Colonel Swinton's diary, all "v. hush-hush".

On the morning of the 20th a party of eight officers set out for London, armed to the teeth with pistols and tommy-guns. They travelled in two private cars, Colonel Swinton driving his own Wolseley containing Lieutenants W. B. Malone, J. McI. Young and P. G. Atkinson-Clark, together with Captain H. H. E. M. Winch in his Lincoln, carrying three Coldstream officers. On arrival at Headquarters London District, Lecconfield House, another conference was held, at which the full horror of the responsibility which they alone were to bear dawned on the senior officers: it was all so "v. hush-hush" that even the Police had not been informed. After the conference Colonel

1. HIS ROYAL HIGHNESS ALBERT, DUKE OF YORK
24th Colonel of the Regiment 1932–1936
and later as
HIS MAJESTY KING GEORGE VI
Colonel-in-Chief 1936–1952

This photograph, taken in 1933, is reproduced by Gracious Permission of Her Majes

2. In the snow with Major H. L. Graham's force near Salangen, April 1940; Lieutenant Rose, Captain Crabbe and Guardsman Wilkie on skis

NORWAY

3. The retreat to Bodö. Men of the First Battalion marching back near Naevernes, 19th May 1940

Swinton held an order group *alfresco* in Hyde Park, the eight officers concerned being seated in a circle on park chairs near Stanhope Gate. Captain Winch was to reconnoitre the route, the selection of which was complicated by the damage caused to the City by the latest series of air-raids. Fortified by luncheon, the conspirators were to set out from the Tower at half-past two.

"At 2.30 p.m. the peace and quietness of the Liberties of the Tower were disturbed by the arrival of a Colonel in a red hat who drove up to the north door of the Governor's House, followed by an ambulance. As a result all idle eyes saw the placing of a stretcher in the ambulance, and its departure followed by the Wolseley." From Tower Wharf Captain Winch led the way in his Lincoln, over Tower Bridge, through Camberwell and Wandsworth, round the Kingston By-pass to Esher, Guildford and the Hog's Back, and on through Tongham and Ash Vale. There were moments of intense unease whenever some innocent on his lawful occasions got between the escort and the ambulance; those in the Wolseley gripped their tommy-guns, set their jaws, and narrowed their eyes in the best Chicago-Hollywood fashion. At a quarter to six the convoy arrived at Mychett and safety; Colonel Swinton and his "gang" had successfully taken the Deputy Führer "for a ride".

For the next ten months Hess was honoured to be guarded by what he called officers of "His Majesty's own bodyguard"; but in February 1942 he was consigned to the care of the Pioneer Corps, and another of the Training Battalion's fatigues was at an end.

In the spring of 1945 Lieutenant-Colonel the Viscount Dalrymple succeeded Colonel Douglas in command, and under him the Battalion carried out its last duties of receiving men for demobilisation and the Third Battalion for disbandment, and taking part in the arrangements for the Victory Parade in London. On 16th July 1946 it was disbanded, and absorbed into No. 2 Guards Training Battalion, under the command of Lieutenant-Colonel E. R. Hill, Coldstream Guards.

IV. THE HOLDING BATTALION

At the end of April, 1940, a large detachment of the Training Battalion moved from Pirbright and Northwood to relieve the 2nd Welsh Guards of the duties at His Majesty's Tower of London. On 1st May Lieutenant-Colonel E. D. Mackenzie arrived to take over command of what, from that day, had become the Holding Battalion, and two days later his Adjutant, Lieutenant the Lord Robert Crichton-Stuart, mounted the Battalion's first King's Guard from the square of Wellington Barracks. "We think it best not to tell the First Battalion," records their diary, "but this Guard was referred to as the best seen

1940

since the beginning of the War." From then on there were few tasks, ranging from the manning of fire hoses to the shooting of spies which did not come the Battalion's way.

At the end of May they were called upon to provide embarkation officers on the beaches of Dunkirk, and the Commanding Officer, Captain R. D. M. Gurowski, and Second-Lieutenants R. G. Rowe and R. H. Bull went out by motor-launch from Dover. After completing their duties they all returned safely, save for Captain Gurowski, who was killed when the ship in which he was a passenger was bombed off Dunkirk. Well known as a leading Army boxer and bayonet-fighter, his death was a severe blow to the Regiment.[1]

The critical situation of the country and the likelihood of invasion called for a more tactical organisation than is usually to be seen in a battalion stationed in the Tower. A "tank-hunting" platoon and a Vickers machine-gun platoon were added to the Battalion's four rifle companies, and in July an armoured element was provided. Two "Peerless" armoured cars, which had first run in 1915, and were reputed to have been in action in the Great War, and to have patrolled the streets in the General Strike, composed this formidable force. Each weighed seven and a half tons, and it is said that the marks they made on the ancient walls of the Middle and Byward Towers as they squeezed in and out can be identified to this day.

In June and July the Battalion manned the defences of Whitehall. At first they took up their positions by night only, but as the danger of invasion grew, the posts were permanently occupied. Companies were sent to such salubrious spots as the southern end of the Blackwall Tunnel, and to guard Kenley Aerodrome. Here on the 18th August were won the first decorations ever awarded to the Regiment for gallantry under fire in the United Kingdom. About thirty low-flying enemy aircraft came in five successive waves. The Detachment Headquarters building was hit and demolished by the first bomb, burying Second-Lieutenant J. D. K. Hague beneath its debris. Once extricated, despite considerable pain from a crushed shoulder, he immediately visited his posts and discovered that in one place burning petrol was forcing the men from the cover of their trenches. Collecting them together into two parties he at once lead them across the open to another shelter one hundred yards away, defying the blast of ten more bombs, which dropped within a few yards of him, and continuous machine-gun fire from the attacking aircraft. Nine Guardsmen were wounded in this attack but heavier casualties were undoubtedly saved by Hague's prompt and gallant action, for which he was awarded the Military Cross. Meanwhile in the face of machine-gun fire from three

[1] Another Scots Guards officer well-known in his particular sport died of wounds received in that campaign; this was Captain M. D. C. Hanbury-Tracy, a leading exponent of the art of *jiu-jitsu*.

aircraft, Lance-Corporal J. Miller maintained his Lewis gun in action to such effect that he shot down one of them, while Lance-Corporal J. Gale, having been blown up by a bomb which broke two of his ribs, rescued a wounded man from the wreck of the Detachment Headquarters and carried him across open ground under fire to safety. They both received the Military Medal.

One week later London had its first long night air-raid and on the 28th the first incendiary bomb fell on the Tower, causing no damage but a great deal of excitement. From then onwards air-raid alarms and bombing became a constant feature of the Battalion's life.

On 10th September the Company-in-Waiting was called out to Cheapside and then on to the Minories, where they saw the Prime Minister, and on the next night they were out again fighting fires at St. Catherine's Dock. On the 16th incendiary bombs set fire to the warehouses on Tower Hill and several high explosives fell uncomfortably close. It was not until 23rd September, during an "Alert" which lasted from dusk to dawn, that any fell on the Tower itself. One, which dropped on the Hospital block, killed Guardsman McKee and wounded two others; the other bomb, which struck empty Warders' quarters, caused no casualties. The luckiest night was that of 1st October, when three 500-lb. bombs fell within the Tower, two almost on top of the Institute block which at the time was full of men. None was hurt, nor were any casualties caused by nine more bombs which fell in and around the Tower during the remainder of the month.

But the Blitz was only the background to the Battalion's proper task: that of providing drafts of trained men when required by the Service Battalions. Men were constantly being assembled for the long sea voyage round the Cape to the Second Battalion in Egypt, and the formation of the Third Battalion in November had disposed of the Kenley detachment, though this was soon replaced by one at Enfield, and later by a guard on Headquarters of Fighter Command at Stanmore. To maintain these detachments, freshly trained men were weekly arriving from the Training Battalion at Pirbright.

The assaults of winter nights left their marks in and around the Tower. On the 8th December twenty-six incendiaries fell in the fortress, and seven high explosives fell within two hundred yards of the Moat, one killing Guardsman Reeve just outside the Wicket Gate. Two more which dropped in the river drenched the Wharf sentries. On the 29th came the Great Fire Raid on the City, during which many thousands of incendiaries fell all round the Tower, and acres of warehouses and offices were devastated. In the Tower itself, one fell on King's House; it was extinguished by Colonel Carkeet James, the Resident Governor, with the aid of Second-Lieutenants Sir Hal Astley-Corbett and C. R. S. Buckle, while another came through the roof of the Officers' Mess and landed on a bed in one of the servant's rooms, where it also was quickly extinguished. Two or three which fell on the roof of Institute block were not so easy to deal with, and owing to the low tide in the river and lack of pressure in the hydrants, the whole block and the NAAFI store of 500,000 cigarettes went up in smoke. As a result the Sergeants' Mess were unable to hold their Hogmanay party.

1941

In January the raids abated, and until their recrudescence in the early spring, life was less troubled. All through the Blitz the Ceremony of the Keys—the nightly locking of the Tower gates—was carried out without interference, but on April 16th for the first and only time there was a slight check. As they were approaching the Middle Tower, the Chief Warder with the Keys and Escort heard the scream of a falling bomb, and a few seconds later the party was flung to the ground by its blast. However, no-one was hurt and, picking themselves up, the command "Escort to the Keys—by the centre—Quick March" was given, and the ceremony proceeded as if nothing had happened. The last serious raid before the Luftwaffe left for the Russian campaign, and that in which the House of Commons was destroyed, came on the 10th May; the Tower was fortunate, the Battalion suffered no casualties, but the Tailor's Shop went up in flames.

On the 17th May the Battalion received its most valuable prisoner. It was no rare occurrence to have some strange captive in the Tower; already there had been a miscellaneous collection of seedy aliens, and a Free French officer who had been awarded "fourteen days in a fortress" by General de Gaulle. But the new charge was unique. He was Rudolph Hess, the Führer's deputy, who had flown himself to the Borders in a misguided enterprise to point out to Britain how much wiser she should be to assist Germany against Russia. For three days he was incarcerated in King's House, where he scribbled on reams of paper provided by the Orderly Room, until his removal, in the manner previously described, to Mychett and the tender care of the Training Battalion.

Another German left the Tower in a manner more in keeping with the mediæval history of that grim place of arms. At Breakfast Roll Call Parade on the 14th August, a firing party was detailed, was quickly marched to the Miniature Range, and as expeditiously shot Josef Jakobs, the first spy to be executed in England during the war.

1942

At this time the Battalion reached its maximum strength of over one thousand four hundred, but it fell rapidly when the Fourth Battalion was formed in September, and this event marked the beginning of the Battalion's decline. On 30th March it paraded at the Tower for the last time and marched under Major J. E. M. Bland to Chelsea Barracks, which it was to share for the next twenty months with a detachment of Military Police.

That summer the Battalion was allowed to venture out of London to train. In May it moved to Ilford for a month's field training, living very comfortably in temporary quarters in Valentine's Park, where Lieutenant-Colonel Bland succeeded Colonel Mackenzie as Commanding Officer. The Battalion returned to Chelsea by "march-route" on 9th June, marching past the Lord Mayor of London at the Mansion House on the way. During September it left London again, this time for Carnforth in North Lancashire, where it went under canvas at Readwell Inn Camp, "better described as a snipe bog". Good weather and extremely hospitable inhabitants made their stay most enjoyable, and after some exhilarating training on the moors, it returned to Chelsea in mid-October.

For the next twelve months the Battalion shrank slowly smaller and smaller, until in May, they "dismounted King's Guard for the last time owing to the fact that every able-bodied officer and man has been picked for draft overseas and there are none to fill their places". In August two officers and 148 men left for the Middle East, taking with them all the Battalion's Pipers and Drummers except two. On the 1st November the remnants marched to Wellington Barracks, where they became a company of the Westminster Garrison Battalion, which found the Public Duties for the rest of the war. There were no more reinforcements to take care of, and the Holding Battalion was formally disbanded.

1943

PART IV

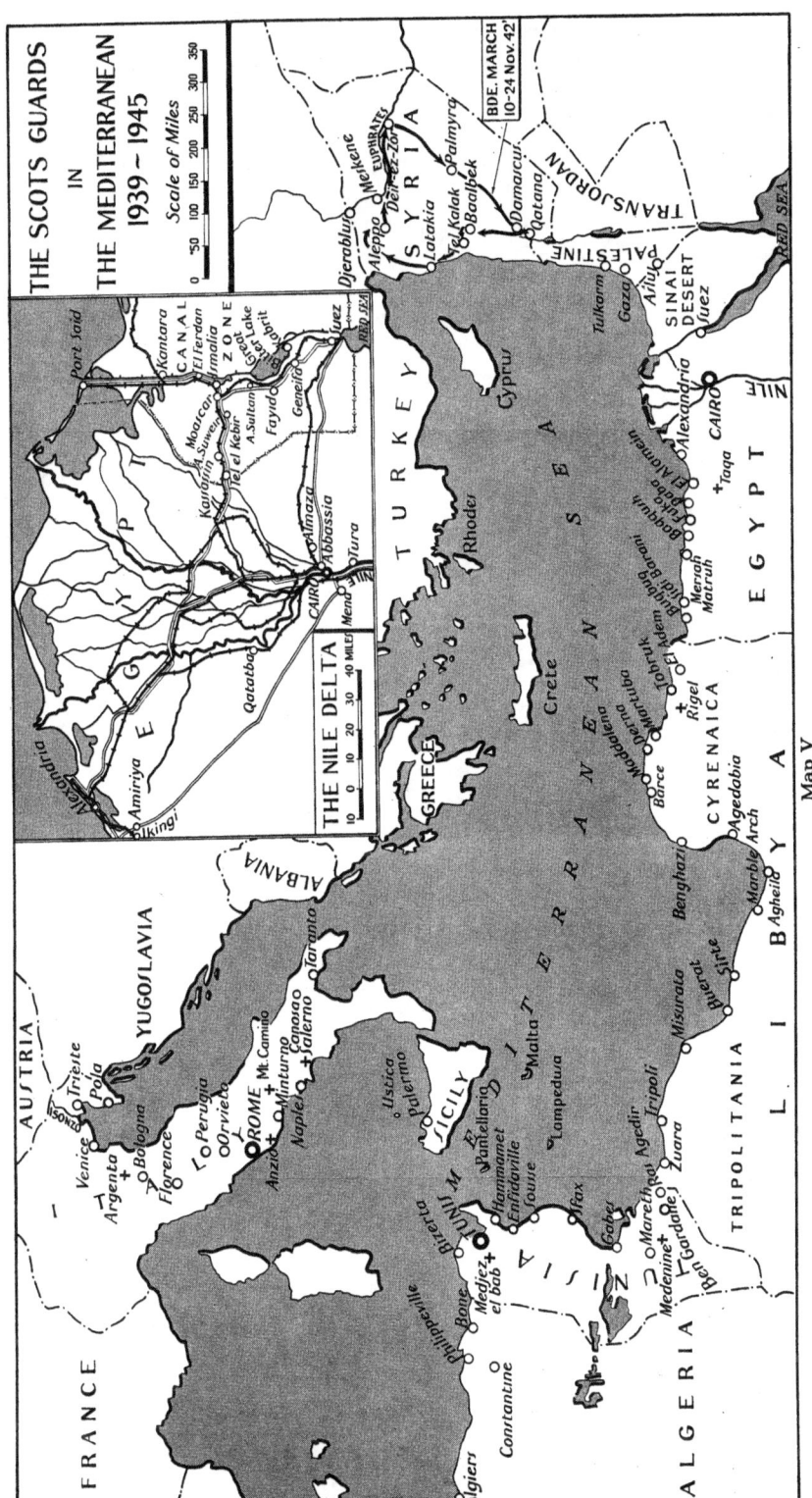

Map V

Africa: 1939–1943

IN the struggle for North Africa, in which the British Army won immortal glory and received grievous wounds, the Scots Guards played a worthy part.

First in the field was the Second Battalion. Denied a share in the early successes against the Italians, it entered the desert in April 1941 when the Germans for the first time appeared at the gates of Egypt. On the Frontier it fought in the abortive summer attacks, and then in November, newly organised as a motor battalion, it took part in General Cunningham's fiercely contested advance, which relieved Tobruk and drove the Germans back to Agheila.

MAP V

From there, the limit of our advance, the Battalion had to execute a hasty withdrawal to the Gazala Line when Rommel advanced in January 1942. In the great battle of Gazala in June of that year the Battalion suffered heavily on Rigel Ridge, north-west of the strongpoint of Knightsbridge, when the companies and anti-tank platoons were overrun by the tanks of the 21st Panzer Division. Reduced to amalgamate into a composite battalion with the 3rd Coldstream, the remnants spent July in the defence of the Alamein positions, to which the Eighth Army had been forced back. After holding this "last ditch" in front of Alexandria, the Battalion was withdrawn to the Delta. It had been in the desert for sixteen months, and in September with the rest of the 201st Guards Brigade was sent to Syria to reform, rest and train.

After the battle of Alamein had been fought and won, the Second Battalion was again called upon in February 1943. An approach march of over two thousand miles along the North African shore brought it—and its 6-pounder anti-tank guns—in the nick of time to Medenine in Southern Tunisia, where revenge was taken on the tanks of the 21st Panzer Division in "a model anti-tank battle". Thereafter it followed up the Eighth Army, through Mareth to Enfidaville, where the advance was stayed at the end of April.

Meanwhile in early March 1943 the First Battalion from home had landed at Algiers as part of the 1st Infantry Division. From there it had gone by sea to Bône and entered the First Army's line at Medjez-el-Bab on the 20th March. After a month's positional warfare, it fought a gruelling fortnight's battle in the great offensive which ended the war in Africa. On the slopes of Gebel Bou Aoukaz on the 27th April Captain the Lord Lyell won the Regiment's only Victoria Cross of the war, in the first stages of the attack which resulted in the opening of the road to Tunis.

When this road had been opened, the Second Battalion, which had been brought round with several Eighth Army formations from the southern front, took part in the final thrust for Tunis, and ended its African adventures by advancing across the neck of the Cape Bon peninsula to Hammamet.

This, in outline, was the Regiment's part in the African war, a war which ended in the annihilation of the enemy. The exciting stories of many individual Scots Guards officers and men who took part in the plethora of small operations and escapades to which the Mediterranean and its surrounding lands lent themselves, are not strictly within the scope of this history. But mention must be made of two organisations in particular.

L.R.D.G.

Perhaps the most remarkable detachment of Guardsmen in the whole war was G (Foot Guards) Patrol of the Long Range Desert Group, which was formed in December 1940 of volunteers from the Second Battalion and the 3rd Coldstream; it was disbanded over two years later when the Desert war was ended.

The Patrol, for which the Regiment found one officer and eighteen men, first went into action on 11th January 1941, under the command of Captain M. D. D. Crichton-Stuart, in a raid on Murzuk fort, the chief garrison of the Fezzan, in south-west Libya. Later in the same operation a New Zealand patrol was ambushed, and Guardsman J. Easton, who was with them, was wounded and left behind; alone, he marched nearly two hundred miles before he was found by some French soldiers, in whose hands he died of exposure. He was the first Scots Guardsman to give his life in North Africa, and the story of his gallantry was broadcast from Cairo Radio and published in Regimental Orders.

This first patrol crossed the whole Western Desert, Libya and northern French Equatorial Africa; it assisted the then Colonel Leclerc in his attack on the Kufra Oasis, the first French operation against the enemy since the fall of France; and it returned to Cairo via the Sudan, with forty-five days of beard on its faces and 4,300 miles behind it. These amazing figures were challenged by G Patrol's final operation two years later, when, under Lieutenant the Hon. B. Bruce, it covered 3,500 miles in thirty-seven days. That patrol started from Hon Oasis in Tripolitania, crossed southern Tunisia, by-passing the Mareth Line: beat off two attacks by Arabs in the best Beau Geste style, entered Algeria, and made the first contact between the First and Eighth Armies. It returned by Fort Flatters, a French Foreign Legion outpost in the Sahara.

But between these two somewhat fabulous extremes there was much valuable work of a less spectacular character. G Patrol was divided into two halves operating independently, one under the command of Captain J. A. L. Timpson; Coldstreamers, Scots Guardsmen and, later, Grenadiers, were represented in each half. Nearly all their operations during the fifteen months of advance and retreat were concerned with the coastal road, the sole artery on land of Rommel's supplies. They took their full share in raiding and sabotage, but their most notable work was probably the Road Watch—"the best thing L.R.D.G. ever did". Night and day, for weeks on end, close beside the road far into enemy territory, they kept an unbroken descriptive tally of every vehicle which passed. Daily their report was wirelessed to Cairo, to become the most reliable and valuable source of intelligence to the Middle East Command. When the enemy came to be aware of those dangerous unseen eyes, they did all they could to hunt them down; in consequence the Patrol's last road watch combined adventure and endurance in a high degree.

Special Forces

G Patrol worked frequently with Colonel A. D. Stirling, D.S.O., the outstanding Scots Guards figure in these outlandish operations. Founder of the Special Air Service, which was formed initially from the disbanded Household Brigade Commando, he became, until his betrayal and capture in January 1943, the terror of German airfields and transport behind the lines. It is remarkable that the exploits which Colonel Stirling planned and led probably accounted for more enemy aircraft than did those of any of the famous Allied air "aces".

Finally, mention should be made of two officers who gave their lives while serving away from the Regiment. In June 1942 Captain R de M. Grant-Watson was drowned in an attempt to rescue enemy pilots who had been shot down in Gazala Bay; and Captain T. C. D. Russell, M.C., who had greatly distinguished himself in the combined raid on Tobruk in September 1942, was killed a year later while on a mission in Roumania.

I. THE SECOND BATTALION

(a) *Eighteen Months' Wait*

The Second Battalion, under the command of Lieutenant-Colonel J. C. O. Marriott, C.V.O., D.S.O., M.C., had been in Egypt just eight months when, at 0030 hours on 23rd August 1939, it received orders to leave Kasr el Nil Barracks, Cairo, and move to war stations in the Western Desert. It entrained at 0600 hours the following morning, and that evening, after passing on the way places to become both

MAP V
1939

familiar and famous—Alamein, Daba, Baqqush—settled down at Matruh to the first of its many wartime nights in the desert. It was already familiar ground to the majority of the Battalion which had been at Matruh for a few weeks early in the year, and three companies in turn had been stationed there since June, and a reconnaissance party, the object of keen suspicion to the Italians, had made an expedition to the frontier at Sollum, where it was accused of going thirty yards into Libya.

The Battalion occupied positions on a two company front at the western end of the perimeter, on the white sand dunes between the sea and the desert proper, and work was at once begun on building defences, of which there were none on this sector. Leave parties from Alexandria and the United Kingdom, the latter crossing the Mediterranean on the deck of H.M.S. *Shropshire*, rejoined the Battalion, and by the declaration of war on 3rd September, the Battalion had settled down to a vigorous routine in which sports and daily bathes in sea or salt lake combined with training to get the Battalion thoroughly acclimatised to the new conditions. The breathing space was valuable, and full advantage was taken of it. But, in Egypt as in France, for the moment it remained a "phoney" war, as there was no enemy in sight.

During November the rains broke, and while the palms swayed like great plumes in the bitter wind the sudden rush of waters flooded the camp, some of the tents being submerged almost up to their canvas eaves. Simultaneously the Battalion read in the newspapers that a Member was asking in Parliament why we had "crack troops basking in the Mediterranean sunshine". A suitable Christmas Card was drawn and sent to him by Lieutenant T. L. Ballantine Dykes on behalf of the Battalion. The stay at Matruh lasted for six months, but it was a Battalion that had "changed from boys to young men", each of whom knew his role on active service and had experienced the cold and rain and dust storms as well as the sun of the Desert, that in March handed over the Matruh defences to the Highland Light Infantry and returned to garrison duties in and about Cairo.

The early summer passed under the burden of increasing guard duties in the heat of Cairo or in Abbassia or at the Tura Caves, and the demands on the Battalion were such that training was virtually impossible. The situation was summed up in an entry in the Battalion Diary for May: "Duty numbers required 294; Numbers available 288; Deficient 6." But somehow fragmentary training was achieved. On 15th May the Commanding Officer left for a Staff appointment—later to command Infantry Brigades in the Sudan—and Major P. H. Catt took over command for a month until the arrival of Lieutenant-Colonel I. D. Erskine. On 10th June Italy declared war, and while the Battalion still sweltered in Cairo the 3rd Coldstream had its first taste of desert fighting on the frontier. To join the Western Desert Force was the predominant wish of all ranks, but they had to remain content with spasmodic training whenever possible—and bear patiently with the eternal duties. The arrival of a substantial draft in September was a welcome reinforcement; it was long overdue, for it had started overland in March, had detrained at Le Mans where it had helped prepare defences, and eventually reached Egypt by way of Marseilles, Ayrshire and Aintree. But still the Battalion was out of the fight.

In December the envy of the Coldstream was at its height; for the Scots Guards had no part in the brilliant victory on the frontier in which "Wavell's Thirty-thousand" destroyed the Italian Army in Cyrenaica, and began the first of the great advances westward—and eastwards—which were to become so prominent a feature of the war in North Africa.

At last, in January 1941, the move from Cairo came. But it was only to employment on A.A. defence of the Canal, where the Battalion fired its first shots at Germans and was responsible for perhaps the longest line ever held by a single battalion; security was poor, and the Battalion were bombed without hurt on the first night in their new camp. On 11th February Lieutenant-Colonel I. D. Erskine handed over command of the Battalion to Major P. C. H. Grant pending the arrival of his successor, and on the 26th the Battalion moved into camp near Kassassin (where the First Battalion had been prior to the advance on Tel el Kebir in 1882), a suitable area for company training, and, it seemed, the first stage on its way to the Western Desert.

1941

Lieutenant-Colonel B. Mayfield arrived to take over the Battalion on 6th March, later than had been hoped, as his voyage took two months, but earlier than it might have been, for "it was too rough to disembark on arrival, according to the Navy, but thanks to the initiative of the younger officers, we hired a tug, got a good wetting and escaped from the ships some three days before anyone else, all for £E1." Training was pushed on—a forty-mile march on hard rations and two nights out with no blankets formed part of the programme—and the Battalion took its place in the newly formed 22nd Guards Brigade under Brigadier I. D. Erskine, its former Commanding Officer; the other two battalions were the 3rd Coldstream and the 1st Durham Light Infantry. Writing just three weeks after his arrival, Colonel Mayfield used words which strangely echoed those of the Earl of Rothes, Captain-General of Scotland, after inspecting four companies of the Regiment 256 years earlier: "I must say that in all my life I never saw better bodies of men, nor better disciplined". "If physical fitness, good discipline, and keenness have anything to do with it," the new Commanding Officer wrote, "the results should be creditable." But there was to be a further disappointment, and for a time the Battalion was at Kabrit, on the Great Bitter Lake, training in bitter cold as part of the 6th Division for a combined operation against the island of Rhodes.

(b) *Summer in the Desert*

Mar. 31   Suddenly on the 31st March, the Germans, led by Rommel, burst upon the African scene. With a speed and daring which took the British—and the German—High Command by surprise, the Afrika Korps overran the weak 2nd Armoured Division in Western Cyrenaica, by-passed the 9th Australian Division in Tobruk, and was making for the frontier. The position was truly desperate, for the 7th Armoured Division was refitting in the Delta, and many of our best Imperial troops and much of our modern equipment had been sent to Greece. The plans for the attack on Rhodes went by the board; the 22nd Guards Brigade was rushed to Matruh, where it arrived on the

April 8   8th April.[1] After many moves the Battalion found itself in position some five miles to the west of Sidi Barrani, and here, on the night of

April 19   the 19th it sustained its first fatal casualty, when Lieutenant H. J.
MAP VI   Stirling was killed on patrol while under instruction with another regiment.

May   By the middle of May, General Gott, who commanded on the frontier, felt himself strong enough to see if he could force the Germans back beyond Tobruk before they could bring up their newly landed 15th Panzer Division. He had the 7th Armoured Brigade, with fifty-five tanks, and the 22nd Guards Brigade.

May 13   On the 13th, after one abortive move, the Battalion handed over its positions at Alam el Dab to the Coldstream, and started its move up the 600-foot high escarpment and westwards to take part in its first attack; it was carried in trucks from the 4th Indian Division. The 22nd Guards Brigade was to advance from Sofafi to the area Musaid–Bir Weir–Capuzzo, and then, if it should be practicable, exploit northwards to Bardia. The 2nd Battalion the Rifle Brigade was to conform along the coastal plain to Sollum village and barracks, while the 7th Armoured Brigade was to operate wide on the western flank to Sidi Azeiz and, if possible, to the Capuzzo–Bardia road. The start line at

May 15   Alam Battuma was crossed at 0600 on the 15th, and C Squadron 4th Royal Tank Regiment moved off to the first objective, the top of Halfaya Pass, and G Company (Major C. A. R. Coghill) was sent after it to mop up and consolidate. The remainder of the Battalion followed the tanks, and after about five miles Right Flank (Captain J. D. C. S. MacRae) came upon a large enemy camp and vehicle park surrounded by a three-foot wall. The enemy was so demoralised by the passage of the tanks that negligible resistance was offered and a general surrender took place as soon as the Company opened fire. Three hundred and twenty prisoners, half of them German, were taken, and after twenty minutes the Company re-embussed and pushed on to occupy the

[1] For Order of Battle, see p. 548.

second objective, the road triangle round Musaid. Here, also, but slight resistance was met, a few more prisoners were taken, and, though later shelled, the Company suffered no casualties. In the meantime F Company (Captain G. C. Rush), after having two men slightly wounded in an unexpected meeting with eight enemy tanks, pushed on and occupied Bir Weir without further loss. The task of Left Flank (Captain the Hon. T. W. E. Coke, M.V.O.), with the help of three carriers, was to mop up and consolidate eastwards to Sollum Barracks. When approaching the barracks the Company came under heavy fire from three machine-gun posts. These were quickly charged and silenced by the carriers under Sergeant F. Riley, which then came under fire from two anti-tank guns. One Guardsman was killed and one carrier put temporarily out of action, but, although his own carrier was hit three times, Sergeant Riley's second charge was also successful and the gun crews surrendered and the advance continued. The Company was in an exposed position at the time, and there is no doubt that Sergeant Riley's speed and dash saved it from suffering heavy casualties; he was awarded the Military Medal, the first decoration for gallantry to be won by the Battalion in the war.

Early the following morning the Battalion was withdrawn—just in time, for a strong force of German tanks swept through its previous position two hours later. It took up a defensive position extending from the foot of Halfaya Pass to the sea, and on the 18th it was relieved by the Coldstream and withdrew to a position south-east of Sidi Barrani. "So ended an action which, even if it did not as a whole fulfil hopes and expectations, the Battalion could look back upon with every satisfaction. All objectives were reached in convincing manner. Casualties suffered were gratifyingly small, namely one killed and four, including Captain P. F. Fane Gladwyn, wounded, figures which paid high tribute to the training of the men. As against these losses, no fewer than 17 German and Italian officers and 385 other ranks were taken prisoner, while the enemy also lost a number killed." Various factors contributed to the almost costless success of the Battalion: careful planning and close co-operation with the tanks, surprise (at least one enemy officer was in bed), and the speed and vigour of the attack itself.

But other units had had a much less favourable time. At the bottom of Halfaya Pass an Italian position held out against the Rifle Brigade, who had no tanks, for the greater part of the day; and the Durham Light Infantry in the Capuzzo area, who lost touch with their tanks and were heavily counter-attacked, lost 11 officers and 185 other ranks. The superiority of the German tank guns over ours had been clearly demonstrated, and the punch of the 88-mm. gun had been felt for the first time.

For a month the Battalion rested, while preparations were made for

May 16

May 18

June

a more ambitious attempt. At the instigation of the Prime Minister a convoy carrying over 250 tanks was hurried through the short and dangerous Mediterranean passage instead of ambling slowly round the Cape; the arrival of this valuable reinforcement at Alexandria enabled a more formidable armament to be assembled in the Western Desert. Lieutenant-General Beresford-Peirse planned to attack with the 11th Indian Brigade along the coast at Halfaya—which had been lost to the Germans on 27th May; along the top of the Escarpment he sent the 4th Armoured Brigade, the 22nd Guards Brigade and the Headquarters of the 4th Indian Division under Major-General Messervy to take Halfaya and Sollum in the rear, and to take Bardia. The 7th Armoured Brigade and the Armoured Division's Support Group under Major-General Creagh he ordered to operate on the left flank. The code-name given to the venture was *Battleaxe*. The object was the repulse of Rommel.

June 14

June 15

At 0105 on 14th June the Battalion left Abar el Arawe, near Sidi Barrani, for the Brigade assembly area at Sofafi, and at 0515 the following day the advance began. The Battalion, less Left Flank which was in front, moved off behind Brigade Headquarters with the 3rd Coldstream on the right and the 1st Buffs, who had replaced the Durham Light Infantry, on the left. About three hours later, when near Rueibit el Warani, gunfire was heard from the direction of Halfaya and at 0900 hours at Qaret Abu Faris, Left Flank (Captain R. A. Orr-Ewing) with one section of carriers was detached to help the 4th R.T.R. to capture Point 206. This attack had to be postponed, for the first tank attack had been repulsed with a loss of two tanks destroyed and others damaged, and it was necessary to await reinforcements. Fourteen more tanks eventually arrived, and at 1900 the attack went in, the carriers following 300 yards behind the tanks, and Left Flank fifty yards behind the carriers. This time the attack was successful. Six officers and 220 other ranks, all German, were captured. No casualties were suffered by Left Flank.

In the meantime much had been happening elsewhere. Capuzzo had fallen to the Buffs and the tanks, the Bir Weir area had been occupied by the Coldstream, and about 1500 the first vehicles of the Battalion had crossed the frontier wire at B.P.43. Here a halt was made and the Battalion suffered its first casualty, Captain H. Knight being mortally wounded by a 50-mm. ricochet. The Headquarters of the 4th Indian Division, of the 4th Armoured Brigade, and of the 22nd Guards Brigade were all clustered together round the wire—fourteen wireless masts were counted in a circle—and the Battalion was situated round them. In the ensuing air attacks several casualties were suffered, Second-Lieutenant A. J. Coats being among the wounded, and whilst passing through the wire after the forward companies, Battalion Headquarters and the rest of the Battalion, except Left Flank, was

4. DESERT RUFFIANS G Patrol of the Long Range Desert Group taken at Kharga Oasis in February 1941 after its first patrol which lasted forty-five days. In the centre are Sheik Abd el Gelil Seif el Nasr and his slave "Midnight"; on the Sheik's right is Captain M. D. D. Crichton-Stuart, Scots Guards, and on "Midnight's" left is Lieutenant M. A. Gibbs, Coldstream Guards. Among the Scots Guardsmen in the group are Lance-Sergeant Roebuck, Corporal Jones, Guardsmen M. Fraser (later M.M.), Pratt, Finlay, Fernbank, Cheetham, Robertson and Wallace

5. THE WHITE SANDS OF MERSAH MATRUH Lieutenant H. J. Stirling's platoon at work on the Three Palms position, September 1939. Note that sun-helmets are still being worn

6. DESERT ORDER GROUP   The Officers of G Company Column receiving their orders in the Gazala Line, February 1942. *Left to right:* CSM Gore, Lieutenants Fergusson-Cunninghame and N. H. Barne, Major Coghill and Lieutenant D. S. Robertson

7. ANTI-TANK GUNS ARRIVE FOR LEFT FLANK   Major J. D. B. Drury-Lowe explaining the gun-drill on the 2-pounder Anti-tank gun to H.M. King George II of the Hellenes at Buq Buq, 14th May 1942

"well and truly shot up" by an aeroplane which had taken off from behind Musaid Fort. Several more casualties were suffered, including RSM F. G. Leiper mortally wounded and Guardsman Connor, the Commanding Officer's driver, killed. There were thirty-three bullet holes in the Commanding Officer's car.

The next stage of the advance was to be an attack by the Battalion, supported by tanks and artillery, on Musaid, and shortly before zero hour, 2000, the companies moved into their assembly area near the Coldstream position at Bir Weir. But the tanks and artillery failed to appear, and the Commanding Officer was left with no alternative but to cancel the attack. However, at 2115 orders were received that Musaid was to be taken during the night: no supporting arms were available; the Battalion was to take the position how and when it could. As reports stated variously that Musaid was unoccupied and that it was a well-defended strongpoint, the situation was far from straightforward. The Commanding Officer, however, decided to deal with it in the most straightforward manner possible, by a direct frontal rush. The event was fully to prove the soundness of his judgment.

At 0440, owing to the darkness ten minutes later than the intended time, the advance began. The attacking force, F Company (Captain Rush) and Right Flank (Captain MacRae), were in line in two waves, with Battalion H.Q. in the centre of the first wave. The remainder of the Battalion was to follow up and help in consolidation or in dealing with any protracted resistance.

June 16

All went well for the first seven minutes of the silent advance across the desert, but then a dog barked and went on barking. "It was pretty obvious that the area was occupied. The advance continued. Suddenly a challenge was heard. No answer was given. It was repeated. We were still advancing, when a heavy fire was opened up from Bredas, machine-guns and small-arms. The noise was terrific and the whole line checked instinctively. The aim was inaccurate and most of the stuff went overhead, but there were enough near misses to satisfy everyone, and a few men were hit. After the momentary pause, the line advanced at a steady double through the fire. After doubling seventy-five yards, the outer defences were reached, a few enemy were bayoneted, some shot, others knocked on the head. The companies then rallied, and charged a further thirty yards into an area of stone sangars irregularly spaced. A few more were killed or wounded, but by this time they were well on the run, and many escaped in the half light to Sollum Barracks."

The attack was remarkable in several ways. It was across open country against an unreconnoitred position of unknown strength. The charge was led by the Commanding Officer with rifle and bayonet and smoking a pipe. For a loss of seven wounded a strongly held position was captured, eighteen enemy killed, and twelve wounded and eighty unwounded captured—to say nothing of the dog which gave the alarm; she was "rather like a smooth Labrador bitch"; the other prisoners were Italian; the dog later escaped. And it was all done "without the assistance of tanks, planes, artillery or any other of the normal 'indispensables' of modern warfare." The only people not satisfied were G Company. But their chance was to come, and with their chance those who had escaped from Musaid were to find that Sollum Barracks was but a temporary haven.

At half-past eight in the morning orders were received that Sollum Barracks, about three miles away, was to be taken. Three hours later, preceded by a quarter of an hour's fire by one Field Battery and five Medium Guns, G Company (Major Coghill) set off, singing, in its 3-tonners across the desert. When about 800 yards from the Barracks, inaccurate machine-gun fire and rifle fire opened up from a spur on the right and from the aerodrome tower on the left. The final 600 yards were covered on foot in the face of additional fire from the Barracks and a post on the left, but the mortars gave effective covering fire and no casualties were suffered. Fire increased as the barrack buildings were approached, Company Headquarters receiving particular attention from a light mortar. However, a certain amount of cover was now available, and the attack was pressed home on the various buildings and posts, Company Headquarters taking part in the capture of thirty Italians with light machine-guns and an infantry gun in a post that was enfilading the approaches to the main gate. In this phase of the attack CSM J. Richmond and Guardsman W. M. Millar[1] showed outstanding leadership and initiative and later received respectively the D.C.M. and M.M. With the fall of these posts the defenders lost heart, and all but a few, who held out in cellars and were dealt with by grenades, surrendered when the Company advanced on the main Barracks. Eleven Officers and 209 other ranks, all Italian, were captured and a further thirty killed or wounded. G Company lost two killed and two seriously and four slightly wounded, and after collecting or destroying various stores returned to the Battalion.

The remainder of the day passed fairly quietly so far as the Battalion was concerned. But much was happening elsewhere, and there was a considerable increase of air activity, the Buffs at Capuzzo and the Coldstream at Bir Weir being heavily attacked. Meanwhile, to the south-west, the 4th Armoured Brigade had crossed the frontier wire and captured Bir Hafid and further to the south the 7th Armoured Brigade had captured Sidi Omar. The first phase of the operation had been completed, and a counter-attack from the direction of Bardia on

[1] In the previous October, Millar had saved three New Zealand soldiers from drowning in the flooded Nile at Cairo, and received the Bronze Medal and Certificate of the Royal Humane Society. He was killed in action in Italy on 22nd October 1943.

the Bir Hafid–Capuzzo area was successfully repulsed. But a strong German force of the 5th Light Division from the west then advanced on Sidi Omar, forcing the 7th Armoured Brigade to withdraw towards the east and the 4th Armoured Brigade to move down to meet this new threat to the flank. Before it could engage the enemy, however, it was thought that the whole of the 15th Panzer Division was about to attack southwards against Capuzzo, and the 4th Armoured Brigade had to turn north again. This left the German armour now advancing from the south-west in a position whence it could either advance to relieve their garrison of Halfaya, which was cut off at the top of the pass, or could drive across the whole lines of communication —and, in fact, it had been reinforced by most of the 15th Panzers. The situation had suddenly changed from the eminently satisfactory to the critical, and General Messervy decided on an immediate withdrawal. The Battalion was the last to be withdrawn, and by the time it moved off at midday on the 17th only a narrow corridor remained. It came under shellfire from Halfaya and a heavy tank battle was in progress on the southern flank, but the withdrawal was completed without loss, thanks to the magnificent efforts of the heavily outnumbered 4th Armoured Brigade, and by way of Bir Nuh, Halfway House Pass and Buq Buq the Battalion made its way back to the Sidi Barrani area and then on to the Baqqush Box, near Matruh. June 17

July 3

Battleaxe had failed; the German armour had won the day. Probably they brought 200 tanks into action against our 180; of these the Germans lost only twenty-five totally destroyed, while eighty-seven of ours were missing. Much more extensive preparations must now be made before we could again challenge the enemy and thus relieve Tobruk. Only this indomitable fortress and Rommel's nightmare of supply stood between him and an attempt upon Egypt. The Prime Minister was bitterly disappointed; General Wavell was replaced in command by General Auchinleck.

By the beginning of July, the Battalion was back at Daba being transformed into a Motor Battalion. "Everyone thought we could do it in a fortnight—quite oblivious of the fact that we had to train from scratch at least 40 carrier drivers and 120 motor transport drivers, apart from the fact that all our signallers had to turn themselves into wireless operators. However we completed it all in a month—not too bad—and took over a large piece of country next door to the enemy." Aug.–
Sept.

This was in the Buq Buq area, and the Battalion was divided into three columns, each with its own artillery under command, and known respectively as FAIT[H] (Major Coghill), HOPE (Major Rush) and CHARITY (CHAR for short), composed of Left Flank (Captain Orr-Ewing) and an Australian gunner battery, the whole under command of a Major Johnson of the Australians—the only time a part of the Regiment served under Australian command in the war. It occupied positions overlooked by the enemy in the shelterless triangle of sand and scrub, of which Sollum is the apex, between the sea and the Escarpment. Seepage made it impossible to dig trenches more than about three feet deep, and movement was virtually impossible by day: August days in Libya are very long.

The result was inevitable. "There has been a lot of sickness in the last month, owing to the heat and general living conditions. Buq Buq has nothing to commend it from the hygienic point of view—sixty men evacuated between 1st and 31st August—rather heavy, but almost unavoidable as we live." Desert sores and heat and flies and dust and dirt were unavoidable. Yet "despite all this we are full of confidence. The prestige of the Battalion is alarmingly high—it is about the only unit which has consistently done what has been required of it and this has been realised in high quarters. The alarming part to my mind is that either we climb higher and higher or there is a fall from grace one day." That last was to be avoided.

Meanwhile the work of the Battalion went on: providing carrying parties for minelaying—"our minefields bag our own and the enemy's vehicles without discrimination, the score being about equal"—manning listening and observation posts by day and night; almost incessant patrolling which all too often only gave the wanted identifications to the enemy. For instance CSM J. Forster was killed on the night of the 23rd August when his patrol got into a fixed line.

With one brief interval, and that far from restful, the Battalion remained in contact with the enemy until 24th September. By 1st September a considerable increase in enemy strength, including tanks, had been noticed, and "a large scale raid" was expected. It was a bit of an exaggeration to write that "the fate of the Middle East depends upon 2 S.G.", but the paucity of supporting arms and the general uneasiness that characterised this period were responsible for this attitude. On the evening of the 14th, when increased pressure above as well as below the Escarpment made the thrust appear imminent and an enemy force of a hundred tanks and five or six hundred other vehicles above the Escarpment started to try to encircle the left flank, the order to withdraw was given.

By daylight on the 15th the Battalion was back in new positions near Sidi Barrani, but in the course of the morning it became apparent that the enemy forces on the Escarpment had been withdrawn, and by midnight the Battalion was back in its previous positions. The possible thrust had proved to be but a reconnaissance in force and our withdrawal had been so rapid and well timed that the reconnaissance had made no further contact.

Three nights later on the 18th a sad loss was suffered when Lieutenant the Hon. J. P. Bowes-Lyon, a nephew of Her Majesty Queen

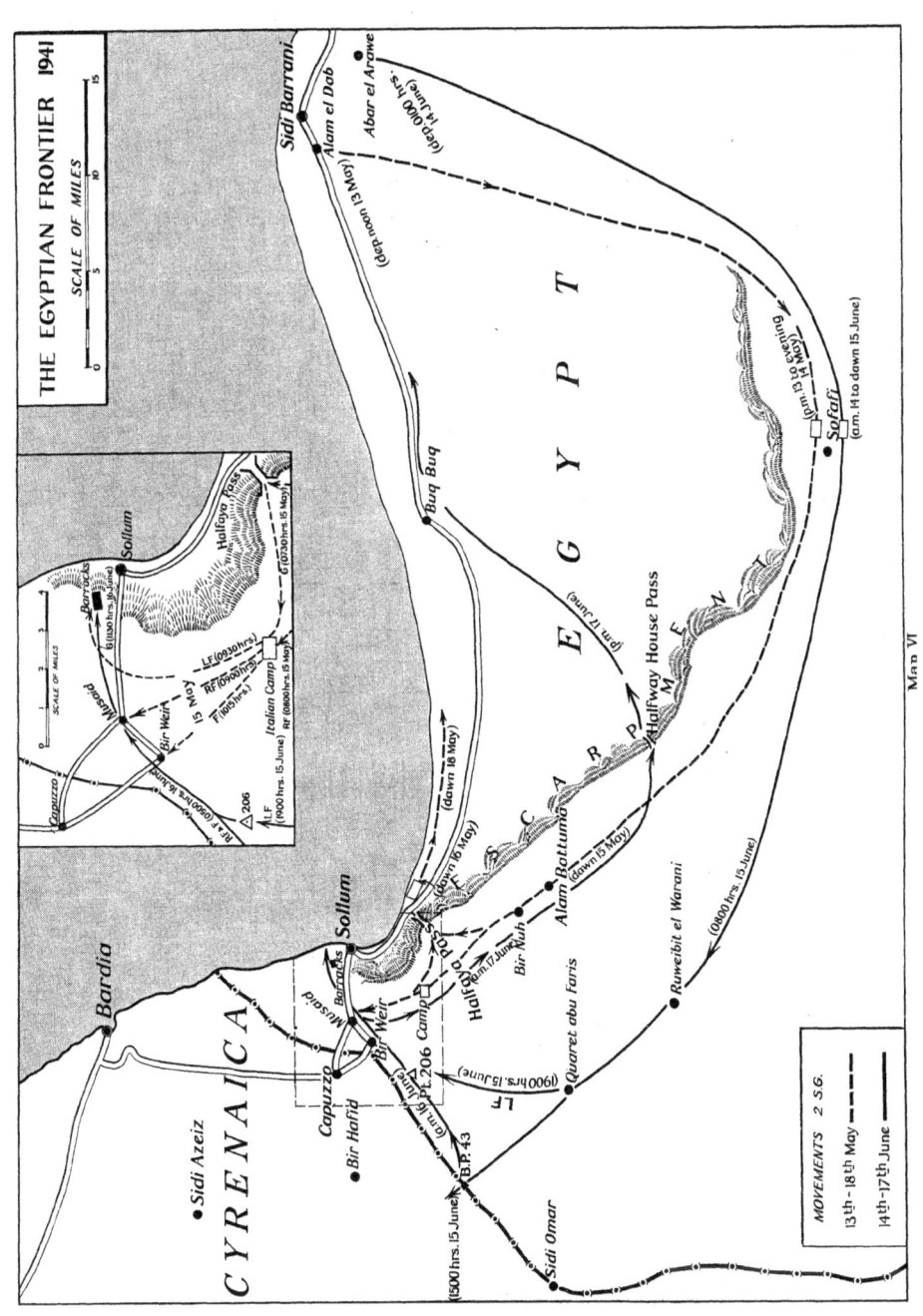

Elizabeth the Queen Mother, was killed while charging an enemy sangar with grenades while on patrol.

On the evening of 24th September the Battalion was withdrawn and on the following afternoon it was back in its old positions at Daba. It was the birthday of the Eighth Army, and a new phase was beginning.

(c) *"Crusader"*

On 20th October Brigadier J. C. O. Marriott relieved Brigadier I. D. Erskine (newly awarded the D.S.O. for his part in *Battleaxe*) in command of the 22nd Guards (Motor) Brigade. There followed a period of training for a new role, and on the 18th November the great offensive *Crusader* began.

The Eighth Army, commanded by Lieutenant-General Sir Alan Cunningham, liberator of Abyssinia, was now organised into two corps. The XIII Corps with the 4th Indian and the New Zealand Divisions and one tank brigade was to attack the German positions on the Frontier, in much the same manner as had been done in the previous offensive; it was then to advance down the Trigh Capuzzo towards Tobruk. But these movements were not to begin until the German armour had been brought to battle. This was the task of the XXX Corps, in which the bulk of our tanks were organised. Lieutenant-General Norrie had the 7th Armoured Division, the 4th Armoured Brigade, the 1st South African Division, and the 22nd Guards (Motor) Brigade. With these he was to cross the frontier well to the south of Maddalena, sweep on northwards towards Sidi Rezegh, engage and destroy the German armour, and relieve Tobruk. The garrison of the fortress was to sally forth into the fight at an opportune moment.

MAP VII

The enemy could field two German armoured divisions, the 15th and 21st, the 90th Light Division, and seven Italian divisions, one of which was armoured. He had fewer tanks, but he had better tanks. He was to lose air superiority, but he had the 88-mm. gun. He was taken by surprise by the opening of the offensive, but he fought a skilful battle and nearly won the day.

The first moves were encouraging; the XXX Corps drove unmolested to the area of Sidi Rezegh. But here it fought a gruelling tank battle on the 21st and 22nd, in which it received harder knocks than it was capable of giving. During this first phase the Battalion was responsible for the protection of B Echelon of the 4th Armoured Brigade; then it was called upon to enter the battle proper. The Commanding Officer described it.

Nov. 18

Nov. 21–22

"Sunday November 23rd was black Sunday for us. We were ordered to join 7 Support Group (Jock Campbell late R.H.A. Commanding) as their two battalions 2 R.B. and 60th had an awful mauling two days previously at Sidi Rezegh aerodrome—the 60th were down to

Nov. 23

8 officers and 170 men and 2 R.B. to $2\frac{1}{2}$ companies.... We set off some 20 miles on a compass bearing to join the Support Group and on the way ran into a South African brigade (in the Charrubet–Bir el Haid–Hareifet en Nbeidat area) who announced that they were going to be attacked by tanks and lorried infantry in half an hour. The Division Commander [General Gott] was there and put us under command of this brigade for the coming battle! Sure enough in half an hour 46 German tanks appeared—you can imagine how much defence we had time to prepare—the sort of hasty defence that is not catered for in the text-books. The digging was hard after two feet anyway, and even the South Africans who had 36 hours there were no more than two feet down anywhere that I saw. This was about 3 in the afternoon, and a most unpleasant encounter took place until it was growing dark at 5.30 p.m.... Although we were intermingling with the South Africans they got the heaviest part of the attack and suffered very severe casualties. The field-gunners and anti-tank gunners did some magnificent work, and there are at least 16 German tanks left on the battlefield, with many dead South African anti-tank gunners and machine-gunners at their posts—this a fortnight afterwards. The Companies got out in the fading light and made off in parties south-east. We were able to keep in wireless touch with them; we were in three parties, my own H.Q. with some odds and ends and a few South Africans, and the others in two different lots. We assembled by midday

Nov. 24 the 24th and had a preliminary roll call, which revealed 130 other ranks and Jimmy Boyle unaccounted for. Never again do I want to be wished into someone else's battle, nor do I want to take a tank attack naked on the ground. A grenade and a tommy-gun seem most inadequate weapons for such an occasion."

Most of the missing were from Left Flank (Major J. D. B. Drury-Lowe). This company had been sent forward again to its original position, where it was surrounded and pinned down. But by the efforts of Major Drury-Lowe, who walked nonchalantly from truck to truck, a move was made at last light, when, led by Captain Crichton-Stuart, Left Flank drove off through the midst of the German vehicles—whose infantry were already too far ahead to interfere; the next day they rejoined the 4th Armoured Brigade. It was at this stage that Lieutenant the Hon. P. J. Boyle got separated, and drove into a German leaguer thinking it to be friendly; eventually he escaped from Italy into Switzerland. Also taken prisoner were CSM Hughes and CQMS Gibson, while CQMS King of G Company was killed.

The stubborn resistance of the 5th South African and 22nd Armoured Brigades had not been in vain. On "Black Sunday" they had inflicted on the Afrika Korps the heaviest losses it was to suffer on any one day of the battle. We now know that seventy of Rommel's 150 tanks were knocked out and that his infantry suffered irreplaceable casualties among its leaders. Nevertheless the Germans could claim to have thwarted the intentions of the XXX Corps in the Battle of Sidi Rezegh. Tobruk was still beleaguered and the German armour was still cock of the walk.

At this point Rommel made his most spectacular move of the Desert War. Disengaging the bulk of the Afrika Korps from around Sidi Rezegh he led them down the Trigh el Abd, across the frontier at Bir Sheferzen and twenty miles on into Egypt. He hoped so to disrupt our communications that General Cunningham would be forced to withdraw. He failed in his purpose, but for five days all was confusion in our rear—a confusion exemplified by the fact that for more than a day Brigadier Alec Gatehouse, who had lost his 4th Armoured Brigade Headquarters and was alone in a wireless truck, was protected by an equally lost truck from the Battalion containing "one young officer, Drill-Sergeant Richmond, and six Guardsmen". *Nov. 24–25*

On the 25th November the Battalion joined the battered 7th Support Group south of the Trigh el Abd. The Group was then forming itself into three Mobile Columns whose purpose was to harass the enemy's lines of communication. Each was a mixed force of artillery, anti-tank guns, and infantry, and each was self-contained and independent. Right Flank (Captain MacRae) and F Company (Captain R. E. L. Harvey) provided the infantry for Mayfield Column under the Commanding Officer, and G Company (Major Coghill) did the same for Currie Column under Colonel Currie, R.H.A.; Left Flank (Major Drury-Lowe) remained with the 4th Armoured Brigade for general protective duties.

By the 29th "Rommel's Raid" had shot its bolt; but it had been the occasion of the relief of General Cunningham by Major-General Ritchie in command of the Eighth Army. The fierce fight about Sidi Rezegh was resumed. *Nov. 29*

The next two weeks were spent in "careering up and down the Escarpment south of the Trigh Capuzzo between el Adem and Sidi Azeiz, and bombarding such targets as offered themselves. It was a most exacting task, as we always had to be on the ground at first light 0615–0630, and this generally meant a four or five mile approach in the dark. It was 5-o'clock Reveille, sometimes earlier, every day, and we were on the go all day, getting into our leaguer for the night about 8 p.m. After that even there was all the replenishment for the next day to be done—so sleep has been short. We did our stuff pretty well, I think, and no doubt helped considerably the clearance of the area east of Tobruk. It was mostly gunner stuff, but the carriers did well and had opportunities for snaffling the odd staff car and other vehicles. John Clarke and Sammy Houldsworth[1] with the Right Flank and F Company carriers were particularly energetic and a 14-hour day was *Dec.*

---
[1] Lieutenant J. R. S. Clarke and Lieutenant H. H. Houldsworth.

continually their lot. They brought in quite a few prisoners and assisted one day at the trapping of three Italian tanks and some transport in some wadis, with the result that the tanks had to bolt for it and two were knocked out by anti-tank gunners, and all the transport."

There is something curiously nautical about those two frantic weeks: the approach through the darkness with the vehicles on either side in convoy barely recognisable silhouettes; the all-importance of the compass; the first chill rays of wintry sun slanting through the dawn mist over a desert as featureless as the sea; the sudden wide expanse of day and an emptiness in which an enemy had to be found and destroyed; the swift hammer-blow, and move, and strike again; the withdrawal for brief rest and preparation for the morrow; the bow-wave plume of sand as the carriers, destroyer-like, hurrying on their business, struck a softer patch. It is to Drake and the Armada that the mind turns rather than to thoughts of armed men on the march.

Certain episodes stood out in the crowded days:

Captain MacRae setting off with three carriers into that emptiness—"anyone can hide themselves at two or three miles distance" —to find out if it was in fact empty. It was not. He had gone about two miles when four anti-tank guns opened fire from less than four hundred yards. One carrier was knocked out, but with the other two he charged the guns. The survivors, two officers and thirty-nine other ranks, surrendered. A 75-mm. gun then opened fire, but without losing a casualty or a prisoner he got back to the column.

The final recapture of a New Zealand hospital, which had already changed hands several times, and the rescue of some wounded members of the Battalion including Lance-Sergeant McConnell of the Pipes whose foot had been run over by a tank. "Sergeant McConnell said they were very well treated by the Germans but very badly by the Italians. A German officer actually apologised to our Brigadier for having to hand over this hospital to the Italians, but said that the Germans had too much on their hands. The Italians pinched their food and water, and when finally relieved, 1,400 wounded in the place had been practically without water for 48 hours."

No. 15 Platoon of G Company, under the command of Second-Lieutenant Crane, Intelligence Officer of the 4th R.H.A., rescuing a party of New Zealanders from a large Italian escort, and Lance-Corporal R. H. Little leading his section away from that attack to cope with what he thought was an enemy force on the flank and returning with another hundred New Zealanders and twelve survivors from their escort. The repeated return, for which Lance-

Corporal Little volunteered, to the scene of the action in the gathering dusk and the rescue of further wounded New Zealanders under heavy machine-gun fire. There was an *Altmark* air about these things. "In all that day," G Company diary records, "about 150 prisoners were taken and about 250 New Zealanders freed from enemy hands."

Two Germans on motor-cycles asking a patrol the way to Sidi Omar, and a German petrol lorry joining one of the columns during a night march.

Amusement over the B.B.C's pronunciation of desert place-names, and the impression it gave that they were towns of some size: "Actually Sidi Rezegh is 'Sheikh's Tomb without a building' which means that it's a heap of stones probably covered by sand."

Currie Column's last day in action, when it woke to find enemy leaguers on three sides of it and ended the day with 159 prisoners and a bag of four field-guns, one tank, six anti-tank guns, and about thirty vehicles destroyed.

The German dive-bombers—the Junkers 87 or "Stuka": "there were often between 30 and 36 of them, and they used to fly very slowly in formation, almost hovering over their target before peeling off and diving to drop their 'eggs' like some vast prehistoric bird. The raids were constant, and therefore unnerving, but they also became quite a joke. If on the move, one often felt one could drive away and avoid the bombs, and good sport was had, when stationary, in shooting at them with all small arms including anti-tank rifles. On the rare occasions when our fighters got among them, there would be terrific cheering from the men and there was always great interest to see how many would turn up for the next raid."

And behind it all was the growing list of casualties, though happily much lighter than might have been expected—G Company had none. And the discomfort of the desert life—no beer and few cigarettes. "There is usually a raging wind all day, and nights are bitter, but we must be pretty hard by now. Water is difficult—$\frac{1}{2}$-gallon per day to include vehicle doesn't go far, especially when hot tea is much in demand. The carrier crews can hardly ever afford a shave—their machines use almost all they get—and many of them are bearded like very old sailors." Leaky tins often resulted in a ration of under half a gallon, and "Tobruk" water was often salty.

But behind it, too, as the Army pressed westwards and the enemy's retreat gained momentum, was the knowledge of valuable work well done. For the rest, the gunners were "jolly good", and "we have all got badly cracked lips which heal up at night, but open again in the morning as soon as someone says anything funny."

Dec. 12 Gradually the Germans were overborne. On the 12th December the XIII Corps attacked them around Gazala; after three days of fighting
Dec. 15 they were in retreat to the west. The 22nd Guards (Motor) Brigade was reassembled south of Tobruk for a thrust south-west behind the 7th Armoured Division.

"I gather we get a few days rest before embarking on another enterprise, full of interest and probable hazard. We could do with a rest and need a refit too." This last was essential, for a number of the vehicles, among other troubles, had broken springs wired together even at the time the frontier wire was crossed and thirty-one 15 cwt. trucks and five 30 cwt. had been lost in those two weeks, "practically all by enemy action, which says a lot for our fitters, both unit and R.A.O.C. How they managed to keep things moving is remarkable—we still have some 1936 Morris trucks with 180,000 miles to their credit."

This much needed rest—which included a move to counter a German thrust—was only to last five days. For the hunt was up, and 22nd Guards Brigade—now only the Coldstream and the Battalion with its supporting troops—set off on its dash across the desert to cut off the enemy retreating down the coastal road.

Dec. 20 At 0750 on 20th December the Battalion crossed the start line, about eight miles north of Bir Hakeim. It had 170 miles to cover on a compass bearing, and its only map, based on Italian survey, was "known to be inaccurate to as much as ten miles, and mostly blank squares at that." Under command were two batteries of 25-pounders, two troops of anti-tank guns, two troops of anti-aircraft guns, a section from a Field Squadron R.E., and a Light Dressing Section. The carriers had been left behind owing to speed of movement and difficulties of petrol and water supply. The first night was spent in leaguer south of
Dec. 21 Hallabet et Ezba and the second at Msus, which proved to be "nothing but an old Turkish fort, a landing-ground, and a horrible deep wadi"
Dec. 22 which had to be crossed in single file. The crossing next morning took nearly two hours, during which minor casualties were suffered from strafing by German fighters, and the Battalion pressed on to the hill-top fort guarding the pass down the escarpment at Sceleidima. This was shelled during the afternoon while the 11th Hussars put in some good work in the plain below, and during the evening the enemy withdrew, which made a ferocious bayonet charge by Left Flank something of an anti-climax, there being no enemy in the fort to
Dec. 23 bayonet! The next day the Battalion moved down the escarpment and
Dec. 24 on Christmas Eve pushed on south to Beda Fomm to try to intercept an enemy column hurrying down the main road from Benghazi. The flank guard, however, dug in about six miles east of the road, was too strong, and Right Flank, after losing Lieutenant M. J. A. Gordon and two guardsmen wounded by 88-mm. guns firing shrapnel which burst thirty feet or so above the ground, was ordered to withdraw.

It was but a trivial setback, but it was symptomatic of the whole situation. For the Eighth Army had outrun its supplies. It had got there for the kill, but it no longer had the killing power, and every day that passed before Benghazi could be reopened as a supply port was the addition of a day in the German stream of supplies, on which they were falling back. Between the Army and the retreating enemy lay the bastion of the prepared positions at Agedabia. If that fell, the battle might yet become fluid again in time.

Christmas Day, during which the Via Balbia gave the Battalion its first sight of a tarmac road and telegraph poles for five weeks, was spent "jogging southwards over vile going—7 miles in 3 hours at one period—arriving exhausted opposite the enemy defences some nine miles north of Agedabia in the evening." The strength and dispositions of the enemy were unknown, but it was known that the defences included eight 105-mm. guns, several 88-mm. and 75-mm., together with the usual complement of Bredas and other heavy and light automatics, and one coastal gun of 155-mm. However, it "looked better infantry country than one expects in the desert, and we were invited to attack it. A daylight attack was out of the question, so a night one was staged for the night 26/27 December. No ground recce. was possible, the map was hopeless. We intended to approach from the north and then take him in the flank from the west. The country we were going over was entirely unknown, and it was a chancy business whether we hit the enemy defences at all." Dec. 25

At 2130 on the 26th the Battalion set off on a bearing of 230°. After two and a half miles the advance was continued on foot, and a five mile march brought it to a position approximately west of the enemy. It was calculated, however, that it might still be slightly too far to the north, so the final advance of six miles was made on a bearing of 95°. Left Flank on the left and G Company on the right led the advance, with Right Flank echeloned to the right rear of G Company. Battalion Headquarters was in the centre to the left of Right Flank. F Company was behind Battalion Headquarters. It was hoped to get four vehicles to the objective, a No. 9 set for communication with Brigade, a No. 11 set with the gunner F.O.O., and two ambulances, but the going, a series of steep sand ridges and wadis running approximately north and south, made this impossible and the vehicles were still nearly two miles away when morning came. To march on foot was an exhausting experience for a battalion which had spent the last six weeks in its vehicles. "There was a strong N.W. gale," the Commanding Officer wrote, "and there were three heavy, icy, rainstorms during the night which soaked us all. We plodded along during the night, getting nearer to our own bombardment. This sounded most impressive—no wonder they hate the 25 pdr. . . . Up to 0630 we had found nothing, but just after this the fireworks began." Dec. 26

Dec. 27

The position at that moment, as cold dawn took the place of bitter night, was nightmarish. The Battalion had struck slightly too far to the north, and the two forward companies, with Battalion Headquarters just coming off the ridge behind them, were crossing a long open wadi the lips of which held the strongly entrenched enemy positions. They were caught in enfilade and, owing to the impossibility of getting the gunners' wireless truck up in time, had no means of retaliation. There was nothing for it but to withdraw. It was "a nasty business as there was no cover for two miles or so. However, they moved off E.N.E. in a very orderly manner, and the enemy shooting wasn't very good to start with."

Meanwhile, about half a mile to the south, Right Flank came up against two enemy posts each of about fifty men with a 75- or 88-mm. gun dug in. With a platoon and a section Captain MacRae and Lieutenant Clarke captured both these positions in spite of heavy cross-fire from light and heavy machine-guns on neighbouring hills. Captain MacRae, immediately appreciating the situation, pushed on over the crest and, with a Bren, covered a long trench packed with enemy, making it impossible for them to fire on the two exposed companies or to man their 75-mm. gun, while the volume of fire from their own side made it impossible for these men to come out and surrender, as they plainly desired. Meanwhile Lieutenant Clarke with Guardsmen R. Wingham and T. C. McAllister stalked and silenced two Breda positions, killing all the crews except two, whom they captured. Captain MacRae, having done all that could be done to cover the withdrawal of the two exposed companies, then himself withdrew.[1] Right Flank, besides saving many casualties to the other companies, had caused seventy to a hundred casualties to the enemy and brought back twenty-eight prisoners: "There would have been more, but their own side shelled them on the way back, and killed and wounded quite a lot. The red and white tracer of the Bredas coming down the wadis was a most unpleasant affair—rather like a very fast bowler on a bumpy wicket, and the batsmen without pads and gloves. The chief difficulty seemed to be to keep the men moving fast enough and to stop them bunching to gossip—I saw four men hit by a mortar shell purely on that account."

The price paid had now to be reckoned. Second-Lieutenant J. G. Critchley, an outstanding Platoon Commander in F Company, had been wounded in the lungs by a mortar bomb early in the action, but despite his wounds he assembled the scattered company, searched fruitlessly for his wounded Company Commander, Captain R. E. L. Harvey, and set the Company on the route for withdrawal; he then fell unconscious and died. Among the thirty casualties to the rank and file, Sergeant D. Douglas, Lance-Sergeants R. Stewart, J. McCall and

[1] He was awarded the D.S.O.

A. Ward were also killed; Captain Harvey was taken prisoner and Lieutenant I. Weston-Smith wounded, as was the Commanding Officer, whose "neat in and out bullet wound above the right knee" did not cause him to leave the Battalion, while eighteen of the wounded or missing got back. The surprising thing in the circumstances was that the casualties were no greater.

Although the attack was a failure, the balance as far as casualties were concerned was heavily on the Battalion's side. And the attack, in the face of difficulties which might well have led to there being no attack at all, very nearly came off. "Actually with a bit of luck with the map, the ground, and navigation, we should have had a cracking big success." Perhaps it was as well that that bit of luck was lacking, for success would have been followed by a counter-attack with tanks. "The whole trouble with this battle has been that we have never really defeated the enemy tanks, and he has constantly produced fresh ones out of a hat. He still has 60 in the field, of which 45-50 are German, and of course, they outgun our own." That preponderance was yet to make itself fully felt. In the meantime, fierce as it was in isolated engagements, the momentum of the battle had been lost, and with it the initiative. From that of an attacking force the role of the Battalion had dwindled to providing escorts to the guns as they put down harassing fire on the enemy. On the 31st an Operation Order was received giving details of action to be taken in the event of withdrawal becoming necessary. Nevertheless throughout the offensive the morale of the Battalion had been excellent—higher, some thought, than at any time before or after. The Battalion could boast that as yet there had been not one absentee, and this despite the fact that they had received no mail from the opening of the offensive on 18th November until the arrival at Agedabia. The year ended in cold and rain. *Dec. 31*

(d) *Retreat to the Gazala Line*

On 6th January 1942, Rommel withdrew his forces from Agedabia. That bastion was no longer necessary. Behind Agheila he had built up forces more than sufficient to cope with anything that could be sent against them. He could bide his time. On the 7th the port of Benghazi was brought into operation. It was too late. On the 7th too, the Battalion occupied Agedabia, where it was found that the Battalion's dead had been properly buried in the cemetery and some unmarked graves were identified. The days passed in wind and rain and desert storms, and the thankless task of ridding the area and the landing-grounds of mines and booby-traps. The task of providing escorts no longer fell to the Battalion, for there were not enough guns, and those available were working with the Coldstream further to the south. There was no defended line for the Battalion to hold, for there were not enough *1942 Jan. 6 Jan. 7* troops to hold the only possible line. It could not take up a proper defensive position on its own, for it had no weapons except small arms with which to defend itself against the tank strength piling up behind Agheila. For all practical purposes it was merely left camping out on the edge of enemy territory, and to it the inevitable was not only inevitable but also obvious. Our 1st Armoured Division, which was new to the Desert, was the only support available. In the meantime the seaside post of Zuetina provided welcome supplies of water and even baths, and the local Arabs were found willing to exchange eggs for tea and biscuits.

At this time came a change in the Brigade's title. At midnight on the 13th/14th it became the 200th Guards Brigade, probably in the hopes of deceiving the enemy into thinking that a fresh Guards Brigade had arrived with the new Armoured Division. The news of the change seems to have taken a long time to percolate even as far as the Battalion, for in mid-February the writer of the War Diary was still referring to the 22nd Guards Brigade, and unofficial correspondents did so well into the next month.

Jan. 21
Jan. 22

On the 21st the enemy began to push forward from Agheila. At 0730 on the next day the forward Platoon reported that enemy armoured vehicles were approaching up the main road, and ten minutes later three German eight-wheeled armoured cars entered Agedabia. A hurried withdrawal was ordered, and in twenty minutes the Battalion was on the move. It had no supporting arms of any sort.

To the west, the enemy streamed up the main road towards Benghazi; to the east, up the track towards Antelat. The essential matter was to get up the escarpment, and the last message received from Brigadier Marriott had been, "Try and meet me at Antelat tomorrow." The question was whether Antelat was occupied by the enemy. Information was conflicting.

Jan. 23

On the morning of the 23rd the Battalion moved east along the track from Beda Fomm. There is little doubt that the perfect desert formation, unexpected in an army in retreat, deceived the enemy as the Battalion moved slowly across the Antelat landing-ground among the burning British aircraft. Lieutenant J. G. Whiteley, heading the column in a Dingo scout-car, drove to the bottom of the Escarpment, while an unknown staff-car drove down from the top of it. The cars stopped a few hundred yards apart; the occupants dismounted and examined each other through glasses; decided they were enemies, and both cars drove back to their battalions! The Scots Guards were wheeled to the left and it was not until the head of the column had begun the climb that the enemy opened fire, and when the Battalion altered course above the escarpment to avoid enemy tanks to the south-east its losses were only one man wounded and seven missing together with eleven reinforcements for the 11th Hussars who had been with the rearmost Company. The evasion was fortunate. Even Captain MacRae's order, long famous in the Battalion, "A little more oil on the anti-tank rifles", could hardly have affected the issue.

The succeeding days of move and counter-move to fit in with plan and change of plan, in the midst of an army sprawled on divergent courses across the Desert, sometimes behind the enemy, always with the possibility that the next as yet unrecognised column might be hostile and that a tank attack might once more have to be taken "naked upon the ground", were so full of incident that detailed record here is impossible. Yet certain things and days stood out. First, barely achieved contact over the air with Corps, and some fragmentary knowledge gained of positions of friend and foe. The Battalion navigation was under Captain M. D. D. Crichton-Stuart, who had joined the Battalion from the Long Range Desert Group in time to take part in the whole advance and now commanded F Company: to be only three hundred yards out at the end of a sixty-one mile march on three different bearings gives a sense of stability in a world of flux. The discovery of an abandoned Ordnance park, and the rescue of an admitted twenty-five new vehicles including two 25-pounder and two 2-pounder guns on the second day of the retreat; "admitted"—for the number was nearer fifty, and practically every rifleman became a driver! It is a wise motor battalion that does not know the extent of its own transport. The arrival that evening at Charruba with petrol almost exhausted, and the exquisite unhurried formality which delayed but, in the face of lack of formality, could not prevent the refuelling. The welcome arrival of eight 2-pounder anti-tank guns to join the Battalion, and their Gunner Officer's exact summary of the situation: "It would all be most frightfully funny if it wasn't so incredibly serious." Renewed contact with the Coldstream and the gradual increase of the attached gunner strength. The discovery of one, then twelve, then eighteen enemy tanks on the Battalion's line of march, and the engagement broken off at nightfall with no casualties suffered. Defensive positions between South Africans and Free French as the retreat coalesced into what was to become the Gazala Line. The minor triumph of ending the retreat with more vehicles than when starting the advance.

Jan. 24–Feb. 5

On 6th February the Battalion moved back to Cherua in the so-called Gazala Line. Companies went out on column work as in the early days of the advance, and parties went out on patrol. The Battalion carriers took part in a scheme and exercise held by the 3rd Coldstream, and there was also a Divisional exercise. Members of the Battalion went back to Almaza and even Palestine on courses—and leave. Fifty men were taken to a bath-house thirty-seven miles away, and when they got there found that the water ration was one gallon in a tin. There was great rivalry between company water-carts to discover

Feb. 6

Feb. 10

Feb. 11

private wells, for the Germans put oil in many of them. Guardsman Balfour, of F, found a well of perfect water, but when most had been consumed two dead Italians were found at the bottom. "Gin and It" was Lieutenant Rose's description! War in the Desert had become static; the line southward from Gazala was continually strengthened.

Mar. 18

March 18th was the Tercentenary of the Raising of the Regiment and, except for the 150 men out with Coghill Column, was a Battalion holiday. "A good supply of NAAFI wares had been collected for the occasion" the Battalion Diary records, "including beer on the scale of six tins per man. Unfortunately the Germans chose this day for an advance in some strength by their tank columns so the issue of beer had to be curtailed."

April–May

April ended with the Battalion starting a much needed three weeks' respite by the sea near its old battle stations at Buq Buq, during which time Captain Drury-Lowe transformed Left Flank into a highly trained Anti-tank Company, armed with 2-pounder guns; each Motor Company had a platoon of Vickers Medium Machine-guns. Lieutenant-Colonel Mayfield, who had led it to increased distinction from the Canal to Agedabia and back had had to leave to take up a Staff appointment. His second-in-command and successor, Lieutenant-Colonel P. C. H. Grant, had served with him throughout the campaign. It was fortunate for the Battalion that there was one of equally wide experience of desert fighting to lead it in the days ahead. It was a remarkable tribute to Colonel Mayfield that "despite our many battles under his command, our casualties were only 40 killed, 50 wounded, and 104 missing, during this long phase in Libya."

On 1st May, H.R.H. the Duke of Gloucester, Colonel of the Regiment, visited the Battalion. All officers and warrant officers present were introduced to him, and other rank representatives of each company. Away to the west the two great armies were preparing to strike. It was "lovely summer weather, with a nice cool breeze from the sea, still pretty chilly before dawn". Rommel's preparations for attack were further advanced than ours.

(e) *Rigel Ridge*

MAP VIII
May 16

On the 16th May the Battalion[1] started to move up to its place with the 1st Armoured Division in the Gazala Line. Its route took it through its old battle area below the Escarpment; up Halfaya Pass, whence it could look back over the area it once so sparsely held, to the white sandhills and the sea, past Capuzzo and its fort, and along the upland wastes to el Adem whence the Trigh Capuzzo led westwards to Knightsbridge and what was to become known as the Cauldron. A

[1] For Order of Battle, see p. 549.

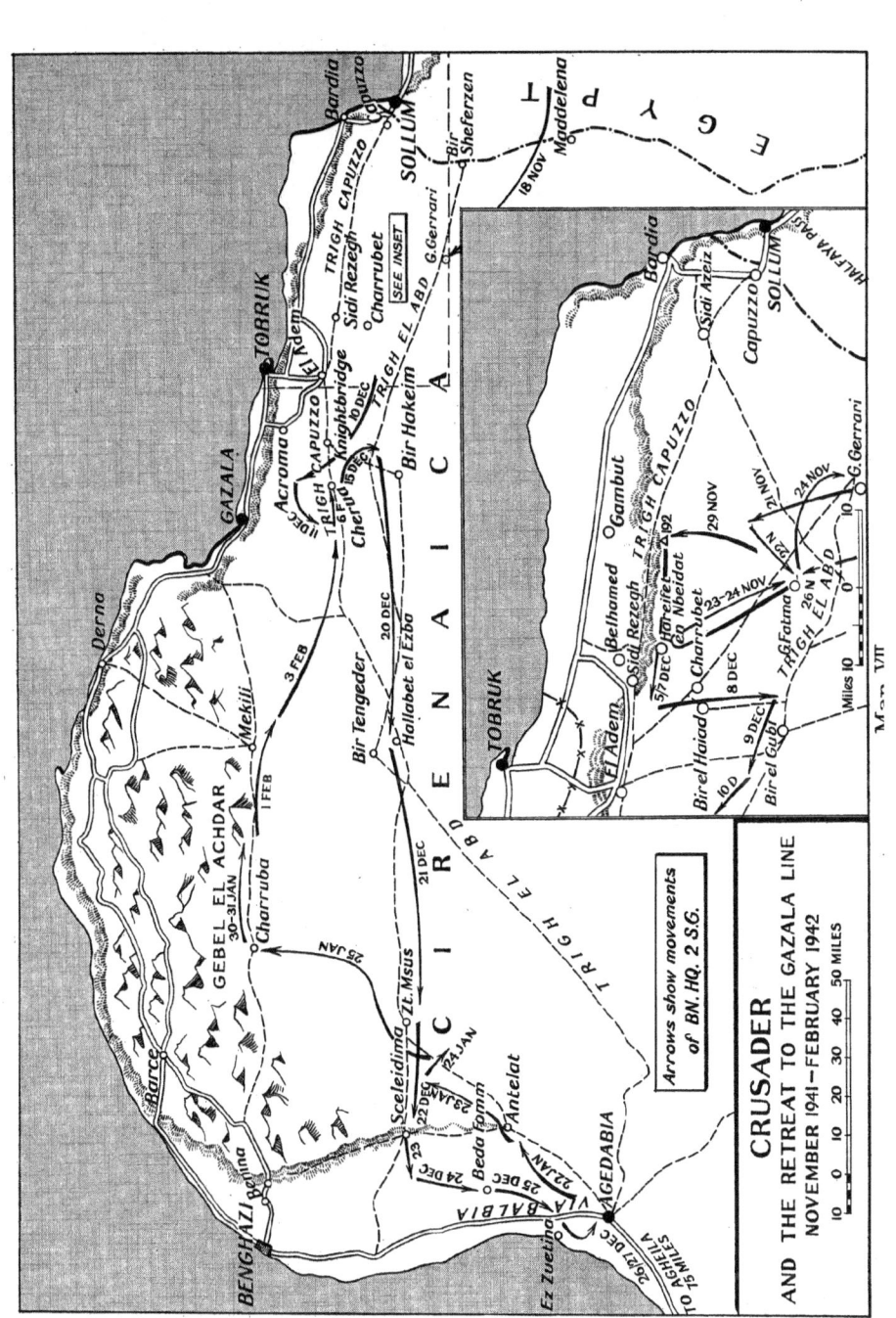

little east of north of the Battalion was Tobruk. About thirty miles to the south-west was Bir Hakeim.

The so-called Gazala Line was well conceived and consisted of a series of irregularly spaced strong-points or "boxes" linked by minefields, one of the most important boxes being that round the track junctions at Knightsbridge about seventeen miles west of el Adem. The importance of the Knightsbridge position was this. It was the key to the Gazala position and had been chosen as such because, so long as it was held, the enemy could win no strategic success. If he were to break through the centre by a frontal attack, Knightsbridge lay directly in his path; and he must either be destroyed on the spot or shepherded away northwards by the armour. In that case he would run on to the Acroma Box and the armour in that area. If he effected a break-through farther north, the right flank of his advance would come under destructive fire from the ridge north of Knightsbridge. If he came round south he could be attacked on his left flank, and his own communications could be cut. Lastly, Knightsbridge commanded all the tracks by which supplies came up to the front. If it were to fall, the whole line from the coast to Bir Hakeim would be untenable. This key position was entrusted to the renumbered 201st Guards Brigade[1] and the R.H.A. Throughout the battle it was the pivot on and around which the armour manœuvred.

The balance of forces was in favour of the British. Five brigades of tanks were matched against the three possessed by the enemy, and the arrival of the Grant tank from America and the 6-pounder anti-tank gun from home had done something to offset the superior quality of the German equipment. How nearly the battle of Gazala succeeded, how the slender breach in the minefield which Rommel had achieved for the extrication of his armour turned into a rushing channel of attack, and why the counter-attack was a costly failure and disaster flooded the whole position like a wave, is part of wider military history. The sole concern of the Battalion and the 201st Guards Brigade was to hold the Knightsbridge position. This it did in spite of overwhelming odds for over a fortnight, and, when the end became inevitable and withdrawal was ordered, the Brigade got everything away with it except two guns.

May 18th was passed in digging in and individual training in the Battalion's position to the south-west of the el Adem Box, and the following day Right Flank (Captain MacRae) and No. 16 Platoon of Left Flank, moved west to join the 3rd Coldstream in making and defending a defensive box at Bir Belefaa (the "Bloody Bir") on the eastern side of the Knightsbridge Box. On the 23rd the rest of the Battalion started work on its new task of defending the passes in the escarpment on the north side of Trigh Capuzzo westwards for about

May 18

May 23

---

[1] The second change in the Brigade's numeral is officially dated 21st May.

7—S.G.H.

ten miles from where it is crossed by the el Adem–Tobruk road. Enemy air activity increased, and nights were disturbed by bombing, and casualties were suffered.

May 27   At first light on May 27th permission was asked and given for F Company's machine-gun Platoon to join the G Company Platoon on the Field Firing Range. At 0820 the order came from Division "Stand-to Instant Readiness". The great armoured drive from the south had begun. Captain A. B. C. Maxwell was hurriedly sent off to recall the machine-guns. "I had only gone 30 miles when I saw black dust and masses of 3-tonners going east like mad. I could not imagine why they were behaving in such an odd way, as I was fifteen miles behind our forward minefield. I stopped and talked to a R.A.S.C. officer and he said 'It looks like a break-through—but I don't believe it'. However, a moment later, at about 500 yards, we made out German tanks and eight-wheeled armoured cars coming straight for us. I immediately said goodbye . . . and by greatest good luck found them in about twelve miles, peacefully starting their practice." By a wide detour and narrowly escaping a tank encounter west of el Adem, the machine-guns got safely back to the Battalion that afternoon, as

May 28   did B Echelon the following morning after being "hunted by German tanks most of the first day and bombed all that night like the rest of us", and owing much to a timely low-flying attack by the Air Force.

May 27   On the afternoon of the 27th the Germans put in their first attack on the Knightsbridge Box. It was the first time that the Battalion's anti-tank guns had been in action and No. 16 Platoon with "ancient weapons . . . killed three brand new Mark IV's" out of seventeen that had attacked it. Its commander, Lieutenant Sir F. H. R. Astley-Corbett, was severely wounded, and had to lie in a trench for five hours before he could be got out by Lance-Sergeant Johnson, who took over the Platoon and set a fine example of bravery and leadership on that and subsequent days, and who three times crossed open ground under tank fire to get trucks, two of them being set on fire as he drove. The

May 28–29   attacks on Knightsbridge went on, and the rest of the Battalion, though as yet free from ground attack, was much troubled from the air by the Stukas, and the unvarying irritation caused by the B.B.C. to the man on the spot rose to the pitch of anger. "The only time we heard the B.B.C. we were all enraged! They calmly said that these last few days had been remarkable for the lack of air activity, which is a wicked and vicious lie. We have never been harried so much from the air, all are agreed, and not only by day but by night as well." On

May 30   the morning of the 30th, when the enemy were in retreat, one bomb destroyed the R.A.P. truck and killed the Drum Major (Sergeant T. M. Longworth) and three other men. "It is practically full moon now and as the nights are always brilliantly clear they have no difficulty in finding any group of vehicles, but provided they are well dispersed they are lucky if they hit one."¹

On the following morning the Battalion, with H Battery R.H.A., moved a few miles to the west to take up a defensive position at Hagiag er Raml, but was almost immediately withdrawn, for during the night Right Flank and the Left Flank Platoon had been sent out with a 2nd R.H.A. Column "to prevent the enemy from escaping west through our minefield, but we ran into a division or so of enemy, and of course failed. A Corps attack would have stampeded the enemy on to our minefield, and saved us our second big mistake of sitting back and watching our people being mopped up in detail, first the 150th Brigade in the Cauldron, and the French". A large-scale counter-attack had been hourly expected, but the force that went out from the Knightsbridge Box was pathetically small. It was still smaller when it returned. The Regiment alone lost Lieutenant B. D. Carris wounded and prisoner and fifty other ranks missing, although only eighteen failed to rejoin subsequently. In the circumstances they were perhaps fortunate. Surprise on both sides may have had something to do with it for they "ran smack into it" in the dark. The remnants of Right Flank and the Anti-tank Platoon rejoined the Battalion in its former position and G Company (Captain Orr-Ewing) and another platoon of Left Flank, with H Battery R.H.A., went into the Box. *May 31*

June 1

One June 2nd the Battalion moved again to Hagiag er Raml and began work on another box. It was joined there by some artillery including all that was left of I Battery 2nd R.H.A. after the night excursion with Right Flank. Thenceforward the Battalion had constantly varying numbers of 25-pounders under command, and in the neighbourhood, the most under command being twenty and the least eight. When the crisis came the guns were at their least. *June 2*

The following day the Battalion was moved west again and was given the task of holding the ridge known as Maabus er Rigel—Rigel Ridge. Its name, meaning "leg of a dog", gives a rough approximation of its shape in plan. The ridge extended westwards from the north-western end of the Knightsbridge Box, the "toe" being to the west, and the purpose in occupying it was to protect the northern flank of the Box and maintain a position from which it was hoped our artillery could neutralise hostile batteries which were proving troublesome. Six-pounder anti-tank guns were issued to the Battalion for the occasion; they were not welcomed by the crews. It cannot be denied that they were more powerful weapons, but nevertheless it was an ill-advised measure for, among other reasons, the gun-crews had confidence in *June 3*

---

¹ An example of how the most imperturbable of men could be momentarily unbalanced by these raids was provided by the Jeeves-like Officers' Mess waiter, Guardsman Fingland; after a particularly unnerving attack, in error he poured the tea into his Company Commander's steel helmet!

their old 2-pounders for close-quarter work, and many of the men were only able to fire one practice shot each before the attack was upon them. This was insufficient to accustom them to the recoil, which was liable to cause the sight to strike the layer in the eye.

To the north and west the ground sloped gently. The southern side of the ridge, about 150 feet high, was steep and cut by wadis. The position on Rigel Ridge, the only one possible for the task, was well placed for covering the flank of the Knightsbridge Box, and gave cover from the south to the guns sited on its northern slopes. But on the other hand an enemy getting on to the ridge further to the east could completely cover both the Battalion and the Artillery positions, and other high ground gave observation over the Battalion positions from various directions, while an enemy getting a footing on the higher ground at the "toe" could effectively command the area. A further disadvantage was that the southern slopes of the ridge were mainly convex, making it necessary for some of the Battalion positions to be placed forward under more direct enemy observation in order to get a field of fire and some defence in depth. For this reason, too, some of the ground in front of the infantry positions remained hidden from the Artillery O.P.s on the ridge. And finally, many of the infantry and anti-tank gun pits on the ridge had to be blasted. As there was only one pneumatic drill available most of the time, and that manned by Indian sappers who would not work it while shelling was in progress, it was not possible to add crawl or communication trenches, and indeed the work on the gun-pits to suit them to 6-pounders and on extending the minefields was never completed. It was clear that the position could not stand alone. In the event of a determined attack with tanks and infantry, it could only serve as a delaying position while a tank counter-attack went in. A box, as has been said, was a pivot for the armour: Rigel was a subsidiary pivot on a box. But when the crisis came the armoured counter-attack could not be mounted in time.

June 4 — On the 4th, G Company and the Left Flank platoon rejoined the Battalion from Knightsbridge, and in the early hours of the following morning the Eighth Army's counter-attack started. Its purpose was to pinch out the enemy bulge defending the eastern end of the ten-mile wide gap he had made in our minefield west of Knightsbridge. The result was the disastrous tank battle in the Cauldron. It was the turning point. With armour still further diminished and with a great gash in the centre through which the enemy could pour supplies, the Eighth Army was now holding a position that had lost its tactical purpose. The cohesion on which the Gazala Line depended had been lost. Thenceforward its strong-points could be tackled one by one, and all this had been achieved without lessening the attack on Bir Hakeim. "During the night" the Battalion War Diary ominously recorded, "there seemed to be a good deal of easterly enemy movement to the south of us."

By the morning of the 6th enemy columns were east and south-east of the Knightsbridge Box, and during the day the enemy overran and practically destroyed the 10th Indian Brigade in its positions to the west. The enemy were closing in for the kill, and in the ensuing shelling Captain A. B. C. Maxwell was slightly wounded but managed to rejoin the Battalion later the same day.

June 6

The next day a strong enemy force of tanks and infantry advanced upon the Knightsbridge Box; the defenders did considerable execution among the infantry and burned out two tanks. The Battalion's guns joined in and had a successful shoot on the enemy transport. But the attack was not pressed; there was no need to suffer heavy casualties: Knightsbridge could wait. From this attack, however, he must have learned one thing, if indeed he did not know it already: that Rigel, although an isolated position, was an integral part of the defences of the Knightsbridge Box. Rigel, too, could wait.

June 7

The 8th and 9th were fairly quiet, but there was much shelling on both sides on the morning of the 10th and some enemy tanks and vehicles were set on fire. "There is plenty of incident," one of the officers wrote that day, "though I think the worst pests are the flies which are now getting into full swing." Hope still remained in spite of the disaster in the Cauldron and the successful counter-attack that never came. "If as seems possible we can clean up Northern Africa in the next few weeks, we shall indeed have been lucky. . . . Everyone naturally is impatient to get on with the job and to charge madly in a westerly direction . . . . Warfare out here," he added mildly, "is most interesting." That night the Free French, after a most gallant defence, were forced to evacuate Bir Hakeim.

June 10

The battle in the Cauldron was a decisive victory for the enemy. The loss of Bir Hakeim placed the initiative once more and unalterably in his hands. The fighting was still fierce, but the diminished and wearied armour could not halt the drive northwards and by the evening of the 11th large enemy armoured forces were to the south of Knightsbridge and concentrating in the el Adem area. Bitter tank fighting continued on the 12th to the south, south-east and east, and the Knightsbridge Box accounted for some Mark IIIs at the south-east corner near Bir Belefaa. But the Germans surrounded el Adem and reached the Raml ridge, a position where, as the War Diary recorded, "they could be most inconvenient to us".

June 11

June 12

The morning of the 13th passed in exceptional quietness as the Battalion waited along its exposed ridge. With it were the eight 25-pounders of the 6th South African Field Battery, commanded by Major J. H. Newman, and two troops of 2-pounders of the 6th South African Anti-tank Battery. It was a pivot: the question was whether

MAP IX
June 13

there was anything to pivot on it, for the 2nd and 4th Armoured Brigades detailed to counter-attack if necessary had been moved some miles to the east the previous day, and were very weak in tanks. At about 1400 a large column of dust was seen moving from south to north and then from west to east towards the right flank of the Rigel position. It then appeared that there were two columns of tanks, one of eight and the other of twenty-nine, and two hundred lorries with infantry and guns; it was, as we now know, the whole of the 21st Panzer Division. The Battalion had about half an hour's warning of what was to come, and then five tanks found one of the three narrow gaps in the western minefield and came through. Three of these were quickly knocked out by the anti-tank guns of No. 17 Platoon and the enemy withdrew. After about an hour the tanks came on again, supported by heavy shelling and followed by the lorried infantry past the western end of the minefield to the south of the western end of the position. This minefield was to have extended from the north-west corner of the Knightsbridge Box to the toe of the Ridge; but it was overlooked by the enemy to the south, and work on it had only been possible at night. There were no mines in front of F and G Companies. Unless our own tanks came, or heavy artillery fire could be brought down, the end was inevitable. The Armoured Brigades were on their way. They came: but not in time. The O.P.s of the supporting artillery in the Box and to the north were blinded by a sandstorm.

In the circumstances it was surprising that Left Flank, F and G Companies, which bore the brunt of the attack, held up the onslaught for so long, for the enemy had been able to get their close support guns and mortars into position and to debus their infantry without ever coming under artillery fire. The weight of the attack was inexorable, and between five and six o'clock "the tanks—looking as sedate as Queen Victoria—rolled over the position". Even then all was not lost. The men in their trenches were pinned by automatic fire from the tanks. Even one supporting tank might have turned the scale and enabled sufficient resistance to be given to the lorried infantry pending further support. A counter-attack in force must almost certainly have succeeded, and indeed had been promised and was the only justification for the Battalion position on the Rigel Ridge. The task would not have been easy, for by then the whole position was thick with dust and smoke. Our tanks got to about three hundred yards of F Company Headquarters, but the intended counter-attack never developed. Their presence, however, certainly saved Battalion and Left Flank Headquarters and Right Flank from being overrun. At 1756 hours the 21st Panzer Division, whose slow progress was causing dissatisfaction to the enemy, reported to the Afrika Korps "Infantry strongpoint on Bir el Rigel taken after stubborn fighting."

The full story of that stubborn fighting can never be known. But certain incidents stood out and have been retained, and from them a sort of flickering picture emerges, both of the action and of the fighting quality of the Battalion.

To have repelled the force brought in to the attack on the exposed position strong and immediate artillery support would have been necessary. The tanks or the infantry alone could have been dealt with. In the circumstances all that could be hoped for was to cause enough delay to enable our own tanks to come, and as one by one the anti-tank guns were knocked out, the time in hand was cut down and down with ever increasing speed. The South African 25-pounders were intended for more distant targets, but events compelled them to join in the anti-tank battle over open sights, and this they did with the greatest gallantry and self-sacrifice. It is possible that the end might have been a little delayed if the Battalion had had its old 2-pounders; the gun-pits were sited for 2-pounders, and their smaller and disruptively painted shields were easier to conceal. But, unless the tanks came, the end could only have been delayed.

The work of No. 17 Platoon under Lieutenant I. Calvocoressi, on which the onslaught first fell, was outstanding, and before its last gun was silenced it had accounted for five German tanks. This last gun was commanded by Lance-Sergeant A. W. MacLeod and on it the enemy concentrated all available artillery and machine-gun fire. But he continued working it with calm and successful accuracy, until it was put out of action and himself seriously wounded; he was captured, but repatriated in the next year. Lieutenant Calvocoressi was finally taken prisoner, but escaped late that night with Major Newman and rejoined the remnants of the Battalion next morning. "When we were in German hands we had to suffer shelling from our own side for a long time, which was unpleasant but had to be. . . . The German soldiers treated us remarkably well and were all charming. The officers on the other hand were bloody and screamed at us. They would not let me get any water for the wounded we had, which could easily be got from our own trucks captured nearby. During the whole time I was a prisoner, no doctor attended to our wounded, some of whom were bad. The soldiers, on the other hand, handed round their own water-bottles to all of us." Lieutenant Calvocoressi's driver, Guardsman A. Watson (whose entry into the Army would have been delayed if his true age had been known), was one of the only two members of the Platoon not to be either killed or captured. In the earlier part of the engagement he was conspicuous in taking wounded South African gunners to ambulances under heavy shellfire, and when the Platoon position was overrun he set off in his truck to report the situation to Company Headquarters. He got through, in spite of a sharp encounter with a German tank, from which he barely emerged with the help of the disconcerting effects of a Verey pistol fired at close range. He then tried to return to the Platoon position, but found that by that time the enemy tanks were too thick on the ground. So he took the place of a casualty on a 25-pounder. Guardsman J. D. W. Boyle was with Watson at the truck before he started and might have gone with him. But he refused to go until he had made a search for Lieutenant Calvocoressi, whose servant he was, and walked back up the hill into the gathering dusk among the shell-bursts.

As the German attack rolled east along the ridge increasing pressure came upon F Company and its meagre support of South African 2-pounders. The shelling, at first, was described as moderate and the machine-gun fire as fairly heavy. But as the anti-tank guns of No. 17 Platoon were silenced, shellfire was concentrated on the South African guns, and the volume of automatic fire also increased as men brought up on the German tanks found suitable fire positions. After some time one of the guns received a direct hit, and the Company Commander, Major T. L. Ballantine Dykes, who had been Adjutant of the Battalion until the beginning of the year, ran across the hundred and fifty yards of intervening ground to the gun-pit where he found one of the gunners seriously wounded. He returned safely to the Command post, but when trying to go back to give further attention to the injured men, he was himself mortally wounded when within ten yards of the comparative safety of the gun-pit. His second-in-command, Captain A. B. C. Maxwell, twice crossed the open to attend to him, and was himself slightly wounded, and Lieutenant H. L. St. V. Rose ordered the crew out of a carrier and himself drove it to where Major Ballantine Dykes was lying, but without being able to get him away. Major Ballantine Dykes' only anxiety to the end was for the South African gunner. His action, and the motive, was typical of one who had long been among the outstanding officers of the Battalion: during the preceding days on the Ridge he had always gone out into the open to visit any of his posts that were being shelled.

Meanwhile the position of F Company was becoming desperate. Captain Maxwell, back in the command post, reported the position over the wireless to Battalion Headquarters and appealed urgently for tank support, and later sent Lieutenant Rose with a carrier to try to lead a tank to the right place. He was still at the wireless set when the German infantry surrounded him; he later escaped with Major Newman and Lieutenant Calvocoressi, and rejoined the Battalion. Major Newman was finally taken in Tobruk.

With the fall of F Company the enemy was able to concentrate his attention on G Company (Captain Orr-Ewing), next eastwards along the Ridge, and on No. 16 Anti-tank Platoon (which had only two guns after the excursion from the Knightsbridge Box), between it and Right Flank at the eastern end of the position. The process was repeated. A fragment of the telephone conversation with G Company Headquarters has been recorded: "Andrew[1] reports twelve tanks coming into your area now—can you see them?" "Donald[2] answering—No, not yet but I can hear their machine-guns." And then, ten minutes later: "Donald calling—enemy infantry four hundred yards off to my right. They seem to have overrun Peter[3]—over." On the northern slope of the western end of the position No. 19 Anti-tank Platoon (Lieutenant A. J. O. Maxtone-Graham) had already been overrun and captured. Only one thing could save the Company: "enemy infantry are meat to a tank's machine-guns". Captain Orr-Ewing sent Captain Robertson off on foot to fetch tanks. He had five hundred yards of open country to cross covered by the German tanks on the Ridge. They found his range with their fourth shell; he was seriously wounded, and later was picked up by our tanks.

Night fell just in time, and at last light the remnants of the Battalion successfully withdrew as ordered, but "bombed and strafed by our own fighters and then shelled by some of our 25-pounders" in the process. The South African gunners fought to the end, and undoubtedly prevented an even more serious disaster. Right Flank got out from the eastern end of the Battalion area with the loss of Lieutenant R. N. Brooke wounded and prisoner and twenty men, and Battalion Headquarters from the lower ground to the north of it. No. 18 Anti-tank Platoon, which had been in mobile reserve near Battalion Headquarters, was successfully withdrawn. Most of the Carrier Platoon of F Company under Lieutenant Rose and one man from Company Headquarters also got away with the Battalion. By the efforts of CSM W. Gore of G Company, five trucks and a few more men were successfully brought down from the Ridge.[4]

It had been "a most unpleasant afternoon and evening", and in addition to those already mentioned the Battalion had lost Captain R. A. Orr-Ewing, Lieutenants J. N. Cochrane-Barnett and P. Dawson and Second-Lieutenants G. P. Burnett and A. M. Archdale prisoners, and Lieutenant C. S. S. Burt of No. 16 Platoon wounded but evacuated. The other ranks lost totalled about two hundred and fifty—an exact figure cannot be given owing to some of the men managing to rejoin in the succeeding days—and the Battalion's total losses since it moved up from Buq Buq were thirteen officers and about three hundred other ranks. Two of the prisoners, Lance-Corporals A. Milroy and W. W.

[1] Captain Maxwell.
[2] Captain D. S. Robertson, second-in-command G Company.
[3] Lieutenant P. Dawson—G Company.
[4] One of the outstanding features of the Battalion organisation from the beginning of the advance was the unfailing efficiency of the signal communications in which the devotion to duty and ingenuity of Sergeant J. Hope played a large part. This was particularly notable during the attack on the Ridge when Sergeant Hope, who was awarded the M.M., operated successfully for four hours in an unarmoured truck in an exposed position under fire. The standard of the signalling was due to the hard work of Lieutenants A. J. Coats and G. C. Lampson, the Signal Officers.

Sutherland, escaped from an Italian prisoner-of-war camp near Tripoli and, after six days in the Desert, got into Tunisia where they were interned by the French and were recaptured after a further attempt to escape. They were both awarded the M.M.

There is no means of assessing the casualties inflicted on the enemy. One of the last officers to be captured on the Ridge counted twenty-one damaged tanks, of which eleven were on fire or otherwise apparently beyond local repair.

June 14   The next day the Battalion was ordered back to el Daba in Egypt. The machine-gun platoon of Right Flank under Lieutenant R. A. Willis and No. 18 Anti-tank Platoon under Lieutenant D. H. Butter (who had concealed the fact that he had been wounded on the 13th) were detached in support of the Coldstream, who had been withdrawn from the Knightsbridge Box during the night and were holding a defensive position on a ridge running west from Acroma to cover the withdrawal of the South Africans into Tobruk. They were immediately called upon to repel two heavy attacks by tanks, during which Lance-Corporal J. D. Stephenson, who had also particularly distinguished himself the prevous day, stopped the advance of three tanks while working his gun single-handed under heavy fire. Outstanding courage and coolness were also again shown by Guardsmen A. Brown and C. McFadyen who, after removing their wounded Sergeant to a truck, returned and successfully worked their damaged gun. On the evening of the 16th, having handed over their four 6-pounders to the Coldstream, the two Platoons rejoined the Battalion at Daba. "We are now having a rest and I expect they will send what remains of us back soon. At least it is nice and warm. It is all rubbish about excessive heat. We play base- and football in the middle of the day, and it is very pleasant; bathing is wonderful."

Meanwhile in Tobruk, where Brigadier J. C. O. Marriott had handed over the reconstituted Guards Brigade to Brigadier G. F. Johnson, also

June 21   of the Regiment, disaster was being piled on disaster. The fall of Tobruk, and the immense and crippling losses in men and material, are a part of wider military history. Thenceforward there remained only the so-called line at Alamein. But to the Battalion it had an added bitterness. Brigadier Johnson, who had commanded the Third Battalion in England until the previous November, was taken prisoner with his whole Headquarters, including two other members of the Regiment, Lieutenants I. M. Tennant and H. R. Wake-Bowell, and also Major R. Dawnay of the Coldstream who, as Brigade Major, had worked in the closest co-operation with the Battalion throughout the campaign. The one gleam in that gloomy episode was the magnificent feat of the Coldstream, of whom fifteen officers and 183 other ranks, under Major H. M. Sainthill, fought their way out and brought with

June 23   them over two hundred from other Regiments. On the 23rd the news

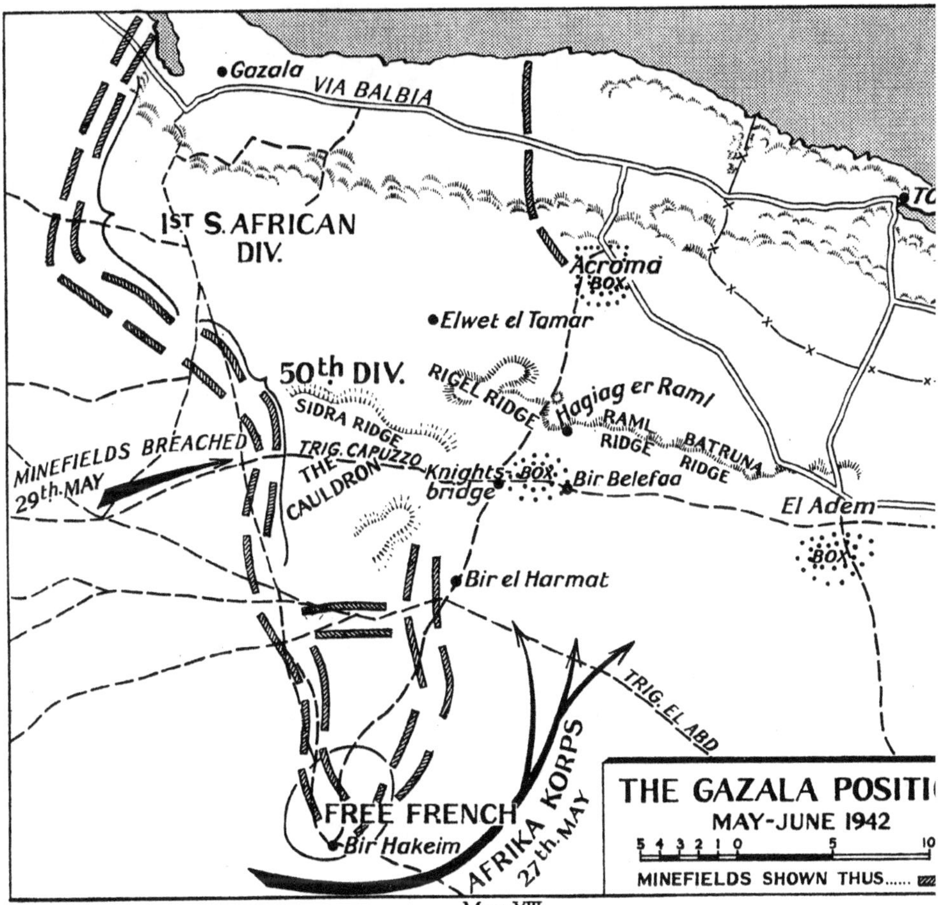

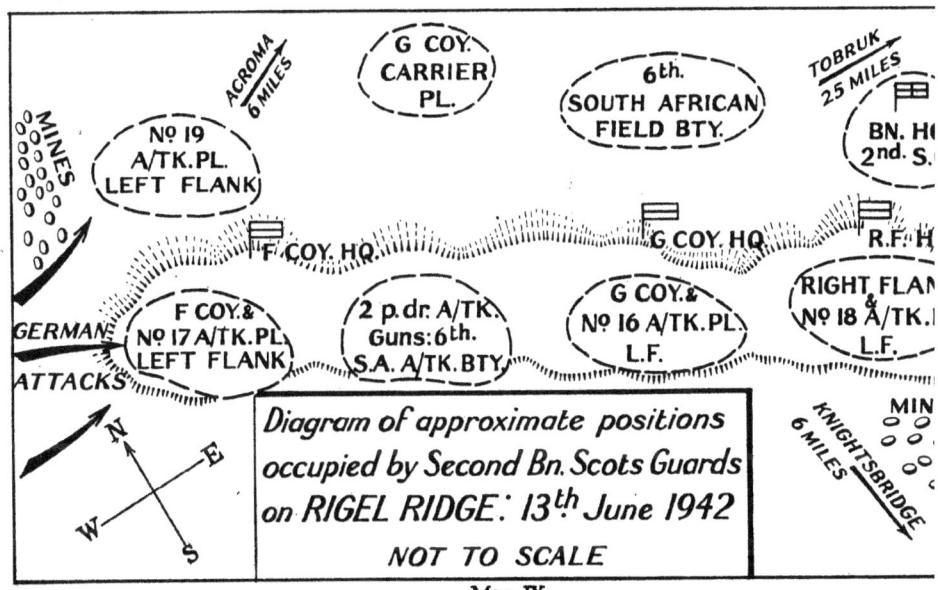

Map VIII

Map IX

was received that this Coldstream party was on its way back to Daba. One member, and one former member of the Regiment are known to have got away from Tobruk. Guardsman D. A. Nockles, Brigadier Johnson's driver, escaped by sea and reached the Battalion at Daba on the 23rd. Lieutenant T. A. Nicol, a former CQMS of G Company and then in the 2nd Cameron Highlanders, walked back bringing much valuable information.

The battle of Gazala and the loss of Tobruk resulted in the greatest disaster ever suffered by a British Imperial Army against a European enemy. The 201st Guards Brigade was in no wise disgraced. Those who fought in the Second Battalion Scots Guards and Third Battalion Coldstream Guards can take comfort from Rommel's own assessment of their qualities: "—almost a living embodiment of the virtues and faults of the British soldier—tremendous courage and tenacity combined with a rigid lack of mobility."[1] But Rommel had failed to appreciate that the "rigid lack of mobility" was ordered from above. Rigel and Knightsbridge were pivots to be held—and held they were, as long as "tremendous courage and tenacity" could hold them.

Major-General H. Lumsden, who commanded the 1st Armoured Division in the battle, summed up the Battalion's part in a letter to Colonel Grant:

"I shall always feel that somehow between us all we ought to have done better and yet of course your losses were not in vain, and, as I told you, our holding on that extra day made all the difference to the 1st South African Division and the 50th Division. Without your great struggle on the Rigel, the evacuation of the Knightsbridge Box would have been a very costly affair to the Coldstream and Brigade Headquarters, as there would have been such a small neck for them to pass through. . . . I look forward to having your Regiment once more under command, as they are the sort one likes to fight with."

In November 1942 Captain N. B. Hanmer, then in the Royal Sussex Regiment, was able to shed some light on the manner in which Rigel Ridge had been defended.

"We were resting at el Adem, after the battle of Alamein, and during my stay there, Rifle Companies used to go out into the 'blue' and camp near old British positions near Knightsbridge which had been overrun in June, 1942. . . . It was an amazing fact that none of these positions had been salvaged by the Germans. Many guns and vehicles were undamaged, even Bren carriers were found needing only a battery to be in good running order. Not one of our men had

[1] See *The Rommel Papers*, edited by Captain B. H. Liddell Hart (Collins), at page 222.

been buried, and driving through a position was like driving through a vast sand model on which some ingenuous "I" Sergeant had constructed, men and guns laid out in defensive positions. It was hard to realise that the men we saw had lived and led the same sort of life that we were living now. The sand appeared to have had some sort of preserving quality and the bodies were hardly decomposed.

A position which impressed me greatly was the 6-pounder antitank positions manned by the Scots Guards. They must have fired their guns until the German tanks were right on top of them. Almost every gun had the body of a Scots Guardsman drooped across the shoulder piece or slumped over the breech.

Several men were still crouching in slit trenches with rifles, as if they had continued engaging the enemy with .303 when their guns had been put out of action. There was an officer[1] lying on his face, his finger round the trigger of a Bren gun.

I don't remember their names or where they came from, they got as good a burial as we were able to give them.[2] We sent their particulars into Battalion Headquarters. But this I do know. The Germans had no easy time overrunning this anti-tank position; they had been faced by men of determination and courage.

It made me feel rather proud to look at those guns and see the dead men by their guns, which they seemed to serve even in death."

(f) *The Alamein Position*

June 1942 marked the nadir of our fortunes in the Middle East. While the New Zealanders fought their great defensive battle at Matruh, every formation that could be collected was moved to the west of Alexandria. In Cairo "the air was full of Bowler Hats and the ashes of secret papers"; at Alexandria what was left of the Fleet began to look for safer harbours.

June 27
June 30

On the 27th June the Battalion started for Amiriya, and on the 30th at Ikingi, preparations were begun for forming a Composite Battalion. The period of rest had been all too short. Rommel had realised that his best chance lay in unrelenting pursuit and attack before a defensive position could be stabilised. "Yesterday the rumble of gunfire reached us again, there was nervousness about the el Alamein Line, the wind whistled through the Eighth Army, and our battered remnants were ordered to take the field."

These battered remnants consisted of Battalion Headquarters

---

[1] A Lieutenant Welch, presumably a South African.
[2] Nine men were buried by this party from the Royal Sussex. One of the men was Guardsman J. Nisbet of No. 17 Anti-tank Platoon. It has been found impossible to trace the names of the others.

(Lieutenant-Colonel Grant, with Major G. C. Pereira, Coldstream, as second-in-command), one strong composite Company (Right Flank) under Major MacRae, with Captain Maxwell as second-in-command, and consisting of two Motor, one Carrier, one Machine Gun, and one Anti-Tank Platoons, and two weak Coldstream companies under Major Sainthill (who received the D.S.O. for his action at Tobruk and was shortly succeeded by Major B. E. Luard, M.C.), and Captain D. R. W. R. Watts-Russell. "It was rather a blow for the chaps as they had been told they were really coming out at last for a spell in the Delta. However, on the whole everyone has taken it very well, and they realise that their presence is badly needed here. When we got back four days ago things did not look too good, but now everyone is much more confident and we feel it will not be long before the tide starts to flow the other way. The R.A.F. have been wonderful, and I reckon that Rommel would now be in the Delta but for them."

July 2

On 2nd July the Composite Battalion was moved sixteen miles in the wrong direction, to the detriment of eleven new carriers and further wear on the old ones, and then immediately despatched west to take its place in the Alamein Line, just north of the Ruweisat Ridge. The word "line" in this connection is apt to be misunderstood, for its association with, for instance, the Siegfried Line tends to give the impression that there was a sort of wall of prepared positions behind which the Eighth Army retired. No such wall existed. The original Alamein Line consisted of the partially prepared Alamein Box and little more than good intentions extending south-west to the Qattara Depression. Except for the Alamein Box, this "line" was never in fact held. The final stand which saved Egypt and changed the whole course of the war was made roughly on where the original support line should have been. At no time did the Composite Battalion occupy a position already prepared, and it may be doubted if any other unit outside the Box did so either.

MAP X

The move, hindered by the softness of the ground and by breakdowns among the Battalion's aged vehicles, was completed by the morning of the 4th, when the Battalion took over protective duties for two Batteries of the 3rd R.H.A. "The going was extremely bad," the War Diary recorded, "And there will be no possibility of withdrawal from this position in face of the enemy. So far there are no mines on our front." In at least one sector it would seem that General Montgomery's famous order—"There will be no withdrawals. Absolutely none, none whatever—NONE"—had been anticipated by topography, and "there followed days noteworthy through the constant noise of shelling, the heat, the flies (aggravated by the unburied Italians in front of us), and the soft sand, in which our undesertworthy vehicles often stuck." It was an exacting life for men already tried, and unnecessary additional irritations made things no

July 4

easier: the occasion, for instance, when orders were suddenly received to send out a "Deep night patrol" with no further instructions than that the direction had better be west or west-south-west, with the only result that Lieutenant Clarke's carrier was hit by a shell from a tank at close range and had to be abandoned: a Coldstream sergeant bringing

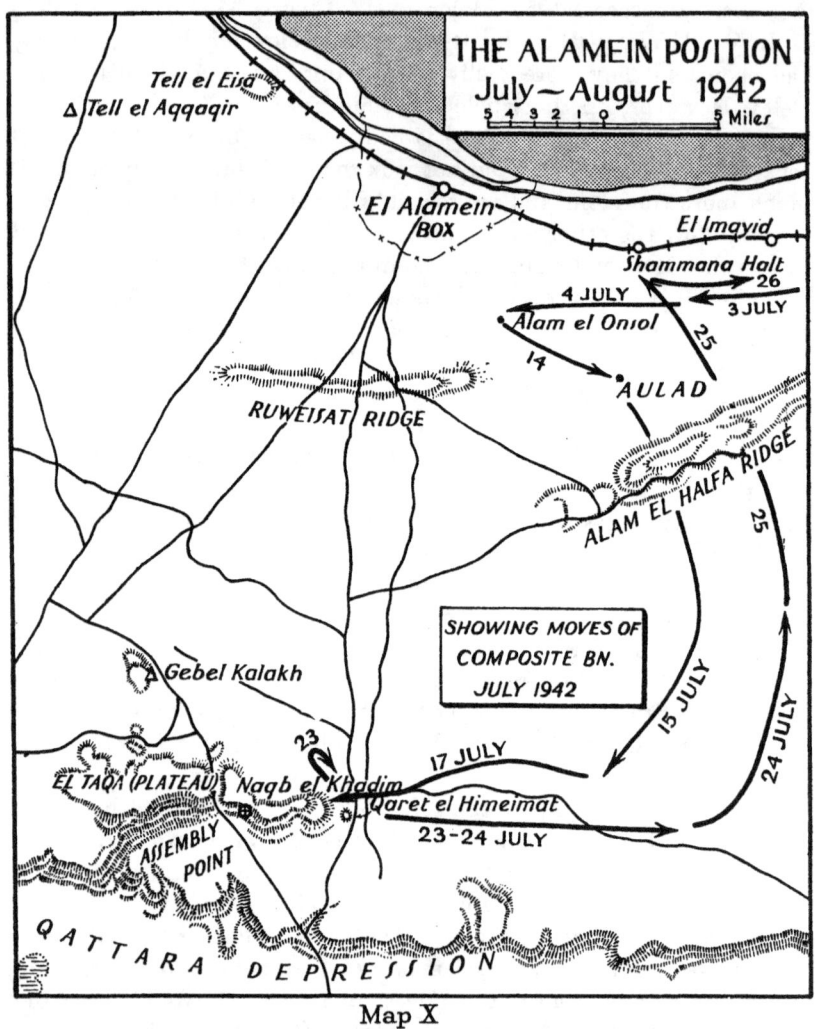

Map X

up some badly-needed men and asking the way and being told to go back towards Alexandria as "The Guards Brigade here is a new one just arrived from Syria". Nor was it clear at times under which formation they were serving. And on top of it all was ever-deferred recall from the Desert and again the growing list of casualties, among them Lieutenant A. Drummond-Hay, who had broken out of Tobruk in the

Coldstream party and was killed by a shell, and Lance-Sergeant A. S. Smith (M.T. Technical Stores) killed in a Stuka raid. But through it all a mood of modified confidence emerged. "All is under control, and if no more mistakes are made we have a great chance of pushing him back some distance. This desert battle will always be a running sore. The supply problem means that we can never get further west than Agheila. Similarly (we hope) they can't get further east than Alamein. All these places are no more than names. There are no buildings there."

On the 14th, orders were received to move south under the 7th Armoured Division with the purpose of harassing the enemy and forcing him to withdraw forces from the centre and north, and two days later the Composite Battalion went into action with M and J Batteries R.H.A. to the north-east of Qaret el Himeimat, a sugar-loaf hill of considerable height, the only distinctive landmark in the area, and much appreciated by the navigators. About fifteen miles further west and just over two miles north of the Qattara escarpment, lay el Taqa, one of many flat-topped hills in that part of the Desert, but important both from its size and its position. It was decided that the surest way to cause the enemy to reinforce his southern flank was to gain a footing on the plateau. *July 14*

The task was formidable, and in the circumstances the attack was one of the finest achievements of the Regiment in the Desert. Except to the north-west, where the ground fell gradually, making ascent to the plateau a simple matter for tanks, the sides of the hill were steep and in places precipitous and the numerous wadis descending from the irregular edge of the plateau made the concealment of defensive positions easy. At the south-eastern corner a single track gave the only possible approach for vehicles. A little below the plateau this track crossed a shelf about forty yards wide before completing the ascent. It was as though the top of a mountain had been sliced off and an attempt to take off another slice had been abandoned as soon as begun. It was clear that this pass and the south-eastern edge of the plateau were defended, but careful observation could not identify any anti-tank gun posts, although a patrol from the Battalion was certain they had drawn the fire of one such gun, a captured Russian piece which the Germans had flown across from the Balkans. The only advantage that the ground gave to the attacker was the presence of a similar though smaller hill, Naqb el Khadim, separated from the eastern end of Taqa by a narrow pass and giving concealed forming up and artillery positions in its re-entrants.

Early in the morning of 19th July, Captain Maxwell was sent out with a fighting patrol to secure the pass on to the plateau for the passage of six of the carriers followed by the rest of Right Flank at first light. The attack was successful in that a German officer and three privates were captured, though it was not made in quite the correct *July 19* place. The proximity of other well-manned enemy posts, however, made it clear that he could not hope to hold the pass with his small party, and he accordingly withdrew with his prisoners. Nevertheless, since no signs of any anti-tank guns had been seen that day, it was decided to continue the assault as planned, and at first light the attack went in. As the carriers got close in under the crest they came under heavy fire from machine-guns and anti-tank guns. The leading carrier was almost immediately hit and its commander, Second-Lieutenant M. F. Beeson, was killed, and the second carrier under Lieutenant Clarke was also hit and set on fire, Lance-Sergeant J. Doran, the wireless operator being killed. The situation was saved from getting worse largely by the quickness and courage of Guardsman S. R. McCormick, who engaged the crew of a 50-mm. anti-tank gun so successfully that they never succeeded in manning their gun and then with a grenade silenced a machine-gun post and enabled Lieutenant Clarke and his driver to get away safely from their burning carrier. The remaining carriers quickly got into action either from hull down positions or with crews dismounted, but the impossibility of dealing successfully with the hidden guns made it clear that the carriers alone could not take the position. Right Flank was therefore moved up in trucks to their left where they quickly got two machine-guns into action to give covering fire, while Lieutenant R. A. Willis brought his platoon up to the crest further to the left. On reaching the crest, Lieutenant Willis' right section was held up by close-range fire from an enemy post set a little way back on the plateau. Major MacRae at once went forward to this point with Lieutenant Willis to see how the situation could best be handled, but was almost immediately killed by a burst of machine-gun fire and Lieutenant Willis was wounded by a shell from an anti-tank gun.

Meanwhile the artillery from the north of Naqb el Khadim continued their efforts to silence such enemy posts as they could see, but the lie of the land gave them only a narrow strip of plateau on which to place their shells, and inevitably their "shorts" fell among our own carriers and their "overs" among Lieutenant N. H. Barne's platoon which had come up on the left of Lieutenant Willis's and was trying to work round the enemy's right flank. The skill and determination of this attack, which entailed the methodical silencing of each post in turn until the flank of the position was reached, was such that Lieutenant Barne was eventually able to work his way on to the plateau behind the enemy's position. During this flanking movement, in which the boldness and initiative of Sergeant A. Turner were also conspicuous, the platoon captured two lorries with anti-tank guns and complete crews, and on its gaining the plateau the enemy retreated and the Company was able to advance and occupy the position. In addition to those captured earlier by Captain Maxwell's party, twenty-nine prisoners were taken and four anti-tank guns, including the Russian 76-mm. and a number of machine-guns and smaller weapons. Two enemy dead were buried.

It had never been intended to consolidate and hold the position, but further action was necessary to cover the evacuation of wounded and prisoners and the withdrawal of the Company. Armoured car O.P.s with the Battalion's four anti-tank guns under Lieutenant Calvocoressi and a troop of South African armoured cars therefore moved out westwards along the plateau, which they had reached by a steep and narrow track, while a carrier patrol with another O.P. went to the northern edge. This anti-tank platoon was the original No. 18 Platoon of Left Flank, the sole survivors of the Rigel battle. One section of two guns mounted on Portees, on the orders of one of the O.P.s, went into action at long range against some enemy field guns. Despite frequent requests for high explosive, the 6-pounders had only armour-piercing ammunition against the field gun's high explosive, so the result was inevitable. Both the O.P.s were put out of action, the crew of one being rescued by Lieutenant Calvocoressi in an unarmoured vehicle. Lieutenant Calvocoressi was soon afterwards wounded when standing beside one of his 6-pounder portees which received a direct hit, but stayed with his guns to deal with an enemy counter-attack led by five tanks until the withdrawal was completed.

The attack on the Taqa plateau was doubly successful in that it achieved its immediate object and also caused the enemy to reinforce his southern flank, and in the circumstances the casualties (two officers killed and one wounded, and one other rank killed, two wounded, and one missing from the earlier fighting patrol) were astonishingly light. But the loss of Major John MacRae was a bitter and grievous blow. Fearless, determined, wise and quick in action, he was a leader such as no Battalion could afford to lose. When his body was brought back on a carrier, the crew would not admit he was dead; they found it too hard to believe. He was buried in the re-entrant on the south side of Naqb el Khadim where his Company had assembled before his last attack, and to commemorate him Pipe-Sergeant A. MacLennan composed a march, which is named after him.

"There followed uncomfortable days of order and counter-order, when much was required and little finally done." In the circumstances it was with something approaching surprise that the Battalion learned on the 21st that, having been to considerable trouble on the 19th to ensure that el Taqa was reinforced by the enemy, its next task was to take part in its recapture. It appeared that the occupation of el Taqa was essential to a scheme to send the newly constituted 4th Light Armoured Brigade round behind the main enemy forces, and that this was to be done on the following day in spite of the two essentials of success, tank support and sufficient infantry, not being

July 21

available. "The men have had a longer innings here than any other unit," one of the officers wrote. "We have only one Company left, and now that the general situation is in hand we should have a rest to get back and form up the Battalion again. The men were magnificent in the last engagement, but I am developing a view about the use of the remnants as Shock Troops." Actually the task given to the Battalion was the comparatively simple one of occupying the western rim of the Naqb el Khadim. But this entailed a night approach followed by the men spending the greater part of the day in shadeless slit trenches, confined by fire from the other side of the pass, under a very hot sun, and with no other sustenance than the warm water in their bottles and the bully that they had carried with them, while two weak battalions of the 69th Brigade put in an unreconnoitred attack that night on the Taqa Plateau. This attack was unsuccessful, and as a continuation of the policy of keeping the enemy's eyes upon the southern end of his line, the Battalion was invited to carry out another attack on the night of the 22nd/23rd, although the last man only got back to leaguer at 2230 on the 22nd.

July 22

July 23

The feature to be attacked was that of Gebel Kalakh, a smaller but more precipitous flat-topped hill about seven miles to the north-west. Fortunately the Commanding Officer was able to get the attack postponed, and the wearied men were able to get a short night's rest before starting off for a morning attack on the Gebel. After advancing about a mile and a half this attack also was cancelled and the Battalion returned to its former position east of Naqb el Khadim. It was perhaps fortunate. An advance over four miles of open country in full view of the enemy before passing through a gap in a minefield into soft sand was not an encouraging introduction to an assault on an unreconnoitred hill so steep that the one track up it was known to be usable only by vehicles coming down. The difficulties in the way of finding the gap in the minefield and attacking and consolidating at night were hardly offset by the advantages of a less conspicuous approach. A night attack, however, was proposed for the same night, but this also was cancelled, and that night the Battalion and 69th Brigade were withdrawn and on the morning of the 25th set off for the north.

July 24

July 25

July 26

By the afternoon of the 26th the Battalion was in its new area south of the railway between el Imayid and el Alamein stations, and later that day news was received that it was to be relieved with the exception of No. 18 Anti-Tank Platoon, which was required in action a little longer. Two days later the Composite Battalion had split up, and the Coldstream had gone to Mustapha Barracks at Alexandria and the Regiment to Cowley camp at Mena outside Cairo.

July 28
MAP V

Aug. 2

The respite was short, and by 2nd August the Battalion (now composed of two motor companies and Headquarters, all of the Regiment) had taken over guard duties on three aerodromes in the Amirya area and had been rejoined by Lieutenant Butter with No. 18 Platoon after fighting a gallant action at Ruweisat Ridge on the 26th and 27th. However, leave once more became possible, and the discomforts of August in the desert and its flies and the additional dust that goes with aerodromes were considerably alleviated by the kindness of the Royal Air Force.

On the 19th the Battalion moved to Qatatba on the edge of the Delta where the unaccustomed green was a solace to the eyes and where there were the additional amenities of a hutted camp and a plentiful supply of water. On the 21st Lieutenant-Colonel M. D. Erskine, who had previously commanded the First Battalion and had come from London District, took over command, and four days later the Battalion moved back to Mena where it was charged with the defence of the desert road to Cairo; the supporting gunners had an O.P. on the Great Pyramid. On the 31st Rommel started his final drive for the Delta. It was a costly failure, and by 6th September, when General the Hon. Sir Harold Alexander, now Commander-in-Chief in the Middle East, visited the Battalion, the German withdrawal was almost completed. The Battalion played its first cricket match since 1939 at Gezira, and on the 15th, now four companies strong again, it left for Syria. That night it rested by the west bank of the Canal at Ismalia. *(Aug. 19; Aug. 21; Aug. 25; Aug. 31; Sept. 6; Sept. 12; Sept. 15)*

It was but a remnant of the Battalion that had been on guard on the Canal nearly two years before that left Egypt on the 16th September. Others were to have the honour of the great break-through and the turn of the tide at Alamein. But the Battalion could at least rest assured that it had played its part in ensuring that there was a tide to turn. It had done all that was asked of it, and more. And if it privately believed that more had been asked of it than of many others, that was but the measure of its own confidence and of the repute that it had preserved and increased. *(Sept. 16)*

Few who served in the Battalion in that eventful year would disagree that three men stood out above their comrades. Thomas Ballantine Dykes and John MacRae were officers of sterling character upon which Regiments are built. The third was the Reverend V. C. Clarke, the padre. He served with the battalion all through the campaign, longer continuously than any other officer. His self-imposed duties knew no bounds and went far beyond his ministerial ones, always untiring and undaunted, and in adversity, always "jogging along". He had twice refused the post of Senior Church of Scotland Chaplain in the Middle East, in order that he might stay with the Battalion; the Guardsmen said his initials ought to be after his name. He was an irresistible influence for good, and it was with the most heartfelt sorrow that those who had served with him heard of his sudden death in hospital in Cairo on 26th September.

Such men had enabled the Second Battalion to give a new significance to "The Sphinx" superscribed "Egypt", which has been emblazoned on the Colours since 1802.

(g) *MAIDAN*[1] *SERENADE*

by Guardsman I. Eames
F Company, 2nd Bn. Scots Guards

Gun-posts, Last Posts, up and down the coast road,
Form fours, Mark IVs, rumours by the score;
Strong tea, P.T., round and round the Maidan,
Scots Guards and desert rats[2] are kin for ever-more.

Tool kit, NAAFI kit, both of them are missing,
Wagon Lines, number nines,[3] remove the signs of war;
Camel tanks, "I" Tanks, scattered round the desert,
Scots Guards and desert rats are kin for ever-more.

Brew up,[4] Start up, make your bloody mind up,
Cold Shai,[5] gun shy; a tin of "swanks" to four,
Wadies, bodies; compass going haywire,
Scots Guards and desert rats are kin for ever-more.

Insects, fair sex, enough to drive you crazy,
"Slap-happy", "Flap-happy",[6] drill parades galore;
Side-hats, Ersatz, dig yourself a slit trench,
Scots Guards and desert rats are kin for ever-more.

Woollen mitts, Messerschmitts, listen to the whining,
Tomahawks, Kittyhawks, always claiming more,
Sandbags, "Jewbags", cap-star needing shining,
Scots Guards and desert rats are kin for ever-more.

Petrol tins, "all-ins",[7] come and get your rations,
Fouling, prowling,[8] on from two to four;
Benzine, Khamseen,[9] sort that petrol stoppage,
Scots Guards and desert rats are kin for ever-more.

[1] Maidan—The Desert.
[2] Desert Rat—Also the now famous sign of the 7th Armd. Div.
[3] Number Nine—Also Scots Guards vehicle number.
[4] Brew Up—Truck cooking in the desert, usually by mixing sand and petrol in a sawn-off petrol tin.
[5] Shai—Egyptian for tea.
[6] Flap-happy—A frame of mind resulting from a series of Flaps, i.e. real or imaginary enemy break-throughs.
[7] All-in—Petrol tin stew containing all rations issued, mixed up.
[8] Prowlers—Night Guards on leaguers known as "prowlers".
[9] Khamseen—Hot desert wind, usually accompanied by sand, capable of stopping more than just petrol stoppages.

Barbed-wire, "Stanna Shwyah",[10] camouflage that shadow,
Tight nut, hard butt, another desert sore;
Scoff up, wrap up, where's my "Jerry" spoon gone,
Scots Guards and desert rats are kin for ever-more.

Pickets, biscuits, bully-beef for breakfast,
Fuka,[11] Stuka, Lunch is bully raw;
Pick-axe, ack-acks, bully stew for dinner,
Scots Guards and desert rats are kin for ever-more.

(h) *Syria and the Great Trek*

The strange sensation of combined relief and nostalgia that comes from the sight of green hills and clear mountain streams after sojourn among sand and the arid hills of the desert lies behind an entry in the War Diary for 17th September 1942: "The Battalion reached Tulkarm West at 1430 hours after driving for 120 miles through the most pleasant country they had seen since leaving England in November, 1938." On the following day the Battalion reached the hutted Camp at Qatana a few miles from Damascus, which was to be its home for the next five months. Even with the accessions received before leaving the Delta the Battalion was still under half its strength, but an intensive training programme was immediately put in hand and the benefits of the complete change of air and scene quickly made themselves apparent, though jaundice did its best to mar the lives of the officers. *(MAP V)*

Activities were not wholly confined to training, and three days after arrival at Qatana Lieutenant M. J. A. Gordon and a platoon of Right Flank were sent off on an expedition to look for two army tractors which had been stolen during the Iraqi rebellion in the previous year and were believed to be hidden somewhere to the north of Palmyra about two hundred miles away. The search might well have seemed hopeless and armed resistance had been considered possible, but two days later he was able to send a report that they had captured the two tractors, fifty tons of hoarded wheat, one sheik, and four hundred tribesmen. The whole episode has a curiously Kiplingesque flavour, even to the tractors being hidden under eighteen inches of soil and the sheik's explanation that they had been buried there since the time of the Romans; the mollifying gift of a sheep (which proved to be very tough); and being taken by the sheikh for a drive in a thirty horse-power Buick surrounded by his heavily armed retainers. *(Sept. 18, Sept. 21, Sept. 23)*

On the 25th a party of eight officers from the Brigade including Lieutenant-Colonel Erskine and Captain Crichton-Stuart, dined with the Emir Fawaz of the Ruwalla: "We sat round a large dish on the *(Sept. 25)*

---

[10] Stanna Shwyah—Egyptian for "Wait a moment".
[11] Fuka—Well-known place between Matruh and Daaba.

floor and ate with our hands, very good food too." The eyeglass of Brigadier J. A. Gascoigne was an object of much interest. But the Battalion pipers were the success of the evening. "A huge black slave of the Emir's carried a lantern to light them. He wore a long scarlet coat reaching from his neck to his ankles, and a dark blue short coat, highly ornamented with gold lace. The five pipers marched in single file with the colossal jet-black slave keeping step and dressing with the second file, the light from his lantern which he held up above his head flashing on his ebony face and on the streamers and uniforms of the pipers." On coming in a second time they played, halted in line, "and the slave holding the lamp kept time with his right foot, exactly like the pipers. When they changed to a time to which they tapped with the toes of both feet, he was a little tied up for a moment but very quickly picked that up, too." On learning that the Battalion was in need of a Drum-Major, the Emir immediately offered the services of the lantern bearer, but the thought of the possible reactions of the Sergeant-Major led to no further action being taken, and the Band not only lost a promising recruit, but also the possibilities of having its first black member for almost exactly a hundred and one years. So impressed was the Emir that when he came to London in 1945 he expressed a particular desire to hear the pipes again. Captain Crichton-Stuart arranged this for him at Wellington Barracks.

Oct. 15 On 15th October the decision was announced that the Battalion, which had been organised in August in four equal Companies each with one Motor, one Motor Machine Gun, one Carrier, and one Anti-Tank Platoon, should revert to three Motor Companies and one Anti-Tank Company; Left Flank was in its familiar role again. Under the experienced eyes of Captain Butter and Sergeant V. N. Mutch, and based on the veterans of No. 18 Platoon, the anti-tank company was formed and trained—to what good purpose will soon be seen. On the
Oct. 23 evening of the 23rd five hundred miles away the Western Desert shook under the great barrage that opened the Battle of Alamein. On
Nov. 8 the 8th November the Allies landed on the coasts of French North Africa, and the advance which was to end in the meeting of the First and Eighth Armies began.

Nov. 10–24 On the morning of 10th November the Battalion left Qatana to take part with the 3rd Coldstream and the 6th Grenadiers in an exercise and "flag-showing" march of the reformed 201st Guards Brigade. By the 24th the Battalion was back at Qatana. Its travels had taken it to Baalbeck, where the pipers played in the main street and the ruins stood out against the background of a red sunset and snowcapped hills; to Tel Kalak, whence a party from each Company was able to visit Krak des Chevaliers in the brilliant sunshine; to Latakia, where the pipers led the Battalion through the town and the whole Battalion bathed in the sea; to Aleppo, where the whole Brigade marched through the town; to Meskene, where the scheme actually started; to Sabkha over appalling roads in the dark; along the Euphrates, "a very dirty, sluggish river", to Dier ez Zor, "an outlandish and very dirty place", where the exercise ended. Here the Battalion "drove past" a French general. As usual the tail of the column sped past in a cloud of dust far faster than the head; the last vehicle was the Officers' Mess 3-tonner, and in the back Guardsman Brownlees casually plucked a duck as he passed the saluting base. Then to Palmyra, doing desert training on the way. The day after the Battalion got back to Qatana the first British ship entered Benghazi harbour. "Lovely weather still, but snow on all the high hills. We are wondering where we shall next be used." Nov. 25

Meanwhile Alamein was passing into history and on 14th December, as Rommel was starting his withdrawal from his Agheila positions, the Commanding Officer left for a tour of the Alamein battlefield. Christmas brought carols in the snow, and the minds of many went back to the last Christmas and the dreary approach to Agedabia. But Agedabia was now no more than a milestone on the way to Buerat. Dec.

Training in January, 1943, was pushed on mostly in rain and cold and mud as the Battalion slowly crept up to full strength. The later arrivals were comparatively untrained and unfit after their long sea voyage, and the Battalion had already been warned on the 30th for a move to an unknown destination before the last of them arrived. The 11th Hussars, companions of the Battalion during the period before Agedabia, had already entered Tripoli. 1943 January

On 4th February two Companies started for Egypt by train and on the 7th the rest of the Battalion moved out along the long flat road towards Palestine with the snows of Mount Hermon glittering in the sunlight to the west. That night, after covering 132 miles, it rested at Tulkarm, and the next night after 120 miles at Asluj, where its arrival an hour and a half ahead of schedule met with some displeasure; its next arrival ahead of time was to be welcomed. Early next morning the Battalion set off on the wearisome 170 miles of Sinai: "We flogged and flogged across nothing. Just sand and more sand. . . . Some brown, some white, some hard, some soft, but all sand. . . . Next morning we crossed the canal and rumbled into Egypt, the country of thieves and flies." Feb. 4 Feb. 7 Feb. 8 Feb. 9 Feb. 10

During the 10th, 11th and 12th the Battalion had a hurried but complete refit at Kassassin. A hundred and thirty-two miles were covered on the 13th, and the Battalion under the command of Major G. A. D. Taylor, after crossing the Nile at Cairo, entered the Western Desert. Then it turned west along the main coast road and "in an incredibly short time we got to Alamein, a frighteningly short time," and then on between the wreckage of German tanks and guns to Feb. 13 Feb. 14

Feb. 15	Daba: 145 miles. The next day was an easy run, eighty-one miles to Mersa Matruh, and the start was in daylight after P.T. and Company Runs. "All along the edge of the road there was a mass of blown up trucks mostly upside down and nearly all enemy stuff. . . . We fairly caught the enemy aeroplanes at Galal and Fuka, and the remains of a huge number were scattered all over the place." That day Major A. E. Cameron, commanding Right Flank, took a large party south to Taqa to visit the graves of Major MacRae and Lieutenant Beeson and
Feb. 16	Sergeant Doran. The next day, after 105 miles through "just the same scrubby country, just the same minefields, just the same bust up Hun and Wop trucks," the Battalion pipers played retreat at Buq Buq, passing Sidi Barrani on the way, "a tiny yellow shambles on the coast," with the Desert beginning to look greener and a few wild flowers
Feb. 17	showing. Then on the next day in brilliant sunshine 118 miles to el Adem, past the bottom of Halfaya, still too heavily mined for use, and
Feb. 18	climbing the escarpment up the steep track from Sollum. The 18th was spent in maintenance and bath parties and in visiting the positions on Rigel Ridge where the grave of Major Ballantine Dykes was found
Feb. 19	and marked. Then on again by Gazala and Tmimi, 105 miles to Martuba, the last part by green and undulating country and a scent of
Feb. 20	herbs. On the 20th eighty-five miles: north-west to the cliff's edge above the sea, then the steep winding descent to the white houses of Derna, "smothered in 'Duce's'", among the trees; back up the cliff and on through the fertile hills past the "nice little white Italian houses with Ente Colonizzione Libya over the door" to Maddalena.
Feb. 21	The next day eighty-eight miles on through the fine country of the Italian colony past Barce and down to the sand of the coastal plain and into the smell and desolation of Benghazi in a gale of wind. It had been hoped to have twenty-four hours there for maintenance, but the
Feb. 22	time could not be spared, and on the next day 130 miles were covered. Breakfasts were eaten on the way and, while a party visited the graves of Lieutenant Critchley and those who fell with him, the Battalion staged about twenty miles beyond Agedabia. Thenceforward the land no longer held memories, and this time there was to be no return.
Feb. 23	On the 23rd another 114 miles of the Via Balbia were covered. The road led on through dull flat sand in which flowers gave an odd look of heather to the rank grass and camel-thorn and a persistent dune hid the refreshment of the sea. The great bastion of Agheila was no more than a name, and Marble Arch no more than a folly in the sand. Carved across the top was NIHIL ROMA VISERE MAJUS[1]: written on the base was "Merry Xmas 1942". Fifteen miles beyond the Arch the Battalion leaguered as a whole for the first time. Another 120 miles
Feb. 24	the next day and the Battalion rested five miles beyond Sirte ("a hundred white houses full of booby traps and a mosque": two trucks

[1] "Rome saw nothing greater than this."

were damaged there on mines), where the Brigade got orders to move on with all speed to Medenine in Tunisia. On again next day 164 miles to Misurata, leaving the coast at Buerat, all through desert except about the last twenty miles where the little white houses of the colonists bore inscriptions such as "We will conquer" and "The Italian people is worthy of victory" and "Let us cultivate the land". On the 26th 142 miles through fine country brought the Battalion to Tripoli where it was met by the Commanding Officer, who had flown on from Cairo, and the advance party. The Brigade was two days ahead of schedule, and the 27th was passed in maintenance and baths. At 0242 on the 28th the Battalion started once more and at 1300 it staged at Ben Gardane. A hundred and thirty-one miles had been covered, and at Ras Agedir the frontier into Tunisia had been crossed. Libya and the defence of Egypt had moved back into history.

Feb. 25

Feb. 26

Feb. 28

Forty-five miles ahead lay Medenine. By dawn on 2nd March the Battalion had moved into position below Tadjera Khir.

Mar. 2

(i) *Revenge at Medenine*

The Battalion had covered well over two thousand miles in twenty-three days, of which three had been spent in a complete refit and only two in maintenance, and the last part of the journey had been made over a road already burdened with the petrol and other supply columns of the Eighth Army. The work of the Brigade and Battalion fitters under Lieutenant A. H. M. Thavenot, the Transport Officer, and Lieutenant Crozier, R.E.M.E., had been such that, in spite of mines and the normal hazards of the road, the Battalion arrived short of one truck only. It was a notable achievement, but even so the journey had been completed only just in time. March 2nd and 3rd were given entirely to digging and mine-laying, and the work was continued on the 4th. On the 5th orders of the day were issued by the opposing Commanders. General Montgomery said that he hoped that the enemy would attack while fearing that they would not, and that they were now advancing for that purpose. Marshal Rommel told his Panzer Divisions that their objective was the high ground dominating the Medenine plain behind the Battalion position, and that if they failed to take it the days of the Afrika Korps were numbered.

MAPS XI and XII March

Mar. 5

The Mareth Line, originally prepared by the French against possible attack by the Italians, occupied an immensely strong natural position in a range of hills, and it ran approximately south-west covering Gabes. Roughly parallel to the Matmata Hills in the low ground and foothills to the east was the road from Mareth to Medenine. Because of the difficulties of supply, General Montgomery had conducted the pursuit from Tripoli with the smallest possible number of troops. The result of this was that on 27th February little more than the 7th

Armoured Division was in contact with the enemy, with the 51st (Highland) Division in the process of arriving. It was not the most opportune moment for creating a diversion, but it was imperative that something be done to relieve the pressure on the First Army and on the Americans at Le Kef, who were undergoing an experience very similar to that of our 2nd Armoured Division in January 1942. The efforts of the Highland Division were almost too successful, and, perhaps mistaking a jab for the beginnings of a break-through, Rommel hurried three Armoured Divisions south to counter-attack from the Mareth Line.

The line of troops which had been hurried forward to face this threat was very thin and could achieve practically no defence in depth. It had, however, plentiful artillery in support and the 22nd and 8th Armoured Brigades were east of the Medenine–Mareth road in the event of the enemy breaking through. The 2nd New Zealand Division held the sector south-west of the road between Medenine and Metameur. The 3rd Coldstream were on their right, and the Scots Guards[1] between the Coldstream and the 131st (Queen's) Brigade. The 6th Grenadiers were in reserve astride the road in a hollow of the high ground known as Tadjera Khir. If Tadjera Khir had fallen the whole Eighth Army position would have been untenable. A German map found after the battle in an enemy tank on F Company front showed that the axis of their advance was to have been through the Battalion position.

When the order came through to complete the march to Medenine with the utmost speed, Major Taylor, then commanding the Battalion, remarked that it was not so much the Guards Brigade that was being asked for as its forty-eight anti-tank guns. Each battalion now had its complement of sixteen guns and, unlike the state of affairs at Rigel, each platoon of four guns was not only trained in its weapons, but also in working with the rifle company to which it was attached. The anti-tank gunners, too, were experienced in battle, for when the Battalion was reorganised in Syria the old soldiers were posted to the specialised work of Left Flank and the new drafts were sent to the rifle companies. It was to be an old soldiers' battle.

The Battalion position, which extended for two thousand yards, was held with Right Flank (Major Cameron) on the right, F Company (Major Crichton-Stuart) in the centre, and G Company (Major R. G. Lewthwaite) on the left. Battalion Headquarters and Headquarter Company (Major D. H. A. Kemble, M.C.[2]), less all the Battalion transport which had been sent well back, save for a few jeeps and wireless trucks, were on the forward slopes of the ridge behind them.

[1] For Order of Battle, see p. 550.
[2] Major Kemble had been awarded the Military Cross when commanding a company of the King's African Rifles in the campaign in Ethiopia in 1941.

The ground rose for about three hundred yards in front of the position and then sank again to the plain in front of the great hills of the Mareth Line.

The position was ideal for anti-tank guns, for no gun could give away its position by firing too soon, and the enemy could not see the guns until they opened fire at close range. The utmost use of these advantages was made by Major Taylor in the siting of the guns, and it is possible that the movement around Battalion Headquarters (which brought a lot of unwelcome attention) led the enemy to believe until the last moment that the defended line was on the higher ground behind. The only weakness of the position lay in the facts that there was neither time nor material to lay a minefield across the front and that some wadis running into the position from the west could not be properly covered by anti-tank guns. It was hoped, however, that the few rather puny Hawkins Grenade mines available would at least have a disconcerting and delaying effect, and that dummy minefields consisting of two strands of barbed wire and some bully beef tins to give enemy detectors something to work on would do the rest. From the Battalion position the ground in front looked flat, but it was in fact cut by a succession of deep wadis running parallel to the front and giving covered forming-up positions to the enemy. As the Army Commander wrote later, "our anti-tank guns . . . were sited to kill tanks at point-blank range: and not to defend the infantry."

The shelling and bombing of the preceding days had not interfered with the digging (indeed in the case of Brigade Headquarters it seems to have expedited it), and by the evening of the 5th everything was ready and a strong tip had been received that the attack would come next day or not at all. Soon after the first light Lieutenant P. H. Gibbs, who had been out all night with an F Company carrier patrol, reported that he was in difficulties with enemy tanks, and in his withdrawal three carriers were lost with two crews. At 0500 the shelling started, and at 0715 reports began to come in of enemy tanks to the south-west moving towards the Coldstream and the New Zealanders. The Coldstream got one tank immediately, and the accuracy of their shooting and the convincing appearance of their dummy minefield caused the Germans to turn north and south and not trouble them again for the rest of the action. Those that turned north worked their way under cover to the part of the line held by G Company. "The rumbling they made was terrific and it gradually got nearer and nearer. . . . Then quite suddenly three of them appeared peeping over the ridge. They were obviously suspicious, rather like a little party of deer, but as they could see nothing they came lumbering on. We let them just get over the crest and then every gun [of Lieutenant F. A. L. Waldron's Platoon of Left Flank] opened up and in ten seconds all three were on fire."

The distribution of one anti-tank platoon to each forward company

Mar. 6

still left one platoon of four guns under Lieutenant J. D. A. Stainton in reserve, and two of these guns were kept on portees throughout the action. Back at Battalion Headquarters, where the view was much more comprehensive, Major J. H. Elwes, M.C., the second-in-command, saw where the first attack was coming and led one of the guns to the spot and scored a broadside hit with his first shot. Thenceforward these guns moved about the front, backing up to the crest wherever danger was most imminent. In their handling the courage and determination of Sergeant V. N. Mutch[1] was outstanding and at least one tank was destroyed by his gun.

In the meantime more and more tanks were moving into position behind the ridge, and shelling on both sides became heavy; "It's incredible how many shells can land within a few yards without so much as driving the flies away. Rather unkindly he punctured most of our water tins. . . ." Men like Sergeant W. Lumsden,[1] Lance-Corporals J. H. Jenkins[1] and J. McComb,[1] all anti-tank gunners, took about as much notice of the shells as did the flies. Battalion Headquarters on its forward slope received particular attention from the enemy's guns and was visited by the Brigade Commander when the shelling was at its height. Concentrated small arms fire added to the din as the machine-guns of the tanks came into action: "My Platoon H.Q. was well dug into a tree and . . . there were so many leaves and twigs falling around us that my Sergeant remarked it was quite like Autumn", and every possible weapon was turned on each tank to ensure that observation was lessened by lids being kept shut.

There was a pause after the loss of the first three tanks, and then they tried again a little further on with much the same result, and an hour later two more tanks were burning in front of F Company, the victims of Lieutenant A. N. J. Gordon's 6-pounders. The general trend of the battle was from south to north, as the tanks groped for a weaker point to break through. There was no weaker point, and a final attempt on the position in line led to the survivors retreating back over the crest.

Meanwhile a platoon of F Company under Lieutenant H. J. H. Eves, which had been detached in support of a battalion in 131st Brigade, was getting an increasing share of the battle as the probing moved north along the front. Its position[2] was far from comfortable as that Brigade's line was further forward than that of the Guards Brigade and the platoon was placed further forward still to enable it to enfilade any infantry attack on the Queen's front. In consequence of this it had nothing between it and any tanks that might try to come over the ridge. It was intended that these should be dealt with by

[1] All awarded the Military Medal, as was Lance-Corporal T. Davies, who manned an O.P.
[2] Marked X on Map XII.

artillery concentrations. They were, and one tank attack was broken up only 300 yards away though still out of sight. In addition to his immediate task, Lieutenant Eves' position enabled him to see down the wadis in which the tanks were assembling on the Regiment's front, and the information he was able to take back led to one attack being broken up by artillery fire before it started.

By midday the attack was over. Four Mark IV Specials, one Mark IV, two Mark II Specials and five Mark IIIs, total twelve, lay abandoned hulks on the Battalion front. Two of them had got to 150 yards of the guns. At least two, and probably three, others had been knocked out but dragged back over the ridge. And it now transpired that all those tanks were from the 21st Panzer Division, the same formation which, nine months before, had overrun the companies on Rigel Ridge. This time the Battalion had one jeep and one anti-tank gun knocked out. Save for one troop with 131st Brigade, our tanks had not been engaged at all.

Infantry attacks had been intended for 1430 and 1630 hours, but in at least one case a wireless intercept gave the assembly area, and the artillery did the rest. The attacks proved to be intended for the 131st Brigade on the right and the 5th New Zealand Brigade on the left. In the latter case the normal artillery support proved insufficient and an additional hundred guns were brought to bear. They fired five rounds each three times. "The result," the War Diary recorded, "was very satisfactory." The work of the artillery throughout the day was superb. It was not so much support as united action, and was only marred by two concentrations falling short, one on Right Flank which caused several casualties, and one on Lieutenant Eves' platoon where one man was wounded.

Away to the north and south attacks by German infantry and the 10th and 15th Panzer Divisions also failed, and, though the possibility of a further tank attack at dawn remained, the great counter-attack at Medenine was in fact over. That night was exceptionally dark, with torrential rain, and patrols—and indeed all the forward companies—although they heard a lot, could see nothing. Reliance was therefore placed chiefly on artillery concentrations on likely areas. These too were successful, and the next day at least two tanks were found with chains attached ready for towing. Two men from one of the Battalion's patrols got lost so decided to sleep where they were and wait for daylight. They were woken about an hour and a half before dawn by German voices shouting orders and the noise of tanks being started and driven away. When daylight came it was clear why no further attack had come in through the dawn mist. Fifty-two tanks were counted in front of the Eighth Army. "It was a grand sight and as the result of the battle the confidence of the Battalion is unbounded." Rommel had lost a third of his tanks.

Mar. 7

The casualties, except for two anti-tank crews knocked out by tanks, were almost all caused by shelling, and in the circumstances were remarkably light. Drill-Sergeant J. Richmond, D.C.M., who was unluckily hit when in a slit trench and who had been one of the mainstays of the Battalion since the early days, three Lance-Corporals and four Guardsmen were killed, and three Guardsmen died of their wounds. Major Lewthwaite was seriously wounded when helping one of his gun crews to move their gun, and nineteen other ranks were wounded. In addition six other ranks from the carrier patrol the previous night were missing, and were later learned to be prisoners.

In the morning General Sir Bernard Montgomery, accompanied by Major-General G. W. E. J. Erskine, who commanded the 7th Armoured Division, made a brief visit to the Battalion; the Army Commander made a speech to as many of the officers who could be collected in the F Company area; in the afternoon came Lieutenant-General Sir Oliver Leese, Bt., who commanded the XXX Corps. On the 8th Major-General Erskine wrote: "I had rather a proud day today. I took Monty round the battlefield and showed him exactly what happened on March 6th. It had turned out even better than I had reported. . . . The men fought magnificently and are absolutely delighted with their success." The Scots Guards had reason to be. They knew that their Battalion had been largely responsible for that success: they had received the immediate congratulations of General Montgomery on its "magnificent performance". Later he was to write that it was "a model defensive engagement and a great triumph for the Infantry and the anti-tank gun." To the Second Battalion it was also a glorious revenge.

For his handling of the Battalion in this critical encounter with its immense effects on the Tunisian campaign, Lieutenant-Colonel M. D. Erskine, who had been with the anti-tank guns throughout the action, received the D.S.O., Major Lewthwaite and Major Taylor, whose tactical handling and inspiring leadership of his Anti-Tank Company was outstanding, received Military Crosses.

(j) *Through the Mareth Line*

For the next week the Battalion remained in the positions it had occupied at the Battle of Medenine, active patrolling took place towards the Mareth Line, and vigorous training was put in hand, one anti-tank practice being stopped by enemy shelling. Life had suddenly changed to the normal of front-line existence and, thanks to air superiority, there was little bombing. "Life is not bad—a bit too sandy—but for the moment food and water are plentiful and good," though, as usual in the Desert, insufficient for a bath. Flies were not too troublesome, and the climate was delightful, but the flower-covered plain with its cultivation and insanitary straw huts produced more than enough fleas: "This morning I bagged nine in the seams of one pair of trousers." Mosquitoes, too, were troublesome. On Sunday, 14th, a service of thanksgiving for the Battle of Medenine was held. Mar. 14

Five miles away to the north-west of where the Battalion awaited the next move was an irregular crescent-shaped formation of hills something under three hundred feet high. This Horseshoe feature, as it became known, was about three miles in front of the main Mareth positions and dominated them; it was believed to be lightly held. In order to cover the flank of the intended attack on the Mareth Line to the north, it was necessary to occupy this feature, and for various reasons, among them the fact that it was looked upon as a simple matter, "Two-O-One", which had had no opportunity for brigade training, was chosen for the task. Lavish artillery support was available, and it was intended that direction should be kept, in spite of the broken nature of the ground and the impossibility of proper reconaissance, by following the barrage on to the objectives.

On the night of 13th March the 6th Grenadiers and the 3rd Coldstream moved to areas about four and a half miles in front of the Horseshoe, and on the following day they moved forward about two miles to positions west of the Wadi Hachana, the Scots Guards moving into the area vacated by the Grenadiers—the last of a tiresome series of nightly moves. On the night of the 16th the attack went in, the Mar. 16
Grenadiers on the right and the Coldstream on the left, and the Battalion moving up in reserve to the eastern side of the Wadi bou Remli which ran across the front of the position and in many places had vertical sides from three to thirty feet in height.

The heroic onslaught of the heavily outnumbered Grenadiers and Coldstream, the capture of their objectives and the impossibility of retaining them, and the withdrawal through the Battalion under cover of smoke next day, are matters concerning their history rather than that of the Battalion. For it was the Battalion's part to wait, under shell, mortar and machine-gun fire, in and around a small grove of figs and olives and palm trees, while astonishing success turned to tragic failure. Although the Battalion was dug in on a reverse slope the enemy guns and mortars did some shrewd shooting, and on the 16th and 17th Majors Taylor, Crichton-Stuart and Kemble were wounded, the latter seriously, wholly losing the sight of one eye; also Lieutenants A. Drew and A. J. A. Weir. All the next day, too, the Battalion was under intermittent shell and mortar fire; in the morning Lieutenant Eves was killed, and in the evening, the second-in-command, Major Elwes. In addition to these casualties, two other ranks were killed, and twenty-one wounded, including CSM W. Gore of G Company who later died, and two other ranks were missing. The Grenadier and Coldstream casualties amounted to the awful total of thirty-four officers and 381 other ranks, killed, wounded and missing; the Grenadiers alone had fourteen officers and sixty-three other ranks killed. Surely this was one of the most terrible nights in the history of the Brigade of Guards. The outpost which they had been sent to attack, and which was believed to be so lightly held that the defenders were insufficient to lay a proper minefield, had in fact been defended by the greater part of the 90th Light Division reinforced by a battalion of Panzer Grenadiers, and had been so heavily mined with three belts that it was impossible for any supporting weapons to be brought forward when the objectives had been reached. Yet the endeavour had not been wasted. The Germans were wholly deceived as to where the main attack on the Mareth Line was going to be delivered, the occupiers of the Horseshoe were unable to go to other sectors where

Mar. 21 their presence was urgently needed, and when on the 21st the news was received that the 4th Indian and 50th Divisions had attacked and made varying progress to the north, and that the New Zealanders and the X Corps had successfully worked round the enemy's southern flank behind the Matmata Hills, the Brigade knew that it had played its part—at a tragic cost.

On the previous day, 250 miles to the north, a third Guards Brigade had entered the line at Medjez-el-Bab; in it was the First Battalion of the Regiment.

Mar. 26 On the 26th the Second Battalion returned to the position it had occupied on the night of the 15th/16th and, in all the discomforts of a khamsin, there known as a Gibli, took over from the 6th Green
Mar. 27 Howards, and the next day it moved south to the Gebel Saikra area
Mar. 28 where it relieved the 1st Rifle Brigade on the 28th and lost Lieutenant R. C. McLeod, wounded, and two other ranks killed and four wounded, in crossing a minefield. That night the enemy evacuated the Mareth Line.

After a brief period of rest and cleaning and after a morning Church
April 5 Parade, the Battalion moved north again, and by the evening of 5th April was in position to support the Highland Division in its attack on the Wadi Akarit defences. This attack went in on the Battalion's left at
April 6 0430 on the 6th, and the only tasks of the Battalion, which had a grandstand view of the whole proceeding, were to put down heavy covering fire and, by means of smoke, give the impression that the Brigade was also taking part in the attack. That night the enemy withdrew, and Lieutenant Weir took out a patrol and returned with one German
April 7 and about twenty-five Italian prisoners. The next day companies were able to send parties to bathe in the sea.

April 10 Sfax was evacuated by the enemy early in the morning of the 10th, and that afternoon after a troublesome march the Brigade by-passed the town, while the Highlanders marched through and were received in a gratifying manner by the inhabitants. The Battalion leaguered in

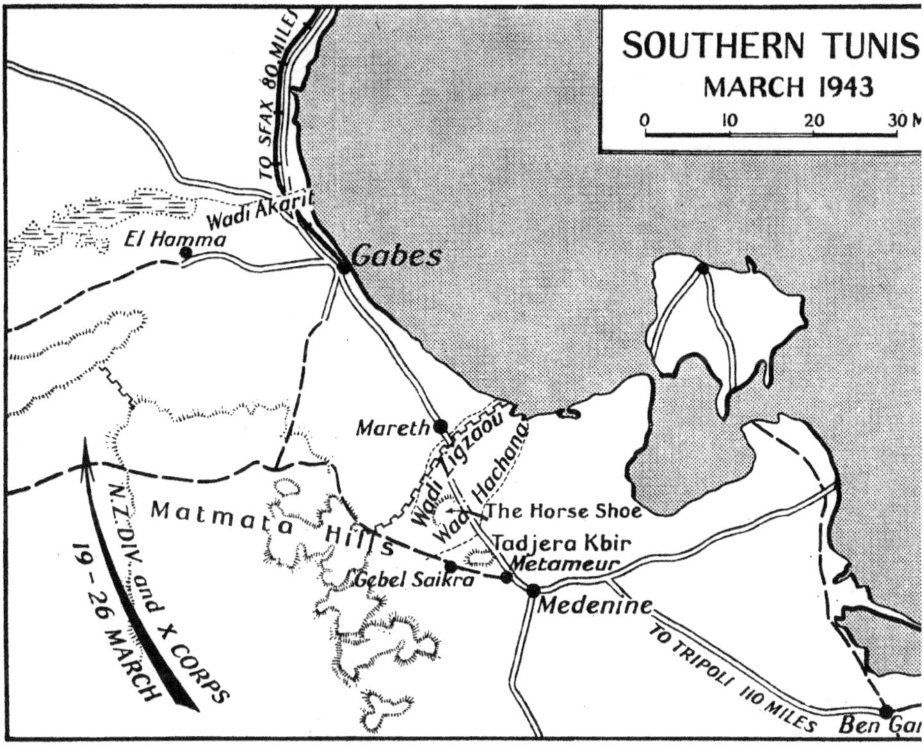

Map XI

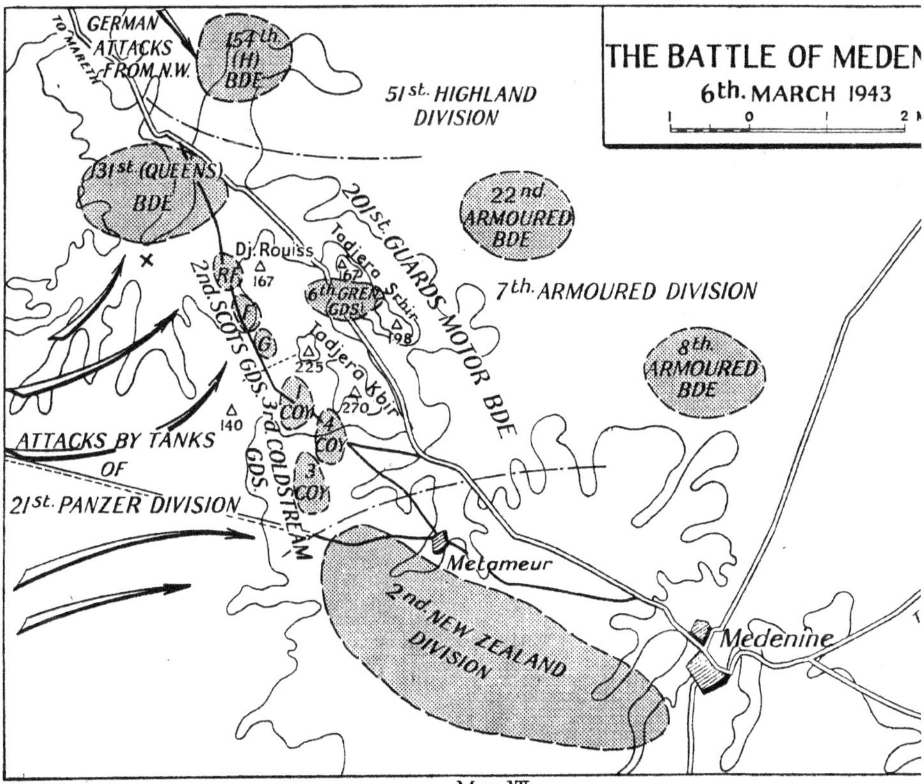

Map XII

a large orchard about eleven miles along the road to el Djem. On the 13th the Battalion moved another couple of miles up the road and camped among olives on a carpet of flowers, and F Company (Major Crichton-Stuart), which had relieved G (Captain J. A. L. Timpson, M.C.) in the boring task of guarding the Djebiniana cross-roads, about twenty-five miles north of Sfax on the coast road, brought to a successful conclusion what was probably the only purely naval action in which the Foot Guards have ever been involved.

April 13
MAP XIV

This action took place off the village of Chebba, where it was found that a fishing boat with a row boat in tow about three miles out to sea had been commandeered by a party of ten heavily armed Italians the day before. A boarding party of two volunteers from each platoon under Captain R. A. Willis was quickly assembled and, armed with an anti-tank rifle, for which it was hoped that a use might at last be found, a Bren, and two Thompson sub-machine guns, put to sea in another fishing boat. "The Italians, who apparently had anchored in the hopes that Chebba would change hands again before their return, promptly set sail, and the chase was on. That was at 1545 hours. By 1605 "Cap'n" Willis had gained sufficiently to fire a warning shot across the enemy's bows. But the enemy, undaunted, held on their course. It may be that in spite of their grossly overladen tow they hoped to be able to escape under cover of darkness. But it was not to be. At 1610 another shot was fired, rather closer, and activity on board was seen to increase. By 1615 "Cap'n" Willis had got within effective range. A little more oil was put on the main armament, and a long burst from the Bren was fired very close indeed. Enemy activity at once became chaotic; the sail came down apparently quicker than intended; a series of splashes showed where their armament was being scuttled; and at 1625 the boarding party swept alongside.

"The return to Chebba was enlivened by the bonhomie of the Italians, who expressed their gratitude at being rescued from further participation in the war by gifts of rations and cigarettes. They were indeed well-found in all essentials, and had enough blankets, boots, and scent to have seen them through a much longer voyage. The sun had set before the boarding party waded ashore with its captives to meet a civic reception and narrowly avoid a civic banquet. The two Italian officers, a captain and a lieutenant, maintaining dignity and dry feet to the last, were, amid loud cheers, pick-a-backed ashore by their men. The boatmen were paid off in boots and cigarettes and the stars shone down on what was once more *mare nostrum*."

The following day the Battalion moved north to the neighbourhood of Bourdjine, and on the 16th it took over a defensive position south of Enfidaville and astride the road from Sousse. The position was painfully reminiscent of that below the escarpment near Halfaya, and once again the Battalion found itself in flat and unpleasant country near

April 14
April 16

the sea where it was overlooked by the enemy and movement by day was virtually impossible. The task of the Battalion was by incessant patrolling to chart the "going", the minefields and the anti-tank ditch, and to push the line ever closer to the enemy, and to the normal fatigues of such an existence was added the interference with sleep caused by a plague of mosquitoes and the fact that mosquito nets were supplied on the scale of two per company—and these two the companies never saw!

April 19   On 19th April the Eighth Army began its attack in the coastal sector and forced the enemy to withdraw into the hills north of Enfidaville. The approaches to Enfidaville were heavily mined, and in trying to find a way through with a carrier patrol Lieutenant N. de P. Henderson-Scott, who had carried out a daring personal reconnaissance the previous day, was killed and Lance-Sergeant J. N. Fraser seriously wounded. The Battalion eventually got into the village on foot and after dark took up a position in the wooded hills about a mile and a half to the north. In the meantime Lieutenant Weir had pushed on with a carrier patrol and not only inflicted many casualties on the enemy but cut the main road to Bou Ficha about five miles north of Enfidaville and prevented it from being mined. The remaining carriers had by now been centralised in two platoons under Battalion Headquarters, and carrier patrols under Lieutenant N. H. Barne, M.C., and Lieutenant Weir were again active next day, and, in the face of heavy shellfire, caused further casualties to the enemy, including the capture by Lieutenant Weir's patrol of two men and a vehicle from an O.P. Both patrols brought back valuable information. Patrols were again active on the 22nd and 23rd April, and in the evening of the latter day the Battalion moved forward preparatory to

April 23   attacking the Djebel Hamadet es Sourah. That advance coincided with the opening of the First Battalion's advance on the Medjez sector.

April 24   Lieutenants Barne and Weir were out again next morning with their patrols, and the former brought in thirteen Italian prisoners whose slit-trenches the carriers had charged and overrun. Later in the day the Battalion was intermittently shelled and Lieutenant R. D. Campbell and Lance-Sergeant Davies of the Intelligence Section were wounded, the latter dying in the evening. At 2200 the advance on Hamadet began. F Company on the right, and Right Flank (Major H. L. St. V. Rose) in the centre, had little difficulty, but G Company came under heavy fire and the position proved too strong for the leading Platoon under Lieutenant W. J. Brown. Captain Timpson then brought up another platoon, but both he and Lieutenant J. S. Cunninghame were wounded by Italian hand-grenades. Lieutenant Brown was also wounded by a grenade, but accounted for the thrower with a shovel, the only weapon to hand, and continued to lead his platoon until the position was occupied and thirty prisoners taken. Throughout the action Lieutenant Waldron and Lance-Corporal T. Howe, who were with the Company to prepare the anti-tank defences on consolidation, gave valuable aid. When the Company was held up Lance-Corporal Howe joined the assaulting troops and, with a Bren gun, led a party in the attack until himself wounded. Contact was with difficulty made with the New Zealanders on the left, on which flank the third platoon commanded by Lieutenant D. R. B. Mynors gained its objective, and by daylight the line was secure. But the position was far from satisfactory as the bare crest between the lines was untenable by either side and the Battalion was exposed to heavy shelling. On the 26th Major J. R. S. Clarke, M.C., was wounded in the arm and was succeeded as Adjutant by Lieutenant the Hon. G. C. Lampson, and on the 27th Lieutenant D. J. N. Bland was killed by a direct hit on his O.P. At last light on that day the Battalion was relieved by the 2nd/7th Queen's, and dug in in new positions preparatory to a further attack. This was cancelled on three successive days, and on the night of the 30th the Battalion was withdrawn and leaguered twenty miles from Enfidaville. It had been decided that the attack from the south by the Eighth Army could not lead to a sufficiently rapid advance through the hills north of Enfidaville. But the attack had done all that was necessary in holding the enemy's forces. The main attack had been switched to the First Army in the centre. The 201st Guards Brigade was on its way to join that Army.[1]

April 26

April 27

April 28–30

II. THE FIRST BATTALION

(a) *Journey to North Africa*

Early in November 1942 a small Allied force under the command of General Eisenhower of the United States Army had landed in Algeria with the intention of taking Tunis and of threatening the Afrika Korps in the rear. The operation failed in its first object, as the enemy managed to build up his forces quicker than did the Allies, and he also controlled airfields which were closer to the front than those in Algeria. The Allies were halted in the bleak, bare hills a day's march from Tunis.

Consequently, while the Eighth Army pushed westward from el Alamein, it was found necessary to assemble a far larger force than that which had at first been despatched. The British element of the force under the command of Lieutenant-General K. A. N. Anderson, was the First Army, a grandiose title for an armament which by early March consisted of the 6th Armoured and the 46th and 78th Infantry Divisions, and an ill-equipped French Corps. Two other British

1942

MAP V

---

[1] The history of the Second Battalion continues on p. 152.

Infantry Divisions were available at home to reinforce the First Army; they were the 1st and 4th, which had been held back at the outset of the campaign as a reserve to counter any move the Germans might make through Spain against the Straits of Gibraltar, a defile through which all Allied communications passed; this threat never materialised. In consequence General Sir Harold Alexander, who from the end of February 1943, as Deputy Supreme Commander to General Eisenhower, commanded the First and Eighth British Armies, the II United States and the French XIX Corps, could count upon the arrival of these two fresh divisions, the 1st in March and the 4th by early April. In the 1st Division was the 24th Guards Brigade, commanded by Brigadier R. B. R. Colvin; in that Brigade was the First Battalion of the Regiment, commanded by Lieutenant-Colonel the Viscount Dalrymple, M.B.E. The other battalions in the 24th Guards Brigade were the 5th Grenadiers, and the Regiment's old friends of the Norwegian campaign and sporting rivals—the 1st Irish Guards.

Nov. 1 On the 1st November at Wanstead, the Battalion had mobilised for service overseas, and soon had moved north by train to Ayrshire, where

Nov.–Feb. it was conveniently placed for speedy embarkation. But a wait of four months had supervened, while the destination remained a closely guarded secret. Meanwhile Battalion Headquarters was at Blairquhan Castle, Straiton; Left Flank and C Company at Dalmellington; B Company at Crosshill; Right Flank at New Dailly; Headquarter Company, less the Carrier Platoon, at Girvan; and the Carrier Platoon at Sauchrie House, near Maybole. Hogmanay was celebrated by the

1943 Regiment in Scotland for the first time for over two hundred years.

Feb. No one knew the Battalion's destination. India and North Africa led the betting. The one thing clear was that a move was imminent. On the 23rd one more Boxing tournament was held against the 1st Irish Guards, this time in the incongruously named Pleasure Hall at Girvan, and ended in a win for the Battalion by six fights to two. On the evening of 25th February it indulged in that great sign of permanence and queller of external rumour, a route march, and by about noon on

Feb. 26 the 26th, after a brief train journey to Gourock, it had begun to embark in the H.T. *Samaria*, then lying about three miles out in the Clyde. For many it was the second time that they had waited there and watched the changing shadows as the light faded over the hills of Argyll and wondered what might lie ahead.[1]

Mar. 1 Near midnight on 1st March the ship moved off in the darkness,

Mar. 2 and next day she was out of sight of land. With her were six other vessels and an escort of three destroyers and three corvettes. The sea was described as "fairly calm, but not sufficiently so for some, and there was at least one man who didn't take much interest in anything connected with the voyage for the next three days." However, it grew

[1] For Order of Battle, see p. 344.

calmer rapidly and the sun began to shine on a blue sea, and P.T. was started. At 1000 on the 8th, rather later than schedule owing to a detour caused by U-boats, the convoy passed Gibraltar, and at about 1700 on the 9th the *Samaria* docked at Algiers. Disembarkation was interrupted by a brief though noisy air-raid, and the Battalion set off to march about twelve miles in a tropical rainstorm and carrying large packs to a Reception Camp near Sidi Bou Zid. Mar. 8
Mar. 9

On arrival in the small hours of the next morning it was found that the camp, perhaps because of a romanticised impression of the Algerian climate, had been pitched in a ploughed field that was rapidly becoming a swamp. The only comfort was the tea which another suffering unit had generously provided. The rain continued, and in the afternoon of the 11th the Battalion, less 1st Reinforcement Company, left its ankle-deep sea of mud and marched to Maison Carrée, about six miles nearer Algiers, where dryness was found in a disused brickworks, and where the Battalion's pipers and those of the Irish Guards beat Retreat in the main square, apparently to the gratification of the populace. A Mobile Bath Unit was fortunately in the neighbourhood, and on the 13th, after sampling the tangerines and smells of Maison Carrée, the Battalion marched back to Algiers and embarked with a party of the 5th Grenadiers in H.M.S. *Royal Scotsman*, a swift packet-boat from the Glasgow–Belfast run, and at midnight sailed for Bône, in cramped and uncomfortable quarters. Half an hour before reaching the harbour the little convoy—one other ship and two destroyers—was attacked by three Italian torpedo bombers. Their torpedoes missed —but only just, and the Battalion safely disembarked. Mar. 10
Mar. 11
Mar. 13
Mar. 14

After a four mile march from Bône they found themselves in a pleasant camp among sand dunes and only about four hundred yards from the sea: "lots of wild flowers everywhere; larks singing— swallows, wagtails—all very peaceful." The NAAFI in Bône provided other amenities: "the ration is one bottle per month and one razor blade per two officers per week"; and the next three days passed pleasantly in bathing and idling and a little training and getting rid of the last of the Sidi Bou Zid mud. Mar. 15–17

(b) *The Medjez Salient*

On the morning of the 18th the Battalion moved off in motor transport in its place in the Brigade column. The destination was a concentration area near Garrdimaou, where it was expected that the rest of the transport and supporting weapons would rejoin, after making a wearisome drive of 500 miles over rotten roads from Algiers. Here the whole of the 1st Division was to assemble, and then to enter the line together. But at this period our troops were thin on the ground, the Germans were making several local attacks, and any MAP XIV
Mar. 18

reinforcements which appeared in the rear areas were liable to be snapped up by hard-pressed commanders and staffs without waiting for the proper ordering of the whole divisional panoply; new troops might well think they were being treated like shuttlecocks.

When the head of the column reached Fernana, about two-thirds of the way to Garrdimaou, an agitated Staff Officer changed its destination to Beja, thirty miles to the east, where the situation was said to be alarming. So instead of turning west, the Brigade kept on to the east; that night the 5th Grenadiers went into the line, while the Battalion lay in a harbour area six miles east of Beja, where its own transport and carriers rejoined it after an even longer forced march than had been expected; the Battalion was now complete. Preparations were made to take over that night, but in the early evening the order came to move again. Now, it seemed they were needed in another sector. The Grenadiers were to stay where they were, while the Scots and Irish were to pile into their trucks again and trundle off to Medjez-el-Bab, a familiar name since the fighting began in late November. Here they were to relieve the 36th Brigade who were needed to counter-attack further north. Medjez was only twenty-five miles down the direct road from Beja, but that road was cut by the Germans, and there must needs be a tiring detour of seventy miles in the dark, by way of Thibar and Teboursouk. By two in the morning of the 20th March the Battalion had taken over a quiet sector of the line from the 6th Battalion Royal West Kent Regiment; they were a few miles west of Medjez and facing north, with the Irish Guards on their right. It was nearly three years since the Battalion had had the Germans in front of it at Bodö; in getting back to the fight they had had a salutary reminder of the flux and bewilderment which accompanies military emergencies. Thereafter the question "Haven't you heard, it's all been changed?" was frequently to be heard—without surprise, but often with irritation.

Three days of very peaceful war followed. "We sit on one ridge and the Germans are opposite on another ridge, and in the middle the Arabs continue their farming." Patrols failed to make contact with the enemy and collected nothing more than mud as they moved through the rosemary-scented darkness.

On the morning of the 23rd the Battalion moved again. Having handed over their positions to the 6th Royal Inniskilling Fusiliers, they marched ten miles to the east to take over the tip of the Medjez salient from the 2nd Coldstream of the 1st Guards Brigade. It was an uncomfortable position, for it had been found impossible to hold Djebel el Ahmera ("Longstop Hill", which had been heroically captured by the 2nd Coldstream two months before) and other high ground to the north and north-west, with the result that it was overlooked and movement by day was, in some places, virtually impossible. The importance of Medjez to the opposing armies could be gauged from the extent of its ruins. On the wall of one hovel used as sleeping quarters a previous occupier had written a quotation from the Book of Job: "And he dwelleth in desolate cities and in houses which no man inhabiteth, which are ready to become heaps." Those heaps were in a salient, and their retention was necessary for the launching of the final attack on Tunis.

For the next month, with the Irish Guards on the left and the Grenadiers on the right, the Battalion lived its strange troglodytic life. By day, as the winter's mud was slowly turned to dust under the increasing sun, and as the vanishing swallows took men's minds with them in their northern flight, activity was almost wholly limited to the air and to artillery and mortar fire. But at night the area came to life and each company sent out its nightly patrols. Sometimes contact was made with the enemy and the quiet was broken by the sudden crash of mortar bomb or automatic fire. But more often there was no contact, for the enemy was lying well back on the hill-tops, and both sides were preparing for the next move. But the enemy was not the only source of danger: "We were practically surrounded by minefields and consequently it was rather dangerous if one missed the gap on returning from patrol." Casualties were few, in spite of air superiority not yet having been achieved and the enemy having considerable latitude in the air: "Nothing much has happened since I last wrote, except that we have been dive-bombed by Stukas. They made extremely bad shots and hurt no-one, but it was a fascinating sight to watch." The fascination waned with frequent repetition, and with the steady toll of casualties. For instance, on the 28th there were two wounded; on the 29th Guardsman Wallace of Right Flank was killed and five were wounded; on 2nd April Captain M. W. Rowe was wounded while out on patrol and on the 3rd Lieutenant J. H. L. Sinclair and Sergeant Bennett. On 13th April there was an accidental explosion while grenades were being cleaned, and one man was killed and six injured, including Lieutenant T. M. F. E. Lowinsky; on the 16th two were killed and four injured by a mine when on patrol. But these losses were trifling compared with the loss of a whole company, which the Irish Guards suffered when they raided Recce Ridge on the night of the 29th/30th March.

Mar. 28
Mar. 29
April 2
April 3
April 13
April 16

On the 8th April the 78th Division on the Brigade's left began an offensive designed to clear the enemy from the hills which overlooked the road from Medjez to Beja. Until this task was achieved it would be impossible to maintain the half-dozen divisions which were to be assembled for the final thrust to Tunis. From its positions, the Battalion could see signs of progress. Bursting shells and bombs, burning farms and fleeting figures told the story of a steady advance. By the 12th the enemy had been ejected from the hills, and his defences now ran south from Longstop through Grich el Oued, and then away to the east. Medjez el Bab was no longer in a salient, our forward positions were pushed out to flea-ridden farms to which previously only patrols had been, the road was clear for traffic—at least by night—and the final offensive could begin.

(c) *The Final Offensive*

The part which the Battalion was to play in the final offensive which resulted in the total defeat of the Axis forces in Africa and the opening up of the Mediterranean sea-route to the East, was long drawn out, exhausting, bloody, but highly creditable. From the night of the 22nd April until the morning of the 6th May the companies were under shell and mortar fire which was as accurate as it was continuous. Stirring incidents, such as the gallant assaults on the heights of Gebel Bou Aoukaz, may tempt the historian to concentrate only on the spectacular; to do so would give a false picture, as it was the continuous nature of this fortnight of battle which most impressed those who fought and survived.

(i) *Preparation*

April 19
On the 19th April the Battalion had been withdrawn from the line to a concentration area in a wadi behind Grenadier Hill south of Medjez, where it lay under desultory shelling, preparing for its first attack of the war. All around the great concentration was taking place; guns, tanks, ammunition, petrol and rations were being marshalled and ordered. Nor were all the troops drawn from the First Army. The 1st Armoured Division had come round from the southern flank to add its punch to that of the 6th; the light desert paint of their vehicles stood out among the darker drab transport newly out from home. The first rumbles of an argument which will still be raging in Chelsea Hospital fifty years hence were noticed by Lieutenant-Colonel M. E. St. J. Barne, to whom Lord Dalrymple had been forced by illness to hand over command of the Battalion. "I have seen several 8th Army vehicles about—one had 'Here is the 8th Army' written on the windscreen! They are horribly above themselves and look on the 1st Army as a lot of amateurs!!!"

This vast concentration was but thinly protected. To the Brigade's right front there lay Banana Ridge; south of Banana Ridge lay a mass of artillery, field and medium, with the ammunition dumped conveniently by the guns. On Grenadier Hill were, suitably enough, the 5th Grenadiers; on Banana Ridge three companies of the Duke of Wellington's Regiment. The risk that the enemy might attempt to upset our arrangements by a sudden spoiling attack had been considered and accepted. It had been impossible to hide from him the fact of the preparations, nor, in the Medjez sector, was it desired that he should be anything but apprehensive. On the evening of the 20th the 10th Panzer and Hermann Goering divisions attempted a blow; "Lilac-blossom" was the code name for their thrust which was intended to forestall our attack.

Early in the night German infantry climbed Banana Ridge and engaged the Dukes. The enemy kept the defenders sufficiently occupied to enable their tanks, supported by another two battalions of foot soldiers to debouch among the guns and to strike westward for the road which runs south from Medjez. At dawn the situation was obscure, and great columns of smoke punctuated by explosions told of local disasters among our gunners. April 20

April 21

During the night the Scots Guards had sent B Company, now commanded by Captain the Lord Lyell, to reinforce the Grenadiers on their hill. In the early morning this company was sent forward to assist the Duke of Wellington's in any counter-attack they might require. It was an unpleasant advance across the open from Grenadier Hill to the Duke's Battalion Headquarters, and Lieutenant-Colonel Gordon-Lennox of the Grenadiers watched them; "it was magnificent to see B Company advancing steadily and keeping their formation exactly, under the heavy mortar and shell fire." They had set out with the expectation of attacking the left hand feature of Banana Ridge, Djebel Hoka, but on arrival, the Duke's with a slight air of injured surprise, said they could manage very well themselves, thanked B Company for coming, and retook their former position without further ado. By noon B Company were back in the Battalion's wadi; their abortive jaunt from Grenadier Hill had cost them two other ranks killed, and Captain A. B. Brown, CSM Gibson and two other ranks wounded. An hour later the enemy withdrew what was left of his force. He had certainly disturbed the serenity of the artillery arrangements, but it had cost him dear; 450 prisoners were in our hands and the hulls of twenty of his tanks littered the plain; the 10th Panzer Division fought the rest of the campaign without any tanks at all.

It had been a night and morning of confusion and alarm. The Battalion was never attacked directly, and apart from B Company's foray, only the anti-tank platoon, with its new 6-pounders, was called upon to take an active part. Brigadier Colvin's resource in collecting a squadron of the newly arrived Churchill tanks, and in their skilful positioning, had preserved the road south from Medjez from any permanent threat; the Grenadiers had had a satisfying machine-gun and mortar shoot at the infantry; all our guns had been recovered. Our attack was delayed; but only for one day. The Battalion spent that day putting the finishing touches to its preparations, rechecking its equipment, and oiling its weapons. April 22

(ii) *The Break-in*

The plan devised for this final blow was as follows. The V Corps, which, from left to right, consisted of the 78th, 1st and 4th Divisions, was to break into the enemy positions in the hills which ran north-westward from the road from Peter's Corner to Tunis; this attack, it was hoped, would draw off German reserves from the main effort which was to be made by the IX Corps, with the 46th Infantry and 1st and 6th Armoured Divisions, directly down the Tunis road. The celebrated Longstop Hill was among the objectives of the 78th Division; the main objective of the 1st Division was the long ridges which culminate in Djebel Bou Aoukaz, soon to be familiar to all as "the Bou". With this hill the 24th Guards Brigade was concerned. From it the enemy had splendid observation, not only over the southern approaches, but also over the country to the east and south-east through which the IX Corps attack was to be made. The importance of the Bou was obvious to both sides.

The summit lay nearly twelve miles distant from our forward position on Banana Ridge. The approach to it, therefore, would have to be made in several stages, to allow the intervening ground to be made good, and for our artillery to move up.

The first stage was to be a dawn attack on the enemy's forward defences which ran eastward from the hovel of Grich el Oued on the banks of the Mejerda along a line of low bald hills. The similarity of these little hummocks, and the inaccuracy of the maps made identification of the objectives in the dark hazardous in the extreme. The Grenadiers were to take Point 134 and the village of Grich el Oued; on their right the Scots Guards were to take Point 130, and then exploit up the gradually rising series of minor summits—145, 151 and 187—which lay south of the Gab-Gab gap. The Irish Guards were to be in reserve in this phase. On the Brigade's right the 2nd Infantry Brigade had a series of similar little hills as its objective; the left hand of these was Point 156.

When the first phase had been concluded, it was the intention that the Grenadiers would assault the western and shorter of the two spurs which ran southward from the Bou; the Irish Guards would take the eastern spur north of the Gab-Gab gap; and the Battalion would go through to take the summit itself. All the way the troops would be under observation from the top of the Bou, and, until its capture by the 78th Division on the 26th April, from Longstop as well. The plain and the first line of little hills were covered in growing corn, which stood some four feet high, insufficient to give cover to a man on the move, but quite sufficient to conceal from help any who fell wounded on the way. To lessen this risk, the Commanding Officer issued an order that the positions of the wounded were to be marked by their rifles stuck bayonet down in the ground; the butts would guide the medical teams to them, and reduce the danger of tanks or vehicles running them over.

At ten o'clock on the night of 22nd the Battalion left its sheltered wadi behind Grenadier Hill for the forming-up position. The night was dark and mist lay thick in the hollows, and the difficulty of keeping direction was increased by mortar fire to the right. Rain soaked the Guardsmen as they swished through the tall crops, and added to the difficulty of those who were attempting to combine map, compass and observation to find their correct line of advance.

At first all went well, but the track which was to have been the axis of the advance could not be found among the corn, and Left Flank (Captain R. H. Bull), aided by Lieutenant C. Lewis, the Intelligence Officer, had to rely on the compass alone for its advance to the first objective. But as the point of departure could not be placed on the map with any accuracy, the compass could do no more than give a very general direction.

At half-past three in the morning of the 23rd April—Good Friday and St. George's Day—350 guns opened up in support of the 1st Division. As the night gave way to the dawn Left Flank hit the German line. It was a hill, but it was not Point 130; in the uncertainty of the night they had gone too far to their right, and the hill they attacked was a shoulder of Point 156, a spur of the larger Point 168 which lay further to their right, and which dominated 156. Point 156 was an objective for the 2nd Brigade. By the end of the day, that shoulder of 156 had a new name; to all the Battalion it was "Tim's Hill", a name inspired by the dash and valour with which Captain Bull led Left Flank into the attack.

April 23

The position proved to be most strongly held, and the leading platoon (Lieutenant R. T. Hunter) came under heavy fire when about three hundred yards from the top. Heavy casualties were suffered, and the Company was for some time unable to advance further. But, as tank support arrived and the half light changed to the full blaze of the day, Captain Bull, although shot through the stomach and with a large mortar wound in the thigh as well as two lesser wounds, organised the final attack in which he "carried out a zig-zag run at a German armed with an automatic on whom he did a Rugger tackle."

In the meantime the other two platoons had worked round to the left, and Right Flank (Captain F. G. Mann), following closely behind, put its leading platoon into the final assault. In this second phase of the attack the leadership of Lieutenant the Hon. D. A. Bethell played a prominent part. At the beginning of the attack his Platoon of Left Flank was to the right rear, when, finding himself unable to advance on his own front, he led his Platoon under heavy fire to the position on the left whence the final assault was delivered. Even the wounded joined in the assault. "I had to think twice," one of the officers wrote, "to realise it was real—the scene in the half light—smoke drifting about—tanks on fire—shells exploding—tracer from A.A. I shall never forget my first view of real fighting."

When, after adding to his brilliant leadership a feat of endurance which astonished the medical officers, Captain Bull was finally evacuated, command of the Company devolved temporarily on CSM J. Lunn, who had already three times gone forward under heavy fire and rescued wounded men lying out on the forward slope. Eventually Lieutenant Bethell, the only surviving officer, was able to leave his platoon and make his way to Company Headquarters, and it was under his command that Left Flank was withdrawn, under a platoon in strength, when finally relieved by C Company (Captain G. C. Rush).

After Right Flank had assisted Left Flank in the capture of Tim's Hill, Captain Mann led them off round by the right to attack what was thought to be their original objective; they occupied it, but in fact it was not the objective, and was also overlooked by 168 to the right. To make confusion worse the Battalion suffered a grievous loss about noon when Lieutenant Lewis was killed; he had given excellent service in the night march, and had served the Brigade well in passing back vital information. Thereafter, Captain J. E. Tyldesley-Jones bore the Intelligence Officer's burden in addition to his other cares as Adjutant; throughout the two weeks of battle he did the staff work of the Battalion in an exemplary manner, despite being severely shaken in the middle of the action when blown up by a mine in a carrier, of which he was the sole survivor. Both Colonel Barne and Captain Tyldesley-Jones were nobly assisted by Major C. A. Fletcher, commanding Support Company, who was usually at Advanced Battalion Headquarters and who "did invaluable work as relief Intelligence Officer, relief Adjutant, relief Commanding Officer, and any other job which came to hand".

Thus at midday the Battalion was lying out in the blazing heat, choked by dust and smoke, and parched by the sun and scarcity of water, with Right Flank forward on the right, C Company on the left, with B slightly behind them. Left Flank, all of whose officers were now wounded, was back with Battalion Headquarters, which lay in what cover could be found in the folds and cornfields at the base of Tim's Hill. The position had been made easier by the capture of the top of 156 by The Loyals, but shelling, mortaring and low-flying air attacks continued throughout the day.

By noon the feature which was the Battalion's next objective had been identified for certain. This was Point 145, the first of the stepping stones which led up to the eastern spur of the Bou. It lay about a mile away across flat and coverless cornfields. Lord Lyell led B Company through C Company's position, and set off on this hazardous march.

The crossing of the open cost them some thirty casualties, mostly from machine-gun fire from their right, but they got there, and occupied the feature, on which they were to remain for the next three days, "cut off from the rest of the world"; there was no shade, there was a scorching sun, there were swarms of flies, and cascades of shells and mortar bombs. The lot of those who were unscathed was trying in the extreme; the sufferings of the wounded were excruciating. Many owe their lives to Lance-Corporal Barber, one of B Company's stretcher-bearers, who lay out in the open with a small party of those who had been hit, feeding them on beans picked in a field and on emergency rations; eventually he got all his charges back to safety.

In the afternoon the Germans mounted the first of their counter-attacks against the Battalion's main position. It was supported by tanks and was directed against C Company below Point 156, where it had already suffered twenty-three casualties. The Loyals on the peak of 156 were pushed off, and three enemy tanks and some infantry occupied the top of the hill. A brilliant artillery shoot directed over the wireless by Captain Rush on information from Lieutenant the Hon. P. H. S. D. Butler with the two forward Platoons, supported by heavy small arms fire, broke up the attack when within 300 yards of the positions.

As the long afternoon drew on, and the torment of thirst was added to that of heat and flies and weariness, the men, sheltering in their hastily dug trenches from constant mortaring and shellfire inter-spersed with frequent attacks from the air, could see, three miles away down the Medjerda valley, the shadows lengthening across the dark bulk of Djebel Bou Aoukaz, a menace and a challenge. After dark, Lance-Corporal Beedie and Guardsman Marshall made their way from Point 145 to Battalion Headquarters and guided the carriers with food, water and signallers—B Company's signallers were by then all casualties—back through the enemy and up the hill. But for their action B Company would have received no supplies. During the night the enemy withdrew from the summit of 156 and C Company put a standing patrol on it.

The Battalion was now in a dangerous salient, and would remain so until the Brigade on the right could make good the dominating ground. The arrival of No. 1 Company of the Irish Guards to thicken up the defences on Tim's Hill had been thankfully welcomed, but the final capture of 168 was the main hope of the Battalion.

At about 0800 the enemy, back on 156, put in a counter-attack supported by tanks against Right Flank. It did not seem possible that that dwindling line could hold. Had it failed, Battalion Headquarters must have been overrun. Secret documents were destroyed and marked maps erased. But with the help of artillery support directed over the wireless by Captain Mann, the attack was broken. In desperation

April 24

Captain Mann brought the fire of our 25-pounders down on his own positions, for the enemy had approached within thirty yards; they left thirty casualties behind them. An attack was then made on B Company, isolated on Point 145, but Lord Lyell was able to bring down an artillery concentration on its forming-up position about four hundred yards away, and the Germans were again forced to withdraw. That afternoon the 3rd Infantry Brigade put in a Brigade attack, taking the high ground about Point 168 to the right forward of Right Flank, whose position then became secure. But in the process the Company suffered further casualties, for its positions had been included in the Brigade artillery plan. That evening Right Flank was withdrawn into reserve. It consisted of Captain Mann and twelve Guardsmen. Among those who had been killed the Battalion mourned especially Sergeant "Sammy" Moorhouse, a fine boxer and well-loved character. He had been killed when a German officer arrived in an armoured car, put his hands up as if to surrender, and was about to be taken by Sergeant Moorhouse, when the driver of the car shot the Sergeant. Moorhouse was the finest type of Police Reservist, and the terror of the Irish Guards in the ring.

April 25   Easter Sunday was passed in the same positions, with the mortaring and shelling occasionally varied by dive-bombing. In the course of it reinforcements were got up to the depleted companies, many of them men whose last sight of their comrades had been when they had gone forward to dig them graves two evenings before. "On Easter Sunday we rejoined the Company with twenty-four reinforcements," one of the Guardsmen of Left Flank afterwards wrote. "What tales we were told. It appears that the Company took the wrong hill and met with very stiff opposition, but the few that were not casualties chased Jerry off the hill with the bayonet, and so won the day. The hill taken by the Company was known to all as 'Tim's Hill'. All the boys were in fairly good spirits after their terrible experiences, and hoped for another smack at Jerry soon." Many leaders in all ranks had been responsible for maintaining this spirit. None of these would deny that first among them was the Reverend James Hamilton, the Padre. He was at the Aid Post with the Doctor, Captain G. C. Hodge, throughout the battle, helping to dress wounds and to encourage the wounded. Many times he went up to the forward companies, searching for the wounded in the corn, and burying those who had been killed. He was a man to be respected and admired.

That evening the Battalion moved across to its original intended line of advance, digging in with Left Flank on the left on Point 130, C Company on the right, Right Flank in the centre, while B Company remained out on Point 145. Here they suffered the unwelcomed attention of our own medium guns; the behaviour of the 19th Field Regiment, R.A., which was in direct support of the Brigade group throughout the battle, was exemplary; only the Germans suffered from their fire.

That day a message was sent out from Brigade:

"The Brigade Commander wishes to say how proud he is of the fine fight put up by the 1st Battalion, Scots Guards, in their storming and tenacious holding of the present line.

"The Brigade Commander fully realises that the Battalion's positions are difficult to hold in the face of intensive enemy artillery fire and mortar fire, but he hopes that within the next 24 hours the position will be greatly eased, as we have now broken and held on to the crust of the German Siegfried Line which was sited between Grich el Oued and Montarnaud."

A considerable amount of reorganisation was necessary—Left Flank, for instance, had to be reformed in two platoons under Lieutenants Bethell and L. E. Widderson—and the work was hindered by steady mortaring and shelling and an occasional attack by dive-bombers, Battalion Headquarters, which by this time had been accurately pin-pointed, receiving particular attention in both its original and its alternative positions. One really satisfactory achievement of a wearisome day was being able to track down the mediums that had been shelling B Company and persuade them to transfer their attentions elsewhere. And in the morning the Irish Guards had gone forward and taken the line of heights which ran northward from Point 145 to the Gab-Gab gap. B Company's siege was raised.

The relief of B Company marks the end of the first stage of the battle for the Bou. The break-in had been a rude introduction for those who were new to the fight; to those who had been in Norway this African battle gave a new hope of ultimate victory, for they saw the vast material resources which could now be deployed in support of the infantryman. But the infantryman also saw what might come back at him. The intensity of the shelling in this battle was to become a legend, and a yard-stick by which future stonks[1] and concentrations were to be measured. "Nothing like the Bou"; "Nearly as heavy as the Bou"; "Just like the Bou"; but very rarely "Heavier than the Bou". "How I hate shells," wrote an officer. "I have seen strong courageous men reduced to whimpering wrecks, crying like children. Some arrive with a long screeching crescendo giving one time to take cover; others come faster than sound and burst without warning. And when one has nothing to do, the fumes and dust and echoed cries of 'stretcher-bearer!' strain one's nerves almost to breaking point. Yet if one goes to ground how incredibly hard it is to get out into the open again to do a job of work! I would sooner have a thousand bullets or

[1] Stonk; an onomatopœic word coined to denote bombardment by mortars, as opposed to guns.

even dive bombers than a day's shelling." The Battalion had undergone four days' shelling; there were nine more days to come.

(iii) *The Bou*

April 26   Throughout the 26th the preparations for the assault went on. Up came the artillery, to place themselves directly behind the Battalion, and to attract more attention from the German artillery and aircraft. Patrols went out that night, but came back with little more valuable information than that there were Germans on the slopes of the Bou.
April 27   In the morning of the 27th, the direct order for the assault came.

The Grenadiers, at this stage of the battle, lay on "Hills Ridiculous" which they had occupied on the 26th; the Irish Guards lay south of the Gab-Gab gap. The plan was that the Irish should cross the gap and secure the eastern ridge which leads up to the summit through Points 212, 214 and 181. Simultaneously the Grenadiers would assault the shorter western ridge about points 106, 154 and 171. Behind them would come the Scots Guards who would march along the Medjerda plain and then assault the summit of the Bou from the west and south. The summit proper was Point 226; to the north was another knoll, 157. The whole advance and attack was to take place in broad daylight, for "higher formation" discounted the enemy's strength. The presence of mines in the plain precluded the use of tanks in support of the Battalion's initial advance.

Despite the capture of Longstop by the tanks of the North Irish Horse and the infantry of the 78th Division on the previous day, it was obvious that the Germans would have an uninterrupted view of our advance across the flat, both from the Bou and from the high ground on the left bank of the river. Such an advance of four miles, followed by an exhausting climb over a rough, boulder-strewn hillside, on which grew a grasping prickly gorse-like bush, and finally an assault on a dominant height, called for the display of all the Battalion's finest military qualities. These qualities were displayed; the summit was taken, and only misunderstanding marred the achievement. The determination of the Battalion that day was described by one of the officers: "David Bethell has broken out of hospital forty miles back, and is back in the line. He still has shrapnel in the hand and chest. That shows you the spirit."

Shortly after noon the Commanding Officer returned from Brigade Headquarters with orders for the attack. Time was so short that these had to be issued verbally, and platoon commanders had to give out their's while on the move. The Battalion was in the wake of the Grenadiers, and ahead of them the hills erupted in fire and smoke as bombers and guns pounded the slopes.

Left Flank led the advance, followed by C Company, Right Flank

8. THE BATTLE Major Taylor, commanding Left Flank, took this photograph from the gun lines just after the 6-pounders of the Second Battalion had knocked out three tanks on the crest of the ridge in front

MEDENINE – 6th March 1943

9. THE BOOTY Sergeants V. N. Mutch, M.M., and J. Stephenson, M.M., examine one of the knocked-out German tanks. It is a Mark IV Special, the most powerful type of tank in the Afrika Korps

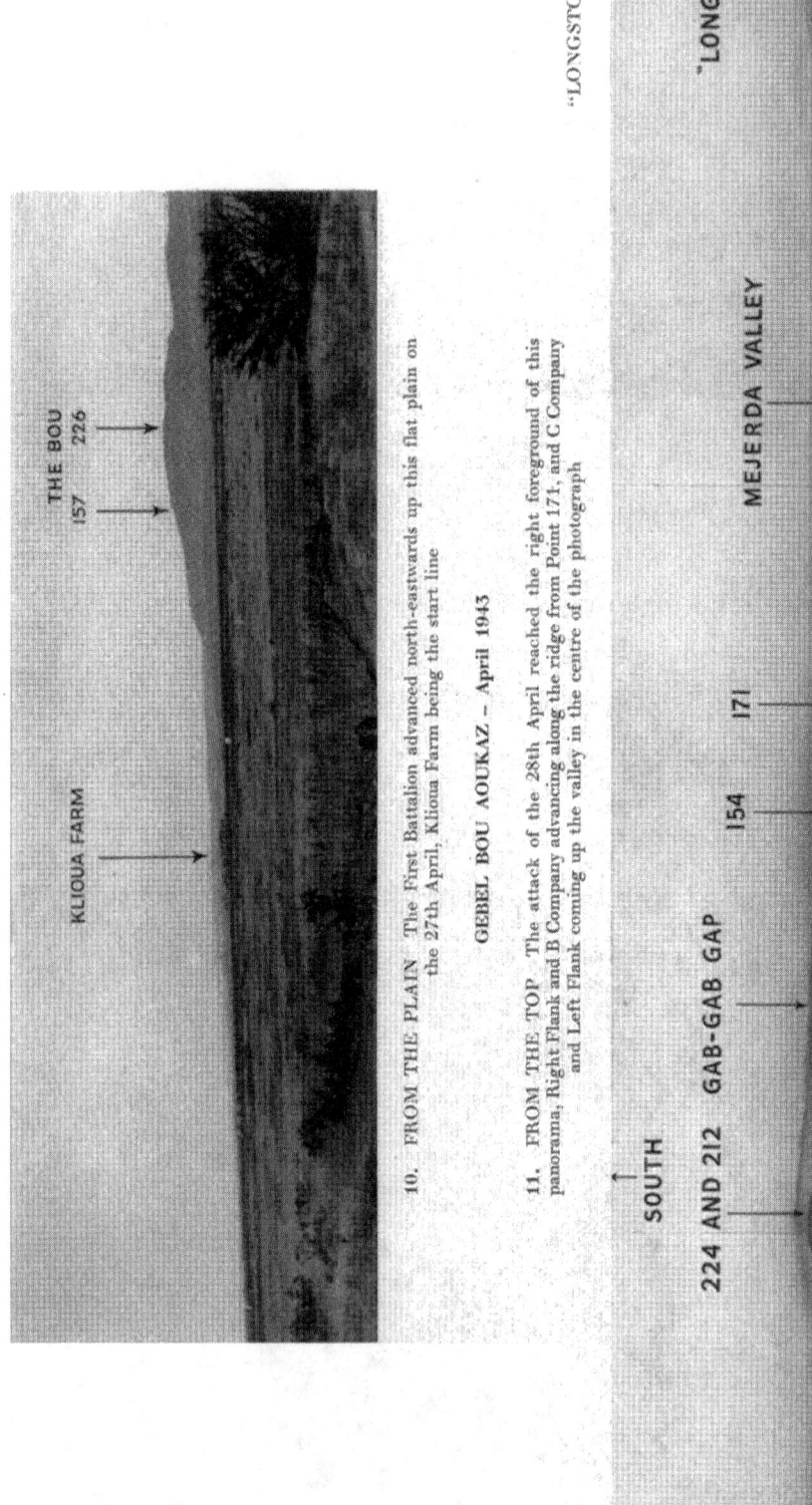

10. FROM THE PLAIN. The First Battalion advanced north-eastwards up this flat plain on the 27th April, Klioua Farm being the start line

GEBEL BOU AOUKAZ – April 1943

11. FROM THE TOP. The attack of the 28th April reached the right foreground of this panorama, Right Flank and B Company advancing along the ridge from Point 171, and C Company and Left Flank coming up the valley in the centre of the photograph

and B Company. The first two Companies were to make straight for Point 157, the second two, when the advance had gone far enough, were to wheel right and attack the Bou itself. "From the Start Line [Klioua Farm] to our objective," one of the Guardsmen of Left Flank wrote, "was about two[1] miles of heavy going through cornfields all the way. After passing the Start Line we were told to deploy to a distance of ten feet between each man. From the moment we started until the time we were held up we were under heavy machine-gun and mortar fire. We hadn't advanced far before we had casualties. . . . This did not deter the other men, who kept the three lines as if they were on a parade ground." The enemy were seen withdrawing in face of this advance, but as the lower slopes drew nearer the volume of fire increased until, when Left Flank was level with the Bou, it came under a heavy cross fire of mortaring from across the river and intense machine-gun fire and sniping from the wadis that cut into the lower slopes of the hill, among them an 88-mm. gun firing over open sights. At this point ten Germans of the Hermann Goering Regiment gave themselves up. Immediately afterwards Captain J. S. Stockton, commanding Left Flank was killed by a mortar bomb that landed at his feet. It was a time for fearless leadership, and one of the Guardsmen who followed him wrote that "he had shown no fear at all, and was a shining example to the other men".

By this time Left Flank, which had only two platoons, had suffered about twenty-six casualties, and the remainder of the Company was so exposed to cross-fire that it was unable to move by daylight. It managed, however, to get into positions whence it could give covering mortar and machine-gun fire to Right Flank and B Company, which had already broken away to the right and started to climb the Bou from the west. C Company, seeing that B and Right Flank were still able to move, left its position behind Left Flank and also moved to the right in their support.

Right Flank (which had already lost CSM D. Fraser, wounded by the 88) and B Company, advancing up the western slope of the ridge below Point 226 at about 1800 hours, came under heavy machine-gun fire from a post away to the left, and were unable to advance further. But Lord Lyell was not pinned to the ground, and realising that further advance was impossible until the post was silenced, collected the only available men—Lance-Sergeant J. Robertson, Lance-Corporal Lawrie, Guardsman J. Chisholm and Guardsman Porter—and ran out into the open. The enemy post was further away than it had appeared, and close to the emplacement in which was the 88-mm. gun that was holding up the rest of the Battalion. Lord Lyell was well ahead of his companions when he reached the machine-gun, and he destroyed its crew with a grenade. At this point Sergeant Robertson was killed and

[1] It was, in fact, a bit farther; it seemed much farther.

Lance-Corporal Lawrie and the two Guardsmen wounded, but Guardsman Chisholm was still able to give covering fire from where he lay, and Lord Lyell ran straight on towards the 88. He moved so quickly that it only had time to fire one more shot before he was in among the crew with the bayonet, killing several before himself being overwhelmed and killed. The survivors of the crew then left the pit, and three of them were killed by Lance-Corporal Lawrie as they retired. Both guns had been silenced, and in the lengthening evening shadows the advance up the long slope went on. For this and other great acts of gallantry, Lord Lyell was awarded the Victoria Cross.[1] Lance-Corporal Lawrie and Guardsman Chisholm received Military Medals. They had freed the pinned-down men, and Right Flank, under Captain Mann, and B Company now under Lieutenant J. D. Forrester, climbed the ridge and pushed on to the summit. At the top, the Battalion's main objective, they began to consolidate.

In the meantime Battalion Headquarters, which had followed B Company in the approach march, was caught by machine-gun fire from the far bank of the river and forced to lie down in the corn, where the only news that reached it was from a Mortar despatch rider who had last seen the companies still fighting on the lower slopes. Wireless communication failed at this time, which was about dusk, when African atmospherics are at their most capricious. In consequence the success of the two companies was unknown to Colonel Barne; soon after dark he reported the situation as he knew it to the Brigadier, and he was ordered to withdraw the Battalion to a position behind the Grenadiers, who were established on Points 171 and 154.

On Point 226 Right Flank and B Company were busying themselves siting positions, building sangars, and scraping what slits they could in the shallow earth. Twenty-five miles away to the north-east the lights of Tunis could be seen; the most formidable hill in the enemy's defence line was in our hands. Then at about eleven, over the wireless, came the order to withdraw. All Captain Mann's efforts to inform the Commanding Officer of the success of the Companies were frustrated by the atmospherics. The two Companies came down; they could hardly do otherwise. The withdrawal began at midnight. "It was an amazing walk back; we had no clear idea where the rest of the Battalion or Battalion Headquarters were, as no-one had got as far as intended. Nor did we know how many Germans might be behind us, as we had all advanced along the plain, and, except for the last half-mile, had deliberately left the ridge untouched. The night was dark; and the ground very rough and steep. We marched in single file as quietly as possible, on a compass bearing towards where we had started from that morning. As far as I can remember we reached the Battalion area just before dawn." By an oversight two Guardsmen were left

[1] For citation, see p. 528.

behind in the confusion of the darkness, and an hour later these were taken prisoner when the Germans reoccupied Point 226 with strong patrols.

By dawn of the 28th the Battalion was established in its new positions in support of the Grenadiers; C and Left Flank were on Point 117, where, wrote a Guardsman, "we had a good sleep and some food". Right Flank and B Company were forward on Point 106, where they had little sleep, and breakfast coincided with the orders for the new attack.

April 28

Inadequate communications had thrown away the fruits of a fine feat of arms. It is useless to speculate on the chances of holding the Bou had the Battalion maintained its position on the top; most probably there would have developed a grim struggle of attack and counter-attack, akin to the epic fight of the Irish Guards on Points 212 and 214 which was now beginning. As it was, the Bou must be assaulted again.

At 1000 that morning orders were issued verbally for a second attack upon the summit. The Battalion was to consolidate along the line of the track between Points 154, 181 and 214, and then, under supporting fire from the 5th Grenadiers, advance to the assault. Reports from the previous night made it seem likely that a route to the right of the Grenadiers was less strongly held, and it was decided to put in the attack at once before the enemy could reinforce this position. Just as the Companies set out, the two Guardsmen who had been left behind on Point 226 the previous night, rejoined. They had escaped from their captors, and brought back the depressing news that a strong force of Germans had been digging in on top since the early hours. At noon the attack began. C Company was on the right; Right Flank, supported by B Company, was on the left; and Left Flank in reserve in a gully near Point 171. After passing Point 171 Right Flank and B Company moved to the left in order to attack the Bou from the west while C Company attacked straight up the wadi.

The reports that C Company's route was but lightly held were not justified. Sniping and machine-gun fire was continuous, and when the right-hand leading platoon got near the top of the wadi it came under heavy fire from Point 181 in its rear. It was clear that there was no hope of being able to work further round from that position, and that the only chance of success lay in an immediate frontal attack. It was taken. But a heavy cross-fire was opened from the left peak and only Lieutenant Butler and Guardsman Alexander reached the summit and survived: every man with them was killed.

Lieutenant Butler then tried to get the other platoon round by the right while Left Flank came up in support. "What difficult country this was for making an attack," one of the Guardsman wrote. "We advanced up what appeared to be the bed of a dried-up stream; there were boulders every other step. We were being sniped all the way up and machine-gunned, and were held up within sight of our objective."

In the meantime to the west Right Flank had almost reached the top of the Bou, but was held up by very heavy point-blank fire from the summit and the flanks; fifty yards from the top snipers took a heavy toll; Lieutenant M. G. R. Nevill and his servant Guardsman Green, two well-known characters in the Battalion, were among those killed. B Company under Lieutenant Forrester moved round to the right to support Left Flank and effected a junction with the remains of that Company and with C Company Headquarters. The combined party then crossed into another wadi still further to the right in an attempt to outflank the enemy, but on reaching the head of the wadi below and behind Point 226 it came under heavy machine-gun fire from both sides and was unable to make further progress. "By now," the War Diary tersely recorded, "the men were suffering greatly from thirst and fatigue." There were not many of them. Another hour was spent by parties trying to work round by both the right and the left, and then the order was given to withdraw, just as a heavy counter-attack came in from the front and right. Somehow the withdrawal was effected—"We were all thankful to come out alive, it was a nightmare while it lasted"—but as the attack on the exhausted men developed, supported by Mark VI tanks, there was grave danger of the whole Battalion being cut off, and it was ordered to withdraw to its former positions. This also was successfully achieved, under heavy supporting fire from the Grenadier and Irish Guards. The attack had failed; the Battalion was sadly reduced. That night the remaining reinforcements were brought up, "many specialists having to be used as riflemen".

April 29

On the morning of the 29th Captain T. F. R. Bulkeley and Captain D. P. M. Malcolm took over command of B Company and Left Flank respectively. The Battalion had moved from attack to defence and the Rifle Companies hurriedly dug-in in the cornfields below Point 117, on which Battalion Headquarters was joined by Battalion Headquarters of the Loyals. With the sanction of Brigade, the Medical Officer, Captain Hodge, whose efforts throughout the battle were characterised as "superb", went out with some stretcher-bearers, an ambulance and a white flag, to tend the wounded, who numbered about thirty, lying under the blazing sun unable to move, near the top of the Bou. Their arrival near the steepest part of the climb coincided with a German counter-attack, and the Doctor and his whole party were captured. The agony of the wounded on the slopes for the next few days was appalling; several died who would otherwise have been saved; one Lance-Corporal of Right Flank, who had been hit in the thigh and shoulder, was given inadequate succour by the Germans, and received no proper treatment until he crawled into our own lines on the 6th May.

Now the Germans sought to restore their position. At noon a strong enemy infantry attack came in from the right against the Irish Guards on Points 212 and 214. If these had fallen, the entrance to the Gab-Gab gap, through which passed a track linking the eastern part of the valley with the Medjerda, would have been virtually open, and the whole Brigade in the foothills would have been in danger of being cut off. Right Flank and B Company were therefore moved towards the top of Point 117 whence they could cover the track. But by that time there was not an anti-tank weapon of any sort in the Battalion, for most of the P.I.A.T.s had been destroyed by shellfire on the trucks, and the 6-pounder guns were brigaded further back outside Colonel Barnes's control; the Companies were helpless against the tanks, which made their way through the Gap and up on to Point 117. They were therefore withdrawn to their former positions in the corn, and an artillery concentration was directed on to the tanks, B Company Headquarters, owing to wireless failure, coming in for its share before it could be withdrawn. "What with Jerry machine-gunning and firing his tank guns and our artillery giving him plenty—it was bedlam," one of the Guardsmen wrote. The enemy tanks remained on Point 117 all that day and late into the night, overlooking the Battalion's positions, and keeping it pinned to the ground. But in the end they withdrew. The Divisional anti-tank guns had put perhaps a dozen of his tanks out of action, but most of them were recovered during the night.

During the night of the 30th what was left of the Battalion moved up to occupy the positions on and about Point 106 from which the Loyals had been withdrawn. Throughout the day it had been continually mortared and shelled, chiefly with air bursts and often with six-barrelled mortars, as it crouched in slit trenches with no shade from the burning sun. It was to suffer this for the next six days while the steady drain of casualties went on. But by May 2nd the situation was beginning to change. The 17-pounders and the Battalion 6-pounder anti-tank guns were brought up into position, and during the hours of daylight a squadron of Churchill tanks waited forward of the position. For the next and final enemy counter-attack there were to be guns that could hit back. *April 30* *May 2*

At 0400 on May 4th it came. Unfortunately the Churchills were late in getting into their daytime positions and were caught while they were still moving up the track in single file by the first German Tiger tanks to appear over the Gap. Two Churchills were quickly knocked out, but the 17-pounders then got into action, and by the end of an hour the Germans had lost six tanks and a tracked vehicle as they came over the Gap. But by that time the Germans had found the 17-pounder positions. The last tank to be knocked out in the Gap fired simultaneously with the gun of BB Battery, 81st Anti-Tank Regiment, gallantly commanded by Sergeant Wells; both tank and gun were knocked out. *May 4*

It had been almost entirely a Gunners' battle, and the Battalion, reinforced by a company of the Irish Guards, had little to do but be spectators in the most uncomfortable circumstances. Only one of the Battalion's 6-pounders seems to have been engaged, and this was knocked out in the first hour.

May 5

May 6

The next day the 3rd Infantry Brigade attacked through the Battalion's positions and went on to take the Bou, and at first light on the 6th the armour, away to the east, followed on its way to Tunis and the end of the campaign; in that final surge went the Second Battalion. But to the men of the First Battalion there was as yet no full knowledge of victory: they only knew that the shelling had slackened, and that for a little while it was possible to leave the constriction of slit trenches and stand erect in air no longer heavy with smoke, and to look down on the sunlit corn, and to have the first wash and shave since going into battle. That evening they were withdrawn about two miles to a position between Point 187 and the river: there were thirty men in each rifle company, including all reinforcements.

May 7

During 7th May the Battalion rested. Even the sound of battle had passed on and was no more than a distant mutter; and that mutter was lost in a sound not heard for many days, nor ever before perhaps in the Medjerda valley. The impact of that moment shines through the brief phrase of the War Diary: "Over the hill, the Pipers came to join the Battalion, piping as they came." And with the pipers came the Quartermaster, Lieutenant Alec Ross, who each night of the battle had himself brought up the rations, ammunition, water and mail, without once failing to find the Battalion in the trackless and ill-mapped plain. It had been a remarkable service, and one requiring courage as well as organisation.

That day those whose inclination led them bathed in the Medjerda: "it wasn't very pleasant, though, because it rained hard all the time;

May 8

however, we felt much better for it". Breakfasts next day were at 0400, and by 1330 hours the Battalion had passed the Bou and the further range of hills and was established among the olive groves

MAP XIV

near Tebourba, crossing the river at el Bathan, whither the Medical Officer and his party had been taken as captives on their way back to Tunis, where a few days later they were to rejoin the Battalion. On the way the news came through that the Germans were on the run, that the forward Armoured Divisions were already in Tunis, that Bizerta had fallen, and that the enemy was withdrawing into Cape Bon. But that withdrawal in fact was not to be effected. That night the Battalion rested in Corps Reserve.

May 9

On 8th May khaki drill was issued, and on the 9th the Brigade, under the command of the 46th Division, was given the task of holding the line of the Medjerda from Tebourba to Djedeida to prevent enemy infiltration. But the task was purely nominal, and in the evening

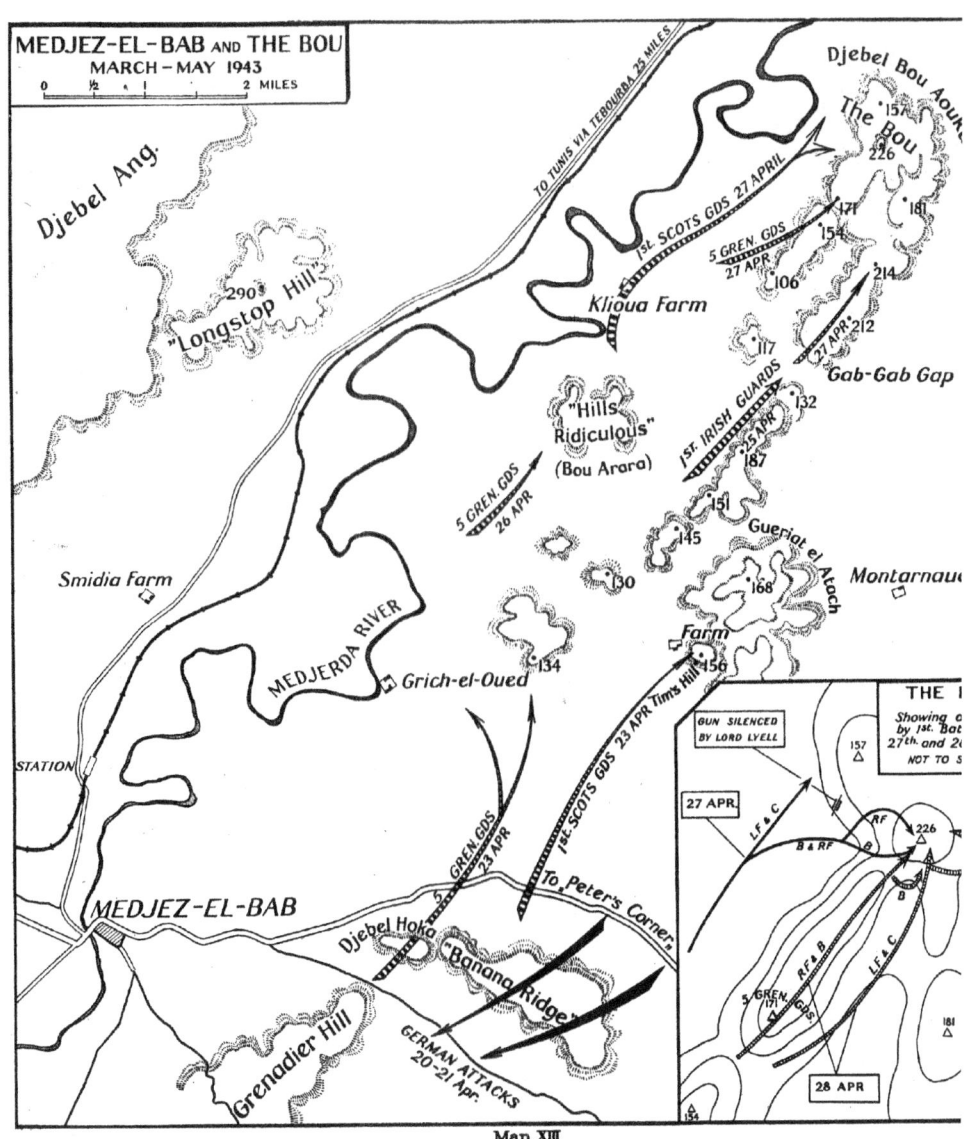

Map XIII

the report came through that all resistance north of the river had ceased. The next day came visible evidence of victory: "vast numbers of Germans passed through during the day on their own vehicles seeking to be made prisoners". There was time to sit back and relax; to absorb the full import of those days. It had been summarised in a message from the Divisional Commander: "Now that this particular phase of operations is over, may I express my very great admiration for the gallant conduct of the 24th Guards Brigade. 1st Division was selected to bear the brunt of forcing an entry through the crust of the enemy to enable the armour to break through. All three Brigades had very strong enemy positions to attack, which they did most gallantly, but the relentless courage, the cheerful sacrifices, and great tenacity of the 24th Guards Brigade was outstanding and, indeed, without it the victory of the First Army could never have been achieved. While it is impossible to differentiate between the gallant conduct of all three Battalions, I think the story of the Irish Guards on Hill 212 will always stand in red letters on the pages of that glorious Regiment's history. Your losses were great and terrible to me, but my heart goes out to you in thankfulness that such courage should produce a reward, the true value of which, at this time, no man can assess." The Scots Guards did not grudge the Irish their hard-won praise.

May 10

The true value of the Brigade's achievement, its effect on the campaign could now be assessed. To the members of the Battalion there was knowledge of great things done, and evidence of victory in the thousands of prisoners, and memory of endurance. "I never knew what *real* fatigue—mental and physical—was, till last week," one of the officers wrote, "and thirst. We were too thirsty and exhausted to eat much." "It was our privilege to go in first," wrote another. "Justice can never be done to the magnificent performance the Brigade put up and I have no doubt that only the Guards could have done it. You must understand that they had to advance over completely open country with not a tree of any sort—just great stretches of corn dominated by a series of rocky ridges—the sort of place that a platoon could hold against a brigade, but they just fought doggedly forward from ridge to ridge through a hail of machine-gun and mortar fire. There was no question of not getting there. They either got there or died. All this was amid tremendous heat and unbelievable dust, and then at last it was over and we had done our job and made the bridge-head from which the final blow could be delivered. It had been a grim struggle, but by sheer guts and gallantry on the part of every man and by brilliant leadership they won through. . . . I have made my H.Q. in a hill where the Germans were for six months and only left forty-eight hours ago. . . . As for future plans we don't know ourselves, but we are all eager to start what I hope will be the last job, though when it will be or where, I have no idea. Until then we shall probably have a pleasant enough time."

"A pleasant enough time" was their just due after fifty days and nights within range of the enemy's guns, in the last fourteen of which it seemed as if every enemy weapon was directed on them. In those fifty days four officers and eighty-one men had been killed, and thirteen officers[1] and more than two hundred and fifty men had been wounded. These casualties were more than thrice those of the defeat in Norway, but they had been suffered to gain an annihilating victory.[2]

III. THE SECOND BATTALION

The End at Hammamet

When the First Army's offensive had opened on the 23rd April, there had been, as we have seen, two Corps engaged. The operations of the V Corps included those of the First Battalion described in the preceding pages; the attack of the IX Corps further to the south-east had been less successful, and it was decided that another substantial reinforcement should be drawn from the Eighth Army in order that the final blow should be delivered by a veritable juggernaut of veterans. To this end General Alexander deprived General Montgomery of the three original formations of the Desert Army; the 7th Armoured Division, the 4th Indian Division, and the 201st Guards Motor Brigade. These were ordered round from the Enfidaville front by a circuituous route to the Medjez sector. When the dominating hills in which the V Corps was fighting had been cleared, the IX Corps, now commanded by General Horrocks and reinforced with these Eighth Army formations, was to strike down the road from Peter's Corner straight to Tunis. This was to be the overwhelming stroke, the *coup de grâce*; as General Alexander wrote, it was to be "a real thunderbolt"; *Blitzkreig* was to be translated into English.

With this mighty force went the Second Battalion.

May 1   At 0700 on 1st May the Battalion moved south along the coast road to the dreary bombed ruins of Sousse where it turned inland along the plain and leaguered a few miles from Kairouan, where the roads were already congested by the 4th Indian Division. About seventy miles
May 2   were covered that day, and on the next about a hundred and twenty: up into the hills by Pichon and on through magnificent scenery of wooded mountains and great cornfields ablaze with poppies—"the country gets better as we go forward and we now feel we have left

[1] In addition to those already mentioned the wounded officers were Captain J. Cumming; Lieutenants H. A. W. Smith, J. Graham, R. T. Hunter, R. O. Stewart, T. C. Lindsay-Peto and D. M. H. Bailie.
[2] The history of the First Battalion continues on p. 155.

the desert far behind us"—past Maktar to leaguer about eight miles east of Le Kef along the road to Medjez el Bab. The next day the Battalion moved east again, left the main road at Le Krib, and leaguered among the wooded hills east of the road from El Aroussa to Medjez el Bab on the edge of the Goubellat plain at the eastern end of which, forty miles away, lay Tunis. That night two posts were put out on tracks leading from the east, for the near-by Hermann Goering Division was known to have what the War Diary described as "offensive habits".

May 3

Nothing, however, happened. The 4th was spent largely in maintenance, and on the 5th, the day the Bou was captured by the 1st Division, khaki drill was issued, and an Order Group held for what was to prove the final battle in Tunisia. Following up the assault of the 4th British and 4th Indian Divisions, the 7th Armoured Division was to thrust down the main road from Peter's Corner to Tunis, and the 6th Armoured Division, to which the 201st Guards Motor Brigade was attached, was to clear and consolidate the Djebel el Mengour to its right. The role of the Brigade was to hold a corridor for the 1st Guards Brigade and the Division's unarmoured vehicles to pass through; the role of the Battalion was to provide an anti-tank screen on a front of about six thousand yards on the right flank facing south.

May 4–5

At 0300 hours on the 6th the final assault began, supported by intense artillery and aerial bombardment. A gap was blasted through the enemy's positions and the Infantry Divisions gained all their objectives and—at last!—the armour passed through. No counter-attack was delivered, and the Brigade never came into action, but had merely to follow in a series of short bounds. That night the Battalion had to take up an anti-tank position south of Borj Frendj facing south. The country was unknown and trackless, and only one Company Commander was able to reconnoitre his position by daylight, but when morning came the line was found to be continuous. But still the expected counter-attack by tanks did not come. Instead, there were rumours of the enemy's collapse and of the Americans having captured Bizerta, as in fact they did that afternoon.

May 6

May 7

During the day the Battalion led the Brigade in a series of short bounds along the main road, and on the next afternoon it reached Fouchana, seven miles south of Tunis, first visible in the distance that morning, where it heard the news that Tunis had fallen. The 9th was uneventful, and was spent in church services, cleaning, and maintenance in preparation for the last lap.

May 8

May 9

With the fall of Tunis the enemy forces had been divided into two. The possibility of the Allied break-through had been foreseen, and supplies of every kind were thought to have been concentrated in the Cape Bon peninsula. From those supplies, and from joining the rest of the enemy forces in a final campaign, the enemy in the north were now cut off. Instead, as the Americans pressed forward from Bizerta and the 7th Armoured Division turned north from Tunis, they found themselves trapped in the Mejerda valley and were forced to surrender. There remained the enemy in the centre and the south. If they could get back from their positions in the hills and cross into the peninsula the campaign might still be prolonged. There was only one practicable route by which they could be cut off: the road that passed through the narrow gap between the sea and the great mass of the Djebel Bou Kournine at Hammam Lif and then on across the neck of the peninsula to Hammamet. That night the 1st Guards Brigade, in a brilliant combined action with the armour in the narrow plain, stormed Djebel Bou Kournine. The way was open and the race was on.

May 9–10

It was still dark, and the action at Hammam Lif was still in progress, when the Battalion moved off. Breakfasts were eaten on the main road about a mile west of Hammam Lif, and then the Brigade passed through the 1st Guards Brigade and took over the task of supporting the armour. The Battalion was not in action but had an excellent view of some of our tanks engaging the retreating Germans and of numerous enemy demolitions. There was a midday halt in a grove littered with Italian armoured cars and then, still in the van, the Battalion pushed on to Gromballa, about half-way across the peninsula, where it passed through the 1st Guards Brigade once more. At the Wadi Chaba, a few miles south of Gromballa, the Division was halted by the blowing of two bridges over a loop of the wadi, just before the arrival of the Commanding Officer and the Brigade Commander. F Company (Major Crichton-Stuart) put in a rapid unreconnoitred attack in the dark on the ridge covering the demolitions, cleared it, and collected 113 prisoners, mostly Italian, who were promptly set to work filling in the gaps again. Then on once more at full speed through the enemy lines in the darkness, with the prospect of being "greeted very warmly as we went round each corner". Even at that eleventh hour a determined ambush might have given time for the enemy to get back from the hills above Enfidaville. But there was no ambush. The enemy had thrown his hand in. Instead of a burst of fire in the darkness, men could be heard talking at the roadside, waiting to surrender. But the Hammamet crossroads might still be vital, and the Battalion could not stop to pick them up.

May 10

May 11

It was still dark when the cross-roads were reached, and one Company position was found to be occupied by Italians; "I routed out about a dozen who were all sound asleep in a dugout, while I was making my reconnaissance for the machine-guns"; but an all-round anti-tank position was taken up without untoward incident. There proved to be no need. Instead of a great thrust for the peninsula, the prisoners came in. By breakfast 1,400 of them had been sent back on foot. "Both Germans and Italians were content to drive in to us in their own transport, and one heavy German gun was driven in with 15 men sitting on the barrel." A message came that no more could be taken further back, and the Battalion's prisoners were set to work building their own cages. Over five thousand men surrendered to the Battalion that day, and great columns of black smoke stained the sky, marking where the enemy was performing his last military duty of destroying his tanks. Apart from the hundreds of vehicles that the enemy themselves brought in, full advantage was taken of the happy fact that Hammamet was an enemy supply area. And if the tenuous line that divides legitimate booty from loot sometimes received insufficient attention, who cared? It was the destruction of an Army; and enemy rations, particularly when eaten to excess, proved a welcome change, and German pistols could be sold to Americans for £15. Lieutenant W. J. Brown acquired "a watch, camera, revolver, etc".

Six hundred and thirty-eight men out of 340,000 escaped from Tunisia—a total victory if ever there was one. It was an astounding reversal of fortune from the dark days of Gazala only eleven months before. It was but justice that the Second Battalion should be in at the kill without bearing the full burden of the Tunisian campaign. It had borne an earlier burden through many months and over many miles of Africa. Now, Rigel was avenged and more than avenged, and with it many things. A victory had been achieved that was more than is commonly meant by victory: an enemy had been eliminated and a war had been ended. The last lap from Tripoli had cost the Battalion four officers and twenty-one men killed; ten officers and some sixty men had been wounded.

At first, the completeness of the collapse could not be believed. During the day it was learned that the Battalion's old enemies, the 90th Light and 21st Panzer Divisions, had surrendered to the New Zealanders. But it was still reported that small parties on foot and in tanks were expected to try to break through from the hills. The line was therefore extended northwards facing west, with the 201st Guards Brigade on the right of the 1st Guards Brigade. The Battalion, with its newly acquired Orderly Room on wheels—"about the size of a London one-tier bus"—and twenty-one Italian typewriters, was on the left. But nothing happened, and on the 13th the War Diary recorded, "The Battalion was concentrated and normal peace-like conditions were resumed". May 13

IV. CELEBRATION AND PREPARATION

The African campaign was over; the victors could now celebrate.

During the final battle the Second Battalion had passed within six miles of where the First lay, but it was not until the 10th May that the two Commanding Officers met. Thereafter many social and sporting May events were arranged, the details of which are lost in the haze they created; the War Diaries cannot even agree on the scores and results of the matches played. Two dinners stand out in particular; the first at Nabeul where 212 officers of the three Guards Brigades in Tunisia dined together, after the massed pipes of the Scots and Irish Guards had played that day at Manouba; the second, more domestic, when Colonel Barne and thirteen other officers from the First Battalion dined with the Second under the moon. Two cases of champagne had been carried three thousand miles from Egypt for that meeting, the first that had been possible since the Second Battalion went overseas in 1938.

On Wednesday 19th May there was a Victory March in Tunis to celebrate the end of the campaign. Detachments from all units in the final battle took part, and on the saluting base in the Avenue Gambetta were General Eisenhower, General Alexander, General Giraud, Air Chief Marshal Tedder, and Admiral Cunningham. They arrived escorted by the Derbyshire Yeomanry, the first of the Allied armies to enter Tunis. There was a bright sun shining, and the route, from pavement to palm trees, was thickly lined with Allied troops.

The French Spahi led, their red cloaks and flashing sabres giving a vivid splash of colour, and the great French column was closed by the Foreign Legion, followed by the bearded and ferocious looking Goums. Then came the Americans, phalanx after identical steel-helmeted phalanx, striding to the strains of Sousa marches, and as enthusiastically received as the French,

There seemed to be a quickening of interest as the bands leading the British troops approached: the pipers of the First Battalion and of the Irish Guards, and a drum and fife band from the Grenadier, Coldstream and Welsh Guards. "It was most heartening", a spectator from the Regiment wrote, "to see the greatly superior marching and smartness of the British soldiers. Artillerymen who had done nought but ply their pieces with shells for months and years, and cavalrymen who had sat huddled in tanks for as long, too; medical orderlies and others—all were swinging their arms, putting their chests out, and marching." The 78th Division led and were followed by the 6th Armoured Division with whom were the 1st and 201st Guards Brigades. Captain Sir Hal Astley-Corbett, Lieutenants F. A. L. Waldron and J. D. A. Stainton, and ninety men marching nine abreast preceded by the Pipers comprised the Second Battalion's contingent. They were all old soldiers and tall men, and marched as though on King's Guard before the war. The men of the 201st Guards Brigade were further conspicuous in that they alone wore service dress caps. As they came by volleys of applause were added to the sound of the pipes, and a Cockney voice was heard to say enthusiastically: 'Those are boys for the job.' They marched as though they knew it. Later in the column came the 24th Guards Brigade with a detachment of fifty-six men from the First Battalion, commanded by Captain G. C. Rush, with Lieutenants A. H. Piper and the Hon. D. A. Bethell. The eye-witness quoted before was bold enough to assert that the contingent from the 24th Guards Brigade was "the smartest and most precise body of soldiers in the whole procession; they also were finely received".

The mechanised troops followed, led by some of General Leclerc's Chad Force. "They came just as they had come those many miles on the caravan routes of the Great Desert—dirty desert paint, ferocious and enormous guns of lavish design mounted in their open trucks, brew-up cans and equipment slung round the sides, and dress 'any order'." The British guns and armoured cars followed, newly painted, and polished, in column of twos in faultless formation, and lastly huge tanks clattering and roaring and dwarfing their surroundings. "They were the climax to what had been a great display of the strength of four conquering armies, one of which had come across 3,000 miles of ocean, from the New World. But we were thinking more of an army that had come 20,000 miles by sea, and 2,000 miles over the desert, to end their saga in this great triumph—even if it was not our pageant, we felt it was—and it was, too."

Cravenly, the historian begs to be excused the invidious task of deciding which was the smarter Battalion contingent; the reader had best follow the instincts of his own prejudices. For no doubt there were differences between the two Battalions, and these differences reflected the contrast between the First and Eighth Armies. The former had trained hard at home for three years, and was primarily part of an army of the European pattern. The latter considered themselves the most experienced veterans in the Allied armies, and as far as the Desert and "pure" armoured warfare went, so they were. Over the years their life of frugal hardships had built up a certain jealousy of those who were thought to be leading a luxurious existence at home; and the scorn of the "Desert rat" was directed at those who came out from home imbued with the new teachings of minor infantry tactics, which had little relevance to a motor battalion's role in the vast, coverless expanse of Cyrenaica, but which had put a new vigour into the Field Army at home, and were to prove more suitable for the later battles in Italy and North-west Europe. To the First Battalion, the Second seemed casual to the point of recklessness, an impression which was heightened by the variety and bizarre nature of their dress.

However, it was possible to dispel most of the Second Battalion's ideas that the First had had an easy time in its short campaign. Visits to the Bou resulted in the return of parties "with an increased respect for the difficulties which the First Army had to face".

June

Distinguished visitors came to pay their tributes to the fighting troops. On the 1st June the First Battalion paraded at La Mornaghia, and was inspected by the Prime Minister, followed by the usual distinguished circus; "we gave him three cheers and he doffed his hat—a large topee—and made the V-sign. It was a very hot afternoon and he did not look very well, but that may have been in contrast to us who are all so brown and weather-beaten. He was NOT smoking a cigar."

On the 2nd Mr. Churchill inspected two divisions lined up along the Hammamet Road. With him were General Eisenhower and Mr. Anthony Eden, General Marshall, General Alexander, and the Chief of the Imperial General Staff, General Sir Alan Brooke. The 201st Guards Brigade received a special compliment, for it was only for the Second Battalion and the Guard of Honour found by the 3rd Coldstream that the Prime Minister got out of his car to walk along the ranks.

On the 17th the First Battalion paraded at Kassar Said, Tunis, with the remainder of the 24th Guards Brigade, and were visited by His Majesty the King.

The rest period in Africa, interrupted by innumerable fatigues and guards on the host of prisoners which were the harvest of victory, was to be short; sterner things were intended on the continent of Europe. The Second Battalion was the first to be called upon.

Second Battalion

The last months of that Battalion's five years in Africa were busy but enjoyable. They were spent under the command of Lieutenant-Colonel G. A. D. Taylor, M.C., who in June succeeded Lieutenant-Colonel M. D. Erskine, D.S.O., promoted to command a Brigade.

Life in the Hammamet encampment, "quiet and peaceful if a trifle boring", passed pleasantly enough in spite of the mosquitoes and a particularly vicious type of fly, for "it is surprising how soon one gets used to them", and there was unlimited fruit and vegetables and eggs; and the sea, with its beach of white sand, was only a mile away. But as always in such circumstances rumours of moves and destinations daily increased. The favourite was that "we are all waiting for the Tartan Funnel"—the ship for home. But on the 22nd orders came that Battalion Headquarters, Right Flank, and Left Flank were to move to Souk Ahras, in the hills south of Bône, and that F and G Companies,

MAP V

under Major Crichton-Stuart, were to go to Philippeville to guard more hordes of prisoners.

That day, too, came the news that the 3rd Coldstream had been ordered to Pantelleria. A new phase of the war was about to begin.

June 23

Both parties set off next morning. The Battalion Headquarters party moved by Tunis, Tebourba, Medjez el Bab, and Beja to Souk el Arba where it leaguered in what had been a staging place of the First Army. The journey to Souk Ahras was completed next day, through superb scenery but over a difficult mountain road with many hairpin bends. The original camp site proved quite unsuitable, and the next day the Battalion moved to a pine forest 3,000 feet up in the hills behind Zarouria and took over the task of guarding a camp of 10,000 prisoners, and a few days later Company training was resumed.

On 2nd July there was a rehearsal by Right Flank and Left Flank, in full view of the prisoners' camp, for the Guard of Honour at the Cenotaph in Souk Ahras in honour of the French dead next day. In spite of a sirocco the rehearsal was such a success that one of the prisoners was heard to remark: "How can we win?" The performance next day was an even greater success, for the French were heard to gasp "Quelle discipline, quelle cadence"; and the Americans asked to borrow the Drill-Sergeant! Later in the month the Battalion again provided a Guard of Honour, under Major H. L. St. V. Rose, representing the British forces in the neighbourhood, for the French National Celebrations. This occasion, too, was a great success, and the Guard was described by General Dillon of the United States Army as a "mighty fine outfit".

July

On the 20th July the detachment from Philippeville rejoined, and next morning the Battalion set off for Sousse. Moving by Souk el Arba and Beja, it leaguered for the night at Medjez el Bab, and by the evening of the 22nd, by Tunis, Hammamet, and Enfidaville, it was in its new camp. Intensive training was at once put in hand. A new phase was beginning. Malaria and damp winds from the sea added to the discomforts.

July 21

On 7th August the Battalion started another move, this time back to Tripoli, which it reached on the 9th by way of el Djem, Sfax, Mahares, Gabes, Medenine, Ben Gardane, and Zuara. Unfortunately a large quantity of small comforts had to be left behind owing to a reduction in transport; the Battalion was being converted from its motorised role, to the less lavishly equipped one of infantry. "The amount of surplus kit that came to light in the process, including over forty 3-ton lorries acquired during three years 'desert-trotting' was highly revealing, and made us realise how repulsive life a-foot was liable to be, after spring beds and electric light in every truck".

August
Aug. 9

Training was pushed on vigorously in all the discomforts of flies and mosquitoes and heat and heavy, moisture-laden air, and with the further disadvantage that the neighbourhood, in places oddly like the Pirbright country, bore no resemblance to the intensive cultivation and great hills that surrounded Salerno. Football, brief leave parties, lectures, and even a dog show ("representatives of all breeds were seen, usually all in one dog") varied the intensive preparation and reorganisation for the very different campaign ahead.

Sept.	By the beginning of September they were ready; other troops had been securing Sicily, Mussolini had fallen, and the Eighth Army was
Sept. 3	springing across the Messina Straits on to the Italian toe. It was time for the Second Battalion to leave Africa, in the wastes of which it had played so distinguished a part for so long.

Perhaps it is not improper at this stage to record an anecdote which illustrates the easy-going confidence of the independent-minded Desert veteran, compared with the more rigid sense of decorum which was still to be found among those more recently from home. On the 31st August the Major-General Commanding the Brigade of Guards, Lieutenant-General Sir Arthur Smith, inspected each Company in turn. After the inspection he addressed the Battalion and, in the course of his address, asked what it was that made a Guardsman finer than any other soldier—and received an instantaneous and anonymous reply from the centre of the Battalion to the effect that it was the process of "spit and polish"—although the speaker used another term for it. The Battalion was delighted to hear that the 6th Grenadiers on being asked the same question had replied "Discipline".

Sept. 5 On the 5th September the Second Battalion sailed for the beaches of Salerno.[1]

First Battalion

The First Battalion had a longer wait, during which they remained under the command of Colonel Barne, though Lieutenant-Colonel C. I. H. Dunbar put in a brief appearance in May, before being summoned back home to take command of the Third (Tank) Battalion.

May–July May, June and July were spent in and about Tunis, doing the work of garrison, and leading the humdrum life of prisoner escorts. The Battalion gradually built itself up from two weak companies to its full strength, as the wounded returned from hospital and drafts came out from home. Rumours and false starts by advance parties created the authentic atmosphere of great events impending, but they had to remain content with a Guard of Honour for General de Gaulle, a private performance by Will Fyfe, a fleeting glimpse of Vivien Leigh, sun, sport and bathing. As was their wont throughout the war, in whatever unsuitable surroundings they might find themselves, the Etonian Officers celebrated the 4th of June with a dinner at which much thought was given to the construction "of a pompous Latin telegram for the notice-board in School Yard".

In July the four rifle companies were reformed, and training predominated from then on. In the middle of August the Battalion moved to the camp at Hammamet lately vacated by the Second Battalion. Here they remained for three months and took part in all the activities of the 1st Division as it prepared for its next fight. It was here

August–October

[1] Continued on p. 167.

12. Lieutenant-Colonel Taylor inspecting the Non-Commissioned Officers of the Secor Battalion in Salerno Stadium, 30th September 1943. Behind him are Major Steuart-Fothringhar Second-in-Command, and Captain Weir, Adjutant

ITALY – Sun and Rain

13. G Company moving up in the rain through the ruins of San Clemente on the way to atta Monte Camino for the second time, 5th December 1943. The Guardsmen are wearing anti-g capes, the British soldier's principal protection against the wet

14. The terraces at the top of Camino. On the left is the rocky peak of 819 and the wood whe F Company fought alongside the Grenadiers. The high peak to the right centre is Monaste Hill, with part of Razor Back on the extreme right. The track on the right is a continuation the Mule Track, and leads to the Monastery; at the time of the first assault this track was n nearly so well developed. Right Flank and G Company were dug in among the scrub and boulde1 The crosses of G Company's temporary cemetery can be seen on the left

MONTE CAMINO

15. The mountain from the south. The left-hand ridge is Bare Arse, culminating in Point 72 with Point 819 and Grenadier Wood to its right. Further to the right is Razor Back, the extren right-hand peak being Monastery Hill (963). In the corrie between Bare Arse and Razor Ba can be seen the white scar of the Mule Track

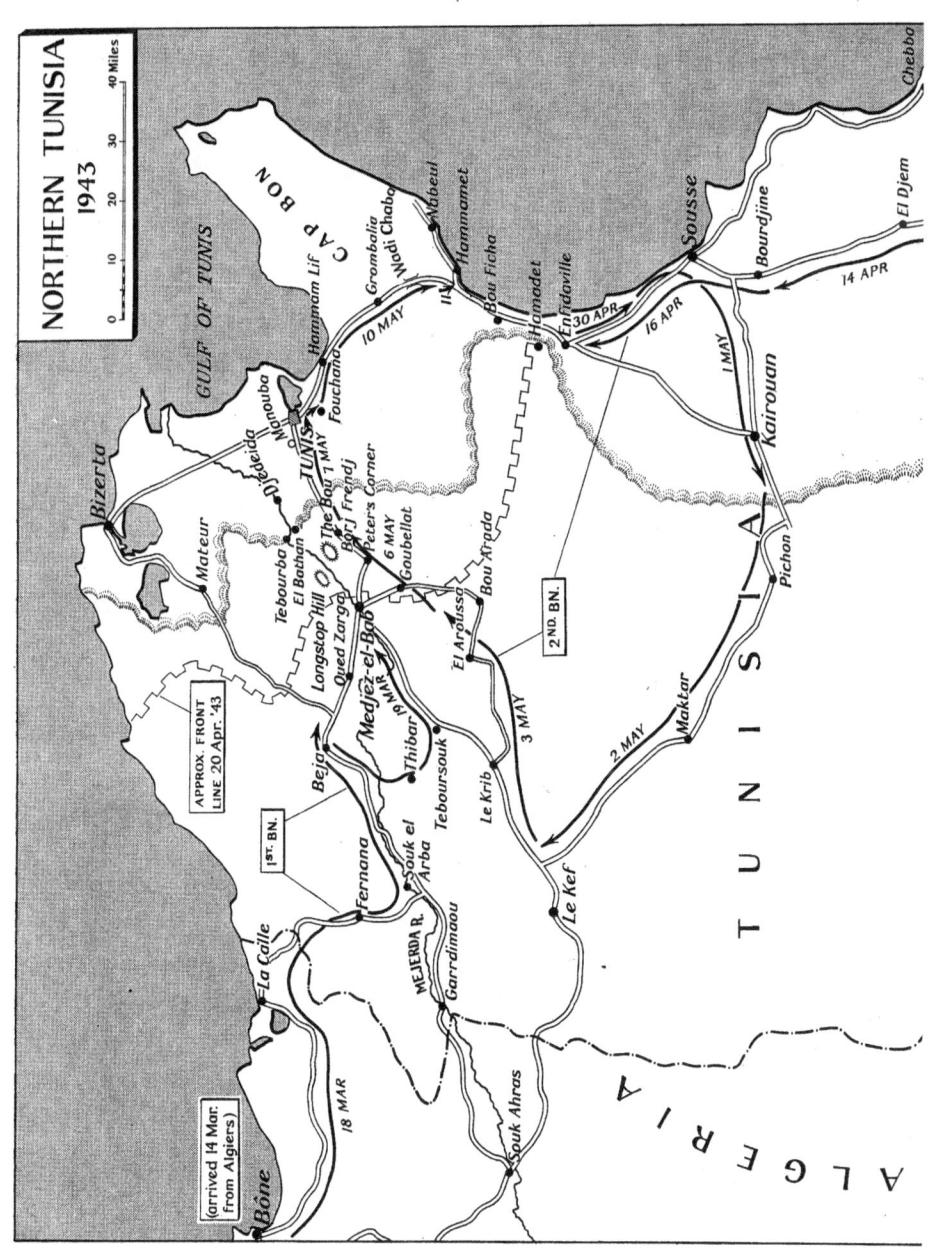

that they heard of the opening of the Italian campaign, with the false rumour that the Second Battalion had landed at Taranto; the real news of the months of hard infantry fighting which followed brought expectations of an early crossing to the continent, but as yet the lines of communication could not support half the troops waiting in North Africa, and, until they were developed, the delay must be patiently borne.

In August Captain D. Traill had succeeded Major Tyldesley-Jones as Adjutant, and the latter had taken command of B Company. In this appointment on the 25th October he presided over a company dinner in honour of the late Lord Lyell, V.C., and of other members of B Company who had won decorations in Tunisia. At the dinner the stick which Lord Lyell had always carried was presented to the Company on behalf of Lady Lyell. It was retained by the Company throughout the war, and is now preserved in the Sergeants' Mess mounted with a silver band engraved with a suitable inscription.

At last on the 22nd November serious and final preparations were begun for the move to Italy. By the 29th the whole Battalion had concentrated in the "Texas Transit Area" at Bizerta, and on the 4th December it embarked on the H.T. *Llangibby Castle* for the voyage to Taranto—and for an arduous eighteen months of fighting which, by way of Anzio and Florence, was to take it to the Po and Victory.[1]

Nov. 22
Nov. 29
Dec. 4

[1] The history of the First Battalion continues on p. 196.

PART V

Italy: 1943–1947

IN the campaign which the Allies waged in Italy from September 1943 to the end of the war, the Scots Guards were engaged throughout. It was a campaign which tested to the limit the virtues of the infantryman. In a country too lightly dubbed the "soft underbelly of the Axis" the harshness of the winter climate, the steepness of the mountains and the demolished state of the roads made physical conditions rigorous in the extreme. But the most trying circumstance of all for those who fought through the whole campaign was that, before their very eyes, they could see their strength being whittled away as division after division left to join the greater Allied force in France.

In September 1943 the Second Battalion in the 201st Guards Brigade took part in the initial landing in the Bay of Salerno, where it fought hard to maintain the narrow foothold the Fifth Army had secured. Then it moved northwards to the crossing of the Volturno near Capua and on over the high ridges to the mountain village of Rocchetta e Croce. From here it approached the mountain which for many symbolised the hardships of that first winter: Monte Camino. Twice its rocky slopes were climbed, the second time to victory. Late in the year the Battalion was transferred to the mouth of the Garigliano river on the west coast, and then, early in the New Year, it spent two dreary months of rain and shelling on the low ridges about Minturno.

The First Battalion, in the 24th Guards Brigade, remained in Africa until December 1943 and then crossed to Taranto, from whence it drove to the Bay of Naples to prepare for an amphibious assault. This came in January 1944 at Anzio, where for six weeks the Battalion was engaged in a stern battle, first of slight advance, then of long drawn-out defence. In March it was withdrawn from the beach-head, and at Sorrento both Battalions were reorganised.

The Second Battalion returned home, leaving behind more than half its strength as reinforcements for the First, which was to remain in Italy. A new and independent company, S, was raised, which served with the 2nd Battalion Coldstream Guards in the 1st Guards Brigade.

The First Battalion re-entered the line in April at Castel di Sangro in the Central Apennines, and then, in the 6th South African

Armoured Division, advanced all the summer months through Cassino, Rome, Orvieto and the Chianti country to the city of Florence, into which it was the first British battalion to enter. On the way north a stout chain of friendship had been forged with the South Africans.

At the same time S Company, in the 6th British Armoured Division, had been fighting its way forward away to the east, from the very ruins of Cassino, past Monte Piccolo, up the left bank of the Tiber, and on through Perugia and Arezzo. In August it, too, stood on the Arno.

In the autumn of 1944 the First Battalion continued the advance north of the river, encountering some of the stiffest opposition of the war on Monte Catarelto; it then sat out the winter in the mountains only eighteen miles short of Bologna. S Company spent the winter further to the east in similar conditions, fighting its final action of note on Monte Penzola.

In March 1945 at Spoleto S Company joined the First Battalion, which was then transferred to the 56th (London) Division on the Eighth Army front. With this division the Battalion fought in the final offensive, skirting the shores of Lake Comacchio, breaking through the Argenta Gap and pursuing the beaten enemy to the Po. On the banks of that river the Italian campaign came to an end—but not all duty, for the Battalion was called upon to help keep the peace in Trieste.

The eighteen months of the Italian campaign was the longest period of continuous infantry fighting in which the Regiment engaged in the war. Inevitably, as the months dragged on, the strain on every officer and man increased. From mid-1944, with few replacements available from home and with the return to the ranks of many who had been wounded more than once, sound leadership both in and out of the line became more and more important. Few who served in that campaign will think it invidious if one group of leaders is singled out for special praise here: the Subaltern Officers. An experienced Company Commander was later to write that "the real burden of those months fell upon the Platoon Commanders, many of them no more than fourteen years old when war began. After an arduous day leading their platoons, it fell to them to take out the patrols and lay the ambushes. As casualties increased and the standards of training and discipline suffered, these young officers showed an example of leadership and devotion to duty which, more than any other single factor, enabled the advance to be maintained and the honour of the Regiment not only to be upheld but enhanced."

In Italy are buried four hundred and sixty-two officers and men of the Scots Guards: just half of all those who fell in action during the war.

I. THE SECOND BATTALION

(a) *Salerno*

On arrival in Tripoli the 201st Guards Brigade (Brigadier J. A. Gascoigne) had become the third brigade of the 56th (London) Division and part of the X Corps, the whole being commanded by General Mark Clark of the American Fifth Army. The conversion to an infantry role was a big task; the establishment was increased by over one hundred, with a far smaller percentage of specialists, drivers and senior non-commissioned officers. Many machine- and anti-tank gunners had to be retained as "honest-to-God infantrymen", and, in the hard physical exercise that this involved, many had to be weeded out as unfit. Flat feet and varicose veins are all very well for careering about in trucks, but they are a decided impediment to the successful scaling of mountains. The cumbersome P.I.A.T. was introduced, and met with some scepticism from those accustomed to the long distances of the Desert; and one practice landing was carried out at Zuara, seventy miles to the west of Tripoli.

On the 2nd September the first part of the Battalion[1] embarked in a Landing Ship Tank (L.S.T.), and spent a baking two days off Tripoli Harbour, riding a gentle swell. On the 4th the rifle companies embarked in their two Landing Craft Infantry (L.C.I.) "groaning under our loads, plus weapons, mortar bombs etc. . . . Very hot and cramped, no bunks, only wooden seats and no chance of lying down. . . . Our ship is amazingly dirty; there's a notice up 'This is the smartest ship in the flotilla, keep her that way', so the others must be a treat to behold. Our White Ensign looks like a dirty handkerchief belonging to someone whose nose bleeds. It's boiling below and the deck—which is made of steel plates—is too hot to touch. I managed to find a spot on the well deck aft to sleep, on my blanket and my Mae West as a pillow." The discomfort was only compensated by the thoughts that the war was moving, and that the Battalion was at last leaving the fly-ridden shores of North Africa. In the early morning of the 5th September the convoy sailed.

By next morning the Cape Bon peninsula was visible to port, and as evening came the sheltered waters in the lee of the land were exchanged for a nasty cross-sea. An L.C.I., like all beach craft, has little grip on the water, and in such circumstances it displays an agility wildly at variance with its squat and solid appearance. The low, unbulwarked decks soon became uninhabitable, and the misery in the airless, crowded holds reached the point when men no longer have heart to grumble.

[1] For Order of Battle, see p. 551.

168 ITALY: 1943-1947

Sept. 7 By the morning of the 7th this trouble was over, and the convoy was moving eastwards in bright sunlight along the north coast of Sicily. About five miles beyond Palermo the vessels anchored in a sandy bay and all had a bathe, the stronger swimmers, including the Commanding Officer, getting ashore. Next morning the convoy joined the others off the island of Ustica, and course was laid for Salerno. As evening came and the first stars appeared over the calm sea unwonted activity among the signal lamps and a faint sound of cheering brought the news that Italy had surrendered. There was an immediate surge of optimism, and discussion as to how long it would take to march to Naples. But further reflection brought realisation that, while the

Sept. 8

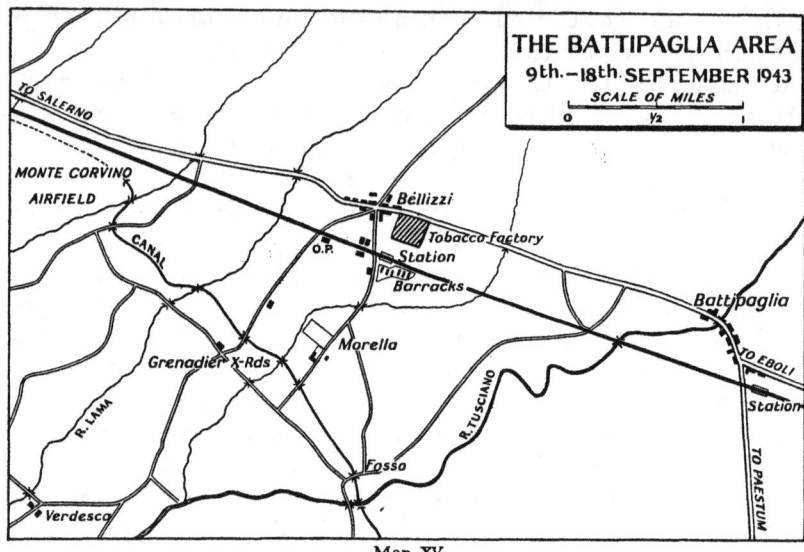

Map XV

absence of the Italian defenders might well make the landing easier, the landing was only a preliminary to meeting the Germans.

MAP XXI The plan was that the American VI Corps was to land in the early hours of the 9th on the southern part of the long narrow plain between the mountains and the sea, and south of the River Sele, the British X Corps in the northern part nearer Salerno. Both forces were then to advance and capture the surrounding hills and then swing north and move on to Naples. In the northern half the 46th Division was to land near Salerno itself, with the 56th Division on its right. The 167th and 169th Brigades of the 56th Division were to do the beach assault, and 201st Guards Brigade was to be in Corps reserve. The crucial question was, as is usual in landing operations, could the force be firmly established ashore before the enemy assembled his armour for a counter-attack?

Sept. 9 September 9th dawned still and cloudless with haze giving promise of increasing heat, and as the day drew on and as the Battalion sweltered in its landing-craft about three or four miles off shore the sound of desultory firing made it clear that, while the landings had been successful, the advance inland had not progressed anywhere near so far as had been hoped. Early in the afternoon the Battalion disembarked immediately south of the River Tusciano and moved to a concentration area about a mile inland, in a field where "sand-soaked Guardsmen were seen picking grass and examining it with interest". That night it crossed the river and moved up to the area of Verdesca within about a mile and a half of a mass of buildings soon to become known as the Tobacco Factory area, south of the road and astride the railway about two miles west of Battipaglia. "The situation in front is fluid, to say the least," the War Diary recorded, "and dawn is awaited with mixed feelings." This fluidity was largely caused by the Germans having taken full advantage of the nature of the ground and left small parties of tanks and infantry hidden in the thick cover provided by the drains, dykes and growing tobacco. These waited until the advanced troops had passed and then indulged in large-scale sniping, a form of warfare disturbing to the hardest troops and tending to unfortunate results in the case of the less well trained. It was this method of defence more than any other single factor that brought the Salerno landing to the edge of disaster. Its effect on the less experienced may be gauged from the occasion when one of the Battalion's officers, who had been directed down the wrong lane when seeking Battalion Headquarters, found himself near a recumbent platoon from another brigade. Their officer shouted to him urgently to get down as they were being heavily sniped from some bushes. In fact they were not being sniped at all, and the bushes on investigation proved to be occupied by a party of Grenadiers peacefully having tea.

MAP XV

Just before dawn on the 10th the Battalion began to move forward to support the 6th Grenadiers who were held up at a cross-roads about a mile short of the Tobacco Factory area. The Grenadiers were then moved further to the right towards Battipaglia, and when F Company (Major Crichton-Stuart) reached the cross-roads it was found that the enemy had withdrawn. Battalion Headquarters then moved up to the cross-roads and the remaining companies passed through F to attack the Tobacco Factory area, G Company (Captain Timpson) keeping straight on up the road which disappeared into thick bushes about a quarter of a mile ahead, and Right Flank (Major R. A. H. Rivers-Bulkeley) and Left Flank (Major H. H. Houldsworth) turning down the road to the right, and then left towards the farm of Morella.

Sept. 10

This so-called "Tobacco Factory" area commanded the enemy's only transverse supply route, the road from Battipaglia to Salerno, and was the key to the whole position. It consisted of a huge agricultural storage depot and its appurtenant buildings south of the road, with a railway between it and a large military barracks composed of huts farther to the south. A naturally strong position surrounded by a spiked iron railing eight feet high, this combined barrack and factory area had been further strengthened by being divided by wire into a series of separate strongpoints. It covered an area of about three and a half acres, and it had to be attacked in daylight without artillery support.[1]

As the attack went in, Battalion Headquarters, behind the houses at the cross-roads, came under fire from an 88-mm. gun which apparently had remained hidden between Left Flank and Right Flank when they turned off the road to the Tobacco Factory. Arrangements were being made to deal with this gun when a shell burst among the officers assembled there. The Brigade Commander and the Commanding Officer were astonishingly unhurt, though the latter was knocked down, but the Adjutant, Captain Sir Henry Astley-Corbett, was killed and Major Crichton-Stuart seriously, and his second-in-command, Captain M. N. Romer, slightly, wounded. Lieutenant A. T. Philipson temporarily took over command of F Company. Elsewhere, the Padre, the Reverend J. M. Gow, M.C., was wounded by a stray bullet.

All three assaulting companies soon came under heavy fire, but all managed to reach their objectives, Left Flank in the centre clearing the barracks and the railway station, where Lieutenant C. P. R. Bowen-Colthurst of the left platoon of Right Flank was wounded, and Right Flank establishing itself beyond the railway where it remained all that night. The tanks of the Greys gave what support they could in this difficult country, one being knocked out on the level-crossing. On the left G Company met with particularly strong opposition, but after some notably fine work, in which successive positions were cleared of the enemy and an 88-mm. and a 20-mm. gun were forced to withdraw, Lieutenant R. S. Dollard established his platoon beyond the railway. But in the absence of artillery support these positions became untenable, and a withdrawal to the line of the embankment was ordered. An O.P. on the railway line, which had been achieved through Lieutenant Dollard's dash and leadership, was, however, retained, and proved invaluable in the later fighting. In the centre the withdrawal was a more difficult matter, for the spiked railings of the barracks had to be climbed under heavy fire. Lieutenant D. I. Fyfe-Jamieson successfully extricated his platoon of Left Flank personally covering this withdrawal with Sergeant W. Lumsden,

[1] It should be pointed out that, although the buildings were marked on the map as *Tabacchificio*, what everyone called the "Battipaglia Tobacco Factory" (1) was *not* at Battipaglia, but at Bellizzi; (2) *never* contained tobacco, which was all sent to genuine tobacco factories at Pontecagnano and Battipaglia proper; and (3) was *not* a factory but a storage depot, with a canning plant attached, where the main crop dealt with was tomatoes.

M.M., but himself slipped and remained suspended by the trousers on the top of a spiked gate that he was negotiating under Spandau fire. Sergeant Lumsden, however, produced a knife and cut his Platoon Commander free and both rejoined their platoon with no worse damage than the loss of a pair of trousers.[1] At last light the companies were withdrawn five hundred yards south of the railway.

Next day sniping by both sides was continuous so long as daylight lasted, and the 65th Field Regiment, which had arrived in support, did magnificent work, G Company's O.P. proving doubly useful as it also enabled Lieutenant Dollard's platoon to do considerable execution with a Bren. During the day orders were received that the Battalion was to attack the Tobacco Factory area that night, and, as it appeared that most of the Germans had left it, the prospects of success seemed good. But when the attack went in at half-past nine in bright moonlight preceded by a heavy artillery concentration, it was found that the garrison had at the last moment been strongly reinforced and consisted of a battalion supported by tanks.

Sept. 11

Right Flank was again on the right, with the main Salerno–Battipaglia road as its objective. G Company was in the centre on the Tobacco Factory itself, and F Company (Captain I. Weston-Smith) on the left directed on the main road cross-roads to the west of the Factory. The volume of Spandau fire from the cross-roads was such that F Company was forced to withdraw after suffering heavy casualties, including Lieutenants W. Beckett and R. C. McLeod killed and Captain Weston-Smith and Lieutenant Philipson prisoners. CSM J. Tulloch took command, and was largely responsible for any men getting back at all; he himself was taken, but later escaped. When the Battalion advanced a week later, there was found lying beside the body of Lieutenant Beckett that of Guardsman Harrold, the oldest soldier in the Company and driver of the Company's three-ton truck. He had no business to be anything like so far forward; he was found still clutching a rifle with bayonet fixed.

In the centre G Company was successful in getting into the Tobacco Factory, which was found to consist of "row upon row of large sheds with lanes between and wire netting everywhere". The platoons "played hide and seek with a mass of Germans in the buildings", and tanks could be heard churning about inside; but the Company had no anti-tank weapons with it. After Lieutenant Sir Nigel Cayzer had been killed and Lieutenant Dollard wounded, Captain Timpson withdrew the remains of his company when ordered to by the Commanding Officer.

Right Flank had a disastrous night. Led by Lieutenant W. A. Elliott's platoon, the Company crossed the railway embankment, taking prisoners and killing Germans, until it crossed the main road,

[1] Sergeant Lumsden was awarded the Distinguished Conduct Medal.

where it met tanks and infantry in the lanes and fields. There a confused mêlée developed, in which Guardsman W. Chadwick greatly distinguished himself,[1] with the Germans making shrewd use of English phrases such as "Is all the Company here?" "Tommy, over here", "Here we are". After the tanks had overrun them, nearly the whole Company, including the three platoon commanders, Lieutenants Elliott, I. J. Fraser and R. T. S. Clarke, were captured. Major Rivers-Bulkeley had several narrow escapes from capture while trying to collect the remnants, but he managed to get back bringing with him his headquarters and Captain R. A. Willis his second-in-command —about a dozen in all. It had been a sad disappointment in view of the early success; in fact Lieutenant Fraser's platoon had already dug in on their objective before they were cut off by the tanks advancing along the road behind it. The attack had failed; Left Flank was not committed.

Sept. 12   In the meantime on the right near Battipaglia the Grenadiers, who had suffered severely from the enemy's infiltration tactics and had been reinforced by two Coldstream companies, had repulsed a counter-attack so heavy that every man in the battalion had to be put in the firing line. Even so the situation remained critical, for there was a gap of about twelve hundred yards between the left of the Grenadiers and the Battalion's right, and the only troops available to fill it were the two remaining companies of the Coldstream, the Brigade's only reserve. It had proved impossible to capture Battipaglia, and it was decided to withdraw from the Battipaglia salient and shorten and strengthen the line. By about midnight on the 12th/13th the withdrawal was completed, after some anxiety about getting the supporting tanks of the Greys and the anti-tank guns and vehicles down the only

Sept. 13   track available. The 3rd Coldstream were on the right in line with the Fosso Bridge over the Tusciano, which was held by the 1st/4th Hampshires, and the Battalion, with F Company and Right Flank amalgamated under Major Rivers-Bulkeley, on a shortened front to their left.

The original assault, which had been intended to clear the hills beyond the Battipaglia–Salerno road and then swing left on to Salerno and through the hills to Naples, had changed to defence of a long thin strip of the sweltering and mosquito-ridden coastal plain. On the right, the Americans had effected a landing, but no more. On the left, the 46th Division was barely clinging to what it had gained. The 6th Grenadiers were the only unit in Corps reserve. No reinforcements could be expected to land until the 16th. The Eighth Army, advancing with what speed they could over demolished roads from the south, could not undertake to be near enough to relieve the pressure until the 17th. The beaches of Salerno were near to being another and, it might have been, less successful Dunkirk. The Prime Minister

[1] He was awarded the Distinguished Conduct Medal.

thought that Wellington's summary of the Battle of Waterloo, "a damned close run thing", fitted the situation.

Soon after midnight on the night of the 13th/14th the last great German counter-attack went in. Perhaps fortunately, they chose the 201st Guards Brigade for the scene of the attempted break-through, and of the Brigade they chose the Coldstream, the strongest battalion. Two German battalions went straight for it in a mad rush of half-tracks followed by about fifty tanks, which after the break-through were to fan out and operate in the congested beaches in the rear. The shooting of the 65th Field Regiment was superb. In the hour and a half that the attempt lasted the Coldstream fired fifty-four thousand rounds of small-arms ammunition. Only one vehicle got through. *Sept. 14*

The 14th was fairly quiet, but G Company and Right Flank had several targets, the latter developing "the technique of 'flushing the birds' with mediums, shooting them up with 25-pounders when they came into the open and then 'flushing' them again when they went to ground with 3·7 air bursts". That day, too, Battipaglia, which had been established less than a hundred years before to house the survivors of an earthquake, was dive-bombed by Mustangs. Two landing strips had been made near the beach and fighter cover was now possible, enabling the excellent rations to be enjoyed in greater peace; "Every night we draw a box of 'Compo' rations for fourteen men; we are ten! Excellent tins which vary from day to day; example, two tins of sausages, one beans, eight tins of steak and kidney pudding, potatoes, tea, jam, margarine, chocolate, cigarettes, boiled sweets, soup and mixed vegetables."

The next morning General Clark, the Army Commander, General Alexander, the Deputy Commander-in-Chief, and Lieutenant-General R. L. McCreery, the Corps Commander, all arrived at Brigade Headquarters in a rather congested jeep, and, after being complimentary about the way the Brigade had fought, urged the necessity for holding on without support for a day or two longer. This proved easier than was expected, for the 29th Panzer Grenadier Division, which had relieved the by now rather tired 16th Panzer, had lost most of its transport in the south and preferred a less mobile form of defence. However, it was active enough to put in an attack which, with considerable loss, forced G Company to evacuate its O.P., and later the house in which Right Flank had established its leading Platoon's headquarters was hit by three salvos of very large shells which killed eleven, including Lieutenant R. A. E. Balfour and CSM Tulloch, and wounded nine. But it was clear that the Germans were withdrawing, and on the next day the Battalion moved forward and occupied the Tobacco Factory, on which nearly ten tons of bombs had been dropped. *Sept. 15* *Sept. 17* *Sept. 18*

The weight of the Allied powers had made itself felt. Heavy

bombers, the 15-inch guns of the *Valiant* and the *Warspite*, and the fighting prowess of the infantry, had combined to secure a firm foothold on the continent of Europe.

Sept. 19
MAP XXI

On the 19th the Battalion moved again, for the Brigade was ordered to take over a position from the 139th Brigade in the mountains immediately above Salerno. It proved an unwelcome change even from the mosquito-ridden Tusciano plain. The lower slopes were cultivated with vines growing on terraces six to ten feet high, and no vehicle or animal could get up to the Battalion's position. Everything, from water to machine-guns, had to be brought up by hand. It was a foretaste of the mountaineering which lay ahead.

Sept. 20

But for a little mortaring and shelling, the next day passed quietly, but was notable for parties being able to go for much needed bathes in the sea and for the sudden arrival in the peach farm which formed part of the line of Lieutenants Elliott and Fraser, "both with nice red beards". They had had an interesting week, which started, for Lieutenant Elliott, by lying hidden in a foot of water in a bramble-grown ditch for an hour and a half before one of the Guardsmen with him got a fit of coughing. His knowledge of German later enabled him to have some converse with his captors, whose "morale was excellent and they still thought they were going to win the war. They had been in Russia. The mess cooks were Russians captured at Stalingrad, wearing German uniform and quite happy in their new role". The next morning some lucky naval shelling caused confusion in which he and Lieutenant Fraser managed to get into a different ditch from their escort. After an enthusiastic welcome at a farm and a cold night on the mountainside they made their way to a village where Lieutenant Fraser, speaking Latin, convinced the inhabitants that they were English, and they were then passed on to the care of the Italian Army hiding further up in the hills, "in a sort of lost world in the middle of nowhere", where they were well looked after and "ate, slept and waited for the next advance". Their return was unfortunately marred by Lieutenant Fraser being badly wounded in an air attack early next morning, in which Pipe-Major J. Raeburn was killed. That day, too, the Battalion lost six killed, including Lieutenant J. P. Carpenter-Garnier, when his patrol ran into a German standing patrol outside Brignano.

Sept. 21

Sept. 21 –25

Except for undergoing some shelling and further losses the Battalion took little part in the operations of the next four days, being content to follow up the Grenadiers and Coldstream in the hills to the left of the road running to Avellino, and providing a flank guard in the area of San Severino. On the 26th Salerno harbour was used for the first time and a heavy rainstorm gave an unpleasant foretaste of the Italian winter, and next day the Battalion was brought back into Salerno to rest and refit.

Sept. 26

Sept. 27

The first stage in the campaign in Europe was over, and a great reputation had been maintained and increased. In the early critical days of the landing a wounded officer from the Battalion was "tended and shaded from the blistering sun on the deck of a Landing Craft by one of the crew who told me that he had heard that things were not going well ashore, and asked what my Regiment was. I told him, and he said: 'I reckon we'll be O.K. if the Guards are there'." In ensuring that they were so the Battalion had lost six officers and forty-five other ranks killed or died of wounds, six officers and forty-six other ranks wounded, and three officers and eighty other ranks missing, nearly all of whom were subsequently reported as prisoners of war.

(b) *Across the Volturno*

On 1st October, the day Naples fell, the Battalion regretfully left the pleasant ease of Salerno for the hills once more, and moved to an area between Fisciano and San Severino Rota, on the main road to Avellino. The fighting had moved northwards, and the Brigade was following until it should again be required. On the 4th the Battalion moved again, through Nola to Cimitile, whence some took the opportunity to climb Vesuvius, and three days later through Caserta to San Prisco where the Battalion became responsible for a stretch of the River Volturno east of Capua, between the Grenadiers on the left and the American 30th Division on the right. On the opposite bank was the Hermann Goering Division.

Oct. 1

Oct. 4

Oct. 7

There followed nights of rain and discomfort and shelling and patrolling by both sides on both sides of the river, in the course of which the Battalion suffered several casualties including Captain M. J. A. Gordon, second-in-command of Left Flank, killed on the 8th, and Lieutenant T. C. H. Thomson by shellfire on the 10th within an hour of joining the Company.

MAP XVI

The assault on the line of the Volturno took place on the night of the 12th/13th, and the Americans to the east, who had taken over part of the Battalion front for their bridging operations, and the 46th Division to the west, successfully established bridgeheads. The Queen's Brigade of the 56th Division failed to cross west of Capua; the Guards Brigade's task was purely diversionary.

Oct. 12–13

G Company carried out a raid across the river; the night before the officers dined in relative state in "the poky little dining room lit by guttering lights" of the Restaurant Faust in Santa Maria di Capua. One hundred and fifty guns supported them as they set off towards the banks, and fired some three thousand shells at the far bank—over thirty shells for each man engaged in the raid. The Company scrambled down the steep bank into the river, which came up to the armpits at its deepest, and began to wade to a low island half-way across. A few ill-directed bursts of tracers came from the enemy shore, but there was no strong force on the other side, or the Company would have had more to contend with. Two platoons went on from the island to the far bank, and the opposition became a bit fiercer, but no-one was hit. The platoons pulled themselves up the muddy banks, and lay for the best part of an hour, replying to the German fire, and listening to the Carrier Platoon "charging up and down the road, banging trays and pretending to be tanks—not very successfully". After counting the

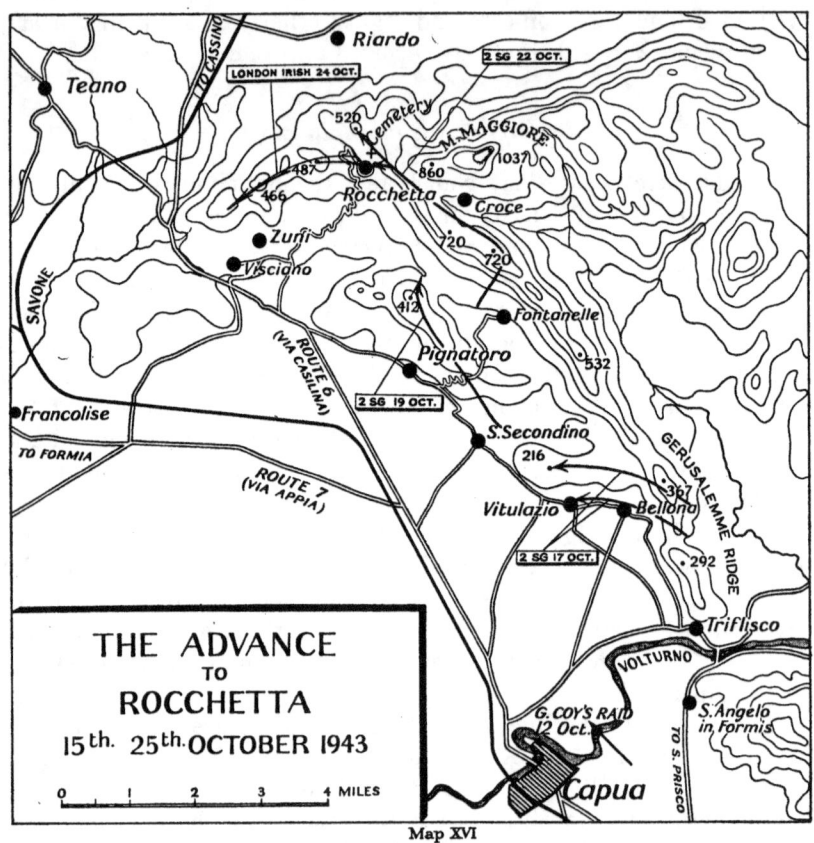

Map XVI

casualties caused by the bombardment—ten sheep and two goats—at the appointed hour of ten they stealthily withdrew. The raid was over; there had been no losses.

"I admit," wrote a platoon commander, "that I felt fairly scared all day thinking about what we had got to take on all alone. Yet on the march to the forming-up point I felt quite confident, and this confidence and a sense of security never left me during the advance and paddle. I hated that hour's wait on the far bank; I felt like a coconut—and a rat in a trap, too, for we all knew that if the Germans could get even one Spandau covering the river with the moon as it was, we were in for a jolly time crossing back. The relief I felt when I reached the home shore was an experience in itself, far greater was it than any similar feeling I have ever had. I wanted to jump for joy. We were all laughing and joking and smiling, so no doubt others felt the same reactions."

Left Flank made another raid on the 14th, while the Americans were extending their bridgehead, and further casualties were suffered from mines, including Lieutenant R. A. M. Reyntiens, who lost an eye when Captain G. L. S. Pike trod on a mine but was himself unhurt. Oct. 14

The role of the Brigade during the next few days was to act as flank guard to 56th Division while the Americans pressed forward up the valleys to the right. On the 15th the Battalion crossed the Volturno by an American bridge under shellfire as reserve to the Grenadiers and Coldstream while they occupied the Gerusalemme ridge running north from the river about five miles north-east of Capua. On the 17th the Battalion moved forward between the other battalions and, after a stiff climb in a rainstorm and losing several casualties, successfully occupied the villages of Bellona and Vitulazio and the ridge to the north of them. Oct. 15
Oct. 17

At Bellona their reception was typical of many in Italy. "The reception we got was superb, a real ovation. There was no doubt we were welcome. The little dirty streets were crowded with even dirtier Wops, all clapping their hands and cheering. Every other person offered glasses or even jugs of vino—that repulsive acid raw red wine—and dried figs, apples and grapes were literally showered on us from balconies and windows. Old women threw their arms around my neck, and I was even given a bouquet of lilies!!"

The neighbouring lanes were heavily mined, and the village blocked by demolitions, and the 18th was given up to achieving a practicable route. This was done by careful reconnaissance and the use of bulldozers and by successful mine-clearance by the carriers under Lieutenant H. Brooking-Clark. Oct. 18

That night the Battalion had to move again: a march of about five miles followed by a steep climb to the crest of the ridge above San Secondino prepatory to attacking the next ridge at first light. This ridge proved to be unoccupied, and the only casualty was Lieutenant G. F. Mundy, injured by his own machine-pistol in a fall. But the ridge was bare and digging was impossible, and it was overlooked by higher ground to the right. Three men were killed and fifteen wounded before the Battalion moved down into the comparative peace of Fontanelle during the night of 20th/21st. But the rest was all too short, and at ten the next night the Battalion started to climb two thousand feet up the almost precipitous line of hills on which the Oct. 19
Oct. 21

12—S.G.H.

Grenadiers were established. Everything had to be manhandled, and the Coldstream and many others, including some flighty Basutos, acted as porters until supply dumps were built at the top. The Battalion then turned north along the ridge behind the Grenadiers, the intention being to turn west along another ridge when the Grenadiers had taken their objective, Point 860, and to capture the village of Rocchetta on its rocky pinnacle overlooking the Savone valley.

The Grenadiers were successful in their main attack on Point 860, but had to divert the company which should have taken Point 520 near to and dominating Rocchetta. The Battalion's line of attack had therefore to be changed hurriedly to include this hill. Left Flank was to attack Rocchetta and G Company 520. There was heavy artillery support, but no time to gain more than the most general impression of the enemy's positions. The enemy took full advantage of this and waited until both companies had advanced to a cemetery well round the shoulder of a steep hill before opening heavy fire with Spandaus and mortars, not only from the objective but also with two Spandaus from behind and from below. Left Flank was immediately pinned near the cemetery and was unable to move until dusk two hours later when a smokescreen laid by the gunners made withdrawal possible. It had lost Lieutenant J. S. Cuninghame and four others killed, and twenty-four wounded including the Company Commander, Major H. H. Houldsworth, whose injuries were very severe, and whose journey back to the R.A.P. took nearly twenty-four hours. G Company, slightly higher up the hill, found some cover, but lost five killed and four wounded without being able to reach Point 520.

At dusk the attack was continued with more artillery support. F Company was directed on Rocchetta, and after a brief period of Spandau fire on fixed lines the enemy withdrew and the village was occupied without further opposition. On 520 the enemy continued to resist strongly, and Right Flank (Captain A. M. Balfour), passing through G Company, came under fire from about eight Spandau posts on the hill. However, the enemy broke and fled in the face of a bayonet charge led by Captain Balfour; "they went up the side of 520 with a shout that gave me the willies. God knows what the Germans thought! Anyway, after a short scrap the Germans ran, shouting 'Aus, Aus!!', and we had got the objective." Lieutenant R. G. Rowe was wounded in this attack, and later in the night Lieutenant D. E. Loder was killed when out on patrol from F Company. Nine other ranks were killed that day, including Lance-Corporal W. M. Millar, M.M. One of those who was later to die of his wounds was Lance-Corporal J. McIlhargey, M.M., who had lost a foot when attempting to rescue a comrade in the open. In the agonising journey back across the ridge he had done much by his cheerfulness to encourage others in less grave plights. The remainder of 520 was cleared next day by Right

Flank, and the next morning the London Irish of the 168th Brigade took the long spur to their west. This the Battalion took over on the 25th, looking north and north-east over the Savone valley and the much-bombed town of Teano towards the great hills. Those hills held the Gustav Line. Oct. 24

By now the winding road up the hill to Rocchetta was cleared of mines and the Battalion at last saw its transport again and got some of the amenities of life. But the drain of casualties continued and on the 27th Left Flank went into abeyance. Even so the Battalion was eighty men short of three full companies. Oct. 27

Ten days had been spent in "terrific feats of mountaineering, with the men desperately tired towards the end, and having to be kept awake with benzedrine tablets". Every item of food and ammunition had to be carried up by porters, and the cold nights had to be spent wrapped in anti-gas capes, without so much as one blanket to give warmth. Rain fell often, and the dew was heavy, but by day the last of the autumn sun dried out the filthy garments which the Battalion now wore. Mules were beginning to appear, which promised better supplies on the heights, but they could hardly provide the comforts for which all were longing; "there are things like clean clothes, a bath, good food, lights after 5.30 p.m., which would be lovely. . . . Funnily enough one gets a good chance of reading in this type of warfare, as so often by day one has to live in a slit trench overlooked by the enemy, when a book is grand. I keep a special place for *Blackwood's* in my pack."

The next few days passed quietly, as the 167th and 168th Brigade with little difficulty, except that of supply, occupied the Division's next objective: Teano and the hills around it. On 5th November Major P. Steuart-Fothringham, the second-in-command, took over from Colonel Taylor, who had to return home to attend a course, and late in the day the Battalion moved forward to a forest of chestnuts (a welcome addition to the rations) on the northern slope of a ridge facing the next objective. On the left lay the valley of the Garigliano, strongly held by the enemy who had made all preparations for flooding it at the first signs of advance. To the right the road leading to Mignano was crowded with American traffic connected with the bitter battle to clear a way through the hills to the plain below Cassino. In front and to the left of this road lay the great mountain mass of Camino, a bastion of the Gustav Line. Frontal attack only was possible. The 201st Guards Brigade had been chosen for the task. Three days earlier Guardsman Chadwick[1] had rejoined the Battalion in civilian clothes after escaping from capture and making his way through the Gustav Line. He brought with him much information, and it was found that "his description of how the Germans were gelignting themselves Oct. 28–30
Nov. 5

---

[1] See p. 172.

into the solid rock in and around the Camino feature was illuminating, but never very encouraging".

(c) *Camino—"first time up"*

MAP XVII

The Camino feature consisted of three main summits forming a flattish triangle with its apex to the south. The first two summits were known respectively from their heights in metres as 615 on the west

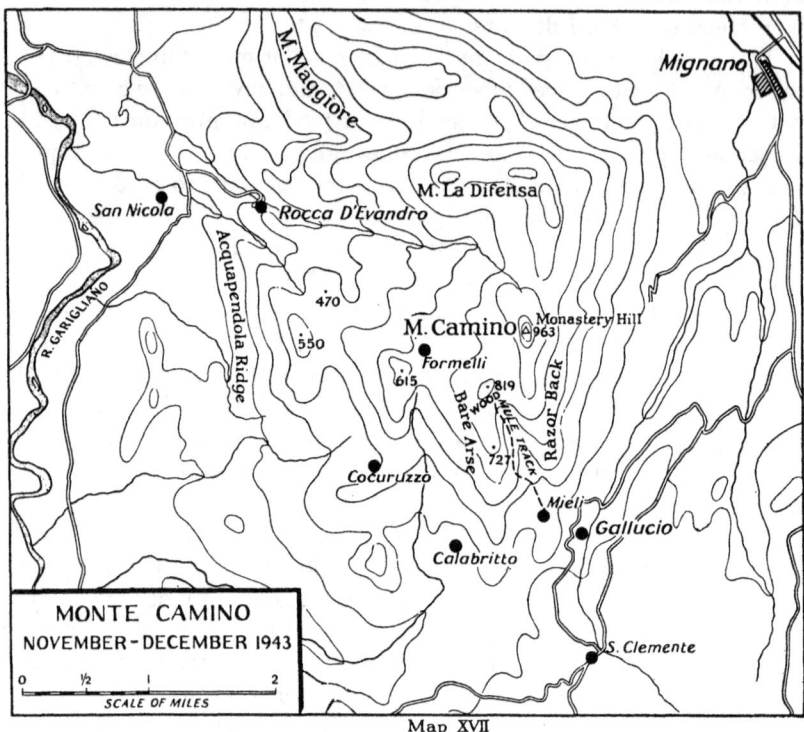

Map XVII

and 819 to the south. The eastern summit, 963 metres, had a monastery on top and was known as Monastery Hill. From each summit rocky ridges sloped steeply southward to the valley. The narrowest and most regular of these, that from Monastery Hill, was known from its conformation as Razor Back. The ridge from 819 at first sloped gradually and then, after rising to Point 727, descended in precipitous slippery rocks towards the village of Calabritto. It was known as Bare Arse. Between Razor Back and Bare Arse a steeply shelving corrie with a rock-strewn mule track led to the col between 819 and Monastery Hill. Between the head of this track and 819 there lay what was to become known as Grenadier Wood, a low rocky ridge sparsely covered with trees. 727 commanded the corrie. 819 commanded 727 and Grenadier Wood. Monastery Hill commanded them all except the corrie. From the valley to 819 was a climb of over 2,000 feet.

The plan adopted was for the Coldstream to form a firm base by capturing the village of Calabritto to the west of the lower slopes of Bare Arse and the Cocuruzzo spur towards the end of the ridge. The Grenadiers would then attack up Bare Arse, capture 727, 819, and the top of the corrie, and send a company to 615. The Battalion was to be in reserve. Camino was defended by the 129th Regiment of the 15th Panzer Grenadier Division, the formation which was to be the Second Battalion's final adversary in Germany a year and a half later.

The Coldstream attack in the evening of 6th November was only partially successful, chiefly owing to heavy casualties from mines, but sufficient was secured to enable the Grenadiers to attack, and after an arduous moonlight climb, mostly in single file, the companies established themselves on 727, 819 and in Grenadier Wood just before daylight. Movement then became impossible, and no further attempt could be made on 615 or the head of the corrie. A heavy thunderstorm added to the discomfort but made it possible for those of the Grenadiers still on Bare Arse to move into comparative cover nearer 727. That night counter-attacks were added to the continuous mortar and machine-gun fire of the day.

Nov. 6

Nov. 7

It had been intended that the Battalion should climb the mountain that night and go on to attack 615, but owing to a patrol from another brigade reporting the corrie track unusable, and to torrential rain adding to the difficulties of Bare Arse, the attack was countermanded. In the meantime F Company (Captain H. S. N. Rathbone) had been detached to support the Coldstream against an expected counter-attack, with orders to follow the Battalion up the hill later. The orders countermanding the attack never reached F Company, and at eleven that night, already soaked by the rain, with no blankets, and with only four boxes of rations instead of the intended ten, it set off in single file to climb Bare Arse. "The going was terribly hard mainly over great sharp-edged boulders and sometimes long grass growing amongst it. One had to choose each foothold and sometimes climb with hands and knees. It was necessary to have frequent rests. Two hundred yards or so was as much as we could manage at a time, especially towards the end when we were all getting very tired. There were heavy rainstorms most of the way up and a biting north wind."

On arrival at the top after about five hours of this climbing, F Company came under command of the 6th Grenadiers and was given a position facing mainly west and south-west covering their Headquarters below 727. There was just time to build very rough stone sangars before daylight, after which movement was impossible. It was bitterly cold and wet, and they made a poor breakfast owing to the shortage of rations.

Nov. 8   During the next day the German pressure increased, particularly on the cold and weary men of the two Grenadier companies in their isolated positions on 819 and in the wood. Their only water supply now was from the bottles of the dead. Eight attacks were beaten off during the day, but the last cut off and captured a platoon, and it was apparent that unless reinforcements could be sent the end was near. F Company was chosen for the task, and at last light it moved into the wood and linked up with the survivors of the Grenadier companies, who were holding a roughly circular position about sixty yards in diameter at the corrie end of the wood, commanded by Captain R. M. C. Howard, who was already seriously wounded in the legs. Of the two companies only three officers and about forty men were left. It was not known if any of No. 2 Company were still holding out on 819 but it seemed unlikely, for 819 overlooked No. 3 Company's position which was under Spandau fire from that as well as other directions. A hailstorm and a small earthquake added to the unpleasantness.

Nov. 9   At about seven in the morning of the 9th, after an almost sleepless night of cold and hunger, the combined company position came under heavy Spandau fire from 819 and other unidentified posts, and this and sniping and mortar fire caused many casualties, including Captain Rathbone killed and Lieutenant Fyfe-Jamieson, M.C., wounded. Captain R. L. Coke, the only surviving officer, took over command of the company, and at nine o'clock the German attack developed from the west and north-west. It was successfully repulsed after about an hour and a half, but the fire continued, and but little movement was possible in preparation for the next attack. This came in just before noon from the west and south-west, and the Germans, making use of dead ground previously covered by men who had become casualties in the last attack, got to within grenade throwing distance and summoned the defenders to surrender. "This was greeted by loud cheers followed by No. 36 grenades. The Germans then most unexpectedly withdrew, for no apparent reason except presumably that they had had enough." That was at about two o'clock, and there followed a respite during which it was possible to reinforce the weaker places from the stronger and issue the last reserves of ammunition. After about two hours the bombardment restarted, but no attack followed. Instead, there came the welcome news over the wireless that help was on its way. It was time. There was little water and almost no food—the Grenadiers shared their dwindling rations with the Company—and no hope of getting the seriously wounded away. When it got dark the worst cases were collected and made as comfortable as possible on the available stretchers, but pitifully little could be done, and several died of cold and exposure that night.

Nov. 10   In the small hours of the morning it was clear that help could not arrive that night, and, as things remained quiet and there was time to reach the Grenadier Headquarters before dawn, those wounded who could still walk but were incapable of taking further part in the fighting were told that they could try to make their own way back. Lieutenant Fyfe-Jamieson and about fifteen men made the attempt; Fyfe-Jamieson, who was able to give valuable information on his arrival, died of his wounds two days later. With daylight the firing was renewed and continued intermittently all day, shelling by our own mediums and 25-pounders, who thought the Germans already in occupation, being an additional trial. But no attacks developed, and evening found the companies still in what was nominally a wood but was in reality a rocky outcrop adorned with some small chestnuts giving almost no cover. It was a grim position: the promised reinforcement of a Grenadier platoon the night before had been unable to get through; ammunition was down to the last reserve, food was almost exhausted, and many of the men, tired and wet and cold, had had nothing to eat all day. But a message had come through on the wireless that help was on the way, and the sound of Bren guns firing from the corrie in the morning had "raised everyone's spirits tremendously . . . the men were very cheerful, and amused themselves by making wild guesses as to what was happening". The Brens, in fact, were those of Right Flank and G Company making their way up the unusable track up the corrie and taking nine Spandau posts in the process. On the 8th Captain J. D. Henderson had taken a patrol up the track; and on the 9th Lieutenant J. S. Burn-Clerk-Rattray had demonstrated that it was usable after all "by the simple expedient of taking a mule train up it until he came under fire near the top".

Right Flank (Captain R. S. P. Home) led the night advance up the corrie, followed by G Company (Major Timpson) and Battalion Headquarters. Movement was slow, and Right Flank came under heavy fire near the head of the corrie. These Spandau posts were dealt with one by one, and by first light on the 10th the Company was established on its objective, the fields in the rim of the corrie. The dash and vigour of its attack, ably assisted by the two scouts, Guardsmen G. H. Connor and H. J. Spraggon, were such that it suffered only two casualties and took seventeen prisoners. In the meantime G Company had occupied the left part of the rim and made contact with the rear companies of the Grenadiers near 727. A firm base, the object of the attack, had been established.

The base, though firm enough, was far from comfortable, for many of the positions were under observation from higher ground and sniping was continuous. One post on Razor Back—"the Bloody Spandau"—was found to cover the whole Battalion position and the mule track up the corrie. It was properly captured with nine of its occupants by a platoon from Right Flank, but it could not be maintained as the Germans were able to pick off every sentry who was posted. "Then began several days of sitting about in the clouds (literally) and shooting like hell, which was not much fun, as our only protection from the weather was the clothes we wore. It was much too hard to dig, but we made quite efficient sangars with rocks which saved a great many lives. . . . It was tiresome not being able to wash or cook but we didn't do so badly. . . . "

That evening a start line was taped for the Oxfordshire and Buckinghamshire Light Infantry who were to attack 819 at three in the morning of the 11th, and the news of the relief was got through to the survivors of the Grenadiers and F Company in the wood. The two last boxes of rations were immediately opened, and the men were able to settle down to face the night and the long trek down the hill less hungry than they had been for days. "The rest of the night German patrols were very busy all around our position and there was a good deal of Spandauing, etc., but no direct attacks. In addition an occasional shell from our own gun was dropped amongst us. The Ox and Bucks turned up at 0340 hours on the 11th. They had no idea we were there and were very surprised to find us." F Company had gone up the hill three officers and a hundred and five other ranks strong. Captain Coke and fifty-seven other ranks came down unhurt. On many occasions during the war Scots Guards Companies were attached to battalions of other regiments of the Brigade. This was the first time in close battle. A standard had been set which was to be maintained.

Nov. 11

The remainder of the Grenadiers had been relieved by the Coldstream earlier in the night. The Grenadier battalion was four hundred and eighty-three strong when it began the attack on Monte Camino. Two hundred and sixty-three returned.

The attack by the Oxfordshire and Buckinghamshire Light Infantry achieved part of its purpose in that it enabled the survivors of the stand in the wood to be withdrawn. But it failed to gain complete control of 819 from which they could have covered the area whence came most of the fire on themselves and on Right Flank and G Company, and in the evening they were driven off what they had gained and withdrew to G Company's area. At the same time as the Light Infantry had made their attack, a platoon of Right Flank had tried to get on to Razor Back; in the attempt, which failed, Lieutenant P. H. Tunnard was wounded. That night a patrol under Lieutenant T. N. Douglas, who was wounded, was unable to return before daylight and was caught in an exposed position. An artillery concentration was put down to enable them to get back, and during it a mortar bomb landed in G Company Headquarters. Two signallers were killed and one wounded and Major Timpson, and his second-in-command, Captain N. H. Barne, M.C., were also wounded. Captain Home, who had done "terrific work in mopping up machine-gun posts and producing prisoners, thirty-four by his Company alone, or corpses like rabbits

Nov. 12

out of a hat", was also wounded that morning; Captain Henderson took over Right Flank and Lieutenant the Hon. A. R. H. Erskine took over G Company. That night, too, a fine soldier was lost when CSM R. Little, M.M., of G Company, was killed while directing a burial party.

By the next day it was clear that, while the footing on the hill could be maintained, progress was impossible without further reinforcements. Reinforcements, beyond a platoon of Cheshire machine-gunners and a company of the Royal Fusiliers which had arrived that morning, were not available, and a withdrawal was ordered for the following night. Shortly after this decision was reached, Brigadier Gascoigne was severely wounded by shellfire in Mieli, and for the remainder of the battle Lieutenant-Colonel W. H. Kingsmill of the Grenadiers took command of the Brigade until succeeded by Brigadier R. B. R. Colvin. Apart from these things the 13th was chiefly remarkable for a new cure for fatigue and a troubled stomach successfully tried by the Commanding Officer: "a whole tin of treacle duff followed by another of rice; he was thereafter himself again", an unruffled figure who gave a steady air of calm and confidence to all around him.   Nov. 13

It was in this uncomfortable situation that the Corps Commander, Lieutenant-General McCreery, twice ascended Camino to see for himself the difficulties and hardships of the assaulting troops. Somewhat less necessary, perhaps, though equally dutiful, was another visitor: "At night we find a stranger in the signallers' trench at Battalion Headquarters, who turns out to be a Colonel ——, a 61-year-old hygiene expert from the War Office, who has flown out to see we are taking our mepacrine[1]—poor soul! He has left a dinner party at the General's to visit us up the mountain. We discuss ants and Italy, he gives me Oxo cubes and chestnuts, and takes a note to my mother. . . . " No doubt the hygiene expert's visit was duly recorded in the social column of the newspaper *Camino Griff* which was written by Lieutenant Buckle and published by the Intelligence Section; five copies in all—"the lowest circulation at the highest altitude!"

The shelling of the Company positions continued on the 14th and Right Flank had eleven casualties including Lieutenant H. Brooking-Clark, who was wounded. The evening was one of mist and rain, and the withdrawal was so successful that the Germans were still firing on the positions forty hours later, long after the Battalion, after a weary night's march, had reached its destined place in the pouring rain, an area succinctly described as one in which there was "neither comfort nor accommodation". The next day, still in pouring rain, it dragged itself out of its mud patch and found some sort of shelter in Grottola and adjacent villages north-east of Roccamonfina. There followed three days of struggle to get dry and keep dry, while leave parties set   Nov. 14

Nov. 15

[1] An unpopular, bitter tasting yellow pill, designed to prevent malaria.

off for a Rest Camp at Naples and it was possible to look back in quiet on the nightmarish episode of the first battle of Monte Camino.

"This last fortnight has seen some pretty ugly goings on, on the tops of hills, where I think I may say that the Brigade has done quite magnificently. . . . I just can't think how we ever got up or how we managed to stay there. . . . It hasn't stopped raining for four days and nights. Before I left our position on the hill, I had to move one platoon's position because a river of good spate colour, four inches deep and two feet wide, was rushing through their trench. . . . All these Italian hills are equally stony, steep, bloody and muddy when it rains as it often does. . . . The Grenadiers did quite superbly, they definitely made history and I hope that the world will hear about it in due time as it certainly should."

"I think," wrote another, "the reputation of this Regiment in particular, and the Brigade as a whole, is as high, if not higher than it's ever been in its whole history. The Generals apparently think the world of us, but the trouble of course is that they will use us the whole time, and for the toughest jobs. . . . According to the old soldiers who have been all through with the Brigade, the severity and discomfort of the fighting in Africa has been absolutely nothing in comparison to this. The men have been splendid, and there is no doubt we have done well. . . ."

Nov. 21 On the 21st the Battalion moved again to Zuni and Visciano in the valley below Rocchetta where quarters were more comfortable and included a slightly dilapidated monastery largely furnished with Nov. 24 packing cases containing the National Library of Naples. On the 24th leave parties were stopped in order that training might be uninterrupted, and other recreations took their place, including concerts and cinemas and a visit from the Band of the Irish Guards. The month ended with a conference to outline future operations and once more the name Camino was heard.

(d) *Camino—"second time up"*

Dec. 2 On 2nd December, the Battalion left Zuni and set off for the second attack on Monte Camino. This time the attempt to force a way to the plain below Cassino was not to be left to one Brigade. Instead, two Corps were involved. That night the Battalion slept in the open just short of San Clemente while an enormous artillery concentration paved the way for attacks by the 167th Brigade on the village of Calabritto, Bare Arse, and 819, and by the 169th Brigade on Razor Back and the Monastery. At the same time the Americans were putting in a large-scale attack on the hills to the east and north, and the 46th Division was advancing on the west between the Garigliano Dec. 3 and the Camino feature. Many Germans surrendered next morning rather than face another such bombardment. The thought of facing Camino again was about as dismal a prospect for those who now prepared to ascend it once more.

The Battalion remained without shelter in the rain until the small hours of the 4th, when the Grenadiers moved up the corrie, and it was possible to occupy their billets and get dry. That morning the Coldstream captured the Cocuruzzo ridge running north from the west side of Bare Arse, but they remained under fire from the flanks; the Monastery still held out, and shelling continued on the mule track and its approaches. Farther back the Battalion's Liaison Officer at Brigade Headquarters, Lieutenant the Master of Erskine, was wounded by shellfire and Brigadier Colvin was so shocked that Colonel Kingsmill had again to take command of the Brigade. At midnight the Battalion set off for the hill; this time they carried rucksacks on their backs. They contained three days' rations, a blanket, ammunition, gas cape and spare clothes, and proved so great an improvement for mountaineering that it was a pity that they had not been available before. The Battalion moved up the mule track, and leaving 819 on its right, was hurried by mortar fire across the top of Bare Arse in daylight to its position behind the Coldstream ridge and below 615. There things were far from comfortable, for the mortar fire continued and the position was also heavily sniped. But from the top of the ridge there was a clear view of the Battalion's objective about a thousand yards away: the southern part of the great Acquapendola ridge, the last ridge of the Camino massif. Beyond it lay the Garigliano valley.

Dec. 4

Dec. 5

Twenty minutes before the advance started, while making his reconnaissance, Captain W. B. Malone, commanding Right Flank, was killed by a mortar bomb, which also mortally wounded Lieutenant K. B. Mackenzie; Captain J. D. A. Stainton took over command. Major Pike was also slightly wounded at this time, but remained in command of G Company. During the advance across the low ground between the ridges further casualties were suffered through shelling, including Lieutenant W. M. C. Duberley, who died of his wounds two days later. The steep climb up the side of Acquapendola was unresisted, most probably because there were very few Germans on the feature; on the right the Grenadiers also successfully occupied their part of the ridge. Further to the north, however, the Germans remained in strength in the broken and precipitous ground between them and Rocca d'Evandro.

From Acquapendola the next morning, the enemy could be seen withdrawing transport along the road by the Garigliano, and that day Monastery Hill was surrounded and captured by the Queen's. On the 8th F Company (Major Rose) was sent down the hill about 1,500 feet to cut off any enemy who might be trying to retreat northwards. The Lincolns, of the 4th Division, were engaged on the same task.

Dec. 6

Dec. 8

Dec. 9 Resistance was strong, and at nightfall F Company was still heavily engaged. The Commanding Officer then took Right Flank down to help, F Company was withdrawn to replenish, and Right Flank pushed on through the Lincolns. The next morning, moving in thick mist, F Company advanced again, passed through Right Flank, and captured the village of San Nicola, where CSM W. Lumsden, D.C.M., M.M., again distinguished himself.[1] They then cut the road leading down from Rocca d'Evandro, the enemy's supply base for the whole of Camino. The Germans in front of Rocca, who had withstood all attempts by the Grenadiers to advance the previous day, then withdrew, their escape being facilitated by the mist and the broken ground. Away to the north-east the Americans were occupying Monte Maggiore; the Mignano gap was forced; the second Battle of Camino was over. The two battles had cost the Battalion five officers and twenty-three other ranks killed.

There was to be a unique aftermath. In the spring of the following year some Moroccan Goums of the Corps Expeditionaire Françaises went to Monte Camino for training. In the course of their exercises they came upon the bodies of several soldiers and buried them with full military honours. The Goums were mountaineers and realised the implications. The bravery of men who could storm such a hill impressed them so greatly that they carved a plaque to their memory out of the rock of 819. It was unveiled on the morning of 2nd May. The Commander of the X Corps, Lieutenant-General Sir Richard McCreery, who had twice visited the positions on the hill during the first battle, was present at the ceremony, and also General Guillaume:

AUX COMBATTANTS BRITANNIQUES
TOMBES GLORIEUSEMENT AU MONTE CAMINO
NOVEMBRE–DÉCEMBRE 1943
LES GOUMS MAROCAINS

Dec. 11 The 11th passed with intermittent shelling but no casualties, and that night the Battalion was relieved by the Lincolns, and after a weary journey, partly in the rain, got back to its former billets in and about Grottola on the morning of the 12th, on which day Lieutenant-Colonel F. H. H. B. Harris took over command from Major P. Steuart-Fothringham. The past days had been bitter, but the sadness of war and loss was shot through with a gleam of gratification. For the 201st Guards Brigade virtually unsupported had very nearly achieved what had eventually to be done in a combined operation of two corps, and in that final success it had borne its full share. More than in any other battle in Italy the dangers and discomforts of Camino impressed themselves upon those who took part. To have survived that

[1] He was awarded a Bar to his Military Medal.

first gruelling, and then to be invited to return to the scene of it, was stretching a weary battalion to the limit. Those who come after will find inspiration in the achievement, but difficulty in emulating it.

(e) *Across the Garigliano*

On the 14th December the Brigade moved to Mondragone, between Monte Massico and the sea, and had another taste of Italian rural life "in a frightful little village, the streets of which serve all known purposes, from sewage disposal to ordinary traffic. The Mess is in a grubby little barn which one approaches through a small and utterly filthy back yard. This yard contains a midden, two pigs, a number of hens, endless children and some frightful toothless old women. They scratch unceasingly and it is presumably only a matter of time before we start doing the same." However things might have been worse, for, though the mud remained, it had stopped raining. On the other hand a wintry sun had a stimulating effect on the flies, and most of the turkeys died that had been bought for fattening for Christmas. Three days later the Brigade moved again, to its new area between Monte Massico and the lower reaches of the Garigliano, in a vast flat plain, dominated by the Germans on the hills to the north and northwest. The Grenadiers were forward on the right, the Coldstream on the left, and the Battalion in reserve. Leave again became possible, and the extensive marshes gave excellent snipe and duck shooting. *[Dec. 14, MAP XXI]* *[Dec. 17]*

The respite from rain was short, and it rained incessantly the day the Battalion relieved the Coldstream. However, billets were possible for all except G Company who were in bivouacs on the sand dunes, where its supplies had to be manhandled to it owing to the floods. The chief duty of the Battalion was to maintain a twenty-four-hour standing patrol at Puntafiume, near the mouth of the river, and just before midnight one night this was attacked by a stronger German patrol and forced to withdraw to G Company positions. Lieutenants Sir David Moncreiffe and J. V. Rowe, the latter out under instruction, were wounded, and a Gunner officer and five other ranks were missing. A platoon counter-attack was put in about two hours later but failed to dislodge the Germans, and lost Lieutenant I. McC. Tait and two other ranks killed and three other ranks prisoners. This was the basis of a Reuter report which caused some amusement in the Battalion a few days later. "British troops of the Fifth Army are fighting strongly to throw back a powerful German counter-attack launched at mouth of Garigliano river. Thrusts were directed against positions at Puntafiume on the south bank. Fighting is going on in the town." The "town" consisted of four houses! *[Dec. 22]* *[Dec. 27]*

At last light on the 29th F Company (Major Rose), with Right Flank (Major W. D. M. Raeburn, M.B.E.) in support, moved forward *[Dec. 29]*

Dec. 30   to drive the Germans out of Puntafiume (from which in fact they had already withdrawn) and then turn left along the river bank and hold it prior to crossing to form a bridgehead through which the 9th Commando could withdraw. The movements were successfully carried out, but F Company and a platoon of Right Flank came under mortar fire for the rest of the night and were unable to retaliate for fear of hitting the Commandos who did not appear until half-past four in the morning. A number of casualties were suffered, none of which was fatal, and the Commando then formed its own bridgehead and ferried itself back

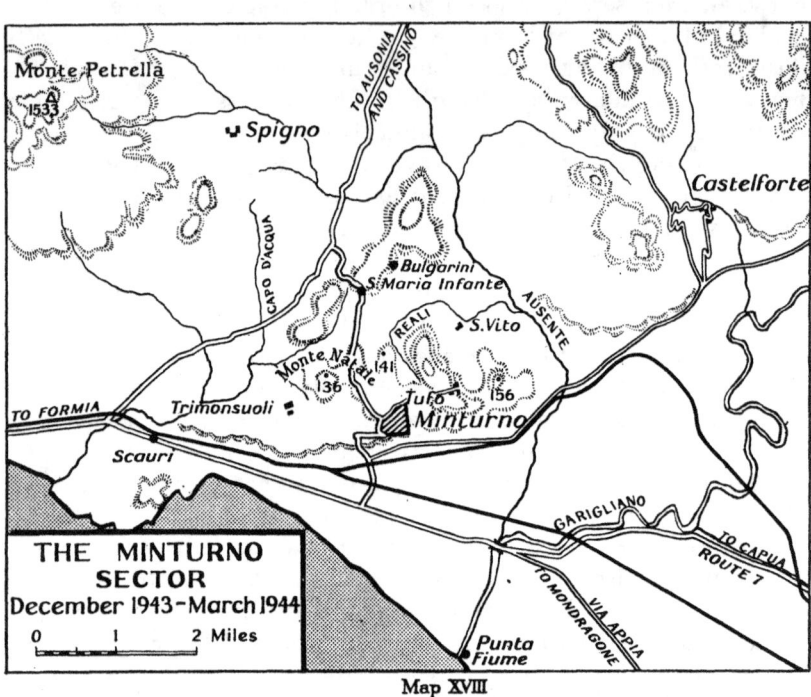

Map XVIII

across the mouth of the river. By seven o'clock everyone had been withdrawn from the forward areas, and the ensuing mortaring and dive-bombing did no damage except to the houses. On the evening of
Dec. 31   the next day the Battalion was relieved by the 2nd/7th Queen's, and in torrential rain made its way back to the by now even less attractive quarters in Mondragone. There had been no Christmas celebrations, and the wetness of Hogmanay was of an undesirable kind.
Jan. 1   New Year's Day was marked by a gale of such force that it blew walls down and uprooted olive trees—fortunately without injuring anyone—and by the arrival of the Africa Star ribbon, which a large number of the Battalion were proudly able to wear. Christmas was celebrated on 2nd January, and Lieutenant and Quartermaster A. Greenwood produced dinners that included tomato soup, turkey, pork,

plum pudding, hot punch, beer (two bottles for each man), and as much "vino" as could be absorbed. His successful efforts in the face of overwhelming difficulties to get supplies to the men in the line, and to arrange that the greatest possible comfort should await them when they came out, had long been a feature of the Battalion's life. On this occasion he surpassed himself. That afternoon orders were received to move next day into Corps reserve at Lusciano near Aversa on the main road from Naples to Capua, and while an advance party went on to look at the area another party went duck shooting in the marshes between the Battalion's former positions and the enemy. "It was quite safe except for shelling as long as one cleared out quickly after the evening flight before the German patrols came out." The duck were unperturbed by shelling, but rose at once to the sound of a shot-gun. The troops resident in this part of the line were less favourably inclined to these diversions; they got the shelling. As a result, when Hogmanay was celebrated on the 5th, each of the forty-nine officers who sat down to dine, among them Major-General G. W. R. Templer, commanding the 56th Division, and Brigadier Colvin, had half a roast wild duck. The rest of the evening was spent in the traditional manner, and the next day leave parties started for Salerno, and all those who had served abroad for over five years left for Naples and the ship for home; these "Five Year Men" numbered 141.   Jan. 6

Now another determined attempt was made to break the German winter line. Combined with the landing at Anzio, of which much more will be heard later, on the 18th the X Corps attacked across the Garigliano with the 5th, 56th and 46th Divisions; further to the north Cassino was assaulted. The 5th Division on the coastal sector made a successful crossing, and broke into the line of low hills which rise out of the marshy plain through which the river runs, and captured the ridge from Trimonsuoli to Tufo, including the little town of Minturno. They could make no further progress, for the enemy had perfect observation from the great mass of Monte Petrella which dominated the triangle of small wooded, rocky hills, lying in the triangle formed by the Capo d'Acqua and Ausente rivers and the coast. This triangle was to be the Battalion's last battle-ground in Italy, and one memorable for the abysmal nature of the weather and for the persistence of the shelling.   Jan. 18 MAP XVIII

On the night of the 20th January the Battalion crossed the Garigliano by the new Bailey bridge on the main road and moved to a concentration area between Minturno and the sea. The plan was now that the Grenadiers should go for part of the Scauri peninsula, east of Formia, while the Scots Guards attacked Scauri village and the Coldstream remained in reserve at Trimonsuoli. But this attack had to be postponed, for it was discovered that a counter-attack was forming up in Scauri. Early in the morning a shell hit a house occupied by Battalion Headquarters; the Adjutant (Captain M. J. Fitzherbert-Brockholes)   Jan. 20

Jan. 21

and the Signals Officer (Captain L. D. Cambridge; *aet*. 37, and grandfather to most officers) escaped untouched, but four signallers were killed and five wounded. At dusk the counter-attack came in. The York and Lancasters were driven off Monte Natale north-west of Minturno, and F and G Companies were moved into defensive positions. The counter-attack was continued at dawn (the day the First Battalion landed at Anzio) and Right Flank was moved up to consolidate on Point 141, a bare and rocky hill to the north of Minturno. This counter-attack was held and the Battalion was not immediately engaged, but there was a continuous drain of casualties through harassing fire, including Lieutenant V. M. Gordon-Ives killed while reconnoitring his platoon position on Point 141. In the meantime the mortar platoon was engaged in Trimonsuoli to reinforce the Coldstream mortar platoon which had suffered heavily, and itself had six men wounded before it moved out.

The situation was far from comfortable. The crossing of the Garigliano, which had been undertaken to conform with activity by the Americans and French near Cassino, had resulted in a wedge into the German lines in the foothills. The only supply route, the main Capua–Formia road, was commanded by the hills about Minturno, and of these hill positions, Monte Natale formed a bulge facing north-west towards the towering bulk of Petrella, and the Tufo position faced northeast towards the German-held village of Castelforte in the hills above the right bank of the Garigliano. The Monte Natale and Tufo positions were each exposed to fire almost from the rear from enemy facing the other, and inaccurate rounds aimed at Minturno itself tended to pass over the hill into the area of Battalion Headquarters, Support Company and A Echelon near the main road. An attempt by another brigade to recapture Monte Natale on the 23rd was unsuccessful. Further counter-attacks were expected that day, for the 90th Panzer Grenadier Division had come to reinforce the 94th Division, but they did not materialise. Shelling, however, was continuous, particularly on Right Flank on its bare hillside. Right Flank had seven men wounded that day, including the Lance-Corporal of the Signal Section in the morning; Guardsman R. Perks immediately took over the Section and, working continuously in the open under fire, maintained communications intact throughout the day. This shelling continued during the ensuing days. On the 24th Captain T. Marsham-Townshend, then attached to Brigade Headquarters was mortally wounded there, and two days later Lieutenant P. G. Atkinson-Clark was killed by a shell in almost the same place and circumstances as Lieutenant Gordon-Ives. Patrols were continuous as the shelling. They involved all junior officers, and most men of the rifle companies, and they enabled a valuable store of knowledge of the terrain to be built up, as well as causing trouble and sleepless nights to the enemy.

The morning of the 25th brought an unusual experience to the Carrier Platoon which had just taken over the position on the hill west of Minturno. A German officer appeared, walking towards them from the direction of Monte Natale. With great presence of mind they remained quiet, and waited for him. It turned out that he was from a tank squadron in Formia, and had just returned from a week's leave. He had been sent out to examine the country with a view to a tank attack, but had forgotten to ask where the respective lines were. *Jan. 25*

The situation became less tense on the 27th for a company of Welsh Guards under Captain R. G. D. Buckeridge had arrived the night before, and with four companies to hold three company positions it became possible to organise proper reliefs. In addition, shelling on the Minturno sector was reduced as the Germans began to concentrate on the Grenadier and Coldstream positions by the little hill village of Trimonsuoli about a mile to the west. Although the shelling abated, the visit of Colonel E. D. Mackenzie, Lieutenant-Colonel commanding the Regiment, on the 29th was far from peaceful. *Jan. 27*

This comparative respite was but short, for on the next day the Battalion changed over with the Coldstream, who after a long and unpleasant spell had carried out, in conjunction with the Grenadiers, a successful advance of about seven hundred yards the previous night. The new company positions were on the forward slopes west and below Trimonsuoli with the reserve company and Battalion Headquarters actually in the village, some of whose houses gave excellent observation over the forward positions and the fertile lowlands of Scauri to Formia and Gaeta. No further immediate advance was planned, and life settled down to the nerve-wracking routine of continuous patrolling and shelling and countershelling in the discomforts of an Italian winter—the possession of a small dugout was a rare luxury, even when shared with the flea-ridden livestock of Italian peasants. Patrolling casualties were fortunately light, and even what appeared to be rocket-propelled bombs weighing about 250 lb., visible in transit and travelling with a disquieting sound, inflicted no worse damage than making large craters; they were the fruit of the 28/32-cm. Nebelwerfer. But it was a wearying existence, and the Battalion was tired enough when it was relieved by the Grenadiers on the night of 5th February and withdrew to Nocelleto about twelve miles inland from Mondragone. *Jan. 30*

Feb. 5

On the evening of the 10th the Battalion started back for the line, with a new Left Flank (Major R. E. L. Harvey) fresh from England and the Fourth Battalion, taking the place of the Welsh Guards company. The whole situation had changed, and instead of relieving the Grenadiers at Trimonsuoli as had been expected, the Battalion took over from the 9th King's Own Yorkshire Light Infantry on Monte *Feb. 10*

Natale. The whole front was being thinned out and becoming static, for the 56th Division was leaving for Anzio, and in consequence all three Guards Battalions were to remain in the line. The take-over was made doubly depressing by the weather which had turned to heavy rain with a bitterly cold wind, and by the fact that the K.O.Y.L.I. had prepared their positions for the fine weather that they enjoyed, with the result that the trenches were rapidly filling with water. Difficulties of feeding were added to the other discomforts, for some of the platoons were in exposed positions on forward slopes, and the next day it was arranged that in the daytime only sentries should occupy these positions, while fires in two of the houses on the main road enabled parties to dry themselves in relays. That night Lieutenant R. A. Carnegie, newly up with Left Flank, was wounded by mortar fire.

Feb. 14 On the 14th, "after a few days of comparative discomfort but relatively little danger", the Battalion was relieved by the York and Lancasters and moved to the road below Minturno where it was intended that it should have four days' rest while under shellfire and Feb. 15 held in readiness for a counter-attack. On the 15th Sergeant A. D. Forsyth, for long Signal Sergeant, and two Guardsmen were killed Feb. 16 while mending a line on the main road, and the next day the Battalion was ordered to move to more restful quarters in Sorbello, an unusually clean village about nine miles beyond the river. The idea was sound, though belated, and the Battalion's brief rest was further curtailed by traffic confusion on the main road making the night journey take Feb. 17 four and a half hours instead of about thirty minutes. However, baths Feb. 18 and a cinema became possible, and on the 18th, after one undisturbed night, the Battalion returned and took over the Tufo position from the 2nd Northamptons. This was far preferable to Monte Natale, for the hill was covered with olives and ilex and movement and cooking became possible.

The Battalion's task was purely defensive. Patrolling became continuous, and the days passed under frequent shellfire, in the usual discomfort from cold and mud among sandbags, wire and mines. At night there were raids to carry out, mine-laying parties to be escorted, and ambushes to be laid. By day the search for information went on and none was more assiduous in the hunt than Lieutenant Buckle, the Intelligence Officer, who combined a thirst for knowledge with a hankering after more varied rations. "We decide at breakfast that, as we are ambushing the track junction below San Vito tonight, I might take the Brigade interpreter, a corporal of Italian origin, to question an old peasant about the German habits. Set off with him and Sergeant Lewis (F Company) down the track from Tufo about 9.30. Take Tommy-gun and small bag for eggs; Sergeant Lewis takes a rifle. Find three biggish dogs who bark at us and run away at the bottom; also five long-dead Germans in the stream . . . , all with bare feet, socks and boots taken by the Italians. The old man in San Vito proves unprofitable, cannot walk, never leaves his garden, has seen nobody. Give him bully and cigarettes; he gives me three eggs. So on to another farm where I find an old woman of 84 and her deaf and dumb daughter, about 40, living alone in considerable boredom. She talked only of her family, and had nothing to tell. The Germans obviously left these people as they could be of no use to us. Went on with Sergeant Lewis along the Bulgarini track to where it crosses the Reali, and look at the side of the Pimple for dugouts, and up the Bulgarini slope, but see no signs of life. Break two of my eggs and return for lunch." Eggs were not the sole commodity Lieutenant Buckle collected; a brother officer alleged that he "walked over to the German lines in daylight, rummaged about at will, and usually returned with odd curious books, abstruse and pornographic. One day he returned with a bridal dress which he wore for dinner in the evening."

On the 20th three Guardsmen in G Company were killed and two wounded, and on the morning of the 22nd a concentration of about a dozen shells fell around Battalion Headquarters, mortally wounding Lieutenant-Colonel Harris, and less seriously the Medical Officer, Drill-Sergeant Parkes, and Lance-Corporal Ross. On the 25th the Battalion suffered its last loss in the campaign, Lance-Corporal J. Bryson, who had won the D.C.M. when with the First Battalion in Norway, being mortally wounded.

By midnight on 7th March the hand-over to the Americans was completed. Just south of the river transport was waiting, and before dawn the Battalion was met by the Quartermaster on the road near Carinola, on the eastern side of Monte Massico, with hot soup and tea and rum. Even the famed Falernian wine, which is said to have come from that neighbourhood, would not have been more welcome in the circumstances. By five o'clock the Brigade column had been formed and the Battalion was on the move once more, and, as a little warmth crept into the bitter air and the snow-topped mountains sank towards plains already brightening with spring, the "long muddy column wound slowly back along the coastal road through Naples to Sorrento. Black berets and stocking-caps moved past as the mortar-carriers rumbled along behind battered portees that had followed the German retreat all the way from Medenine. For the last time officers in jeeps went by wearing the corduroy trousers and sheepskin Hebron coats of the old Desert Eighth Army." That night the Battalion slept in billets that seemed doubly luxurious after what had gone before. Two miles away the First Battalion also was in billets, with the remains of the 24th Guards Brigade, back from Anzio. The Second Battalion had fired its last shot in Italy; it was now bound for home.

Mar. 7

II. THE FIRST BATTALION—ANZIO

(a) *Preparing for a Landing*

MAP V
Dec. 7

Dec. 8
Dec. 9

Dec. 12

Dec. 14

Dec. 22

Dec. 24

Dec. 25

MAP XXI
Dec. 31
1944
Jan. 3

On the 7th December 1943 the First Battalion disembarked at Taranto from the H.T. *Llangibby Castle,* after an uneventful crossing from Bizerta. It landed near the ancient castle, appropriately adorned with the Germanic Imperial Arms. "It is nice," one of the officers wrote, "to be in Europe again." The following evening it entrained outside the town, and on the 9th, after twenty hours in the train, it reached Canosa di Puglia and moved by motor transport to a tented camp, "wet, cold, and very muddy", about five miles south of the town; here it was joined by its own vehicles, which had made the passage from Bizerta to Naples. Three days later the Pipe Band and the bands of the 5th Grenadiers and the 1st Irish Guards beat Retreat in Barletta, whose streets had once echoed to the very different nocturnal music of the silver-voiced Manfred and his two Sicilian accompanists. In the meantime the Second Battalion were at Mondragone on the coast north of the Volturno, and on the 14th Major D. V. C. McBarnet, the second-in-command, set off to visit it there.

In the ensuing days the bands of the Brigade beat Retreat in Cerignola, Canosa, Barletta and Andria, and on the 22nd the Pipe Bands of the Battalion and the 1st Irish Guards played at Bari, where the Pipe Majors were introduced to General Alexander. To a populace accustomed to the music of the wandering players from the Abruzzi the sound of the pipes cannot have been wholly strange: but the wheel had gone full circle since, little over a year before, men of the Second Battalion, taken in the disaster at Rigel, had spent days of hunger just outside the town on their journey to the north.

But this peaceful interlude was drawing to an end. On Christmas Eve a warning order was issued for a move to the Eighth Army front on the 28th. Christmas Day was passed in climatic conditions that at home would have been described as traditional. Nevertheless, "it was a great success. The cooks produced a wonderful dinner under difficult conditions. We had pork and plum pudding, and the local red wine was made into a very potent punch." That day the move was postponed until further orders. But the sergeants were not to be caught by a simple one like that, and that evening held their Hogmanay concert as arranged. Officers from the Brigade, and many others, were present, and it was a success of the kind described as roaring. On the last day of 1943 the Advance Party set off for Avellino.

On 3rd January the Battalion left Canosa by road, and fourteen and a half hours later, having crossed the snow-capped Appenines, threaded with rivers in spate, in bright sunshine under a cloudless sky, moved into four schools and a factory in the unattractive town of Scafati near Pompeii, soon to be rendered even less attractive by another eruption of Vesuvius. The following day Colonel Barne attended a conference at the vast Royal Palace at Caserta, the headquarters of the Fifth Army, on Operation *Shingle*: the landing at Anzio.

Jan. 4

This landing had been planned at Tunis in the previous month. Its purpose, by threatening the main enemy supply line from Rome to Cassino, was to break the virtual deadlock that existed from the Garigliano in the west to the Sangro in the east, and, by expediting the northern advance and the destruction of the German forces, to enable the Italian front to be greatly advanced, and, if possible, made fluid, before the opening of the assault on northern Europe. Tactically, the site chosen for the landing could not have been bettered. The beaches were suitable and the long double coastline of Italy and the weakness of the enemy in numbers made continuous beach defence by the German forces impossible: an expanse of low-lying scrubby country gave promise of easy deployment; an advance of only twelve miles would cut the supply line on which the enemy's right flank depended.

MAP XXIV

Two courses were open to the landing force. The first was to push on quickly and, by giving an appearance of greater strength than was possessed, spread alarm among the defenders, and in so doing to risk perhaps irrevocable disaster or win the greatest prize. The other was to consolidate within a small perimeter until such time as a breakout and advance in force could be achieved. Owing to commitments of landing-craft elsewhere, the force that could be put ashore was smaller than that originally intended. Even so, there can be no doubt which course would have been adopted if, for instance, the old Afrika Korps had been given a similar task. Lieutenant-General J. P. Lucas, the Commander of the VI U.S. Corps who was in charge of the expedition, chose the second course, no doubt influenced by his experience at Salerno where he had with difficulty maintained his lodgement. But in the days that followed, when the initial lack of opposition was met by stagnation, and the initiative passed to the enemy, and the fate of the whole Anzio beach-head trembled in the balance, the minds of many turned to a landing thirty years before on the Gallipoli Peninsula, when another elderly General played for safety and even safety was barely achieved.

For the first phase the Battalion, of which Lieutenant-Colonel D. S. Wedderburn had assumed command on the 8th, was withdrawn from the 24th Guards Brigade, which was not to land until after the assault, and was placed under command of the 2nd Infantry Brigade, which was to disembark about six miles north of Anzio in the initial landing.

Jan. 8

MAP XXI

Jan. 15

The ensuing days were filled with hurried and complex preparation, made no easier by the possibility of "literally falling between the two stools of the two Brigade Majors and Staff Captains", But by the 15th all that could be done was completed, and a Commanding Officer's Parade was held on the square in front of the school. "We had all been so busy in our own small ways that a Commanding Officer's Parade was exactly the tonic necessary to take our minds off our immediate worries. The morning was a great success; Colonel David addressed the Battalion, which then marched past. Everyone was trying their very hardest, the men looked fit and clean and well turned out and it gave me no little pleasure as Adjutant to hand over such a Battalion to our new Commanding Officer."[1]

Jan. 16

On the next day, the transport started to move. Anti-tank guns and Jeeps were loaded on the D.U.K.W.s which had been supplied for the operation, and the first forty vehicles (of the total fifty-six allowed) went off that

Jan. 17

day to their assembly area. The assault party of infantry left on the following day and embarked at Naples on the L.S.I. *Derbyshire*—a well-found Bibby liner with every convenience and comfort.

On board ship we were fed and quartered in the most comfortable circumstances and we felt that everything was being done to make our voyage a happy one. We spent our days in practising boat stations, climbing in and out assault craft, and for the most part studying the maps and photographs and laying detailed plans. We had to thank the Officer Commanding Troops, Lieutenant-Colonel Dryden, for his kindness in giving us the sole use of the Operation Room on board. It was a real boon—beautifully lit and appointed, and just exactly right for our purpose. Colonel David held all his Order Groups and Conferences in that room, and Harry Keith[2] enjoyed himself thoroughly pinning charts and photographs on the walls and desks for us to study. There was much peering through stereoscopes and magnifying glasses, and after a few days we felt we all knew the objectives as if we had actually lived there for some time.

Jan. 18

We had only one practice landing—which took place on the very beach where the Second Battalion landed just below Salerno. Exercise *Oboe*, as it was called, proved a complete success—everything (so far as the Battalion was concerned, at any rate) went like clockwork and, for the most part, we landed dry shod. From a tactical point of view the exercise finished at about

Jan. 19

four in the morning, and after that time we lit the most enormous fires and cooked breakfasts and dried ourselves. We re-embarked in the *Derbyshire* at noon.

[1] The account of the First Battalion's part in the Anzio battles is based mainly on one written contemporaneously by the Adjutant, Captain D. Traill, assisted by the Signal Officer, Captain D. J. Forbes. Various small alterations have been made in it to give continuity, and some technicalities omitted, but the historian has changed it as little as possible, as he feels the spirit and atmosphere of those days in the Beachhead are far better described by one who was there, than by any account which he can write now. For Order of Battle, see p. 545.

[2] Lieutenant H. S. Keith, Intelligence Officer of the Battalion throughout the campaign in Italy.

We set sail from Salerno that night and moved up the coast to the harbour of Pozzuoli where we again dropped our hook, and lay in the placid calmness of a Mediterranean bay. The weather was still superb—sunshine and blue skies but very cold at night. We fully expected rain to fall at any moment, but, thank goodness, it never came.

Thursday was a very quiet day, nothing to report and food still quite excellent—more study of photographs and another conference. It was late on that day when we discovered that D day was to be the following day—Friday. The landings would begin at two in the morning of Saturday, 22nd January, and go on throughout the rest of the day. Jan. 20

We had become so used to the idea of what we were there for that no-one was in the least surprised—rather the reverse in fact, for we all wanted to get on with the job. This time was not without its qualms and fears—you can well imagine how our thoughts were running—the embarkation for the last time in our assault craft—the silent run into the shore—the opening up of the enemy machine-guns—wire—mines—and the assault over the beach itself. Still, I don't think many people actually worried about it—strange as it may seem.

And so at last the hour came round and we were "piped" on deck for the last time—every man carrying a full load, grenades all primed and a round up every "spout". As we were lowered from the davits on to the water the loud hailer on board wished us "Good luck", and off we went. Jan. 21

(b) *A Quiet Landing*

It is difficult to describe one's feelings on that journey. It was a beautiful starry night, moonless but with just that suggestion of breeze which made small waves lap noisily on the flat-bottomed bows of the craft. Everyone was very silent, we were packed like sardines in a tin, and the men rapidly got restive and stood up to relieve their cramp. We were all carrying a very full load, and these craft are not designed for Guardsmen! However, we managed somehow to stow ourselves away, together with the wireless sets, the Bren guns and all the other things we had to carry.

We went in on the second flight, that is thirty minutes after the original assault. As H approached we were listening apprehensively for the sound of the defensive fire which we thought was bound to follow. But everything was quiet—the stillness broken only for a few minutes by the firing of the rocket shells from a ship lying close by. H passed, and we ourselves landed at the appointed time only a few hundred yards from the spot originally planned. Surprise had been complete, the beach was deserted of enemy and we found ourselves able to move about, form up and generally conduct ourselves as if we were on an exercise. Looking back, it all seemed ridiculously easy but it did not appear so at the time; we thought that we were liable to be attacked at any moment. Some poor unfortunates on our left stumbled into a minefield—number of casualties not known—but apart from that incident there was no warlike display on the enemy side. Jan. 22
MAP XIX

The Battalion landed in two waves at fifteen minutes' interval. By the time the second wave had arrived, the first two companies, Right Flank and B, had formed up and were ready to move off to their objectives. We spent little time in getting C and Left Flank into position and moved off from the forming-up place towards the road about four hundred yards distant. It was there that we definitely placed ourselves, for the track we followed from the beach joined the main road immediately opposite a house

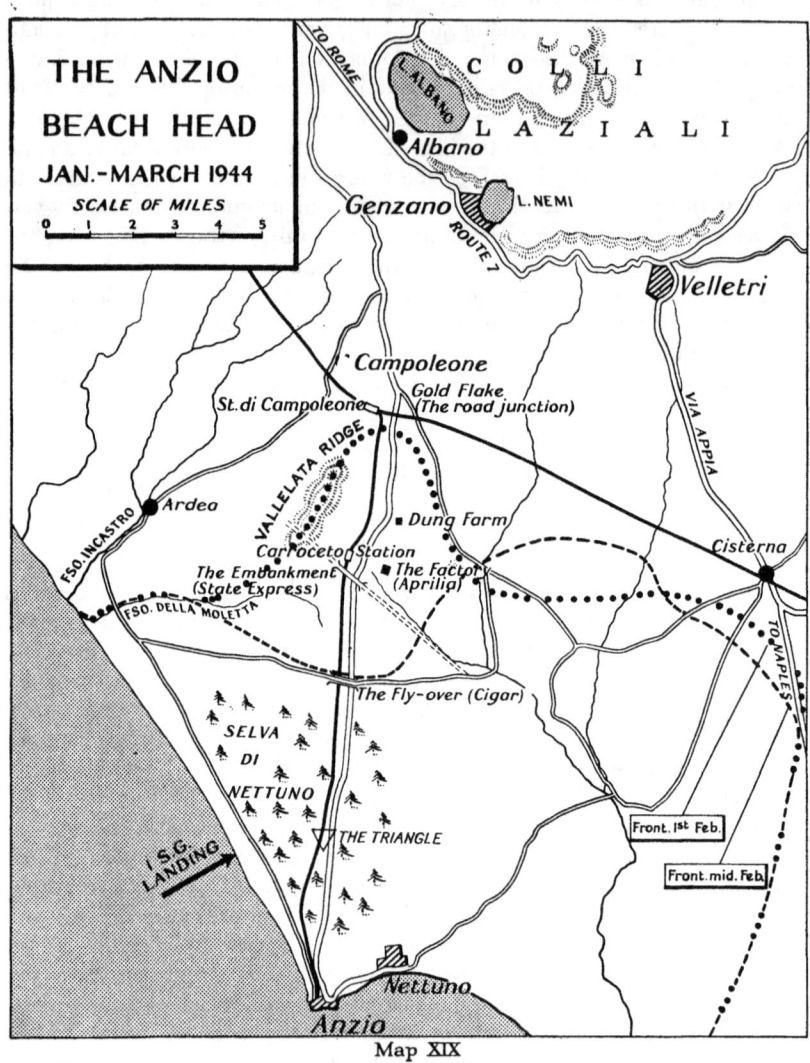

Map XIX

and tower which we all immediately recognised from our study of the oblique and vertical photographs on board ship. The Company Commanders had all been so carefully briefed beforehand that it was only a very short time later that they set off towards their objectives. No opposition was encountered and within two hours of our first landing the rifle companies were in position and digging commenced.

Tim Bull[1] claimed first contact with the Germans, an extremely well-placed shot killing a pillion rider on a motor cycle which appeared along the road from Anzio. The motor cyclist himself got away, no doubt to fall into the bag very soon afterwards.

It was now getting on for first light and I went back to the track from the beach hoping to contact Kit Fletcher[2] and his Support Company vehicles and weapons which we expected to land at about six-thirty. D.U.K.W.s were already streaming up from the beach; but so far no sign could be seen of any Scots Guards vehicles. But very soon afterwards Tony Tuke[3] appeared riding on a D.U.K.W. containing his Jeep and trailer. The 6-pounder guns followed soon afterwards and the process of "DE-DUKWING" commenced. It was remarkable how smoothly it went, despite some rather nasty shelling from an 88-mm. gun which had suddenly awakened to the fact that we had come ashore and was now registering the road at the point where the vehicles came on to it. But all went very smoothly; again we suffered no casualties, and the guns were in position in a very short space of time. Battalion Headquarters was established on the beach road running from Anzio northwards towards the beach on which we had landed. Digging was comparatively easy, for the ground was sandy with no rock. No opposition had been encountered on any of the Battalion's fronts and it can safely be said that the landing had been a complete success on all sides. News came through of the fall of Anzio and of the success of the American landing parties on the beaches to the south.

General Alexander made a tour of the beach-head that morning, wearing his red hat and riding in a jeep followed by the usual retinue. We were again reminded of the likeness of the operation to an exercise—the Chief Umpire visiting the forward positions and finding things to his satisfaction.

Our supporting arms at this point consisted of our usual battery of 25-pounders. We also had a FOO (pronounced as spelt and not in individual letters) who had on call the naval guns of two destroyers lying out in the bay. Each destroyer had six 4·7-inch guns and I have very distinct recollections of young Monk (the FOO) coming to us throughout the morning and pleading for targets which, unfortunately—or fortunately as the case may be—we were unable to supply.

The 24th Guards Brigade (Brigadier A. S. P. Murray) consisting of the 5th Grenadiers, 1st Irish, the balance personnel and vehicles of the Scots Guards, and Brigade Headquarters landed on the beaches at almost midday, and we reverted to their command.

The Grenadiers had been ordered to take up positions further to our right, that is between ourselves and Anzio, while the Irish Guards were to take over our positions, and we meanwhile would push forward towards the right centre of the perimeter that had been formed. We received this instruction with little enthusiasm—merely because we didn't relish the idea of digging trenches for the use of the Irish Guards. Still we did have the satisfaction of pushing forward and thereby enlarging the beach-head. We moved during the late afternoon and took up positions on the main

---

[1] Major R. H. Bull, M.C., commanding Left Flank.
[2] Major C. A. Fletcher.
[3] Captain A. F. Tuke, Anti-tank Officer.

road running north from Anzio in what we called the Triangle. B Company were the farthest north straddling the road; Right Flank occupied positions on the right of the road; C Company were in the woods on the left; while Left Flank, Battalion Headquarters and Support Company were dispersed in the woods between the road and C Company. It wasn't a very satisfactory position—we could only see a very short distance by reason of the trees and scrub—but we had command of the road leading from Anzio towards the north, which is what really mattered.

We were subjected to a little shelling that evening and Right Flank sustained some casualties including one killed. But apart from that all was very quiet and we heard encouraging reports from the beaches of the stores and supplies that were being landed and made available. Reports of American progress on the right were also received. It is not too early for me to stress how difficult it is to obtain an accurate picture of what our allies are doing. No one ever seems to know for certain. We continually hear rumours of successes or reverses, with wild estimates of numbers of enemy and tanks, etc., involved. These generally have proved to be grossly exaggerated, so we always treat American reports with a great deal of reserve. It is annoying that it should be so, for it has given Harry Keith a great deal of extra work in ferreting out information which should otherwise come to us as a matter of course in the form of Intelligence Summaries and Reports.

Jan. 23   Sunday found us still in the Triangle with no news as to what the general intention was to be. There was a little shelling, but no casualties. Enemy aircraft began to show a certain amount of attention to us—particularly at about last light—and we were treated to several displays of anti-aircraft gunfire with a certain measure of success.

(c) *The Advance*

Jan. 24   Late on Monday night we received orders that we were to move next morning. The road that we straddled ran due north for about twelve miles almost in a straight line. About three miles from our present positions was a road bridge of a "Fly-over" nature, with consequently a large embankment at the point where it crossed the main road. This embankment was called *Cigar*. About three miles still further on was another bridge across our road; this was a bridge which carried no more than a railway "bed" —the lines had not yet been laid.[1] Again a considerable embankment was there, but, whereas the *Cigar* embankment crossed the road at right angles, this second embankment, called *State Express*, crossed at a slight angle running from north-west to south-east. The next point on the road was about six miles still further ahead near Campoleone. At this point the north road joined a main artery leading from the coastal sector of the Fifth Army Front to Rome. There was also a railway running parallel with the north–south road. The point where the Anzio–Albano road joined this other road and railway was given the name of *Gold Flake*.

The intention was that the Brigade would advance in a mixed column,

---

[1] It is now (1955) a large main road.

i.e. marching troops and transport, up the road towards Albano, making good the two bounds *Cigar* and *State Express*, with a Brigade objective at *Gold Flake*, there to form what the Brigade Commander called a "Brigade Pivot". It was an ambitious plan, but with scant information about the enemy, who seemed non-existent in the area, it looked very much as if it would be successful. Not only would it take the Brigade more than halfway to Rome, but our occupation of *Gold Flake* would substantially cut the communications of the German Army at present facing our Fifth Army.[1]

Such an advance at this stage I am sure had not been contemplated. But now it seemed to be made possible by the absence of enemy resistance and the complete surprise which had been obtained in the landing. The original intention had been to secure a beach-head and hold it with the troops landed in the initial assault. Later more fresh troops were to be landed, who would exploit and make good further ground. Still, the plan looked workable, although it appeared at first sight to leave our communications dependent upon one single road which might be cut at any time by an enemy thrust on either flank.

The advance started at about first light on Tuesday—the Grenadiers leading, followed by the Irish and Scots Guards in that order.

Jan. 25

At about midday we were informed that the Grenadier Guards had made contact with the enemy at a "Factory" situated just to the right and beyond *State Express*. It was made the object of a company attack, but stronger opposition than was at first expected was encountered, and eventually a battalion attack was considered necessary with considerable artillery support. While the attack was being made Colonel David held an Order Group on the Embankment at *Cigar*—it having been decided that, if the Grenadier attack on the Factory should prove successful, the Brigade would consolidate on positions astride the road and remain there for, at least, the night.

MAP XX

After the Order Group we watched the progress of the Grenadiers from our vantage point on *Cigar*. The mediums and 25-pounders put up some very creditable shooting, and with the aid of glasses we could clearly see large holes appearing in the Factory building. Here let me explain that this Factory covered a very large area—comprising not only a large factory building but also a model village for the workers, complete with cinema, shops, and storehouses; [its real name was Aprilia, and it was a show-place of Fascist planning].

The assault was launched at about two-thirty and news soon came through of its success. The Grenadiers lost approximately one company in this engagement. They consolidated their position in the Factory while the Irish Guards took up position on the railway bed at *State Express*. The Scots Guards were again behind the Irish in a position straddling the road, Left Flank and C Company on the left, with B and Battalion Headquarters on the right. Right Flank was put under command of the Grenadiers, and took up position in front of the Irish in and around the station at Carroceto. Battalion Headquarters were established in a small house about a hundred yards off the main road—everything very dirty and squalid, but still a roof with reasonable protection against shell and mortar fire—or so we thought

[1] Fully to achieve this object would require the cutting of the Via Appia; this was the task of the Americans advancing on Cisterna, eight miles further east.

at the time. We settled down quite happily; the Companies quickly dug themselves in, and with the Factory in our hands we felt reasonably secure. The Buonriposo ridge overlooked us from the left, while in the far distance we could see the hills behind *Gold Flake*.

No contact was made with the enemy that night. The Companies were fed from the cookers, which came up soon after dark and rations were issued for the next day. Support Company established themselves under an embankment of a road running off to the right behind Battalion Headquarters. We decided to keep the very minimum of transport and sent back all the unessential trucks and jeeps, keeping only the carriers and one or two other vehicles, e.g. the Signal truck, which we were able to tuck away in a cowshed next to Battalion Headquarters.

Jan. 26 The night was very quiet with no alarms and excursions, but just after first light we were subjected to shelling and mortaring which seemed to come mainly from the ridge to our left. The shellfire was particularly insistent and carried on throughout the whole day. Our house was hit three times, once by high explosive and twice by solid shot. Numerous other shells fell on the garden around us, and the Companies soon began to suffer casualties. It was on this day that Lieutenant R. O. Stewart was killed; a shell exploded in a tree just above his slit trench and had the effect of an air-burst, killing him instantaneously.

As a result of this shelling Colonel David decided to move position slightly. B and C Companies remained unchanged; Left Flank was withdrawn some two hundred yards behind a reverse slope, and occupied the top end of a wadi which provided good protection. Battalion Headquarters moved back about half a mile to another house, less conspicuous and therefore better suited for the purpose. We also established a Command Post in the same embankment as Support Company and seemed relatively secure. The night was quiet and the move seemed completely justified by the absence of shelling in our new positions.

Further forward, the Grenadiers beat off strong counter-attacks on the Factory, and in doing so the Scots Guards anti-tank guns, which had been despatched to their support, knocked out two tanks. In this action Lance-Corporal R. R. Bates greatly distinguished himself, personally accounting for both the tanks. After heavy shelling six enemy tanks had appeared and had started to shoot up the positions. Despite heavy fire Bates left the safety of his slit trench and engaged the tanks. One of the guns of the platoon was knocked out, but nevertheless Bates stood to his gun, knocking out one tank and damaging another; the remainder withdrew. Later in the day in another attack, Lance-Corporal Bates loaded, laid and fired his gun single-handed, and knocked out the second tank. He was awarded the Distinguished Conduct Medal.

Jan. 27 On the following morning Colonel David and myself visited the Companies, and later called at Colonel Andrew's[1] Headquarters at the Embank-

[1] Lieutenant-Colonel C. A. Montagu-Douglas-Scott, D.S.O., commanded the 1st Irish Guards.

ment, and plans were discussed for the further exploitation of the bridgehead along the axis of the road.

The information regarding the enemy was, to put it briefly, that his main line of defence would not be contacted until we reached *Gold Flake*, and that any positions held by him between there and our present positions would be largely in the nature of outposts. The opening of the main road was of course of paramount importance, and the absence of strong resistance made the general plan an inviting one. It would naturally leave the flanks of this "pencil point salient" very much exposed, but we had news of the Americans who would come up on our left and right. After all the factors had been appreciated, it was decided that the Battalion would go forward from its present area that night and take up a defensive position on and forward of the higher ground on which stood the Agricultural School Farm Buildings [henceforward to be referred to as Dung Farm—though at the time it had an even less complimentary name].

The Grenadier Guards had a company approximately halfway between our main line and this new position—stationed in fact in the left-hand house at M 25. Meanwhile the Irish Guards had sent forward a mixed patrol of infantry and carriers to a cutting in the road which overlooked our proposed positions. They reported to us that no enemy had been contacted and this information, together with Colonel Andrew's assurance that this patrol would stay out until we occupied our new position, meant that we would move in as quickly as possible after last light.

The Divisional Commander[1] arrived in the middle of the conference and the proposals were put forward to him for consideration and approval. He appeared enthusiastic about the whole plan, but decided not to commit himself to a definite order. We were to prepare for the move, but had to await orders from Division before vacating our present positions.

Meanwhile we were being shelled very heavily, and the Germans had made no mistakes in their registration of the Embankment near which Colonel Andrew's Headquarters were established. We had one particularly anxious fifteen minutes when a shell scored a direct hit on an ammunition dump in a ditch some fifty yards away. The stuff started to smoke, and then to blaze, and we all felt quite sure that an enormous explosion would soon follow, when an Irish Guardsman ran across the open road, seized the offending boxes and threw them into a puddle close by. He was a very brave man, for no-one was in any doubt as to what would inevitably happen should the fire continue. Having done this he started to return and I have a very vivid recollection of him jumping a good two feet into the air when a shell landed some distance away. The nervous reaction on the man must have been simply enormous. Anyhow you can be certain that we all heaved a deep sigh of relief and gratitude.

The conference finished at about half-past two and Colonel David, anxious to make the most of the daylight and the Irish Guards protective patrol, went off on his jeep to have a look at the ground, leaving me to organise an order group to be in the area of the road cutting (where the Irish Guards patrol was established) in thirty minutes' time. Kit Fletcher

[1] Major-General E. W. S. Penny.

went with him, and together they set off up into the farm, having first formed a protective screen with a section of Irish Guards to go ahead in case of trouble. All went well. Colonel David returned with Kit and gave out the orders. Company Commanders were shown their positions, and platoon commanders were called up for the Company Order Groups. All this happened in a sort of no-man's land, for we were never quite sure when and where the enemy would rear his ugly head. However, we were left in peace and we were very grateful indeed for the wonderful opportunity afforded for such a detailed daylight reconnaissance.

The plan was briefly this: Right Flank (Major A. J. A. Weir, M.C.) was to revert to our command from the Grenadiers, and was to take up position at last light in the area of the farm itself, and cover our occupation of the olive groves beyond. Left Flank (Major Bull) would move through the farm and take up positions on the high ground in the olive grove overlooking the plain to our right and forward. B Company (Major J. E. Tyldesley-Jones) was to occupy a similar position on Tim Bull's left overlooking the road, while C Company (Captain D. P. M. Malcolm) would stop short of the farm and take up position dominating the Y-junction near the cutting.

Meanwhile Kit Fletcher went forward with his platoon commanders to show them where their support weapons were to be disposed; when coming back along the track at the foot of the slope an enemy Spandau opened up at short range, killing Kit instantly. It was such bad luck and was the only black spot to spoil an otherwise perfect afternoon of reconnaissance and planning. Kit was such a grand chap in every way and an integral part of the First Battalion. One could always rely on his sound judgment, and I, for one, always went to Kit when I wanted advice or consolation. Yes, we suffered a grievous loss that day.

We got back safely to Battalion Headquarters and had a good meal. We were very hungry and thirsty, for we had been out since breakfast, and I have seldom tasted more delicious tea or bully. What the British Army would do without tea I really do not know. The Compo rations on which we were feeding were most excellent, and can be made to produce the most palatable and yet solid diet that a soldier could wish for. We were fortunate, too, in having an adequate supply of "Tommy Cookers" which, together with the tea, sugar and milk powder supplied with the Compo ration, ensured that we could always get a cup of hot tea at short notice.

Although the order to move the Battalion had not yet reached us, Colonel David thought it advisable not to interfere with his arrangements for the occupation of the farm buildings by Right Flank. This was carried out at last light according to plan. John Weir soon reported that he was in position and that no opposition had been encountered. The Irish Guards patrol remained out in position at the road junction during all this time.

With all arrangements complete, all we could do now was to wait until we received the order to move. We were so anxious to get away and make the utmost of the hours of darkness for digging and the like that we were all most impatient for the order to arrive. The hours slipped away and still no orders had arrived. We made repeated inquiries from Brigade. I am not quite sure what caused the delay, anyhow we could but wait.

The long-awaited order did in fact arrive at about ten-thirty and C

Company started off. All went very smoothly, although the rate of advance was naturally slow by reason of the darkness. C Company were soon in position and started to dig. Left Flank passed through the cutting successfully and so on to the olive grove.

After the two leading companies had gone through, a most unfortunate accident occurred. The B Company carrier, while crossing a trough in the road, which all the previous vehicles had successfully negotiated, blew up, killing Major Tyldesley-Jones, Lance-Corporal J. E. S. Gale, M.M., and two others, and wounding eight. It transpired later that a box of Hawkins grenades had fallen off the carrier while crossing the dip, and that they had detonated on striking the ground. This was not known at the time and the search for a possible minefield by the Pioneer Officer, Lieutenant H. A. W. Smith, and the clearing of the debris by Right Flank delayed the rest of the Battalion. However, the Signals Officer, Captain Forbes, found another route round the obstruction, and the column could proceed. Also lost in the confusion was Sergeant Maugham, the Intelligence Sergeant, who disappeared and was captured while searching for an alternative route; and later Lieutenant Smith was wounded when another of the grenades exploded.

By one in the morning of Friday all the Battalion had passed through; Battalion Headquarters took up its position at Dung Farm, and began to dig.

Jan. 28

At about six o'clock, just as the Companies were getting fairly well below ground, the Germans decided to put in an attack. Colonel David's first job on establishing his Headquarters had been to arrange the Battalion SOS and DF[1] tasks with the Battery Commander, Freddie Mills, so all was in order and fire was brought down in double quick time. In addition to a battery of 25-pounders, we had under command a battery of eight Self-Propelled guns. So we had a very reasonable amount of fire power at our disposal. The Companies replied to the fire to which they were being subjected, and for about an hour the exchanges were quite fierce. The SOS tasks had the effect of sending the enemy scuttling back, only to be brought under the fire of the DF tasks. So the attack proved to be entirely without success and quite a number of Germans were accounted for.

The Germans continued to harass us throughout the day but the threat was never serious—probably two or three small sections of men each with a Spandau and several belts of ammunition. But the position was so well sited and our field of fire large enough, that we felt we were in no real danger.

A glance at the map will show you how exposed were our flanks. We were ordered to send out a daylight patrol to a house out on the ridge on the

[1] Pre-arranged artillery shoots capable of being fired at the shortest notice. An SOS task could be fired immediately the order reached the gun positions, for, when not firing, some guns were kept permanently laid on each SOS target. The DF (Defensive Fire) tasks, which were normally further from our own troops, could be fired in a few seconds. See p. 214.

left. John Sinclair[1] led this patrol, made contact with the enemy in the house, had a bit of a battle and eventually broke off contact. It was impossible to get the men away in daylight so they lay up in a culvert after their battle and came in at night.

Just about last light a further attack was put in on our positions, but again the guns put up a good show and the Germans were forced to withdraw.

Alec Ross[2] with the maintenance train continued his previous practice and arrived nightly at about seven-thirty with hot dinners, and rations and water for the next day. I cannot stress too highly the way in which Alec carried out this all-important, nerve-wracking duty. On not one single day when the Battalion was in the line and in contact with the enemy did he fail us with our hot dinners, rations, mail, etc. I know he set that record in Tunisia and I feel it is worth recording that he maintained it at Anzio. On the nights when Alec himself did not appear, his place was most ably taken by RQMS Watts. Altogether the Quartermaster's staff was worthy of the highest praise.

Jan. 29 The next day we remained in the same positions, having almost continual contact with the Germans. Our casualties had been very small. B Company and Left Flank bore the brunt of the attacks, for they were the forward companies. C Company had been asked the day before to provide a strong patrol to occupy a house—known as "Clo"—on the left for the following reasons. The Grenadier Guards were to advance from their positions in the Factory and around M 25 and occupy the ridge on the left of the main road with "Clo" as their forward position. Their occupation of this ridge would mean that the road would be dominated by our fire from both sides and our position would be made considerably easier. It was during the Grenadier's reconnaissance of this area that they suffered a terrible disaster. Instead of turning into our Headquarters from the main road, the whole party went straight on and ran into an enemy position on the road just beyond our forward left-hand positions. The enemy let them get close up and opened fire with Spandaus, killing three officers and capturing another, who was wounded. One or two others managed to get away and eventually found their way to our Headquarters. They were badly shaken by their experience, but unscathed.

Meanwhile David Malcolm's patrol from C Company went out to occupy "Clo", there to await the occupation by the Grenadiers. They remained there all night, no Grenadiers appeared, and eventually we learned that their orders to move had been cancelled, and our position with two open flanks remained as it was.

(d) *The Night Attack*

In the evening we received orders to make an attack that night with our furthest objective as Point 105. Again you will have to consult the map. Roughly speaking the Battalion was to advance about a mile due north from its present positions. To hold Point 105 was an obvious advantage.

---

[1] Captain J. H. L. Sinclair (Right Flank).
[2] Captain and Quartermaster A. Ross, M.B.E.

16. Rocchetta seen from Point 520, which was taken with the bayonet by Right Flank. In t foreground is the temporary grave of Guardsman W. McGuigan. Neat wooden crosses similar this one were erected by all battalions of the Regiment. Guardsman McGuigan now lies in t Minturno War Cemetery, his grave cared for by the Imperial War Graves Commission

ITALIAN HILL DWELLINGS

17. Minturno from the east. Around this little town the Second Battalion spent its last mon in Italy

18. Men of Left Flank about to leave Scafati. They are wearing leather jerkins, with stocking Field Service caps. In the left foreground, armed with a rifle, is Lieutenant R. O. Stewart

EMBARKING FOR ANZIO – 17th January 1944

19. The First Battalion boarding the *Derbyshire* in Naples docks. The Guardsmen were ashore by the small assault landing craft seen hanging from the davits

Briefly the plan was as follows. The Battalion was to advance on the right of the road, and the Irish Guards were to make a similar advance on the left. Left Flank was to occupy Point 105; Right Flank was to occupy a track junction three hundred yards south-east of Point 105; B and C Companies, in that order, were to advance up the road, clear it, and take up positions to the south-west of 105. The whole object of the attack was to secure the start line for the 3rd Brigade to pass through and capture Campoleone Station, just short of *Gold-Flake*. The attack was to go in half an hour before midnight after considerable artillery preparation. Then on the success signal being received, the supporting arms would come forward along the road, which by that time should have been cleared.

We had no Sappers under command. But we did have considerable support in the shape of anti-tank guns from the 81st Anti-Tank Regiment, Vickers machine-guns from the Middlesex Regiment, and four American M 10 Tank Destroyers who had been with us since the occupation of this position.

The track running along to the right had not been considered suitable for the supporting arms, for it was very much open to enemy attack from the right flank, and no troops would be there to prevent such an attack. Tim Lindsay-Peto[1] had led a patrol supported by carriers and mortars into this area on this very day. He had located enemy in a house to the right of the track and, after a brisk engagement in which casualties were suffered on both sides, he came back and reported enemy in considerable strength in that area. With the troops at our disposal it was impossible to do much about this threat, except to engage the area with artillery and mortar fire. This was done, but for all we knew, when the attack went forward to Point 105 the threat from our right would still remain.

During the hours of darkness before the attack started all was very quiet. Ten minutes before zero hour the artillery barrage opened. A careful programme had been worked out—after ten minutes of very close support the guns lifted, and the Companies began their advance.

With so much close artillery fire the air rapidly became filled with smoke, and from our very near front the enemy machine-guns opened up in every direction. Resistance seemed to be strongest on our left—but of course you must remember that my own position did not change throughout the battle, so I was in no way able to tell exactly what was happening. The wireless was working well and Colonel David with his own set was out quite a little way in front of the control and Headquarters sets.

B Company [now commanded by Captain E. A. G. Balfour] and C Company on the left rapidly became very heavily engaged. They reported strong enemy positions on the right of the main road, with wire and many machine-guns. From the noise to our left it seemed that a tremendous battle was in progress. German light machine-guns fire a very high percentage of tracer, which is always rather terrifying, but on the other hand one can see the general direction of the bullets, and the tendency at night

---

[1] Lieutenant T. C. Lindsay-Peto (Right Flank).

seems to be to shoot high. Left Flank and Right Flank reported good progress and advanced steadily.

Jan. 30 The trouble on the left became acute, and Eustace Balfour and David Malcolm were unable to make any headway in that direction. The wireless net was working perfectly, and the Commanding Officer had to make a very quick decision. The progress that Right Flank and Left Flank had made on the right opened up the possibility of switching the attack and coming in on the Germans from a flank. This in fact he did. B and C Companies were brought back to the Start Line, sent off in the wake of Right Flank and Left Flank and reached their first objectives after some very stiff fighting, but with many less casualties than they would have suffered had they persisted on their original axis.

Nevertheless Lieutenant P. H. Shaw-Stewart, of B Company, was mortally wounded in the fighting, and Lieutenant D. M. H. Bailie, of C Company, was killed while going in with the bayonet to attack a house covered by a German tank. In the advance Sergeant F. C. Bennett greatly distinguished himself in command of the leading platoon of B Company. Personally he led sections in attacks on four enemy posts, being wounded in the shoulder, arm and side in the capture of the final objective. Despite his wounds, with one other guardsman he escorted back some forty prisoners through territory as yet not clear of the enemy. For his gallantry he was awarded the Distinguished Conduct Medal.

The problem now was the road. The ultimate success depended entirely on the bringing up and establishing of supporting arms, particularly anti-tank guns, before first light. Our objectives were in our hands; but the road had not been cleared and, though virtually cut off, the potential German resistance there was strong. The hours of darkness left to us grew shorter and shorter.

Colonel David, Harry Keith and Lance-Sergeant Bell, the Commanding Officer's wireless operator, by this time were right forward with the Companies. It must have been about four o'clock when the situation first became desperate. The Germans used many flares to light up the battlefield, and all the indications were that very shortly the inevitable counter-attack would come in, supported by tanks. Colonel David knew only too well the difficulties that faced the Battalion at this time. The transport was already formed up waiting for the word to advance, and still no road was open. The only solution to the problem was to have support from our own tanks—if we could get them. These we knew could have an admirable run through the country we had just covered, and there was still sufficient darkness left for them to be brought up and put on the ground. But we had no tanks under command, and although we knew they were in the vicinity, we had to ask for them through Brigade.

In the course of the request for tanks Colonel David had emphasised how vital it was to get up our own supporting arms. No road was open to us, and if they were to be taken up on to the battlefield, the only possible route was the track on the right. So Gervase, Mike Jardine, Harry Keith and myself[1] set off to the transport to organise the party to go up this track. Gervase organised every man he could find to act as infantry protection—police, servants, sanitary men and the like were all impressed and briefed for the task of protecting the column of supporting arms which was to go forward up the track on the right.

The transport was already formed up, but facing to the main road, and certain adjustments had to be made to get the head of the column on to the right track. This was just being carried out, all engines were running, and we were just setting off, when an 88-mm. began to shell us. It was still dark and it was a most unlucky shot, for we could not possibly have been observed, but the first shell landed on one of Tony Tuke's portees which immediately burst into flames. Six-pounder ammunition and 2-inch Mortar bombs on the portee started to explode, and altogether it was a most unpleasant party. As soon as the truck started to blaze the Germans put down a concentration on the spot, so you can readily understand what an inferno it was. I certainly will not forget it in a hurry.

The scene as viewed in the light of the blazing vehicles was not a pleasant one. There were several men lying on the ground—some dead, others badly wounded—the driver of the portee was still in his seat, but I'm sure he was killed instantly. Just then the next vehicle started to blaze. I cannot truthfully say whether it was hit by another shell or by the exploding ammunition. It was at this point that young Mac Hayward[2] ran across, and regardless of the danger to himself, got into the next vehicle and drove it to safety, thus making a gap in the column and thereby saving the remaining transport. His was a most outstanding case, but there were others, drivers of vehicles, who behaved equally gallantly, especially Guardsman Duff. Altogether the behaviour was quite first class.

In the meantime Captain Blois had managed to organise a party of six anti-tank guns, and had set off up the track towards the battlefield proper. His own vehicle became ditched, but he found an American Tank Destroyer, in the opinion of its driver hopelessly bogged, got it moving again under shell and machine-gun fire, and guided the driver across country towards Right Flank. At first light he found a disabled German Tiger tank and captured the crew. He then pressed on and after several more engagements, during which another enemy tank was hit and forced to retire, and two 88-mm. S.P. guns and one 75-mm. Semovente knocked out, his Tank Destroyer was hit and disabled and he led its crew back on foot—"in time for some breakfast!"

Interest now centred on Left Flank at Point 105. About a quarter to four in the morning they had beaten off one enemy infantry attack supported by tanks, and soon after dawn they reported that another

---

[1] Captain G. R. E. Blois, commanding Headquarter Company; Captain M. J. Jardine (second-in-command of Right Flank), who was wounded later in the night; and the Intelligence Officer and the Adjutant.

[2] Lieutenant F. McL. Hayward, Transport Officer of the Battalion throughout the Italian campaign.

attack was upon them. It seems that in the darkness they had slightly over-shot their objective and were in rather an exposed position on its forward slope, out of touch with the rest of the Battalion and overlooked by the higher ridges to the north. At a quarter-past seven they reported jubilantly that the enemy were in full retreat, and that they had knocked out a large tank; ten minutes later Major Bull's voice was heard on the wireless with the news that they were "surrounded, and looked like being overrun. After that—complete silence". Major Bull, a truly brave man, was killed, and the remnants of the company were taken prisoner. Not until the next day, the 31st, was Lieutenant P. G. Henderson, the only other officer in the company, picked up; he was seriously wounded. It is not now possible to apportion to the Companies the losses sustained in the night attack and in the subsequent counter-attacks. But on that day, besides the three officers already mentioned, forty-two other ranks were killed, the largest number of Scots Guardsmen to fall on any one day of the war. These included CSM J. C. Begg of Right Flank, four Sergeants and seven Lance-Sergeants, among them G. A. Cashmore and R. N. Miller, both of whom had won the Military Medal in Tunisia. Also killed was Guardsman G. Patience, a well-known cross-country runner.

The Irish Guards on the left of the road had had an equally sticky time and had not yet reached their objective. Tank support was promised; in fact the tanks had by this time arrived, and were prepared to go forward in support of them. But the Irish Guards still had a lot of ground to gain before they conformed to our positions on the right. An attack [by a company of the King's Shropshire Light Infantry properly supported by tanks] was prepared and went in during the first few hours of daylight with complete success. Artillery was still very active on both sides but the concrete results of the night's work soon began to show in the shape of droves of prisoners coming in from the battlefield—a very cheering sight.[1]

With the capture and consolidation of the Brigade objectives, the plan had been for the 3rd Infantry Brigade to go through us and attack the railway at *Gold Flake*. The preparation for this was proceeding according to plan. The K.S.L.I. occupied the positions we had vacated, and lay there waiting for the signal to move through us on to their objective. Their Commanding Officer came to see us in the farm at about ten o'clock. The attack was timed to go in half an hour later, but did not in fact take place until about two hours later. Nevertheless the tide of war steadily receded from our positions and, when afternoon came, all was quiet on our front, and prisoners were still being collected and sent back. C Company moved up to Point 105.

We were all very tired after the excitements of the previous night and morning, but the fact that our attack had been successful in every way had the best possible effect on all ranks. The one black spot was the loss of Left

[1] To all save the Intelligence Officer, who noted some from divisions which had last been heard of in France and Jugoslavia. The Germans had found troops from outside Italy to contain the beach-head.

Flank. We could not quite understand what had happened. Events that morning moved so quickly that it was only in the evening when things were quiet that we could collect our thoughts and try to reconcile the events of the day. Gerard Hodge and the Padre[1] had had a busy night and day in the R.A.P. They were favourably placed in that there was a huge wine cellar under one of the farm buildings, which gave Gerard an admirable place to work. Not only were men of our own Battalion treated there, but many others from various units which passed through us.

I prepared to sleep in the straw of a big barn round which was grouped Battalion Headquarters. I don't know how long it was since we had slept, but I do know that the thought of a night in the straw was quite the most acceptable thing that ever happened. Just before I dropped off to sleep, I remember thinking on the following lines: Three things can happen to me: (1) a shell can hit the roof and a slate fall on my head; (2) the barn can go on fire; (3) a shell can hit the wall of straw bales behind me and bring them down on top of me. At about five in the morning I was awakened by a shell exploding nearby—and the third of the three possibilities happened! I was smothered in straw, but fortunately none of the bales which fell on me struck a vital spot!

Jan. 31

The next day the situation remained unchanged. The Sherwood Foresters were reported to be on *Gold Flake*, and apart from one or two minor attacks from the flank and almost incessant shelling, things were fairly quiet. During the afternoon we were told that we would be relieved by the 6th Gordons. At about four o'clock their advance party arrived; guides from companies were there to meet them, and the relief was complete at about six. It was just getting dark when the Battalion moved back, leaving the Gordons in possession of the ground we had won—and right glad we were to be relieved. We took over positions around M 25 and started to dig again.

Further to the east the American Rangers had attacked towards Cisterna and had been repulsed with heavy losses. Neither Campoleone nor Cisterna were in our hands; the prime purpose of the expedition had failed. The line reached on the 31st January proved to be the limit of the advance.

(e) *Defence*

Although we had moved about two and a half miles back, you will remember how long and thin the axis was on which the whole British force was operating. We saw little of the Americans, although we did hear that they were going to conform on our right. In actual fact the position we now occupied at M 25 was every bit as much exposed as the one we had just left. The Buonriposo and Vallelata Ridges dominated our positions from the left, but our tails were so well up that it didn't seem to matter.

We were just settling down in M 25 when some news came through from Brigade regarding a potential threat from our left. Colonel David lost no time in laying on an extensive artillery programme, mediums and

[1] Captain G. C. Hodge, M.C., the Doctor; and the Rev. J. Hamilton.

25-pounders. I do not think that anyone could have used artillery to better effect than he did. Many, many times the Battalion was undoubtedly saved by his foresight, his skill in reading a map, and generally anticipating the movements of the enemy, so that every possible forming-up place and vantage point was registered. We had things so well organised that we could call down fire on any part of our front in anything from thirty seconds to three minutes. DF tasks were legion—we would have as many as eight separate DF tasks in front of one Company. We were limited to two SOS tasks, but Colonel David's plans for building up a fire plan were always accepted by the gunners. SOS tasks when called for were always developed into the surrounding DF tasks. Even on paper you can get a good idea of what happened. The Germans would attack our positions; SOS fire would come down perhaps only 100–200 yards in front of our positions: the Germans would withdraw to reform, only to run into the "built-up DF", and so on until the attack was completely smashed.

Colonel David insisted on his gunner officers giving their fullest co-operation and if they wouldn't "play" to his liking, he sacked them. It may seem a little cold-blooded to put it like that, but he demanded the very highest standard of artillery support and there were one or two gunner officers who felt the sharp side of an otherwise gentle and easy nature. The mediums were the guns he liked to have. We had in support a battery of mediums from the 80th (Scottish Horse) Medium Regiment, and none of us can speak too highly of their efficiency. They seemed only too pleased to be serving a commander who knew what he wanted, and who could talk with knowledge on their own particular problems. We had one or two outstanding gunners attached to us. Wright of the 19th Field Regiment was one; Fraser of the Scottish Horse was another.[1]

The programme which Colonel David had worked out for the night was put down according to schedule. He had considered all the factors; the nature of the ground; likely lines of approach; estimated enemy timings based on distances to be covered from known locations, together with first light, etc. No attack developed. Perhaps it was never intended—I prefer to think it was smashed to pieces in the earliest stages.

Feb. 1–6   For the next week the Battalion remained in different positions to the west of the road, frequently shelled and moving every now and then as the situation required.

Feb. 1   On the 1st February they handed over their positions around M 25 to a battalion of the 504th U.S. Parachute Regiment, and, in broad daylight, moved forward a thousand yards to positions on the Vallelata ridge, with the inevitable result that they were accurately shelled, and very soon the Companies were found less exposed localities on the same ridge.

Thus the general position at the beginning of February was that the 3rd Brigade attacking *Gold Flake* was halted astride the road north of where it was crossed by the railway to Campoleone. The Irish Guards, south of the railway, held positions to the west of the road;

[1] Captain P. A. Wright, R.A., and Captain J. A. Fraser, M.C., R.A.

on their left the Battalion was on the Vallelata Ridge with the American Parachute Battalion to its right rear about M 25; and the Grenadiers behind it along the line of the *State Express* embankment west of Carroceto. Behind the Grenadiers the North Staffords, detached from the 2nd Brigade, which had been unable to advance to the right of the Guards Brigade, held the Buonriposo Ridge. Shelling was heavy and almost continuous, and there was a steady drain of casualties, which included Lieutenant D. G. S. McMurtrie killed. Frequent minor moves added to the fatigue. The more fortunate had some sort of shelter, howsoever squalid. "Other inmates [of a dugout occupied by five people] are a white rabbit, which we rescued from some rubble, and a very raucous, bomb-happy hen which was in residence when we took over. It will insist on sleeping on our beds in turn, an untidy and messy habit. We kick it around more than somewhat, but it seems to prefer this to braving the big world." _{Feb. 2}

By the 3rd it was clear that the attempt to break out of the beachhead had failed, that the initiative had passed to the enemy, and that powerful counter-attacks were imminent. Wire and mines were hurriedly procured, and shortly after midnight the first assault came in. It fell upon the Irish Guards and the Gordons. The left-hand company of the Irish Guards was eventually overrun and a wedge driven so far behind them that thenceforward the road near M 25 was under small-arms fire. On the right the positions held by the two forward companies of the Gordons were lost, and the Irish Guards, virtually surrounded, came under heavy fire from that now exposed flank, and the whole 3rd Brigade was cut off. But the Irish Guards held on and a counter-attack by the London Scottish of the 56th Division, which was now arriving in the beach-head, retook the Gordon's position, and the 3rd Brigade was able to withdraw into reserve followed by the Irish Guards. This left the Battalion at the point of the salient, and it was pulled in a little to get in touch with the Americans at M 25 and to hold an area north-west of Carroceto Station; the forward companies—Right Flank and C Company—not far north of the railway bed about a hundred yards from the road, and B Company further to the right, near the railway west of M 25. Battalion Headquarters was established in a pink house in the area of Carroceto Station; Support Company in the station itself.

Feb. 3

Feb. 4

It was at this far from comfortable juncture that the Lieutenant-Colonel Commanding the Regiment, Colonel Mackenzie, came from England to visit the Battalion. He arrived on the 4th and stayed with the Battalion for three days, during which time he saw most of the officers and many of the men; a welcome and much appreciated visit.

On the 6th February active preparations were commenced for the stabilisation of the line as it then stood. Mines and wire were laid covering the area between B Company and the railway embankment. Altogether it

Feb. 6

was a quiet day—not too much shelling and no direct attacks on our positions.

That night Lance-Corporal Bates and another member of the Anti-tank Platoon captured a German Volkswagen. It contained a German Battery Commander of Nebelwerfers, who was out on a reconnaissance for an observation point. They had misread the map and ran down a road near one of our anti-tank positions. Harry Keith was tremendously excited. There was a large quantity of documents, and even marked maps showing proposed dispositions. The Germans had wonderful maps—very much better and more accurate than our own. The prisoners were sent off to the Brigade for interrogation, and we managed to retain the car and some of the loot.

Feb. 7
The next day was also quiet. Companies were well established in their positions. Rations and mail, water and ammunition, came up regularly throughout, and Ross continued to maintain his unbroken record of a hot meal every night.

That afternoon arrangements were made to take over M 25 the same night from the American Parachute Battalion with Right Flank and C Company; B Company was to remain *in situ*. No. 4 Company Irish Guards (Captain D. Drummond) came under command and was to be placed north of Carroceto Station, in which Battalion Headquarters itself was to be established. There was a most adequate cellar in the station and the top floor, which had been the stationmaster's house, provided excellent O.P.s on every side. Battalion Headquarters vacated the Pink House at last light and occupied the station. It made a very good Command Post indeed and we found that wireless worked perfectly from the cellar itself. It was almost impossible to keep the telephone lines open. Shelling has the most devastating effect on cables. Linesmen were out nearly all night mending cables. They would come back and report as many as fifteen breaks between Battalion Headquarters and one of the Companies. It was most heartbreaking for Donald Forbes, but the main thing was that communications were never broken for anything more than a short period. As Colonel David put it, "The No. 18 Set always *just* managed to work".

(f) *Carroceto Station*

Feb. 8
On the 8th a determined enemy attack was launched on both the Grenadiers on our left, and on the right on the London Irish Rifles, who were holding the Factory. The latter failed to hold the Factory and the Grenadiers were forced back from their flank positions, and withdrew to behind the railway embankment at *State Express*. This left us very much exposed, for it meant that we had literally no protection on our front and right and left flanks. The ridge on the left was in German hands and dominated our positions. The Factory on our right was filled with German infantry and tanks, and there was an open gap of five hundred yards between our Companies at M 25 and Battalion Headquarters. Several days before this attack we had been ordered by Brigade to draw a three days' supply of ammunition, rations and water. The ammunition was dispersed in small dumps in the numerous ditches around us. The rations and water were stored in a room in the station itself, under guard. We felt reasonably secure, despite our

exposed flanks and front. The Companies were well dug in, though scattered, and we could maintain ourselves without help from outside should the necessity arise.

That day the Germans started to move on our front. It was in the early afternoon, when an observer in the O.P. facing northwards reported enemy movement in a hollow, about six hundred yards distant and almost level with Right Flank. We went up to have a look, and through glasses could plainly see some Germans, in quite considerable strength, forming up in a long black ditch in the hollow. This ditch ran in the same direction as we were looking and we could see every movement. It was an ideal target for a medium machine-gun shoot, so we quickly got one up into position at the window, and in the meantime gave the target to the gunners and also to our own mortars. Pat Butler[1] mounted it on a table, with some bags of grain under the tripod legs, to keep it steady. He opened fire as soon as he was in position and by this time there were about two platoons of Germans in the ditch. It was a most extraordinary performance altogether; mortars, artillery and Vickers all firing together caused many casualties and many Germans came away from the place, and disappeared from view towards two houses which were a short distance away. You can imagine our surprise when a short time later the same performance was repeated, and the same trench was again filled with Germans. Down came our fire on them again and once more they retreated towards the houses. Then appeared a small party carrying a large white flag, with the Red Cross on it, and they went down to the place presumably to attend to their wounded. Some of the Germans who were still there congregated round the flag and by their appearance they seemed to indicate that they wished to surrender, so the Commanding Officer made a quick plan for a party to go out from Right Flank to bring them in. There was still a certain element of doubt as to their intentions, so the supporting arms were kept trained on the spot ready to fire should there be trouble. John Sinclair, who was commanding Right Flank, chose to lead the party himself and went out with a small patrol of about ten strong. We could see them plainly as they made their way across the fields and saw them approach the Germans. The latter were quickly rounded up and doubled back across the field at the point of the bayonet. In all, twenty-five Germans were taken away. The enemy stretcher bearers were left to attend to the wounded who could not move. Then a most peculiar thing happened. The party of prisoners were fired upon by other Germans whom we could not see, and eight of the twenty-five were hit. However, a net total of seventeen were brought back to Right Flank Company Headquarters. It was a most successful raid, marred by a tragedy which happened after it was all over. John Sinclair had got back into his slit trench and was about to get out again when he was killed by a stray bullet. He was the only casualty we suffered and it seemed so unnecessary.

I really don't know what the Germans were thinking about, but a very short time afterwards, the Red Cross flag disappeared and once more they came into the ditch. We opened fire again, inflicting more casualties, and

---

[1] Lieutenant the Hon. P. H. S. D. Butler, Machine-gun Officer.

then the Red Cross people appeared as before. This time there was little doubt that they wished to surrender, and David Drummond, the Irish Guards Company Commander, went out with a party and brought them in. There were not so many this time, about twelve, I think. A German Warrant Officer [who was captured by Captain Traill] told us that a whole company had been accounted for. He estimated their casualties as eighty, which wasn't a bad afternoon's work. A captured Operation Order, taken from the same Warrant Officer, showed that the Germans were intending to launch an attack on a large scale at four the following morning. Amongst their documents captured was a very comprehensive trace showing lines of approach and objectives for the attack. It did not develop.

At that time we had in support of the Battalion, a troop of Shermans and four M. 10 Tank Destroyers. The latter are fitted with a 3-inch naval gun and are, potentially, very powerful support. For the most part these tanks and M. 10s were tucked away, either behind odd houses in the immediate vicinity, or behind the railway embankment with the Grenadiers at *State Express*. Even so, they were not any more than three hundred yards from our Battalion Headquarters. Apart from the previous battle on 31st January, they had done very little but it was a comfort, or so we thought, to have them with us. An American Liaison Officer from the M. 10s lived with the Battalion—in rather in the same way as the Battery Commander or FOO would do. He was a pleasant chap and promised support whenever we might require it. Unfortunately, though, he had no communication between us and his M. 10s, but the distances involved were so short that we did not consider this a serious disadvantage. Normally his communications consisted of a wireless set fitted into a jeep which was tucked away in the station yard outside Battalion Headquarters, but on 9th February a shell struck this vehicle, which was burnt out, and the set rendered unfit for duty. So he went back to his headquarters, intending to return with a new radio, but whilst there he was ordered to remain and did not rejoin us.

Feb. 9 Wednesday was for us a fairly quiet day, apart from some unpleasantly close shelling. Despite the fact that the Germans were all around us, we were not troubled unduly, and the shelling, such as it was, did little damage and there were very few casualties. The Pioneer platoon trenches in the station yard had one or two direct hits and it was extraordinary that no-one was killed or badly wounded. The Pioneer platoon under Sergeant Pirie are a good lot and it was always a sense of comfort to know that they were responsible for the immediate defence of Battalion Headquarters.

The O.P.s in the upper window of the house reported movement all around us, and whenever we saw Germans they were either sniped at, mortared or shelled, according to the numbers seen. They weren't so far from us, in two houses on the ridge on the left and behind. B Company occupied most of their attention on that side. These houses had been occupied by the Grenadiers until the attack of the previous day, but now appeared to contain quite a large number of Germans. Arthur Piper[1] arranged for a second Vickers gun to be put into a room in the station commanding these houses. Sun-blinds outside our windows permitted a

[1] Major A. H. Piper, formerly Carrier Platoon Commander, now commanding Support Company.

certain amount of movement inside the rooms in the station, but did not interfere with the siting and firing of the weapons from well inside. The station house was modern and well furnished, but, by the time we occupied it, everything was in dreadful disorder. But the walls were reasonably stout and stood up well to mortaring and shelling—in fact they withstood 88-mm. shells from normal ranges. There was a large hole just above the stairs, made by a 105 or larger gun.

Activity in the two houses mentioned previously seemed to increase and the Commanding Officer decided they must be cleared. A plan was made, and it was arranged for a raid to be carried out by a platoon from the Irish Guards company under command, supported by tanks. The Troop Commander of the Shermans came up to Battalion Headquarters to be briefed, and I must say it seemed to take an extraordinarily long time for him to assimilate the details of a perfectly simple plan. At last it was decided to send in one Sherman which would advance up a sunken road towards the houses, closely followed by the infantry. It was the early afternoon when the raid was made. First, the houses were shelled and mortared—then the tank went forward, and, firing solid shot from a range of about two hundred yards, tore the first house to shreds. Then the Irish Guards platoon went in and cleared the house. An unaccountable delay followed, and we, who were watching the progress of the party from the windows of the station, found it difficult to explain. However, the tank did eventually move forward slightly and engaged the second house. The Irish Guard's platoon went forward again and had soon occupied the place. They returned soon afterwards, but suffered several casualties themselves. Their Company Commander, David Drummond, had elected to lead the party himself and took with him another officer from his company, Colin Dodds.[1] Colin did not return with the others. David Drummond stated that Colin had gone off with one or two men in pursuit of some Germans who had fled over the ridge. He had seen Colin drop to the ground as if hit and disappear on the spot. We could only assume that he had been wounded.

The houses having been cleared of enemy, the Commanding Officer considered it was a justifiable risk to send out a carrier carrying a Red Cross flag with a couple of stretcher bearers to bring in the wounded if they could be found. The carrier proceeded up the sunken road and disappeared from sight over the ridge. We never saw any of the crew again, and had to face the hard fact that they had been taken prisoner despite the Red Cross flag on the vehicle and the armbands of the stretcher bearers. Later that evening, after last light, Colin Dodds walked into our Headquarters. He was unscathed, but had found himself cut off, so dropped into a shellhole and stayed there until darkness. Another Irish Guardsman came in with him. Naturally we were all delighted to see them, but grieved over the unnecessary loss of our Medical Sergeant, stretcher bearers and carrier driver. On the whole the party had been a success. The houses had been cleared and our casualties had not been heavy. But shortly afterwards the houses were again occupied by Germans and exactly the same situation was present as before. Pat Butler had several good shots with his two Vickers guns, and

[1] Lieutenant J. C. Dodds, Irish Guards.

Martin Lowinsky[1] did some good close range work with his mortars. We must have accounted for quite a number of enemy that day, too. Right Flank and C Company at M 25 had a quiet and relatively peaceful day.

On the previous day we had had considerable close bombing support. It must have been most terrifying for the Germans. A large number of fairly heavy bombs were dropped only a few hundred yards in front of us. The noise was deafening and the whole ground shook. On the following day, when the enemy were much closer and also in possession of the Factory, we hardly saw our planes at all. But at least we were not troubled by the Luftwaffe at this stage. What we would have liked to have seen was a large-scale bombing raid on the Factory, which by this time was in German hands and filled with troops and tanks.

That night (9th/10th) the rations arrived as usual and we recounted our experiences of the day. The only difficulty was how to feed B Company, which was virtually cut off. The roads were wet and muddy and the track leading to B Company position was impassable, even to jeeps. The other way round ran past the two houses before mentioned and was therefore out of the question. Michael Baillie[2] had come up with a fresh platoon to reinforce B Company, but could not possibly get to them. So Colonel David made them occupy the positions at the Pink House (between us and B Company) and they reached this place without incident.[3]

We had received written orders on that day that we were to hold the ground north of the Embankment until further orders. We had suffered several casualties in the last few days, and the Commanding Officer decided to do some regrouping of his forces in order to hold the ground to better advantage. Quite unexpectedly we were reinforced by three platoons of Sappers of the 23rd Field Company, who had been ordered to act as infantry under our command.[4] You may gather from this that we were running very short of men on the beach-head generally.

It had been intended to reorganise the Battalion into a smaller area during the night, and great difficulty was experienced trying to find a passable track for the anti-tank guns which were out with B Company. While discussion was going on about this, a German tank appeared from the direction of the Factory, and, from very close range, started to machine-gun the Company positions. It was supported by other tanks and infantry, numbers and strength considerable, but which could not accurately be estimated. Had any of the Companies been moving when the attack started, there would have been a most dreadful shambles, but they were all still in the same positions.

It was then midnight, and on the left B Company faced and held off the assault of the 4th Parachute Division, driving down towards the station. On the right the 65th Division debouched from the Factory and attacked past the Battalion's exposed right flank, completely by-

---

[1] Lieutenant T. M. F. E. Lowinsky, commanding the Battalion's platoon of 3-inch mortars.
[2] Lieutenant M. E. V. Baillie.
[3] Marked PL on Map XX.
[4] They were placed in the position marked RE on Map XX.

passing Right Flank and C Company, and driving straight down towards the Regimental Aid Post which was overrun within half an hour, Captain J. Hamilton, the Chaplain, and Captain G. C. Hodge, M.C., who had both given long and invaluable service to the Battalion, being taken prisoner. In B Company Captain E. A. G. Balfour and Lieutenant the Hon. C. H. B. Pease had been wounded, and in C Company Captain A. M. Balfour, M.C., had been killed.

The enemy advanced on Battalion Headquarters and, coming up the side road leading to the station, the leading tank came to a halt not more than forty yards from our front door. We could just discern its ugly shape looming through the darkness of the night. It looked immense, some say it was a Mark VI [Tiger], but I doubt if that was the case—probably a Mark IV. **Feb. 10**

It immediately opened fire on the building we were in, systematically going over each window and doorway with Besa (or equivalent) fire. All bullets seemed to be tracer and from the incredibly short range they ricochetted all over the place. We suffered fairly heavily in dead and wounded; Besa fire eats through brick walls. It was here that Drill-Sergeant Standing was hit in the knee. He was badly burned by the phosphorus in addition to the wound itself. He must have suffered a lot of pain, but on being put down in the cellar sat up and still kept a grip on things. As soon as anyone opened fire, he was replied to by a burst from the tank. It was all very unpleasant. Then to add to our trials, he started to shell the house from point-blank range, using solid shot which tore great holes in the walls and brought the staircase tumbling down over our heads. This was even more unpleasant. The cellar where the Rear Link wireless was situated rapidly filled with dead and wounded. Fortunately the set was still working, both forward and to Brigade.

As soon as the attack started, Colonel David had decided that that was the time to call on the support of our M. 10 Tank Destroyers. They were only a matter of three hundred yards away behind the Embankment, but we had no Liaison Officer now; nor had we any wireless contact with them. So the Commanding Officer decided that personal contact was the only means of communication, and he and Arthur Piper set off into the night, dodging the bullets and shells, and eventually got to the Embankment in safety. There they contacted the M. 10 commander, also the Troop of Shermans. The tank outside our doorstep was a sitting target; all that was required was for the M. 10s to come through the railway bridge, and, by using a road up to the left, get a most excellent cross-shoot at our most unwelcomed visitor. We in Battalion Headquarters felt sure that the tanks would soon be seen off and waited for our deliverance. Meanwhile Brigade kept up a steady conversation with us on the Rear Link. Companies were active, too, calling for DF, which we had to pass over the Rear Link to the Gunners on the same net. It was a pretty hectic night which I won't forget in a hurry.

For *four hours* the Commanding Officer pleaded, cajoled and even threatened those in authority over the tanks; but at last he had to admit defeat in this battle with his own side; the War Diary recorded that he "returned at 0430 having met with little success". Ten years later an officer wrote, "At the time we were livid, and I still think we had reason to be."

It was nearly daylight when the Commanding Officer decided that Battalion Headquarters must be pulled out behind the Embankment, the conditions in the station making it impossible to function properly; the move started at about half-past five. The journey along the railway track occupied some ten minutes; we had very little distance to go, but we had to move with extreme caution.

Daylight was now upon us; and there was considerable confusion which took some time to sort itself out. This was difficult enough, as we had arrived in small groups carrying what we could. Tony Tuke was unable to extricate his anti-tank guns from either Right Flank or B Company positions, but all the crews got back after rendering the guns unserviceable. C Company under Johnny Graham[1] was strongest and was ordered to support a Grenadier company on the west of the railway line behind the Embankment. Few of B Company appeared and we assumed they had been overrun, for we had had no contact with them since half-past three.[2]

At long last Colonel David bludgeoned the tanks and tank destroyers into an attempt to help out those who were trapped, at day-break. This was made about seven o'clock. Eventually twenty-five of Right Flank appeared under cover of this diversion; and many were the personal hand-to-hand fights they had had before reaching the Embankment, in particular Tim Lindsay-Peto's fight with a German officer, which earned for him the immediate award of the Military Cross; the German did not live to tell the tale. Of the 23rd Field Company, R.E., who had been sent to us the previous evening three platoons strong under Major Hornby, only one platoon managed to extract themselves. Major Hornby was not amongst them; this was a sad loss to us, for he had been a very good friend to the Battalion. The Irish Guards company remained to defend the station until Battalion Headquarters had left. By first light they had not followed us and we had to presume them overrun. This fear was confirmed when they did not appear under cover of the later diversion. The whole operation was very difficult and a great deal of credit goes to those commanders who extricated their men from serious positions.

At this stage, with C Company in the houses to the west of the railway, the twenty-five men of Right Flank and the platoon of Sappers to the east of the road, with Battalion Headquarters in the centre, the resultant strength of the Grenadier and Scots Guards was sufficient to hold out there for the day. Buonriposo Ridge was in enemy hands; they had also penetrated some miles behind us further to the west, whilst information about our right flank was almost non-existent. We were therefore under direct observation from all sides and suffered continual shelling and mortaring, throughout the day. Battalion Headquarters was with the Grenadier's R.A.P. which was catering for us at the same time. It was an unpleasant place; the

[1] Lieutenant J. Graham.
[2] Lieutenant A. J. Blackett-Ord, commanding B Company, was wounded and captured.

stretcher bearers were continually being called for and sniped, whilst the Doctor was kept permanently busy. Just to round off the party it began to rain very hard, which transformed the R.A.P. dug-out into a foot of mire. I remember thinking that one could hardly have been beset by more miseries at once, on top of which it *had* to rain.

Shortly after the tank diversion, a combined raid was planned on the station. A composite platoon of Grenadier Guards and Scots Guards, led by Lieutenant the Hon. J. R. B. Norton, Grenadier Guards, attempted to reoccupy the station with artillery and mortar support. They reached the outbuildings under heavy fire, but had to return without reaching the station proper. They suffered heavily, as German tanks were in dominating positions around their objective. Whilst this was in progress, C Company on the left were kept fully occupied. The Embankment levelled out four hundred yards to the west of the road and became a gully. This was used by infiltrating Germans as a forming-up place. Mortars, machine-guns and snipers were kept busy trying to check this steady flow into the salient they had made south of Buonriposo Ridge. Other than this, and the heavy mortaring and shelling on the Embankment, there was little aggressive action made by the enemy in the station area.

"In my view," one of the officers wrote, "the importance of the Battalion's counter-attacks at this time cannot be overestimated. Captured War Diaries of the 4th Parachute Division later revealed that they caused alarm and confusion and considerable casualties to the enemy, and may well have deterred them from further attacks which we were in poor shape to resist. I have always thought that Colonel Wedderburn's action in ordering these counter-attacks was one of the major proofs of his supreme qualities as a commander." Nevertheless the enemy was confident of success that day. Captain Tuke escorted to Battalion Headquarters a tall, fair-haired, typically German Parachute officer, who asked in a gutteral accent, "Where is the sea?" The direction being pointed out to him, he said, "Thank you very much. I just wanted to know, since you will all soon be in it." At the time it seemed difficult to resist the opinion that the German was right.

All troops were behind the slope in a confined area with O.P.s on the forward ridge. Casualties were heavy, due to this restricted area, and movement was fatal. It became increasingly apparent that new positions would have to be dug when daylight failed. Our daylight positions on the Embankment would have been a perfect target at night without observation and tanks to help us.

About four-thirty a reconnaissance party from the Duke of Wellington's Regiment arrived with the welcome news—it was news to us until they actually appeared—that they were to relieve us that night, the take-over to begin at eight. We were extremely thankful for this news as we were by now very tired; it put new heart in us. The positions were reconnoitred and taken up by us at last light. The Dukes arrived actually at nine-thirty hours, a delay we had anticipated, for they had not been given much more notice than we had received. Mac Hayward had transport to meet us four miles down the road—he was not allowed to bring it closer. In consequence we were all very tired when we reached it. There were about one hundred and twenty of us.[1]

(g) *In Reserve*

Feb. 11–12
MAP XIX
Feb. 13

The 11th and 12th February, with a severe nocturnal air attack in between, were passed in reorganisation, and it was found that enough riflemen remained to make one full company. The following day, Sunday, after another air attack at night, Brigadier M. D. Erskine, D.S.O., a former Commanding Officer of both the First and Second Battalions of the Regiment, who had temporarily taken over command of the 24th Guards Brigade, addressed the Company at what should have been a Battalion Church Service but for the Battalion's Chaplain being a prisoner and the Chaplain of the Gordons being too heavily engaged elsewhere.

Although withdrawn to it for rest, B Echelon was a rest area only in name. The whole beach-head down to the docks was in range of German artillery, and on the 12th the Embankment at *State Express* had fallen to the enemy, who then proceeded to put a Division, heavily supported by tanks, into an attack down the east side of the road against the Fly-Over at *Cigar*. It once got within a hundred yards. But as the beach-head contracted, the more concentrated became the artillery and air support.

In the afternoon orders were received to start digging defensive positions to the west of *Cigar* and to produce another company. With considerable difficulty a second company of two platoons was gathered together, made up of the remnants of Support Company and of men employed on administrative duties arbitrarily decreed "non-essential". Command of these companies, which had virtually no supporting arms and were known as Flank and Centre Companies, was given repectively to Major Weir and to Major the Hon. F. Fermor-Hesketh, who had arrived in the beach-head four days earlier.

Feb. 14

On the morning of the 14th the Commander-in-Chief, General Sir Harold Alexander, visited the Battalion and met all officers and warrant officers and later spoke to the assembled companies, congratulating them on their performance in the recent bitter fighting. But meanwhile the situation further forward was becoming critical, and it seemed likely that the Battalion's position to the west of the road in the "Long Stop Line" would have to be occupied. That day and night digging and wiring were pushed on rapidly, and by the following morning the positions were virtually ready.

Feb. 15

[1] Since the opening of the German attack on 8th February, thirty-eight other ranks had been killed.

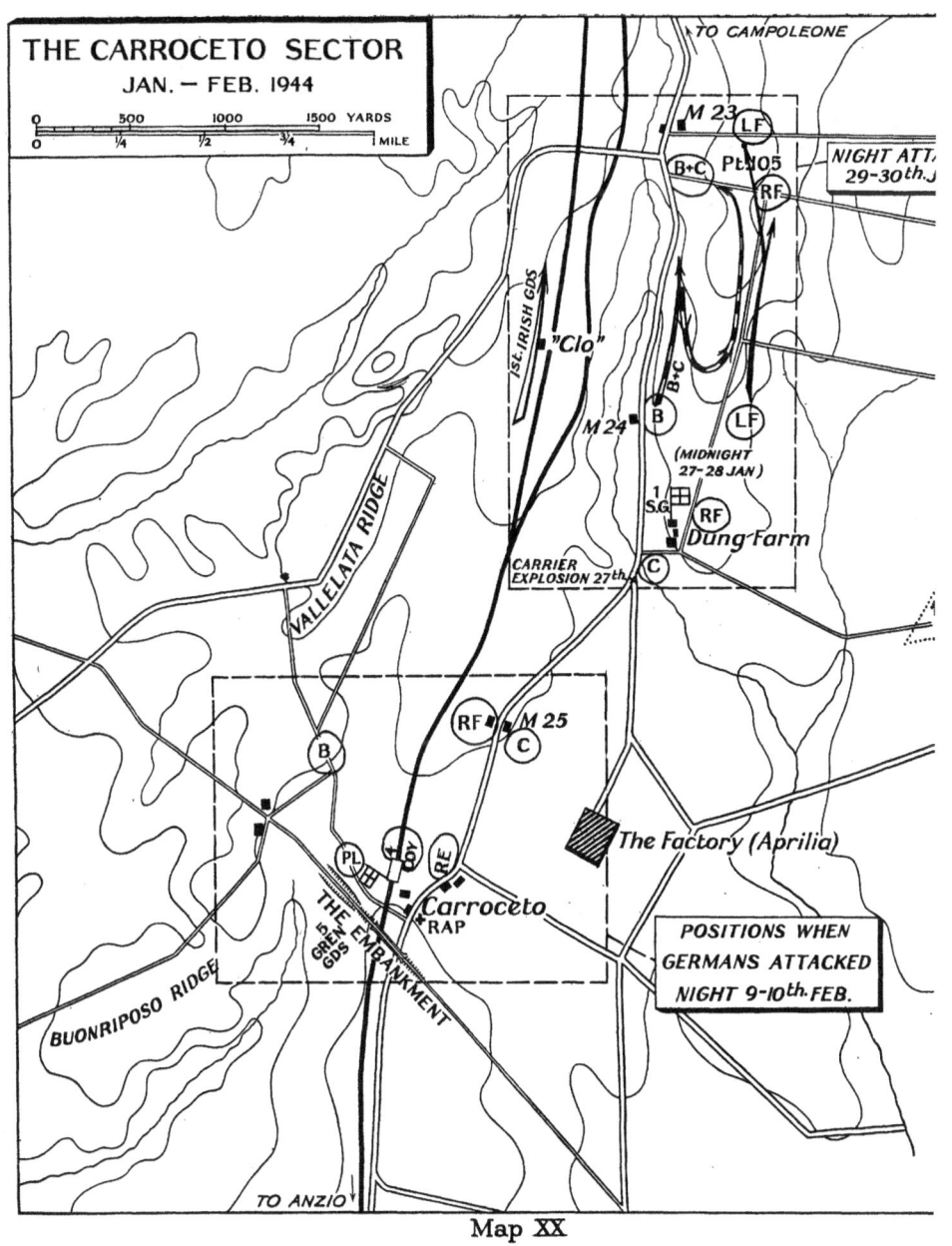
Map XX

20. THE BATTLEFIELD OF CARROCETO

Looking north from the top of the Embankment called *State Express*. On the left the ground rises slightly towards the Vallelata Ridge. Immediately ahead is the station, occupied at the time of the German attack of 9/10th February by Battalion Headquarters. On the horizon are the Alban Hills, which gave the enemy perfect observation over the whole bridgehead. The main road to Rome runs towards the hills across the right-hand part of the panorama, and along it in the middle distance can be seen the small houses about M25. Farther on and in line with M25, but not discernible in this photograph, was Dung Farm from which the night attack of the 29/30th January was launched. On the extreme right is "The Factory", otherwise Aprilia, and beyond it the Lepini Mountains.

The photographs were taken by Major R. A. Abercromby, M.C., in the summer of 1944. At the time the First Battalion fought at Carroceto the buildings were, of course, in a much less ruinous state

21. CASTEL DI SANGRO   Men of B Company looking out across the valley of the Sangro, 21st April 1944. The village on the far side was in German hands

ITALIAN SCENES

22. PATROL IN THE SUN   Men of C Company returning from patrol to the village of La Vergine, 17th September 1944. The leading man is armed with a ·45 "Tommy Gun"; he wears a camouflaged smock, with a camouflage net around his neck, and on his head he has one of the hideous "Caps G.S."

At eight in the morning of the next day the order came, and by ten the Companies were in position, Centre Company to the right near the Fly-Over, with night positions north of the lateral road, and Flank Company slightly forward and to its left. Shelling and dive-bombing, the close support of the German attack, was heavy during the move in, and Lieutenant Lowinsky was killed by a bomb near Battalion Headquarters. Shelling was nearly continuous for the next forty-eight hours, but no physical contact was made with the enemy, whose line of attack was down the east side of the road towards the positions held by the Loyals. In spite of the shelling the only incident recorded of the night was the collapse of the shanty near which Battalion Headquarters was situated: "not unnaturally, as its main supports were slowly but surely being removed to make dug-outs and sangars". *Feb. 16*

The following afternoon, the Battalion was relieved by the 6th Gordons, and the Companies moved back to reserve positions about two miles to the south. As these positions were just behind the gun area, they received a liberal amount of the counter-battery fire as well as night bombing. But the casualties were fairly light; for "all had shelters of some description, and doors from Anzio were at a premium". They were to be needed and occupied off and on for the next three days while the German attacks to the east of the Fly-Over reached and passed their climax. This came in the early hours of the 19th when the stubborn resistance of the Loyals to the main German thrust formed what proved to be the turning point of the battle for the beach-head. *Feb. 17* *Feb. 19*

On the afternoon of the next day the new Brigade Commander, Brigadier A. F. L. Clive visited Battalion Headquarters, and on the following day the Battalion was ordered to relieve an American unit in positions just north of the Fly-Over. As the headquarters of this unit was hidden in the middle of a wood, and as Battalion Headquarters had to share the site of its former shanty, now completely disappeared, with the headquarters of the Gordons, the absence of landmarks added to the difficulties normal to such a proceeding. But the relief was completed by three in the morning of the 22nd, and that night Flank Company, on the right and in front of the Loyals, beat off an enemy patrol. One Guardsman was taken prisoner by two Germans dressed in American uniforms and speaking English. "He went off with them, and was never seen again. Which only goes to show that you cannot be too careful." But apart from the shelling there was little aggressive action by the enemy. The skill of the Commanding Officer in picking suitable places for artillery concentrations, and the whole-hearted co-operation of the 19th Field Regiment, nullified any attempts that the Germans may have made to form up for an attack. The main difficulty was supply, owing to the inaccessibility of the Company positions. But Captain Ross, as usual, remained master of the situation. *Feb. 20* *Feb. 22*

Feb. 25	In the evening of the 25th the K.S.L.I. arrived to relieve Centre Company. Flank Company, in an exposed position in front of the Loyals, had to wait a little longer to screen the relief of the Loyals by the Buffs of the 18th Brigade, now under command of Brigadier
Feb. 26	Erskine. This was completed early on the 26th, and the Battalion concentrated once more in its former rest area. "Again we were very tired, and seemed to become so more easily, which in the light of the past month was hardly surprising."

On that Sunday evening at B Echelon about three miles north of Anzio to the west of the main road, the glad news was received that the Battalion was to leave the beach-head to reform and reorganise. But the following day the Battalion was to receive its saddest and most shattering blow.

Feb. 27   Battalion Headquarters was in an almost oval glade with the officers' tents at one end, the tents of the Commanding Officer and Major McBarnet being sited end to end near two outstandingly tall trees. At about five o'clock the Commanding Officer was talking outside his tent to Major Weir, when a shell came over and landed outside the clearing and in the direction of the road. A few seconds later Major McBarnet appeared with the news that this shell had severely wounded Lieutenant J. W. Stuart-Menteth. On hearing this Captain Ross left his tent and started towards the Commanding Officer. At the same time Lieutenants Butler and L. E. Widderson approached the group to announce their success in finding a NAAFI. At that moment two shells landed in the tent area, and, it is thought, hit the tall trees, which turned them into air-bursts. Major McBarnet, Major Weir, Lieutenant Butler, Lieutenant Widderson, and Corporal Wood, the Commanding Officer's driver, were all killed. The Commanding Officer, who had just gone back into his tent, received critical injuries, and Captain Ross and his driver and RQMS Watts were also wounded.

For a time hopes were held out that the Commanding Officer might
Feb. 28 recover. But on the following evening he grew worse, and shortly
Feb. 29 after midnight, in the midst of a heavy air-raid, he died. The loss to the Battalion was summed up in a letter from the Commanding Officer of the 1st Irish Guards: "The whole Division is absolutely miserable; the General, C.R.A., and G.1 left the battle to pay their last respects when we buried him. He had done wonders for the Battalion. His own personal success was outstanding—it is so wicked to think he got over all these dangers to catch it back here.[1] Barney [Major McBarnet], too, was a first-rate asset to the Battalion and had done more than people realised during the difficult times. John Weir was probably the best Company Commander in the Brigade." It is not surprising that

[1] Colonel Wedderburn had been recommended for the Distinguished Service Order before his death, and so he was awarded the Order posthumously.

the Adjutant, after describing the disaster, wrote: "If ever morale was to touch rock bottom, it did so that afternoon."

Fortunately, Lieutenant-Colonel the Viscount Dalrymple, M.B.E., though still too ill for permanent command, was available in Naples, and that evening he arrived with four more officers and thirteen other ranks, and took over command. "Their arrival was the best tonic for the morale of the Battalion", and they "received their initiation into the spirit of Anzio, when the area was heavily bombed that night".

On 2nd March, while attacks in the American sector were being repulsed in torrential rain, the Battalion started handing over kit and vehicles to the various dumps, and on the 4th orders for the move to the docks were received. On the following afternoon the advance party left. The Battalion moved off early on the morning of the next day, and in the assembly area it was addressed by the Divisional Commander who congratulated it on its performance in the beach-head. At noon in American trucks it moved off and embarked in two L.S.T.s, some 238 strong. It had lost 15 officers (including six of Field rank) and 122 other ranks killed or died of wounds, 9 officers and 303 other ranks wounded, and 4 officers, including the Padre and Doctor, and 213 other ranks missing, mostly prisoners of war.[1] Its total casualties were almost exactly the average of the Brigade.

Mar. 2
Mar. 4
Mar. 5
Mar. 6

III.—PRELUDE TO THE SUMMER ADVANCE

(a) *Reorganisation*

On the 7th March the First Battalion disembarked at Pozzuoli, and drove round the Bay of Naples to the Sorrento Peninsula. Here on the next day they were joined by the Second Battalion, newly relieved from its two months' tour in the Minturno sector of the Fifth Army front. Social gatherings, very similar in character to those which had marked the end of the African campaign, were quickly arranged between the two Battalions, but there were sad gaps in the ranks of those who had celebrated round Tunis and Hammamet but nine months previously.

Mar. 7
Mar. 8
MAP XXI

The hard infantry fighting in the Italian mountains and on the lowlands of Anzio had made great inroads into the reinforcements of the Regiment, and into those of the whole Brigade of Guards. No longer was it to be possible to maintain in the Mediterranean theatre three complete brigades, totalling nine battalions. In a few months the long

---

[1] In addition to those officers already named there were also wounded Lieutenants P. R. Methuen (8th February) and T. C. Lindsay-Peto (21st February); Lieutenant E. L. T. Cumming was taken prisoner on 10th February.

awaited new front in north-west Europe was to open, and then the Guards Armoured Division and the 6th Guards (Tank) Brigade would be in action, requiring a steady flow of new men for their seven armoured battalions, and probably a torrent of men for the Division's four infantry battalions. Plainly the Brigade could not maintain twenty battalions in the fight—and certainly the Scots Guards could not maintain three—at the rate of casualties that had recently been incurred.

Since September 1943 the Second Battalion had had 20 officers and 147 men killed, 23 officers and 286 men wounded, and 3 officers and 84 men taken prisoner—a total of 46 officers and 513 men, all in six months. In six *weeks* in the Anzio beach-head the First Battalion had lost 26 officers and 638 men, making the terrible sum of 72 officers and 1,151 men for the whole Regiment. In the next few months many of the wounded would return, but these would do little more than balance the further loss sustained by sickness, in particular jaundice and malaria, and the return home of the 141 men of the Second Battalion who had been overseas more than five years. Already the Fourth Battalion had been broken up to sustain the First and Second; now the Second was to return home as a cadre, to reform and train for a different role.

The 201st Guards Brigade was to take home the 6th Grenadiers, 2nd Scots and 1st Irish Guards. In Italy were to remain the 1st Guards Brigade with the 3rd Grenadier, 2nd Coldstream, and 3rd Welsh Guards; and the 24th Guards Brigade, with the 5th Grenadiers, 1st Scots and 3rd Coldstream, this last battalion being kept in the pious, though improvident, hope that the Coldstream could maintain three infantry battalions in action in two theatres during the coming summer.

Before the skeleton of the Second sailed, there were many to be transferred to the First. In principle all those who had come abroad after 1st June 1942 were transferred; in fact 17 officers and 480 other ranks joined the First from the Second, including the whole of Left Flank under Major T. C. Harvey, which thus served as a body in three different battalions. Lieutenant-Colonel Taylor was appointed to command the First Battalion[1]; Major Steuart-Fothringham, who had frequently commanded the Second Battalion in the line and who had won the confidence of all ranks, remained in command for the voyage home.

Mar. 18 In the last six months the men of the Scots Guards had seen to the full what man could do with liberated fire and energy; now Nature was to treat them to an even more awful sight. On the 18th March (the day that a large party from the Second Battalion visited the Isle of Capri and found it "strongly held by the Americans") Vesuvius,

[1] For Order of Battle, see p. 546.

which had been without its plume of smoke for some days, started to erupt. By nightfall the red glow above the crater was matched by great lines of molten lava moving down the mountainside and reflected in long lines across the waters of the bay. Overhead a huge unending billowing cloud of ash, rising, it was said, to twenty thousand feet, pressed on towards the horizon. By the 24th the ash was falling. The streets became strangely quiet as after a fall of snow, and rapid movement on the parade ground as elsewhere stirred up the dust in clouds. By the 1st April the worst of the eruption was over, and most of the Second Battalion went for baths to Castellammare di Stabia, whither the inhabitants of Pompeii had unsuccessfully tried to fly for refuge from the volcano's most famous endeavour. The town was as dusty as Sorrento but possessed "lavish supplies of medicinal waters curative of many ills from which the Battalion was not suffering".

Meanwhile on the 27th March the First Battalion, with its host of new faces, had moved away from the spring paradise of Sorrento to the less salubrious district around the village of Pontelandolfo, some forty miles north-east of Naples, where training began in earnest with an exercise prophetically entitled *More Bullets*. Before it had set out the Battalion said an affectionate farewell to the 1st Battalion Irish Guards, trusted comrades-in-arms in three short but exacting campaigns. Mar. 27

The Second Battalion was sent on its way early in April. On the 5th the commander of the Eighth Army, Lieutenant-General Sir Oliver Leese, addressed the men of the 201st Guards Brigade, recounting their long and proud record in the field and wishing them well on their journey home. With him were three members of his staff, all former officers of the Battalion in the Desert: Major the Hon. B. Bruce, M.C., Captain D. H. Butter, M.C., and Captain I. M. Calvocoressi, M.C. April 5

On the evening of the 9th the Battalion, together with the 6th Grenadiers and the Irish Guards, returned to Castellammare. This time a train was waiting, filthy with evidence of occupation by mules and barely big enough to carry even the reduced Brigade, but heading in the right direction. A light drizzle was falling as the Brigade entrained. There followed the normal apparently interminable and objectless delay; and then the train moved out into the gathering dusk. Jerkily and with definite leisure it crept on through the night. By dawn the twenty miles had been covered and breakfast eaten in the Naples sidings. As soon as it was light the Battalion marched down to the docks where lay the long-awaited "ship with the tartan funnel". The next day, early in the morning, the *Cape Town Castle* sailed for home.[1] April 9
April 10
April 11

---

[1] The history of the Second Battalion continues on page 395.

S Company

During March, in consequence of the amalgamation, large numbers of Scots Guards reinforcements had been collecting in the "God-forsaken village of Rotondi" in the hills not far south of Pontelandolfo, where was situated the 1st Battalion of the Infantry Reinforcement and Training Depot (I.R.T.D.). The Scots Guards Company there contained some four hundred fit men, and a hundred of these had been in the care of Captain A. S. Neilson, who had recently come from the Training Battalion's Battle Camp in North Wales. He brought with him the ideas and enthusiams which emanated from the School of Infantry at Barnard Castle and which had permeated the Fourth Battalion, in which Captain Neilson had previously served. His hundred men were energetically trained as a company; most of them already knew him from the Battle Camp and were thoroughly receptive to his teachings. Envious eyes were cast on this new unit.

It so happened that the 2nd Coldstream (Lieutenant-Colonel H. R. Norman) of the 1st Guards Brigade (Brigadier J. C. Haydon) had had a particularly unpleasant and expensive introduction to the Italian campaign on Monte Ornito in February, and was already reduced to three companies. With the customary reassurances from Authority that the attachment was purely temporary, it was arranged that the new Scots Guards Company should join the 2nd Coldstream to complete it to full establishment. On the 28th March, now commanded by Major H. D. Cuthbert, S Company joined their new comrades at San Potito, fifteen miles north of Capua. The "temporary arrangement" was to last until 1st March 1945. "There were misgivings on both sides about the success of this combination," records the Coldstream historian,[1] "but in a few days the Scots Guardsmen settled down happily, and the succeeding weeks and months dispelled every doubt."

Mar. 28

A word should here be said about the title of this celebrated company. Normally the companies are lettered alphabetically in seniority throughout the Regiment. At the date of the new company's formation, the letters V, W, Y and Z were vacant, due to the disbandment of the Fourth Battalion; letter S was borne by the centre Squadron of the Third Battalion. However, the proper ordering of things escaped those in Italy, and S Company it became, the result of selecting the initial letter of the name of the Regiment to which the men belonged in order to distinguish them from the Coldstreamers with whom they served. Months later when the title was questioned from home, it was

---

[1] The historian is indebted to Messrs. Michael Howard and John Sparrow, joint authors of *The Coldstream Guards 1920–1946*, and to their publishers, the Oxford University Press, for permission to quote from pages 216–247 of that book, which cover the period of S Company's service with the 2nd Coldstream. Orders of Battle of the Company will be found on p. 558.

agreed to allow the anomaly to remain, for by that time even the Army Commander knew it as S Company.

* * *

Therefore, for the next year of the Italian Campaign there are the deeds of two distinct bodies of Scots Guardsmen to be followed; those of the First Battalion, for the most part in the 6th South African Armoured Division; and those of S Company in the 2nd Coldstream, in the 6th British Armoured Division.

And there was nearly a third body. In July 1944 Regimental Headquarters heard with dismay that Captain R. G. Rowe was in the process of forming W Company at the I.R.T.D., and that the hard-pressed Coldstream coveted this also. Fortunately the plan came to naught. As will be seen, the supposedly rich store of reinforcements was soon consumed away: by November the First Battalion had to disband B Company for want of replacements, and remained on this reduced establishment until S Company took its place in the Battalion in March 1945.

(b) *Castel di Sangro*

The grand strategy of the Italian Campaign was once again directed at an attempt to drive the Germans out of their tremendously strong positions which dominated the entrance to the Liri Valley at Cassino. It was considered of prime importance that Rome should fall to the Allies before the opening of what at home was called the Second Front; those in the Mediterranean liked to think of it as a Third Front. When the great descent on the Northern French coast had been made, it was intended that a second landing should be made in the south of France; the troops for this operation would in the main be taken from Italy, so General Alexander had urgent reasons for pressing his offensive before all the French and some of the American divisions left his armies. MAP XXIV

Neither of the Guards Brigades took part in the initial assault. The plan for the attack involved moving the bulk of the Eighth Army from the eastern part of the Italian Front to the Cassino sector. In consequence the central sector in the Apennines was to be left very thinly guarded. The 24th Guards Brigade was giving a holding role in a sector of this mountainous region in the area of Castel di Sangro.

On 12th April the Brigade relieved troops of the Polish 3rd Carpathian Division on a front of about thirty miles. Complete secrecy was essential, for the Germans must have no inkling that the Eighth Army was side-stepping to its left. The Brigade must keep them thinking that the Poles were still in Castel di Sangro. Brigadier Clive April 12 wrote of the period in this sector that it was one of "hard physical effort up terrific hills, with supplies mule-borne, and continual alertness on everyone's part". It also enabled the Battalions to make acquaintance with the supporting arms of the Brigade Group.

The First Battalion put B Company out north of Castel di Sangro and Right Flank into the town itself. Here Major F. G. Mann, M.C., sported the grandiloquent title of Fortress Commander and Captain E. A. G. Balfour became Town Major, though it had to be admitted that the real power resided in the local priest who filled with efficiency the role of a somewhat dictatorial Poo-bah.

At first C Company occupied the battered village of San Pietro Avellana, but they were soon relieved by companies of the 5th Grenadiers. Thereafter the companies alternated in the positions around Castel di Sangro and guarded the mile-long tunnel which ran east and west through Monte Pagano, and formed the main line of communication between the Battalion and the Grenadiers; all supplies came up through this tunnel. The nightly convoy was a dramatic affair, especially during the relief of the Poles. Vehicles were carefully counted on entering and leaving the tunnel, and at the Castel di Sangro end a curtain had to be drawn back to allow the trucks to pass out into the darkness. The surrounding country was served by execrable roads, and Brigade Headquarters was over twenty miles away. In front lay a broad mine-strewn no-man's-land, through which ran the headwaters of the Sangro river.

The Battalion, which was in the closest contact with the enemy, saw few of them, but shelling was frequent, particularly in Castel di Sangro, interspersed with propaganda leaflets in Polish—a measure of the success of the security arrangements. Casualties were light and the main activity was patrolling deep into no-man's-land to mark enemy positions with a view to offensive raids. From one of these, Lieutenant J. Graham, M.C., an outstanding platoon commander, did not return, and it was not until months later that it was discovered that he had been taken prisoner; on capture he had given his identity as a private soldier in order to assist his chances of escape. In exchange the Battalion was able to welcome several escaped Allied prisoners to our lines, besides an Italian general who was carried across the Sangro on his A.D.C.'s back.

May 12 — As the days passed the enemy's artillery fire increased, though it did little damage, and on May 12th a warning order to move was received, and a fire plan to keep the Germans apprehensive was carried out. That day saw the opening of the great attack in the Liri Valley, prelude to the fall of Cassino and the opening of the road to
May 17 — Rome, and by the early morning of the 17th the relief of the Battalion by the 12th Lancers was complete. Less than twenty-four hours later the last German had left Cassino.

(c) *Cassino*

A week after joining the Coldstream, S Company entered the line at Cassino, in front of which the Allied armies had been held up ever since the capture of Monte Camino in December 1943.

April 5

The Coldstream were allotted the central sector of the Brigade front, holding that part of the ruined town facing the Continental Hotel in which there were known to be a number of enemy and at least one German tank; the two reserve companies, of which S was the left hand, occupied positions about a mile to the rear behind the Rapido river. From their almost impregnable positions on the heights of Monastery Hill above the town the German Parachutists commanded perfect observation over the whole of the Brigade area and for many miles beyond. All movement in and around Cassino had therefore to take place at night, and, in the forward areas, the darkness had to be deepened by smoke. No vehicle could cross the Rapido river without the noise of its engine bringing down a hail of fire upon the mile-long, dead straight road which ran into the town; porters had to carry forward all rations, water, fuel and ammunition, and all the wounded had to be carried back, along this "Mad Mile". During the first week S Company remained behind the Rapido it supplied thirty porters under Lance-Sergeant Davidson. So hazardous was their work that every effort was made not to use the same men more than once every other night, but there were many occasions when this was not possible. During the month spent in Cassino five of S Company's porters were wounded, but they never lost so much as a tin of bully-beef.

During the night of 13th April S Company moved up along the "Mad Mile" and relieved No. 2 Company in the left forward position; the area had been hard enough to find in the dark among the heaps of rubble, but when morning came it was little easier to pinpoint it on the very detailed maps provided. Landmarks could not be identified; in their place were broken walls, decaying corpses and shellholes full of water. The Company lived in sangars built of the rubble, or in cellars—where they could be found intact. The stench of corpses was nauseating; it was a place of desolation. By day, each post could observe only the shortest of distances, and often no further than a man could throw a grenade. The horizon was a jagged mass of churned up masonry behind which any number of Germans might be lurking. Posts could be visited or relieved only by night; wounds and meals had to wait for the darkness—and longer if there was a moon, or when the enemy were particularly active. As yet the sun was not too hot, although it was hot enough in the Company Headquarters cellar for Major Cuthbert to be able to claim that he spent most of his days without his trousers!

April 13

April 23	On the 23rd the Company was relieved by the Black Watch, and returned to San Potito to rest and train. Within a fortnight it was back again under the shadow of Monastery Hill. At first the Company was again in reserve, but three days later it was back in its old familiar ruins. On the way there Lieutenant E. M. Sharp, who had joined only the week before, was killed by shellfire.
May 5	
May 8	
May 11	On the evening of the 11th May the nightly smoke-screen was fired over the town, but the usual porters did not come forward under its cover. For this was the night of the great offensive. The forward companies had already built up three days' supply of food in their positions lest they should be cut off. The 1st Guards Brigade's orders were to sit still in Cassino and "make faces" at the enemy, while the II Polish Corps to the north and the 4th British and 8th Indian Divisions to the south attacked on either side of them. For a week they sat in their ruins while the battle raged around them, nagging at the enemy with continual harassing fire and with a few small raids on his forward positions.
May 18	Early on the morning of the 18th the Monastery of Cassino surrendered to the 12th Podolski Lancers of the 3rd Carpathian Division, and patrols of the 4th Division entered Cassino from the south. By midday the Company found its position overrun by press-photographers, war correspondents and a whole crowd of enthusiastic sightseers who wandered happily, and it seemed, irreverently, over ground which only a few hours before had been firmly in the hands of the Germans. To the Guardsmen it was incredible that so many people could be interested in so disagreeable a place; the "swanners" thinned out rapidly after two Press men had trod on a mine. Later in the day when S Company marched back down the Mad Mile in unaccustomed daylight, it left the stinking rubble of Cassino almost deserted.

IV. THE ADVANCE TO THE ARNO

(a) *The Road to Rome*

MAP XXIV From now on the fortunes of the two Guards Brigades in Italy were linked to those of the two Armoured Divisions of the Eighth Army. In view of the mountainous nature of the terrain General Leese thought it essential that each Armoured Division should contain an additional Infantry Brigade instead of the normal establishment of one; he selected the two Guards Brigades, not only with an eye to their reliable quality, but also in an attempt to avoid heavy casualties which could not be replaced. In the five months of relentless and often strongly contested advance which followed, they were subjected to a

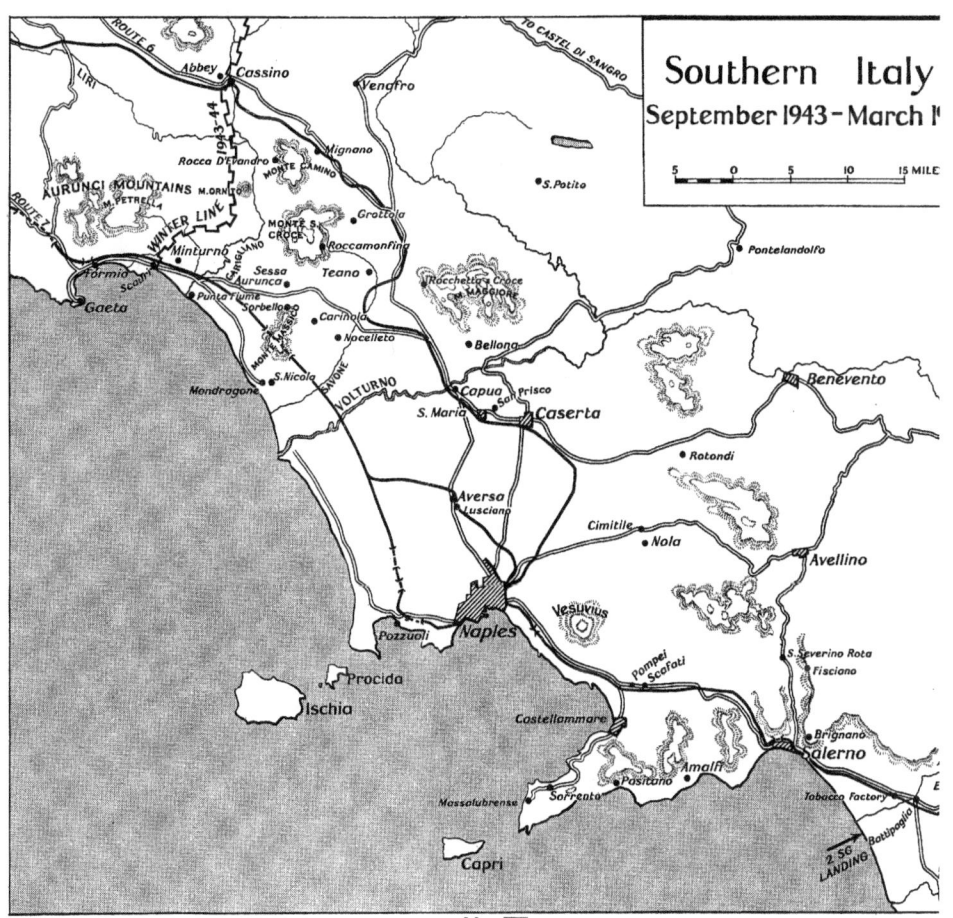

Map XXI

steady drain, but they were spared the stiff, sanguinary set battles which were the lot of the Infantry Divisions, particularly on the east coast.

First Battalion

The First Battalion joined the 6th South African Armoured Division (Major-General W. H. E. Poole) on the 19th May a few miles east of Caserta, and there began what can safely be described as the happiest association of the campaign—if not of the whole war. The regiment of tanks with which the 24th Guards Brigade was chiefly concerned was the Pretoria Regiment (Princess Alice's Own), commanded by Lieutenant-Colonel A. H. Johnstone; the Battalion worked in the main with A (Rhodesian) Squadron commanded by Major F. D. Wade. During the next months of mobile fighting the Guardsmen came to look upon the South African tankmen as their trusty friends, and it is no idle boast to claim that the Pretoria Regiment held similar views about the Guardsmen. Never before had the Battalion worked in such close co-operation with armour, and the resource and agility of the South Africans in getting their tanks on to hills which would have seemed inaccessible to mere mechanics, gave the infantry confidence and won their unstinted admiration. Other South African units in the Brigade Group were B Support Group of the Royal Durban Light Infantry, armed with Vickers medium machine-guns and 4·2-inch mortars; an anti-tank battery of self-propelled M.10s of the 1/11th Anti-Tank Regiment, South African Artillery; and a detachment of the South African Military Police. The service given by these units was all of a piece with that given by the Pretoria Regiment.

The Battalion found equally trusty friends in the British units of the Brigade Group; the 23rd Army Field Regiment R.A., the 42nd Field Company, R.E., and the 550th Company, R.A.S.C. The latter were particular friends, for they carried the Battalion in their 3-tonners wherever they went. Infantry Brigades in Armoured Divisions were allotted sufficient transport to carry the whole at one time, a luxury the 24th Guards Brigade had not previously enjoyed.

While the introduction was being effected the armies were striking hammer blows at the enemy on all sectors of the front. On the left the Americans attacked out of the Anzio beach-head; in the coastal sector they advanced through the mountains; on their right the French swept across the Aurunci Mountains; the British attacked in the Liri Valley, and the Canadians passed through to break the Hitler line at Pontecorvo. The fall of Cassino to the Poles had unlocked the door to Rome. So great had been the German casualties that Field Marshal Kesselring realised there could be no serious stand south of Lake Trasimene, and that even here there could be but a temporary halt. His main concern was to salve what he could from the wreck.

May 19

236   ITALY: 1944

Both armoured divisions played their part in the advance which followed.

S Company

May 26
MAP XXII

On the 26th May the 1st Guards Brigade supported by the tanks of the 17th/21st Lancers were advancing down the Via Casilina (Route 6) which runs generally north-westwards from Cassino to Rome; they were the leading troops of the Eighth Army. S Company rode on the Sherman tanks to within a mile of the town of Arce, when the column, led by the 3rd Grenadiers, was held up by the enemy ensconced

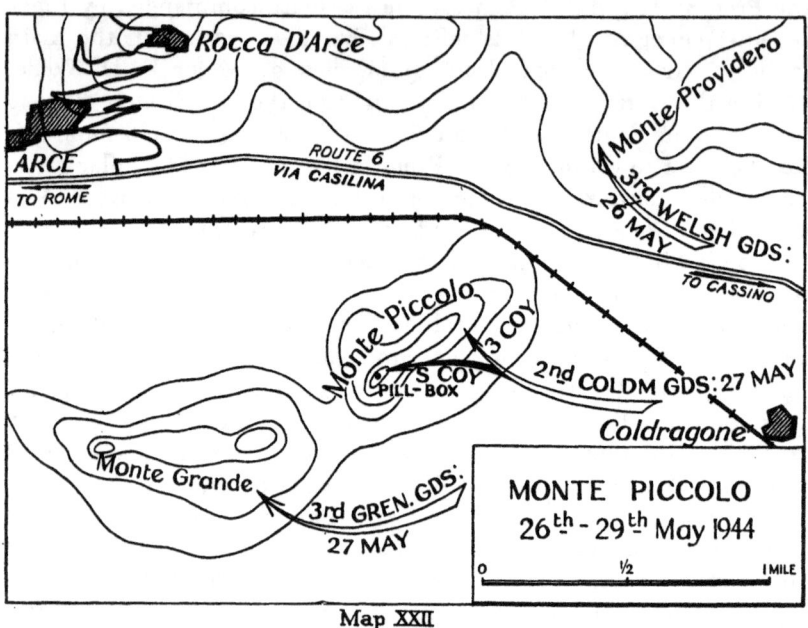

Map XXII

on hills to the left and right of the road. The hill nearest to the road on the left was Monte Piccolo; on it, S Company won its spurs against the German 1st Parachute Regiment.

The ridge on the left of the road was divided by a saddle into two halves, each about a mile in length, Monte Piccolo to the east and Monte Grande to the west. That evening the 3rd Welsh Guards reached the lower slopes of Piccolo and managed to occupy its neighbour, Monte Providero, on the right of the road. The armour sought out fire positions on the following morning and at 4 o'clock in the afternoon orders were given out for a night attack. The Grenadiers were to go for Monte Grande, while the 2nd Coldstream were to capture Monte Piccolo. There was little daylight left for an adequate reconnaissance, and when the advance began at nine it was map and compass which gave direction. No. 3 Company went for the right-

May 27

hand half of the hill; S Company's objective was the highest point, on the left-hand half.

Captain Neilson (who was commanding in the absence on leave of Major Cuthbert) made the Company follow the barrage as close as was possible, closer than seemed safe, "and it seemed a miracle there were no casualties". As they went up the hill the Guardsmen shouted to each other to keep direction; this soon developed into a "noise like dervishes", and one officer, who was himself greatly heartened by the din, was, on reflection, not surprised to find that "in the all-important Pill-box [a demolished concrete emplacement which marked the summit] a Spandau pointed downhill, belt in the breach, and not a round fired". The top of Piccolo was in our hands, and all began to scrape and build, for the ground was too rocky to dig.

On Monte Grande the Grenadiers had also reached the top, but just before dawn they were pushed off by a determined counter-attack. This placed the Coldstream left flank, that held by S Company, in a precarious position, and after daylight they too were attacked, and No. 3 Company fifteen minutes later. Both companies were subjected to a hail of grenades and Schmeisser fire from very short range before the enemy could be driven off. Lieutenant H. R. Bridgeman was killed and Captain Neilson wounded. Despite the fact that he was losing a good deal of blood, he would not be evacuated while the company was engaged with the enemy, and he spent the remainder of the battle walking about on the bare hillside, regardless of his own safety, and encouraging everyone by his example.

May 28

All morning the enemy attempted to infiltrate over the crest and into the Company positions. In the Pill-box Lance-Corporal T. Smythe and Guardsman F. Munday were instrumental in thwarting these efforts with Bren and Tommy-gun. Throughout the morning they and others held this key point, and at midday in the blazing sun a lull enabled water and ammunition to be brought up, and the wounded to be taken back; Captain Neilson was persuaded to go with them, only to return as soon as his wounds had been dressed, despite the strong remonstrances of the doctor. No sooner had he completed the stiff climb back, than a second and even more determined counter-attack came in. The Pill-box was knocked out by a shell from a self-propelled gun. This was the crisis of the battle; for if the Germans established themselves in it they could command the whole of the reverse slope of the Scots and Coldstream positions. "Corporal J. England went to the ridge and began flinging aimed grenades at the enemy, whereupon a fanatical adolescent type with a Schmeisser got into the remains of the Pill-box and killed England. Had he been joined there by a Spandau—or even managed to remain there himself—things would have been sticky indeed. But Sergeant D. Bailey ran round the *far* side of the Pill-box—which was the most vulnerable side—and with his Tommy-gun killed the youth. In doing so he got three Spandau bullets through his clothing. If he hadn't killed the creature in the Pill-box the whole day might have ended differently." As it was there was confused fighting all over the Company position; Captain Neilson was at last overcome by loss of blood and taken to the rear, when the command devolved upon Lieutenant H. F. C. Charteris, who since early morning had been the only unwounded officer in the Company; almost at once he was severely wounded in the head.

Command now devolved on CSM T. Brown, who rallied the remnants in one final overwhelming charge at the crest, and drove the Germans down the northern slope. In that final charge Lance-Sergeant P. Jones, who now commanded Lieutenant Bridgeman's platoon, seized the barrel of a Spandau which was actually being fired, pulled it towards him, turned it upon its crew, and killed them.

The German Parachutists attempted no further attacks; CSM Brown consolidated on the Company's original position, which he handed over to Lieutenant J. S. Wilson, who, though sick, had managed to escape from hospital to rejoin the Company. That night May 30 the enemy withdrew up Route 6, and the advance of the Eighth Army was resumed.

This first battle had cost S Company dear; one officer and ten men had been killed, and two officers and eighteen men had been wounded. But they had won a reputation to live up to. For their gallantry Captain Neilson received the Distinguished Service Order, and Lieutenant Charteris the Military Cross. CSM Brown was awarded the Distinguished Conduct Medal; and Lance-Sergeant Jones, Lance-Corporals Downie and Smythe, and Guardsmen Munday and Lingwood, a devoted stretcher bearer, the Military Medal.

June 1 After two days for rest and reinforcement, the Company set off with the Coldstream up Route 6 to Ceprano, and thence, by abominable
June 4 roads, they branched north into the hills. reaching Lake Canterno the
June 5 day the Americans entered Rome. The next day they bumped along in their 3-tonners until they came to rest six miles short of the city. Here they slept, but Rome did not see them yet.

First Battalion

While S Company had been engaged about Monte Piccolo, the South African Division, with the First Battalion, had been champing in the rear. Traffic congestion, caused by the lack of roads, the lavish equipment of the Allied Armies and the skill of the enemy's demoli-
May 29 tions, kept all but a few divisions well behind. For two days the Battalion had to be content with a flank protection task at Roccasecca, ten miles west of Cassino and north of Route 6.

June 2 On 2nd June it moved twenty-five miles on to an area south of

Frosinone, and from there on the next day it began its first tactical move as an advance guard. It set off for about seven miles up the main road, and was then directed northwards on Fiuggi. For the Americans had entered Valmontone, thereby cutting Route 6 behind the enemy, who was making desperate efforts to escape northwards into the hills. Less than three hours after starting, the Battalion was held up by serious demolitions at a gully about five miles south of Fiuggi, where mines caused several casualties and two vehicles were blown up. Further delay and more casualties were caused when shellfire knocked out a bulldozer which had been brought forward to clear the obstruction, but eventually the advance continued. It was not until late that night that it was found possible to manhandle a jeep and trailer past the obstruction and obviate the use of mules. By ten o'clock on the next morning a diversion for tanks had been made, but an intended attack on Acuto, three miles south-west of Fiuggi, was frustrated by the 6th British Armoured Division, who had taken Fiuggi from the east and moved across the Battalion's front. The Battalion had been "squeezed out". That evening a Panther Mark V tank was found undamaged and abandoned—said to be the first untouched specimen to fall into Allied hands—and at about the same time the Americans entered Rome.

"The Hun is definitely very rattled," the Commanding Officer wrote, "though it is by no means a rout yet. Anyway, so far so good, they are going back so fast we can't catch the brutes, but they have left a hell of a lot of stuff behind this time. Also the Air Force have done a very fine job of work straffing. It is fantastic the amount of direct hits on trucks I have seen, and they must have caused the Huns very heavy casualties indeed."

On the next day the Brigade set off again up Route 6, the 5th Grenadiers leading, and the Battalion at the tail of the column. The new plan was adventurous. Rome having fallen the enemy were falling back beyond it in great confusion and little strength. The Brigade, at the head of the Eighth Army, was to advance with all possible speed to seize the first bridge over the Tiber north of Rome. The situation of our own troops was hazy, and that of the enemy unknown, and maps of the area were unobtainable. The Grenadiers set off at a rattling pace, but as they approached Rome the traffic, French and American, became thicker and thicker. It was more like Derby Day than a lightning advance. The American Fifth Army claimed the roads through Rome as theirs, and the Brigade had to be content to wait in its trucks in the heat and dust while the jam got worse and worse. In the middle of the afternoon the "crawl"—for it cannot now be said to have been an advance—began again, this time delayed by the French, and, once again, by the 6th Armoured Division. When the bridge site was reached, it was found to be destroyed—and already held by the French on the left bank and the Americans on the right! At midnight the Battalion went thankfully to sleep.

(b) *The Road to the Arno*

After the capture of Rome came the great summer advance. The German Army had suffered huge losses in men and material in the battle for Cassino and in its subsequent retreat; Field Marshal Kesselring pinned his hopes on the "Green Line" he had been preparing along that section of the high Apennines which runs slightly north of west beyond the Arno river. To this line, known to the Allies as the Gothic Line, the Germans conducted a skilful retreat. All the while the Eighth and Fifth Armies attempted to overtake and break through the enemy rearguards, but, save for some hard-won local successes, there was no decisive penetration.

For the Scots Guards it was a period of almost daily movement, over dusty roads, sometimes in a trice turned to a slimy morass by torrential rain, past countless well-sited craters, tumbled bridges, hidden mines, and demolished villages. The Italian valleys and hills afforded admirable positions and observation for delaying tactics; and every attack involved a climb. Accurate information about the enemy's whereabouts was often scanty; friendly peasants had plenty to say, but a healthy scepticism was an asset when extracting the dull truth from their imaginative reports. The desire of the Allies was to get on; therefore a ridge, from which came a few accurate concentrations of 88-mm. shells and several bursts of Spandau fire—"like the ripping of a shirt"—had to be attacked quickly, before the real strength or extent of the position had been fully ascertained. Inevitably, all too often these initial attacks would be made with too small a force, and the leading troops would be halted. Then a more elaborate attack would have to be mounted, only to find that the enemy had withdrawn at the last moment. Thus our advance would have been delayed and the enemy would have gained another few hours' grace. And beyond that ridge was always another.

By the time the two months which it took to get from the Tiber to the Arno had passed, the troops were very tired and badly in need of a rest. For despite the facts that they advanced through some of the most beautiful country in Europe, that the inhabitants were on the whole delighted to welcome them, and that for the most part the weather was excellent, the strain of constant watchfulness, jerky movement and heat was cumulative. But when in the end they reached the Arno the First Battalion had forged a never-to-be-forgotten link of friendship with the South Africans, and S Company had become an integral part of the 2nd Coldstream.

(i) *Over the hills to Florence: First Battalion*

On the evening of the 6th June—the day of the Normandy landings —the First Battalion retraced its steps, and passed through Rome to cross the Tiber. The Commanding Officer found it "a fine city and lots of pretty girls who all seemed very pleased to see us"; he spent the night there, being regaled with brandy in a luxurious villa, while his driver was treated to former Fascist whisky. The Battalion drove through in the dark. *June 6*

For the next four days the 11th South African Armoured Brigade led the Division's advance, which, in the face of a disorganised enemy, went swiftly. In consequence the Battalion's lot was several tiring moves at short notice northwards along the Via Flaminia—in this inelegant age unromantically redesignated Route 3. A few miles south of Civita Castellana it passed by the smouldering caves of Kesselring's former headquarters, burrowed into the rock of Monte Sorrate.[1] At Civita Castellana it branched left off the great highway, following the tanks north-westward through Viterbo. For the next two months the Division, serving in the XIII Corps under Lieutenant-General S. C. Kirkman, was to follow the dusty white roads all the way to Florence; rarely were the vehicles and their bruised passengers to experience the smoothness of tar-macadam. *June 7*

On 10th June on Monte Rosso five miles north of Viterbo the South African armour broke through the German anti-tank screen, and an even more rapid advance seemed in prospect. The Battalion was placed under the Armoured Brigade's orders, but on the following day the Guards Brigade took the lead, and the Battalion reverted to its normal command. The 5th Grenadiers led off on a misty morning in the direction of Orvieto, while the Scots Guards, supported as usual by the tanks of the Pretoria Regiment, cleared woods on the left of the road. They sent many patrols to investigate the multitude of farms and hamlets with which Umbria abounds, and were gratified by the sight of much abandoned enemy equipment. But by the evening the Grenadiers were held up south of Bagnoregio. The assault on this village, perched high on a rocky promentory dominating the road, required a more elaborate plan than could be prepared that day, and so the Battalion dug-in in the dark on the wooded hills a mile south-west of the village. *June 10* *June 11*

On the next day a Divisional attack was intended to coincide with one by the French on the left, but, as so often happens, the preliminary stages went slower than had been hoped, and it was not until dawn *June 12* *June 13*

---

[1] It was while "swanning" through these caves in the hopes of finding something more artistic that the Brigade Intelligence Officer (Captain A. R. A. Hobson, of the Regiment) chanced upon a marked map which disclosed to the Allies for the first time the exact course of the Gothic Line.

next day that the Grenadiers and the 3rd Coldstream went forward to find that the enemy were abandoning the village. By half-past ten Bagnoregio was in the hands of the Grenadiers and the Royal Natal Carbineers, and the Scots Guards passed into the lead, advancing on to the high ridge north of the village after overcoming opposition in cornfields to the west of the road. Here they took prisoners from two of the finest of the enemy's divisions, the Herman Goering Panzer and 4th Parachute. In the afternoon a halt was called, the Brigade formed a firm base, and the 12th South African Motor Brigade passed through to capture Orvieto.

For the next week the Battalion was in reserve moving slowly forward in the wake of the Division through the vineyards, orchards and fields which lie below the magnificent rock plateau on which June 16 stands Orvieto. Rain began to fall heavily, and a jeep-borne platoon of Left Flank with supporting weapons became completely bogged in the deep mud of a remote track. Nor was the Divisional axis much better, for it had deteriorated into a narrow second-class road, and with the news of stiffer resistance in the area of Cetona and Chiusi came rumours of reversion to mule transport. An armoured division with mules! What price your theorist now? In fact the Division was now meeting a sector of the enemy's Trasimene Line, before which Kesselring hoped to delay our advance and thus gain time for reorganisation.

June 21   When the Battalion arrived on the forward slopes of Monte Cetona to relieve the Royal Natal Carbineers it could see three miles ahead the ridge over the crest of which lay the small town of Sarteano; further to the north-east, across the valleys of the Astrone river, rose
June 22   the formidable stronghold of Chuisi. On the next day the Brigade was to seize the Sarteano ridge, which ran generally east and west, was steep and covered with chestnut trees, and at the southern foot of which ran a small stream. That morning the Coldstream moved into Cetona village, and in the afternoon the Scots Guards began their advance towards the ridge.

Right Flank (Major Mann) and C Company (Major Hesketh) were directed on two features at the top of the ridge to the west of where the road winds its tortuous way from Cetona to Sarteano, but they got little further than the stream at the foot of the rise, for fierce machine-gun fire from the higher ground to the left, together with mortar bombs and shells and the difficulties of the terrain, brought the advance to a halt. Nor was the expedient of sending B Company (Captain J. C. Blackett-Ord) and Left Flank (Major Harvey) round left-handed of any avail. The strength of the enemy position was now fully apparent,
June 23   and it was decided that a Brigade attack should be mounted next day against the two enemy battalions which were thought to comprise the defenders of Sarteano. Their position was rendered formidable by

the excellence of the observation the heights afforded them, and the attackers were at a disadvantage through their ignorance of the position of the French advancing up the Siena road on their left, and through the knowledge that on their right the Motor Brigade had not yet come up.

The attack on the 23rd was made by two battalions. On the right the Coldstream objectives were the lower ridge south-east of Sarteano and Point 550 further to the west, which had been one of the Scots Guards objectives of the previous day. On the left the First Battalion was to take another small feature on the crest, but its most important objective was Point 685, from the area of which had come most of the fire which had held up their original attempt. A squadron of the Pretoria Regiment was to support each battalion.

The Scots Guards moved up to their start line in darkness, and at first light the attack began in a thick ground mist, though it was not thick enough to screen the advancing men from the enemy machine-gunners. Almost immediately the Commanding Officer received news that Left Flank had gained Point 685, but this report proved premature, and in fact the Company were held up below the summit for the remainder of the day. By skilful use of the ground and supporting fire from the tanks Right Flank and C Company both attained their objectives on the summit of the lower part of the ridge, as did the Coldstream to their right. This progress, which had been stoutly resisted, was plainly unwelcome to the enemy. About noon he attempted to counter-attack. This took the form of infiltration by small parties armed with Spandaus, but the presence on the ridge of the Sherman tanks of the Pretoria Regiment soon put a stop to any serious progress. Throughout the battle the tanks had done everything asked of them, even though they had often to manœuvre in very close country, and had frequently to go out on to the forward slope in full view of Tiger tanks on the next ridge. The tanks and M. 10s engaged the enemy tanks in Sarteano, claiming the destruction of two Tigers. During this fire fight, the Battalion dug in, harried by continuous shell and mortar fire, which the enemy, still on Point 685, could direct on them with great accuracy. After dark the enemy's strength was tested by patrols, the most satisfactory of which was one from Left Flank which reached the top of 685 in the small hours, and found the enemy gone. Early in the morning Left Flank were on the summit, and the action for the Sarteano ridge was at an end; it had cost the Battalion six men killed and a score wounded. The Coldstream found the village abandoned, and the Grenadiers went into the lead with the intention of advancing across the Astrone.

Rising from the valley of this river, and extending some five miles north-westward from Sarteano ran a massive rambling hill, its slopes deeply indented with gulleys and covered with scrub, which culminated in a thickly wooded plateau, marked on the map as Point 846; its name was Poggio Pietraporciana. On the slopes above the Astrone the Grenadiers met stiff resistance from a fresh enemy battalion and were held up south of the river. While they patrolled and reconnoitred, Brigadier Clive ordered the Scots Guards to send a mobile column round by the left, over the top of Point 846 to La Foce, a small village and road junction near the source of the Astrone, from where it should be possible to outflank the Germans opposing the Grenadiers.

June 24

The column, which was commanded by Major Harvey, consisted at first of about half Left Flank, together with carriers, the Battalion's Vickers machine-guns and four light Honey tanks of the Pretoria Regiment. It set out at half-past nine and soon, about a mile south of the summit, enemy were encountered, which civilians variously reported as being in battalion or company strength. The column was reinforced by two troops of the heavier Sherman tanks, and with their aid the enemy were quickly driven back, retiring in the direction of 846. No further advance was made that day, and, reinforced by the remainder of Left Flank and half the mortar platoon, the column spent the night preparing to attack the heights next day.

June 25

At half-past six in the morning the force was on its way, followed closely by B Company. On and around Point 846 were dug in the best part of three German companies, which constituted an ample garrison for so formidable a position. But here it was that the perfect understanding and confidence between the tanks and the Guardsmen were born. The attack went swiftly and was directed with great skill from one of the tanks by Major Harvey. By ten o'clock the company was on the objective, having flushed the enemy from their trenches, killed many of them, and driven the survivors on to the next hill, with the tanks in pursuit doing great execution. The speed and accuracy with which the tanks had engaged the enemy's Spandau posts directly they had been pointed out by the infantry, gave the Guardsmen that fillip to morale which converts a steady assault into a storming. The enemy reacted strongly to this success, and besides having to beat off the routine counter-attacks the Companies had to deal with many isolated enemy posts which had been by-passed in the woods. Moreover, while Left Flank were consolidating their position on the plateau they were subjected to constant and heavy mortar fire, during which the Battalion suffered a grievous blow. The bombs killed the Commanding Officer, Lieutenant-Colonel Taylor, and Captain the Hon. W. H. Vestey, who was commanding Left Flank in the place of Major Harvey; in addition Lieutenant D. J. Forbes and sixteen men were wounded that day, and two Guardsmen killed. The Battalion was ordered to halt where it was, for until reorganisation and replenishment had been effected, there could be no further move towards La Foce. All the Companies now came up, and by six in the evening the whole

June 26

Battalion was firmly established, having made contact with the French on its left, thus getting the first reliable news of their whereabouts for several days.

The death of Colonel Taylor was a sad event, more especially for those who had served under him in the Second Battalion and had come with him to the First. He had always been most careful of the lives and welfare of his men, and during that first Italian autumn, in a battalion which included many who had been away from home nearly five years, that care had been greatly admired and appreciated. He was succeeded in command by his second-in-command, Major R. D. Cardiff, who in his turn was succeeded by Major J. S. Sanderson.

The capture of 846 had the desired effect of forcing the Germans to abandon their position in front of the Grenadiers, and when next day both Battalions continued their advance, the Scots Guards, in liaison with Moroccan troops on their left, quickly reached La Foce and beyond, while by midnight the Grenadiers had occupied the ridge north of the Astrone which had been denied them for the last five days. Shelling, as usual, took its toll, Captain Blackett-Ord and Lieutenant E. Crutchley, both of B Company, being wounded. *June 27*

On the 28th the Battalion pushed on northwards from La Foce. After a long, hot march against scanty resistance the day's objectives were reached to the sound of demolitions set off by the ubiquitous German sappers. Next day, for the first time for a week, no move forward was made; the previous days of fighting had wearied the whole Brigade, but there could be no relenting in the chase while the enemy was so hard-pressed to maintain his front. In C Company there was little rest, for in the morning a patrol was pushed forward to the pleasant watering-place of Montepulciano, where a handful of Germans was seen, and the inhabitants, longing for their release from fear and danger, reported a score or more. In the evening the Company made another visit, finding even fewer Germans, and taking a prisoner.[1] *June 28* *June 29*

On the 30th the advance was resumed in earnest; in the next five days the Brigade was to cover nearly forty miles. So thorough were the demolitions on the axis road that the Battalion, with B Company in the lead, made a wide detour to the west, passing through the territory of the neighbouring French division, and skirting Pienza, a miniature city on a hill, adjudged by many one of the finest unspoilt examples of early Renaissance architecture. On rejoining the former axis, Right Flank went into the lead and advanced into Montefollonico. From this typical Tuscan hill-village good observation was to be *June 30*

[1] For a fascinating description of the German Army in retreat and of the coming of the Scots Guards to La Foce and Montepulciano, see *War in Val d'Orcia* by the Marchesa Origo, an English lady who, throughout the campaign, gave succour to many escaped prisoners of war, partisans and destitute children.

had towards the Chiana valley to the east. Here the Armoured Brigade on the Guards Brigade's right was some way behind, and German infantry on the move could clearly be seen from Montefollonico. These were smartly engaged with mortars, artillery and machine-guns, and a plan quickly hatched to resume the advance slightly east of north towards Torritta in the hopes of cutting off the enemy facing the Armoured Brigade. Again the demolitions made initial progress slow, and a strong position on the high ground north of Torritta directed accurate mortar fire on to B Company (Captain J. D. K. Hague, M.C.) riding in its transport—an unpleasant experience, for there are better circumstances in which to be shelled than seated in an unarmoured lorry five feet above the ground. The lateness of the hour

June 31 prevented further advance towards Torritta, and in the morning B Company and Left Flank had a noisy but bloodless battle before the tank gunners, with their hawk-like eyes, blasted the Germans off the high places dominating the village. Here the Battalion met the Motor Brigade entering from the east, and at once returned to the Guards Brigade's axis, three miles to the west.

For the next four days the two other Battalions led, and daily the Scots Guards moved up to take over the Coldstream's previous posi-

July 4 tions. On the 4th July they crossed the main Siena–Arezzo road, and at Castelnuovo Berardenga entered the country famous for the Chianti wines. In a month they had come over a hundred and fifty miles from Rome, and more than two hundred and fifty since the great offensive began against Cassino nearly six weeks before.

July 5 At midday on the 5th the Battalion set off up the axis to resume the advance, with Right Flank leading. Little progress had been made before substantial demolitions halted the column; the demolitions, as usual, were under enemy observation, and accurate concentrations fell on the Sapper parties who tried to render them passable. Right Flank and B Company left their transport and continued up the east side of the road, heading for a massive castle, that of Brolio. On their right, the Grenadiers were patrolling forward from the high ridge of Campi; on their left the Natal Mounted Rifles sought out routes to the west; and in the evening the Coldstream came up behind these South Africans. An attack was ordered against the castle for that night. C Company set out on the west of the road from the lower slopes of the Campi ridge, supported by a troop of Shermans. Their progress was slow, for they were in difficult country covered with thick gorse-like undergrowth, and once again the enemy guns made good practice. Half an hour before midnight the Company was up to the gate of the castle.

Castel di Brolio was a massive building. Its origins lay in the late tenth century, and its owners, the Ricasoli family, had held it since the year 1141. It had a varied history of siege, capture, destruction and rebuilding in the wars between Florence and Siena, but the appearance it presented to the Scots Guards in July 1944 owed little to the mediæval military engineer. The Ricasoli were the most famous growers of Chianti wines and the most extensive landlords in the area; in the nineteenth century they had produced one of the leading statesmen of the *Risorgimento* and it was in his time that the castle had acquired its present form. The Chianti baron had built as stoutly as any of the steel-masters who were his contemporaries in Britain; the resulting structure was as falsely military, as undomestic and as indestructable as another, more familiar, castle on the banks of the Dee.

The excellent observation which the castle afforded to the south and west made the approach to it hazardous, but once close up to the fortress it transpired that the main obstacle was a solid masonry wall, many feet thick and forty feet high, encircling the inner keep. This wall was pierced on the north side by one large and one small door, both covered by posts on the ramparts manned by a weak company of German infantry, whose O.P.s could give accurate corrections to the supporting guns and mortars. After a gallant attempt by Lance-Sergeant J. S. Walker[1] to gain an entrance through the strongly-barred gate, C Company were withdrawn, for there was no means of scaling the walls in face of the constant machine-gun and mortar fire directed from the battlements, nor was it practicable to make another approach to the gate.

July 6

While this abortive assault was in progress, General Poole arrived at Brigade Headquarters with the news that the Eighth Army was meeting stiff resistance all along its front. In fact the next line of delay, the Arezzo Line, had now been reached; before it the Army was to pause for more than a week while formations were regrouped and work was pushed forward to clear the demolitions which still obstructed the lines of communication. The divisions flanking the South Africans had made slower progress, so the 24th Guards Brigade had to withdraw slightly to conform with its neighbours; the Battalion was recalled from the assault on the castle and dug in on the lower slopes of the Campi ridge about a mile to the south, but the first positions taken up, particularly by those of Left Flank, proved too exposed to artillery fire, and so a further slight withdrawal had to be made. In these positions the Battalion remained for more than a week while preparations were made for the main attack on the Arezzo Line by the 6th British Armoured Division and the New Zealanders twenty miles to the east. The Brigade's orders were to make good the ground gained, keep contact with the enemy, but to advance no further.

---

[1] Lance-Sergeant Walker, who was awarded the Military Medal, was taken prisoner during the final stages of the Battle of Monte Catarelto in October, and was later killed by the Germans while attempting to escape.

For the Battalion these orders meant busy preparation for the capture of Castel di Brolio which had been designated as its primary objective when the advance should be resumed. These preparations manifested themselves in numerous patrols designed to glean information about the ground over which the advance was to be made and also to establish the truth or otherwise of the conflicting reports, emanating from partisans and peasants, of the strength and composition of the garrison of the castle. The only occupant of whose presence there was no doubt was the Baron Ricasoli himself; he and his home experienced a distressing few days in which they were the target for fighter-bombers, medium and field artillery, M. 10s, mortars, tanks and lesser weapons, all of which made remarkably little impression on the solid walls. Equally disturbing to the Baron were the nocturnal visits from patrols. The most notable of these was that led by Captain R. A. Carnegie on the night of the 9th/10th July. That afternoon our observation posts had noticed white sheets being raised and lowered in the castle, and at the same time civilians reported that the enemy had gone. After dark, accompanied by four men of C Company and an Italian guide, Captain Carnegie approached to within a few yards of the outer wall. Near the main gate he observed two German sentries, who he killed with his Tommy-gun. The continued occupation of the castle was thus confirmed, and in the retaliatory fire which this exploit provoked the Italian guide was wounded.

July 15   On the 15th the hard work of reconnaissance was put to good use. That morning, at the same time as the 1st Guards Brigade attacked Monte Lignano in the Arezzo Line, the Battalion resumed its advance northwards. The two Flank Companies moved forward on to the high ground to the west of, and level with, the castle, while C Company was again charged with the task of forcing an entry. On arrival at the main gate Major Hesketh found no defenders, for the Germans had at last withdrawn. But the great door was still as tightly shut as ever. A barrier which might have withstood for many weeks the *condottieri* of yesterday was of no avail against the weapons of today. From point-blank range a Sherman tank of A Squadron of the Pretoria Regiment fired one 75-mm. high-explosive shell; the siege of Brolio was at an end. Within, the garrison was now found to consist solely of the Baron Ricasoli, who, as Lieutenant Keith in his laconic style recorded, "was extremely annoyed". That afternoon C Company went on to a wooded peak to the north-east, where it captured an outpost of eight stalwarts of the *Wehrmacht* preoccupied in a game of cards; B Company moved up to a position half a mile south of the castle; and in the evening Colonel Cardiff moved his Headquarters into Brolio, which was without a doubt the most impressive building it occupied in the whole war.

July 16   The Coldstream now went into the lead towards Gaiole, the duty of the Scots Guards being that of protecting the right flank of the

Brigade by picketing the heights, a task which involved much mountaineering, but little action, save for Right Flank, which in establishing itself on one summit captured two Germans who had been Baron Ricasoli's unwelcomed guests for the last few days, and who were the cause of all his dilapidations—towards the repair of which he submitted an official claim to the Allied Command!

Even now[1] one scar of war has yet to be effaced from the masonry. Those who visit the castle today, bent no doubt on tasting the incomparable Chianti which bears its name or on enjoying its sweeping vista to the tower of Siena and beyond, can see within the gateway on the right-hand wall the deep scar where the tank's shell exploded. In the gardens a few overgrown slit trenches dug by the defenders can be identified, while in the ditch to the left of the main gate can be seen the now empty graves of the two sentries shot by Captain Carnegie. Any attempt to extract from the guide details of the events of 1944 receives little satisfaction; instead he would rather talk of happier days and less turbulent visitors. Set among the pine trees and towering above the famous vineyards, Brolio is again one of the most peaceful places in the land.

The 24th Guards Brigade now entered on the most mountainous part of its journey to Florence. The road which was the Division's axis ran over the top of the Chianti Mountains. These were steep and thickly wooded, and through them for the next twelve miles the narrow white road wound its tortuous way. It was to take eight days to force a passage, for to the physical difficulties was added the stout resistance of the enemy, who had pressing orders to stand and fight. Although the 715th German Division turned a deaf ear to these exhortations, the orders were obeyed to the letter by the soldiers of the 356th, an experienced division whose morale and fighting qualities had steadily improved in the course of its long and successful withdrawal. Progress against these defenders and over these hills was inevitably slow, as each height on both sides of the road had to be scaled, assaulted and consolidated as a separate operation. Nevertheless far better speed was made than might have been expected, certainly much better than the enemy intended. Indeed it was reliably reported that the enemy's programme for his withdrawal north of the Arno was upset by forty-eight hours. The Scots Guards were quick to give credit for this success to the Pretoria Regiment, whose uncanny ability to get their tanks up the most precipitous slopes and on to every objective had a devastating effect on the Germans.

On the 17th July the Coldstream captured the first height north of Gaiole, and on the next day the Grenadiers seized the summits of Monte Majone and advanced further northwards along its ridge. Then came the turn of the Scots Guards; Colonel Cardiff received orders to take Monte San Michele.

July 17
July 18
July 19

[1] September 1954; the only guide book is in German!

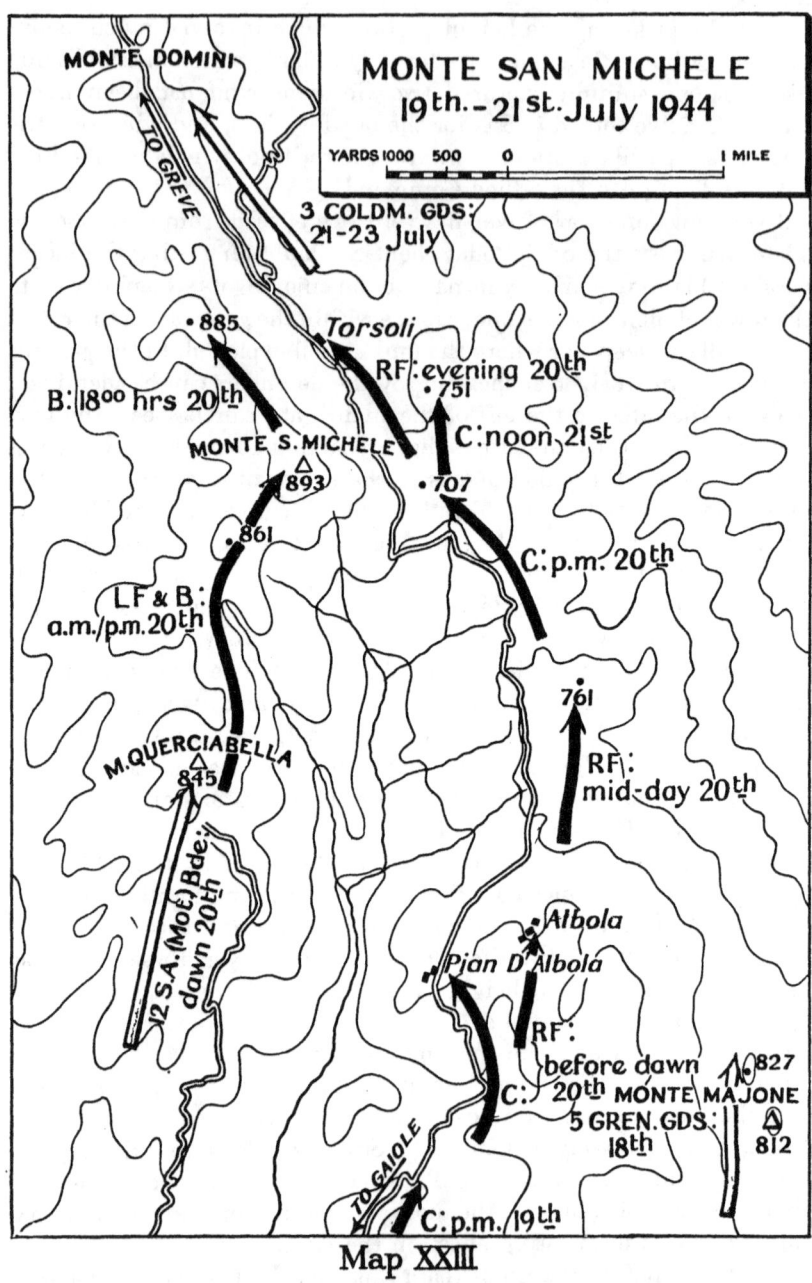

Map XXIII

MAP XXIII   The road northwards twisted and turned along the side of great ridges, nearly everywhere exposed to observation from the German positions, and in every way suitable to those devastating craters with which the enemy Sappers rendered the Italian mountain roads impassable. C Company set off up the road, followed by Left Flank, with the intention of occupying the hamlets of Pian d'Albola and Albola which lay below the northern ridge of Monte Majone. Soon C Company came under heavy fire from guns and mortars, suffering several casualties, including its newly ennobled commander, Major the Lord Hesketh, slightly wounded. During daylight it was plain that further progress was impossible, for the demolitions prevented even the Pretoria Regiment from getting their tanks into suitable positions for support. Plainly the task of assaulting Monte San Michele straight up the road was going to prove extremely uninviting. But fortunately a far better prospect presented itself on the left. At first light the next day the Motor Brigade was to assault Monte Querciabella, and it seemed a far preferable course to cross into their territory and then to attack along the ridge which led from Querciabella to San Michele. This course was at length agreed to, and once again Major Harvey was placed in command of half the Battalion for this purpose. He was to take Left Flank and B Company in their transport with two troops of the Pretoria Regiment, on a wide detour to the west, and then, early in the morning, to pass through the Motor Brigade on Monte Querciabella and from there assault the summit of Monte San Michele. During the night the other half of the Battalion was to continue up the road, and then take the high ground on the right of the road level with San Michele.

The night advance was achieved without opposition, and by first light C Company was established in Pian d'Albola and Right Flank in Albola. Great difficulty was still experienced in surmounting the road demolitions, during which the tireless 42nd Field Company suffered several casualties on the mines laid in the debris.

The assault by the Witwatersrand Rifles/De la Rey Regiment on Monte Querciabella was successful, and by six o'clock in the morning Major Harvey's force, with Left Flank in the lead, was passing through to assault the main objective. At first progress was slow over the trackless, scrub-covered hill, and it was not until the early afternoon that contact was made with the principal defences. These consisted of a strong company, who had had little time to prepare their positions, and who had received accurate attention from the artillery; against the tanks they had no suitable weapons except two Bazookas. Indeed they can be excused for not having expected to be attacked by tanks from that quarter; their consternation at the appearance of the Pretoria Regiment on the summit was evident. It was certainly the tanks which decided the issue, and by half-past three Left Flank was on the highest point, 893. There was still "mopping up" to be done, for several machine-gun posts remained on the south-eastern and northern slopes; these were soon silenced by the tanks and by the Battalion's mortar platoon. Two hours later B Company went on another mile to take the next crest, Point 885, whose defenders had

July 20

been thoroughly shaken up by two concentrations from the Divisional artillery. While digging in on the objective one of the platoon commanders, Sergeant J. J. C. Hill, M.M., was killed by shellfire; he had been an outstanding leader and had already been twice wounded, but even the loss of an eye had not prevented him rejoining the Battalion.

Meanwhile the right half of the Battalion had also achieved what was intended. Here the Companies had the help of the tanks of the Natal Mounted Rifles who supported them on to the series of heights which were their objectives. By two o'clock Right Flank had gained Point 761 unopposed, and, at about the same time as Point 885 fell to B Company, C Company reached the top of Point 707. Here the defenders had to cope with not only the tanks of the Natal Mounted Rifles to their front but also with the menace of those of the Pretoria Regiment to their right rear. To see hostile tanks charging about on high ground covering the only line of retreat is unsettling to the steadiest troops; the enemy left their positions in haste. To complete the day's advance Right Flank was sent forward to the village of Torsoli. Thus all was ready for the Coldstream to pass through to attack the inevitable next hill—Monte Domini.

The Battalion and its supporting tanks had fought a most successful battle, in which once again the decisive factor had been the mutual confidence between Infantry and Armour. At the cost of less than a dozen casualties (which included Lieutenant T. R. Bland, of Left Flank, wounded and two killed), some twenty prisoners had been taken and an important penetration had been made in the enemy's positions. The importance of the success can be measured by the pains the enemy took to reinforce the defenders of Monte Domini, and also by the effect on the progress of the neighbouring British formation on the Brigade's right. For some days the 4th Division had been held up, but the fire which the tanks could now direct into the valley below enabled them to resume their advance. But perhaps the most gratifying event of the day had been the first sight of Florence; twelve miles to the north the city could be seen from the top of Monte San Michele. It was the prize of which all had talked since leaving Rome.

July 21   The next day was fixed for the attack on Monte Domini. Early the Companies were under shellfire, in which Lieutenant J. E. Baxter was wounded, and the advance of C Company to Point 751 was hoped to mark the end of the Battalion's spell in the front line. But when the Coldstream attack went in in the afternoon it made little progress; shelling on the road prevented the clearing of the obstacles, and the attack was called off, still leaving the Scots Guards with no-one between them and the enemy. To the Battalion's disappointment this was to be the situation for the next two days, during which there was little rest, for the enemy attempted to infiltrate back on to some of the ground he had lost, and a larger gun than those to which the Brigade was accustomed began to lob heavy shells into the Battalion area. On the 23rd, after two unsuccessful attempts from the low ground, the Coldstream took Monte Domini, and the Battalion at last experienced relative tranquillity. On the 25th the Grenadiers made a deep penetration along the narrow Hog's Back-like ridge, and, to enable them to push on to Monte Collegalle, B Company and Left Flank were moved forward two miles to form a firm base; during their march forward, among the casualties they suffered from shellfire were three killed and Captain R. A. Carnegie wounded. That day the Carrier Platoon, too, was active, supporting the Reconnaissance Troop of the Pretoria Regiment in spying out the roads to the north-west, and on the next day two sections of carriers gave valuable fire support to No. 3 Company of the Grenadiers in its successful defence of the farthest point reached on the long ridge. By dark that day the Scots Guards were concentrated once again on the road. The fighting in the Chianti range was at an end, but, as usual, there was to be yet one more ridge for the Battalion to attack before Florence could be entered. *July 23* *July 25* *July 26*

From looking at the map Higher Authority appeared to think that the country ahead did not present any special difficulties for tanks, nor was there any knowledge of defensive lines similar to that which the Brigade had just breached. But in fact both these assumptions were errors. Monte Collegalle had been an important buttress of the enemy's *Olga* line covering the approaches to Florence, and behind *Olga* stood other buxom *frauleins*. First came *Paula* shielding Strada in Chianti, and on the great Impruneta feature an anonymous *Mädchen* stood guard. But the existence of these sirens being unknown, an air of some optimism prevailed outside the ranks of the fighting troops, and there was gay talk of a speedy and heroic entrance into Florence.

On the 27th the Armoured Brigade set out in an attempt to advance north-westward from Greve, and, on the Guards Brigade's front, for the first time since the summer offensive began, the Pretoria Regiment led the advance fighting as a complete armoured regiment. It was not long before they came face to face with the powerful array of weapons at *Paula's* disposal: Tiger tanks, S.P.s, 88-mm. and smaller anti-tank guns covering a well-sited minefield. These were deployed to defend Strada in Chianti, and when the tanks breasted the Poggio a Mandorli (known more familiarly as Point 302) it was plain that independent armoured advance was impracticable. *July 27*

Point 302 was part of a flat bare ridge, the crest of which lay a mile south of Strada. The Coldstream in support of the Pretoria Regiment immediately made to occupy it, but the intensity of the mortar fire and the determination of the defenders, of whom many had been by-passed by the tanks, made the position of their forward companies precarious in the extreme, particularly that of No. 4 Company which

July 28 — was cut off from all supplies of food and water and from medical assistance on the southern slope of 302. In the early morning B Company was ordered to relieve No. 4 Company. It was hoped that, with the tanks as an advance guard, this would prove a relatively easy matter, but this time even the Pretoria Regiment were unable to do the trick quickly. Although the tanks engaged them with every weapon, the 356th Division fought fanatically, and individual Germans were seen standing on top of 302 firing their Spandaus from the hip at the advancing tanks. Eventually in the early afternoon, when proper liaison had been established with the tanks, Captain Hague led a bayonet charge and got his men up on to the ridge, where they dug in just below the summit in close proximity to the enemy and in a position which unfortunately gave good targets for the German snipers. The charge had been most strongly opposed, young Germans firing their automatic weapons to the end; not one was seen to surrender or to retire. After dark Right Flank took over the Coldstream company's position, and Left Flank went on to the top to

July 29 — reinforce B Company; on the next evening C Company came up on Right Flank's left. From its original weak strength of eighty men B Company lost twenty killed and wounded, the latter including one of the platoon commanders, Captain J. V. Rob, who was badly hit. There were still enemy on the crest of the ridge firing down over the slope which our men occupied, and the *Paula* line was in no wise broken. The Coldstream had been relieved in one of the bitterest battles of the advance, but there were yet to come three days of most uncomfortable war on the bare ground south of Strada.

Apart from the stoutness of the resistance to the immediate front, the main reasons for the lack of progress lay on the flanks. On the left the Armoured Brigade had been unable to take the high ground about Impruneta, and on the right the even higher mass of Monte Scalari still withstood the 4th British Division, who were coping with a harpy named *Lydia*. From Scalari the enemy could direct with accuracy his artillery on to the exposed positions of the Scots Guards on the ridge, and from their posts near the Battalion his infantry could prevent the laying of mines which would give protection against any counter-attack supported by tanks. Plans for the Grenadiers to pass through to take Strada were abandoned; the ordeal must be patiently endured.

July 30 — During the 30th the hostile artillery gradually slackened, and on that day it became possible to replace B Company on the top of the ridge with a company of the First City/The Cape Town Highlanders. That day also Colonel Wynne Finch, now commanding the Regiment, visited the Battalion to see for himself the difficulties with which it was faced. That night it became clear that things were beginning to

July 31 — move on other sectors; the next day the New Zealanders away to the left made rapid progress towards the city; and heavy explosions during the night told of destruction by the retreating enemy. On the morning of the 1st August they had gone; the Natal Mounted Rifles and the Pretoria Regiment went forward to Strada; and at the same time troops of the 4th Division, which had finally overcome Monte Scalari, entered the village from the east. The fight on Point 502 had been a severe test for a battalion by no means at full strength and one which, since arriving before Sarteano six weeks ago, had been in almost continuous contact with the enemy. Great credit goes to Colonel Cardiff and all who led it in that trying advance, and in particular, on this occasion, to Captain Hague, who, for his gallantry with B Company before Strada, was awarded a Bar to his Military Cross.

August 1

It fell to the Grenadiers to subdue the *Mädchen* on the Impruneta ridge, and to the Coldstream to cover the next three miles before the outskirts of Florence were reached. On the evening of the 3rd five huge explosions were heard, which marked the destruction of all the Florentine bridges save the Ponte Vecchio, but including the beautiful Trinitá. Half an hour before midnight Colonel Cardiff gave out his orders for the last lap of the advance into the City of Flowers.

Aug. 2

Aug. 3

The enemy had declared Florence an open city, and General Leese had no intention of continuing warlike operations which would result in further damage to so famous a centre of civilisation. The main force of the Eighth Army was now being regrouped eastwards for the assault on the Gothic Line near the Adriatic coast, and therefore there was no great military urgency to push on to occupy the whole of the city, the greater part of which lies to the north of the Arno. In that part of Florence a state of anarchy prevailed; it was the last hours of Mussolini's Fascist Republic. Rival bands of partisans, representing the several factions into which Italy was rent, roamed the streets, cloaking in the guise of summary justice the settlement of personal and political vendettas. The mass of the population cowered in their houses, longing for the arrival of the Allies with law and order in their train; but wider military requirements and the desire to spare the architectural beauties of the city precluded an immediate crossing to the north bank. The bitterness which many Florentines felt at this—to them—inexplicable delay has not yet entirely evaporated. It left them to the mercy of a reign of terror such as had not been seen in Italy for many centuries.

On the morning of the 4th August the city on both sides of the Arno was quiet and still as the Scots Guards moved in through the southern outskirts. The Companies were posted on the last ridge overlooking the Pitti Palace, San Miniato and the suburb of Ricorboli. From the Torre al Gallo, once used by Galileo as an observatory, the Intelligence Staff and the gunners had an uninterrupted view over the city to the hills beyond. Although it proved impossible to depress sufficiently the astronomical telescope, another large glass was brought

Aug. 4

to bear, and with its aid the gunners engaged enemy transport seen moving northwards on the roads running to Bologna through Prato and Fiesole. The sole remaining bridge, the Ponte Vecchio, afforded no passage to the other bank, for, though they had spared this celebrated mediæval relic, the Germans had taken good care thoroughly to demolish all approaches to it by blowing down the adjacent buildings. First to reach the Arno had been patrols from the Imperial Light Horse/Kimberly Regiment, and when Right Flank pushed one of its platoons to the water front between the destroyed bridges of San Niccolo and Alle Grazie, Lieutenant H. N. Snell was killed and others of his platoon wounded by a single Spandau firing from across the water. That day, too, the Battalion suffered another grievous loss when the Pioneer Officer, Lieutenant H. A. W. Smith, was blown up in his jeep by a mine. Up to that date, for the only time in the whole campaign, fatalities among the junior officers had been notable by their absence; it was a vicious fate which claimed these two on this penultimate day in the line.

Aug. 5 By darkness sections had been established at several places near the river, Right Flank placing one near where Lieutenant Snell had been killed, and from which he was valiantly avenged by another of his company's officers. Armed with a sniper's rifle Lieutenant Sir David Moncreiffe posted himself at the window of a house with a good view of the far bank, and his patience, courage and marksmanship were rewarded by a bag of no less than five of the enemy killed and by a

Aug. 6 very considerable reduction in enemy activity. When on the 6th the Battalion handed over its positions to the Royal Canadian Regiment, quiet had once again descended on the Arno. The advance from Cassino was at an end.

The Battalion drove south to another famous Italian city: Siena, for so long the bitter rival of Florence. Here the Scots Guards rested for an all too brief fortnight, and here, in the intervals between leave, sports, concerts and "smokers", they could number their losses and measure their achievements. On the road from Cassino four officers and thirty-four men had been killed, and eight officers and a hundred and sixty men had been wounded; the whole Brigade Group had suffered just over one thousand casualties, of which eight hundred had fallen on the three Guards Battalions and one hundred and fifty on the Pretoria Regiment. The incidence of casualties is notoriously a matter of luck, but it was observed by one independent witness that those of the Scots Guards were considerably smaller than those of the other two battalions, a gratifying circumstance he attributed to the excellent tactics and eye for country of the commanders of the rifle companies. It was their men who had borne the brunt of the losses, and it was to their credit that the Companies had retained their fighting qualities to the end of the advance.

Of the achievements there could be no doubt. Perhaps they were not very sensational in the journalistic sense; as far as hard work went the Brigade had done its full share. It had taken 370 prisoners, and killed and wounded some hundreds more of the enemy. In two months the Division had come nearly three hundred miles as the crow flies; as the roads and diversions took it, it had come 601. The field and tank gunners had fired 200,000 rounds of 25-pounder and 75-mm. ammunition, and the Sappers had constructed sixty-four Bailey bridges, and had surmounted 196 major road demolitions. Plainly the advance had been a triumph of all arms in concert, and none had worked in greater harmony than the British and South African soldiers of the 24th Guards Brigade Group.

The Regiment could take a special pride in Brigadier Clive's staff, for the entire Operations Branch of his Headquarters was found from its officers: Major T. F. R. Bulkeley, Brigade Major; Captain C. P. Whitehead, GSO III; Captain A. R. A. Hobson, Intelligence Officer; and Lieutenant A. L. Logue, Liaison Officer. These officers saw to it that the traditions of their Regiment were occasionally maintained in the mess. One evening, to entertain some Italian guests, they produced Lance-Corporal J. Roe to play the pipes round the table after dinner. In order that their guests might be acquainted with the names of the tunes, the programme was translated by the Italian Liaison Officer. Strange-sounding phrases which would have confounded the judges at Inverness or Portree made all crystal clear to the Italians; among the tunes were *Le colline di Mar* (The Braes of Mar); *Venendo via il grano* (Coming through the rye); *Il vento che fa ondeggiare il grano* (The wind that shakes the barley); and, perhaps, most exotic of all, *Il gonnellino e il mio orgoglio*, which is to say, The kilt is my delight.

(ii) *Up the Tiber and down the Arno: S Company*

While the First Battalion had been crossing the hills to Florence, S Company had been following the river valleys. The 6th Armoured Division, at first in the X Corps under Lieutenant-General Sir Richard McCreery, drove up the Tiber to take Perugia; later the division was transferred to the XIII Corps under which it took Arezzo and fought its way down the valley of the upper Arno.

The first stage of the advance under the X Corps was up the Via Salaria towards Terni. Whereas the 24th Guards Brigade had gone up west of the Tiber, the 1st went up the eastern bank. On the 7th June the 2nd Coldstream began to move slowly forward in the wake of the 3rd Grenadiers, and it was not until two days later that it was their turn to go into the lead. After crossing the River Farfa below the Monti Sabini, the column, which included tanks of the 17th/21st Lancers, came to a halt before a narrow and easily defended gorge

June 7

June 9

through which passes the road, railway and river. The infantry had to seize the hills dominating this defile; at dusk S Company took part in the advance, reaching its particular hill on the right of the gorge against little opposition save from shelling. Later in the night other companies passed through, and for the great majority of the Company

June 10 the advance of the Grenadiers and the 3rd Welsh Guards next day marked the end of the danger of the Farfa crossing. But further back near Poggio Mirteto station, Lieutenant-Colonel Norman's headquarters came in for a brief bout of extremely heavy and accurate shelling in which five officers, including the Commanding Officer, and five other ranks were hit; among the killed was CQMS A. McDade, who had given sterling service to S Company when the problems of supply were at their most difficult and dangerous in Cassino. In the reorganisation which followed Major R. E. J. C. M. Coates succeeded to the command of the Battalion, which he retained for the remainder of S Company's stay with it, and CQMS J. McLay joined the Company.

The advance was now resumed by the other Brigades in the Division, the 26th Armoured being supported by the Green Jackets of the 61st Infantry. Behind these S Company moved in daily, jerky bounds up the Via Flaminia, leaving the Tiber to pass by Narni and Todi, and later rejoining the river a few miles to the south of the ancient and

June 17 learned city of Perugia. Four miles south of this city on its hill the advance was brought to a halt, for the Division here came up against Kesselring's Trasimene Line of delay, with which the First Battalion also was about to contend thirty miles away to the west at Sarteano.

Perugia itself was not included in the enemy's defensive lay-out, but two days of patrolling and of flanking advances were to pass before

June 18 it could be entered. On the night of the 18th two patrols from the Company attempted to enter the outskirts from east and west, but before they could reach even these, they both ran into enemy in strength; in the confusion of one of these fights Sergeant Bailey and

June 19 two others were taken prisoner. The next day was memorable for a
June 20 depressing deluge, but early on the 20th the forward Coldstream companies found the lower part around the railway station to be clear, and later in the morning patrols entered the upper part of the city whose inhabitants expressed their joy at their liberation with gratifying enthusiasm. But though the Germans had left Perugia they had not left the higher hills immediately to the north of it, which they intended to retain as long as was necessary to their scheme of retreat.

All three battalions of the 1st Guards Brigade were given tasks of seizing various summits from which the Germans had good observation over Perugia and the wide plain beyond: Monte Pacciano was the height which concerned the Coldstream. In the late afternoon S Company led off, and after a brief encounter with some enemy sections, established itself some three hundred yards from the top.

Next afternoon, on which two Scots Guardsmen were killed by shell-fire, the Coldstream companies came up in positions of support, and a plan could now be hatched for the final clearing of the summit. To this end numerous patrols were required to spy out the land and the strength of the enemy, the chief centre of interest being a wooded gully which ran between the Coldstream and the Welsh Guards on the left. In this gully on the 25th a Coldstream patrol got into difficulties, and a patrol from S Company under Lieutenant the Hon. C. J. Dalrymple was sent to succour it, and itself brought back valuable information of the enemy's defences. Late on that evening a platoon of the Company occupied a large white farmhouse which gave protection to the Battalion's forming up area, and half an hour after midnight the advance of the Coldstream companies began. In the small hours against considerable opposition from Spandau posts all three Battalions of the Brigade reached their objectives, and the Germans were denied their observation over Perugia. After their week on Monte Pacciano S Company were grateful for a couple of nights in that almost undamaged city.

_{June 21}
_{June 25}
_{June 26}

On the 2nd July the Battalion was off again, moving round the south of Lake Trasimene to Castiglione Fosco, a rear area from which the first leave parties left for the Coldstream rest camp newly established in Perugia, and which S Company were kindly invited to share. Then by short marches the column moved up the west shore of the lake until on the evening of the 6th July it harboured beneath the prominent rock of Cortona; here a week was spent preparing for the next assault.

_{July 2}
_{July 6}

The XIIIth Corps, to which the 6th Armoured Division had been switched, was now facing the Arezzo Line, and on the 78th Division's sector Monte Lignano was its chief bastion. This and other hills to the east again gave the Germans perfect observation over the advancing British, and on Lignano were battalions of one of their best divisions, the 15th Panzer Grenadiers. The 2nd New Zealand Division was to be brought up to attack the summits of Lignano and of other hills to the east, while the 1st Guards Brigade had come up to attack the north-western ridge of Lignano and another smaller hill on the left of the main road north of the junction with the Siena road. The pass through which the road ran to Arezzo would then be forced, and the tanks of the Armoured Brigade could go through to take the city.

The week which was required to get the New Zealanders forward from the Liri valley allowed ample time for reconnaissance, and during it every section commander was shewn the objectives from a convenient spot on the floor of the Val di Chiana, and every Company Commander was able to fly over the ridge in an artillery spotting aircraft to examine its peculiarities at closer range. Captain Neilson, D.S.O., who with Lieutenant Charteris, M.C., had now rejoined S

Company from hospital, made one of these flights. Air photographs and sand models were also used in this thorough briefing.

July 14

On the night of the 14th July the move forward for the attack began. The 2nd Coldstream, which now had but three rifle companies, Nos. 2, 4 and S, lay out that night in the lower slopes of Lignano, while in

July 15

the darkness the Grenadiers made the first assault on the hamlet of Stoppiace and the feature known as Point 575, both about half a mile north-west of the summit of Lignano, which was simultaneously under attack from the New Zealanders. Just before dawn the Grenadiers reported themselves on their objectives, and the companies waiting lower down the hill hauled themselves to their feet, and began the arduous climb to the battlefield. No 4 Company went first, arriving about eleven o'clock, in time to assist the Grenadiers retake Point 575, off which they had been pushed by a counter-attack. The situation being restored it was now possible for S Company's part in the battle to begin. At about the same time, twenty-five miles to the west, the First Battalion was knocking down the gate of Castel di Brolio.

From Point 575 a long undulating ridge ran north-westwards down to the main road. This ridge was covered with farms and cultivation, and the task of the Battalion was to take several successive features on it. No. 4 Company led and took the first objective, Point 565, after which S Company was called upon to pass through to take the next feature, Point 501. Before it had passed through the Coldstreamers Captain Neilson stepped on a *schu*-mine and was mortally wounded. About half-past three Lieutenant Charteris took command and led the Company into its hardest attack.

The Panzer Grenadiers fought stubbornly. S Company wormed its way up the slope, using grenade and bayonet to subdue the defenders; it reached the top of 501, but the fierceness of the fire encountered from the reverse slope prevented any advance beyond the crest. Lieutenant Charteris was severely wounded; CSM Brown, D.C.M., Lance-Sergeant Jones, M.M., and four others besides were killed, and ten more wounded. The depleted Company stuck doggedly to its gains under Lieutenant Wilson, the sole surviving officer. Heroic work was done that day by Sergeant W. Young and Lance-Sergeant A. MacPhail, on both of whom devolved the command of platoons. Sergeant Young was untiring in siting Bren guns in positions from which they could do the greatest damage to the enemy, in passing back information about targets for the supporting artillery, and in encouraging his men under the trials of heavy mortar and shellfire. In the initial assault Lance-Sergeant MacPhail had commanded the leading section and at a range of but twenty yards had silenced with two bombs from a P.I.A.T. a dugout which was a nodal point of the German defences.

While the struggle progressed, for two hours, Colonel Coates had no news of the Company, and it was not until after dark that it was possible for him to send No. 2 Company through S Company to clear the reverse slope of 501. Just after ten o'clock the Coldstreamers found the Germans gone, and early next morning the Welsh Guards passed through and down the ridge to clear the whole feature as far as the road and to occupy the smaller hill beyond it. At dawn the 16th/5th Lancers rattled up the road; by ten o'clock they were in Arezzo.

_{July 16}

By the death of Captain Neilson the Regiment sustained a severe loss.[1] There can be no doubt that it was he who imbued S Company with the dash and fighting spirit which carried it to its objectives on Monte Piccolo and Monte Lignano, and with the grim determination which kept it on them. It had been no easy task for one with no previous battle experience to bring into a Battalion with the traditions of Dunkirk and "Longstop" behind it a new company, the training of which was based on the theories of a Battle School at home. Although the experienced Coldstreamers may at first have smiled indulgently at S Company's disruptively painted equipment and at its bursting, almost naive, enthusiasm, Piccolo and Lignano had proved that the ideas which permeated the Company were sound; and to these ideas was now added an invaluable tradition of its own, a tradition which did not die with Captain Neilson and CSM Brown.

For his gallantry in the action Sergeant Young was awarded the Distinguished Conduct Medal, and was promoted Company Sergeant-Major; Lance-Sergeant MacPhail received the Military Medal. To command the Company came Major R. L. Coke, M.C., who had commanded F Company alongside the Grenadiers on Monte Camino; he was to command S Company for the remainder of the war.

For the ten days following the capture of Arezzo the 2nd Coldstream remained at rest in the valley below Monte Lignano. On the morning of the 26th the Company had the honour of finding part of the Battalion contingent which lined the road for the visit of His Majesty the King; in the evening came a move forward towards the front again.

July 26

For the next three weeks the 6th Armoured Division advanced slowly down the Arno towards its junction with the Sieve at Pontassieve. The river ran through a green and fertile valley, to the west of which rose the Chianti Mountains; to the east rose the great watershed of the Prato Magno. It was to the lower slopes of this mountain that S Company was called forward. For nearly a week it was in static positions to the north-east of Montevarchi, acting as flank guard to the Division. This proved an unexacting task, and one which was succeeded by greater activity on the night of the 1st/2nd August.

[1] A month previously his mother had been killed in the Guards' Chapel disaster.

Aug. 1	On that night the 1st Guards Brigade, now commanded by Brigadier C. A. M. D. Scott, took over from the Green Jackets five miles south of Cancelli, and then began a week of slow and difficult advance supported by tanks of the Derbyshire Yeomanry and the 2nd Lothian and Border Horse. Opposition from enemy infantry was slight, and the main difficulties came as usual from the wiles and destruction of the German sappers, and from the observation posts of the enemy's mortar and artillery batteries. The main road to Florence lay on the left bank of the river, so that on the right the advance was confined to narrow, third-class tracks which wound their way from village to village through the luxuriant crops, nearly ripe for the harvest. It was slow work, and unspectacular, this progress from one village to another. In the matter of casualties S Company were luckier than the others; nevertheless Lieutenant J. F. W. Lloyd-Johnes was severely
Aug. 5	wounded by shellfire while firing a P.I.A.T. at the enemy during the attack on Santa Agata, and CQMS McLay was killed and his
Aug. 6	driver wounded when the Company carrier was blown up on a mine while bringing up the rations. By the end of the week, the Battalion had made little progress beyond Santa Agata, and it was with thank-
Aug. 9	fulness that it retired to a large villa in the valley to rest. In this
Aug. 13	"gigantic and extremely vulgar" billet it was left for three days, before returning for a final spell of four days in the line south of
Aug. 18	Rignano. On the 18th August it was relieved in these positions, and drove back to the neighbourhood of San Giovanni for a longer period of rest and refreshment. S Company's part in the summer advance was over; now at last some managed to see Rome, which had been bypassed in so tantalising a fashion two months before.

The road from Cassino had been a hard one, and a bloody one. In the Company, the full, though rarely attained establishment of which was five officers and one hundred and twenty men, three officers and twenty-four men had been killed, four officers and about forty men had been wounded, and five men had been taken prisoner. These casualties, amounting in three months to two-thirds of the establishment in other ranks, show at what cost was created, maintained and handed on the traditions of S Company.

V. THE APENNINES

MAP
XXVIII   In late August 1944, on every front, the war seemed to be moving towards an early conclusion. In the east the Russians were at the gates of Warsaw; from Normandy the armoured divisions were racing towards the Rhine; in the South of France French and American troops were marching up the Rhône; in Germany the July revolt of the General Staff officers had exposed to the people the pessimistic view these experts took of the future. In Italy huge losses had been

Map XXIV

inflicted on Kesselring's armies, and it seemed that a break-out into the flat valley of the Po was imminent. In this supposedly easy country it was hoped that the six Allied armoured divisions would at last reap the harvest of mobile warfare. Despite their weariness the armies were infected with spirits predominantly optimistic, although the more cautious were quick to qualify confident predictions of an easy conquest of the Apennines with a rider that it would be gratifying if hostilities ended before General Alexander called on them to storm the Alps. Those who had experienced the cold and wet of the previous Italian winter had no desire to spend another in either range of mountains. Thus when in October it became clear that the winter was indeed to be sat out in the mountains and on the river banks below Comacchio, the troops were swept by a wave of disenchantment.

The main reasons for the autumn failure were two. The first was the deprivation of the American Fifth Army of more than half its strength; the divisions which were marching up the Rhône had come in the main from the Italian front, and with them had gone the remarkable French mountaineers who General Alexander had hoped to send across the Central Apennines to Bologna in like manner as he had sent them across the Aurunci Mountains to the Liri valley earlier in the year. In consequence there were sufficient resources for one army only to attack at any one time. That first attack was mounted by the Eighth Army at the Adriatic end of the Gothic Line, and, in a month of bitter fighting, the line was broken, but at such a cost of casualties, exhaustion and ammunition that it could go no farther. Moreover, the plain the Army reached proved not to be the paradise for tanks that had been hoped. The south-eastern part of the Po valley resembles in many respects the more familiar lowlands of Holland, being intersected with numerous dykes and water-courses, now brim-full with the autumn rains. The soggy fields off the embanked roads were impassable to a mechanised army. In the mud of the Romagna, as in the fens of Holland, the hopes of August were submerged.

The activities of the Scots Guards that autumn and winter were confined to the mountains. They took no part in the direct assault on the Gothic Line, but the First Battalion was heavily engaged in the subsequent attempt to reach Bologna by the shortest route on the Fifth Army front. When that attempt was halted, the Battalion spent the winter at its furthest point of advance in the southern slopes of Monte Sole. When relieved in February it had been in the line almost continuously for six months. S Company's last months of independent existence was spent on the higher mountain tops farther to the east, and included another of those smart assaults at which it could justly claim to have become expert.

(a) *The Autumn Advance*
The First Battalion

August
The fortnight the First Battalion had spent at rest near Siena had been welcome and necessary, but annoyingly brief, and, in reality, insufficient. With the Eighth Army about to assault in the east, in the west the line of the Arno was to be held from Pontassieve to the sea by the Fifth Army. On the right was the British XIII Corps; in the region of Florence the American II Corps; and extended from the outskirts of Florence to Pisa was the American IV Corps. These three corps were under orders from General Clark to tie down in front of them as many enemy divisions as they could, and, when the moment seemed opportune, to attack the mountain section of the Gothic Line. It was intended that the II Corps should make the main effort northwards from Florence, but in the event all three were involved in heavy fighting. It was to the thinly-spread IV Corps (Lieutenant-General W. Crittenberger) that the 6th South African Division was called forward to hold a stretch of the Arno from Florence to the Fucecchio marshes. The 24th Guards Brigade was given the western part of this

Aug. 24
line, and by midnight on the 24th August, having driven forward by way of Poggibonsi and Castel Fiorentino, the Scots Guards had relieved a battalion of the United States 85th Division on a mile and a half front north of the village of Bastia. It was the first time since Anzio they had relieved Americans in the line, a circumstance in which British troops always felt themselves compensated by the quantities of discarded rations and equipment Uncle Sam's prodigal nephews were wont to leave behind.

Aug. 25
The Battalion lay with three companies up, each a few hundred yards back from the river bank. There were still a few German pockets used as patrol bases holding out on the south bank, where the ground was flat and very enclosed. Consequently the only effective observation for the forward troops was from the upper storeys of the numerous farms and villages: from the *casas*, as the troops called them. On the north bank there ran a range of small rounded hills, none of them more than a couple of hundred feet high, on which the enemy had his inevitable observation posts controlling the fire of his guns and mortars. As usual these proved to be his most troublesome weapons, inflicting a dozen casualties on the companies in the coming week. Further to the north, some fifteen miles away, could be seen the first ridges of the Apennines: along their skyline, three thousand feet above the plain, ran the Gothic Line.

Before the main defences could be approached it was painfully obvious that the Arno would have to be crossed. In consequence the activities of the Brigade were directed to clearing the remaining Germans from the south bank, and to reconnoitring the river for crossing places suitable for men and vehicles. The very night after the Battalion's arrival an enemy patrol tried to penetrate its positions, and by day cautious observers recorded enemy defences to the north. Strict instructions not to disclose to the enemy the relief of the Americans by the South Africans were somewhat compromised when over-friendly civilians in San Miniato replaced a prominent Stars and Stripes with an equally prominent Union Jack; but perhaps more revealing of a change of tenure was the bombardment by the Battalion's mortars of a party of Germans seen bathing in the river. Plainly the previous tenants of the Scots Guards' sector had had some tacit arrangement whereby the naked were immune from the horrors of war! Aug. 26

There was one particular enemy post on the south bank which occupied Right Flank's attention. One night a small patrol under Lieutenant the Hon. D. A. Bethell, M.C. had crept to within fifty yards of it, but there Lieutenant Bethell trod on a mine, the explosion of which wounded him severely and more slightly two of his men. There had been a painful crawl back to safety, and Lieutenant Bethell was brought back by a stretcher-bearer party protected and led by Sir David Moncrieffe. The enemy post was not left in peace for long, for early in the morning of the 31st the Pretoria Regiment attempted along the south bank an armoured sweep, which floundered about in the minefields and close country. Decisive results were achieved later in the day when Major Mann led two platoons supported by a tank against the position; in the dark the garrison was chased back across the Arno, leaving one prisoner to compensate for another two men wounded. That evening came the order to cross on the night of the morrow. Aug. 29 Aug. 31

On the 28th news had been received of the initial success of the Eighth Army's attack; all the divisions of the Fifth intensified their efforts to keep occupied the enemy on their respective fronts. An opposed night crossing of the Arno by the South African Division was contemplated, but, to the relief of all, on the 1st September it was clear that the enemy was withdrawing; the Coldstream and Scots Guards were ordered to send patrols to the north bank without delay. In the early afternoon platoons waded across the shallow, yellowish river; there was no opposition. The remainder of the Battalion followed, carefully picking its way through the numerous minefields the enemy had sown in the banks. By teatime the low hills from which the Germans had dominated the companies on the south bank were securely held all along the Brigade front, and a further half-mile was covered before darkness fell. That night patrols probed deeply forward, one from the Battalion finding Cerreto Guidi, the Brigade's central objective in the crossing operation, clear of enemy. Soon after dawn the village was occupied in force, patrols renewed their Sept. 1 Sept. 2

explorations, and B Company was despatched as flank guard to Vinci, birthplace of Leonardo.

At Vinci Major Hague acquired a fourth platoon. This was composed of a band of Russians who had deserted from the German army some months before, and which was led by a French-speaking officer. During the two weeks of their attachment the Russians performed their military duties efficiently, though the punishments with which their leader enforced discipline may have erred on the side of severity. Two men, one who got drunk and one who went to sleep on sentry, were shot out of hand. On joining B Company there had been seventeen Russians, but how many had been "disciplined" since deserting the Germans was never discovered.

For the next week the Brigade advanced across the flat plain south of Montecatini, overlooked on the right by the Monti Albano, of which the South Africans took care, and bounded on the left by the marshes, which were impassable and thus took care of themselves. The real hard work fell on the Natal Mounted Rifles; behind their armoured reconnaissance screen the Guardsmen moved forward with stately leisure, more in the manner of an army in the aristocratic days of Louis XIV than of one designed for the vulgar bustle of the *Blitzkrieg*.

Sept. 7

By the 7th the line of the demolished arches of the *autostrada* had been reached, and numerous contacts had been made with the partisans, who were already in control of the ancient city of Pistoia, the spa of Montecatini, and the town of Monsumano, in whose nearby caves Kesselring had made his headquarters after being chased by the South Africans from his previous hideout on Monte Sorrate.

The partisans the Battalion had dealt with previously had been of varying quality; but there could be no doubt of the patriotism and military value of those it found in the Val d'Arno. Here was a region with a long tradition of civic pride, and a cradle of modern civilisation. The hatred which its inhabitants felt towards the *Tedeschi* from the north had been intensified by the recent barbaric massacre of four hundred Italian hostages on the road south from Monsumano. It was greatly to the credit of the enraged Italians that they handed over to the Allies the prisoners they took, instead of disposing of them in summary fashion, as too often happened in their quarterless battles behind the German lines. Furthermore a live demoralised prisoner was a more trustworthy source of accurate intelligence than was a cock-a-hoop desperado. From the jig-saw of captured maps and men, of loquacious partisans and silent air-photographs, a clear picture of the next obstacle began to emerge. The Gothic Line in the hills beyond the *autostrada* now claimed the Brigade's attention.

Sept. 8

On the 8th the Battalion began a fortnight of steady ascent up the great chestnut-covered ridges which led northwards to the dreaded line. Patrol bases were established in the stout stone villages and farms; from these garrisons, both by day and by night, small parties sallied forth to spy out the land ahead. It was a period which imposed a very heavy strain on the company officers and non-commissioned officers, and, to make life even more burdensome, the ascent into the mountains coincided with a break in the weather and the coming of colder nights. Cold and rain had to be endured in summer clothing. Instead of the relatively lavish comforts obtainable from motor transport in the plain, the forward troops "on the hill" had to make do with the more frugal capacity of the mule. The company positions were on the spurs and in the valleys, running approximately north and south, while the enemy sat on the high ground at the head of the rise. The two main features with which the Scots Guards were concerned were the ridge of Feminamorta and the lower slopes of Monte Bersano a mile to the east, both of them rising to more than three thousand feet. From every source of intelligence it was clear that Feminamorta was a main bastion of the line, and great was the consternation throughout the Brigade when it was suggested from on high that here might be a suitable place to break into the defences by a frontal attack, apparently with no additional support other than a fourth battalion. All the efforts of the Pretoria Regiment to get their tanks high enough up the steep, treacherous slopes were in vain, and without their close support the prospect seemed bleak indeed. But it all came to naught, and the Brigade was spared to fight another day.

In the second week it became clear that there was considerable enemy movement on the front, and since this was thought to indicate that the defenders were thinning out to reinforce their Adriatic flank, the Brigade was goaded on to yet more aggressive patrolling. This effort was satisfactory from the point of view of the wider plan; on a local level it attracted some unwelcome neighbours. For some days there had been disquieting rumours of the arrival in the area of the 16th SS Panzer Grenadier Division. It was vital to discover the truth or otherwise of these reports, and a Company raid by Right Flank was ordered to secure a prisoner. While Major Mann and Sir David Moncreiffe were engaged near the top of Feminamorta in the final reconnaissance for this raid, they chanced upon a German. The third member of their party, Guardsman Copland, Sir David's servant, shot the German dead. The need for the raid had passed; the body was that of an SS man. The reaction of Authority was to prepare against a spoiling attack by this high-class formation justifiably suspected of "offensive habits", both military and political. But again panic subsided.

Sept. 14

Sept. 21

It was events further east which dictated the enemy's movements. By the 21st September the United States II Corps had stormed the Giogo and Futa Passes on Route 65 to Bologna. The latter pass had been guarded by some of the most formidable defences in the whole line, and its loss, combined with the Eighth Army's penetration in the east, finally convinced the enemy that the whole Gothic position must be abandoned. The only hope remaining was that of holding the Allies in the foothills but fifteen miles south of the Via Æmilia. All Kesselring's efforts were now concentrated on this object; by dogged fighting and skilful generalship he succeeded until the spring.

Sept. 23 From the 23rd the main task of the Brigade was to protect the left flank of the Motor Brigade advancing up Route 64; later it was expected that the Guards would conform up Route 66. For the Battalion this meant that now they alone were concerned with
Sept. 25 Feminamorta, and on the 25th, Left Flank penetrated to the very wire of the defences without encountering any opposition save a "stonk" on the return journey. That afternoon the Company held positions very near the top. Only feeble rearguards had been left to
Sept. 26 watch from the once-vaunted Gothic Line. The next day the Scots Guards side-stepped to their right to relieve the Grenadiers, who were
Sept. 27 to head the proposed advance up Route 66, but the morrow brought a fresh change of plan. One night's rest, including time to don the winter battledress, was all that was allowed them before they were precipitated into their fiercest action since Anzio.

* * *

The idea of advancing up Routes 64 and 66 had proved impracticable due to the thoroughness with which these two roads had been demolished. But on Route 6620 north from Prato the United States 34th Division had made remarkable progress, penetrating beyond the prepared defences to Montepiano. The South African Armoured Brigade had made equally good progress on the left of the road, and the leading troops of this brigade had reached Castiglione dei Pepoli, being charged with the duty of protecting the left flank of the II Corps. It was to reinforce the South African armour that the Guards Brigade was despatched up the road, and the battalion most readily available to head the column was that of the Scots Guards. Brigadier Clive and Colonel Cardiff set off at once to the Armoured Brigade's Headquarters, leaving instructions for the Battalion to follow early the next day.

When the two officers arrived at Montepiano the situation was by no means clear. The South Africans were out of touch with the enemy, nor had the Americans any more certain news, though they had penetrated a further couple of miles on the right. That the enemy had retreated was certain, but there was no indication as to how far, and it was even thought that he might be retiring completely from the Apennines, in which case the Brigade might have the pleasure of an almost unopposed entry into Bologna, the Mecca of Italian gastronomes. A few stragglers from the German 65th Division had been picked up, and no information was available of other German formations in the area. The "fog of war" seemed murky enough; it was rendered murkier still by a thick natural mist and heavy rain which had set in during the day, making visual reconnaissance of the ground ahead impossible. But what the two officers had seen of the road on their journey north convinced them that, until repairs could be effected, it was but a tenuous strand on which to maintain a force of any size. Also it was clear to them that there was nowhere south of Castiglione where a battalion could be deployed off the road, and that in that little town, facing up a ten mile valley, there was insufficient cover should the weather clear and the enemy be able to see the place from the hills to the north. Already he had put some large 210 mm. shells into it, and no doubt a worthwhile target would attract more. In order that the whole Brigade could deploy it was intended to deny the enemy observation over Castiglione. For the reasons previously given it was deemed unsafe to send forward the whole of the Scots Guards; therefore Colonel Cardiff called forward half the Battalion, with the intention of directing them on to Pallazzo, a hamlet near the crown of a wooded hill at the southern end of the ridge which culminates in Monte Catarelto. MAP XXV

The two Flank Companies, Battalion Headquarters, a proportion of the supporting weapons and a troop of the Pretoria Regiment set out from the well-earned comfort of a convent near Pistoia early on the morning of the 28th September. The journey to Castiglione was about thirty-five miles, but the previous pessimistic view of the road's capacity was confirmed; the column took eight hours to cover the distance, arriving in drenching rain at about four o'clock. Battalion Headquarters was established in the town, and at about dusk the two companies left their transport and set off for their objectives. These were some two and a half miles ahead, visibility in the mist was down to a hundred yards, the advance was over ground neither of the company commanders had seen before, and there was no knowing what enemy might be met. Major Harvey led Left Flank northwards following the line of the road, and by half-past six, having encountered but scanty opposition, he had established the company on the lower slope of the ridge dominating the road a thousand yards south-west of Pallazzo. Further east Right Flank's advance was more difficult. Major Mann had been directed to follow the line of what appeared from the maps to be a long straight track keeping to the highest part of the ridge leading up to Pallazzo; but the "track" was nowhere to be seen on the ground—which was hardly surprising, since in reality it was the longest railway tunnel in Italy, which carried the *direttissima* railway from Bologna to Florence, and which was one of the showpieces of Fascist engineering! But at length Right Flank reached Pallazzo about ten o'clock that night, having had to contend with Sept. 28

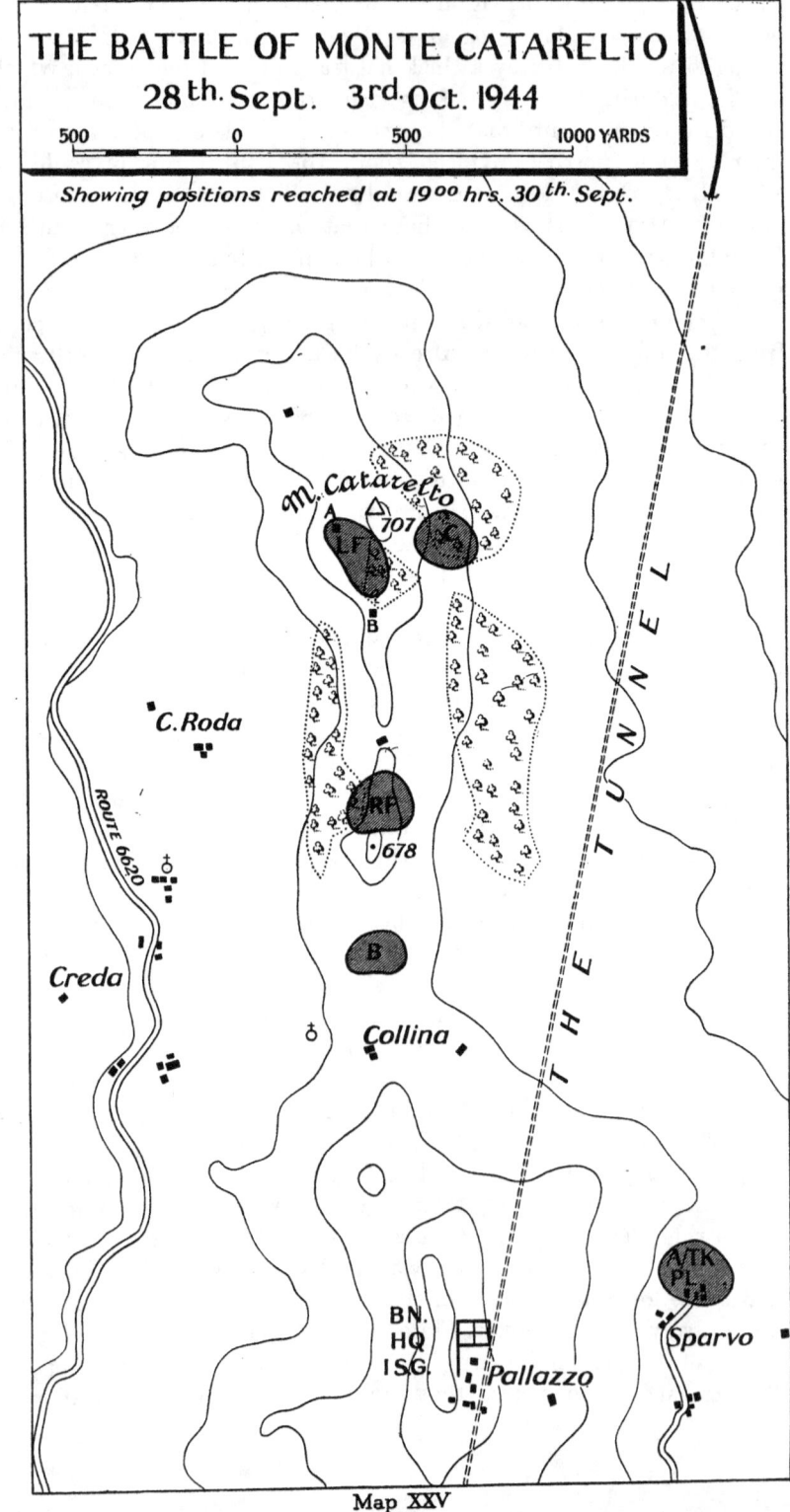

muddy slopes, scrubby woods, pitchy darkness, but no enemy. However they did manage to secure one more deserter from the 65th Division. Across to the west of Route 6620 an Indian battalion (the 4th Battalion 13th Frontier Force Rifles) had been placed on the high ground a little to the left rear of the Scots Guards, and it was now considered safe for the remainder of the Battalion to come up to Castiglione. It was to arrive at eleven the next morning, when the Battalion would be complete and ready for battle.

The wider Brigade plan envisaged the capture of the summit of Catarelto by the Scots Guards, then an advance by the 3rd Coldstream to the Bucciagni spur level with Catarelto on the left of the road, and finally an advance by the freshest battalion of the Brigade, the 5th Grenadiers, to Monte Salvaro, a hill of some 2,700 feet six miles further down the valley. In view of what was known at the time of the enemy's dispositions this did not seem over-ambitious; but what was known was soon to be proved seriously at fault.

In the morning visibility had greatly improved, and soon after dawn Left Flank was engaged by mortars and machine-guns from the slopes between it and Right Flank, and also from the neighbourhood of San Rocco. Right Flank on the higher ground quickly spotted the enemy, and with the aid of the Gunners' Forward Observation Officer drove the Germans back; they retired to the houses of Creda and to the woods of the next summit on the ridge, Point 678. Half a mile beyond 678 could be seen the highest point of Catarelto, Point 707, and here the observers could see busy activity. Thus early in the action the 166th (Newfoundland) Field Regiment, R.A., had given proof that it was well qualified to replace the trusted 23rd Field Regiment, which had departed with reluctance from the Brigade Group at Siena. But as yet only one of the three batteries had come up, and the eight guns of this 136th Battery were furnished with but two hundred rounds apiece, a poor supply with which to open a prolonged engagement. *Sept. 29*

The whole Battalion would have been committed to an immediate assault had not Sir David Moncrieffe, of Right Flank, made an important discovery in an abandoned post near Pallazzo. The find was a marked enemy map, which, on being interpreted by Lieutenant Keith, yielded valuable, if depressing information. The marks disclosed that to its front lay the Battalion's former opponents on Feminamorta: the 16th SS Division. This must have made a hasty move eastwards to plug the dangerous gap developing south of Bologna. Furthermore the map revealed that Catarelto was part of a main line of resistance. Thus far the whole hierarchy of Intelligence Officers was agreed; but as to the detailed dispositions of the German division there was no unanimity. The Divisional Staff was inclined to think that only one of the SS division's two regiments was manning the whole South African front, with the other still back in the Po valley, and that, anyway, the map was out of date. Lieutenant Keith was inclined to the opinion that the map showed both regiments in the line, with two battalions on Catarelto alone, and another in reserve behind them. The more optimistic interpretation was allowed to prevail, with what unfortunate consequences will soon be seen. However, even this view made it plain that a more thorough preparation would have to be made. The assault was postponed until the morrow.

Meanwhile Colonel Cardiff brought his headquarters up to Pallazzo, where the new Adjutant, Captain A. L. Logue, fresh from the comforts of Brigade Headquarters, was rudely reintroduced to the rigours of Battalion life. All supplies had now to be brought over the wet, steep hills by mule, and the headquarters received some unaccustomed shelling. On arrival in the evening B Company (Major Hague) was posted in Sparvo to guard the right flank; C Company (Lord Hesketh) was ordered to occupy Point 678. In the face of heavy small arms fire they were unable to gain it, and dug in on the saddle to the north of Collina. Early in the night a patrol from Right Flank investigating the ridge near Point 678 found many enemy at work, and narrowly escaped capture. But it was a German patrol that produced the night's best evidence. An enemy party engaged B Company in Sparvo, losing in the scrimmage one dead; that dead man wore an SS uniform and was found to have belonged to the 35th SS Panzer Grenadier Regiment.

The task confronting the Battalion was extremely difficult. On the credit side was the fact that from Pallazzo there was excellent observation northwards all along the ridge to Point 707, enabling artillery and mortar fire to be put down with accuracy; also the position was admirable for the Vickers machine-guns, which could engage with direct fire any movement which might be seen; and, lastly, the progress of the attacking companies would be easy for the Commanding Officer to follow. Against these advantages had to be set the strength and determination of the enemy troops holding the feature. It had been universally agreed that they could scarcely be in less than company strength and that probably they were very much stronger. They were for the most part tough and fanatical Nazis who had been out of the serious fighting since July and were probably spoiling for a fight. Furthermore the Battalion's exposed flanks and lack of support made it necessary to maintain a firm base around Pallazzo, precluding the employment of the whole strength in the assault. To strengthen this base, Point 678 must be taken and firmly secured before any advance could be made to Point 707. Finally, there was no prospect of the comforting close support of the Pretoria Regiment's Shermans up the sodden hill.

At half-past eight in the morning Right Flank led off to attack Point 678; B Company followed, having been relieved in Sparvo by the Anti-Tank Platoon, acting as infantry. When Right Flank started the ascent it was met with heavy small arms fire from the wood to its front and also from Creda to its left rear; the enemy's artillery also came into play. But B Company, and C Company from their over-night position in the saddle, managed to silence the Germans in Creda, who made off towards Point 707. Right Flank wormed its way forward, being nobly assisted by Sergeant T. Taylor, who organised highly effective covering fire during the assault. The Germans began to withdraw to their main positions on 707, and Right Flank, without requiring the assistance of B Company, reached their objective and held it safe for the remainder of the action. The Company had twelve men wounded in the attack, and were to suffer further from shelling and mortaring in the next two days, during which CSM W. Robertson, who had been wounded on the first day, gave his usual splendid example of cheerfulness and endurance, refusing to leave the Company until the end of the battle.[1]

Sept. 30

Some 4·2-inch mortars of the Royal Durban Light Infantry had by now been brought into play to augment the Battalion's 3-inch weapons; all these made good practice on the reverse slopes of Catarelto throughout the action. In addition, part of the Reconnaissance Troop of the Pretoria Regiment had managed to penetrate beyond Sparvo and was able to give some support, though at long range. Finally B Company relieved C Company in the saddle, for the assault was to be made by the latter and Left Flank. It could now begin.

The two assaulting companies set off at three o'clock with Major Harvey in the lead. He took them through the woods on the eastern slope of the ridge, getting quite close to the summit before being detected, and thereby avoiding most of the defensive artillery fire which fell close behind. By half-past five Lord Hesketh had C Company firmly established in the woods on the eastern shoulder of 707, and half an hour later Left Flank, which had met stiffer opposition, had reached a track which ran along the north-western end of the wood immediately south of the summit. The SS men withdrew before the advancing Guardsmen, moving with a casualness and deliberation which, for several, can only be described as suicidal; the Machine Gun Platoon saw to that. The lack of caution displayed by the enemy throughout the action was exceptional, being one of the main reasons for their heavy casualties, and, it must be conceded, for their success. Beyond the woods lay open, harvested fields. The summit itself was rounded and coverless, save for heaps of stones which the peasants had

---

[1] At the end of the war, for the many conspicuous services he had given as Company Sergeant-Major of Right Flank the whole way from Castel di Sangro to the Po, CSM Robertson was awarded the Distinguished Conduct Medal.

removed from the fields and piled up in the manner of rough walls. In these walls and in a sunken track the SS Spandau gunners had entrenched themselves; on the reverse slope others could with ease make the bare summit untenable. Nevertheless Major Harvey led a bayonet charge which reached the crest, putting the enemy on it to flight, but to hold it in face of the fresh fire of the Germans beyond was, in the conventional if officially deprecated infantryman's phrase, "not on". Left Flank withdrew to the wood south of the summit. But some progress was maintained beyond the wood, for a platoon under Captain R. T. Hunter charged across a hundred yards of open ground to capture a small house[1] to the west and immediately below the top. This proved to be the limit of the advance. Good intentions of continuing the attack at first light next day were frustrated by the counter-attacks of the coming night. Henceforth the battle was one of defence.

Oct. 1

Left Flank were not left in peace for long. Shortly after dark the enemy started his attempts to infiltrate into the position. By midnight several counter-attacks had been launched at the platoon in the isolated house, but all had been beaten off. In addition there were diversionary movements round the rear of the Company which boded ill for the future. At midnight the platoon in the house had to be withdrawn into the wood, and for the next two hours there was some diminution in the cascade of rifle grenades and mortar bombs which had been falling among the trees. During this lull some much needed ammunition was brought forward, an undertaking of great difficulty and hazard. Its arrival was timely, for at two in the morning a more deliberate attack was launched from two directions; from the house recently vacated and from the cover of a wood to the south-west. This fell upon the left-hand platoon, which was forced to give ground further into the wood, joining up with the remainder of the Company in the southern part. The enemy now penetrated to another house[2] between the two Flank Companies, from which they could be most troublesome. When at first light they attacked in force from the west and south-west, they had the advantage of covering fire both from this house and from the north. This was the most formidable attack of all, and it called on all the fighting qualities of the depleted company to repel it. Major Harvey, by now wounded in the thigh, inspired his men to beat back the two companies which beset them: his example was taken up by many. For instance Lance-Sergeant C. H. Starkey from a shallow slit which afforded him but little protection passed back most valuable information which enabled the Newfoundland gunners to plaster the attackers with the greatest accuracy, even to within

[1] Marked A on Map XXV, which shows the positions the Companies had reached at this stage.
[2] Marked B on Map XXV.

twenty yards of our men; and Guardsman W. G. Cocker, one of the platoon runners, performed prodigies of valour with a Bren gun he had acquired; when the Bren was destroyed by shelling he was equally untiring with rifle and grenade. In the end the early morning attack was halted, that from the west by the gunners, whose whole Regiment was now in action, and that from the south-west by the small arms fire of the Company. But the position was now precarious in the extreme for the Germans were established between the Flank Companies in greater strength than before and were beginning to infiltrate between Left Flank and C Company. To complicate things still further both Left Flank's and the Gunners' wirelesses were now put out of action, whereby communications with the Commanding Officer and the Field Regiment were severed.

Though there could be no speech with Major Harvey, it was clear that his situation was desperate. B Company was ordered up to support him and, if necessary, to relieve him. Major Hague led it forward, but soon after starting it was caught by heavy defensive fire, causing casualties and disorganisation. It could not reach Left Flank, and instead joined C Company in its wood and there dug in. At half-past ten Major Harvey ordered Left Flank to withdraw, for the steadily mounting toll from sniping and mortaring had reduced the Company to but forty-five men, and he considered that the enemy penetration could be held no longer. He brought back all the survivors, and only when he was satisfied that all were accounted for did he have his wound dressed. For his gallantry on Monte Catarelto Major Harvey was awarded the Distinguished Service Order.

The withdrawal of Left Flank left B and C Companies isolated. But fortunately the enemy were smarting under the heavy shelling and mortaring, and, after a taste of Left Flank's close range fire, seemed not disposed to face that of the united Centre Companies. The SS men were content to consolidate their gains.

The Scots Guards were not now fighting alone. At dawn the Coldstream had begun to advance on Bucciagni on the far side of the road, and from the slopes of that feature the tanks were at last able to intervene in the Catarelto battle, though still at long range. The Coldstream found themselves opposed by the other regiment of the SS Division, the 36th, which identification fully confirmed the Battalion's original interpretation of the captured map, though it left those who had been in the right throughout with little more than the hollow and belated satisfaction of having told others so. The Grenadiers, too, were now at hand, and these Brigadier Clive decided to send against Catarelto the following day. In order that their supporting fire should be unimpeded, he ordered the withdrawal at last light of B and C Companies. B Company went back to its former trenches in the saddle, while C Company, which had sat tight for twenty-four hours in its allotted positions despite all the efforts of the enemy to shift it, descended to Creda. Right Flank remained on Point 678.

Oct. 2   On the 2nd October the Grenadiers went forward by much the same route and met much the same difficulties as had the Scots Guards two days before, and it was not until the Germans withdrew
Oct. 3   during the following night that the top was finally secured. An hour later Bucciagni also was reported clear and the battle of Monte Catarelto was at an end.

A careful inspection of the battlefield now revealed the true extent of the defenders' strength. A full battalion reinforced by an additional company had originally attempted to hold the mountain: a force numbering perhaps four hundred men. Further companies, making the ultimate strength about two battalions, had been brought forward during the battle. Forty bodies were found on the field, from which figures, allowing for others removed for burial before the end of the action, a conservative estimate of the total casualties was put at two hundred and fifty. It was now clear that Catarelto had been a main bastion between the SS Division and the 4th Parachute to the east, and the value of its capture was shown by the rapid advance the Americans of the II Corps were now able to make.

In numbers the Battalion had lost heavily, particularly in Left Flank. Captain R. T. Hunter, CQMS A. Coonie and twenty-two men had been killed, fifty-eight had been wounded, including Major Harvey, Lieutenant D. Tylden-Wright, CSM Robertson and CSM F. Hall, and nine men had been taken prisoners of war. The Companies were brought back for rest in Castiglione, where they received several visits of congratulation. Generals Crittenberger and Poole came to thank them for the great fight they had put up against superior odds. The Battalion had in fact been called upon to attack too strong a position with too small a force. What it had been asked to do was, in the event, probably beyond the powers even of a fresh battalion, and certainly beyond those of a tired one. Throughout the action those supporting arms it had been possible to deploy had been used to great effect. All their crews had given of their best and had undoubtedly saved the Battalion many casualties. But even if it had been possible to deploy more heavy weapons it is doubtful if one battalion alone could ever have taken Monte Catarelto.

*　　*　　*

The last three weeks of October were busy ones for the Battalion. The stay at inhospitable Castiglione lasted a week; it was in no wise to be compared to lounging in a luxurious leave-camp, for daily the idle hands were claimed for road mending on the shattered axis. Here
Oct. 8   the Battalion was visited by the Major-General Commanding the Brigade of Guards, Lieutenant-General Sir Charles Loyd, who could

judge for himself how well, despite their long period in the line, the Guardsmen had maintained their standards since he had last seen them at Sorrento six months before. The whole army in Italy was now showing the strains of repeated wounds, sickness, weariness, and long absence from home. The prospect of winter in the shelterless mountains was dismal. In every regiment both the leaders and the led had to grit their teeth and summon up their final reserves of courage and endurance to keep themselves going forward.

For this was the time of the greatest strain, when the weaker wills were mercilessly exposed. A very few men deserted to the tempting hiding places among the teeming population. While the loyal soldier who "stuck it" for month in and month out fully understood that the strain of war-weariness affected some much earlier than others and that some were made of sterner stuff than others, he had little sympathy for the tiny hard-core of ne'er-do-wells, and only contempt for those who he suspected of evading front-line duty in comfortable billets far to the rear. Politicians at home would have been surprised at the vehemence with which all ranks expressed themselves on the need for exemplary punishment for those who they thought had let them down. That the influence of the faint-hearted was not wider reflects the greatest credit on the Non-Commissioned Officers and Guardsmen, and especially on RSM Hamilton and his outstanding team of Warrant Officers, for their task of maintaining morale was far harder than that of their opposite numbers in the 21st Army Group. During the Italian winter of 1944–45 the cumulative effects of five years' Mediterranean campaigning became apparent throughout the army; as yet the campaign in North-West Europe was but five months old.

The task of the Guards Brigade was now subsidiary to that of the Motor Brigade. The latter was to attack northwards along the line of heights to the west of the road: first Monte Stanco, then Monte Salvaro. The Guards, in the valley of the Setta, were to conform to this advance. But five miles ahead at the narrow gorge of Vado there stood a mountain dominating the valley: Monte Sole was already in the planners' minds, and the 24th Guards Brigade had been nominated to attack it. For this attack Brigadier Clive intended to keep fresh the Grenadiers and Coldstream; in consequence the lion's share of the work on the approach march was to fall to the Scots Guards. *MAP XXVI*

On the 11th October the Battalion re-entered the line, taking over from the Coldstream in positions south and west of Pian di Setta. Two days later the South Africans opened their attack on Monte Stanco; in conjunction Right Flank occupied Grizzana Station, near which they picked up an SS deserter, evidence that these tough soldiers were still facing down the valley. But on the next day when B Company and Left Flank advanced to Veggio they captured a *Oct. 11*
Oct. 13
Oct. 14
Oct. 15

member of the 94th Division, a pleasant indication that the more blatant Nazis were moving away eastwards. However, it was still the SS who defended Poggio when it was attacked on the 16th by Left Flank. A stiff battle had to be fought for the possession of the houses, in which Lieutenant J. E. Baxter was killed; he was well to the fore of his platoon when he grappled with a German who suddenly confronted him round the corner of a house; in the struggle the German

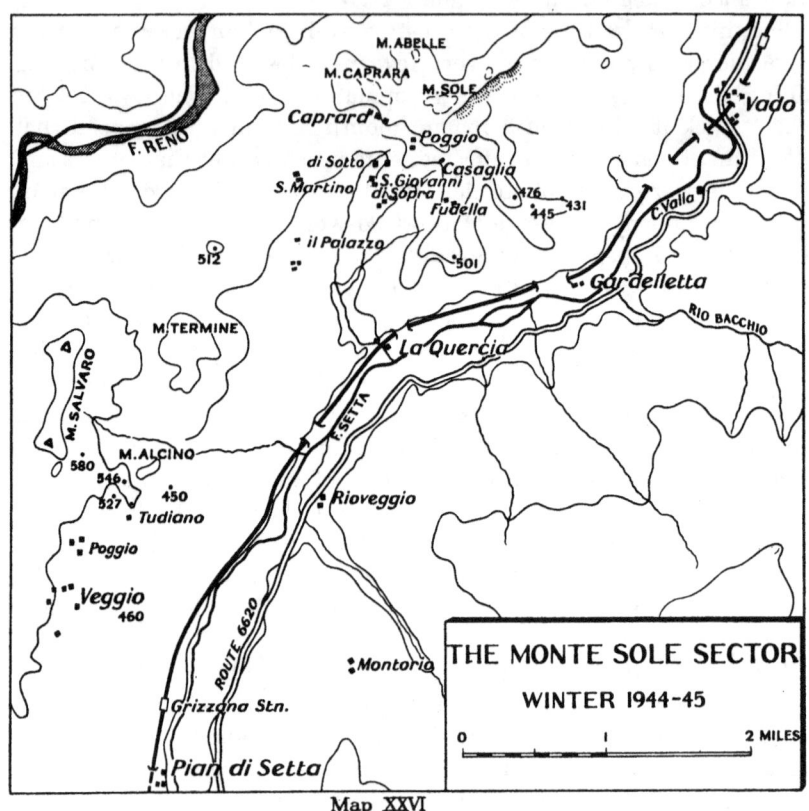

Map XXVI

dropped a grenade, which exploded, killing them both. Some measure of revenge was taken that night when a patrol of B Company killed two of the enemy in Tudiano.

The Battalion's next target was now within range, but it was not to be attempted until the Motor Brigade had reached the southern summit of Monte Salvaro. Early on the morning of the 19th that condition was fulfilled, and the preliminaries of the attack on Monte Alcino, a spur of Salvaro, began.

It must be said that, from the first, things did not go as well as had been hoped. The reasons were several. First, officer casualties in the Battalion due to sickness and battle had of late been considerable; in particular a serious loss had been the wounding by mortar-fire on the previous day of Major Hague. The weather was heart-breaking, for a solid wall of mist and rain surrounded the forward troops almost the whole of the time. The ground was most difficult, consisting of steep, muddy gullies. The rain was hated more than anything, and little sleep could be snatched in the intervals between attacks. These factors were not conducive to raising morale.

Oct. 18

At eight o'clock two platoons set out for Alcino. Soon the platoon from Left Flank was dispersed by fire from our own medium guns and had to return. The platoon from C Company had better luck, establishing itself in Tudiano by midday, where it was joined by the remainder of the Company. The hill in front seemed to be firmly held by the enemy. B Company (Captain R. A. Readman) set out at half-past three to attack Point 546, but almost at once came under heavy small arms fire, suffering casualties in a difficult defile between Points 546 and 527. The leading platoon was badly dispersed and the Company was withdrawn to positions near Tudiano. The losses of this weak company were serious, for the killed included Sergeant J. Clement, M.M. and Lance-Sergeant R. S. Dougall, M.M., both of whom were commanding platoons.

Oct. 19

The next day it was planned that the Battalion should not only clear Monte Alcino, but also go on to Monte Termine. At four in the afternoon Right Flank and B Company moved off, after very heavy artillery preparation. On the left, Major Mann led Right Flank well up on to the high ground, and came down on Point 580 from an angle the defenders had not expected. Before the swift assault, in which Lance-Sergeant A. Bremner led the leading section with conspicuous dash, the enemy retired in disorder, leaving behind their arms and equipment. But again B Company, this time reinforced by a platoon of C Company, was less fortunate. It had again been sent at Point 546, and again had run into heavy fire. Although a few men reached the objective, they could not consolidate it; the Company was again withdrawn, after what had been an exhausting failure in which five men had been killed.

Oct. 20

Right Flank's position on 580 was valuable, but uncomfortable. Overlooked though it was by the enemy on the northern summit of Salvaro, the Company was able to make life equally uncomfortable for the Germans lower down on Point 546. These were subjected to all forms of fire, including that of tanks from the far side of the valley, and the combined effect was to prevent any supplies coming forward, so much so that prisoners later reported that they were reduced to living on nuts! So precarious had the enemy's position become that on the night of the 21st/22nd he withdrew and by midday all Alcino was in the Scots Guards' hands. For his leadership and skilful tactics on Monte Alcino, on a par with those he had displayed throughout the

Oct. 21

Oct. 22

summer advance, Major Mann was awarded the Distinguished Service Order. It was men of similar spirit and courage, though of taller physical stature than Major Mann, who were responsible for a story with which the SS men had made the 94th Division's flesh creep. Prisoners said that the SS had told them that they were opposed to a specially trained Guards Division, members of which were Scottish shock troops, all giants! The Germans' morale in consequence was rather low.[1]

Oct. 23 The attack on Monte Termine depended on what progress the South Africans might make to the northern summit of Salvaro, for the artillery would not be available until this dominating peak had been taken. By two in the afternoon the Imperial Light Horse/Kimberley Regiment were on the top, and the Battalion started off. Avoiding the enemy's defensive fire, which had been drawn and noted by a patrol of the previous day, Right Flank and C Company both made progress, taking some prisoners. But a minefield was found which held them up, and Brigadier Clive ordered the advance to halt for the hours of darkness. That night was one of no comfort, for no supplies could be got over the difficult ground. The Sappers lifted the mines, which were found to be innocuous, for some careless German

Oct. 24 had forgotten to give the order to arm them. Soon after dawn it transpired that the enemy had gone, and Right Flank and C Company, followed by Left Flank, ascended the wooded hill unopposed. Though they did not know it, Termine marked the limit of the year's advance.

Preparations were now pushed forward energetically for the pro-

Oct. 25 posed assault on Monte Sole. While the Grenadiers secured its southern spur, Point 501, north of the Setta, the Scots Guards patrolled and reconnoitred on the south-western slopes, posting Left Flank in a

Oct. 26 miserable position on Point 512. Right Flank, who were to participate in the assault under the command of the Coldstream, returned to Veggio to gird themselves for the ordeal. Attempts to reach San

Oct. 28 Martino by a patrol of C Company ended by the patrol being taken prisoner of war, and it was with relief that the news was received on

Oct. 29 the 29th that the attack was postponed for at least a month. The rains were washing away the roads and the bridges, and the supply of artillery ammunition was running low. The whole Fifth Army, now nearly exhausted, was ordered to halt. The month ended with the glad news that the Battalion was to be relieved in the line by the

Nov. 5 South Africans, and by the evening of the 5th November the Royal

[1] A lasting impression of the huge bulk of certain Scots Guardsmen had been fixed on the minds of the peasants of this valley. When the historian visited Catarelto in 1954 an old woman and two men working in the fields asked him, unprompted, if he was one of the "*grandi Scozzesi*" who they remembered with evident affection. It was a most heartening experience after having been taken by peasants for a German on Monte Camino, and then having been told by them that it was the Americans who had taken it.

Natal Carbineers had taken over. Before Battalion Headquarters had moved out, Captain G. P. M. Ramsay, the Signal Officer, had been wounded by shell-fire while on an urgent errand up the mule tracks. In this he was combining his official business of repairing telephone lines with the unofficial, but highly important, charge of recapturing some stray pigs which were rumoured to have escaped from the isolated farm where, clandestinely, they were being fattened for Christmas.

By the 6th the Battalion had driven south to a bleak carpet factory in Prato for its first rest out of the sound of guns since the crossing of the Arno two months before. A week of sleep, of "walking-out" in Florence, and, for some of the officers, of relaxation at the Villa Medici at Fiesole was drawn on to the full.   Nov. 6

S Company

That autumn S Company went into no great attacks. As with the South Africans, there was no intention that the 6th Armoured Division should be heavily engaged until it could be unleashed on the plain of Lombardy. This opportunity never came, and in consequence the infantry of the Division were called upon to plug gaps in the line as required, thereby once again enabling the 1st Guards Brigade to live up to its nickname of Tunisian days: "The Plumbers".

The first summons was on the 1st September to the mountainous right flank of the XIII Corps front facing the Gothic Line. The 2nd Coldstream moved up the Arno valley to Pontassieve, and then turned right along Route 70 to Consuma. Here, at an altitude of 3,000 feet, they took over on the watershed of the Prato Magno from the 7th Battalion the Rifle Brigade. The drive up had been picturesque but uneventful, for, although large stretches of the road were in full view of the enemy in his line, either sloth or shell shortage delayed the shelling until the vehicles were past. S Company's positions afforded them the most perfect view over the autumn landscape, the vista extending westward as far as the sea beyond Pisa. All save the most forward sections could find accommodation in farms and villas, for in this part the Germans were in no significant strength. Patrols and the sifting of civilians and partisan intelligence were the staple fare of this week of little danger. Perhaps the greatest danger came from a band of friendly bravos, styled the *Riconoscenza Folgore*, meaning, roughly, The Lightning Squad. They were armed to the teeth on the scale of two or three weapons per man, and carried no equipment other than water-bottles full of Chianti. One night some hundred of them sallied forth to patrol towards the Gothic Line; the next night a somewhat half-hearted attack was delivered against S Company by men who sounded most Italian; the night after the *Folgore* returned elated, admitting they had got a little lost, but claiming to have attacked the Germans and "probably" to have inflicted casualties!   Sept. 1

282 ITALY: 1944

Sept. 9   It was with regret that the Battalion came down from this pleasant sector to Pelago to prepare for the second of their autumn tasks.

Sept. 10 This was to participate in the advance up to the Sieve valley, later to be diverted north-eastwards up Route 67 leading to Forli. After a brief halt in Dicomano, the Coldstream were directed up the road towards San Godenzo, keeping to the left while the Grenadiers kept to

Sept. 12 the right. Early on the afternoon of 12th September, at a time when the Company was in the lead, the first close contact with the Gothic Line was gained. The enemy could be seen strolling about their positions, hanging their blankets out to dry in the sun. It was also easy to see that the defences were in a far worse state than rumour would have them; the barbed-wire was dishevelled and rusty, the camouflage was peeling off the pill-boxes, and many of the trenches full of water. Patrols which reached the wire that evening neither saw nor heard much of the enemy; within a few days it became clear that on this sector also he had withdrawn. It was a most popular retreat. But now, to assist the II Corps attack north of Florence, the Brigade was

Sept. 15 required to "lean upon the enemy". For S Company this meant a short advance across country through the defences and down to the outskirts of the village of Villore. There was no opposition, the real danger being from the thickly sown mines. One day one of these very nearly claimed Major Coke and Lieutenant I. J. Fraser, when Fraser trod on one of the smaller "anti-personnel" variety. "We knew we had four and a half seconds in which to do something before the little horror jumped into the air to scatter its load of ball-bearings at all and sundry." They both dived for cover, one behind a rather slender tree, and the other behind an entirely inadequate bank; before they were on the ground the mine jumped. "I saw its shadow—and then it just fell down again. It was a most awful anti-climax and I imagine that we owe the intactness of various parts of our anatomy to some nameless Czech who kindly omitted the detonator."

MAP XXIV The Xth Corps now claimed the services of the 1st Guards Brigade.
Sept. 17 Driving back down the Arno valley along the road they knew so well as far as Arezzo, the Brigade turned north up the eastern side of the
Sept. 19 Prato Magno to relieve the 10th Indian Division, which had been called away to the great battle on the Adriatic coast. There the Company went up to the forward slopes of Monte Penna, arriving in position half an hour before midnight, after a three hour climb to more than 2,500 feet. Here the mules were again essential, and one dark night several of them fell over a cliff. If anything, these unfortunate animals had a more unpleasant life in the mountains than did the humans. There could be no great battles in this inaccessible area, and again it was patrols to the still occupied defences of the Gothic

Sept. 22 Line that provided the main work. On the 22nd it became clear that there was nothing to fear on this sector, and the Brigade was relieved

S COMPANY   283

by a light Anti-Aircraft regiment, now acting as infantry, for there
were no more enemy aircraft to claim their attention.

The final call of the autumn came to the most dangerous and   MAP
uncomfortable position of all. It had been expected that the Division   XXVIII
would be kept in hand for the break-out which now seemed about to
be accomplished, and the Brigade moved up from a rest area near   Sept. 27
Arezzo to Pelago to await the call forward. On the 2nd October the   Oct. 2
call came, but it was not for armoured action, but to take over from
troops of the United States 88th Division on Monte Battaglia, a precipitous mountain they had carried in a swift assault. It lay on the
northern fringe of mountains but twelve miles from Imola. In
pouring rain the Brigade drove forward along the road which runs to
the east of the Futa Pass, through Firenzuola and down the valley of
the Santerno. The convoy halted two miles short of the village of
Castel del Rio by the side of the swollen river and there, huddled
under groundsheets in the lee of their vehicles, the Company ate the
hottest meal they were to get for almost three weeks. Thus refreshed
the Guardsmen set off soon after dark on the long walk up the slippery,
rainswept mountain track which led to their concentration area,
where, under the persistent downpour, they slept the night in some
sodden upland fields, where even the voice of Miss Vera Lynn, "The
Forces Sweetheart", crooning over the wireless, "Thanks for the
Lovely Week-end" was unable to bring solace. Next morning there   Oct. 3
was some delay until the Americans had repulsed a German attack,
but shortly after midday the two Coldstream companies went forward
to take over the advanced positions on Monte Battaglia, leaving S
Company behind to help with the mules. During some scattered
shelling S Company suffered a grievous loss when their devoted
stretcher-bearer, Guardsman J. Lingwood, M.M., was mortally
wounded. By the 6th October the Scotsmen too had gone forward.   Oct. 6
The unpleasantness of the siutation became apparent to all.

"Battaglia was a ridge some 2,400 feet high, running from south
to north and culminating at its northern point in a ruined castle. From
this castle two ridges, Cornezzano and Poseggio, radiated to east and
west, both bending round to the south, so that the whole feature
resembled an anchor with its head towards the enemy. The castle and
central ridge were held by the Brigade; Cornezzano and Poseggio
were still in German hands and had been used as bases for desperate
counter-attacks to regain the Battaglia ridge."[1] At the outset two
Coldstream companies took over positions on the south-eastern slopes
of Battaglia; the Welsh Guards held the main ridge; and the Grenadiers protected the Gunner O.P. in the castle. All these positions were
overlooked by the enemy from three sides and were pounded night
and day by his guns and mortars, so that sleep, except from sheer

[1] The subsequent extracts are taken from *The Coldstream Guards 1920–1946*.

exhaustion, or existence at all outside a slit trench, were barely possible. On top of all this never before had the Company experienced such rigorous weather. It had originally been intended that the Brigade should hold Battaglia for but forty-eight hours, but eventually the first spell there was no less than twenty-four days, during every one of which rain fell upon the mountain. Slit trenches filled to a depth of many inches of icy water, clothing and blankets became so wringing wet that there was no hope of drying them, and the paths up which all supplies had to come were soon deep in slimy, treacherous mud. "The platoon areas were filthy with old ration tins and excrement, and all around there spread a waste of mud and rock and shell-scarred tree stumps, scattered with shell-holes and the unburied corpses of German and American dead. Cooking was possible only on Tommy-cookers, and of these there were very few."

Throughout the three weeks of this misery, the problem of supply was one of the greatest. "Mule-head" was at a farmhouse four miles from the summit of Battaglia and the tracks which led between the two were accurately registered by the German guns. Matters were made no easier by the attitude of some of the Indian muleteers, who, only too often, would think nothing of dumping their loads and riding the animals themselves, even despite the fact that it was quite common for a laden mule to slip in deep mud and fall down one of the many precipices. The evacuation of the wounded, too, was most laborious. The stretcher-bearers, mostly Italians, would often take as long as seven hours to reach the ambulances on the main road, and then only after braving the persistent shellfire and struggling to keep their feet against the howling storms which lashed about them.

Oct. 7
For the first nine days of this ordeal, the Company remained in a position on the right flank. Patrols went out to probe the enemy positions almost every night and one of these composed of Lance-Sergeant Wilson, Guardsman Mellor and Bruno Salveti, an Italian partisan who was attached to the Company, was ambushed on the slopes of Cornezzano and all were captured. Salveti managed to conceal his nationality from his captors. He escaped from Imola back through the lines, but before he passed through the British outposts he carefully hid his signet ring in a churchyard, later explaining, somewhat cryptically, "I know the British Tommy!" Disregarding this slander, Major Coke presented Salveti with a Scots Guards cap star, which he proudly wore.

Oct. 10
S Company were not called upon to play an important part in repelling the main German attack, an attack which ended disastrously for the enemy after making a deep penetration behind the forward positions.

Oct. 14
On October 14th the Coldstream exchanged their battered area for that of the Castle, and prepared for an attack on Cornezzano. Life was

a bit quieter in the new positions, but these were more difficult than ever to supply; rations had to be sent up in haversacks and handed up the steepest places. A welcome improvement in the weather made the mountain more tolerable. On the 15th the Company took over positions on Battaglia West and sent out almost nightly small patrols to examine the enemy defences on the Cornezzano ridge opposite. These were usually only very small parties, and one consisting of Lieutenant P. J. Blandy and one Guardsman, spent most of a night listening to a conversation between two German sentries on the top of the ridge. The attack to which these patrols were meant to be the prelude was, however, "rained off". Oct. 15 Oct. 20

Next morning two Divisional Commanders, Major-Generals Murray of 6th Armoured and Laver of the 1st Infantry, accompanied by the Brigade Commander, the Commanding Officer and all the Company Commanders, appeared in the Company area to view the ground ahead and to concert plans for an attack. Such a gathering of distinguished visitors is always wildly unpopular with front-line troops and, sure enough, within a few minutes of the departure of this galaxy of "Sun-rays"[1] S Company was briskly shelled for ten minutes and the departed visitors roundly cursed for as many more. In fact the conference had decided that, weather permitting, Monte Cornezzano should be taken on the following night, but again the weather prevented the plan's execution. A patrol went out, and confirmed signs that the enemy were withdrawing along the whole front; the German positions were empty. The next night other troops took over Cornezzano and on the following day the Company was relieved. Transport was waiting at Castel del Rio to take it to billets in the little village of Casa Melina several miles back along the main road, where the accommodation was "far from luxurious, but after Battaglia a pigsty would have been welcome". Oct. 21 Oct. 22 Oct. 23

After nine days out of the line, the Company went forward to positions overlooking the valley of the Senio, the next valley to the east of the Santerno. It took over positions on Monte Cornezzano, arriving there just before midnight after the usual gruelling march up from Castel del Rio in pitchy darkness and pouring rain. The mules were defeated by the gradient and the mud and had to be left behind until morning. Here there was much less shelling, and even better weather, in fact "lovely fine sunny days, but cold at night". Save for nocturnal prowlers, the position was vastly preferable to any other the Company had occupied near Battaglia. One night came the herald of winter, a cold wind blew across the mountains and with it came the first snow—two inches, which soon disappeared. Nov. 2 Nov. 7

On the night of November 11th the Welsh Guards relieved them and the Company tramped back the eight weary miles to the road, Nov. 11

[1] *Sun-ray*: code word in Wireless Procedure for a Commander.

286 ITALY: 1944

Nov. 12
arriving at four in the morning, cold, hungry and utterly exhausted. Mobile baths and a change of clothes appeared later in the day and soon afterwards came the welcome 3-ton lorries. Few remembered the bumpy journey back over the watershed to Borgo San Lorenzo. By nightfall, with all settled into billets about twenty miles from Florence, their sleep was that of the just.

(b) *The Winter Months*

The main concern of the Scots Guards during the Italian winter of 1944–45 was to exist as comfortably as possible. It is true that the First Battalion spent two anxious months before the proposed attack on Monte Sole was called off and that S Company actually attacked and took Monte Penzola; but nevertheless it was the problems of living, not of fighting, which were uppermost in men's minds.

The life in the front line was predominantly an open-air one. Hence the weather was the most important factor of all. Rain meant mud, wet clothes and feet, slippery tracks, uncertain supply, leaky dugouts and waterlogged trenches. Snow and frost were much preferred, for with them came crisp invigorating air, more passable tracks, dry clothes and better visibility by night. Patrolling in the snow was a new experience. Patrols sallied forth clothed in white, but any movement always made what seemed a tremendous noise on the crackling surface, and the danger of ambushes was greatly increased by the telltale tracks in the snow. Moreover the intense cold prevented prolonged periods of lying up and listening. During the white months the forward companies were supplied with kapok sleeping-bags, windproof smocks, heavy socks, mittens, pullovers, scarves and all the various comforts which came from kind-hearted and industrious womenfolk at home; rarely was there sufficient winter clothing for all, and the article which was found to be the least adequate was the standard army boot, which proved unable to withstand the alternate strains of mud and frost.

In this period perhaps the most important, and certainly the most welcome, occurrence was the advent after dark of the Quartermaster with his train of jeeps or mules. Captain J. Quinn, M.B.E. for the Battalion, and CQMS S. Kiddle for S Company, kept those in the line well provided with all that could legitimately be obtained, and also with those "extras" which were the spoils of the bloodless and unrelenting *guerrilla* conducted against all stores, dumps and NAAFIs; at Christmas, of military necessity declared a movable feast, the fare was sumptuous. On many occasions little would have reached the forward companies had it not been for the mules. Sometimes no bigger than Great Danes, sometimes far nobler characters than their polyglot muleteers, these wretched creatures were essential to survival in the mountains. For all the alleged comforts of Battalion Headquarters, no company officer envied the Pioneer Officer, Lieutenant R. M. C. Nunneley, his charge of the Battalion's mules. Cursing, kicking, heaving and groaning, nightly the caravan of men and beasts made its way forward, burdened with food, clothes, water, rum, ammunition, wireless batteries, and, to be received with joy and to be read with avidity, the mail. Often progress was interrupted by shelling and machine-gunning; sometimes there were ambushes laid by an aggressive enemy; often their path was lighted by the "artificial moonlight" produced by reflecting the glow of searchlights from the base of the clouds. This illumination was more popular with the domestics than with the tacticians, for those on patrol required a more sombre darkness in which to approach the enemy.

The morale of the army that winter was the special care of all commanders, from General Alexander downwards. All realised that the troops had passed through a prolonged period of severe strain culminating in a frustrating stalemate. To revive flagging spirits for the battles which were surely coming in the spring was the mission of every officer. To this end a deliberate attempt was made to allot divisions permanent sectors of the winter line, which could then be divided up in such a way as to ensure a rota of regular reliefs. Static bases were established well to the rear, to which it was hoped the fighting soldiers would make regular visits. S Company came back several times to the village of Strada, but the Companies of the First Battalion were less fortunate in the frequency of their visits to Prato. During the eleven weeks from the beginning of December to mid-February no part of the Battalion came further south than Castiglione; the periods out of the line had to be passed in the bleak farmhouses of the Setta valley. Here, at the Battalion level, a heavy burden fell on the shoulders of the Padre and the Doctor. In all conscience it had been a hard enough task to succeed Captains Hamilton and Hodge, who, it will be remembered, had "gone into the bag" at Carroceto; but during the advance from Cassino the Reverend A. A. MacArthur and Captain H. N. Mansfield had proved themselves worthy successors. The former was untiring in his care for the welfare of the Guardsmen and in his help over their home troubles, caused by the separation and disturbance of war; the latter by his skill and devotion instilled in all his prospective patients a confidence which all Harley Street would have envied. Another familiar figure came to remind the Guardsmen of a far-off square among the pine trees; Captain L. C. Archer, M.B.E., M.M., of Pirbright fame, was now Quartermaster at the I.R.T.D., and the only method by which he could maintain his own morale was to visit the Regiment whenever opportunity offered. On one such visit it was recorded that he went by night to every section post in the line: his coming was like a visit from

ITALY: 1944

another world, and the effect of it on the troops of far greater immediate benefit than was that of a party of equally well-intentioned Members of Parliament. That winter there were many who helped to restore the army to fighting pitch, and the aforementioned were not the least of them.

There remains but to chronicle briefly the events of those months.

The First Battalion

Nov. 14   The Battalion drove northwards from Prato on the 14th November.
MAP XXVI During the rest period the most notable event had been the departure for home of the first leave party: small as it had been, it had done something to counter the erroneous idea that troops in Holland and Belgium were able to return home at regular intervals. The Battalion returned to the line with but three rifle companies, for battle casualties, sickness and the need to give adequate leave made it impossible
Nov. 16   to maintain four at sufficient strength; for the winter months B Company became a reinforcement company. On arrival in the valley of the Setta the Battalion found that the 24th Guards Brigade was now commanded by one of its former Commanding Officers; Brigadier Clive had been succeeded by Brigadier M. D. Erskine, D.S.O., who was to command the Brigade for the next three years.

Until Christmas the Battalion's thoughts were dominated by the proposed attack on Monte Sole. To attack this mountain which overlooked the whole Brigade area in the valley and which was defended by the same 35th SS Regiment which had fought on Catarelto, was plainly a formidable undertaking, an undertaking made no less formidable by prolonged contemplation of the objective. The task assigned to the Battalion was, in the preliminary phase, to clear the houses and farms on the ridge running northward from La Quercia, roughly in the area of Fudella and San Giovanni di Sopra. The other two battalions would then attack the summits of Sole and Caprara, after which the Scots Guards were to be ready to exploit eastwards, and perhaps to attack the third summit of Mont'Abelle. Therefore, until the attack was finally called off, it was the La Quercia sector which the Battalion occupied, and from the forward positions on the spur above the village (Point 501) many patrols went out to build up
Nov. 18   as accurate a picture as possible of the German defences. From one of these, to San Giovanni di Sotto, Lieutenant K. A. P. Monfries did not return; many months later his grave was found in the garden of the house where he had been killed by the defenders; he had been with the Battalion only a few days. Otherwise the enemy's persistent harassing fire caused but few casualties, which included Captain R. A. Carnegie wounded for the third time in the campaign. At night preparations for the attack were pushed forward with vigour; tracks had to be improved to take jeeps and, it was hoped, tanks; ammunition

had to be stored forward in convenient, if risky, dumps; mines had to be lifted, ambushes had to be laid, and the enemy's knavish tricks had to be frustrated. And all the while, every night, the domestic chores of a battalion in the line had to be performed. Fortunately, once the railway and its many tunnels had been opened up as a road, all stores could be brought up to La Quercia in motor transport, which could also get as far as the other sector based on Gardelletta.

At the end of the month the Battalion again went down to rest at Prato—for the last time, as it proved, but on this occasion the period of rest was peremptorily interrupted by the supposed imminence of the attack. The Battalion came back in a hurry to La Quercia ready to set out on the first stages of the operation the next day. Again the start was postponed, and after a week of unprofitable scrapping by the Grenadiers and Frontier Force Rifles for features on the spur above Gardelletta it seemed as if the attack was put off for good. But good intentions die hard. After a brief rest in the valley the Scots Guards spent the last fortnight of December around La Quercia while conflicting rumours daily changed the date of the assault. At last, on Christmas Day the irrevocable word was given to halt all offensive operations on the Fifth Army front: the 24th Guards Brigade was never to attack Monte Sole. The shortage of ammunition, the need to conserve strength for the spring and the temporary rout north of Lucca of the United States 92nd Negro Division, all combined to frustrate the aggressive plans of both armies. The Battalion received the news with unalloyed pleasure.

Nov. 29

Dec. 3

Dec. 10–14

Dec. 25

Christmas was spent in the reserve billets in the valley, with the ground thick with snow, but, as if to try all Scotsmen to the limit of their patience, on New Year's Eve the Battalion was made to take over an unfamiliar sector of the front from the dismounted men of the Natal Mounted Rifles. The new posts were to the east of the Setta opposite Gardelletta, with one forward company along the road a mile south of Vado and north of the Bacchio, and another on the high ground to the south of the stream. These positions were under the direct observation of the Germans on Sole, so that movement by day in the forward platoons was much more restricted than in the positions to the west of the Setta. For the month they remained there the Guardsmen experienced the rigours of snow warfare, and in the first part of the month they had also to contend with enemy troops of high quality: the 4th Parachute Division. Towards the end of January it became clear that these tough customers were departing, and it was urgently desired to know who had taken their place. In consequence the Battalion marked its own departure from the sector with a small raid designed to secure a prisoner. Lieutenant E. H. L. Wallace with fifteen men of Right Flank and a 20-lb. pole-charge attacked Casa Valla under cover of a diversionary party of Left Flank commanded

Dec. 31

Feb. 1

by Lieutenant D. A. Colquhoun. Casa Valla proved a mare's nest, and, save for the wounding by shellfire of the man carrying the pole-charge, the heated dispute among the unwounded as to who should have the honour of planting the infernal machine against the cottage wall, the intensely satisfactory explosion which resulted, and the unnerving tiptoe back across a snow-covered minefield, the raid was

Feb. 2 unproductive. But when the next day the Scots Guards left the sector, they heard that the Frontier Force Rifles had secured the wanted identification: the Parachutists had gone, and a more docile Mountain Division had arrived.

Feb. 8 On the 8th February the Battalion entered the line in the Apennines for the last time. It took over the third sector of the Brigade front, that based on the village of Gardelletta and extending up the lower slopes of the spur that culminated in Point 476, on which the Germans

Feb. 10 were still firmly ensconced. Save for a fruitless attempt by a Psychological Warfare Unit armed with a monstrous loudspeaker to persuade the Germans to desert, the week spent around Gardelletta was

Feb. 14 uneventful. On the 14th the Frontier Force Rifles came to take over: the period of the 24th Guards Brigade's service with the 6th South African Armoured Division was at an end.

Feb. 17 The Brigade drove south a hundred and eighty miles to the un-
MAP XXIV damaged city of Spoleto, where all the Guardsmen in Italy were assembling for a second reorganisation. For the last time the battered vehicles wound their way up the road which climbs out of the Setta valley through Castiglione, that inhospitable village in which the Flank Companies had arrived on a misty afternoon five months before. In the lower part of Castiglione, with what must, on a clear day, be one of the finest prospects in all Italy, lies the Divisional cemetery, now neatly ordered and carefully tended by the Imperial War Graves Commission. The view northwards reveals Stanco and Salvaro, with the high peak of Catarelto concealing from sight the dreaded Sole. But more impressive than the view are the diverse inscriptions to be read on the headstones of the fallen; here alongside each other lie both Guardsmen and South Africans without any formal separation into Regiments or nationalities, save for the one long homogenous row where the score of Scots Guardsmen who fell on Catarelto are buried. The munificent gift of £5,000 subscribed by all ranks of the South African Division towards the rebuilding of the Guards' Chapel in London and the blue-red-blue flash of the Brigade Colours with which the troopers of the Pretoria Regiment now back their cap-badges, might be thought evidence enough of the alliance between the Guardsmen and the "Springboks"; but in centuries to come it is these mingled graves which will bear the proudest witness to months of happy comradeship in a famous partnership from Cassino to the Apennines.

S Company

Before S Company settled down to the winter routine it carried out an attack, at once highly skilful and successful.

The 6th Armoured Division was to spend the winter in the Santerno valley and on its flanking hills. Across its front, barring the way to Imola and the plain, in the same way that Monte Sole barred the way to Bologna, ran a great chalk cliff, the Venna di Gesso, which crossed the road just to the north of Tossignano. Hope of breaching this line had not yet been abandoned, and as a preliminary to the proposed capture of Tossignano by the 61st Brigade, it was thought necessary to capture the 1,300 foot peak of Monte Penzola (Point 411). This little Matterhorn rose sheer from the cliff face of the Venna di Gesso and a frontal attack on it would have been impossible. But to the west our troops already had access to the ridge from the mass of Monte Verro, on the most easterly feature of which, Monte dell'Acqua Salata, S Company had spent the last ten days of November in acute discomfort. From Acqua Salata a good view was to be had over the northern slopes of Penzola, and from here the attack could be launched. Once Penzola was captured, the enemy would be denied close observation over the road south to Castel del Rio, and work on developing the road to maintain the Tossignano battle would be greatly simplified. Disregarding this cogent argument an officer of the Company, in the usual manner of experienced infantrymen, was content to say that Penzola was "to be taken at all costs, for some reason or other best known to the Generals, etc". The task of capturing Penzola was entrusted to the 2nd Coldstream; S Company was charged with the assault on the summit.

MAP XXVII

Nov. 19–29

The day of the attack was one of low cloud which grounded the intended air support, and of rain squalls which made the muddy slopes yet muddier. However, the whole Divisional artillery was in support, and as soon as the light began to fail the guns began their opening shoots, keeping up an incessant fire for the next three hours. The plan of attack was simple. Starting from the eastern slopes of Acqua Salata No. 2 Company was to secure a position on the ridge to the west of Penzola in the region of Casa Budriolo; at the same time No. 4 Company was to occupy the Famosa spur to the north of Penzola. Once the Coldstream companies were secure, S Company was to pass through No. 2 and, making a wide sweep to the north-east, to assault the peak from the north, taking its defenders in the rear. Immediately after dark the three companies moved up on to Acqua Salata under protection of the Lothian and Border Horse, who were divorced from their tanks in an infantry role. The Coldstreamers crossed the start line at a quarter-past nine, and for an hour the Scotsmen waited, unable to hear anything of the infantry advance, since the noise of the artillery predominated—particularly the noise of one cretinous

Dec. 4

gun which was persistently off-target and which pitched its shells far too close for comfort. At a quarter-past ten No. 2 Company reported itself firmly established at Casa Budriolo, and, though there was no news from No. 4, Colonel Coates gave the word for Major Coke to set off.

The moon had now risen and in its pale light the pinnacle of Penzola looked even more perpendicular and unscalable than it had by day. The Company made its way eastwards along the ridge, past Casa

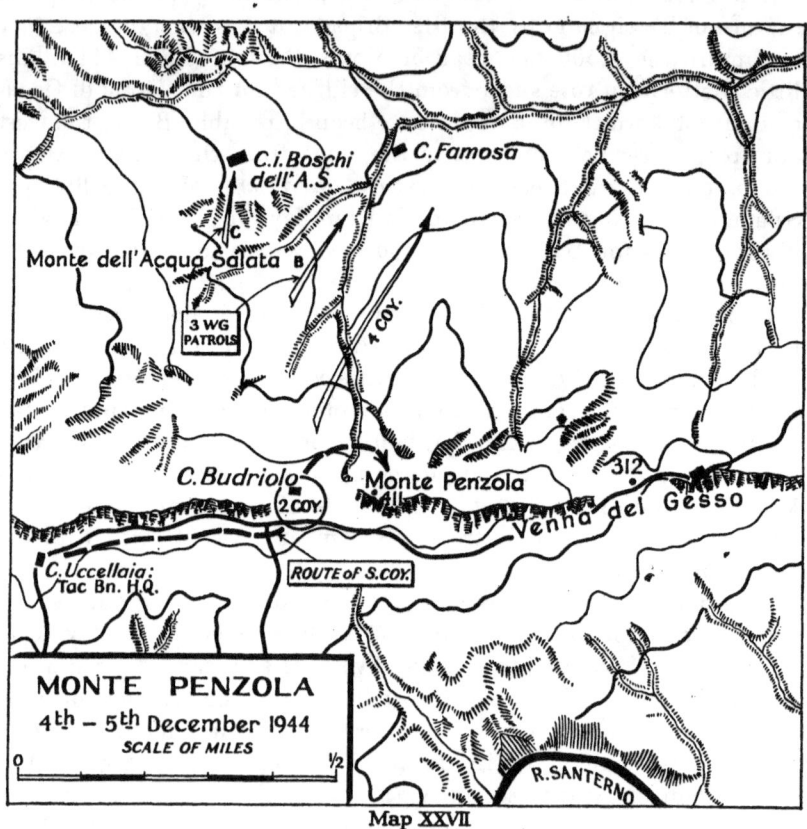

Map XXVII

Budriolo, over ground which was very muddy and was intersected by even muddier ravines. The passage of this poor going in extended order, carrying all the impedimenta needed for the assault and consolidation, was exhausting to the Guardsmen, and when they reached the foot of Penzola proper there was sweat on their brows despite the coldness of the night. The final climb was precipitous; at times men were crawling on their hands and knees, and several, with their heavy burdens, slipped backwards among the rocks and bushes. Six were wounded by enemy shellfire as they scrambled upwards, and it was midnight before the Company was assembled and ready for the final assault.

The enemy had been taken completely by surprise by the direction of the attack; most of them, including their sentries, were lurking snug and safe in the bottom of their slits and dug-outs. But they quickly awoke to their danger and a fierce hand-to-hand battle soon raged among the rocks. The fight was especially fierce about the German company headquarters where the lieutenant commanding the company put up a determined resistance with his pistol, wounding several of the attackers, including Lieutenant J. H. Inskip, the leading Platoon Commander, in the eye. He also hit Guardsman H. Rush in the arm. "This made Rush very angry, and he changed his Tommy-gun to his left hand and the German officer duly paid the price with the contents of a magazine in both legs." Still angry, Rush also wounded another of the enemy who was trying to escape, and then assumed charge of his section in place of his wounded commander, refusing to leave despite his painful wound until the position was firmly consolidated several hours later.

Dec. 5

Fighting died down as quickly as it had begun, and it transpired that the best part of a weak German company had been destroyed. But there was no time to relax, for it soon became clear to the enemy on the other parts of the ridge that Penzola had been taken, and the fire of their guns and mortars came down in earnest. The lot of the wounded was miserable; the danger from a field of *Schu* mines seemed likely to prevent their being carried down before dawn, so they had to steel themselves for a night of discomfort on the frozen windswept ground, wrapped in as many captured greatcoats as could be found for them. Fortunately, just before first light, a clear route down was found. It avoided the minefield, but entailed carrying the stretchers down an almost perpendicular face with a drop of fifty feet or more for any who should lose his footing. Somehow the stretchers were got down, mainly through the brilliant work of Lance-Corporal A. McMinn, the senior stretcher-bearer; despite the weariness of himself and his men, he spurred them on in their merciful work, and brought all his charges to safety.

Soon after the departure of this first batch of wounded, and after a sharp bombardment, the enemy delivered his expected counter-attack. The Germans came along the ridge from the north and east, and with the aid of automatic fire and many grenades managed to effect a penetration into the position. After a few anxious moments, during which Guardsman R. Tinlin led his section with great dash, they were thrown out again, losing more prisoners and suffering more men killed, but not before they had killed Lance-Sergeant A. Dyson and Lance-Corporal J. Imrie, and severely wounded CSM Young, D.C.M., who was subsequently to lose both a foot and a hand; for the remainder of the night until he could be taken to the rear, the Company Sergeant-Major gave a splendid example of cheerfulness to all around him. After the repulse of the counter-attack an attempt was made to exploit our gains eastwards along the ridge to Point 312, but the enemy was found to be too firmly established to allow for any reasonable prospect of further success.

When darkness again fell Major Coke ringed his position with "Bee-hive" mines and stood-to, prepared for another counter-attack, but none came. Save for some desultory mortaring the night and following day were uneventful, until after dark No. 2 Company relieved the weary men, and they slithered down the slopes they had carried by assault two days before. Two days later in pouring rain the Welsh Guards relieved them "after a charming spell of twenty-one days' bloodiness". The Company waded and heaved its way back through the mud to Castel del Rio, and then drove south to comfortable billets in Strada.

Dec. 6

Dec. 8

The achievement had been a very real one. At the cost of two men killed and an officer and thirteen wounded, far lighter casualties than any had dared to hope, the Company had captured an important feature of the enemy's defence line, taking prisoner an officer and twenty-five men and killing and wounding at least a further score. Major Coke received the Distinguished Service Order for his gallantry and leadership, and Lance-Corporal McMinn and Guardsmen Rush and Tinlin the Military Medal. The loss of CSM Young was greatly to be deplored, but a worthy successor to him was found in Sergeant T. Taylor, M.M., from Right Flank of the First Battalion.

Lack of space forbids a detailed account of the next two months of positional warfare in the Santerno sector. The Green Jackets' attack against Tossignano turned out a costly failure and marked the end of offensive operations. What Captain Dalrymple described with some cynicism as a "Merry Christmas" was spent in a reserve position on Monte Verro, living in the pigsties underneath farmhouses: "Quite revolting, but safe". Rations were supplemented by the butchery of roaming sheep and too-trusting chickens, and, for Lieutenant Fraser, a whole guinea-fowl, since his Platoon were suspicious of so rare a bird! On New Year's Eve the Company moved up to the forward positions on Monte Verro, where the Coldstream platoon attached to it lost two prisoners when the Germans carried out a raid in force on the night of the 2nd January. That night the Scots Guards platoons, too, saw some brisk action, in which Lance-Corporal J. Heap, although slightly wounded, was instrumental in seeing off some aggressive Germans bent on a similar mission; Heap's determination prevented the loss of any prisoners and won for him the Military Medal. In January and February there were four more spells of duty on Monte Verro, and when the 2nd Coldstream left the Santerno valley for the last time, the

Dec. 25

Dec. 31

1945

Jan. 2

Feb. 14

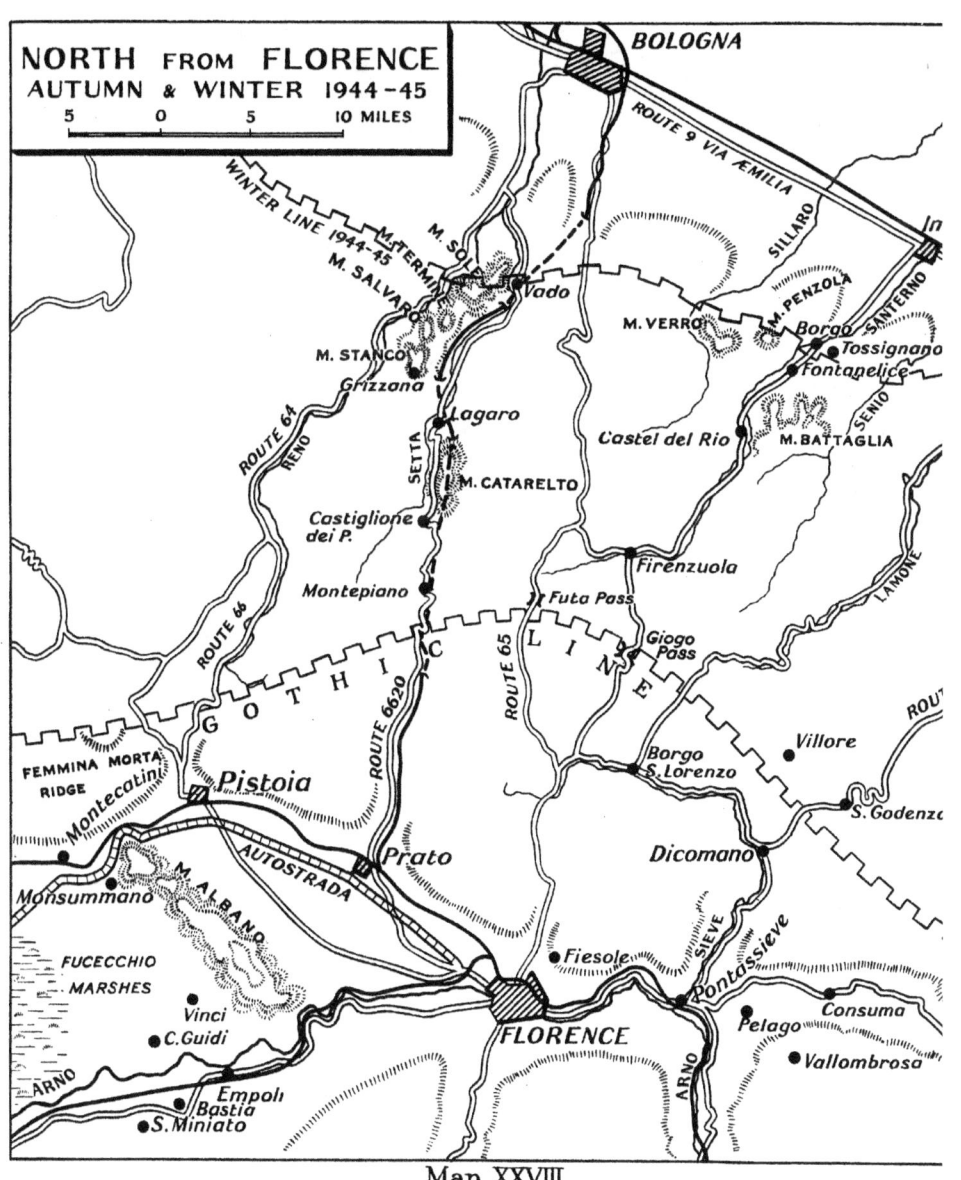

Map XXVIII

thaw had set in, spring was on the way, and the days of S Company as an independent body were numbered. The 1st Guards Brigade joined the 24th at Spoleto, and reorganisation was again the order of the day.

It would be wrong to pretend that there was great enthusiasm in the Company at the prospect of joining the First Battalion as its new B Company. The ties which had grown up between the Company and the Coldstreamers were based on mutual trust and admiration arising from ten months' hard campaigning. Just as the 24th Guards Brigade was loath to leave the South Africans who had treated them as guests, to join a British division where they would be considered nothing very extraordinary, so S Company were sorry to leave the Coldstream. There was a very real appeal in being a member of a unique organisation, and the wrench of parting from old friends was made more difficult by the loss of that exclusive status. But off to the First Battalion the Company had to go, and under its new letter worthily maintained its reputation.

The record of the men who wore the most colourful set of shoulder badges in Italy was indeed a remarkable one. S Company sported the blue and gold Regimental titles, the scarlet II of the Coldstream Battalion, and the black and white of the 6th Armoured Division's Mailed Fist. They had also an unofficial company colour, devised by some Roman ladies, of red and blue silk, emblazoned with a large Regimental star, the Thistle of which had to be conceded "rather a miserable affair; possibly a Roman Thistle, not a Scottish one". But these gaudy trappings did not display their honours. These were recorded on the signed presentation cards which Colonel Coates gave to each officer and man who served with the Company, and to the next-of-kin of those who had been killed. Decorated with the Stars of the Thistle and the Garter, and framed in scrolls listing the eight principal engagements[1] in which the Company had taken part, the cards bore the legend "In appreciation of the excellent fighting spirit and splendid record of S Company and in remembrance of those who have fallen whilst fighting with 2nd Bn. Coldstream Guards." Below were listed the names of those who had been decorated: two Distinguished Service Orders; one Military Cross; two Distinguished Conduct Medals and ten Military Medals.[2] It was a remarkable score. None could deny that each decoration and each tittle of the Company's reputation had been won the hard way. Finally, on their own memorial in the Anglican Church of the Holy Trinity at Florence, the Coldstreamers recorded the names of the three officers and twenty-nine men of S Company who had fallen on the road from Cassino to Penzola.

[1] Cassino, Piccolo, Perugia, M. Lignano, Advance to the Gothic Line, Gothic Line, M. Battaglia, M. Penzola.
[2] In April 1945, as B Company, members of the former S Company won a further two Military Crosses, one Distinguished Conduct Medal and two Military Medals.

VI. TO THE PO AND VICTORY

In April 1945 the Eighth and Fifth Armies destroyed the German Tenth and Fourteenth Armies in Italy. Under their new Commander, General Mark Clark, the Allies were not content merely to contain the divisions facing them; south of the Po they annihilated the enemy's fighting troops and forced on General von Vietinghoff the first capitulation in Europe. This victory was won with resources even smaller than those that had been available in the previous autumn. Not only had the I Canadian Corps and the 5th British Division departed for North-west Europe, not only were two other divisions under orders to follow, but also the II Polish Corps had reserves sufficient for only one major battle, and the unpopular decisions taken at Yalta as to the future boundaries of Poland had produced in the ranks of the Poles a mood of acute despair—a mood they most gallantly overcame. The troubles in Greece had made further inroads on the troops available to Field Marshal Sir Harold Alexander, now Supreme Commander in the Central Mediterranean. In Italy reserves of men and ammunition were perilously small. The problem was to fight and win a short, decisive battle, and thus avoid a succession of set-piece river crossings—of the Po, the Adige, the Brenta and the Piave—and also the storming of the Alps beyond. The relentless infantry battle fought towards Argenta and Bologna by the Eighth Army (Lieutenant-General Sir Richard McCreery) and the subsequent break-out and pursuit from the Apennines by the Fifth Army (Lieutenant-General Lucian Truscott) solved the problem and crowned the achievements of the Italian campaign.

The victory would not have been possible had not the most meticulous attention been paid to the morale of the troops. The Eighth Army's infantry divisions, which, on the road from Salerno, had been shot to pieces time and again, were revitalised by a programme deliberately designed to show their men that they were not members of a "Forgotten Army"—that glib headline title British troops are all too quick to take upon themselves when, for the moment, their front is not that which attracts the main attention of the sub-editors of the more sensational press. To this end a mass of new equipment was procured and this was demonstrated to all divisions, whether they were going to use it or not. Newer marks of Churchill tanks, more heavily armed Shermans, "Crocodile", "Wasp" and "Lifebuoy" flame-throwers, "Ark" bridges, "Kangaroo" armoured troop carriers, and, for the division on the flooded Comacchio flank, amphibious "Buffalo" and "Weasel" tractors. All these dispelled the idea that the Italian front took the place of Cinderella in the queue for equipment.

Allied command of the air was unchallenged, and if the Desert Air Force's fighter-bombers were not quite so up-to-date as were the Tactical Air Force's rocket-firing Typhoons in Germany, it was but a very minor deprivation. The enemy could do nothing to hinder the huge columns of vehicles as they waited to pass the bridges over the numerous water obstacles; but for him road traffic by day was well-nigh impossible. And, for the only occasion in the Italian campaign, an offensive was prepared, launched and concluded without interference from the weather. In that April the heavens made ample recompense for their previous out-pourings of rain and churnings of mud.

(a) *A Final Reorganisation*

The two Guards Brigades met at Spoleto for the final reorganisation of the campaign. The Grenadiers and Coldstream each amalgamated their two battalions, sending home as cadres the 5th and 3rd respectively. Henceforward the 1st Guards Brigade, now commanded by Brigadier G. L. Verney and still in the 6th Armoured Division, consisted of the 3rd Grenadiers, the 3rd Welsh Guards and the 1st Battalion The Welch Regiment. The 24th Guards Brigade consisted of the 2nd Coldstream, the 1st Scots Guards and the 1st Battalion The Buffs; this Brigade was transferred to the 56th (London) Division (Major-General J. Y. Whitfield), the infantry division with which the 201st Guards Brigade had fought its Italian battles of 1943. S Company returned from the 2nd Coldstream and became B Company. Since there were in Italy barely fifty fit Scots Guards reinforcements, plans were made to have available one of the two Coldstream companies which were held in reserve at the I.R.T.D., but fortunately the campaign proved too short for the Coldstreamers to be called upon to settle their outstanding account for the loan of S Company. To command the First Battalion came Lieutenant-Colonel R. G. Lewthwaite, M.C., from the Staff of the 21st Army Group, and to be his second-in-command came Major T. F. R. Bulkeley from Brigade Headquarters.[1]

MAP XXIV
Feb. 19

Mar. 1

Mar. 15

At Spoleto (where the Battalion was billeted in a huge orphanage, the walls of which were covered with outmoded Fascist slogans) the three weeks' stay was predominantly one of recreation. Leave, entertainments, social gatherings and sport were the main occupations. At Rome Prince Doria, appointed by the Allies Mayor of the city on its capture, most generously lent to the Battalion his own beautiful Villa Doria-Pamfili, set in a peaceful park behind the Janiculum Hill; thither went over eight hundred men, some of them getting their first real leave since the previous March. In the Opera House at Spoleto was produced a mammoth revue, *As Improperly Dressed*; under the experienced direction of Captain Buckle the amateur

---
[1] For Order of Battle, see p. 547.

talents of the two Brigades played before enthusiastic audiences. In the Messes entertainment was open-handed; the Scots Guards Sergeants held their delayed Hogmanay party. Taken all in all, when Mar. 9 on the evening of the 9th March the Battalion climbed into a convoy of 3-tonners driven by sleepy Indians, it was smarter and more alert than it had been at any time since passing through Cassino.

Mar. 10 The Battalion drove northwards through the mountains, skirting Ancona, and on up the Adriatic coast. It staged for breakfast at Fano, MAP XXXA whither the I.R.T.D. had moved up from Rotondi. Then on to Forlì, a dirty, dusty, overcrowded town in Mussolini's home province of the Romagna, and at this time the Armentières of the Eighth Army. Here the Brigade joined the 56th Division, and donned its sign of a homely Black Cat; but it must be admitted that it was some weeks before the yellow and green triangle of the South African Division finally disappeared from all shoulders, for several loyal spirits surreptitiously reassumed that popular mark when on leave. However, the Battalion quickly settled down in its new formation, getting off to an encouraging start by winning both the Association and Rugby Football championships of the Division.

Intensive training now succeeded recreation. In accordance with the Army policy, the Guardsmen trained with the "Kangaroo" troop carriers, being visited by General McCreery during the exercise. Signal procedure, night attacks, street fighting, assault-boating were all rehearsed. It was unfortunate that there was no opportunity of making the acquaintance of the various regiments of tanks which were to support the Battalion in action. Here was one of the usual handicaps of the Infantry Division, and one which seemed doubly unfortunate to a battalion which had maintained such close liaison with its previous supporting armour.

Mar. 26 At the end of the month a large party from the Brigade, including three officers and forty men of the Battalion, motored the hundred and fifty miles to Lucca to bid a formal farewell to the South Africans. At a parade on which every tank and vehicle of the Pretoria Regiment was drawn up Brigadier Erskine presented to Colonel Johnstone a pennant of the Brigade colours to be flown from the aerial of his tank. In return the tankmen presented to each battalion of the Brigade a fine impala head, suitably inscribed and mounted.[1]

The event at Forlì which caused a few days of the greatest consternation was the descent on the Brigade of the Inspector of Army

[1] It would be more accurate to say that Brigadier Erskine *attempted* to present the pennant. In his speech the Brigade Commander described a pennant of the Brigade colours as something not easily to be given away. This proved all too true, for the Staff Officer charged with bringing the pennant to Lucca had left it behind at Forlì! A temporary substitute had hastily to be fashioned from the one on the bonnet of the Brigade Commander's car. The Staff Officer concerned was *not* an officer of the Regiment.

Equipment. From time immemorial every soldier has known that the scale of equipment allowed by the War Office is totally inadequate for the comfortable, if not efficient, performance of his duties. Any fool can be uncomfortable, and no self-reliant soldier has ever allowed himself to become so through too rigid an adherence to the scales laid down. In the Second World War the most glaring examples of over-equipment were to be found in the realm of mechanical transport. Every regiment in Italy possessed clandestinely acquired vehicles, and it must be confessed that the Battalions of the Brigade of Guards were notable offenders on this score, especially since to them had been bequeathed the surplus vehicles of those battalions of their Regiments which had gone home; and the Second Battalion Scots Guards had never been noted for travelling light. To the Quartermaster-General's minions it seemed inequitable that the First Battalion should be the proud possessor of, among other desirable items, nineteen jeeps, when the permitted number was eleven. Some hard bargains had to be struck, and some surplus equipment had to be disgorged. Total disaster, however, was narrowly averted. By great good fortune the Inspector had pounced first, unheralded and with his piquets of Military Police, upon the luckless Coldstream; before his arrival at the Scots Guards several heavily laden vehicles had made a hurried exodus to the remote foothills; after his departure they returned, and life went on much as before.

On Easter Sunday, attempting to cover its trail by leaving behind the Pipe Band and all outward signs of occupation, the Battalion drove quietly out of Forlì to bivouac in the ancient pine woods which skirt the coast north of Ravenna. That afternoon it carried out training in the sea with the newly arrived American "Buffaloes", which had been renamed "Fantails" in the hope of concealing their identity from the enemy. Originally designed for crossing the coral reefs and hard beaches of the Pacific, these amphibious tractors were as yet unproved on the steep dykes and in the flooded rice-fields which bounded the shallow Comacchio lagoon.   *April 1*

That night the preliminaries of the great offensive began.

(b) *The Spit*

Before the main Eighth Army attack was launched, there were two amphibious operations to be mounted in the south-east corner of Lake Comacchio. The first was the seizure of the sandy Spit of land which separates the lake from the sea; the second was the capture of an area of flooded fields and dykes north of the Reno known as the Wedge. The seizure of the Spit was entrusted to the 2nd Commando Brigade, supported by the 24th Guards Brigade, and was designed to draw enemy reserves to the north-east corner of the lake; the second was entrusted to the 167th Brigade of the 56th Division, and was designed to provide a springboard for further water-borne ventures to the north-west. On the night of the 1st April the Commandos made their attack. After experiencing the most appalling frustrations with the "Fantails", which proved unable to surmount many of the obstacles in the lake, the Commandos, by a superhuman feat of reorganisation, carried out their attack at dawn in shallow-draft storm-boats. During the next three days they captured all that part of the Spit lying to the south of the Valetta canal—Lake Comacchio's main outlet to the Adriatic. They took over nine hundred prisoners from the 162nd (Turkoman) Division, a low-class formation composed in the main of renegade Russian prisoners, well led by a sprinkling of Germans. On the afternoon of the 4th the Coldstream and Scots Guards moved up over the Reno with orders to cross the Valetta canal that night, and thereafter to exploit north-westward round the top of the lake. But there was inadequate time to mount this attack, and instead the battalions relieved the Commandos in the line, the Scots Guards taking over the left-hand sector with B and C Companies forward. Already intelligence had been received that the capture of the Spit had had the desired effect of drawing German reserves to Porto Garibaldi, the small town on the north bank of the canal, dominating the lower ground to the south; full-blooded Germans of the "Kesselring" Reconnaissance Unit of the 29th Panzer Grenadier Division and of a battalion of the 42nd Jaeger Division had come down to stiffen the shaken Turkomen. The news of these reinforcements did little to raise hopes of success when the order came for the two Battalions to make diversionary raids across the canal on the night of the 5th to coincide with the attack by the 167th Brigade against the Wedge.

April 2

April 4

April 5 Early in the morning, after a night of patrols which reported no German defences south of the canal, the forward companies were withdrawn to a line nearly two miles to the south of Porto Garibaldi, which then received three heavy raids from medium bombers. At dusk the Centre Companies reoccupied their positions, and the advance of the Flank Companies to the canal bank began.

The operation of that night was to be a "Chinese" attack. It was plain that the artillery and Sapper resources were insufficient to sustain a strongly opposed crossing, and strong opposition could certainly be expected from the first-class troops now manning the north bank. If the enemy was found in strength and alert, the orders were that the crossing was not to be pressed. It was hoped that Left Flank (Major A. F. Tuke) would cross at Porto Garibaldi, and B Company (Major Coke) at the hamlet of La Posta, half a mile to the west. Right Flank led the advance to the canal bank opposite Porto Garibaldi, passing through the heaviest defensive fire the Battalion had experienced for many months; miraculously all went through unscathed, except for Major Mann who received a slight wound in the face in the early stages.

The Company reached the bank without further trouble, only to find the surface of the canal brilliantly illuminated by the real moon and also by the artificial light of the searchlights to the Brigade's rear. Behind Right Flank came Lieutenant Nunneley's Assault Pioneers sweeping the tracks for mines, making safe the way for Lieutenant Hayward's convoy of jeeps and trailers carrying the assault boats; as quietly as possible these were deposited in the Boat Assembly Area some three hundred yards south of the canal, where the Support Company Commander, Major A. H. Piper, was dug in with a wireless set to maintain communications. So far no Spandau had fired from the north bank, and it was now time to try for a crossing. Left Flank lay under mortar fire behind Right Flank waiting for the word, and one of the Platoon Commanders, Lieutenant D. A. Colquhoun and his servant, Guardsman Whyte, made a courageous attempt to cross the canal in an inflated rubber reconnaissance boat to examine the far bank for a suitable landing place and to search for mines and wire. When the boat was halfway across the water, an illuminating flare rose from the north bank, the enemy machine-gunners opened fire, and the boat and its occupants disappeared from view. Plainly the enemy was still alert and prepared to defend the line of the canal, and, it seemed, he was not demoralised by the bombing. For Left Flank to attempt a crossing now would be to invite a bloody disaster. Further to the left B Company also had been thwarted by the brightness of the night. In the small hours Brigadier Erskine gave the order for both battalions to be withdrawn.

April 6

In its wider context of a diversion to assist the 167th Brigade's successful attack on the Wedge the "Chinese" attack could be adjudged profitable, though the deaths of Lieutenant Colquhoun, Guardsman Whyte, and Lance-Sergeant Nesbit (also of Left Flank and killed by a mortar bomb) seemed to the Battalion a heavy price to pay for so little immediate result; in the sixth year of a war "operations in aid of a Corps plan cut no ice". Nevertheless Colonel Lewthwaite was able to write home that he had been very pleased with the performance of the Battalion, and was also pleased to find "that everyone knew his job very adequately".

There was now no prospect of further successful offensive operations across the main reach of the Valetta Canal, as daily heavy weapons in support of the Spit sector were withdrawn. Patrols went nightly to the canal bank and B and C Companies made some abortive forays across the western reach into some salt-pans, where it proved impossible to clear all the houses due to the coverless nature of the approaches along the raised causeways. One stormy night Lieutenant P. J. Blandy and Guardsman Lillico of C Company (Major D. P. M. Malcolm) when returning from patrol were accidentally wounded when fired on in error by a sentry who did not hear the password, and another night Guardsman Forbes of the same Company was hit by a burst of enemy fire. The Battalion took over the whole sector on the 8th, and the next night its supporting weapons took part in an elaborate diversionary shoot, for that afternoon the Eighth Army had launched the main attack across the Senio. The only Scots Guardsmen who took part in that assault were the men of the "Wasp" flame-thrower section (Lieutenant T. N. Douglas), which supported troops of the 8th Indian Division across the high flood-banks—or, as they were called in Anglo-Indian jargon, bunds. With the whole front now in action the Battalion could not expect to be left for long basking in the warm sun among the gorse bushes. On the night of the 10th the Spit was handed over to the 43rd (Royal Marine) Commando, and the Scots Guards returned to the Pineta north of Ravenna. The 56th and 78th Divisions, under the V Corps commanded by Lieutenant-General C. F. Keightley, were about to storm the Argenta Gap.

(c) *The Argenta Gap*

Whereas to the south of the Reno the Poles, New Zealanders and Indians had to contend with a succession of embanked rivers—the Senio, the Santerno, the Silaro and the Idice—to the north the obstacles were of a different nature. Here the Germans had breached the dykes, flooding the low-lying reclaimed land. There remained but two narrow funnels of dry, tank-bearing ground, known collectively as the Argenta Gap. Through the wider and more southerly funnel ran the main road from Ravenna to Ferrara (Route 16), passing the large village of Argenta from which the gap took its name; at its narrowest this funnel was about a mile wide, and its close cultivation afforded some cover, though it restricted visibility and movement. This funnel was the concern of the 78th Division, and, if it was opened before the line of the Idice further to the south had been breached, it was through here that the 6th Armoured Division was to make its decisive thrust north-westwards towards the Po crossings. Three miles farther to the north across marshes impassable to vehicles, in completely open country where only waterlogged ditches gave cover, was the second and narrower funnel; this was the concern of the 56th Division. Along the top of a dyke skirting the waters ran a minor road, the Strada della Pioppa, roughly parallel to Route 16. At its narrowest the northerly funnel was about half a mile broad; at this point a substantial drainage canal ran athwart the road: the Fossa Marina. The fight for the crossing of this canal was the Battalion's main effort in the forcing of the Argenta Gap.

The capture of the Wedge at the outset of the battle had provided an admirable jumping-off place from which to launch a right-hook attack across the floods. On the 11th the 169th (Queen's) Brigade had made a successful attack over the waters to the Strada della Pioppa in the neighbourhood of Menate, and confidence in the "Fantails" was temporarily restored. It was now the turn of the 24th Guards Brigade, which was ordered to seize the crossings of the Fossa Marina by a water-borne assault, and, in conjunction with the 2nd Parachute Brigade which was to be dropped two miles north-west of the canal, to threaten Argenta from the north-east. But three factors marred the execution of the plan. First, at the last moment it appeared that the enemy had got wind of the proposed parachute descent, which had then to be abandoned. Secondly, to bolster up the battered 42nd Jaeger Division, he had brought up from reserve the major part of the 29th Panzer Grenadier Division, together with some Tiger tanks. And thirdly, once again, the going proved too difficult for the "Fantails".

April 11

At dawn on the 13th the Buffs and the 9th Commando attempted an assault landing on the Strada della Pioppa near the mouth of the Fossa Marina. Many hazards of navigation were encountered, and severe casualties were sustained in the stranded "Fantails", particularly by the Buffs. Few of the original objectives were reached, and those that were reached were all south of the Fossa Marina. The Buffs displayed the greatest gallantry in their desperate situation, taking and holding against all counter-attacks the important bridge called Ponte Ovaretta. Among those subsequently decorated was Guardsman J. Wade, a "Weasel" driver of the Scots Guards attached to the Buffs for the landing. When his "Weasel" was knocked out, instead of remaining in the rear as he might reasonably have done, Wade joined an assaulting company and gave such a good account of himself in a house-to-house battle that Lieutenant-Colonel G. E. F. Oliver of the Buffs recommended him for the Military Medal. By dawn on the 15th the Coldstream and the Commando had cleared all the ground to the south of the Fossa Marina, but an attempt by the Commando to cross the partly destroyed bridge which carried the road over the canal had been unsuccessful. By this time the Battalion had come up through Menate and B Company had been attached to the Commando to support them if necessary; but save for some risky reconnaissance patrols to the canal bank, the Company had not been seriously involved. At midday came orders for the Scots Guards and the 9th Commando to cross the Fossa Marina that night.

April 13
MAP XXIX

April 15

The first attempt to cross the canal met with no success. Immediately darkness fell patrols set out towards the Fossa Marina and towards the Scolo Parato, a minor canal which flowed into the Marina from the south and into which it was intended to launch the assault boats. No Germans were found south of the Marina but many mines were discovered, the clearance of which took several hours before the boat assembly area could be declared safe. When the Battalion's pioneers had done their dangerous work, the Companies began their forward move. C and B Companies went first, and, with their assault boats, moved across the flat open fields towards the Parato about

April 16

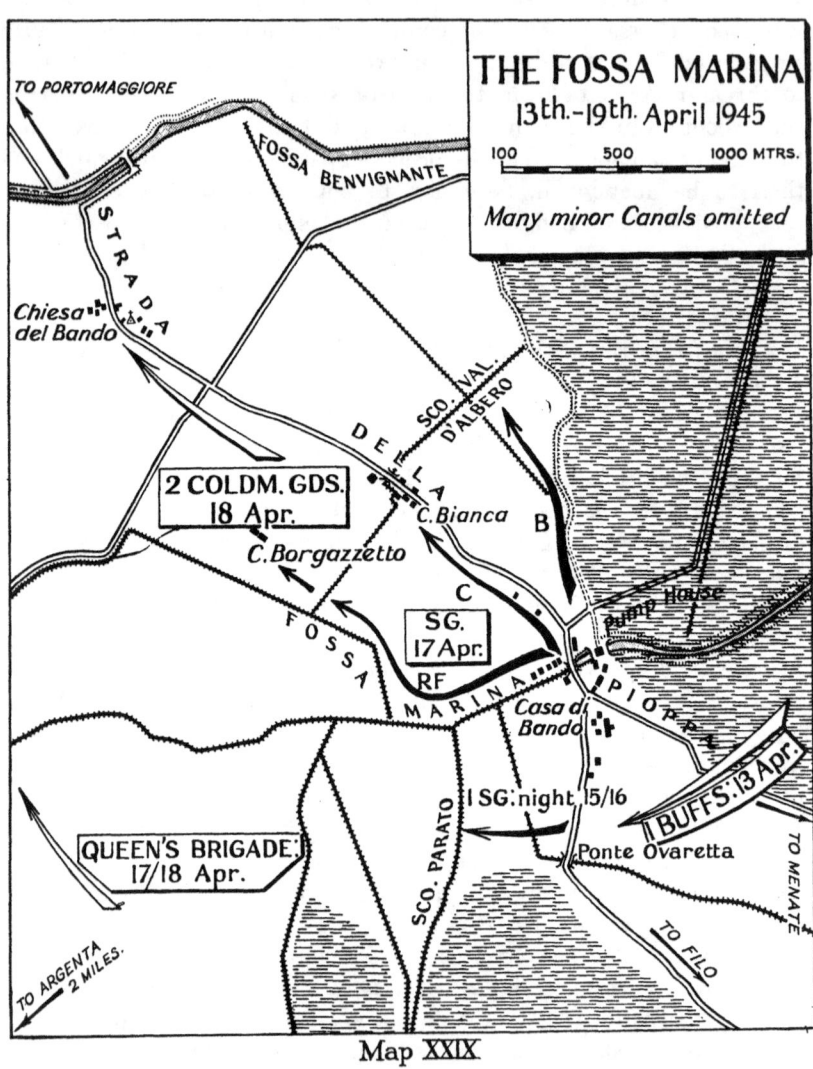

Map XXIX

three hundred yards south of the Marina. Despite heavy supporting fire from medium and field artillery, from tanks, M. 10s and machine-guns, the Panzer Grenadiers dug into the bunds and emplaced in the houses on the north bank were in no wise subdued. The glare of searchlights away to the south, which was of great assistance to the

78th Division, again proved a decided impediment to the advancing Guardsmen, revealing them to the enemy in sharp silhouette. Heavy Spandau fire met them, and several of their canvas boats were punctured before many yards had been covered. Moreover among the houses on the north bank lurked several powerful S.P. guns which, in the darkness, our tanks and M. 10s were unable to locate, let alone silence. One of these guns fired with disconcerting accuracy at the house in which Captain Mansfield had set up his Aid Post, hitting it with six shots; at the same time a Spandau on a fixed line was putting bursts of tracer in at the front door and out at the back. By half-past five in the morning it was clear that there could be no crossing before the dawn revealed the unprotected Guardsmen spread out on the bare ground; the attack was abandoned and the Battalion withdrew to rest and plan anew. On the right of the Strada della Pioppa the Commandos had met with no better fortune.

In daylight, while medium guns and the aircraft of the Desert Air Force allowed the enemy no respite, Major-General Whitfield, Brigadier Erskine, and the Commanding Officer carried out a close reconnaissance of the Fossa Marina, the result of which was an order to attempt a furtive crossing by a small party into a pump house which had been one of the Commando's objectives the previous night. This pump house, between the road and the lake, stood in the middle of the canal joined to either bank by sluice-gates topped by substantial bridges, the southern span of which had been demolished, leaving a gap of twenty-five feet between the pump house and the south bank. At first a small bridge of assault boats was to be floated in the gap, then a party was to cross it to take the pump house, and then a company was to form a bridgehead on the north bank. In order that tanks and anti-tank guns should be promptly available in case of a counter-attack, an "Ark" (a turretless Churchill hull with ramps attached to either end) would then be driven into the canal, and the vehicles enabled to cross. Later a larger bridge would be built on the site of the demolished road bridge. The First Battalion was ordered to make the crossing, and soon after dark the Guardsmen took over the positions immediately to the south of the pump house.

Fortunately the enemy had posted no-one in the pump house itself, considering either that it was too exposed a station or that any advance in that direction could be prevented by fire from the houses and bunds further back. At about eleven a Sapper officer swam out to the house, and on his return reported that the proposed bridge of boats was feasible. Immediately after his reconnaissance the Germans plastered the pump house and its approaches with rifle grenades and small arms fire, so that, before bridging could begin, the area had to be obscured by smoke, put down by the Gunners and by the Battalion's two-inch mortars. In an opaque cloud and to the deafening noise of a April 17 bombardment the bridge was successfully completed at four o'clock. Led by Captain E. I. Ll. Mostyn a party of Left Flank got into the pump house, and later the whole company crossed to the north bank to form a shallow bridgehead. B Company followed at half-past five, clearing by assault the houses and bunds to a depth of two hundred yards. Here Sergeant J. Allardyce led the platoon he was commanding with especial dash across dead flat ground against an enemy well dug in, and cleared buildings and captured prisoners in handsome fashion. Later Right Flank hurried across. Once again Major Mann was in command, having quickly recovered from his wound "lest his beloved Right Flank might win the war without him". This Company turned to the left, and with the awe-inspiring support from the south bank of a "Crocodile" flame-thrower, cleared the houses along the north bank to the west of the road. By seven o'clock C Company was safely over, the "Ark" bridge was in position, the armour was beginning to cross, and a score of prisoners had been taken. Among these were identified men from both the regiments of the 29th Panzer Grenadiers and they disclosed that their division was fully committed along the Fossa Marina.

All now seemed set for the Battalion to advance to the Scolo Val d'Albero: the "next canal", a phrase as common that April as had been the "next ridge" the previous summer. An advance in daylight across the open ground was bound to result in heavy losses, and the only cover to be had was in the ditches and along the bunds which flanked the road and the canals. The task would have been much easier had a sufficient number of tanks been able to cross the Marina, but after the leading troop of A Squadron of the 10th Royal Hussars had got across, an M.10 of an anti-tank battery missed its footing on the "Ark" and toppled into the water, so tilting the contraption that it was temporarily of no further use for vehicles. The three tanks which had got over were allotted to Major Malcolm to support C Company in its advance up the line of the road, for here, for a part of the way, a string of small dwellings gave the tanks some shelter from the powerful self-propelled guns along the Val d'Albero.

Accustomed as the Battalion had been to long-standing close liaison with a whole Squadron of the Pretoria Regiment, and accustomed as it had been to fighting in undulating country where the skilful use of ground could enable both tanks and men to approach an enemy unobserved, the support of a single troop from an unfamiliar Regiment in these coverless fields seemed most inadequate.

During the day the Battalion fought its way forward on a three-company front. On the right, skirting the floods, B Company did well to worm up the ditches and dykes, and, at times, to dash across the open, but it took all the daylight hours to cover the thousand yards to the Val d'Albero. Once again one of the platoon commanders,

Lance-Sergeant G. S. Dudgeon, displayed outstanding leadership, greatly encouraging his men, who by now had had no proper sleep for the two previous nights; he was later awarded the Distinguished Conduct Medal.

On the left flank Major Mann led his company along the line of the Fossa Marina towards its junction with the Val d'Albero. Before reaching this goal the company was heavily mortared while lying on the canal bank, and some dozen casualties were suffered in Lieutenant Wallace's platoon. The seriously wounded were got away by the gallant action of the Medical Sergeant, Sergeant Barber, M.M., who was himself wounded on the journey to the rear. Sergeant Barber brought up to Right Flank an assault boat flying a Red Cross flag, which did not prevent the enemy shelling the boat the whole way up the Marina, and the whole way down again to the Scolo Parato. When the wounded were disembarked at the end of the journey they were again shelled, one of them, Lance-Sergeant Gill, being killed. This boating trip marked the climax of Sergeant Barber's splendid service to the wounded throughout the war.

It was C Company on the axis of the road which met the stiffest resistance. The Company began its advance by a series of forward rushes under the cover of smoke and with the support of the tanks, one of which was almost immediately put out of action by a bazooka. One by one the houses were occupied, but determined resistance from all manner of German "frightfulness" was encountered at one of the numerous Casa Biancas. Here the leading platoon under Lieutenant G. Godfrey-Isaacs was pinned in the ditches, the slightest movement drawing the fire of enfilading Spandaus. But the advance was put in motion again by a spirited attack led with outstanding bravery by Lieutenant A. O. Worthington-Wilmer. Covered by a patchy smoke-screen, Lieutenant Worthington-Wilmer led his platoon in extended order across completely open ground, assaulted and cleared Casa Bianca, and held it in the face of close-range fire from three sides. In this he was assisted by the two remaining Sherman tanks, but their effectiveness was gravely reduced when the Troop Leader was killed by a sniper. By now it was four in the afternoon, and pressing orders were coming from the Brigade Commander for the Battalion to clear the whole line of the Val d'Albero as soon as possible, in order that the Coldstream might pass through to attack the village of Chiesa del Bando. For C Company this involved assaulting a prominent house on the north bank, which could only be reached by scrambling over the remains of a demolished bridge. In the house and on the banks the enemy were still in strength. Under cover of the fire of Lieutenant Worthington-Wilmer's platoon two sections of Sergeant E. Robbie's platoon made a gallant attempt to cross the blow, but they were met by a shower of grenades and a stream of bullets, being forced back with loss. By now there remained in action but one tank, and this was running short of ammunition. It had carried out many shoots at the houses on the north bank, and had been itself the frequent target of the enemy anti-tank weapons as it dodged about among the houses.

April 18

When darkness fell the demands from Brigade Headquarters to push on became more insistent, and, through heavy defensive fire, Left Flank was brought up from the pump house. Captain Mostyn carried out a detailed close reconnaissance of the houses north of the bridge, and in the small hours he was able to report no sign of the enemy; by three o'clock Left Flank were over and the way was clear for the Coldstream to cross to resume the advance. On the right B Company had more difficulty in approaching the canal, sustaining casualties from fire from another house on the north bank, but this was later subdued by our artillery, and the canal from the lake to the road was reported clear. To the left of the road Right Flank had already reported its sector of the far bank to have been abandoned by the enemy.

When the Coldstream went forward at four in the morning, Right Flank was charged with the protection of their left and with the capture of the houses at Casa Borgazzetto. Major Mann was unable to receive his orders before dark, nor could he receive them personally from the Coldstream Commanding Officer, Lieutenant-Colonel W. L. Steele. In the darkness and smoke of battle the identification of the houses proved extremely hard. The Company ferried itself across the Val d'Albero in a leaky boat, found by chance lying half-submerged in the canal. It then formed up on the far side and moved off towards the supposed objective. It proved almost impossible to find, and everyone got very tired searching for it in country intersected with numerous ditches. But by first light all had been put right, and the Company was disposed in its intended positions, without loss. Touch had now to be gained with the Queen's Brigade to the south-west. This Brigade had crossed the floods north of Argenta on foot, and was now up to the line of the Fossa Marina. Lieutenant Wallace found the Queen's outposts, but had a few anxious moments before he convinced the sentries that he was not a German in disguise; only a flow of uninhibited English preserved him from being shot out of hand.

The advance of the Coldstream went well, yielding many prisoners, but for the Scots Guards it meant an unpleasant period of shelling and mortaring as the enemy attempted to hinder the construction of a bridge over the Val d'Albero. By eleven Chiesa del Bando had been taken, and B Company and Left Flank were patrolling forward over the ditches and fields on the right of the road towards the next substantial water obstacle, the Fossa Benvignante. It was hoped that at dusk the Coldstream might "bounce" the bridge over this canal north of Bando, and that the 167th Brigade would then pass through to debouch from the Argenta bottleneck. But by a few minutes the

Coldstream were denied their bridge, a failure which was doubly disappointing since the Queen's Brigade had succeeded in a similar mission further west, and therefore it was through that Brigade that the 167th was committed. After dark B Company and Left Flank reached the Benvignante, from which it appeared the enemy had pulled back, and in the morning B Company, unopposed, sent a patrol to the north bank. Save for the loss on a mine of a patrolling carrier and its crew, the Battalion's part in the action was at an end. The Argenta Gap had been forced.

April 19

The Scots Guards contribution to that victory had cost them nineteen killed and forty-seven wounded, nearly half the casualties falling on C Company. In three exhausting days and nights they had forced two substantial obstacles against first-class enemy troops ensconsed in strong positions and equipped with weapons as good as any in Italy. In the words applied to the wider battle by the Short Official History[1] the enemy's "best troops in a series of well defended positions of very great natural strength, had failed to prevent the Eighth Army's veteran divisions from breaking his line: within forty-eight hours the victors and the vanquished would be racing for the Po." The Scots Guards had done their share of breaking this line by sheer determination and courage in the open, for in the naked flatness of the Comacchio flank manœuvre and guile had been of little assistance.

From every other sector came good news, for by the 20th both Armies were in full cry. The 78th Division had taken Argenta, and the 6th Armoured Division had passed through and was thrusting south of Ferrara towards the Po; the Poles had defeated the Parachutists, their old antagonists from Cassino, and were on the eve of their triumphant entry into Bologna; and the Fifth Army had burst out of the Apennines and was racing forward almost unopposed. But the news which gave the greatest pleasure to all was that of the storming by the 12th South African Motor Brigade of the three forbidding peaks dominating the Setta valley: Sole, Abelle and Caprara. It came as no surprise to the First Battalion to learn that, in the course of that bitterly contested assault, three South African tanks had reached the heights.

(d) *The Chase to the Po*

The Battalion was granted a night's rest before resuming the advance. In the interval the V Corps had moved forward with ever increasing rapidity. On the 56th Division's axis canal after canal had been crossed, until, with the capture of Portomaggiore and the forcing of the Condotto Brello by the 167th Brigade, it could be said that the enemy's left flank had been unhinged from its Comacchio pivot. The race to the Po was on. To that river the enemy was now in full retreat

April 20

[1] *The Campaign in Italy*, by Eric Linklater (H.M.S.O.), p. 438.

in the vain hope of retiring across it with some, at least, of his heavy weapons; but the remorseless attacks of the Desert Air Force and the disruptive thrusts of our mobile troops frustrated all but a very few of his divisions. The 56th Division was given the task of protecting the Corps' right flank, and at the same time of making all speed to the north. For the next week the First Battalion was engaged in darting advances on foot and in transport, and in dogged scraps with stubborn rearguards. The landscape had now changed from wide vistas of flat fields to close cultivation, which allowed little visibility either to the flanks or ahead; but still the main obstacles were the numerous canals and their demolished bridges.

On the afternoon of the 20th the Battalion moved up through Portomaggiore and the 169th Brigade with the intention of driving eastwards across the rear of the enemy confronting the Buffs and the Coldstream, who were held up along the line of a succession of canals. But it soon became clear that these Germans had pulled back, and there came new orders to advance with all speed to the north. Right Flank, supported by Churchill tanks of the 12th Royal Tank Regiment, led on unopposed through the night, collecting a miscellaneous assortment of stragglers, whose unkempt and hungry appearance displayed all the symptoms of an army in dissolution. Speed was now more than ever essential. Swift strokes in the halflight might well prevent the destruction of bridges and culverts, and the capture intact of even the smallest of these was of the greatest advantage to the tanks and to the overworked Sappers. B Company claimed the first notable success when at first light it took the lead and, with the aid of a troop of Churchills, "bounced" a substantial bridge. Pushing on without delay it seemed that Major Coke might penetrate far into the enemy's rear and capture many prisoners. But at ten o'clock two Spitfires made an error of recognition and machine-gunned the column, killing one of the tank drivers, and causing such a delay that surprise was lost. In the afternoon, also, Left Flank (Major Tuke) experienced a characteristic check when the armour leading its column was engaged by two anti-tank guns, an 88-mm. and a 75-mm. Despite the presence of Churchills and armoured cars it took nearly two hours in that close country to take these German guns, demonstrating once again the paralysing effect these weapons could still exert upon the tanks. However, both guns were overrun, and with them were taken more prisoners. After dark Right Flank and B Company moved forward again, with orders to reach the next major obstacle, the Po di Volano, as quickly as possible. Air reconnaissance reports about the bridges here had been optimistic, but on arrival none was found intact, nor were any Germans to be seen. Early in the morning B Company clambered over the remains of the main bridge at Finale di Rero, clearing the village, and taking stragglers and vehicles. Soon bridge-building was under way, for it was now decided that through here the whole Division was to pass, and across this bridge were to come huge quantities of ammunition and equipment for the assault crossing of the Po. In two nights and a day the Battalion had covered some dozen miles, they had crossed some dozen canals and streams, and had taken a dozen score of prisoners. These came from no less than five different divisions, the mixed bag indicating the chaos which now reigned in the enemy's rear; and, indicating the fate of his heavy weapons, was the presence in that bag of sixty men of a Tiger tank battalion: they were Tiger-less and on foot.

It fell to the Coldstream to head the advance for the next twenty-four hours, a period of great optimism at the prospect of a rush to the Po and of an immediate crossing by the other Brigades. General McCreery and Mr. Harold Macmillan, the Minister Resident at Field Marshal Alexander's Headquarters, came to Finale di Rero, adding to the sense of urgency. But though the enemy was disorganised, the innate military qualities of the German soldier were once again to be manifested by a determined rearguard.

The Coldstream, despite the loss in an ambush of a complete company and its transport, had passed through Copparo to the village of Cesta by the morning of the 23rd. Away to the west at dawn that day, *April 23* the 6th Armoured Division had reached the Po beyond Ferrara, shortly to be followed further to the west by troops of the Fifth Army, who made the first unopposed crossing that night. Back on the front of the 56th Division, in the afternoon the First Battalion was ordered to cover the final four miles to the river.

It was plain that, once again, success would depend upon good fortune with the bridges. The first one of importance lay about half a mile to the north of the village of Coccanile, spanning the Canale Bianco, the largest obstacle now remaining between the Battalion and the Po. To the north of the Bianco were two smaller canals, the Montecchio and the Andio. Colonel Lewthwaite planned to capture the Bianco bridge from two sides at once. Left Flank, with Churchill and Honey tanks and followed by the main body of the Battalion, was to advance from Cesta through Coccanile by the direct route, coming upon the bridge from the south-west; C Company (Captain T. C. Lindsay-Peto, M.C.), with some of the Battalion's Vickers machine-guns and a troop of Churchills, was to make a wide sweep to the east and to come down upon the bridge from that direction.

C Company made its detour, gaining much assistance from the armoured cars of the 27th Lancers patrolling wide on that flank. By eleven at night the Company had wormed its way westward along the banks of the Bianco, and had launched a spirited assault on the houses dominating the bridge. These were swiftly cleared, the success owing much to the leadership of Sergeant W. A. Hill, whose valour won him the Distinguished Conduct Medal. The bridge also was seized, and a tight bridgehead formed to the north of it. But unfortunately the bridge was found to have been partly demolished and to be incapable of bearing tanks. The enemy had been taken by surprise, and several unsuspecting parties and vehicles were shot up as they approached the Company; Lance-Sergeant C. Ogg and his section had some easy close-range targets.

April 24

Left Flank, which had cleared Coccanile, passed through C Company just before midnight, pressing on as fast as possible to the next canal, the Montecchio, which ran parallel to the Bianco five hundred yards to the north. An attack was quickly mounted, and, after wading the canal, the Company took the bridge and the house to the north of it in the face of some resistance from the surprised Germans and at a cost of three killed. Normally it was an axiom of tactics that infantry should never be separated from adequate anti-tank weapons. But in a chase such as this with very little likelihood of meeting enemy armour, this cautious rule was often disregarded. This time the gamble did not come off.

The capture of the Bianco bridge had been most unwelcome to the enemy, who, as we now know and as some suspected at the time, had intended to hold the line of that canal until dusk on the 24th. When Left Flank penetrated beyond the Montecchio he became really alarmed, and energetically set about restoring the situation. The 98th Volksgrenadier Division—which had as its sign a somewhat more emaciated cat than the plump animal worn by the 56th Division—assembled a battle-group of about three weak companies, supported by a battery of six small S.P. guns of Italian manufacture, each mounting a short 75-mm. gun. This force came rapidly down the road, loosing off its weapons in all directions. The presence of the S.P.s, which in the darkness were taken for tanks, decided Major Tuke to withdraw to the south bank of the Montecchio. Leaving a section in the upper storey of the house on the north bank to cover the retreat, the two platoons withdrew to the houses south of the canal where they joined the third platoon. Here, while searching for some men who had gone astray in the dark, Major Tuke had the misfortune to run into a party of the enemy and to be taken prisoner. Two of his signallers also fell into enemy hands, as did the seven men left north of the canal. The remainder of Left Flank was now withdrawn on to C Company, which held firm to its bridgehead and thus denied the enemy his main objective of destroying the Bianco bridge. In the confusion of the night the officers and non-commissioned officers of Left Flank had done well to get their men to the rear in good order, Lieutenant S. C. M. Bland and Sergeant Ferguson especially distinguishing themselves by ensuring that every man in their platoons was accounted for. CSM R. H. Thomson, who with Captain Mostyn was the sole remaining member of the Company to have come abroad with it from the Fourth Battalion, took a firm grip on the remnants, reorganised them on the line of the Bianco, and in all respects exhibited that steadfast courage which had been such a feature of his long service in Italy: he was later awarded the Distinguished Conduct Medal. Soon after dawn B Company took over the bridgehead from C Company; that Company had remained steady during several hours of severe mortar fire and the unsettling withdrawal of Left Flank. Its casualties in performing this sterling service included Captain Lindsay-Peto mortally wounded.

Plans were now laid to attack again, but it was plain that there could now be no deep advance until adequate anti-tank weapons could be got across the Bianco. From the air the enemy S.P.s could be seen lined up along a thick hedge immediately to the north of the Montecchio, but all attempts by fighter-bombers to destroy them proved unavailing. To fill the gap in the bridge fascines were dropped into the canal, and at last the Churchills began to cross. As at the Fossa Marina, the first tank got safely over, but the second failed to keep to the middle and fell into the water, once more rendering the bridge impassable to vehicles. Thus our own heavy weapons achieved what a gallant German officer had failed to do: armed with a bazooka he had ridden down the road at speed in the sidecar of a motor-cycle, only to be severely wounded and captured within a few yards of his goal. But without waiting for the tanks, B Company had already begun to advance northwards, the platoons of Lieutenants I. J. Fraser and P. W. Bartholomew being directed on a group of houses a hundred yards south of the Montecchio bridge. These houses fell only after stiff fighting, and after a wild charge across the open by Lieutenant Bartholomew's men covered by the fire of Lieutenant Fraser's. Both platoons then fortified themselves in the houses, to which the solitary Churchill now came forward. Hardly had it arrived and begun to poke its nose round the corner than an unlucky shot from one of the S.P.s hit it in the track, immobilising it where it could give no support. A further advance was once again out of the question.

Meanwhile the third platoon of B Company had been engaged in a fierce battle on its own. Along the banks of the Bianco westward from the bridge there were still nests of aggressive machine-gunners, and the winkling out of these proved costly. While attacking one of them Lieutenant E. F. Winter was killed by a grenade.

The security of the two forward platoons depended on the destruction of the S.P. guns in the hedge. There seemed little chance of the bridge being repaired for several hours, and the platoon commanders at once took the solution into their own hands. Both Fraser and Bartholomew crawled out into the open and secured hits on two of the guns with P.I.A.T. bombs; the range was long and the fire positions were exposed, but these gallant actions enabled the Guardsmen to get the upper hand. All the while German infantry had been active in the bushes round the houses. Foremost in the fight against these had been Lance-Sergeant J. Moir, whose section chased off a party of fifteen from the left rear and also killed two daring men armed with bazookas who were crawling up a ditch towards the houses. By now a platoon of Right Flank had come forward as a reinforcement, and this also took part in the defence, Lance-Sergeant A. Black performing a similar feat with a P.I.A.T. against a third S.P. It was at this stage that the frustrated Guardsman Morris, of Right Flank, whose duty it was to carry and to fire the ungainly weapon, was heard to complain that "You can't get a —— shoot for the —— officers and sergeants!" The snipers, however, got their best shoot for many days, picking off several of the enemy as they fled to the north; but undoubtedly their most difficult targets were the crews of the S.P.s as they jumped from their weapons like scalded cats when the P.I.A.T. bombs struck home.

By the early evening the enemy fire had slackened, and when B Company was finally relieved by the remainder of Right Flank the dangerous part of the battle was nearly at an end. Major Mann brought with him two Churchills and two M.10s, for the bridge was at last April 25 repaired. With this overwhelming support, soon after midnight Right Flank crossed the Montecchio by a rickety plank to the west of the road, finding all the enemy gone and his smoking S.P.s abandoned. The Company pushed on to occupy the houses and farms immediately to the north and also to seize intact the bridge over the Andio, "positively the last water obstacle before the Po". Blocking the bridge was another burnt out S.P., and yet another was found undamaged in a barn nearby. With the mopping up of weary prisoners and the unopposed advance up the road of the Coldstream, the First Battalion concluded its last day of fighting in Hitler's war. On that last day it had taken 150 prisoners at the cost of two officers, Lance-Corporal Heap, M.M., and eight others killed, twenty wounded, and the prisoners already noted from Left Flank. Also on that last day, unknown to the troops, a German SS general had arrived in Switzerland with full authority from General von Vietinghoff to negotiate the surrender of his armies.

Since leaving Forlì on Easter Sunday the Battalion's total losses had amounted to three officers and twenty-nine men killed, and three officers and eighty men wounded. These casualties, which might be considered relatively light in view of the fierceness of the battle, were nevertheless sufficient to consume all the Regiment's reinforcements in Italy. The reserves had only just lasted out.

The Battalion was content to learn the details of the last weeks of the war from the B.B.C., from the *Eighth Army News* and from Captain Keith's huge world information map displayed outside the

Intelligence Office. Deadly arrows pointed at the heart of Germany, and already a ring of Russians encircled Berlin. In Italy the war was to last but one week more. On the night of the 25th the Coldstream sent their companies over the Po without hindrance, and then the other two Brigades of the Division carried on the advance through Rovigo and on to Venice. Far away to the west and north the final seal was being put upon the fate of von Vietinghoff's armies as Americans, South Africans and New Zealanders sliced through his rearward areas, forcing with unexpected ease the well-prepared defences on the Adige and the Brenta. Already on the afternoon of the 25th the reason for this feeble resistance had been explained—by a German general. Lieutenant-General the Graf von Schwerin, commander of the LXXVI Panzer Corps, surrendered to the 27th Lancers with dignity and the remains of his champagne. His Corps had been opposed to the V Corps throughout the battle, and now, he said, he could no longer fight with a few Divisional Headquarters which had no troops to command. The troops were in the cages, and their smouldering equipment littered the fields to the south of the Po. Those of the First Battalion who had felt the lash of the *Luftwaffe* five years before in Norway, saw in the havoc wrought by the Desert Air Force a stern and just retribution.

As the battle, such as it was, receded, the Scots Guards rested. With the news of victory coming from every front, a few, foreseeing perhaps an early return to the fields of commerce, occupied their time in the catching of abandoned German Army horses, and in selling them to unwary peasants. The sellers, of course, passed no good title to war booty, and loud were the protestations of the purchasers when Authority relieved them of their dearly bought animals. A "receipt" inscribed "This Wop paid me 2,000 *lire*: he's had it" and signed "Harry Lauder" or "Donald Duck" was found to give no protection.

The 29th, the day the terms of surrender were agreed in secret at Caserta, brought a move to the north of the Po. The Companies marched to the bank, and, peacefully in D.U.K.W.s, crossed the broad, brown stream of which they had talked for so long. The transport made a wide detour to the great bridge erected north of Ferrara. With this column went, it must be admitted, more vehicles than ever before. Captured German lorries swelled the numbers, which, doubtless to the rage of the Inspector of Army Equipment had he known, now included the twentieth Jeep. By the evening the Battalion was billeted among some squalid farms to the east of Rovigo. Here on the next day Major Tuke and the captured Left Flankers rejoined, having been liberated in Padua by a partisan rising; they, too, could testify to the effectiveness of the air attacks to which they had been subjected during their eighty-mile march to the north.

On the 2nd May the final capitulation of all German forces to the west of the River Isonzo came into force. The campaign in Italy had ended, but an intricate tangle on her frontiers had now to be unravelled.

VII. TITO AND TRIESTE

MAP V

To the east of the Isonzo the Germans were not yet ready to surrender. Here they were withdrawing from the Balkans before the advance of Marshal Tito's Jugoslav Partisan Army of National Liberation; before laying down arms General von Loehr was anxious to get Allied troops between his men and the "Jugs"—as the Partisans were called by the troops. Already Tito's men had penetrated into Italian territory, overrunning the whole frontier province of Venezia Giulia, and in some places crossing the Isonzo into the purely Italian province of Friuli, where they were eager to settle accounts with several thousand fleeing Chetnicks and Ustashi, their Serb and Croat opponents in the bitter civil war. Several months previously in Belgrade Field Marshal Alexander and Marshal Tito had agreed that any Partisans who might cross the Italian frontier would come under Alexander's command, but now, flushed with success and finding that his army had got much farther to the west than he had expected, Marshal Tito went back on his word. The first of Europe's post-war trouble spots had erupted.

The dispute was primarily one for politicians, not for soldiers. In short, there were four main interested parties. The Jugoslavs, with the tacit consent of the Russians, laid claim to all Venezia Giulia including the predominantly Italian cities of Trieste, Pola, Gorizia and Fiume, basing their case on the presence of a Slovene majority in the interior, on just demands for reparations from Italy, and on the stark fact of conquest. The Italians could point to their overwhelming majorities in the cities, and, somewhat unmindful of their behaviour in 1940, they looked to Britain and America to protect those territories which had been Italy's reward for entering the war on the Allied side in 1915. The inhabitants themselves were the third party to the dispute. Cosmopolitan and commercial the Triestini were undoubtedly opposed both to the Slavs and to Communism, for all their culture and traditions tied them to the west. But not all favoured inclusion in Italy; many, including the Catholic Slovenes, hankered after the vanished days of Austro-Hungarian rule, or saw a solution in the status of an autonomous port, akin to that of Danzig between the wars. Finally, the Western Allies' point of view was the simplest of all: the problem of Italy's frontier must be settled round the conference table and not by force. As Field Marshal Alexander wrote in an explanatory message to his troops, the Jugoslav conduct was "all too reminiscent of Hitler, Mussolini and Japan". It was in support of this allied policy that the First Battalion was to spend the next two and half years in and around Trieste. It saw the southern end of the Iron Curtain come clanking into position between East and West.

Late in April the XIII Corps (Lieutenant-General Sir John Harding) had been charged with the task of capturing Trieste and of checking the partisans' westward advance. Soon the 2nd New Zealand Division (Lieutenant-General Sir Bernard Freyberg, V.C.) reached the city, and, to the disgust of the Jugs, accepted the surrender of the German garrison. It was considered urgent that token forces from Britain and the United States should join the New Zealanders to "show the flag"; the First Battalion was selected to perform this duty on behalf of the United Kingdom.

April 28
May 2

Already the Battalion had moved up over the Brenta, and on the 5th had arrived immediately to the west of the Isonzo at Saciletto. The next day, "with all webbing equipment scrubbed and whitened" and every man with "a fully-charged magazine and ten rounds spare in the pocket", the Battalion motored along the magnificent cliff road into Trieste. Everywhere there was evidence of Communist rule: Jugoslav flags displayed Red Stars, walls were daubed with Slovene inscriptions in red paint, and grim, grey, soldiers, both male and female, stood guard. The sullen demeanour of the Partisans and the brutal behaviour of their military government soon alienated the fund of goodwill they had built up among the Allies by their heroic fight against the Germans: to the Triestini, from the very beginning, they were no more than barbarians from the east. The citizens' joy at the presence of British troops was unconfined. The simplest evolution by the sentry outside Battalion Headquarters in the Hotel Savoia-Excelsior on the waterfront brought rapturous applause from the crowd, and the nightly beating of Retreat by the Pipe Band in the main square attracted an audience of many thousands—to the chagrin of the Jugoslavs who glowered even more grimly over their Spandaus covering the square. Language proved an insuperable obstacle to friendship. British troops, especially Scotsmen, were quick to pick up a tolerable fluency in Italian, but Croat and Slovene defeated everyone. What intercourse there was was confined to one football match against the *Smrt Fascismu* (Death to Fascism) team of the 9th Assault Division, in which the Battalion was severely defeated. Dark rumours circulated that several first-class players had joined the Division from Belgrade only the night before; the prestige of totalitarian sport, it seemed, was a serious matter. But there was no clash of arms. What shooting there was took place on VE Night to celebrate the final defeat of Germany. Long bursts of tracer rose into the sky from the Spandaus, while from the Allies Verey lights and mortar flares ascended. One flare fired from the Savoia-Excelsior fell upon one of H.M. Motor-gunboats in the port, setting her on fire; fortunately the crew was still

May 2
May 5
May 6

May 8

in possession of sufficient of their senses to extinguish the flames. After the celebrations the situation remained as tense as ever. Plans were made for all eventualities; for fighting in Trieste, for fighting a way out and for evacuation by sea. Tension was at its highest when one morning a dead Partisan was found in one of the Company areas. Marshal Tito, with the support of the Russians, was refusing to withdraw. The Western Allies decided that only an overwhelming show of force would shift him: the XIII Corps reorganised for battle.

May 20
May 22

On the 20th the Battalion left Trieste to rejoin the Brigade on the Isonzo, and two days later the forward move of the Corps began. Three divisions, supported by more tanks and guns than the Jugoslavs had ever seen before, drove up on to the low Carso hills to the north-west of Trieste and there established themselves in commanding positions.

May 25

On the 25th the Battalion also moved up, pitching its tents in rocky fields at Prepotto among the shells of Slovene villages burnt by the Germans after the rising of 1943. The Jugs were over-awed, and slowly the implications of the manœuvre began to sink in. While the Battalion basked in the sun, despatched its first men for demobilisation[1] and began its post-war educational programme, the negotiations went on. In the middle of June a compromise was agreed. Until the final peace treaty with Italy, Venezia Giulia was to be divided by the "Morgan Line" into two zones. Zone A, including Pola and Trieste with its hinterland, was to be occupied and administered by an Anglo-American Military Government. Zone B, which included all the eastern half of the province, was to be governed by the Jugoslavs. The disappointed Partisans withdrew behind the Morgan Line and for the time being the threat of armed conflict was removed.

June 12

July 26

When the Battalion moved back into Trieste it went to a substantial Italian barracks; it was the first barracks the Battalion had occupied since leaving London for Norway in April 1940. It took some weeks to remove the last filthy traces of Jugoslav occupation, but once this had been done the Guardsmen began to enjoy the delights of their new station. Trieste, almost undamaged by the war, was a city "devoid of ancient monuments, but boasting every modern convenience, including blondes"; and there was no "non-fraternisation" order here. Tastes for swimming, yachting, rowing, cricket, football and athletics could all be indulged. Back in Friuli elaborate racecourses were laid out, on which many thousands of *lire* were won for loyal punters by *Colonna* and *Fliap* ridden respectively by Brigadier Erskine and Major Bulkeley. Leave was taken all over Italy, and in Austria as well, but it was the road home which was the most popular. Immediately hostilities had ceased overland leave to Britain began. The first small parties went the whole way to the Channel ports by lorry, but soon

[1] These included Pipe-Major A. MacDonald, B.E.M., who had been Pipe-Major since 1931. He was appointed piper to His Majesty.

the railways were in use again and the numbers getting leave at home rose rapidly. Despite many wearisome guards on docks and dumps, Trieste was a most popular station.

Other events of note during the Battalion's second stay in the city included a spectacular searchlight Tattoo at which Field Marshal Alexander made his final appearance as Supreme Commander, receiving a tremendous ovation, especially from the Italians. In October Lieutenant-Colonel C. I. H. Dunbar, D.S.O., arrived from the Third Battalion to assume command of the First; he was later to be followed by large drafts from his former command. In November, on the occasion of the anniversary of the Italian occupation of the city in 1918, violent anti-Jugoslav riots broke out, and the duty companies were kept standing by to aid the civil power. But fortunately the local police, trained and led by men from Scotland Yard, proved equal to the task. In December the Colours were brought out from home, but the parade at which they were to be formally received by the Battalion had to be abandoned, for the Bora, the biting north wind from the Alps, blew so hard that it was impossible to stand upright on the square. *Oct. 6*

In the New Year the Battalion moved out into the country north of Trieste to assume control of part of the Morgan Line. The main body was billeted at the former Hapsburg riding school of Equile Lippizzano, with companies manning road blocks on the Line. This was not very clearly marked on the ground, nor was the standard of Jug map-reading very high. In consequence several members of the Battalion were apprehended by the Partisans as trespassers in Zone B, on one occasion even the Commanding Officer and second-in-command (Major R. A. Orr-Ewing) spending an uncomfortable day's detention in Jugoslav hands. In the early summer great care had to be taken to avoid provocation on the Line, for at that period a "Fact Finding" delegation from the Allied Foreign Ministers was in Trieste, and tension rose sharply. Early in June tactical dispositions had to be taken up on Monte Castellaro and Monte Cocusso, two hills vital to the scheme of defence. The summit of Castellaro, affording a magnificent view over the whole of Istria, became a favourite vantage point for "swanners" and senior officers, including no lesser personages than the new Supreme Commander, General Sir William Morgan (after whom the line was named), and the Commander-in-Chief of the Mediterranean Fleet, Admiral Sir Algernon Willis. So serious was the threat of war at this time that the Colours were despatched under guard to Venice for safe keeping. But, as before, the tension relaxed, and undivided attention could once again be given to the extensive rifle range constructed by the Battalion on the lower slopes of Castellaro. *1946 Feb. 14* *Mar. 26* *June 9*

Early in September the Battalion drove seventy miles to the south to carry out garrison duties in Pola at the tip of the Istrian peninsula. *Sept. 2*

Here was another Italian town isolated in Jugoslav-occupied territory. Prior to 1918 it had been the main base of the Austrian fleet, and now the landscape was one of battered forts and exploded magazines. The Battalion was billeted at the water's edge in the former Italian Submarine School, a convenient situation in which to give and receive hospitality between the warships which were the sole visitors to this remote outpost. It was tantalising to be separated by only two miles of blue water from the forbidden island of Brioni. Once the luxurious playground of the capitalist classes, it was now reserved for the exclusive enjoyment of the Communist Dictator and his cronies.

1947
Feb. 1

The Battalion was thankful to return to the barracks in Trieste in February 1947 for its third and final stay in that city. On its first visit to Trieste the single sentry at Battalion Headquarters had received the plaudits of the Triestini. Now, before the Battalion's final departure, the citizens were treated to a larger and more stately spectacle. In the

May 2

presence of Colonel G. F. Johnson, D.S.O., Lieutenant-Colonel Commanding the Regiment, the Regimental Colour was trooped on the Trieste Racecourse on the occasion of the second anniversary of the surrender of the German garrison to the New Zealanders.

Aug. 16

Early in June the Battalion once more moved out to the Morgan Line, being based on the Slovene village of Sesana. Here Lieutenant-Colonel H. N. Clowes, D.S.O., assumed command, and it was under him that the Regiment's final duties in Italy were performed. Rumours of a settlement of the Trieste problem were in the air, and the Battalion was warned that it would shortly be joining the 4th Guards

Sept. 11

Brigade in Germany. Early in September the Battalion moved back over the Isonzo to Palmanova, coming under command of the United States 88th Division. The permanent frontier between Italy and Jugoslavia had now been agreed, save for the question of the city of

Sept. 12

Trieste itself.[1] By the 12th September the Companies were strung out along a mountainous fifty-mile sector of the new boundary to the north and east of Gorizia. The Jugoslavs advanced to this line on the

Sept. 16
Sept. 17
Sept. 28

16th and the next day the Scots Guards handed over their posts to the Italian Army, returning at once to Palmanova. A week later, in a brand new train provided by the Italian government, the First Battalion left the country in which it had served for nearly four years. Its destination was not Germany, but home. Travelling by the Hook

Oct. 2

and Harwich, the Battalion reached Pirbright on the 2nd October. It had been abroad four years and eight months.

[1] It was not until 1955 that the administration of Trieste was finally handed over to Italy.

23. MONTE SOLE, SEEN FROM THE SETTA VALLEY JUST NORTH OF LAGAR(
AUTUMN 1944 On the extreme left the ground is rising up to Monte Salvaro. Next is th
wooded mound of Monte Termine. In the centre, the lighter left-hand mountain is Caprara, th
lower peak next to it is Abelle, while Sole, the highest of the three, is to the right. Behind and
the right of Sole is Monte Santa Barbara

ITALIAN LANDSCAPES

24. COMACCHIO FLOODS, APRIL 1945 It was in country like this that the First Battalic
fought its way across the Fossa Marina. The pump house in this photograph is similar to th:
captured by Left Flank at Casa di Bando

25. The attack on Chênedollé, 11th August 1944. Churchills of Left Flank in the bocage; the burning tank is that commanded by Lieutenant The Lord Bruce

NORMANDY

26. Major Fitzalan Howard addressing the tank crews of Left Flank before the attack on Estry, 6th August 1944

PART VI

North-west Europe: 1944–1946

THREE Battalions of the Scots Guards were represented in Field Marshal Viscount Montgomery's armies which fought from Normandy to the Baltic. They entered the fight in a reversed order of seniority, and fought both as infantry and as armour.

1946

In late June 1944, X Company, the surviving unit of the Fourth Battalion, was the first to be engaged on the Normandy battlefield, and the company fought alongside the Irish and Welsh Guards Battalions of the Guards Armoured Division from the Bocage to the Rhine.

A few weeks later, in the independent 6th Guards Tank Brigade, the Third Battalion, mounted in heavy Churchill tanks, was launched into battle in Normandy in a famous assault at Caumont. The autumn and winter were spent in frequent attacks in the Low Countries, and ended with a month of the fiercest fighting between the Maas and the Rhine. The Battalion played a prominent part in the break-out across the Rhine and in the subsequent advance into the heart of Germany. Finally it penetrated to the Baltic Sea.

The Second Battalion, refreshed and recruited after its African and Italian campaigns, re-entered the line in February 1945, first seeing action in the battle which cleared the western bank of the Rhine. In the following month it advanced with the Guards Armoured Division through North-western Germany, fighting stiff battles alongside the tanks of the 2nd Battalion Welsh Guards against some of the enemy's most determined troops. Finally, the Second Battalion reached the North Sea at Cuxhaven and provided the garrison of the island of Heligoland.

Before describing these operations something must be said about the formation, training and equipment of the Third and Fourth Battalions.[1] They formed part of what was certainly the best-equipped army which has ever left these shores; that army was also, with the exception of musketry in which it must yield the palm to the Expeditionary Force of 1914, the best trained. The early history of these two Battalions is bound up with the story of Guardsmen in tanks and with the formation of the Guards Armoured Division. In the new

---

[1] An account of the reforming of the Second Battalion will be found at p. 395.

experimental armoured role the Scots Guards Battalions were always to the fore, and they can make fair claim to have been among the best-trained Battalions in a magnificent armament.

When all is said and done, it is the genuinely unsolicited testimonial which carries the greatest weight. The reasons for the German defeat were summarised in a staff diary of the 15th Panzer Grenadier Division a doughty formation which was opposed to British troops both in Italy and in this campaign, and which, in the last weeks, fought against the Guards Armoured Division and, in particular, against the Second Battalion.[1] The first reason, wrote the Germans, was the thorough preparation and planning of all attacks, especially the co-operation between the ground and air forces. The second was the overwhelming amount of material. The third reason, and to our troops by far the most complimentary, was "better trained men, especially as individual fighters".

I. THE YEARS OF PREPARATION

(a) *The Third Battalion*

1940

Even before the *débâcle* of Dunkirk plans were afoot for the raising of a Third Battalion of the Regiment. At the same time as the First Battalion was struggling in the snows of Norway, steps were being taken to raise a battalion which was to be at full strength by the 1st August. Lieutenant-Colonel J. S. Coats, Coldstream Guards, who had commanded the short-lived Fifth (Ski) Battalion, went to Chamonix to confer with the Chasseurs Alpins on the organisation of the new battalion; the intention was to train it for mountain warfare, and later as ski troops; training was due to begin at Blair Athol in mid-June. But again events overtook intentions, and the disasters of the summer put the plans back in the melting-pot.

The Regiment had raised a Third Battalion on two previous occasions. At the outbreak of the South African War in 1899 it had been formed for the first time and held the reinforcements and recruits for the two senior Battalions while they were serving abroad. In 1901 it had received Colours from King Edward VII, and had continued in existence until disbanded in 1906. In October 1914 it was again called into being as the Reserve Battalion of the Regiment, and was stationed in London where it fulfilled a similar function throughout the war. The same pair of Colours was again taken out, only to be returned to Buckingham Palace for safe-keeping when the Battalion was disbanded in 1919.

Oct. 16

On 16th October 1940 the Third Battalion was formed at Chigwell in Essex by Lieutenant-Colonel G. F. Johnson.[2] It was on the normal

[1] See p. 455.
[2] For Order of Battle, see p. 553.

establishment of an Infantry Battalion, with a Headquarter Company and four rifle companies, namely Right Flank (R), S, T, and Left Flank (U), which joined complete from the Training and Holding Battalions. Major J. A. Burns was second-in-command; Captain J. L. Harvey, Adjutant; Lieutenant W. J. Dorman, Quartermaster; and RSM E. C. Gray, Sergeant-Major.

The Battalion formed part of the 30th Guards Brigade commanded by Brigadier A. H. S. Adair; the other Battalions were the newly raised 4th Battalions of the Grenadier and Coldstream Guards. The operational role of the Brigade at this critical stage of the war was the defence of the eastern perimeter of London north of the Thames.

The winter of 1940–41 was spent in good billets on housing estates and in large private houses, but the darkness was nightly rendered hideous by the raids of the German air force. The inhabitants of Chigwell, who suffered the same dangers as the Battalion, were most hospitably disposed towards the Guardsmen. Dances, baths and entertainment in their homes were the main features of this happy relationship. Later, when stationed in remoter camps, many looked back with nostalgia to Chigwell; not a few men married there. The degree of hospitality enjoyed is shown by the answer of one Guardsman who went to have a bath in a private house. Asked if it had been satisfactory he replied, "Fine, sir, thank you; I had two teas!"

When at the end of January 1941 H.R.H. the Colonel paid his first visit to the Battalion it was well on the way to reaching the standard of training traditionally demanded by the Regiment. The area of its billets was ill-adapted for field training of a realistic nature, and companies had to travel far for shooting and field firing. Exercises with the other battalions of the Brigade and with the local Home Guard gave experience of larger-scale operations, and during these months a foundation of sound infantry knowledge was laid, which foundation was invaluable when the Battalion eventually took its tanks into battle in support of an infantry division. The smartness and drill of the Battalion was never neglected; spring drills in March were enlivened, though not interrupted, by two German land-mines, which appeared to be allied to the slothful, for they blew out the windows of the Drill Sergeant's bunk!

1941

By the early summer the Battalion felt itself fully prepared for action. The sooner intensive training is followed by action, the better for the morale of any body of troops; for endless repetition can only bring boredom and a loss of sense of purpose. Having taken the trouble to train themselves to a fine pitch as infantrymen, the Battalion was taken aback when the astounding news arrived that it was to be converted into armour.

May

After the great German victories in Poland and France, armour was acknowledged to be Queen of the Battlefield. Infantry, in its then state of equipment, was at a discount. The triumph against the Italians in North Africa, and the subsequent counter-attack by the highly mobile Africa Korps further depressed the Infantry's reputation. At the outbreak of war there had been but one embryo Armoured Division in the British Army, and what few tanks there were had either been lost in France or despatched to the Middle East. By mid-1941 production of tanks was at last increasing, and effect could be given to plans which had long been in existence for the expansion of the Armoured element of the Army. Previously this had been the preserve of the Royal Tank Corps and of the unhorsed Cavalry regiments; now these sources had been exhausted, and other arms had to be drawn upon. Moreover, early in 1941, before the Germans had disclosed their preoccupation with Russia, it was thought that there was still a real danger of an attempted invasion of this country in the spring of 1942, and it was considered an urgent necessity that there should be two more Armoured Divisions available to meet this threat. By the standards of the time the Army was top-heavy with infantry formations, and many of these were being converted to other arms: gunners, engineers, and searchlights. Other battalions, six of the Brigade of Guards among them, were converted to tanks. The Guards Battalions were not to form part of the newly constituted Royal Armoured Corps, under which all other armoured troops were administered, but were to retain inviolate their Regimental identities and their own training establishment. A Guards Division was to be formed; and it was to be an Armoured Division.

The idea was, of course, novel and, inevitably, to some, shocking. It seemed a waste to uproot from their traditional role battalions of the steadiest infantry in the world. Some felt that the prestige of armour was unnaturally high, and that before long a more realistic sense of values would reassert itself. Some thought that already the Brigade of Guards was becoming too big, and that, should fighting be prolonged and heavy, it would be impossible (as, in fact, it subsequently proved) to maintain the increased number of Battalions at effective strength; to add the complication of armour to this problem would render the task of reinforcement even more precarious. Some said that the physique of the Guardsman was quite unsuited to the cramped quarters of a tank. There were even some who thought that the Brigade, both in its commissioned and non-commissioned ranks, did not possess the mental equipment to master the technical skills required in armoured and mechanical warfare.

This last objection was fatuous. There were, of course, in any infantry battalion, many individuals who were unsuited, mentally and physically, to armoured warfare. But why, it may be asked, should Guardsmen in general be thought less adaptable to the mysteries of mechanical vehicles than had been the grooms and amateur jockeys of the Cavalry regiments? The similarities in tactics of armoured warfare of the 1940s to those of the cavalry warfare of the old era before barbed-wire and machine-guns (an era that had long since passed!) were at best superficial, and the problems of equipment, communication, weapon-training and supply were totally different. There was an equal, if not greater, fund of suitable men in the infantry, and in all ranks, particularly among the younger officers, there was a burning desire to take part in the war with the most effective equipment and in the most modern style. As regards the Scots Guards in particular, why should there be any misgivings about a tank battalion recruited from the most famous race of mechanical engineers in all the world?

The truth is that it is a vulgar fallacy that the Brigade of Guards is incapable of adapting itself to new roles. Any one can question the *wisdom* of converting excellent infantrymen to another untried arm; to scoff at the *adaptability* of the Guardsman is to fly in the face of all the evidence. In recent years this has been proved in Malaya; in the war years it was proved by the host of distinguished leaders of novel ventures both at home and in the Mediterranean. It was proved by the Guards Armoured Division. And, it may be claimed, above all it was proved by the 6th Guards Tank Brigade, which was composed of battalions trained first as infantry and then as tanks; their role was to support the infantry, and they knew what they were about. Not only did they prove adaptable to the new task; in it they were pre-eminent.[1]

On the 30th May the Adjutant brought from London the authentic news of conversion to armour. For several weeks the rumours had been circulating; now they were confirmed. Few had ever seen, let alone been inside, a modern tank. The number of wireless operators, drivers, gunners, fitters, electricians and storemen that would be required far exceeded the meagre numbers in an infantry battalion. Selection and planning began at once, for the new establishment would be over three hundred men fewer than the old, and soon the surplus would have to be disgorged.   *May 30*

On 11th June His Majesty the King inspected the Battalion on parade, complete with its establishment of infantry weapons. Almost immediately afterwards the first of a host of officers and men left for courses arranged by the Royal Armoured Corps at Bovington and Farnborough. From that time on the Battalion began rapidly to absorb the new knowledge. The 17th/21st Lancers at Cambridge—the nearest tanks!—gave noble help in introducing the men to their new weapons, but it was very much a nominal change when the title "Third (Armoured) Battalion Scots Guards" was assumed. The four rifle companies were changed into three squadrons, Right Flank, S and   *June 11*   *Sept. 15*

[1] See p. 466 for Field Marshal Montgomery's views on this aspect of the matter, and p. 488 for Field Marshal Sir John Harding's.

Left Flank; T remained as a training squadron for the remainder of the Battalion's stay in England.

Sept. 18 Three days later the Battalion left Chigwell for Tilshead Camp, near Salisbury, where it joined the Guards Armoured Division (Major-General Sir Oliver Leese, Bt.). The Brigade changed its name to the 6th Guards Armoured Brigade, and took its place in the order of battle alongside the 5th Guards Armoured Brigade and the Support Group.

On arrival at Tilshead there were but three tanks, against an establishment of sixty-one! At that period all available modern tanks were shipped off to the Middle East, and the requirements of new formations at home had to take second place. But by Christmas the Battalion had twenty-seven Covenanters to play with, and with these fast, but under-gunned and thinly armoured cruiser tanks they began their elementary armoured training. Many distinguished persons came to see developments. Among the visitors were Her Majesty Queen Mary, H.R.H. the Colonel, Lieutenant-General the Hon. Harold Alexander, then commanding Southern Command, and Colonel Balfour, Commanding the Regiment. The latter was treated to a ride in a tank driven by his son, Second-Lieutenant P. E. G. Balfour; the Regimental Adjutant reported much crashing of gears.

Nov. Early in November Lieutenant-Colonel Johnson was promoted to second-in-command of the Divisional Support Group, and was succeeded in command of the Battalion by Lieutenant-Colonel the Hon. H. K. M. Kindersley, M.B.E., M.C., who was to command the Battalion for the next eighteen months. At the same time, the Battalion moved to B Camp, Codford St. Mary, an uninviting collection of Nissen huts and sheds on the edge of Salisbury Plain. This dreary area of mud was to be the Battalion's home for a year and a half, and energetic steps were at once taken to make the mud and water passable for both humans and vehicles. Rubble had to be fetched from the ruins of Bristol, and soon something had been done to mitigate the foul condi-

1942 tions which prevailed in the winter months. As the weather grew
Mar. 18 better, so the training intensified; even the Tercentenary of the Raising of the Regiment was not allowed to interrupt the courses of
April gunnery, of wireless, and of driving and maintenance. In April the whole Battalion gave a demonstration tank battle before the Prime Minister and the United States Chief of Staff, General Marshall, after which Mr. Churchill inspected the tanks. Visits to the Field Firing ranges at Linnie Head gave the Squadrons their first practical experience of gunfire.

There were several changes in the chief appointments, especially that of Major C. I. H. Dunbar, who relieved Viscount Dalrymple as second-in-command on the latter's appointment to command the First Battalion; and that of Captain R. C. Whigham, who relieved Captain Harvey as Adjutant.

To attract keen candidates for commissions in the armoured half of the Regiment, several parties of Public School boys, soon to be called up, were given instruction in the Battalion's tanks and other armament; they enjoyed themselves hugely, and the Regiment got its recruits.[1] A unusual attachment was that of Second-Lieutenant Ling-chieh Kung, of the Regiment, a nephew of Generalissimo Chiang Kai Shek. This officer had seen something of the German Army's attack in 1940, and had later passed through Sandhurst and had been commissioned into the Regiment, which took pains to show him every activity. The Third Battalion felt he must have profited greatly from his stay at Codford, for later in the war it was strongly rumoured that he was commanding an Armoured Division in China!

While the training of the Division was being rapidly advanced, a new organisation for British Armoured divisions was evolved. It had been found too great a strain on communications for a Divisional Commander to control two Armoured Brigades and, also, the infantry of the Division, which had previously consisted of motor battalions only, had proved insufficient. The establishment was reduced to one Armoured Brigade and one Lorried Infantry Brigade, together with an armoured Reconnaissance Regiment and one Motor Battalion. Therefore, in the Guards Division, one Armoured Brigade had to go and an Infantry Brigade had to be brought in. In November, the 6th Brigade, in which was the Third Battalion, went; already in May the 32nd Guards Brigade, in which was the Fourth Battalion, had come in to provide the Lorried Infantry.

Nov.

There were a few weeks of uncertainty until the new destination of the Third Battalion was known. It was to involve another change of equipment and role. From the cruiser tanks, in which they had expected to perform in the dashing manner of the Panzer drives of 1940, the Battalion was to change to heavy tanks to support infantry in the assault. They were to give up the Covenanter and get instead the Churchill. From the Guards Armoured Division they were to go to the 15th (Scottish) Division. This division was to be a "mixed" division of two infantry brigades and the tank brigade. At the same time Brigadier Adair left to command the Guards Armoured Division and Brigadier G. L. Verney assumed command of the re-christened 6th Guards (Tank) Brigade. The Battalion became the Third (Tank) Battalion Scots Guards.

At this stage of the war the British cruiser tank had a very poor reputation, due to being outgunned in the long ranges of the desert; no better was the reputation of the Churchill, which possessed the same main armament, had a dismal history of mechanical unreliability,

[1] The historian, *aet*. 17 (who did *not* subsequently serve in the Third Battalion) removed the door of a bread van in the streets of Devizes while driving a scout car under the instruction of a justifiably apprehensive Piper.

and so far had seen action only on the beaches of Dieppe. It seemed that all that had been learnt about swift armoured advances was to be shut out of the Battalion's mind, and it was to be condemned to waddle along at 16 m.p.h. in forty-ton monsters armed with a 2-pounder pop-gun. But the Battalion rose above its disappointment, and set about the task of re-thinking its tactics and getting to know its new weapon. On second thoughts the Churchill proved a better proposition; in the result it proved an excellent tank and a magnificent support for the infantry.

With the detailed history of this tank we cannot be concerned at length, but briefly, it arose from the necessity of having, from the late months of 1940 onward, some form of heavily armoured tank for the defence of Britain. Vauxhall Motors, who had never before been engaged in the production of tanks, designed and produced the early models in a fantastically short time straight from the drawing-board—without the refinements of prototypes. Inevitably there were teething troubles of the most complicated sort. The best that could be done was for the Vauxhall men to learn from the troops in whose hands the tanks were and to modify the later tanks as they could. Thus each new mark of Churchill was an improvement on the last, and in the end the Battalion was able to go into action with tanks in which, as far as mechanical and cross-country performance went, they had every confidence. In view of the turbulence of the Churchill's conception, birth and upbringing this represented a remarkable achievement on the part of Vauxhalls and, it is fair to say, on the part of the troops to whom the tank was supplied.

1943
March
April

In March 1943 the Duke of Gloucester visited the Battalion at Codford and presented to the commander of each tank a pennant of the Brigade colours to be flown on the wireless aerials. In April the Battalion left Codford for the Hawes area of Yorkshire; Battalion Headquarters and Headquarter Squadron were at Simonstone Hall, while the Tank Squadrons found themselves, for the first time, on their own, Right Flank at Hawes, S Squadron at Bainbridge and Left Flank at Gayle. Although the area provided but mediocre training grounds, the next six months saw constant activity, during which the basis of trust and confidence between the Tank and Infantry Brigades was laid. Great pains were taken, especially by Major S. J. Cuthbert, to devise suitable drills for tank/infantry co-operation, and, as will be seen, these tactics stood the test of battle.

About this time the organisation of the Battalion crystallised, and thereafter remained the same, save for minor alterations, throughout the war. At Battalion Headquarters there were four Churchill tanks; each of the three Squadrons had three tanks at Headquarters and five Troops of three tanks each, though later casualties reduced the number of Troops to four. Thus each Squadron had eighteen tanks, making a total of fifty-eight Churchills for the whole Battalion. In addition in the early stages there was in Headquarter Squadron an anti-aircraft troop of converted Crusaders, and later the Reconnaissance Troop of scout cars was strengthened by the addition of six light Honey tanks. At home additional tanks were available to T Squadron for training purposes. In all the establishment totalled thirty-eight officers and 632 men.

Each troop was normally commanded by a Subaltern officer, who commanded his own tank as well; the other two tanks in the Troop were commanded by the Troop Sergeant and Troop Corporal.

In each Churchill there were five men. The *commander* of the tank was in the turret, and to him fell a multitude of tasks; he had to direct the driver; he had to give fire-orders to the gunner; and he had to take heed of his superior commander or inferior tanks over the wireless. In the turret with him was the *gunner*, whose duty it was to aim and fire the main armament, at first the 2-pounder, later the 6-pounder, and, finally, the 75-mm. gun; he had also to fire the belt-fed Besa machine-gun mounted co-axially with the gun. Also in the turret was the wireless *operator* whose duty was to keep in touch with the outside world by wireless, and with the commander over the inter-communications set; he had also to load the gun with either High Explosive (H.E.) shells or with Armour Piercing (A.P.) solid shot. In the front of the hull, with visibility limited to the ground immediately ahead, sat the *driver*; beside him sat the *co-driver*, whose duty was to assist the driver and to fire the second Besa mounted in the hull. Of these five men, only the Commander, who usually kept his head out of the turret, had much idea of how the battle was progressing beyond the confines of the tank.

Two important events took place during the stay in Yorkshire. First, Lieutenant-Colonel Kindersley left to command an Air Landing Brigade of the 6th Airborne Division; in this appointment he was severely wounded in the D-Day landings. The shell which wounded him also hit Brigadier the Lord Lovat, then distinguished as a Commando leader, and a former officer of the Regiment. Lieutenant-Colonel C. I. H. Dunbar succeeded to the command of the Battalion, of which he had been second-in-command; he had recently been despatched to command the First Battalion in Tunisia, but was recalled to command the Tank battalion, which he held for the rest of the war. *May*

The second event was of a most disturbing nature. Nine battalions of the Brigade of Guards had fought in the Tunisian campaign which had been brought to a glorious conclusion in May, but at a heavy price in casualties. The reinforcement outlook was gloomy, and word got round that the 6th Brigade was to be disbanded and its men dispersed as reinforcements. Every argument was deployed, every legitimate string was pulled, and at last, after the Prime Minister himself had been appraised of the situation, the Brigade was reprieved.

Thereafter the most notable event of the training season was *Sept.*

exercise *Blackcock*, which was arranged under the auspices of the VIII Corps, and lasted for ten days at the end of September. It was the largest and longest exercise in which the Battalion was engaged, and many parallels were later to be drawn between this exercise and the first operation of war in which the Battalion was engaged, *Bluecoat*. At the conclusion of the exercise the Battalion concentrated at Thoresby Park in the Dukeries. Here the Tank Brigade was removed from the order of battle of the 15th Division and was replaced by a third infantry Brigade; the 6th Brigade became Second Army troops. The "mixed" division had been found to be an extravagant luxury, and in future Tank Brigades must be available to whatever Infantry Division needed them. But later when the 6th Brigade went into action, staffs took good care to put them in support of the 15th (Scottish) Division whenever that was possible; fortunately this proved to be the case in the Third Battalion's first battle.

1944

Apart from a now legendary officer's dance of happy memory, the winter at Thoresby was hard and monotonous. Captain Whigham[1] was elevated to Brigade Headquarters, and Captain V. F. Erskine Crum took his place as Adjutant. In February the Brigade and the Regiment suffered a sad loss when the G.S.O. III, Captain the Earl of Chichester, was killed in a road accident. Brigades of the 51st (Highland) Division, newly returned from Africa and Sicily, came to train with the Churchills, and in March His Majesty reviewed the entire Brigade in Thoresby Park; the tanks drove past nearly two hundred strong, a stirring sight of three battalions in column of squadrons. The simplest strategist could detect signs of the coming invasion. On the 30th April, in deepest secrecy, the Battalion moved south to Eastwell Park, near Charing, in Kent.

April 30
MAP XXX

Once again, concealed from the eager tank crews, a crisis in the Brigade's existence had been met and overcome. The casualties of the Italian campaign, and especially those of the 24th Guards Brigade at Anzio, when added to the pessimistic forecast of those likely to be suffered in North-west Europe, again forced those responsible for reinforcements to cast envious eyes upon the 6th Guards Tank Brigade. To those "in the know"—and they were but few—the dismal fate of disbandment seemed inevitable; a counter-proposal from Regimental Headquarters that the Third Battalion should be re-numbered the Second, converted to Sherman tanks, and added to the Guards Armoured Division, fell on deaf ears. Once again it was the Prime Minister, with his unrivalled flair for recognising a good thing when he saw it, who rescued the Brigade;[2] the tidy-minded planners were put to flight, and the Third Battalion was saved to go forward to its triumphs. The

[1] Major Whigham was killed in a traffic accident in Germany soon after the end of the war.
[2] See *The Second World War*, by Winston Churchill, Vol. V, pp. 618 and 619 (Cassell & Co. Ltd.).

crisis delayed those triumphs, for its effect was to take the Brigade out of the force which was to make the initial landings, and to relegate it to the status of Army Group Troops. Many water-proofing measures which had been put in hand now became unnecessary, and the modern Mark VI tanks mounting 76-mm. guns had to be handed over to another Brigade, in return for which the Battalion received vehicles armed with 6-pounders. Eventually in the weeks before sailing, a rapid conversion to 75-mm. was made, and Troops set out armed with two 75-mm. and one 6-pounder tank each. In addition, with each Squadron Headquarters were two tanks mounting 95-mm. howitzers, designed for the close support of the infantry.

The final crisis surmounted, it now remained but to get into action. On 30th May the whole Brigade attended a deeply moving "Service before Battle" in Canterbury Cathedral. Archbishop Temple preached, and the service was conducted by the Dean, Dr. Hewlett Johnson; assisting him were the Chaplains of the Brigade, including the Rev. G. H. T. Reid, Church of Scotland padre to the Battalion, whose sombre black habit and flaming red hair made a notable contrast to the gorgeous vestments and white locks of the Cathedral Clergy. The Band of the Regiment played, and after the service led a march-past of the entire Brigade. — May 30

On the 6th June the landings began. A week later came the flying-bombs, which struck a sad blow when one of them killed almost a third of the Brigade's R.E.M.E. Workshops' staff; the Battalion lost many good friends in that disaster. But of battle there was still no sign, and the Scots Guards had to rest content with "Eyewitness" in the form of Captain C. O'M. Farrell, who had been treated to a brief attachment to the XXX Corps in Normandy. — June 6, June 24

In the interval between D-Day and the Battalion's crossing to France, there was staged a most realistic exercise, by name *Sizzle*. After protracted negotiations this was allowed to be held in the Stone Street training area, which consisted of very close farm land intersected by high hedges and deep ditches, very similar to the Norman Bocage in which the Battalion was to fight its first battle. The tanks did tremendous damage to the countryside, which was compensated by the experience their crews acquired—and by the harassed Claims branch. Just as *Blackcock* had introduced the Battalion to the Staffs under which it was to fight, so *Sizzle* gave it a valuable foretaste of the type of country it was to encounter.

On the 16th July the move to the embarkation area began.[1] — July 16

(b) *The Fourth Battalion*

On 28th September 1941, a Regimental Order was issued intimating that His Majesty had graciously approved the formation of the Fourth — 1941 Sept. 28

[1] The Third Battalion continued on p. 340.

Battalion Scots Guards. At this date men were coming into the army fast, casualties had so far been light, and the conversion of the Third Battalion to armour would mean the removal of some three hundred men from that Battalion. No-one seriously contemplated the prospect of four Battalions in action simultaneously; this number would have been far beyond the capacity of the Regiment's resources. But the best way to train and keep occupied the reserves which were accumulating was to form them into tactical Battalions. The Fourth Battalion went through its life with the threat of dispersal constantly in the background.

The command was to have been given to Lieutenant-Colonel J. E. M. Bland, but ill-health prevented him assuming his post, which was filled by Lieutenant-Colonel A. V. C. Douglas. Major F. H. H. B. Harris was second-in-command; Captain O. Priaulx, Adjutant; Lieutenant J. Quinn, Quartermaster; and RSM A. Wilford, Sergeant-Major.[1] The Battalion assembled on the 11th October in the Wanstead area of North-east London, not far from Chigwell, which the Third Battalion had left three weeks before. The companies were well spread out and changed their billets several times during the next seven months; Headquarter and X Companies were in the Royal Wanstead School; Right Flank (V) and W Companies were at Little Heath and Aldborough Road respectively, while Left Flank (Y) disported themselves in the Leytonstone Girls School. The Battalion was part of the 32nd Guards Brigade (Brigadier L. Bootle Wilbraham), and on its flanks stood the 6th Grenadiers and 5th Coldstream.

Oct. 11

Shortly after their arrival at Wanstead, His Majesty the King visited the Battalion, inspecting them on parade and later watching a lively demonstration on the Assault Course. The news that His Majesty had been much impressed by all he had seen gave considerable encouragement to the young Battalion. This was a suitable tonic, for the next five months were taken up with a long series of exercises which tended to become monotonous, one of which, starting on March 14th, prevented even limited celebration of the Tercentenary of the Regiment. The Pipes and Drums were, however, able to take part in a special B.B.C. broadcast commemorating the event a few days later.

Nov. 21

1942
Mar. 14

Mar. 18

May

Early in May the Battalion moved from Wanstead to Mortehoe Camp, North Devon, for battle training on Exmoor, and the Companies spent three strenuous weeks fighting each other over this excellent training area. The Mortehoe camp site was very exposed, and the rock too near the surface to allow the tent pegs to get a proper grip, thus when a great gale sprang up soon after the Battalion's arrival the whole camp was blown completely flat; the Officers' Mess accounts were scattered for miles.

It was also at Mortehoe that the Battalion heard the welcome news

[1] For Order of Battle, see p. 556.

that, together with the rest of the 32nd Guards Brigade, they were to join the Guards Armoured Division as Lorried Infantry, and at the end of the month they moved to Marston Bigot Camp, near Frome in Somerset, to train for this new role. Here they were unlucky with their training, for at the end of June two men of W Company, Lance-Sergeant J. Porter and Guardsman M. Hughey, were drowned during a Battalion river-crossing exercise; this unfortunate accident in no way deterred the remainder of the Battalion, and when it came to the turn of Battalion Headquarters they swam across accompanied by Colonel Douglas, who was handicapped by the fact that he had lost a leg in an air accident before the war, and now sported a metal one.

May 30

June 25–26

Training went on day and night. The "Training Bee" was introduced; experts in every form of training from all departments of the Battalion each had a booth, in the manner of a fair-ground. In each booth a different activity was demonstrated, such as wireless, 3-inch mortars, decontamination of a vehicle after a gas attack, the anti-tank gun. The men circulated in small parties, changing booths on the blast of a whistle at the conclusion of each period; it took three days for everyone to cover every activity, and at the end of it every man had a rudimentary idea of all sorts of jobs which might be useful to him in an emergency, and of which he had had no previous knowledge.

In October Right Flank and X Company marched seventy miles to Exmoor for a fortnight's field training, while W and Left Flank went north to Achnacarry in Inverness-shire, where the instructors of the Commando School were astounded at the fitness and agility of the Guardsmen; in fact, the companies were secretly proud of having outstayed the Commandos in endurance. Headquarter Company with the supporting weapons followed Right Flank and X to Devonshire. They went to Lynton, a popular resort on the North Devon coast, but not to lounge about. They dug positions and took part in the rifle companies' exercises, sometimes acting as enemy, sometimes in support. Live ammunition was used as much as possible, not only to simulate the noise of battle, but to give men confidence in their weapons under active service conditions. Before returning to the Division, the officers entertained the Mayor of Lynton to dinner, which prompted Pipe-Major Bain to take a liberty with the tune's title and to include "The High Road to Lynton" [*sic*] in his set for that evening. After leaving Lynton, they moved to another camp at Longbridge Deverill, where in November the Battalion was inspected by Brigadier J. C. O. Marriott, a former Commanding Officer of the Second Battalion and now commanding the 32nd Guards Brigade.

October

Nov.

At Longbridge Deverill occurred one of the memorable weeks in the Battalion's history: the Night Week. In order to fit in as much night training as possible into a limited period, day was turned into night, and *vice versa*. Reveille was sounded at 6.30 *p.m.*, and Lights Out at

10 a.m. Consequently there was no need to give extra time in bed to those who had taken part in a night scheme under the usual conditions, and officers were able to use the early morning for the purposes of reconnaissance and administration. By concentrating the night training in this manner, the men were given an adequate chance to accustom themselves to moving and living in the dark, invaluable on active service. A night raid on Brigade Headquarters brought the week to an end; it had been highly instructive, but few were found who would admit to having enjoyed it.

1943

At the end of January a new War Establishment was promulgated, and Left Flank was disbanded, X Company temporarily becoming the Left Flank company. On this three-company organisation the Battalion took part in the extensive exercise *Spartan*, a title descriptive of its character; other than the discomfort of constant movement, this exercise was chiefly notable for the victory of Major T. C. Harvey, of Right Flank, who was successful in a correspondence competition culled from the pages of *Titbits*. The moves of *Spartan* landed the

Mar. 15

Battalion at Eastcote in Northamptonshire, and on the 15th March they moved with the remainder of the Division to Hunstanton in

April 24

Norfolk. Here His Majesty paid a second visit on the 24th April; and here the Battalion mobilised at the end of May.

June

In June the first of many drafts left the Fourth Battalion to reinforce the First and Second in North Africa; four officers and 270 men, under the command of Captain W. B. Malone, made a great gap in the Battalion's ranks; W Company and Left Flank were entirely denuded of Guardsmen. Nothing daunted, Colonel Douglas arranged a special course with Brigadier H. Houldsworth, of the School of Infantry at Barnard Castle, on which two complete cadres down to section leader were trained in all the latest tactical doctrines that magnificent establishment had to impart. Thereby it was hoped to provide a healthy competitive spirit between the "old" and "new" halves of the Battalion should sufficient men be available to reform the two companies.

July

But, alas, the men were never to come. As the officers and NCOs from Barnard Castle were returning to the Battalion, they met Colonel Douglas on York station, on his way to Pirbright to take command of the Training Battalion; later many of them were to follow him there, and to become the leading lights at the Battle Camp which was established at Llandwrog in North Wales; and many were to make their mark in companies in other battalions. In particular Captain A. S. Neilson carried the torch of Barnard Castle with him to S Company in Italy, as has been seen in an earlier part of this history, and the initial success of that company can be taken as sufficient proof that the methods and ideas of the School of Infantry were basically sound.

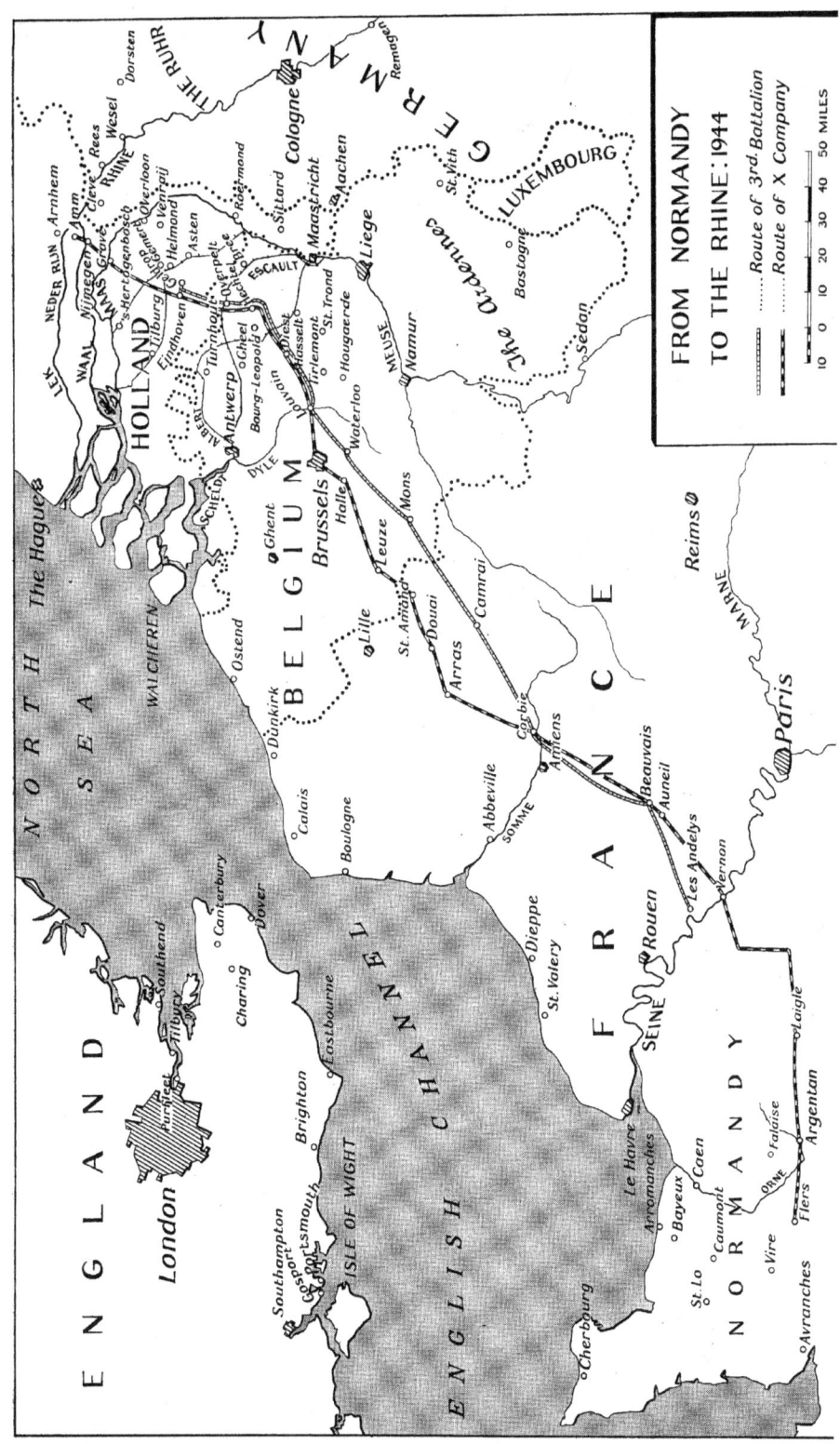

27. A Churchill ("Lyon") of Left Flank followed by a carrier belonging to the infantry, followed by a Honey, followed by more Churchills. Note the track plates welded on to the hull of the leading tank to give extra protection. The vehicles are passing through a gap in a minefield in front of the Siegfried Line, 8th February 1945; the white tape marks the limits of the swept passage

THIRD BATTALION WEAPONS

Honey tanks of the Reconnaissance ᴐop on the way through the woods to lzen; 13th April 1945. These light tanks, ᴐ known as Stuarts, were of American nufacture. They were armed with one ·mm. and three machine guns, and were manned by a crew of four

29. A scout car ("Macbeth") follow a medical half-track in the floods Kranenburg, 12th February 1945. I light-coloured coat is Major Whi Second-in-Command; the face over his shoulder is that of RSM Brown; and (back of the scout car is the Padre Reverend George Reid

30. ON THE ROAD TO TILBURG   Men of the 2nd Bn. the Glasgow Highlanders dismount from the tanks of S Squadron near Moergestel, 25th October 1944. In the turret of the leading tank are Lance-Sergeant Hurd and Lieutenant Stevenson

WITH THE 15th SCOTTISH DIVISION

31. ATTACKING THE SIEGFRIED LINE   Third Battalion tanks with the 2nd Bn. the Argyll and Sutherland Highlanders, 8th February 1945. Note on the roofs of the turrets the fluorescent panels used as a recognition mark for our aircraft.

Meanwhile the Battalion had moved to Yorkshire with the Division, and it was at Malton that Colonel Douglas left for the Training Battalion, and handed over command to Major F. H. H. B. Harris. In the same month a company of the Irish Guards arrived for attachment to the Battalion, and soon after another of Coldstreamers. Despite strenuous attempts to secure the substitution of the Fourth Battalion for the Second, the day of disbandment was clearly approaching. On the 25th July a further two officers and sixty-six men left on their way to Africa. The 3rd Battalion Irish Guards had been similarly reduced to provide reinforcements, and on the 3rd September Right Flank and X Company, plus twenty additional men, were added to that Battalion. The remainder of the Fourth Battalion Scots Guards travelled south to Northwood; on the 4th October all ranks were transferred to the Training Battalion at Pirbright, and the Battalion was formally disbanded.   July 25 / Sept. 3 / Oct. 4

Right Flank and X Company proved to be numerically larger than the whole of the 3rd Irish, and so Mahomet, in the shape of Lieutenant-Colonel J. O. E. Vandeleur, was obliged to come to the Scots Guards mountain and set up his headquarters at Malton. But by Christmas a further call came from Italy, and Right Flank in a body left for the Second Battalion, which they joined on the Garigliano and became Left Flank of that Battalion. There remained but X Company, and this company was the sole Scots Guards unit to fight in the original Order of Battle of the Guards Armoured Division, now commanded by Major-General A. H. S. Adair. In May they moved south to Sussex as part of the 32nd Guards Brigade, now commanded by Brigadier G. F. Johnson, who had made good his escape from Italy after being captured in Tobruk while commanding the 201st Guards Brigade. At Eastbourne the Company waterproofed its vehicles and waited for its turn to follow the leading waves across the Channel.   1944 / May

The Fourth Battalion had been denied the chance to prove itself in battle as a unit; but those who had served in it carried with them a proper pride in its achievement. To measure that achievement it is sufficient to examine the history of Right Flank, which fought in Italy as the Left Flank Company of both the Second and First Battalions; S Company which was trained and, in its early stages, led by Fourth Battalion officers; and the story of X Company[1] which is to be told in the pages which follow.

II. NORMANDY

(a) *Goodwood*

X Company crossed the Channel with the 3rd Battalion Irish Guards seventeen days after "D-Day". On the 16th June they had   MAPS XXX & XXXIV

[1] For Orders of Battle, see p. 558.

June 16	moved from Eastbourne to Netley Common near Southampton, where
June 20	four days later they embarked in the *Llangibby Castle*, the same transport which had carried the First Battalion from Africa to Italy seven months before. For three days they swung at anchor off the
June 23	Isle of Wight, until the morning of the 23rd when they sailed for France, disembarking in the famous Mulberry Harbour at Arromanches that afternoon. In the rain they moved to a staging area a mile south of Bayeux, where for four days they sat in the dripping orchards, where they got their first whiff of Camembert cheese, their first warmth from Calvados brandy, and where they were rejoined by their transport, which had sailed independently from Tilbury.
June 28	On the 28th June the 32nd Guards Brigade entered the line for the first time. The Brigade took over the left-hand corner of the salient to the west of Carpiquet airfield, which lay three miles to the west of the ancient Norman city of Caen. Here X Company sat, patrolled, were shelled, were mortared, and were gradually acclimatised to the noise and stench of war. Nearly every man in the company was new to it all, with the important exception of the Company Commander, Major P. Steuart-Fothringham, whose experience and shrewdness soon gained for him the distinction of an oracle among his fellows in the Brigade. "Major Feathers"—as he was known to all ranks on account of the Crimean proportions of his whiskers—won from his inexperienced company in Normandy the same loyalty and devotion which he had extracted from the battle-wise Second Battalion in Italy.
July 11	The Company remained in positions about the airfield and the farm of La Bayeud until the 11th July, when, having been spectators of a costly Canadian infantry attack and of a raid by 400 bombers on Caen, they were withdrawn to rejoin the armoured element of the Division in the orchards round Bayeux. They had tasted defence; now they were to sample attack.

Cherbourg and Caen were now both in Allied hands, and—to those at home, at least—the time appeared ripe to break out from the beachhead. But for General Sir Bernard Montgomery, who at this stage commanded all the Allied troops ashore in France, the time was not yet come. His strategic intention was by threats and concentrations to draw to the Caen sector the main weight of the German Army, especially its armour, and then, and only then, to let the Americans effect the decisive break-out in the west. The attack which he ordered east of Caen, known by the code-word *Goodwood*, was another step forward in this scheme. At the time many thought the operation had wider ambitions, a belief which was nurtured by talk of "classic tank country" in the rolling plains south and south-east of Caen. In consequence its apparent failure disappointed observers in the field, and particularly those at home. Now that the operation can be seen in true perspective, it can be said to have achieved its strategic intention, though at a heavy cost in tanks, balanced on the credit side by added experience.

Since D-Day the 6th Airborne Division had been holding the crossing over the River Orne known as Pegasus Bridge, five miles northeast of Caen; *Goodwood* required the three British Armoured Divisions—the 7th, 11th and the Guards—to cross this bridge, swing south and break through the German defences. The weight of their armour was to overwhelm the defenders, and it was understood they were to go on to Falaise. That was the limit of the General's intention. The 11th Armoured Division was to lead; the Guards were to swing left on to Vimont; the 7th was to go for Falaise.

With the wider story of the immediate failure of this attack we cannot deal at length. Suffice it to say that on the 18th July the Allied Air Forces struck a massive blow with 2,000 bombers, a blow which pulverised the foremost German defences, but which failed to eliminate the screen of 88-mm. guns and heavy tanks on the ridges and in the cornfields farther south. Against this barrier the waves of British armour beat in vain. *July 18*

For the infantry the first day was spent in a deadly, dusty, crawling procession of transport, bumping along through gaps in minefields, feeling indecently exposed to bursting shells, and wondering why those in front did not get more of a "move on". At about tea-time they saw the reason; X Company's section of the column came up with the burnt-out wrecks of the 11th Division's tanks. Now the Company left their trucks, and, with the Irishmen, continued the advance on foot. Crossing open fields bounded by thick hedges they reached the blazing ruins of La Prieurie Farm, a solid stone farmhouse built on the site of an ancient priory; here, under impartial shelling from both sides, the Company took its first prisoners. Then they dug; in an hour they were well below ground, and were immediately ordered forward to Frénouville, to the chagrin of all save Lieutenant I. N. Thorpe who, with an eye for the caprices of authority, had selected a former gravedigger as his runner.

It was now almost dark, and, with little idea of what was going on around them, the Battalion formed up in a paddock near the burning farm, and set out on a compass march across country. The leading Irish companies were well under way when Colonel Vandeleur received a wireless message altering the route of advance to Frénouville; he was now ordered to take his Battalion by way of the village of Cagny. The companies in the lead were beyond recall, so Colonel "Joe" set off for Cagny with only X and No. 4 Companies at his heels. At two in the morning the battered village was reached and No. 4 Company took the lead from X Company, heading for Frénouville. Unexpected opposition forced yet another change in the axis of advance, this time to the east of the main road. Winding their way *July 19* through standing corn on their new route, the two companies had gone but 300 yards when they hit the enemy again. Not only German missiles, but British ones as well, were fired at them. Fortunately, it was soon discovered that in the confusion of the night they had passed through the screen of tanks of the 2nd Armoured Battalion Irish Guards; therefore the companies were ordered to dig in where they were, about half a mile south of Cagny. Dog-tired, they dug fast and deep.

"When dawn broke," wrote Colonel Vandeleur, "the Battalion looked like a crowd at a football match, but by the mercy of Providence the leading elements were about three feet behind the reverse slope." For the next three days X Company sat in these hastily dug positions, soaked to the skin by steady rain, bitten by mosquitos, and "stonked" by mortar bombs. On the 22nd the 51st (Highland) Division relieved them—and they were glad of it.

July 22

To those engaged *Goodwood* appeared a failure; but it had taught X Company a lot. Major Fothringham wrote that "whoever trained this company was bang on the right lines"; a modicum of experience added to a thorough grounding of realistic training more than doubles the value of a soldier.[1]

(b) *The Churchills cross to France*

While the Guards Armoured Division had been engaged in the battle of Cagny, the 6th Guards Tank Brigade (Brigadier G. L. Verney), with the Third Battalion of the Regiment, had been arriving in France.

July 16
July 19
July 20

On the 16th July the Battalion had moved from its concentration area in Kent to Bentley, near Southampton. On the 19th the tanks and trucks began to embark in Tank Landing Ships from the Hards at Gosport; on the evening of the 20th, after a rough crossing, they disembarked on "Jig" Beach on the Norman coast, half a mile east of the artificial harbour at Arromanches. After landing, the Battalion began to assemble in the orchards of Esquay, two miles east of Bayeux. The crossing had been successfully accomplished—save for the disappearance of part of S Squadron.

"S Squadron, the L.A.D., and some of the wheeled vehicles of Headquarter Squadron, arrived at the Hards at Gosport on July 20th to find three L.S.T.'s waiting to be loaded. Two of them were new ships, but the third had apparently spent a long and eventful war. So much was evident to the casual observer, for she had lost the folding doors in her bow. Moreover, her number, LST 413, aroused adverse comment amongst the more superstitious Guardsmen.

[1] X Company's history continues on p. 351. During *Goodwood* two officers of the Regiment at Headquarters Guards Armoured Division had become casualties; Captain J. W. Burden had been killed and Lieutenant Sir Anthony Meyer, Bt., wounded.

However LST 413 was to be our ship all right, so on board we went. The chains on the tank-deck were incomplete, much worn and very rusty. This was understandable, for we learnt from her crew that the ship had been in continuous use since the first North African landings. We also learnt that she had never yet carried heavier tanks than Shermans, and that most of the chains were of the lighter type intended for cruiser tanks.

We chained up, lay off the Isle of Wight until after dark, and at midnight set sail for Juno Beach at Courseulles. There was a heavy sea running, and soon the ship had a roll on, which was accentuated by her flat ramp in place of the bow doors. *July 21*

At about three in the morning those of us who were asleep (and not out of action through sickness) were roused by a series of thuds from the bowels of the ship. It was clear that some of the tanks had broken loose, and all tank crews immediately went below to investigate. The eight Churchills farthest aft had snapped their chains and were sliding about, hammering the hull, first on one side and then on the other every time the ship rolled.

For the next three-and-a-half-hours we struggled to chain the tanks down again with such pieces of chain that remained. While the ship drove on the ventilators had to remain uncovered, and only a dim blue light was allowed below. The task was hopeless—and extremely dangerous, for there was every likelihood of men being crushed between the tanks as they slid. Eventually the ship was hove-to head to wind, the ventilators covered and the lights switched on, and we chained the tanks as best we could. Meanwhile the Captain decided that, as the ship could not be expected to take much more hammering from a dead weight of over three hundred tons, it would be best to put back.

On arrival once again at Gosport we drove the tanks off and assessed the damage. One bogey had been sheared off, but, apart from this, the injuries were limited to smashed mudguards and infantry telephones. The ship's hull was somewhat dented, but otherwise she, too, was all right. New chains eventually arrived, the tanks were again chained up and once more we started off for France.

There was still a heavy sea running, but this time we were luckier. Only the two rear tanks shifted and these caused no damage. When we went ashore at Juno Beach we had been on board for over fifty hours." *July 22*

Wireless silence had forbidden any news of these vicissitudes reaching the Battalion and it was a very anxious group of officers who stood on the sands on 22nd July to watch LST 413 arrive.

The completed Battalion lay in its orchards for the best part of a week, paying social calls on veterans of six weeks' standing, sampling the products of the countryside, practicing *parlez-vous* with the inhabitants, and taking a professional, if lugubrious, interest in the wrecks of Allied tanks in a nearby tank graveyard. Soon the instinct of self-preservation spurred the crews into purposeful activity, as they welded spare track-plates on to turrets and hulls to give additional protection against the power of the 88-mm. gun.

July 28   At seven in the evening of the 28th came an unexpected order to move; by nine the Battalion was on the march for Ste. Honorine-le-Ducy, a village three miles behind our forward position on the ridge of Caumont l'Evente—"Windy Caumont" to its inhabitants, so called from the fury of the autumnal gales which lash the heights. That move marked the end of training; after three years this was, at last, the "real thing".

(c) *The Battle of Caumont*

Although, as we have seen, the attacks by the British and Canadians to the east and south of Caen had failed to break through the German positions, they had succeeded in effecting General Montgomery's predominant intention, of attracting to that sector of the front the bulk of the German armour. In the west, therefore, the enemy could confront the Americans with infantry alone, and when on the 25th July General Bradley had attacked about St. Lo he harvested the fruits of the battles of attrition fought around Caen. The German front was breached at several points, the war of manœuvre seemed about to begin, and it was essential that the enemy should not be allowed to reform his front.

One of the main features of Norman topography is a great ridge which runs east and west some five miles south of Caumont. To the east this culminates in Mont Pincon, the highest point in Normandy; to the west the ridge ends about the Bois du Homme, a feature nearly as high as Mont Pincon, affording magnificent observation, and providing a defensive position of great natural strength on which it was feared the enemy might attempt to hinge his left wing. If he could hold this ridge he might be able to swing back his left in good order; if the hinge was broken the fluidity of the battle would be maintained and all ideas of a "front" in France would be at an end. To break this hinge was the first objective of operation *Blue-coat*.

MAP XXXI   Three British corps were to take part in the attack. In the centre was the VIII Corps, commanded by Lieutenant-General Sir Richard O'Connor, and among the formations under his command was the 15th (Scottish) Division (Major-General G. H. A Macmillan), which was to be supported by its old friend of training days, the 6th Guards Tank Brigade. The Scotsmen and the Churchills were to make the initial attack southwards from Caumont on to the Bois du Homme.

On the left flank of the Division there was to be an attack by the 43rd Division, which was under the XXX Corps; on the right the 11th Armoured Division was also attacking. When the Bois du Homme had been secured, the 11th and Guards Armoured Divisions were to press on down the main road to the town of Vire.

Between the ridges of Caumont and Bois du Homme was an expanse of farm land. This was of the now famous Bocage type. It comprised small arable fields bounded by high banks, stoutly built of earth and of stones, which generations of peasants had removed from the fields. On the top of these banks grew tall, thick hedges. Orchards, meadows and copses alternated with the fields, and in the hedges grew many tall trees thickly clad in creeper. Narrow farm tracks ran through the area, affording but poor communications, for they were sunk between the banks of the fields, and were impassable to most military vehicles. Dotted here and there were solid stone farmhouses and hamlets, easily converted into infantry fortresses. Seldom in Europe can troops have fought in closer country, which, in the full leaf of summer, was admirably suited to small arms defence. Positions could easily be dug and concealed in the banks, snipers could be hidden in the ivy of the trees, artillery observation was severely limited, and any commander could be excused for thinking that this was not, in the accepted sense, "tank country". Already the Sherman tanks had found the majority of these banks unsurmountable. So far they had to rely on armoured bulldozers, gunfire and an ingenious plough devised by an American sergeant. None of this paraphernalia was required by the Churchills.

The Battalion[1] arrived in its concentration area behind the Caumont ridge at about 0830 the next morning after an all-night march. It had moved in two columns, one of the tanks and the other of the wheeled vehicles. For the "tracks" in particular it was one of the most exhausting moves of the whole war. The ill-defined cross-country route of some fifteen miles was shrouded in an opaque dust cloud, and great credit was due to those who led and those who drove. Praise was also due to the staff of the VIII Corps whose duty it was to assemble the formations at short notice. On arrival at Ste. Honorine-le-Ducy the crews snatched what rest they could between their duties of maintaining their tanks and assimilating their orders. For commanders at all levels there was precious little rest as they hurried to and fro between the various Order Groups and their commands. In fact, few of the leaders got more than an hour or two's sleep between the morning of the 28th and the conclusion of the battle on the evening of the 30th.

July 29

The attack was to be made by the 227th (Highland) Brigade supported by the 6th Guards Tank Brigade, and these Brigades were to move up that evening to the reverse slope of the Caumont ridge.

[1] For Order of Battle, see p. 554.

On the morning of the 30th the 2nd Gordon Highlanders and 9th Cameronians, supported by the Grenadiers, were to take Lutain Wood and the hamlets of Le Bourg and Sept Vents, in order to free the main road for the 10th Highland Light Infantry and the Coldstream, who

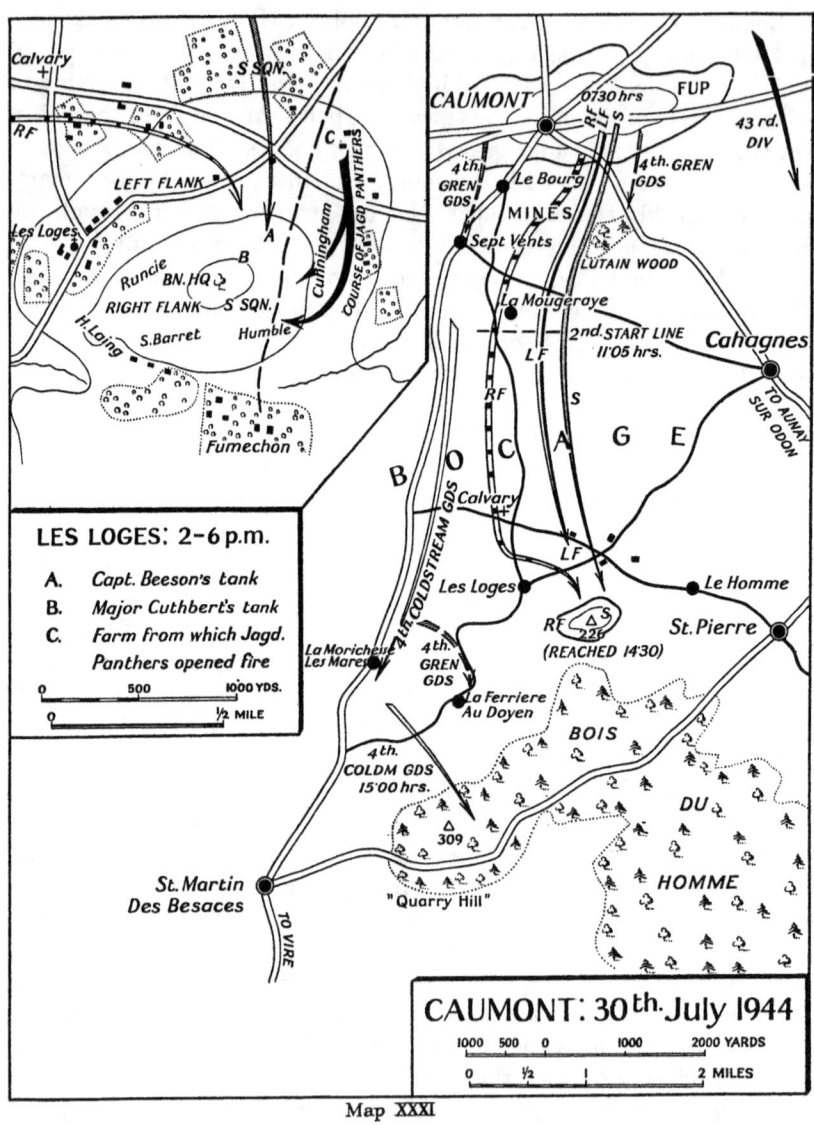

Map XXXI

were to advance down it towards St. Martin des Besaces. In the centre the Scots Guards were to support the 2nd Argyll and Sutherland Highlanders southwards through the Bocage. It was intended that at about eleven in the morning the Scots Guards and the Argylls would attack the first slopes of the Bois du Homme ridge, close to the village of Les Loges. From here, if all went well, they would push on still farther with the 7th Seaforth Highlanders to the westernmost of the summits on the ridge; Point 309. For the first phase of the attack there was to be an airburst barrage advancing at the rate of a hundred yards every four minutes.

The enemy was known to be holding that sector of the front with six battalions of the 361st Division, troops of average quality; but the real interest from the armour's point of view centred on a battalion of self-propelled guns of the 2nd Panzer Division which was thought to be close at hand. There were known to be anti-tank mines about Le Bourg, and the usual complement of anti-tank weapons with the German infantry.

The Battalion moved up on the evening of the 29th and harboured in some steep fields under the Caumont ridge, just east of the town. The night was warm, and quiet too—except for the British guns; but at dawn the enemy sent over a few shells and mortar bombs, which fell further down the slope and gave little trouble. The Grenadiers set off over the ridge for their part in the attack, and the Battalion sat listening to the noise of their battle, which was at one stage drowned by the roar of 500 heavy bombers; these could not be seen for the low cloud which hung above the battle, but the noise of their engines and of their bombs put added confidence into a Battalion which was going into action for the first time.

July 30

The Grenadier attack went well but took longer than expected and it was not until 0730, twenty minutes late, that the Scots Guards were allowed to move forward over the ridge and into the smoke-filled valley. As they did so, the leading Squadrons, Right Flank (Major the Earl Cathcart) on the right and S Squadron (Major W. S. I. Whitelaw) on the left, ran into mortar, shell, and machine-gun fire, and at first the strength of the enemy positions between Le Bourg and Lutain Wood made fast progress impossible.

An officer then in S Squadron describes the tactical method employed: "We advanced with the infantry right round us, to protect us from Bazooka men and snipers, and from hedge to hedge, making each hedge a bound. Each hedge was practically a tank obstacle anyway, as they were always on top of very high earth-banks. As we came through a hedge we made the infantry look first to see if there was a Panther in the next field. If not, we went through into the middle of the field, brought the supporting Troops up to the hedge behind, and then settled down to a quarter of an hour's speculative shooting-up of the next hedge, H.E. into any likely looking places, and Besa everywhere, including the tree-tops. All this you must imagine happening under intense mortar fire and very considerable small arms fire, mostly Spandau, coming from all over the place but from nowhere where you could pinpoint it. Every house we brewed up with H.E. fire at once. This may sound a very slow method of advance but it paid time and time again. Of course, if there was no return fire against the infantry, we went straight on, so it was not really as slow as all that." One of the greatest problems was "the Spandau which you couldn't locate, and which completely prevented the infantry from advancing. The extraordinary part was that from beginning to end you probably saw no more than two to three actual live Germans at the most, and later I was in attacks where I saw none at all. Yet afterwards, we always counted large numbers of German dead in the area we had covered, generally in the bottoms of the hedges. After the first attack we did, during which I never saw a German at all—apart from people surrendering—there were over 400 picked up. This method was all based on our own carefully worked out technique of tank–infantry co-operation, and in the Bocage it was extremely successful. The armoured divisions tried it but never really got hold of it, because, having always looked down on tank–infantry co-operation as being not quite the thing, they were a little slow in understanding what was wanted. Also their tanks weren't good enough, and couldn't stand up to heavy mortars."

It should here be explained that the German weapon referred to as a "bazooka" was not in fact similar to the American rocket-launcher from which it took its popular name. Whereas the American bazooka could fire any number of bombs in succession, the German variety, called by them *Panzerfaust*, was a single-shot weapon which could be used but once. It was more in the nature of an aimed grenade. For all that, it could cause serious damage to a tank, and the flash made by the great bulbous bomb would usually start a fire. Normally this weapon was used by a team of men, who would seek to ambush a tank at the closest range, the "bazooka boy's" *kamerads* covering his withdrawal and picking off the tank's crew as they "baled out". Altogether it was an unpleasant and efficient weapon when used by determined men in close country.

Two hours after the start the Argylls and the tanks were still fighting in the same area and it became obvious that if the second start line south of La Mougeraye was to be reached on time and proper advantage taken of the artillery barrage things would have to be speeded up. Colonel Dunbar[1] therefore ordered the tanks to crash on as fast as the opposition allowed and to leave the infantry to follow in their wake. By this stage two tanks of Right Flank had been blown up on the expected minefield near Le Bourg, but otherwise the Battalion was intact, although several tanks, including the Commanding Officer's, had been hit by artillery fire.

[1] Colonel Dunbar had the only reliable map. This was made up from recent air-photographs and was far superior to the printed maps, which were virtually indecipherable in the roadless Bocage.

Using their Besa machine-guns and high explosive shells to great effect amongst the many pockets of enemy resistance on the way, the leading Squadrons reached the second start line by 1105, only five minutes late, and fought on towards Les Loges preceded by the barrage.

At about 1215, having advanced well over a mile and sent back scores of prisoners, the tanks were so far ahead of the Argylls that Colonel Dunbar ordered a halt to wait for them to catch up. While waiting, S Squadron was shot at from some cottages, but these were soon dealt with by the Troops of Lieutenants R. Humble and C. R. T. Cunningham, which engaged the houses with high explosive at point-blank range; the infantry later found the ruins littered with corpses.

By 1315 it was clear that the infantry were so far behind—in fact they had not crossed the second start line until one o'clock—that unless the tanks went on at once the effects of the barrage would have worn off and the opportunity of reaching Les Loges without serious opposition would be past. The position was explained to the Brigade Commander, who immediately gave permission to the Commanding Officer to push on alone, and S Squadron, moving with remarkable rapidity, reached the eastern slope of the Les Loges ridge at 1430. Right Flank, unwilling to pass through the village without infantry support, turned left and followed S Squadron on to the ridge. The position was then consolidated with Right Flank on the right, S Squadron on the left, and Left Flank (Major the Hon. Michael Fitzalan Howard) behind them in support.

Meanwhile the Argylls struggled on through the Bocage, mopping up infantry which the tanks had by-passed. By 1615 the leading Company had cleared Les Loges and two more had gained the ridge alongside the tanks. Unfortunately their transport and anti-tank guns were far behind.

So far so good, and the two Battalions were now ready to go on to the final objective, Point 309. Colonel Dunbar made an urgent appeal for permission to advance, but General Macmillan, mindful that the Les Loges ridge commanded the main Vire road which was to be his division's axis, ordered the Scots Guards to stay where they were. Instead he ordered the Coldstream with the Seaforth on to the high ground from the north-west, a task which they accomplished with great speed and success, and thereby crowned the day's achievements.

Thus the Battalion's right flank was fairly secure but of the progress of 43rd Division to the east nothing was known, nor could anything be discovered, as the country was far too rough for anything but a Churchill to reconnoitre. The Battalion was a good four miles inside enemy territory and holding an extremely bare and exposed ridge, overlooked from the front and hedged in by thick bocage to the left and rear. No anti-tank guns had yet come up, and the infantry were, not surprisingly, somewhat reluctant to sit in the open among the tanks, exposed to every type of fire. They preferred to remain in the village on the reverse slope. Any counter-attack seemed most likely to come from the dominating ground to the south, so the leading Squadrons kept their tanks hull down on the ridge, and waited for something to happen from that direction.

About six o'clock, just as the B.B.C. News of the battle was coming over the air, the enemy put down a heavy shell and mortar "stonk" which forced the tanks to close down, and shells hit Captain N. W. Beeson's tank twice, the second killing him as he was attempting to rescue his wounded hull gunner. A few minutes later a hail of shot from what was evidently an outsize high-velocity gun poured on to the ridge from out of the depths of a thick wood some 300 yards to the left rear —that is, from an entirely unexpected direction, and from an area which, according to the plan, should by then have been reached by the 43rd Division. But, alas, they were still struggling through the Bocage three miles behind.

The first three rounds knocked out all three tanks of Lieutenant Cunningham's Troop, which was the guardian of that flank. Then two enormous self-propelled guns emerged from the wood and, covered by a third from behind a house, lumbered up the hill into the centre of S Squadron's position. They were Jagd Panthers, mounting extra long 88-mm. guns, the largest machines of their type in existence and never before encountered by the British in action. Their tactics were highly successful.

One monster advanced under cover of a hedge through S Squadron from the south-east, skilfully keeping itself screened from Left Flank to its rear, whilst the other came in from the north. Between them they destroyed eight more Churchills at point-blank range before slipping out of sight southwards over the ridge, leaving on the position a mass of blazing hulks. Days later two of these giants were found abandoned nearby, and one, which had been hit in the track by a shell, was credited to the gunner of Lieutenant D. L. Bankes' tank, who had originally claimed a hit with a 75-mm. H.E.

The whole attack had taken no more than five minutes and was unsupported by infantry—but it had been a heavy blow; the more so as Major S. J. Cuthbert, second-in-command of the Battalion since Yorkshire days, had chosen that very moment to move up on to the crest in his tank to look at Left Flank. He must have met the enemy head on, for his tank was found penetrated through its heaviest frontal armour with the turret blown clean off. He and Lieutenant Humble were both killed in this short onslaught, and Lieutenant Cunningham was wounded. The Battalion's total other ranks casualties for the day amounted to twenty-one killed, including Sergeant E. Thorn, who commanded No. 7 Troop of S Squadron, and eighteen were wounded.

As soon as the Jagd Panthers had made good their escape Major Whitelaw quickly reorganised the remnants of his squadron, and the tanks remained on the ridge, expecting more trouble. At about 1930 our own S.P. guns arrived. Once they were installed the Battalion withdrew to "forward rally" at the eastern end of Les Loges, leaving the ridge in the sure hands of the Argylls. As they moved back in the dark to find a suitable harbour area they fell in with A Echelon coming up under Major Sir Charles Maclean, Bt., and a harbour was made in the nearest field. No sooner had the tanks been filled with petrol and ammunition than the cooks had a hot meal ready, but most were too tired to eat.

The Battalion's first day of battle had been at once glorious, tragic and exceptional. There was the glory of a deep penetration of the enemy lines, the virtual destruction of an enemy division, and the receipt of a host of congratulatory messages. All this had been won in co-operation with the 15th Division, the formation with which the Brigade had trained so hard in the previous year. The mutual confidence between the tanks and the infantry sprang from that period, though the crews could not fail to notice the sad gaps, particularly among the junior leaders, which had occurred in the ranks of the Scottish battalions since the date of their landing.

The tragedy of the day lay in the losses suffered by S Squadron on the ridge of Les Loges. Tank Battalions are usually more fortunate than their infantry comrades in the proportion of their losses. At Caumont, on that one first day of battle, the Battalion suffered one-third of all its fatal casualties of the whole campaign in Europe; and all save four of the killed and wounded were from S Squadron. The loss of Major Cuthbert was an especially heavy blow; he had been one of the chief innovators in the realm of infantry and tank co-operation, and his energy knew no bounds.

The exceptional feature of the battle was the loss of so many Churchills, and in particular the fact that those destroyed on the ridge caught fire with such apparent ease. In none of the Brigade's subsequent battles were tank losses to be so heavy, nor was the incidence of fire to be so frequent. It was well known that the Sherman tank was prone to burst into flames all too easily; in fact, the enemy nicknamed them "Tommy cookers". But fire was a bogy which rarely troubled the Churchill. It seems that the special 88-mm. gun and ammunition carried by the Jagd Panther, when fired at such close range, had an altogether exceptional power of penetration and explosion, and that the combination of circumstances was never again repeated.

Reflection after the battle did not point to any serious error in the disposition of the Squadrons having allowed the enemy an easy success. Rather it was his brilliant tactics and his audacity which won for him that final triumph. On the Battalion's part, battle experience was lacking, and the resulting infinitesimal hesitation by the rearmost Squadron in realising that it was enemy, and not friendly, armour which was crossing its front proved a costly delay.

One's admiration of the crews is heightened by the knowledge that they shrugged off these losses, and looked only at the other lessons of the battle. The most heartening was the amazing cross-country performance of the Churchill tank; another was the tremendous morale effect of the concentrated fire of a squadron on the defending infantry. It was more than a consolation to learn that the Germans labelled the combination of the 15th Scottish Division and the 6th Guards Tank Brigade "Churchill's Butchers".

What was it like to fight in one of these mobile steel fortresses? One who commanded a troop from Normandy to the Baltic has described it:

> Living in a tank for days on end under battle conditions turned out to be something very different from spending a few hours in the driving seat or in the turret during an exercise at home.
>
> To crash straight across country ignoring the easy route, taking in Churchillian strides small woods, buildings, hills, valleys, sunken roads and, worst of all, those steep high banks which divide up the Norman Bocage like the ridges on a monstrous waffle; this was something for which we were not quite prepared by our training in the Dukeries.
>
> There was no luxury and little comfort about the Churchills, save when driven slowly along a road: in the small fields of Normandy, among the cider orchards, every move during the hot summer brought showers of small hard sour apples cascading into the turrets through the commanders' open hatches; after a few days there might be enough to jam the turret.
>
> Five men in close proximity, three in the turret and two below in the driving compartment, all in a thick metal oven, soon produced a foul smell: humanity, apples, cordite and heat. Noise: the perpetual "mush" through the ear-phones twenty-four hours each day, and through it the machinery noises, the engine as a background, with the whine of the turret trainer and the thud and rattle of the guns an accompaniment. The surge of power as the tank rose up to the crest of a bank; the pause at the top while the driver, covered with sweat and dust and unable to see, tried to balance his forty tons before the bone-jarring crash down into the field beyond, with every loose thing taking life and crashing round inside the turret. Men, boxes of machine-gun ammunition, magazines, shell-cases— and always those small hard apples.
>
> The skill of the driver, and indeed of all those men in the crew, was remarkable: the operator struggling to keep the wireless on net

and the guns loaded: the gunner with eyes always at the telescope however much the turret revolved and crashed around him; the hot stoppages in the machine-guns; the commander, with his head only above his hatches, choked with dust, not quite standing, not quite sitting during all those long Normandy days: always the wireless pounding at his ear-drums.

After dark was the time for maintenance, when the 3-ton trucks from the echelon came up with petrol, ammunition and food; then the guns had to be cleaned and all repairs finished before first light and stand-to. Thanks to the tanks, repairs were not many, but crews could not go on for very long without a rest.

A brief rest, in the course of which three more guardsmen of S Squadron were killed by one of our own shells, was now granted to the Battalion. Major Whitelaw became second-in-command, and Major C. O'M. Farrell succeeded him in the command of S Squadron, which withdrew to B Echelon to reform. Brigadier Verney was promoted to the command of the 7th Armoured Division, and was in his turn replaced in command of the Brigade by Sir Walter Barttelot, Bt., who had commanded the Coldstream in their dashing attack on Point 309. Now the battle developed: down the Caumont–Vire road passed the Guards Armoured Division.[1]

(d) *Infantry in the Bocage*

The break-through achieved by the 6th Guards Tank Brigade set the British front in motion. As the Americans fanned out from the breach they had made on the coast, the British pressed on through the thick Bocage, ever southwards, still tying down the bulk of the German armour and thus preventing any large scale concentrations against the American columns. Now it was the turn of the Guards Armoured Division to enter the Bocage.   MAP XXXIV

After *Goodwood* X Company had rested in Colombelles, an industrial suburb north-east of Caen. On the day of the Third Battalion's attack they moved by way of Bayeux and Le Tronquay to an area three miles north of Caumont, where the infantry companies of the 3rd Irish "married up" with the tank Squadrons of the 1st Armoured Coldstream to form a "Bocage Battle-group". The close country ahead could be successfully traversed only if there was the most intimate co-operation between foot and armour, and these groups were the genesis of the four regimental groups which were to be a unique characteristic of the Guards Armoured Division for the remainder of the war. On the morning of 1st August the Division set off down the Caumont–Vire road. For the first two days the Groups pressed on   July 30   Aug. 1

---

[1] The history of the Third Battalion continues on p. 353. At Brigade Headquarters Lieutenant R. E. Heywood-Farmer had been wounded on the 30th July.

through the close country. The work was hot and slow, and the Guardsmen were glad of the flagons of cider with which the Normans welcomed their liberators. In a vast game of leap-frog the Division passed through the battered villages of St. Martin des Besaces, St. Denis-Maisoncelles and Le Tourneur. X Company arrived at St. Charles le Percy at dusk on the 2nd, and received orders to mount an attack that night.

Aug. 2

Aug. 3 Soon after midnight they set off across country for the little villages of Montchamp and Maisoncelles, three miles away. At first they were in rear of the Irish companies, but at four in the morning they took the lead to the hamlet of Courteil, which lay on their route to Montchamp. Four hundred yards short of Courteil they met determined resistance from troops of the 10th SS Panzer Division; for a day they fought these worthy opponents at close quarters in the hedges, banks and fields. First-class leadership added to sound training was needed to counter the sudden emergencies which arose in this war of small battlefields, confused noise and rumours of "snipers"—a term which the Company Commander reported was used by others to denote any "noisy German with a Spandau who tries to draw fire, and, if a man tells you he has been sniped all day, he often means he can hear small-arms fire which he *thinks* may be in his direction". To "read the battle" in these circumstances required a cool head and an ear for the characteristic noises made by friendly and enemy weapons. The carrier driver, Guardsman Floyd, could properly claim to have been "sniped"; for as he drove up to the company's position he had to dodge well-aimed shells from a self-propelled gun; he made it, having driven at high speed with one track overhanging a ditch, and having been irritated by the loss of one driving-mirror which the "sniper" had removed with a solid shot.

Aug. 4 At midday on the next day, the Company was enabled by the arrival of a troop of Coldstream tanks to advance through Courteil, and they wheeled south on Maisoncelles. Here Captain E. J. Hope (who was commanding in the absence of Major Fothringham, temporarily in command of the Battalion) led the Company in a determined attack which all but gained their main objective, a small cross-roads. He sent two platoons round the rear of the enemy, and with P.I.A.T.s they drove off two German tanks which formed the mainstay of the enemy defence, and captured a third intact; its crew were too busy trying to repair some mechanical defect to notice what was in progress around them, which was fortunate, as the tank was "undoubtedly formidable and had a gun stretching from here to Sunday week".

It soon became plain that the loss of Maisoncelles was unwelcome to the enemy, and steps were quickly taken to reinforce the company with a platoon of the Irish Guards, some 3-inch mortars and two 17-pounder anti-tank guns of the 21st Anti-Tank Regiment R.A. This reinforcement was timely, and suitably composed. Just after dark four German tanks, of which one was a Panther, clanked out of a wood to the right, and drove along a track not fifty yards in front of the forward trenches. The anti-tank gunners were lying by their guns, resting after their exertions of getting into position, but they sprang to life and let fly at point-blank range. In a few seconds four blazing wrecks illuminated the battlefield, and in the light of these funeral pyres a company of German infantry was seen advancing on the position. Scots Guards bullets, Irish Guards mortar bombs and the Gunners' shells saw these off, too. Later in the night a misdirected enemy supply convoy ran into the Company's defences, and in the morning wrecked vehicles and a bloody German Dressing Station were evidence of the havoc the defenders had caused. It had been a close melée, in which Captain Hope had had to call the defensive fire of the supporting 25-pounders on to his own positions to ensure the victory. At dawn the enemy resigned himself to the loss of Maisoncelles, and for the next two days X Company did little but exchange shots with fleeting figures in the hedges and houses of Montchamp. At midday on the 7th they moved away to the east to secure a new gun area for the 15th (Scottish) Division who were engaged about the village of Estry, supported by the 6th Guards Tank Brigade. On the move the Company were heavily mortared, and suffered their first officer casualty when Lieutenant Thorpe was slightly wounded.[1]

Aug. 5

Aug. 7

(e) *The Tanks at Estry*

For three days after the battle of Caumont the Battalion remained in the harbour area near Les Loges, ready to go out in a counter-attack role at short notice. These fine summer days were spent maintaining and repairing the tanks and salving what they could from those that had been knocked out. On the afternoon of 3rd August, with "Wee Jocks" of the 2nd Glasgow Highlanders and 10th H.L.I. riding on the tanks, the Battalion, less S Squadron, which was still reforming, drove round the Bois du Homme feature and took up positions about the village of La Mancellière at the foot of its southern slopes.

Aug. 3

Two days later the advance continued to Montcharivel some seven miles to the south-east. Meeting no opposition Right Flank, supporting the 2nd Argylls, pushed on to the hamlet of La Motte a mile beyond the village, where they harboured for the night in an orchard, while Left Flank with the H.L.I. reached Au Cornu a mile farther on where they, too, harboured, but under heavy shellfire.

Aug. 5

MAP XXXII

At dawn on Sunday 6th August the Battalion received orders for its

Aug. 6

---

[1] X Company's history continues on p. 363.

23—S.G.H.

second battle, which was to take it to the south-west to establish a
firm base in and around the village of Estry and its important cross-
roads. As at Caumont a week before, the Gordons with a squadron of
Grenadier tanks were to start the day by driving down the main road
from La Caverie to capture Estry. As soon as Estry was in our hands,
they were to be followed by the H.L.I. with Left Flank in support,
who would pass on to Le Theil, a mile or so to the south-east. Meanwhile Right Flank with the Argylls would push down the Vassy Road,

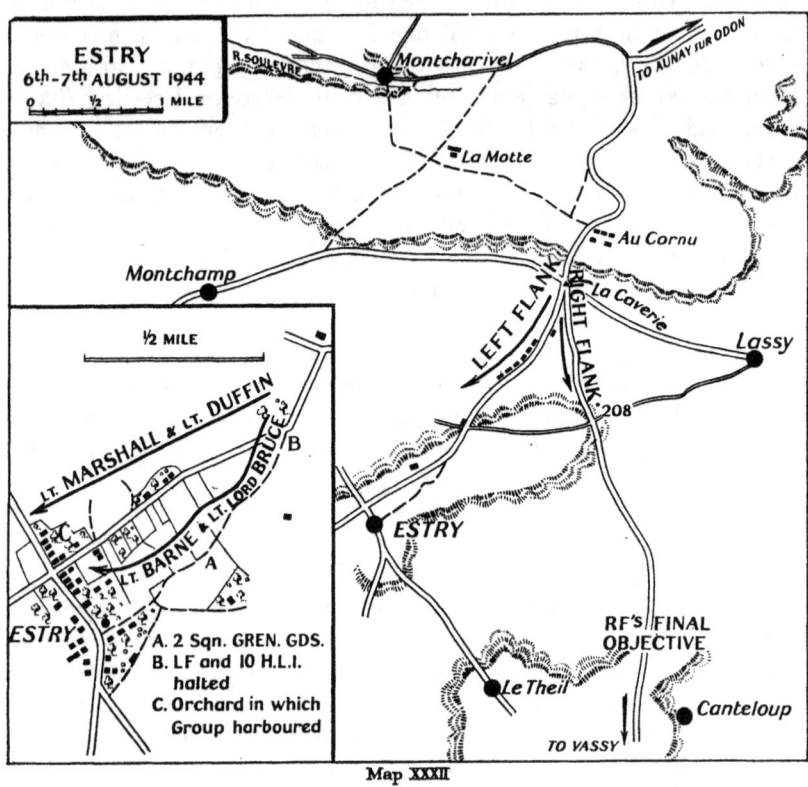

Map XXXII

due south from La Caverie, to occupy Point 208, and then the high
ground above Canteloup, which formed the eastern summit of the
Le Theil ridge. The enemy were thought to contemplate retreat, and
there was an optimistic reconnaissance report of weak resistance.

Thick morning mist delayed the start, and the Gordons and Grenadiers were moving off from La Caverie cross-roads as Right Flank
arrived there to pick up the Argylls. While the Churchills were still
nose to tail on the road, an enemy tank, which had moved up from
the direction of Lassy, began to shell the cross-roads from a range of
about a thousand yards. As soon as our tanks had got off the road, its
position was spotted by Lieutenant A. I. D. Fletcher's Troop, which

quickly moved to engage it. Unfortunately it was able to fire several rounds before they could do so, one of which, an H.E., hit Captain D. G. Mathieson's scout car, killing him and wounding Guardsman Houston, his operator. Once engaged, the enemy, now recognised as a Tiger, swiftly withdrew, but at the same time artillery and mortars began to plaster the area of the cross-roads and this shelling was kept up intermittently throughout the day. Right Flank, who were deployed to the right of the road waiting to advance towards Canteloup, spent an unpleasant morning under this hail of shot and shell.

At about 1130 Left Flank and the H.L.I. passed through this unsalubrious spot in the wake of the Gordons, led by an advance guard of one company supported by two Troops under Captain P. E. G. Balfour. As soon as this advance guard had passed over the cross-roads it deployed on the left of the Estry road and carried on for a mile until they came up with the Gordons and Grenadiers, who were fighting their way forward astride a sunken road against growing and tenacious opposition. This was not what had been forecast; nor was it realised at the time that the 9th SS Panzer Division, troops of the highest quality, had turned Estry into a strong-point and were intending to hold it at all costs. Two or three companies of an SS Regiment, a dug-in tank, 88's, bazookas, mines and Nebelwerfers were there, and plenty of artillery and mortar support as well. By the afternoon the Grenadier Squadron had lost its Squadron Leader killed, four officers wounded and all but four of its tanks disabled. Shelling was continuous on the road behind, and casualties amongst the infantry were mounting fast, not only among the Gordons, but also among the H.L.I., who, with Left Flank, were halted behind them.

Sitting on a road under shellfire with nothing to do is trying in the extreme, and, as soon as it was confirmed that the Gordons were unlikely to make anything but very slow progress, Left Flank and the H.L.I. were ordered to deploy and make a firm base around the point where the sunken road branched off to the left from the main road. In doing this Captain Balfour ditched his tank in the sunken lane and, despite the efforts of Lieutenant H. W. S. Marshall's Troop to recover it under fire, it had to be left there. At about the same time an enemy bazooka team crept up on Lieutenant C. J. R. Duffin's tank, but were spotted in the nick of time and their purpose thwarted; one of them was disintegrated by an H.E. shell at five yards' range. Throughout the late afternoon shells and howling Nebelwerfer bombs continued to fall in the area and Sergeant Tranter's tank was knocked out, the Sergeant being wounded.

By the evening the Gordons had made little progress, and a plan was therefore made for the H.L.I. and Left Flank to assault Estry down the main road, after the village had been blasted by a concentration of medium guns.

The attack formed up with a company and two Troops on either side of the road, Lieutenants Marshall's and Duffin's Troops on the right, Lieutenants J. M. Barne's and Lord Bruce's, on the left. The artillery programme was not fired, and at 1915 the attack began without it. By late evening tanks and infantry had fought their way beyond the cross-roads on the right and to the neighbourhood of the church on the left.

Marshall and Duffin had met little opposition on the right, though Marshall's tank was blown up on a mine, which killed his co-driver, Guardsman Finch, as was Captain Balfour's when the reserve Troop and Squadron Headquarters moved up to join them.

On the left, it had not been so easy. The H.L.I. were held up in very thick country by heavy machine-gun fire, which eventually was dealt with by fire from the tanks, directed by the infantry. As Lieutenant Barne emerged from the last orchard before the church, he spied a Panther hiding in a shed 200 yards to this right. He fired and hit it with an H.E. shot, but before he could re-load with armour-piercing, the Panther replied, setting his Churchill on fire and forcing the crew to "bale out". Two of them were hit by bullets before they could get to cover, but Barne himself was unscathed and was able to withdraw the remainder of his Troop under cover of smoke to where Lord Bruce and Sergeant Coleman were being called upon to surrender by a party of SS men. Lord Bruce's reply to this impudence was to shoot their leader with his pistol; the rest were despatched by Besa fire. Lieutenant Barne then went off on foot and collected the M.10 self-propelled guns which were following up in support, and directed them on to the Panther, which they quickly destroyed. He then went on to guide the leading platoons of the H.L.I. into the village, and was of great assistance to the leading Company Commanders.

Aug. 7

Night was now coming on, and still the enemy showed no sign of yielding. If an SS man put up his hands to surrender it was usually in order to distract a tank crew's attention from some bazooka party trying to creep up from the opposite direction. They were "wonderful soldiers"—a phrase used in their letters home by many officers when describing these fanatics. The casualties which they had caused amongst the infantry had been very heavy. The H.L.I. were therefore withdrawn into the orchards on either side of the cross-roads for the night, and there, along with the Gordons, they dug in, with Left Flank and the M.10's forming close squadron harbour to protect them. The infantry had just got below ground when the enemy swept the orchards with a heavy concentration of medium artillery. It was a nasty night: and until ordered to withdraw to Montcharivel on the following afternoon, Left Flank remained with the infantry in these orchards under heavy close-range mortar and machine-gun fire. It was under this heavy fire that Major Fitzalan Howard personally directed the forming up for the move to the rear.

We must now return to the previous day to follow the fortunes of Right Flank, who we left sitting under steady fire around the La Caverie cross-roads. To their relief (for it is stuffy and uncomfortable to remain "closed down" in a tank for hours on end), the advance down the Canteloup road began at one o'clock. Their battle was to be no easier than that of Left Flank. The road was thought to be mined, mortar and machine-gun fire were constant, and trouble was experienced from dug-in tanks and S.P. guns on the high ground to the east, which, had the plans of others gone properly, should have been cleared earlier.

The Squadron moved on the right of the road and soon came up to a good fire position from which they could cover the Argylls' advance on to the first objective, Point 208. As they reached it, heavy shellfire came down on the luckless infantry, and every tank in the Squadron now engaged the forward slope of the objective with Besa and H.E. to cover the Argylls forward, but owing to the incessant shelling they were unable to make use of it. For a short time communication between their Commanding Officer and Lord Cathcart broke down when the former left his wireless to reorganise his battered forward companies; but after separate, and eventually successful, attempts to locate him by Lieutenants Bankes and A. G. Laing, personal contact was again established, and a smoke-screen put down by the gunners also relieved the situation.

During the shelling Lieutenant Fletcher, who had two tanks only in his Troop, and whose Troop Sergeant, Sergeant T. Hislop had already been badly wounded, observed a poorly camouflaged tank on the road at the top of Point 208. The first round blew off its screen of netting and foliage to reveal a Panther, and a fierce fire fight ensued, in the course of which Sergeant Hislop's tank, which had continued in the battle under the joint command of Guardsmen Small and Millar, was knocked out; Small was killed and Millar wounded. Although the petrol tank was penetrated the Churchill did not catch fire. The Panther evidently had had enough, and reversed over the ridge.

The Argylls, now reorganised into two companies, began their assault on Point 208 closely supported by the Troops of Lieutenants Laing and D. W. Scott-Barrett. As Lieutenant Laing approached the crest he saw a Panther sixty yards away, slowly traversing its gun on to his own tank. To his horror he quickly discovered that, owing to the steepness of the hill, he was unable to depress his own gun sufficiently to shoot at it, but luckily for him the Panther gunner was a bad shot and missed this sitting target with his first round, although with a later shot he hit another Churchill, killing Corporal Stewart, its commander. Lieutenant Laing was therefore able to reverse out of sight down the hill and, dismounting from his tank, he collected a section of infantry with a P.I.A.T. and went forward on foot to try and knock the monster out. After the first shot from the P.I.A.T. the tank withdrew, but this was not noticed by Guardsman Drummond, the driver of Corporal Stewart's tank, which had been holed through the turret, for he also dismounted and under heavy fire directed Lieutenant Scott-Barrett's Troop to where he thought that the Panther still was. Finding what he had thought was "a number of Tigers" to have disappeared, he ran back to his own tank and, driving it down the hill to the road, helped to cover Captain J. P. Mann's Churchill which had slipped into a ditch and was now being heavily mortared; Captain Mann's tank had only been saved from the Panther owing to the fact that, in his case, it was the Panther which could not sufficiently depress its gun. Drummond was awarded the Battalion's first Military Medal.

By the evening the northern slopes of Point 208 were in our hands, and it was decided not to go farther before morning. The tanks were therefore withdrawn a short distance to refuel and replenish with ammunition, and since the morning attack never materialised they remained where they were in a counter-attack role, until finally withdrawn to Montcharivel thirty-six hours later.

Aug. 7

Throughout both the Squadrons' battles not least of the difficulties was the evacuation of casualties, all of which had to pass over the dangerous and shell-swept La Caverie cross-roads. The Battalion R.A.P., operating under Captain A. T. MacKnight, R.A.M.C., coped magnificently in this unpleasant area, giving succour to the infantry until both Squadrons were withdrawn, and was very lucky not to have been hit by the many shells and mortar bombs which crashed around it. Casualties during the engagements amounted to twelve killed, including Captain Mathieson, and eight other ranks wounded. In addition Lieutenant E. C. H. Warner was severely wounded by shellfire while in command of A 1 Echelon, subsequently losing a leg.

Estry later withstood a full scale attack by another Infantry Brigade with the whole Grenadier tank battalion, flame-throwers, aircraft and a great deal of artillery to support them, and this assault could claim less success than that carried out by Left Flank and its gallant Scots infantry. The village was not captured until advances on other sectors forced the SS finally to withdraw.

(f) *The Tanks at Chênedollé*

Aug. 7–9

The Battalion remained at Montcharivel for the next three days, basking in a hot sun and scrubbing off the filth of battle under the showers of a mobile bath unit. Typhoon fighters could be seen harassing the enemy to the south with their spectacular rockets, and the fact that the Battalion was in a gun area made the rest much less quiet than it might have been, for the gun makes more noise at the despatching end than does the shell on arrival. On 8th August the reconstituted S Squadron rejoined and to celebrate the occasion a memorable officers' dinner was held which ended in the dark with cow-back exercises. Perhaps this was a kinder fate than that which was suffered by many of these placid animals; their carcasses made the air of Normandy noisome that summer.

On Thursday 10th August the Battalion was placed under command of the 32nd Guards Brigade of the Guards Armoured Division, and thus under its first Commanding Officer, Brigadier Johnson, for an attack on the high ground near Presles, two and a half miles to the south-west of Estry, and for a subsequent advance as far as the village of Chênedollé, or "China Doll" as the Guardsmen called it—3,000 yards further south. The news that they were to support the infantry of the Guards Division was received by all ranks with pleasurable anticipation.

Aug. 10
MAP
XXXIII

The Battalion was required to concentrate near Cavignaux, due west of Estry, and to get there involved a long and tortuous march, which was needlessly enlivened by a friendly four-engined bomber of disputed nationality which suddenly appeared and dropped its bombs on the column. Luckily the aim was poor, so there was neither damage nor casualty, save for Lord Cathcart, who dislocated his shoulder when diving for cover under his tank. Like Captain R. W. O. Burnett, who was suffering from throat trouble, he was evacuated to the rear for treatment and at the base hospital found to his consternation that the doctors were intending to send him back to England. The doctors were deprived of their prey when both Captain Burnett and Lord Cathcart fled forward by devious routes, and recuperated at the Battalion's B Echelon.

The field over which the Battalion was to fight its final action in Normandy was clad in the familiar Bocage vegetation. But in this case it was to be an attack up a steep hill. Looking from Presles southwards across the valley of the small river Allière a sharply rising ridge could be seen. In the bottom of the valley was a substantial hummock; next there came an abrupt slope on which our forward infantry were dug in and, over the top of its false crest, lay the village of Le Bas Perrier; from Le Bas Perrier there was a steady ascent to the most prominent feature, Point 242, just south of which, and slightly lower, was the larger village of Chênedollé. Behind Chênedollé ran, east and west, the main Vire–Vassy road, crossing the high point of Le Boulay-aux-Chats.

The plan for the battles of the 11th August involved the Battalion in two distinct phases. In the first, S Squadron (Major Farrell) starting at 0630, were to support Nos. 2 and 3 Companies of the 1st Welsh Guards in attacks upon two hamlets on either side of and slightly beyond Le Bas Perrier, whilst Left Flank (Major Fitzalan Howard), starting three-quarters of an hour later, were to support No. 4 Company of the same battalion in an advance to the east to an important track junction north of Houssemagne. This was not expected to take

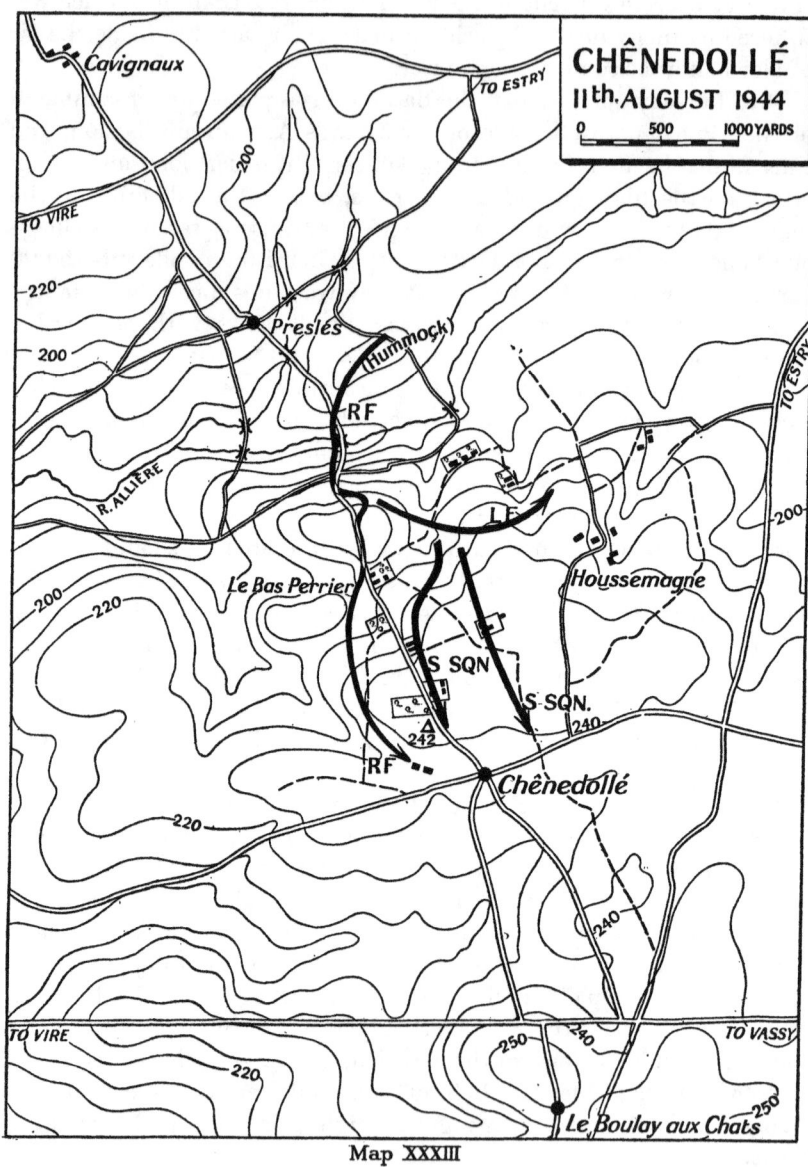

Map XXXIII

long, and in the second phase the 5th Coldstream were to be supported on the right by Right Flank (Captain J. P. Mann) and on the left by S Squadron in an attempt to form strong positions either side of the village of Chênedollé. There was also a third phase which involved exploitation across the main road, but this did not include the Battalion, and, as frequently happens, never in fact materialised.

The Battalion left its concentration area and began to move along the narrow road to Presles at three o'clock in the morning. There was a great deal of anxiety lest an enemy shell, of which there were a fair number flying around, should coincide with a tank and block this tricky defile. Fortunately no such disaster occurred, and the Battalion was in position on and around the small hummock beyond Presles by first light. Aug. 11

S Squadron's attack opened on the dot of half-past six, with Major Farrell and two troops supporting the Company on the right and Captain W. P. Bull with two more troops supporting the Company on the left. No serious opposition was met by the latter party and by half past seven they were on their objective with the infantry digging in. On the right, however, it was a different story, and Major Farrell with No. 3 Company took no less than three and a half hours to cover some four hundred yards. The reason for this was the presence of an SS company entrenched in the thickest of bocage with at least four Panthers in support and plenty of artillery on call.

The main battle, therefore, was on this flank. It started inauspiciously when the enemy replied to our opening barrage with a heavy rain of mortar bombs which caught the Welsh Guards as they were forming up in the open, and cost them twenty casualties. With the aid of the tanks' Besas and shells the Welshmen edged slowly forward, winkling out no less than nine separate Spandau posts before the objective was reached. Early on, a Panther showed itself amongst the hedgerows just long enough to hole Lieutenant M. Law's tank through the engine at the shortest range, and then disappeared before anyone could reply. Not long after, Lieutenant E. P. Hickling, peering through a thick hedge to his front, spotted several more enemy tanks near a barn in the area of the objective. They had not seen him and so, wisely holding his fire, he reported their position to his Squadron Leader, and remained where he was to observe. Major Farrell realised that Captain Bull's tanks on the other flank could get broadside shots at the enemy. He therefore ordered a troop to cross the road and stalk up as close to the barn as possible. By great good fortune—and by what might be called "bocage-craft"—Lieutenant P. M. Ward's Troop was able to get within a 150 yards, and were rewarded with the sight of three unsuspecting Panthers. Unfortunately one moved away as the Troop appeared but they scored a quick "right and left" on the other two, Lieutenant Ward getting one and Sergeant P. MacFarlane, his Troop Sergeant (who was killed later in the day), the other. These were the first Panthers to be destroyed for certain by the Battalion, and they were sweet revenge for S Squadron. By nine-thirty the infantry were almost on the objective, and the Squadron received orders to detach themselves and to carry on with the second phase.

Meanwhile Left Flank had met their company of Welsh Guards and had formed up just below Le Bas Perrier. "H-Hour" was to be at 0730, but half an hour before that time the early morning mist in the low ground had combined with some thick enemy smoke put down to annoy S Squadron; visibility was so poor that the infantry asked for the attack to be postponed. But the sun broke through by half-past seven and the attack was able to start as planned. Right Flank sat on the hummock in the valley to give fire support if needed.

Left Flank advanced with two troops "up" and with a platoon working with each. Their attack was to the east and at right angles to that of S Squadron. The first opposition came from a platoon of SS men in two cottages, but stopped abruptly after these buildings had been demolished about their occupants' ears. The country became more difficult as the advance pressed on, the fields became smaller and the hedges thicker. Soon a second enemy platoon was encountered and as swiftly dealt with and, shortly after, the right-hand Troop and platoon were on the objective. The left-hand infantry were held up, and, in an effort to assist them forward, Lord Bruce was ordered to take his Troop out on the extreme flank and to shoot the Welshmen in from there. Whilst doing this his tank was bazooka'd at close quarters, severely wounding him and killing his operator, Guardsman Brand. The other members of his crew managed to get him out of the tank before it was enveloped in flames, and after seeing him off to the rear on the back of another Churchill, they joined the infantry and continued to fight on foot with their pistols.

The whole objective was gained by nine o'clock. Left Flank remained in support of the infantry until 1530 during which period there was plenty to occupy them. The first excitement was the arrival on the right flank of an enemy tank which quickly knocked out three Shermans of the 2nd Armoured Irish Guards. However, Captain Balfour and Lieutenant Barne avenged this loss by stalking the German with some M.10s of the 21st Anti-Tank Regiment, and it was effectively silenced. Next a suspicious house was engaged with H.E.; the house blew up with a shattering explosion and was found to have been an enemy ammunition dump. The report of a Tiger in the area kept all on the alert, and artillery fire was quickly obtained through the Commanding Officer, who was at Brigade Headquarters. A concentration, directed with great accuracy by Major Fitzalan Howard was put down in the suspected locality. Finally, Left Flank had the satisfaction of killing a bazooka man who, it was discovered from his pay book, had been awarded the Iron Cross for knocking out a British tank during July.

We must now return to S Squadron, now engaged on the second phase, and pushing slowly forward without undue incident with their company of the 5th Coldstream. By one o'clock they were firmly established to the east of Chênedollé village, and there they stayed until five. Right Flank had an equally easy advance, during which they preceded their infantry, keeping close behind the artillery barrage. In this manner they were able to do great execution among the Germans, who attempted to emerge from their trenches the moment the barrage had rolled over them. Once on the objective the tanks took up positions to cover the exits from the village, and to their delight a Panther soon appeared down the road from Le Bas Perrier. Tanks armed with 6-pounders were quickly brought up and S Squadron across the road were warned of the prey. To mix a metaphor, the Panther was a sitting bird—if ever there was one; but to the disappointment of the gunners its crew, realising the hopeless position, drove off the road into a barn, in which the machine ignominiously committed *hari kari* by setting itself alight.

That evening the Battalion concentrated at a "forward rally" to the north-west of Le Bas Perrier. Shelling was intermittent, and at about half-past seven an unlucky round came down among S Squadron, wounding several men. At the same time a concentration fell around Battalion Headquarters while Brigadier Johnson was holding an Order Group there, but the tight armoured box formed by the Headquarters tanks gave a reassuring sense of security to those within. Far more unsettling than the shelling was the appalling stench emanating from a whole herd of dead and now bloated cows, in the middle of which the Command Post had been injudiciously sited. It was to be an unlucky night also, for later a scout car coming up to the Battalion through Presles was hit by shells and Lance-Sergeant Lindsay and Guardsman Donald were killed. In all, the Battalion's casualties in the fight for the Chênedollé ridge were four other ranks killed, and one officer and thirteen wounded. These were relatively light losses, and the Battalion could find consolation in the tribute written by one of the Welsh Guards Company Commanders—"Never had we had such splendid support".[1]

(g) *Sourdevalle*

While the Third Battalion had been engaged before Chênedollé, a mile away to the north-west X Company had occupied the most uncomfortable position they were to meet in Normandy. On the 10th August the 3rd Irish had taken over the tip of a salient the 11th Armoured Division had driven into the German lines; that tip lay about a mile and a half north of the Vire–Vassy road, and its centre was the farm of Sourdevalle, which faced south across a deep valley, down the middle of which ran a small stream. Above the stream lay the Germans, who had perfect observation of the slope down which any attack would have to be made, and in addition the enemy also had

MAP XXXIV

Aug. 10

[1] Third Battalion continued on p. 365.

observation from the left rear of Sourdevalle, from high ground which was not taken until the day of the Chênedollé attack. Constant mortar and machine-gun fire made movement impossible, even in what would normally have been the reserve positions on the reverse slope of the Sourdevalle ridge. X Company were in one of these reserve positions, and were thus spared an infantry attack by the enemy on the night of the 10th, nor were they called upon to take part in an assault
Aug. 11 across the stream on the next day in conformity with a Coldstream attack farther to the left. They remained the compassionate spectators of its bloody repulse; later in the day they did what they could to succour the wounded Irishmen as they lay out in the exposed cornfields, at last mercifully obscured by the smoke-screen which wider tactical requirements had previously precluded.[1]

That brief thirty-six hours of extreme danger brought X Company's fighting alongside the Irish Guards to a close. As the Battalion reformed, the enemy were making their final effort in the west to stem the on-rush of the American tanks into the heart of France. That effort
Aug. 13 had failed by the 13th, and the great retreat to the Seine was on. Normandy and all France were the fruits of the unrelenting pressure with which the British and Canadian armies had engaged the enemy.

At Le Busq X Company left the 3rd Irish and was transferred to the
Aug. 23 1st Welsh Guards. The "Micks" gave them a farewell party—"the best and largest party given in Normandy since the days of William the Conqueror". "Everyone," wrote Major Fothringham, "was very doleful when we left the Irish Guards, as we got on so splendidly with them, and they treated us so wonderfully. Colonel 'Joe' has always treated us as something special (better than we deserved). . . . So far, we have given him nothing but three cheers, which were the loudest and heartiest I have ever heard."

Later Colonel Vandeleur had special cards printed, and these were presented to every officer and man who had served in the Company in Normandy. They bore the stars of the Thistle and St. Patrick and the words "In commemoration of eleven months' enjoyable service at Home and Abroad", and the names of the principal engagements— La Bayeud, Cagny, Maisoncelles and Sourdevalle; and, fittingly, "Quis Separabit".

X Company's new hosts were as hospitable as had been the Irish. To Lieutenant-Colonel J. F. Gresham the Scotsmen were a welcome and experienced reinforcement, which immediately set about making firm friends with the Welshmen, not only among the infantry of the 1st Battalion, but also among the tank crews of the 2nd Armoured Reconnaissance Battalion, which formed the other half of the Welsh Guards

---

[1] While trying to gain contact with the assaulting Irish companies, Lieutenant A. Drew of X Company was wounded.

Group. This latter battalion was equipped with the speedy Cromwell tank, and with it in the following year the Second Battalion Scots Guards were to fight in Germany.

These alliances between the three Celtic regiments of the Brigade of Guards had a literary parallel, which, if distant in time by 500 years, can at least be claimed to be drawn in the same province of the fair land of France. When King Harry went forth to war against Harfleur, Captains Jamy, MacMorris and Fluellen, for all their wordy disputations, were trusty comrades-in-arms, skilled in the "disciplines of war".[1,2]

(h) *Refit and Refresh*

Chênedollé and Sourdevalle marked the end of the fighting in Normandy for the Third Battalion and for X Company. In that fighting the Third Battalion had suffered two-thirds of the fatal casualties it was to incur in the whole war; four officers and forty-three other ranks had been killed or had died of their wounds, and four officers and forty other ranks had been wounded. Nearly all these losses were suffered by the tank crews in the course of one brief fortnight. Nor were these battle losses all the Battalion had to bear; on the 2nd September the Quartermaster, Captain W. J. Dorman, M.B.E. and the Electrical and Mechanical Engineer Officer attached to the Battalion, Captain C. E. Pring, were killed in a road accident. This was a sad blow; Captain Dorman had been Sergeant-Major of the First Battalion in Norway, and Quartermaster of the Third Battalion since its formation. He was temporarily succeeded by Lieutenant H. E. Brown until the arrival in October of Captain and Quartermaster F. Morley, M.B.E. Another tragedy which was keenly felt by all was the death of the Brigade Commander, Brigadier Sir Walter Barttelot, Bt., who was killed on the 18th August when his scout car blew up on a mine. It had been due largely to his bravery and initiative that the 4th Coldstream had made their dashing advance to Point 309 in the Caumont battle; the loss of this experienced commander was rendered doubly sad by the unnecessary manner of his death. Brigadier W. D. C. Greenacre, late Welsh Guards, was appointed to command in his stead, and under him the Battalion served for the remainder of the war.

A loss of a different kind was experienced when Major Fitzalan Howard was spirited away to the appointment of Brigade Major of the 32nd Guards Brigade; he was succeeded in command of Left Flank by Major J. P. Mann.

In the latter half of August the tide of war receded rapidly from

---

[1] It must not be thought that the historian sees the Anglo-Saxon Regiments of the Brigade in the characters of Bardolph and that arrant coxcombe Pistol!

[2] X Company continued on p. 367.

Normandy. The Battalion was concentrated round Roullours, near Vire, and, except for a brief foray by Right Flank, there was no call on their services from the 3rd Division, under whose command they were now placed. The time was spent in the everlasting maintenance, repairs and cleaning. Expeditions were made to gather military intelligence from the wreck of the German Army which littered the battlefield centred on the Falaise gap; expeditions of a less official character were made to gather the good things of life which France has to offer; it did not take long for the troops of the Second Army to acquire the urge to "swan", a form of predatory tourism long since practised in the Eighth. The gastronomical acquisitions were more successful than the mechanical. When one of the Panther tanks which had been knocked out by S Squadron at Chênedollé was found to be in running order, an attempt was made to enlist its services against its former owners. On its way to the Battalion the engine seized up, and the tank had to be abandoned. Crestfallen, its captors had to admit they had neglected to ensure that there was water in the radiator!

The lessons of battle were under constant discussion; to one officer, there were three main lessons: "The first is that in close country all attacks must be properly laid on tank–infantry assaults. Secondly, that the tanks must support the infantry, and not *vice versa*. This is where everybody else went wrong. Tank crews can very easily get into an attitude of mind where they think that, not only does the whole battle depend on them, but that, if they suffer losses, they are so important that they need not go on. Also that once they have captured ground all their responsibilities are ended. Now all our reputation, which is considerable, is based on the fact that we fought against all of these ideas, and for this the credit goes to Colonel Claud [Dunbar]. We were lucky in arriving after a certain amount of experience had been gained, and Colonel Claud very quickly realised the sort of thing that was going on. If you can once convince the infantry that you will see them on to the objective at any cost, that you will not desert them the moment a German tank appears, and that once you have got them there, that you will stay and see that nobody pushes them off, then the battle is as good as won. Of these, easily the worst was the last, since it often entailed remaining in the tanks for twelve hours or so at a stretch, which is very uncomfortable. Also when once you have got an objective there is a pause of about twenty minutes, after which another completely different battle starts, coming the other way this time, but usually with fire only, plus a few Panthers which try to stalk you from a flank. Other lessons are 'Beware of the SS', and be very suspicious of the order 'Advance to contact', which generally means that there is practically no advance at all—and far too much contact."

Training was resumed with the 3rd Division in co-operation with the infantry. Rafting, and passing over the Churchill bridge-layer were practised, concert parties were welcomed, baths were indulged in, and rivers were bathed in. But all felt out of it; for now the leading armoured divisions were racing across the old battlefields of Marlborough, Wellington and Haig, and the burning question was whether the Battalion would see action again before the war was brought to a glorious conclusion before Christmas. The speed of the advance over country in which all communications had received unrelenting attention from the Allied Air Forces was indeed amazing. But these communications could support but few divisions. To alleviate the supply difficulties, formations well back in Normandy formed transport units from their own 3-ton trucks and, under the command of Lieutenant Scott-Barrett the Battalion provided a platoon of thirty vehicles. Their operations were supervised by Captain Griffin of the 229th Company R.A.S.C., and they carried forward ammunition, rations and men in a successful attempt to keep the advance in motion. "Keep moving or get off the Road" was their watchword; they moved the sinews of war from Normandy to Holland.

On the 7th September Brigadier Greenacre began to move his Brigade forward, with the intention of getting over the Seine, and thus being more readily available when the call came to go forward to the Low Countries. The move had to be made without the assistance of tank transporters, which were all engaged with the forward divisions, so for three days the tanks clanked along the roads to the Seine on their tracks, at a maximum speed of twelve miles per hour. The complete absence of mechanical trouble gave further proof of the mechanical efficiency of the tank crews. On the 12th the Battalion crossed the river on a pontoon bridge at Les Andelys, and by tea-time were encamped near the Paris–Rouen road. Here they spent a fortnight of rest and entertainment, punctuated with a few searches for German stragglers in the woods. The feeling of being out of the fight began to grow more and more acute, but, with the revival of enemy resistance along the great river barriers of Holland, the call came at last on the 26th September.

Sept. 7

Sept. 12

Sept. 26

Before continuing the story of the Churchills,[1] we must follow the fortunes of X Company in that momentous September, and watch them in their hardest battle.

III. THE LOW COUNTRIES

(a) *Brussels Liberated*

In the early hours of August 29th the Guards Armoured Division left the orchards and hedges of the Bocage for the last time to join in the great advance.

Aug. 29
MAP XXX

[1] Page 379.

Sept. 1

Moving via L'Aigle, where they spent the night, X Company, with the Welsh Guards, crossed the Seine at Vernon, fifty miles from Paris, "on a rickety pontoon bridge in miserable weather" and drove on through Beauvais and Corbie, until they harboured for the night in the outskirts of Arras. The reception they received in each successive town and village was all a victor and liberator could desire, and the column of vehicles was frequently brought to a halt by cheering crowds. An order had been issued in the Company that females were not to be allowed on to the vehicles, but, to the amusement of all, this very quickly broke down at the seat of discipline itself. Whereas Monsieur was content to stand and stare in open-mouthed envy at Major Fothringham's whiskers, with occasional gasps of "C'est formidable", Madame was not so restrained, and vied with her sisters to stroke its luxuriant expanse. Major "Feathers" suffered these indignities with the patience of one who had seen worse terrors.

Sept. 2

The greatest welcome was at Arras, for here the Welsh Guards, who were the first British troops to enter the town in 1944, had also been the last to leave, after a gallant defence, in 1940, and X Company found themselves involved in the grateful rejoicing, which was followed by "Reveille at 0900 hrs."—a testimony to the hospitality of the liberated.

Sept. 3

Douai was reached by the following evening, and here General Adair gave out his orders for the morrow. "My intention," he told his Order Group, "is to advance and liberate Brussels," adding, amidst laughter, "and that is a grand intention." It was just short of seventy miles to Brussels, and two centre lines were chosen for the Division to drive on; the Welsh Guards Group was to lead on the right, the Grenadiers on the left. The "off" was given at seven o'clock on the morning of 3rd September, which dawned fine and clear and later turned into a glorious day. It was the fifth anniversary of the Declaration of War. With armoured cars of the Household Cavalry in front the tank squadrons and their attendant lorry-borne infantry set off as they were to end—flat out. The Belgian frontier was crossed at about half-past ten, and no serious resistance was encountered until the leading squadron bumped into an enemy rearguard well inside Belgium, at Leuze, but this was dealt with within the hour and the column raced on, fearful that this delay would deprive them of the honour of reaching Brussels first.

According to Captain A. N. B. Ritchie, of the Regiment, a Staff Captain at Divisional Headquarters, who followed up on the Welsh Guards centre line, "the Belgians' welcome was even more spontaneous than the French, and the flowers and fruit in my scout car were sufficient to start a shop". At 1815 there was another short hold-up at Halle, only ten miles from Brussels, but an hour later the Welsh Guards Group were in the suburbs with only two miles to go, and by

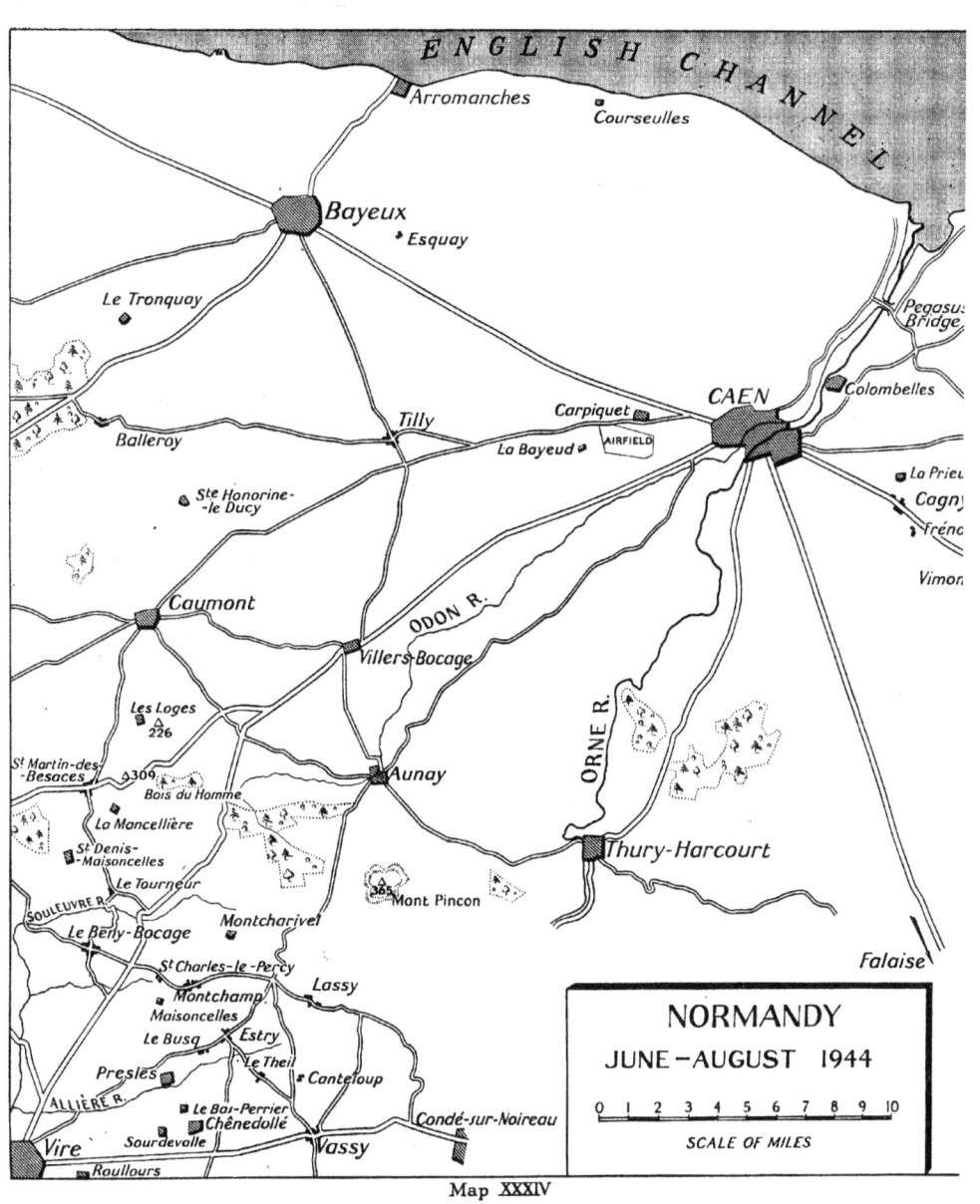
Map XXXIV

eight o'clock they had reached the centre of the city itself. The Grenadiers, who were at that moment entering the western outskirts, had been "pipped on the post".

Resistance in the city streets came mostly from the delighted Belgian crowds—they were impenetrable. Thousands and thousands of wonderfully happy people packed the streets, showering gifts on the troops and singing "Tipperary" and "God Save the King". The cobbles literally flowed with brandy and champagne and the tanks and vehicles were brought to a complete standstill and boarded by children and pretty girls. Tank guns were stuffed with plums and pears, and almost every tank had at least one girl in the turret shouting "Vive les Anglais" over the wireless.

As darkness fell the rejoicing capital was lit by a full moon and by the flames of the burning Palais de Justice, which the Germans had set on fire before they left. Several days later a London newspaper published a photograph of "the patriotic citizens of Brussels rescuing the archives" from this burned building. X Company, who, sometime around midnight harboured in the Boulevard Waterloo nearby, knew better. The "archives" were cases of wine stored in the Palais de Justice by the Germans; the equally patriotic Company helped in the "rescue". The "archives" refreshed them after "an armoured dash unequalled in this or any other war".[1]

On the following morning—there is no mention of the time of Reveille in the Company diary—the Battalion moved from the Boulevard Waterloo to the outskirts, where they remained for the next two nights. On the 5th, X Company went out with the Prince of Wales Company to mop up a small pocket of resistance on the Louvain road, but the tanks alone dealt with the enemy, and the infantry returned to Brussels unused.

Sept. 4

Sept. 5

(b) *Hechtel*

After the fall of Brussels and the capture of Antwerp by the 11th Armoured Division, Sir Bernard Montgomery, newly promoted Field Marshal for the triumph of his armies in Normandy, made a determined effort to force the great river barriers, and to carry the war into Germany. Between Brussels and the Rhine there were no less than nine major water obstacles, and by the 6th September only the crossing of the Dyle at Louvain had been secured.

The Guards Armoured Division set off up the road to the east from Brussels on 6th September, with the Welsh Guards Group in the van. At Louvain and Diest they met only cheering crowds, but at Beeringen on the Albert Canal they were greeted by machine-gun fire, and

Sept. 6

MAP XXXV

---

[1] In fact there had been longer armoured advances in one day. Probably the record is still held by Rommel for his advance to Cherbourg with the 7th Panzer Division on the 17th/18th June 1940, an advance of 150 miles.

24—S.G.H.

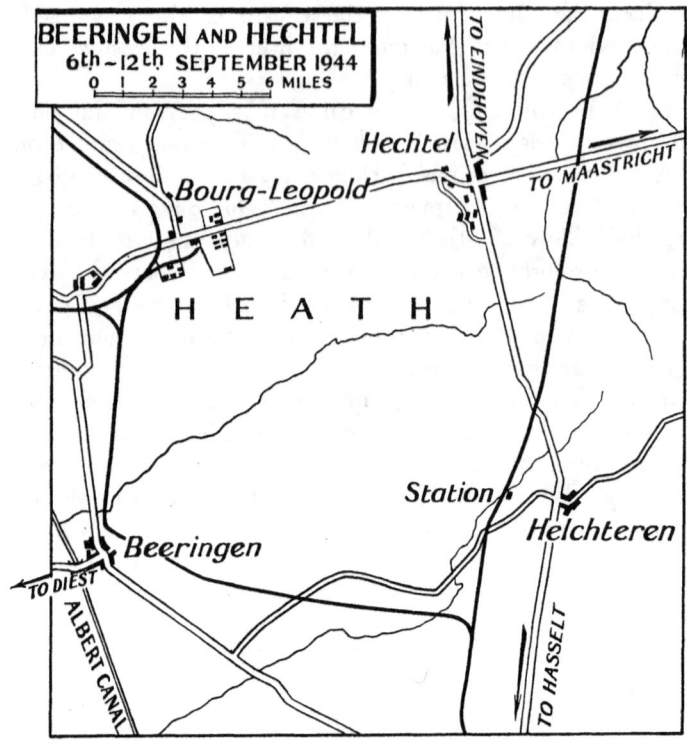
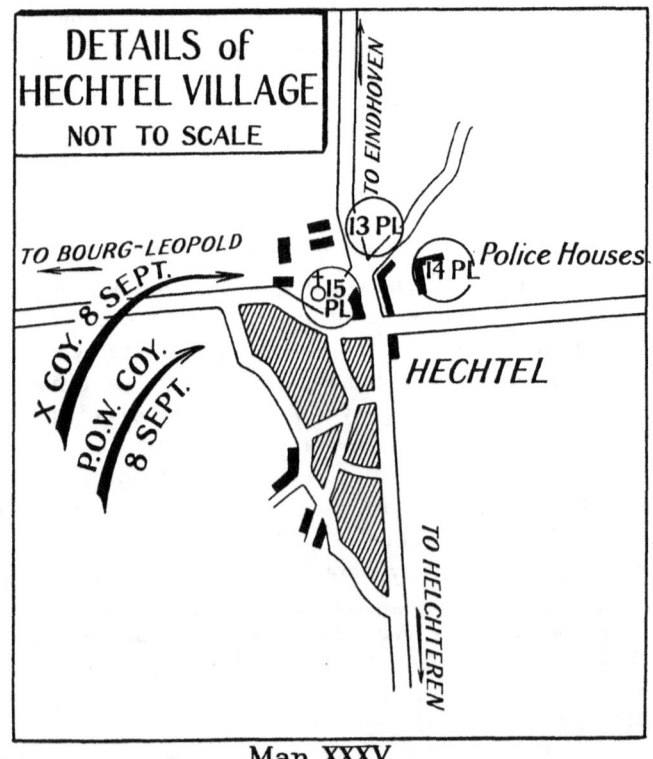

Map XXXV

found that the canal bridge had been partly demolished. The enemy were soon pushed back and, under increasing shellfire, the Sappers set-to to build a temporary bridge, which they finished that night. X Company, who until now had been in reserve, crossed behind the tanks at "first light" on the following morning and moved into Beeringen town, where the Welsh Guards Companies, who had crossed the day before, were having to deal with stubborn resistance. Anti-tank guns on the west of the town were reported to be holding up the leading tanks and the Company was ordered to "de-bus" and investigate.

Sept. 7

Lieutenant Thorpe took out a patrol and soon found an S.P. gun in a street; with two men and a P.I.A.T. he set off to stalk it. He was just getting into position for a shot when the quarry moved away out of range. Several further stalks were unsuccessful and, finding that he was now so deep into enemy territory that there were German posts on three sides of him, he dropped a grenade on to one of them from an upper window, and withdrew.

On this information Lieutenant the Hon. J. L. Vernon was at once sent out with his Platoon to prevent the enemy from getting a further hold on the houses at the western end of the town. Large numbers of enemy infantry were caught by his fire in the open and suffered heavily. Meanwhile the Germans were increasing their shelling, but in spite of this an O.P. was established in an upper window, from which the two Company snipers, Guardsmen Harley and Gibson, did accurate execution, accounting for three of the crew of an S.P. gun, which Lieutenant A. D. G. Llewellyn was chasing with a patrol. By midday most of Beeringen had been cleared, at a cost to X Company of two killed and seven wounded. At this stage the Irish Guards Group took over the battle to allow the Welsh to disengage in order to continue their advance.

Opposition beyond the town was nearly as strong as it had been in it, and the tanks had to deal with machine-gun posts and men with bazookas all the way to the next village of Helchteren, where their route turned left towards Hechtel and the north. Dusk was already falling when the leading Squadron ran into a strong position on the outskirts of this second village and the advance was halted for the night. X Company, who had been following up in reserve, spent it in Helchteren railway station.

Next morning a plan was made to capture Hechtel, and at midday X Company and Prince of Wales Company moved forward to attack, leaving the remainder of the Battalion at Helchteren to guard against expected counter-attacks, which soon began. Unfortunately, before the Company set out Lieutenant Vernon was accidentally wounded when his Sten gun went off in a fall; the Sten, a cheap and elementary weapon, was the cause of many such casualties.

Sept. 8

Hechtel is built around an important cross-roads, the arms of which point to the cardinal points of the compass. On the previous evening the Welsh Guards tanks had attacked up the road from the south, but now the method chosen was for the two companies to by-pass the strong-point which the tanks had encountered and to advance on the village astride the main road which runs into it from Bourg Leopold to the west. Bourg Leopold is the Belgian Aldershot, and its surrounding country is of the familiar Pirbright sort. The attack was to be supported by artillery and tanks shelling from the south, but owing to the precarious state of the Beeringen bridge, few guns had been deployed. The difficult going on the left also resulted in a delay which lost the effects of what artillery support there was.

X Company were just getting to their assigned place on the north of the Bourg Leopold–Hechtel road when enemy troops were seen to be running into the village across the open fields to the east and the whole of Company Headquarters opened fire spontaneously and with some effect. At this moment a convoy of enemy transport came down the road at high speed from the west, the first three vehicles passing right through Lieutenant Llewellyn's Platoon as it was in the act of crossing the road. The first two managed to speed on into the safety of Hechtel, but the third was shot up, and crashed; the crew, who jumped out, were sniped by Guardsman Harley. Another seven trucks heard the firing and stopped before they reached the Company, thus causing Major Fothringham the added anxiety of having to keep an eye over his shoulder throughout the attack.

The advance on Hechtel began through fairly thick and enclosed country. The first enemy to be encountered appeared with a towed 88-mm. anti-aircraft gun. They were just over a wall in front of Lieutenant Llewellyn's Platoon, No. 14, and were spotted by Guardsman Pettigrew through a hole in a door; without thought to the extreme danger involved he at once loaded his P.I.A.T., and fired a bomb *through* the wood of the door, setting fire to the gun and killing several of its crew, and thus confounding the training manuals which stated that a P.I.A.T. bomb would explode on the first contact after firing. The Platoon then made for the road fork to the north of the main cross-roads in Hechtel and there destroyed a second 88 with the help of No. 15 Platoon, which, since Lieutenant Vernon's accident, was now commanded by Sergeant Dannfald. Lieutenant Llewellyn, who had been slightly wounded in the face, took No. 14 Platoon on a further 150 yards to the south-east and dug in round a row of houses and hedged gardens.

Meanwhile, Lieutenant Thorpe, with No. 13 Platoon, had advanced through growing opposition to his objective in an orchard and backyard on the corner of the same road fork, having knocked out at least one enemy vehicle on the way. All platoons dug in on their objectives and by the evening things were quieter, and Sergeant Dannfald's Platoon was moved to a position to the west of the church, where they could defend the Mortar Section and Company Headquarters. Prince of Wales Company on the right had been unable to get on to their objectives and so drew back after dark and dug-in in a small area close to the X Company Headquarters Group. Unfortunately, this meant that Lieutenants Llewellyn and Thorpe were now isolated, and both Platoons spent a restless night, continually firing on small parties of enemy who were infiltrating into the village. One party got into the next garden to the rear of Company Headquarters, but after one of their number had been killed and another captured, they withdrew. The Company's casualties for the day amounted to nine wounded.

Early next morning the enemy, now known to be a battalion of the Hermann Goering SS Parachute Division, put in an attack on the village, but were beaten off with heavy casualties. Later in the day another Welsh Guards Company came forward on the right of Prince of Wales Company in an attempt to clear up the very confused situation which existed on that flank, but they too were held up in the western outskirts and could get no farther than the area of the church. Sept. 9

The enemy who had infiltrated into Hechtel during the night now made it well-nigh impossible to get from Company Headquarters to either of the forward platoons.

No. 13 Platoon was now commanded by Sergeant McClelland. "It was plain to see," he wrote afterwards, "that the enemy intended getting control of various vantage points, such as high windows in the surrounding houses, for the purpose of pinning us down, but with some really good shooting from the Platoon small arms most of these were denied to them. They were, however, trying very hard to obtain entrance to a house in our rear and Mr. Thorpe decided to take two men into the house to investigate if they had in fact gained possession. I went up to the attic window of a house opposite to watch the various windows and the door to the north. After Mr. Thorpe had been in the house for some time one Jerry appeared at the door, walking right into the sights of my rifle. It appeared to me that something had gone wrong and so I ordered Lance-Sergeant Hogg and some of his section to investigate. They found two wounded enemy in the house and came back with the information that Mr. Thorpe had been killed and Guardsman Burnett badly wounded. It appears that they had gone upstairs and the enemy had come in at the bottom." Sergeant McClelland realised that he was now isolated, but yet in a strong position from which he "would take some moving", and he sent back with intelligence of the situation Guardsman E. Gibson, who, although suffering from a wound on the forehead, had volunteered to go. With the aid of a phosphorous smoke grenade Gibson dashed across the main road which was covered by Spandau fire and managed to pick a hazardous path through the enemy outposts to Company Headquarters. Later in the day Gibson went back over the same dangerous ground with the message for the Platoon to withdraw. It was only after he had guided them to their new position that he allowed anyone to dress his wound. Sergeant McClelland had by now established an O.P. in an upper window which commanded an excellent view across the open country to the east, and from here he saw many enemy infantry gathering for another assault, and these he engaged with a Bren.

Shortly afterwards a troop of Welsh Guards tanks was sent round by the north to make contact with the isolated Platoons. These tanks found both Platoons firmly established though under constant fire, and Lieutenant Llewellyn's in particular, who were being engaged from the south as well as from the east and north, were suffering casualties. The tanks delivered ammunition and food, but anti-tank fire soon forced them to withdraw. Glad as the platoons were to receive food and ammunition, the presence of their suppliers proved to be a mixed blessing, for they attracted enemy armour to within 200 yards of No. 13 Platoon's position and, thus supported, a company of German infantry were able to get across the main road to the north. Things were getting hotter, and it appeared as if an infantry Battalion at least was forming up for an attack about three hundred yards to the east of Sergeant McClelland's position. An S.P. gun now appeared, at which Lance-Sergeant Henderson had two unsuccessful shots with his P.I.A.T., and with a burst of Bren, Guardsman Samson managed to knock an accompanying motor-cyclist off his machine. Lance-Sergeant Henderson next directed his attention on to three large armoured vehicles which had approached from the east to within fifty yards of the Platoon's slit trenches; he crawled through a house with his P.I.A.T., and blew up the leading one with his first bomb. The explosion coincided with the start of the assault, for at once a hail of fire came down from all quarters and under its cover the enemy infantry began to close in. No. 13 Platoon was now reduced to twenty men, and Sergeant McClelland, realising that they would inevitably be overrun, decided to withdraw to Company Headquarters. Although the lines of withdrawal crossed two roads which were under heavy fire, by skilful use of smoke he managed to get the whole platoon back without the loss of a man. Guardsman Burnett, who was too badly wounded to be moved, had to be left behind with three wounded prisoners, and he was captured.

Lieutenant Llewellyn's 14 Platoon had spent a similar day, dug in among the gardens of a line of police houses; he himself had been wounded for a second time and was now too weak to walk. During the afternoon he sent a patrol back for orders under cover of smoke, and shortly afterwards (about the same time as Sergeant McClelland's retirement), when the situation was becoming hopeless, he ordered

Sergeant Dunderdale to take back the remainder of his men, now only twelve in number. With great skill Sergeant Dunderdale, assisted by Guardsman Brown, Lieutenant Llewellyn's servant, successfully carried out this withdrawal over open ground in full view of enemy armour and infantry, and arrived at Company Headquarters intact. Lieutenant Llewellyn insisted on remaining where he was in order not to encumber the withdrawal of the remainder. With three other wounded Guardsmen he was cared for by some civilians in a cellar, and he also kept with him the crew of a 6-pounder anti-tank gun which had been sent up to him on the previous night, and which he hoped to be able to send back to safety as soon as it got dark. However, the enemy over-ran his position almost as soon as his Platoon had retired, and he and all those with him were taken prisoner.

All that remained of X Company now consolidated in the area to the west of the church in very close contact with the enemy. No. 15 Platoon under Sergeant Dannfald had been there all day, and by their steady and accurate fire were able to drive off the determined attack which came in on the position from the north just behind the two retiring platoons. Throughout the day Sergeant Dannfald had maintained an O.P. in a house which was continually struck by enemy 75-mm. shells, and from which he was able to give most valuable warnings of impending attacks. At the same time he directed the fire of the mortars, the Company snipers and some attached 17-pounders.

Guardsman Floyd, the Company carrier driver, once again distinguished himself by deed and example. On being told to take his carrier back to Battalion Headquarters with the wounded and not come up again until ordered, he pleaded that he was too tired to drive and sent his spare driver instead—his only object by this manœuvre being to remain with the Company to continue his own "private war", and for the next two days and three nights he dashed about the Company Headquarters area entirely on his own, bristling with captured enemy weapons, and usually with a box of grenades under one arm. An enemy fire position had only to be discovered, and Floyd was there in a trice, engaging it with Spandau, Schmeisser or Luger, and it was undoubtedly owing to his constant energetic actions that many casualties were caused to the enemy.

When darkness fell, the enemy, now accurately stated by a prisoner to consist of three battalions, renewed their efforts to dislodge the Company and sent in strong patrols which moved around the position all night, apparently not knowing exactly where it was. Guardsman Michie of No. 15 Platoon wiped out one whole party of eight at no more than a few yards' range with his Bren, and Sergeant Dannfald later went out under heavy fire into the area in which they had been and brought in four Spandaus. This platoon claimed that not one German passed its position that night without being either killed or wounded, and in the morning the area was littered with enemy dead, some within five yards of the slit trenches. X Company's own casualties for the day amounted in all to seven killed, eleven wounded and eight missing, all of whom were later confirmed as prisoners, the three men of the anti-tank gun crew being the only ones unwounded.

Sept. 10 Next morning as it was getting light, the noise of a tracked vehicle was heard at extremely close quarters, and an S.P. gun, escorted by a small party of enemy infantry, was seen to be coming down the road between the Company Headquarters area and No. 14 Platoon's garden. Sergeant Dannfald at once seized a P.I.A.T. and crawled forward to close the range for a shot, but no sooner was he in position than Major Fothringham, who did not know about the P.I.A.T., opened fire on the infantry with his own rifle, killing one of them, whereupon the whole party and their gun withdrew in haste for a short distance up the road and thus deprived Sergeant Dannfald of another opportunity. The S.P. gun now fired straight down the road into the Company position, and destroyed two mortar carriers before it was driven off by the 17-pounders, firing indirectly on instructions from Sergeant Dannfald's O.P.

While this was going on, more enemy infantry were seen to be digging in amongst the gardens to the north, and the guns of a troop of tanks were quickly brought to bear on the area. Their extremely accurate shooting at once threw the enemy into confusion, during which Guardsman Harley had a sniper's field-day, seeing no less than eight victims fall to his rifle. He had remained all the time in the O.P., which had gaping holes in the walls and roof, and was constantly under fire of one kind or another for most of the battle; during the five days of its duration fifteen of the enemy were seen to fall to his shots and there were two more probables. On this occasion it was mainly owing to his shooting that the infantry withdrew, a fact which was later confirmed when Sergeant Dunderdale worked forward with another troop of tanks and found the area to have been abandoned, but strewn with enemy dead.

Five more men were wounded during this third day of battle, including CSM A. Law, who subsequently died of his wounds.

Sept. 11 The enemy continued to resist strongly during the whole of the 11th, and the Company remained pinned to their positions and subjected to every type of fire. The remaining Welsh Guards Company attacked from the south during the morning and managed to link up with No. 3 Company but, like its predecessors, could get no farther. Since the enemy were still fighting hard it was decided to lay on a two battalion attack on the village with proper artillery preparation; as a preliminary to this, all companies were withdrawn from Hechtel during the night. X Company, who had had two more men wounded on the 11th, were in
Sept. 12 reserve for the attack on the 12th, and had little to do but collect prisoners.

Five hours after the attack had been launched Hechtel was finally taken, and among the ruins were found 160 German dead. Six hundred more were taken prisoner during the day, of whom 200 were found to be wounded. Even without the unknown figures of dead and wounded which the enemy must have evacuated during the battle, these numbers were impressive testimony of the fury of the whole five days' fight. And if more proof were needed of the bitterness of the battle, Major Fothringham, when examining the area after it had been cleared, came upon two slit trenches of Lance-Corporal Forster's Section of Lieutenant Llewellyn's Platoon with four dead Guardsmen in them, surrounded by a ring of enemy corpses, some lying as close as five yards.

The fight at Hechtel has been described in greater detail than can normally be included. It marked the end of easy optimism after the great rush forward, and it was X Company's hardest battle. In the five days it lasted the Company lost one officer and eight other ranks killed and died of wounds, one officer and twenty-six wounded, and one officer and five were prisoners, all of whom were wounded. The death of CSM Law was a sad event; he had been Sergeant-Major of the Company since 1942, and could claim to be largely responsible for the excellent spirit and discipline of the men. He was an Army footballer. His place was successfully filled by Sergeant McClelland who, with Sergeants Dannfald and Dunderdale, Guardsmen Floyd, Harley and Gibson, received the Military Medal; Lieutenant Llewellyn was awarded the Military Cross. Of Major Fothringham, already "a by-word throughout the Division for valour and determination", it was written after Hechtel that "his Company regarded him as something superhuman: they knew rightly that he would always be there when dangers and difficulties were greatest, and his presence inspired them to the tremendous deeds which they have done".[1]

(c) *The attempt to reach Arnhem*

While X Company had been fighting at Hechtel the remainder of the Guards Armoured Division had by-passed them to the west and pushed on to capture intact the bridge over the next water obstacle, the Escaut Canal, at Overpelt. Here the Welsh Guards spent the five days following the final capture of Hechtel; and here, owing to their losses, they were forced to disband one of their companies, and X Company received a platoon of Welsh Guardsmen under Lieutenant D. J. C. Stevenson, as a reinforcement.

On September 16th orders were given out for the next stage of the

MAP XXX

Sept. 11
Sept. 13
–17

---

[1] The early death of Major Steuart-Fothringham in 1952 is recorded with deep regret.

attempt to force the river barriers. Airborne Divisions arriving by parachute and glider were to seize the important bridges at Grave on the Maas, Nijmegen on the Waal, and at Arnhem on the Rhine, and to relieve these landings the Guards Armoured Division was to dash forward up the road which runs to these three objectives northwards from Eindhoven. It was not the turn of the Welsh Guards Group to

Sept. 17 lead, and so on the following day they sat by their vehicles, watching the great air armada drone overhead towards Holland. Eventually they

Sept. 18 left Overpelt on the morning of September 18th, and after a slow and unspectacular drive through the Dutch countryside in the wake of the leading Grenadier and Irish Guards Groups, they rolled across the

Sept. 21 great bridge at Nijmegen on September 21st, the day following its gallant capture by the Grenadiers and Americans. They harboured about a mile to the north of the bridge, and here they remained for

Sept. 21 the next two nights.
−23

The ground which lay between them and Arnhem, in the outskirts of which the 6th Airborne Division was cut off, was known as the "Island"—and a miserable place it was. The distance between the Rhine and the Waal at this point was ten miles and in between lay an expanse of dead flat fen land overlooked at every point from the enemy-held hills to the north of Arnhem. The only good road, which was the centre line, was built on a causeway raised above the level of the surrounding countryside so that any traffic on it could be seen for miles around and, owing to the steepness of the bank, could not hope to get off it if attacked.

The enemy resisted stoutly all attempts to enlarge the bridgehead

Sept. 26 on the Island. On September 26th the Company took over a position
MAP XLI guarding the Aamsche Bridge, the farthest point reached towards Arnhem at this stage of the campaign; that day the remnants of the Airborne Division were withdrawn across the Rhine, and the attempt had failed. For the remainder of the month and for the first week of October the Company occupied a series of depressing water-logged

Oct. 7 positions until finally relieved on the 7th. Five of its number had been killed on the Island.

For the whole of October they rested at Graves and at Malden, a suburb of Nijmegen. The billets were comfortable, the natives were friendly, and there was leave to Brussels. Reinforcements came out and the Company could once again field three platoons. It was here that Major Fothringham left them; he had been unwell for some time and now the doctors removed him from the field. Captain Hope succeeded him, with Captain Ritchie taking his place as second-in-command.

The season of great advances was over for that year; now ground which had been gained must be made secure.[1]

[1] X Company continued on p. 391.

(d) *The Churchills come up*

The Third Battalion set out from Les Andelys on the Seine on the 27th September. The Battalion travelled as usual in two parties; the wheeled vehicles, and the tanks on their transporters. The first delights of liberation had not yet left the population of Northern France and Belgium, and there were many enthusiastic bystanders to cheer the Battalion on as it traversed this dull flat land of large fields, brick houses, pitheads and factories. The places they passed through were famous on the Colours of the Regiment; Mons and Waterloo have special significance for all who value and maintain the traditions of the British Infantry. But at Cambrai the traditions of infantry and tank-men are fused, for it was here that tanks in large numbers first went into battle. What advances in design and reliability there had been since that winter day in 1917!

After three days, having passed through the Regiment's most recent battlefield at Hechtel, the Battalion began to enter Holland. Here they found the population less demonstrative; in those early months the nearer the front, the more afraid the people appeared to be to show outward signs of gratitude and hospitality. This was soon realised to be the aftermath of the rigorous German occupation, and of the threats of the departing enemy of what they would do on their return. Thus the Dutch (except, as will shortly be seen, in the first flush of liberation) were taking no chances. Later the people extended every kindness to the troops, and it is no exaggeration to say that that part of Holland in which the Second Army lived and fought in the winter of 1944–45 is the area of Europe in which all things British are most popular today. By the 30th the last of the tanks on its transporter had arrived. There had been many breakdowns on the way, which was hardly surprising in view of the pitch at which the transporter companies had been working during the last month. The Battalion settled down in a wood outside Geldrop, a few miles east of Eindhoven.

The great advance of September had resulted in a narrow and vulnerable salient being thrust northwards into Holland. This salient was too narrow for the safety of the army's communications, and early in October it became clear that all thoughts of further advance would have to be abandoned until this danger was eliminated. Also the port of Antwerp, though captured intact in the early days of September, could not be brought into operation until the Germans had been cleared from the islands and river banks of the Scheldt Estuary. In addition, from the Island above Nijmegen there were calls for more troops, and also the enemy must be cleared entirely from the west bank of the Maas before there could be real security.

380   HOLLAND: 1944

The Battalion was caught up in the web of most of these operations—or intended operations—and became extremely proficient at coping with the sudden and entirely unexpected moves required of it; the inhabitants of the town nicknamed them the "Eindhoven Wanderers".

"The last [alarm] was the best," wrote Major Whitelaw. "We thought we were going some distance south (to the Maas opposite Roermond). We had looked at the new place and all was set. About 6 p.m. one day we were told that all that move and operation was off. About 1 a.m. that night Chips [Major Sir Charles Maclean] and I were sleeping peacefully when Vernon [Captain V. F. Erskine Crum, the Adjutant], woke us to say that we were moving at 8 a.m. to an entirely new place some way north [Overloon]. I shot off with the advance party at about 7.30 and the Battalion moved off somehow about 8.0.... Then yesterday, with a little more notice, we were off again back towards our original place. Now we are sitting here [near Gemert] waiting for the next move."

In the intervals between these excursions, which occupied most of October, the Battalion again trained with their old friends, the 15th (Scottish) Division, but apart from the bombardment of an enemy O.P. some four thousand yards off on the banks of the Maas from a position in the 6th K.O.S.B.'s area, nothing of an active nature resulted.

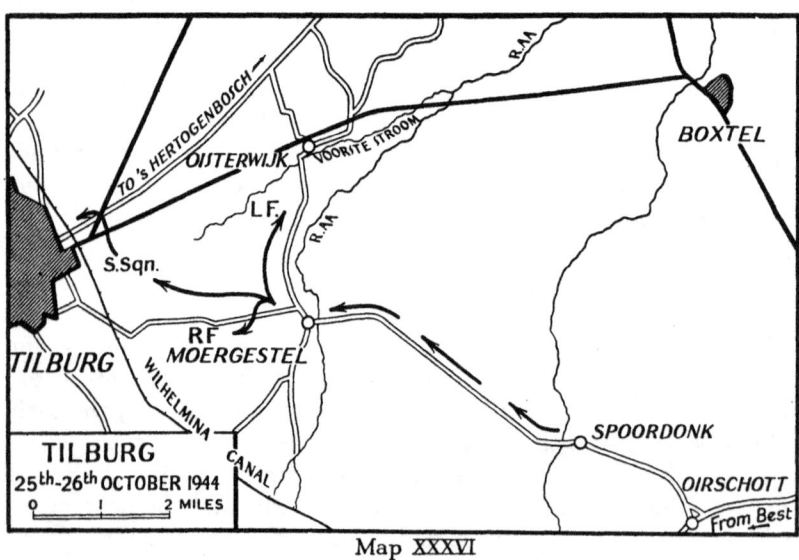

Map XXXVI

(e) *Tilburg*

MAP
XXXVI

By mid-October it was decided to widen yet further the corridor which ran up to Nijmegen by an attack to free Tilburg, one of the largest industrial cities of Holland. Accordingly, the XII Corps, specially reinforced for the operation by the old and happy combination of 15th Division and 6th Guards Tank Brigade, was ordered to mount an attack, seasonably named *Pheasant*, for the capture of the town.

The Battalion, which had arrived at Zon on the 24th, received orders to strike west in support of the 46th Highland Brigade to secure the village of Oirschott, some ten miles from, and on the most direct road to, the town of Tilburg itself. However, no sooner had the plan been made than word was received that the enemy were withdrawing, and had abandoned Oirschott to another brigade without a fight. An "advance to contact" was therefore substituted for the original plan, and on October 25th the Battalion set off at a brisk pace, with Right Flank in the lead, down the wide main road to the west, with infantry of the Glasgow Highlanders riding on the leading tanks.

Oct. 24

Oct. 25

All went well until the head of the column reached the outskirts of the village of Moergestel, where the road bridge over the little River Aa was found to have been completely demolished. It was thought that there might well be an enemy strong-point at Moergestel and, expecting a hail of armour-piercing shot at any moment, Lieutenant Fletcher, who commanded the leading Troop, nosed his tank forward to the obstacle with the greatest of caution. To his relief, on the far bank of the chasm where once the bridge had stood he saw, not a troop of Panthers as he feared, but the whole population of Moergestel cheering and waving as if at a football match. The sight of their would-be liberators at close quarters provoked renewed applause and soon orange flags began to appear in every window, and men started to wade across the gap, laden with food and drink. One woman with two small twins clinging to her skirts whisked them away and produced them again a few minutes later dressed in orange blouses and blue trousers, the colours of the Royal House of Nassau. When the initial excitement had subsided, Lieutenant Fletcher inspected the river bed with care. The population grasped the situation. Led by their priest, they began with feverish haste to roll boulders, throw stones and to heave whatever objects they could lay their hands on into the stream in an effort to bridge the gap. So great was their energy and enthusiasm for the task that it soon became dangerous to stand on the opposite bank. Eventually Lieutenant Fletcher decided that it was time to test the results of these labours, and drove his tank down into the river bed. To the intense disappointment of the audience, *Montrose*[1] just failed to gain the farther bank, and slid back ungracefully into the mud. Meanwhile a bridge-laying tank had been called

[1] The armoured vehicles of the Battalion had all been given names, which were painted on their hulls. A complete list of these will be found in *The 6th Guards Tank Brigade*, by Patrick Forbes, at pages 237 and 238.

forward and very shortly after *Montrose's* unsuccessful attempt, one of these extraordinary vehicles appeared on the scene. The watching crowd was hushed in awe as the great girder bridge poised itself in the air, but as it slowly descended to bridge the gap, they broke, with one accord, into their National Anthem. It was very moving. They continued to sing with fervour until the first Churchill had crossed. By half-past three in the afternoon the whole Battalion were over the river.

Contact with the enemy had still not been made, and so Captain Pember with the Reconnaissance Troop was ordered to dash on as fast as he could, carrying a Company of infantry. He was to seize the bridge over the Wilhelmina Canal on the outskirts of Tilburg before it became dark. Unfortunately the traffic jam in Moergestel village delayed the tanks, and the infantry never appeared; the Honeys, therefore, eventually raced on alone in the deepening twilight. Some four hundred yards short of the bridge the light failed completely, and they found themselves in the dark in the middle of what appeared to be a German company position. A brisk engagement followed during which much damage was thought to have been done to the enemy and to the nearby farmhouses which he was holding. But after three Honeys had been bogged the remainder of the Troop withdrew, to report the bridge firmly held. The bogged tanks were later extricated under heavy fire, two that night and the third on the following morning.

While Captain Pember was thus engaged, Left Flank, with the 7th Seaforth mounted in Kangaroos, had come up behind Right Flank with the intention of branching right and pushing up the road which led northwards to Oisterwijk and their objective—the road bridge over the Voorste Stroom just below that village. The presence of this second squadron made the traffic block in Moergestel worse. Such was the confusion that at a late hour only four tanks of Left Flank had managed to get through the village, and it was quickly decided to send on Lieutenant G. Cameron's Troop alone, as the only hope of seizing their objective intact before it got dark. Major Mann's tank was the fourth, and he followed behind the Troop.

Lieutenant Cameron's three Churchills set off at once with all speed through thick unreconnoitred woods and were able to drive, without incident, to within a short distance of the stream. Here they found a road block of felled trees, through which they managed to burst despite heavy mortar and Spandau fire directed at them from the slight rise on which Oisterwijk stands. Pressing on to the river bank they found the bridge blown and the stream to be an obstacle to tanks. A fierce fire fight now ensued, during which most of the nearest houses in Oisterwijk were set on fire and the church tower, an obvious O.P., demolished. During this battle, Lance-Sergeant Marsden, the

Troop Corporal, bogged his tank near the bridge, and was killed when a mortar bomb burst squarely on the top of its turret.

Meanwhile the remainder of Left Flank, having extricated themselves at last from the chaos of Moergestel, came up from the south and deployed in a wide half circle along the river bank. The tanks, combined with the smoke of the burning houses, provided an admirable screen behind which the Seaforth were able to alight from their Kangaroos and advance to the stream with very few casualties.

During that night, while Right Flank and S Squadron sat with their infantry along the Wilhelmina Canal opposite Tilburg and Left Flank remained in front of Oisterwijk, a plan was made to capture the latter place as soon as it became light.

A footbridge had been discovered intact across the Voorste Stroom to the right of the demolished road bridge and another light bridge had been found still farther to the east. A Seaforth company was to go over each of these bridges at dawn covered by Left Flank. Half an hour before first light, the Churchills began to leave their harbour area and to close up to the river. As the crews were mounting, an 88-mm. gun, which had been shelling the area the evening before and occasionally during the night, put two rounds of air-burst into the midst of the Squadron, killing Lieutenant J. S. M. Ramsay and wounding SSM A. Price.   Oct. 26

As dawn broke the Squadron was in position opposite the two bridges and for twenty minutes every tank blasted the enemy across the river with all its weapons. At the same time an artillery concentration came down on Oisterwijk itself, and at about twenty minutes past seven the Seaforth rushed the bridges with great boldness and swept on into the houses on the other side. By midday, assisted by the Glasgow Highlanders, they had driven a German battalion out of Oisterwijk, and Right Flank was moved up into the area south of the village in support. Left Flank had been withdrawn as soon as the infantry were well into the town, and it was only then, after he had seen to the usual requirements of petrol and ammunition for the whole Squadron, that SSM Price admitted his wound. He had fought his tank throughout the morning with a large hole in his right hand and splinters up the length of his arm. He was later awarded the Military Cross, the only Warrant Officer of the Regiment to receive this honour during the war.

While Left Flank were engaged at Oisterwijk, S Squadron supporting the Cameronians had advanced to the large bridge which carried the main 's Hertogenbosch road over the Wilhelmina Canal into Tilburg, only to find that this too had been destroyed. On the following morning their infantry managed to crawl across the debris and to get patrols into Tilburg against little opposition. The Reconnaissance Troop also spent that morning in the same area, patrolling the ground   Oct. 27

between the canal and the railways north-east of the town and found little to oppose them.

News from within the town soon confirmed that the Germans had withdrawn during the night, and the only opposition was coming from apprehensive Dutch SS men. During the afternoon Left Flank picked up the Seaforth near Oisterwijk and carried them to the canal on the north side of the 's Hertogenbosch road after which, having watched them cross unopposed, they retraced their tracks to the Battalion harbour east of the demolished road bridge, where all three squadrons spent the night. It was frustrating to hear the sounds of rejoicing emanating from liberated Tilburg and yet be unable to take part.

(f) *Through the Peel to the Maas*

MAP XXX

Immediately after the capture of Tilburg the Battalion was involved in another alarm; this time it was one with some substance behind it.

Oct. 27

As had been feared the failure to clear all the country up to the Maas had enabled the Germans to mount an attack towards our communications. One Parachute and two Panzer Divisions had forced back the thinly spread American 7th Armoured Division; they had captured Meijel, and were thought to be advancing on Helmond through the Peel, a tract of heath and bog in which movement off the road was extremely difficult. Rumour increased the German threat a hundredfold; some thought that the presence of the Second Army Headquarters in Helmond gave an added air of panic. There was, in short, a "flap".

Oct. 28

On the afternoon of the 28th the Division issued orders for the Third Battalion and 227th Brigade to start off for the east as soon as possible. The remainder of the Division and the other two tank Battalions would follow in the morning. Passing through Eindhoven and Geldrop, the Battalion reached a point just west of the small town

Oct. 29

of Asten in the small hours of the morning and, as soon as it was light, the three squadrons moved out to the south and east of the town, each in support of an infantry battalion.

The day was full of vague and sensational rumours, mostly emanating from the Americans, but no enemy were seen near Asten. It was disturbing for a previously "Ever Victorious Army" to learn that Army Headquarters were preparing to bolt from Helmond, a good fifteen miles to the rear; it would have been all in the day's work in Africa!

Oct. 30

The following morning the Infantry Brigade and the tanks moved farther down the road from Asten to take over positions from the American Armoured Division, which was being withdrawn. On their way they passed the Brigade's guns, who for the past twenty-four hours had been blazing away, well out in front of their infantry.

Now the guns, S Squadron and the 2nd Argylls were all concentrated in a position astride the road at Heusden; Right Flank were about a mile farther on with the H.L.I. in a large wood to the right of the road; Left Flank were with the Gordons, dug in on the opposite side almost level with the H.L.I. That night the H.L.I. were attacked, and in support of them Right Flank formed up in a line, and opened up with every gun firing tracer.

At dawn Lord Cathcart pushed the Troops commanded by Lieutenants Fletcher and R. A. K. Runcie forward about a mile into the woods, where they saw many shadowy figures moving past their position to the east, and assumed that they were our own infantry of which no-one had bothered to warn them. As it got lighter, it soon became apparent that these had not been British infantry at all, but a German company making good its escape; they had shared the wood for the night.   Oct. 31

During the afternoon Lieutenant Cameron's Troop of Left Flank supported a company of Gordons in an attack on an occupied farmhouse and, without casualty to his Troop, brought back twenty-three prisoners and an anti-tank gun. The prisoners were not the same type the Battalion had fought in Normandy; one glance at them was enough to see that. They were small and underfed, and willing to raise their hands early in the fight. The expected German attack never materialised, although there was quite heavy shelling and mortaring. The enemy had lost the initiative, and from now on the attacks were directed at him.

Apart from the shelling, two peaceful days were spent around Heusden. On November 2nd, the Reconnaissance Troop, patrolling across the heathland beyond Right Flank, discovered an enemy company dug-in in a peat bog. As soon as this news was passed back to Battalion Headquarters a company of Argylls and Lieutenant Hickling's Troop of S Squadron were quickly despatched to the area. Unfortunately, the ground was quite unsuitable for heavy tanks, and very soon two Churchills were hopelessly bogged. The infantry had been badly caught in a mortar concentration, and when Lieutenant Hickling put down smoke to cover the extrication of the bogged tanks they took it for a prearranged signal to retire and returned to the start line. This left the tanks unsupported in the gathering gloom, and the enemy promptly attacked them with infantry.   Nov. 1–2

Months later while the Battalion was sorting prisoners in Schleswig a German, who claimed to have been in this battle, volunteered the information that during this infantry attack on the tanks about one hundred and thirty men were hit in a very few minutes. He also said that an S.P. gun, which had fired a few H.E. shells into the area during the action, would have opened up on the tanks with armour piercing had it had any left. Whatever the truth of these statements, a

25—S.G.H.

Nov. 3 — fierce defence was put up by the Troop, and having beaten off the infantry and blown up an ammunition dump which they found in a peat bog nearby, the Troop withdrew in the dark, abandoning one tank which they had been quite unable to move. But the enemy also withdrew, and an Armoured Recovery Vehicle was able to pull the undamaged tank clear of the bog on the following day without being molested.

Nov. 4 — By November 4th the shelling had died down, and the Battalion was moved back to comfortable billets in a factory and some private houses in Helmond; Army Headquarters had left vacant some most "desirable residences".

Here for the first time since leaving England the officers were able to have a Battalion Mess. There were sad gaps in the group which had left Southampton in July, but an officer wrote home: "Every time I

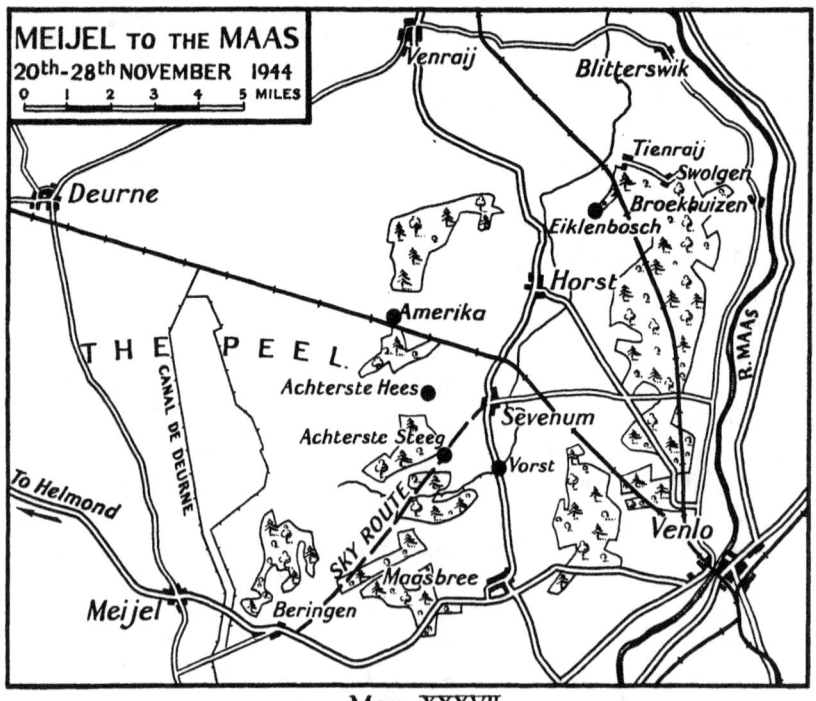

Map XXXVII

see an infantry battalion that I know well, I am appalled at the number of new faces, but we have remained substantially unchanged from the beginning. There is no doubt it is much safer in a tank, even though at times you think that everything in the world is firing at you." Safer, perhaps, but the winter was coming on, and with it new hardships. The shortening of the days meant that the hours of active operations were less, and maintenance could more easily be carried out. But life in a Churchill in winter was not one of ease and comfort.

As in summer the tanks were stinking ovens so in winter they became ice-boxes surrounded by freezing metal, every breeze a draught, and every rainstorm a series of cataracts that poured through the hatches and down the necks of the occupants.

Though better than most British tanks at that time, even the Churchill bogged down in the sodden winter fields of Holland, and after a few unbogging operations the inside of the tank became as muddy as the infantryman's trench. In snow and on ice the tank behaved like a forty-ton toboggan, sometimes going the way commander and driver wanted, sometimes not. But in snow and ice, rain or sunshine, the Churchill tanks, in the idiom of the Guardsmen who fought in them, generally "got there".

During these peaceful days at Helmond the Battalion occupied itself mainly in maintaining its vehicles and keeping fit, and with a few unfamiliar drill parades. Leave to Brussels was always welcome. At Battalion Headquarters Captain P. E. G. Balfour took over the appointment of Adjutant from Captain Erskine Crum, who left for the Staff College via Divisional Headquarters.

Plans were now made to clear the enemy from the wide stretch of country which he still occupied west of the Maas. Opposition from the enemy was trouble enough; but now the weather broke in earnest, and what was to prove the wettest Dutch November on record reduced the Peel to the consistency of soggy sponge. Once again there was to be tank fighting in what, to the purist, was obviously not "tank country". MAP XXXVII

Orders for Operation *Nutcracker* were received on the 13th. Once again the Battalion was placed in support of the 227th Highland Brigade of the 15th Division. "We have settled down to become almost an extra Battalion in this Brigade and the Squadrons really regard themselves as extra Companies of the Battalions they work with. It is all a very satisfactory arrangement." Nov. 13

The line of the 227th Brigade's attack was to take them in a north-easterly direction from Meijel, right across the heaths and bogs to Tienraij, and on to the banks of the Maas beyond—a distance of some twenty miles. Rough tracks would have to serve for roads, and supply promised to be the greatest of all difficulties.

Preparations for the advance included the clearing of the large minefield in front of Meijel, in which the Reconnaissance Troop assisted; on the 19th Captain Pember's scout car struck a mine which injured both him and his driver, Piper Taylor. On the previous evening the Reconnaissance Officers of S Squadron and Left Flank (Captains C. S. R. Graham and Bankes) accompanied patrols of the H.L.I. to examine the ground and determine the tank "going" between Meijel and the Canal de Deurne. Despite the downpour of the past few days the going was found to be suitable, and signs of enemy positions near the canal were observed. Nov. 19

Nov. 20 *Nutcracker* opened on November 20th. At 7 o'clock on that morning the Battalion left Helmond in pouring rain and, passing through Meijel, crossed the Deurne Canal and formed up with their infantry on the north side of the main Venlo road not far from the village of Beringen.

Plenty of opposition was expected, and to assist in the advance against it, the Battalion had been given a generous supply of assorted mechanical devices, known collectively as "funnies". These included a Squadron of Flail tanks of the Westminster Dragoons to assist in penetrating the minefields, a Battery of S.P. guns, a Troop of A.V. R.E., including a bridge, and two Churchill bridge-layers. The Flails and S.P. guns were shared out—one Troop to each tank squadron, whilst the remainder followed up behind Battalion Headquarters, looking for all the world like a herd of prehistoric monsters.

While deploying, the Battalion was sharply shelled by an S.P. gun, but suffered only one casualty. At 1145 Left Flank and the 2nd Gordons headed off up what the Division had named "Skye" route, a muddy track which led across flat and wooded country towards Sevenum.

They had gone about a mile when several Spandaus and the whine and crash of mortar bombs began the battle. This halted the infantry; but Left Flank, ploughing on through the muddy fields, dealt swiftly with the houses from which the fire was coming, killing about twenty Germans and sending back fifty more as prisoners. "What makes me really angry is the way they fight like hell till you get up to them and then come out grinning all over their faces, expecting to be taken prisoner." Nevertheless, it was better than SS Bazooka men who fought to the last, as at Estry.

So far it had been relatively easy, but as the infantry were coming forward, two German S.P. guns opened up on Left Flank from thick woods, first from the right and then from the left front. Seventeen empty cases were later found in one of their positions, and it was only through Major J. P. Mann's skilful handling of his squadron that more casualties did not result. As it was, three Churchills were hit before the enemy were forced to withdraw. Two of these sustained little damage, but the third was completely knocked out, and its commander, Lieutenant J. Wilson, and two of the crew wounded; Lieutenant Wilson died that night. Also wounded was Lieutenant I. L. Thorpe, who received a Spandau bullet in the face.

Elsewhere during the afternoon two other tanks had been lost. A Churchill of Right Flank struck a mine which killed its driver, Guardsman Grieve, while in support of the 44th Lowland Brigade to the north-west, a task which involved no action; and a Honey of the Reconnaissance Troop went off on a patrol into the woods ahead and did not return. Some days later it was found abandoned with a broken track, surrounded by every sign of a terrific struggle. Lance-Sergeant Fenton and its crew had been taken prisoner.

As soon as darkness fell Left Flank withdrew to "forward rally" on the left of the track, while S Squadron harboured with the Argylls on the right. Right Flank and Battalion Headquarters spent the night near Beringen.

At first light next morning the advance continued through the glutinous mud and streaming rain, with Left Flank and the Gordons still in the lead. About two miles beyond the scene of the previous day's battle they came up to a canal where the bridge had been demolished, but which was not defended by the enemy. The A.V.R.E. bridge and a Churchill bridge were soon in place and tanks and infantry pushed on to form a bridgehead beyond. No sooner were they across the canal than they came under heavy shell, mortar and nebelwerfer fire, which forced the infantry to ground on the sodden earth, and there they spent an unpleasant afternoon. By evening the ground around the canal crossing had become so bad—and the incessant rain was making it much worse—that it was decided not to pass over any more tanks that night, but to wait until the morning when the bridges could be shifted to better sites. Left Flank therefore stayed out in their bridgehead alone for the second miserable wet and muddy night of almost twelve dark hours, lit only by the light of burning farms. *Nov. 21*

At dawn next day the bridges were shifted, and Right Flank was able to cross by nine o'clock. This squadron pushed on with the H.L.I. to capture the village of Sevenum without opposition. The Brigade Group, now so far forward that they were only just in range of their own guns, spent the night round this village under intermittent shellfire. *Nov. 22*

The enemy were now withdrawing with some speed, and on the following morning when Right Flank continued the advance they were able to cross the Helmond–Venlo railway and enter Horst with no opposition—except from the population, who held them up with the now familiar liberator's welcome and handed over five frightened prisoners. The rain continued to come down in torrents, and added enormous difficulties to the administration. Eventually the "Skye" track became so bad that it had to be abandoned and all that was required came up to the Battalion from A Echelon at Heusden via Deurne, and down the railway line to Amerika—a most circuitous route. These difficulties delayed the Battalion in Horst for two days, until on November 25th the advance continued. *Nov. 23*

Right Flank went forward with the H.L.I. to Eiklenbosch, while S Squadron and the Argylls attempted to assault the village of Tienraij, only to find their attack unopposed, and they were established there by midday. Left Flank with the Gordons passed through, and by *Nov. 25* nightfall reached the village of Swolgen, only two miles from the Maas. During the night the Squadrons harboured around these three places under shelling from the heavy German guns on the far side of the Maas and the Reconnaissance Officers of Right Flank and S Squadron went out with patrols to inspect the going up to the river bank. During a particularly heavy bombardment on Left Flank's harbour area a shell burst directly under Lieutenant H. W. S. Marshall's tank, the usual and the safest place to sleep, killing him, Guardsmen Petty and Irvine, and wounding the other two members of his crew.

Nov. 26 At ten o'clock in the morning Right Flank and the H.L.I. were off again with the intention of finishing the operation by reaching the Maas at Blitterswijk, but they were halted just outside the village by a water obstacle which prevented all but two of Lieutenant H. Laing's Troop from getting forward. These two Churchills managed to silence what Germans had been left there, and Blitterswijk, too, was in our hands. Two Troops of Left Flank had meanwhile assisted the Gordons into Broekhuizen, and the 227th Brigade Group had achieved its objective. As if discouraged by this success, the weather now gave up the struggle it had been waging on behalf of the Germans; the rain stopped, and for eight days it was comparatively fine. Save for a sortie by a Troop of Left Flank under Major Mann to assist the Gordons into Kasteel, and also to help to demolish some booby-trapped houses around Broekhuizen, the Battalion's part in clearing the Peel was over.

Nov. 28 On the night of the 28th the Adjutant was disturbed in his billet by RSM Brown, "who came in, saluted and said—'I'm sorry, Sir, I've been blowed up', drank half a pint of neat rum, grinned broadly and retired quite unmoved. When I examined his scout car I found that it had almost ceased to exist. How he survived I don't know."

Nov. 29 The next day the Battalion was withdrawn to their old billets in Helmond where it quickly set about removing the mud and dirt accumulated during the last week. Here it was honoured to receive a visit from the Supreme Commander, General Eisenhower, who, with the Army Commander, Lieutenant-General Sir Miles Dempsey, walked round the Battalion area during a maintenance parade and talked to a large number of officers and men. General Eisenhower was accompanied by his British Military Assistant, Colonel J. F. Gault, a former officer of the Battalion.

(g) *The Pause and Alarms of Winter*

MAP XXX After their battle across the Peel the Third Battalion rested in Helmond, and hoped they would still be there to celebrate Christmas and Hogmanay in their comfortable billets. Pleasurable anticipation was troubled by a plan which would send them into the line as infantry. It seemed as if there would be little use for a Churchill tank brigade during the coming months, and the infantry divisions needed all the rest they could get. It was learnt that the Battalion would take over a sector of the Maas, which promised little fighting, but which threatened an uncomfortable life. Gritting their teeth in the face of the inevitable, the Battalion began to oil its rusty knowledge of infantry tactics.[1]

For the orthodox Scots Guards infantry contingent November in Holland had been a period of drudgery. X Company guarded the Nijmegen bridge, went to help the 11th Armoured Division at Veulen near Venraij, and later rejoined its own division forty miles to the south near Sittard, where they were the first Scots Guardsmen of the war to enter Germany when they took over a sector of Birgden village, sharing it with German out-posts and countless booby traps with which the retreating army had ensnared this bastion of the Fatherland. [MAP XXXVIII]

On the 16th December the blast of the great—and final—German offensive in the Ardennes blew the Scots Guards out of the doldrums, and at the same time wrecked all previous plans for a Merry Christmas and peaceful New Year. The German Panzer armies, secretly assembled and led with their old skill and daring, struck at a weak American Corps, broke its front, and were rumoured to be able to reach the Meuse at will. The 21st Army Group in the north moved formations south to counter any attempt at a deeper penetration, but the valiant fighting qualities of the Americans held the thrust, and the Regiment saw no fighting—but movement in plenty. [Dec. 16, MAP XXX]

On the 17th X Company, with the rest of the Division, drove south into Belgium, and were billeted in and around the brewing town of Hougaerde, near Tirlemont, a station made popular by the hospitality of the inhabitants. It seemed a good place to spend the holiday period, but the Germans disposed otherwise. [Dec. 17]

The Company Clerk, Guardsman Hannah, recorded in the Diary: "Christmas Eve—Football v. 2 Sqdn. 2 W.G.; 'O' Group at 2200 hrs.—Bn to be prepared to move at first light. All food which had been drawn for the Christmas dinner returned to Q.M." The Guards Armoured Division was rushed to Namur to block any threat to Brussels. Rising on Christmas Day far earlier than they had intended, the Company moved off in bitter cold towards the fortress, the name of which is the Regiment's first Battle Honour, and there they breakfasted a few hours later. Panic now subsiding a little, during the afternoon they moved out of Namur to take up a position in the ruins of Fort d'Anoy, which had withstood the German onslaught in 1914. On Boxing Day, after a fifty per cent. "stand to" all night due to the complete absence of intelligence, the Company held a very successful [Dec. 24, Dec. 25, Dec. 26]

[1] The Third Battalion continued on p. 393.

shoot through the nearby woods, much to the chagrin of the owner's daughter, who, appearing in the middle of one drive, expostulated that when the Germans had shot over her father's ground they had hit nothing; but now "Vive le sport, and—pouf—no more pheasants."

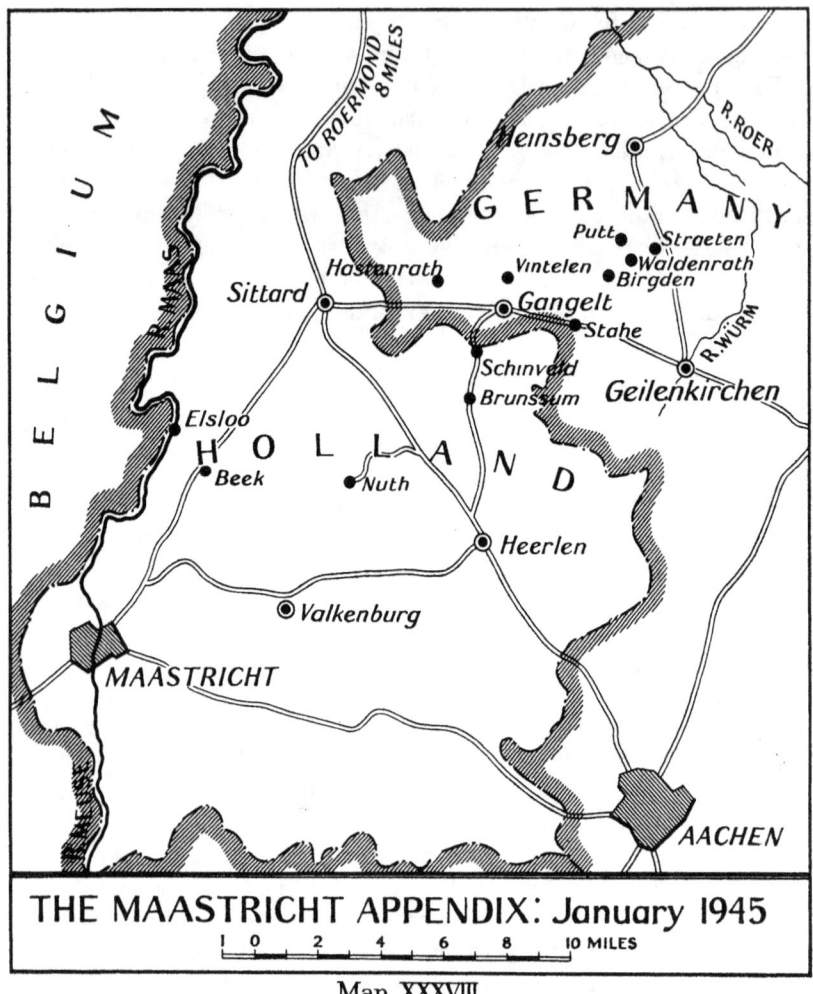

Map XXXVIII

Dec. 27   The next day they were relieved by the 6th Airborne Division, and returned to their billets around Hougaerde. When they arrived that evening, the inhabitants were much alarmed; they thought that the troops had been driven back before the exaggerated threat of the German offensive. Once more preparations were made for the Christmas festivities, and this time successfully. Hogmanay was celebrated
Dec. 31   in traditional fashion only two nights later, and was attended by officers and sergeants from all over the Division. Suitable quantities

of the "necessary" had been provided by Major H. H. Houldsworth of the Regiment, who held some appointment of immense influence at Headquarters 21st Army Group. For the whole of January the Company remained at Hougaerde, and there they must be left while the fortunes of the Third Battalion are followed.[1]

1945
January

When the German offensive had opened, a strict embargo had been imposed on any news of its progress. Until the 20th the Third Battalion had remained at Helmond, while the fog of war was illuminated by the wildest rumours; on that day they received orders to move to Bree, thirty miles to the south in Belgium. During the next twenty-four hours the Brigade found itself under the command of three different Armies in succession, First Canadian, Second British and Ninth American. On the 21st reconnaissance was carried out in the Louvain area, where it was thought the Brigade would cover the approach to Brussels, but in the early hours of the next day the Battalion found itself on the road for Maastricht going in a diametrically opposite direction. At one time such was the confusion of orders and plans that the tanks of the Scots Guards, moving to the east, passed those of the Coldstream, moving to the west, on the same road! Thus, save for extensive reconnaissance for possible counter-attacks, the Battalion took no part in driving back the German armour in the Ardennes. The Maastricht Appendix proved to be its next battle-ground.

1944
Dec. 20

Dec. 21

Dec. 22

Around Valkenburg, where the Battalion found billets, the inhabitants treated them as guests. One, a baron with an excellent cellar of port, on whom Lord Cathcart and his Squadron Headquarters billeted themselves, claimed that a Sir Alan Cathcart had also billeted himself there in 1415 whilst in command of a Scots Brigade. This friendly atmosphere, combined with a spell of fine frosty weather, enabled the Battalion to enjoy a splendid Christmas and later a very successful Hogmanay. "The Dutch," we need not be surprised to learn, "were much astonished by the playing of what they called the 'doodlesack' in the early hours of the morning."

MAP
XXXVIII

On December 27th the Brigade were placed under command of 43rd (Wessex) Division and were put at six hours' notice to move in a counter-attack role should the enemy attack again north of "The Bulge". During the next fortnight many plans were evolved to deal with possible developments round Sittard, and as far south as Eynatten, below Aachen; but the Battalion sat and waited. The area was full of American troops, some of whom were coloured, "with very itchy trigger fingers at night, so that life is apt to be dangerous after dark"; the only other danger came from occasional German jet aircraft. The Luftwaffe's final effort on New Year's Day did no damage to the Battalion, although they had a grandstand view of a perfect

Dec. 27

1945
Jan. 1

[1] X Company continued on p. 420.

demonstration of ground attack by fighters on other units in the neighbourhood. Much more excitement was caused by the draw of the ballot for leave to the United Kingdom, which was to start on 1st February. In an atmosphere reminiscent of the draw for the Irish Sweepstake the officers' ballot was won by the E.M.E. (Captain R. Owen) and that for the other ranks by one of the despatch riders.

With the New Year came a break in the weather, and heavy snow Jan. 8–9 began to fall which, on the 8th and 9th of January, amounted to a blizzard. This inopportune moment was decreed suitable for the Batta-Jan. 12 lion to leave the warmth of their billets on 12th January, and move up over the frontier into Germany to support the 43rd Division in the area around Geilenkirchen. Such was the state of the roads that this journey had to be made across country. S Squadron found shelter in the cellars of Gangelt, about six miles to the east of Geilenkirchen; two of the Troops were pushed forward into the villages of Hastenrath and Vintelen. Right Flank dug in their tanks on the Gangelt–Geilenkirchen road in the area of Stahe; and Left Flank, after waiting one Jan. 13 day with Battalion Headquarters on the Dutch side of the frontier at Schinveld, moved into the battered snow-covered ruins of Geilen-Jan. 17 kirchen itself. After four days the whole Battalion joined them there. Here the tanks were whitewashed, covered in discarded parachutes or even, it must be confessed, in some cases with "liberated" German linen, to give a suitable winter camouflage.

The Battalion now took part in a plan to support an attack of the 43rd Division north-eastward from Sittard towards Heinsberg. The object of the attack, which was given the nostalgic codeword of *Blackcock*, was to push the enemy back beyond the River Roer, and provide a better jumping-off place for the expected spring offensive. The Battalion was to be employed in an artillery role, and was required to obliterate by concentrated fire from their guns the three German villages of Straeten, Waldenrath and Putt as a preliminary to their capture from the west. This shoot was known as "Pepperpot"; it was meticulously planned by the Adjutant, Captain Balfour, who had been Gunnery Officer of the Battalion at home.

Jan. 21 After an initial postponement, the operation was ordered for 21st January. On that day the tanks moved up on to the icy and windswept ridge about a mile to the east of Geilenkirchen where they stood almost track to track along the crest. As soon as they were in position the shoot was once again postponed, this time until the following dawn, and the tank crews spent a miserable night bivouaced in the snow or in the Jan. 22 ruins of a neighbouring factory. At dawn the shoot was fired as planned, and, at a range of about four miles, until half-past seven in the evening every tank pumped shells into the three villages, following the complicated details of timings on the programme.

The tanks then returned to Geilenkirchen, but no sooner had they reached their billets than word was received that the infantry attack had been delayed by mines, and that a further "Pepperpot" would be required. Before the tanks could turn round, their billets in the town were subjected to a brisk attack by four R.A.F. fighter-bombers who raked the houses with machine-gun fire and dropped eight bombs. Fortunately, apart from frayed tempers, no casualties or damage was caused to the Battalion. From their ridge the tanks repeated the mixture as before. But yet it was not enough, and the infantry were again held up; more fire would be required in the morning.

At dawn, after a second bitter night, the Battalion began to fire a third "Pepperpot" on the village of Straeten; this lasted until 0930, by which time all ammunition had been exhausted. In all, 12,000 rounds had been fired by the 75's—a total weight of about twenty-eight tons; prisoners taken a few days later at Heinsberg confirmed the accuracy and effectiveness of the shooting.   Jan. 23

A rehearsal for a proposed attack with the 5th D.C.L.I. was carried out on January 25th, but the intended objectives were taken by others, and an attempt to use Left Flank in support of infantry holding these newly-won positions also came to naught owing to the perilous condition of the roads and the many mines sown in the verges. By January 27th the last village on the south bank of the River Roer above Roermond had been captured. The Battalion moved back from Geilenkirchen to Valkenburg, their task in the south completed. Two days later the tanks slithered their way into Waterscheide in Belgium where they were loaded on to transporters for a long trek which eventually brought them, on February 3rd, to their old friends of the 15th Division at Nijmegen.[1]   Jan. 25 / Jan. 27 / Jan. 29 / Feb. 3

(h) *The Second Battalion re-enters the Field*

The time had now come for the Second Battalion to enter the fight again. We last left them steaming out of the Bay of Naples on board the *Capetown Castle*, bound for home after five years abroad, during which they had fought their battles in Africa and Italy. The story must be carried back to the spring of 1944, before the Normandy landings.   1944 April 11

The voyage home was uneventful, and by the morning of 22nd April the *Capetown Castle* had entered the Mersey which was looking as grey and as sodden as the Bay of Naples eleven days earlier. The day was passed lying out in the channel waiting for the tide to allow the ship to come alongside. In the evening the Battalion disembarked, and the next morning it entered Wellington Barracks. It had been away from England since 1938.   April 22 / April 23

There was an immediate disappointment. Instead of the leave to

[1] The Third Battalion continued on p. 400.

which everyone had been looking forward, the Battalion found itself in quarantine for three weeks owing to a case of small-pox on board ship. However, many activities filled in the time, including finding King's Guard for the first time for nearly six years, and everybody got his leave in the end and by the beginning of June was ready for the next stage.

May 20
June 10

On 20th May Lieutenant-Colonel H. N. Clowes took over command from Major Steuart-Fothringham, and three weeks later the Battalion moved to Stobs, near Hawick, among the sheep-clad hills of Roxburghshire: "a wilderness of army huts, muddy grass and, later, snow, reminiscent, if only in aspect, of a previous hutted camp, far away now in the mountains of Syria". Four days earlier the great invading armies had crossed to the coast of Normandy.

By this time the lack of men in England was becoming acute, and in June and July it was found necessary to transfer 1,500 men to the 201st Guards Brigade from the R.A.F. Regiment. Of these men about three hundred came to the Battalion, and a smaller number were trained by it for the Coldstream.

The successful transfer of men from one Regiment to another is frequently a troublesome matter. When men are compulsorily transferred from one Service to another the possible difficulties are so much the greater, and no higher praise can be given to the keenness and spirit of co-operation of those concerned than to record that it was not a hasty amalgam but an homogeneous Battalion which was visited by H.R.H. the Colonel of the Regiment on 23rd September.

The difficulties in the way of this achievement were made greater by the unsatisfactory state of the camp itself, which had been built for German prisoners in the 1914–1918 war, and presumably had once been fit for human habitation: the rats there were sufficient to provide permanent occupation to two professional rat-catchers. Even the enthusiast who announced obscurely that, if he *had* to leave the Air Force at all, he wanted to go into the Army and not into the Brigade of Guards, can hardly have found it an agreeable introduction to Army life. But the first step in overcoming these difficulties was made by the R.A.F. Regiment themselves who, as far as the other demands upon them allowed, sent only their better men. The generosity in this matter of General Liardet, then commanding the R.A.F. Regiment and a former commander of the 56th Division, was to be justified in the campaign that lay ahead, and a number of former Aircraftsmen were to return to civilian life as Sergeants in the Guards. Much of the credit for the success of the transformation must go to RSM Barnstaple, and his assistants, Drill-Sergeants Fraser and McKirdy; but, despite their efforts, it was said that at any distance an ex-R.A.F. Guardsman could be distinguished from the depot-trained by the way he stood and walked.

On Sunday 24th September H.R.H. the Duke of Gloucester attended a parade service in St. Giles' Cathedral, Edinburgh, in memory of Guardsmen who had fallen in the war. It was the first time that a Battalion of the Regiment had visited the Cathedral in which, in peacetime, hang two sets of its colours. After being inspected by the Colonel the Guard of Honour entered the Cathedral while the Regimental Band played "The Garb of Old Gaul". The service ended with "The Flowers of the Forest", played by Pipe-Major P. Bain, followed by the National Anthem, and after it the Battalion marched through the rain to the Mound where the Duke took the salute at the march past. Before the march past the Band of the Regiment led the parade of former Scots Guardsmen in Home Guard uniform and plain clothes from the Cathedral to its forming-up place near the saluting base. No more critical spectators could have been gathered together, yet none could say that the Battalion was other than it had always been.

One period of training is very like another. The only difference in this case was that it was more concentrated. There was a nucleus of veterans from Africa and Italy. There were drafts of young soldiers from the Training Battalion at Pirbright. There was the R.A.F. intake, forming about a third of the total strength. Somehow these had to be moulded into a unit, and then that unit had to be trained to a pitch at which it could take its place in the Guards Division alongside war-hardened men who had driven the conquerors of Europe from Cherbourg to the Rhine. And all the time, as the too-short days slipped by, the difficulties of training increased as the coming of winter made the camp ever less desirable and snow covered the surrounding hills. But it was done. By the time of the Edinburgh parade the Battalion had become a unity. There followed a concentrated period of tactical training when billeted in Bowhill House near Selkirk. Then the Battalion moved back to Stobs. It was ready. On 13th December the mobilisation order was received. By midnight on the 3rd/4th January 1945 the Battalion had returned from embarkation leave. On the 6th the Sergeants' Mess had their Christmas Dinner and Smoker, at which "the whisky was plentiful, but the beer had to be thawed in the barrels". On the 9th the Battalion was officially mobilised. On the morning of the 25th the Battalion was addressed by Colonel Wynne-Finch, Lieutenant-Colonel Commanding the Regiment. During the previous night the thermometer had showed more than thirty degrees of frost, and at midday the Battalion vehicles under Captains R. A. C. Gordon-Lennox and R. L. Stuart set off through a world of snow and ice on the first stage of their journey to the Elbe.

The Battalion left Stobs for Tilbury in three groups on the 27th. The first difficulty was getting the tracked vehicles to Stobs siding, for the ice made the roads unusable, and even getting the vehicles out of the camp, prior to making the journey across country over

Dec. 13
1945
Jan. 4
Jan. 6

Jan. 9
Jan. 25

Jan. 27

snow-covered hills, was far from an easy matter. However, the first two groups got off not long after the scheduled time. The third party paraded under the Commanding Officer at eleven at night but was warned that the train would not be in until 0050 hours. On arrival at the siding at the amended time in a blizzard it was found that there was no train. It appeared that the engine driver and fireman, perhaps deterred by the weather, had chosen to go on strike at Hawick, and that there was some difficulty in finding deputies. However, the train arrived at last, and at 0215 hours, cold and wet but cheered by departure, they left Stobs to its rats and its memories of German prisoners in 1916.

In the afternoon, and about three hours behind schedule, they arrived at Purfleet where they were met by Colonel Wynne-Finch and other officers of the Regiment, and Right Flank, Left Flank, and G Company went to the Transit Camp. The remainder went straight on to Tilbury and embarked on the ss *Longford* which almost immediately put out to sea. The night was spent anchored off Southend, and early next morning the ship moved off on the crossing to Ostend. It was unescorted, a circumstance superficially disquieting, but gratifying to those who remembered the long sea voyage by the Cape when the Mediterranean was closed and the Atlantic barely ours. The crossing was uneventful, and early in the afternoon everyone was in a comfortable Transit Camp at Ostend, a former naval barracks near the Docks, enjoying the first hot meal since leaving Stobs. The remainder of the Battalion was not so fortunate and had an unpleasant three days' journey of which the first was spent under frozen canvas at Purfleet in a Transit Camp which was succinctly described as "a military crime".

On 2nd February the complete Battalion moved by Ghent to billets in and around Hougaerde, "not exactly luxurious, though the old Italian campaigners say that they are much cleaner than what they were used to"—and the next day attended a demonstration of tank and infantry co-operation by the 2nd Welsh Guards and X Company. That night the Battalion suffered its first casualty, Lieutenant A. N. J. Gordon being shot through the shoulder by an Irish Guards sentry whose keenness apparently led him to believe that a challenge was prejudicial to accurate marksmanship. Lieutenant Gordon's remarks to the sentry were admired but not recorded.

It had been decided that the Battalion should replace the 1st Battalion Welsh Guards in the Guards Armoured Division, for the casualties the Welsh had suffered in Italy and in North-west Europe had been too heavy to permit them to keep one armoured and two infantry battalions up to strength. The Battalion was to work with the 2nd Armoured Reconnaissance Battalion of the Welsh Guards, and what had previously been the Welsh Group now became the

Scots/Welsh Group.[1] From now on a battalion of the Scots Guards would ride on the Cromwell tanks of the Welsh Guards, where before only X Company had ridden. It was a form of warfare wholly new to the Battalion even in training, except in theory, for during the strenuous months of preparation at Stobs no-one had even seen a tank. But much can be learned in a short time when teachers and pupils are equally keen and co-operative. It had been said that eight miles was the physical limit for the transport of infantry on tanks, after which they should revert to their troop-carrying lorries. But this limit was frequently exceeded in practice, for the Cromwell was a more comfortable tank to ride on than was the Sherman. The only drawback to the squadron–company arrangement was the fact that there were four infantry companies, and but three tank squadrons, so there had to be occasional changes in the squadron–company groups.

The 1st Welsh were not to leave the Division until the end of March, so for the time being the Second Battalion found itself a fourth battalion in the 32nd Guards Brigade, and set about getting to know the habits and ways of its new formation.[2]

IV. INTO GERMANY: *VERITABLE*

During February and March the 21st Army Group eliminated the German forces between the Maas and the Rhine. The operation was given the code name *Veritable*, and in it more units of the Scots Guards were employed than in any previous battle of the Regiment's long history. Until this clearance had been completed there could be no advance across the Rhine into the heart of Germany.

MAP XLI

The plan was as follows. On February 8th the First Canadian Army, of which the British XXX Corps would form the larger part, was to attack from the area of Nijmegen south-eastward between the Maas and the Rhine, with the line Geldern–Xanten as its final objective. At the same time the Ninth American Army was to open a complementary attack across the river Roer, from the ground recently captured with the assistance of the Third Battalion, some sixty miles to the south; this advance would eventually link up with the Canadian Army on the Rhine south of Xanten. Meanwhile the depleted British Second Army would hold the ring along the River Maas.

The Third Battalion was to be engaged with the Canadian Army from the outset, and was to spend twenty-four days in the line, engaged in the hardest battle of its existence. X Company and the Second Battalion were to have a holding role until early in March, and then, at Bönninghardt, the Second Battalion carried out its first, and X Company its last, attack on German soil.

[1] Known more familiarly as the Celtic Group.
[2] The Second Battalion continued on p. 412. For its Order of Battle, see p. 552.

(a) *Through the Siegfried Line*

Feb. 1

The Third Battalion was again placed in support of the 227th Highland Brigade of the 15th Scottish Division, which was part of the XXX Corps.

The ground over which they were to fight consisted of the flood plain of the Rhine, bounded to the south by the wooded hills of the Reichswald Forest. Across the marshy plain, and skirting the edge of the high ground, ran the road from Nijmegen to Cleve, some twenty miles to the south-east, passing successively through the villages of Wyler, Kranenburg and Nütterden. Near the last of these villages, it swung away to the north-east to avoid the hills, which here crowd down to the road, and, for its last few miles, steep wooded slopes overhung its right-hand verge up to the outskirts of Cleve itself. Just where the road made its change of direction, and about midway between Kranenburg and Nütterden, lay the northernmost extremity of the Siegfried Line, now strengthened and reinforced from the days of 1939.

It was thought unlikely that the enemy would expect Churchill tanks to be included in an assault across this country, over which the going was expected to be, to say the least, unfavourable. The secrecy which surrounded everything to do with the operation was therefore doubly important so far as the 6th Guards Tank Brigade were concerned. Brigade and Battalion signs were painted off vehicles and removed from battle-dress; no-one except authorised parties were allowed on the roads; and from the 3rd until the 7th of February the Battalion was virtually confined to its billets in Nijmegen.

The Army plan, as far as it affected the Battalion, was as follows. On the left, over what on the map was marked as marshlands but which in fact was a vast expanse of flood water, two Canadian Divisions were to attack between the Cleve road and the Rhine. On the right the 46th Highland Brigade supported by the 4th Coldstream were to seize the heights of the Reichswald Forest, while, in between, the 227th Highland Brigade with the Scots Guards would push straight down the main road to capture Kranenburg by the evening of 8th February. Then the 4th Grenadiers with 44th Lowland Brigade would follow up during the night and begin breaking through the Siegfried Line on the following morning.

Feb. 8

Veritable began punctually at five o'clock on the morning of February 8th with a mighty barrage of no less than 1,334 guns, ranging in calibre from super-heavies to 25-pounders. This exceptional concentration of artillery, which eclipsed that which had preceded the battle of el Alamein, poured destructive fire on to the German positions for the next five hours, after which programmes were fired in support of the different attacks.

The noise was deafening, and as the Battalion left Nijmegen and moved along the road to Wyler the ground shook with its intensity. At a point just short of the hamlet of Berg-en-dal the tanks turned off to the south and moved across country through the gun area to their Forward Assembly Area in the woods. This they reached without incident at half-past seven, an arrival which gave satisfaction, as trouble had been expected on the very inadequate roads and tracks.

At 0915 S Squadron, with the Argylls on their tanks, debouched from the woods and set off for the start line almost a mile further on. Before they could reach it they had to pass through an old minefield laid by American airborne troops after they had landed in the area in the previous September. The open ground was still littered with tattered parachutes and the skeletons of wrecked gliders, but fortunately the Americans had laid their mines on the surface, plain for all to see, and after the infantry had found a gap and taped it, the tanks were able to roll on unharmed. Not so the "funnies" in support. The mud was far too deep for them, and despite the efforts of Left Flank and the Battalion's Armoured Recovery Vehicles, all the precious flail tanks became inextricably bogged on the home side of the start line almost before the battle had begun, and there they remained for the rest of the day.

S Squadron and the Argylls crossed the start line, a track running north from Groesbeek, on time, and immediately behind the barrage. They advanced behind it as far as the German minefield only a short distance beyond. Here it seemed for a moment that the operation might well fail; for there were no flail tanks to cut a path through the mines, very few Sappers were available, and the infantry, who had tried to walk through the minefield, had suffered quite heavy casualties. Meanwhile the barrage was rolling on, and unless something was done rather quickly its benefit might be lost for good. Lieutenant A. R. G. Stevenson, commanding the leading Troop, restored the situation. He had spotted a small track leading through the mines to the east and, taking a chance that this might indicate a gap, he led his Troop along it. It was a gap, and he reached the far side without casualty, his tanks exploding several Schu mines on the way. The remainder of the Squadron and the infantry then followed in his tracks and, apart from two tanks damaged by mines, all got safely to the other side.

The advance now continued against slight ground opposition and shelling, which was negligible as far as the tanks were concerned, but which early on hit every officer in one Argyll company. At 11.40 the leading infantry were up to the German–Dutch frontier on schedule.

During a pause on the frontier Right Flank with the H.L.I. came up on the left and the advance then continued on a two-Battalion front. Right Flank had had the greater trouble with the going, which was now appalling, and had lost two tanks, including Lieutenant Scott-Barrett's, in the minefield before being able to discover the gap, but by swift and skilful driving they managed to make up ground, and were in time to shoot the H.L.I. into the western end of Kranenberg village. Here they made the welcome discovery that the enemy had failed to destroy the bridge on the main road, and Lieutenant Scott-Barrett's Troop was quickly moved over it and into the village to assist the infantry with their mopping-up. The approaches to the bridge were very soft, and, when the remainder of the Squadron tried to get on to the road to cross, no less than eight of the tanks became stuck in the mud. By late afternoon the H.L.I. had cleaned up Kranenberg; the enemy were too dazed by the weight of the barrage and so surprised by the sight of unexpected tanks to offer much resistance.

On the right it was very similar, though it was mainly owing to the determination of Major Farrell and Lieutenant Stevenson that S Squadron managed to get five of their tanks on to the final objective over what was to become quite impossible going.

By five o'clock the infantry had consolidated all their objectives and had sent back 300 prisoners. Although many tanks were so badly bogged that they were never recovered, the Battalion's only other tank destroyed was that commanded by Lieutenant C. Campbell, of Left Flank, which blew up after striking what was thought to be a mine attached to a dug-in aerial bomb; Lieutenant Campbell was fatally wounded.

At nightfall Battalion Headquarters moved up with Brigade Headquarters to the hamlet of Hettsteeg, about a mile to the west of Kranenburg; Right Flank rallied round their bogged tanks near the bridge; S Squadron at Kranenburg railway station, and Left Flank remained with the Gordons behind the start line.

Feb. 9   It had been intended that the Grenadiers should now pass through and assault the Siegfried Line. But mud, floods, and traffic jams further back had prevented them from getting up, and so Left Flank and the Gordons were allotted the task in their stead. This attack on the village of Nütterden was arranged for the evening, but the road from Wyler was found to be so obstructed by mines, road-blocks and trenches that it was almost dawn before the Squadron and its infantry passed through the ruins of Kranenburg, and eight o'clock before their attack went in. They advanced straight down the main road. The anti-tank ditch half-way to Nütterden was crossed with ease, for the Germans, in panic, had failed to blow the bridge, and the village entered with little opposition. By ten o'clock the Gordons had silenced all resistance, and had extracted some two hundred very "bomb-happy" prisoners from large concrete bunkers. Left Flank were thus the first British tanks to penetrate the famous Siegfried Line. On their sector it had been an anti-climax.

That evening Right Flank moved forward on to a spur of high ground called Wolfs Berg, about a mile to the south of Nütterden. On their way through the Squadron was shelled from the forest on the right and the Reconnaissance Officer, Captain J. W. O. Elliot, was wounded. In the rear, attempts were continued to extricate the bogged Churchills.

During the night plans were made for the capture of the fair-sized town of Cleve on the following morning. While Right Flank and the H.L.I. remained where they were at Wolfs Berg, the other two Squadrons with the Argylls and Gordons were to advance across a tongue of the Reichswald to the east and clear the town. Captain Pember's Honeys were to protect the area where the final attack was to join up, which was round a look-out tower on high ground overlooking Cleve.

Accordingly at eight o'clock the next morning Right Flank and S Squadron set out with their infantry up a narrow track, only to find, after advancing a short distance, that their route was completely blocked by the transport of the 43rd Division. That formation, which had been ordered to by-pass Cleve had, in error, driven into its western suburbs; there it was involved in a fierce tussle with some newly arrived and extremely aggressive parachutists. Despite an order to the Division to clear the road, little was achieved, and in the congestion the column found itself advancing into battle headed by an enormous girder bridge. Eventually, after endless delays, just as the leading tanks were about to enter the forest, orders were received to halt and get off the track. Meanwhile the Reconnaissance Troop in their smaller and faster Honey tanks had managed to slip on ahead and had taken up their positions in the intended place. Here they met sharp opposition, including bazookas which cost them two tanks and fatally wounded Sergeant Ramsay. Eventually they were withdrawn, but only after they had killed a number of the enemy and forced him to evacuate several of his positions. The short February day was now ending and, while Left Flank returned to Nütterden and Battalion Headquarters moved up close to them, S Squadron remained where they were for the night near the edge of the forest.

Feb. 10

Early on the following morning an advance on Cleve was ordered once again, but this time down the main road through Donsbruggen. Left Flank and the Gordons were to lead, and were eventually to be passed by Right Flank and the H.L.I., who would clear the town.

Feb. 11

At the start Left Flank had trouble with bazooka parties who fired at them out of the thick cover of the wooded slope on their right, but after Major Mann had sent a Troop up into the wood the enemy soon disappeared. By the afternoon the tanks and infantry had reached the outskirts of Cleve. Right Flank had waited in the rain all day for orders to pass through, but it was not until dusk that the orders came.

Then, with a minimum of preparation, they rumbled down the road and through the Gordons' bridgehead into the badly bombed town. They found little opposition, but plenty of confusion. At one moment there was nearly a brisk battle in the dark between Right Flank on the one side and the Grenadiers coming up from the south on the other. Eventually fighting ceased, and Right Flank retired to a crossroads forward of Left Flank's position on the western outskirts; S Squadron spent the night at Donsbruggen and Battalion Headquarters at Haysenhof, two and a half miles in rear. The first phase of *Veritable* had been completed; it had cost the Battalion one officer and four other ranks killed, and one officer and ten wounded.

Feb. 12–14

For three days after the capture of Cleve no move was made. The Flank Squadrons continued to sit on the outskirts under occasional shelling from the German guns farther south. The enemy had been overcome; now the battle was one of supply and communications with the rear. B Echelon was still at Tilburg, a good fifty miles away; the tank Squadrons were hardly less cut off from their A Echelons which were at Nijmegen. The Rhine floods on the left flank had been rising during the advance and by 13th February the road back to Nijmegen was covered with water to a depth of three feet and over, and the journey was only possible by D.U.K.W. The Churchills which were still bogged around Kranenburg were now almost submerged, and a water Weasel had to be obtained to rescue valuable stores from them before they eventually disappeared below the water. Until the floods subsided Major Sir Charles Maclean and A Echelon kept the Battalion regularly supplied by D.U.K.W. The Battalion despatch riders did fine work making long, difficult and often dangerous detours through the Reichswald to the south. Undeterred by the shortage of maps and the darkness of the nights, they found their destinations at all hours.

(b) *The Advance South-eastwards*

Feb. 15

On 15th February the Battalion was placed in support of the 7th Canadian Infantry Brigade for an advance towards Calcar. Colonel Dunbar and the Squadron Leaders visited the Canadians during the day, and held a final conference at eleven o'clock that night; the Battalion was already on the move through Cleve.

The plan was for Right Flank to advance to the assault and seize the high ground one mile to the south of Moyland, a village about five miles down the straight road to Calcar; then Left Flank, with the Winnipeg Rifles in Kangaroos, was to come up on their right to seize the village of Louisendorf; at the same time S Squadron and the Regina Rifles were to move up on their left, along the southern fringe of the Moyland woods to take a knoll above the hamlet of Rosskamp. The area was for the most part open and agricultural, and was flanked by thick woods, particularly to the north, and dotted with smaller ones.

After an early breakfast the Battalion moved out of Cleve to beyond the village of Bedburg, where they were in position by half-past nine. Thick morning mist delayed the attack and Right Flank were not sent forward until half-past one. Then, advancing across some three miles of rolling, open country, they reached their objective without difficulty; on it they were subjected to heavy shellfire from large calibre guns, including a heavy railway gun from across the Rhine.

On the right, Left Flank advanced with equal ease to capture the village of Louisendorf, but had to hold it themselves for an hour and a half before the Winnipeg Rifles caught up with them. The shelling was now the heaviest that the Squadron had ever experienced, and, at its height, Captain R. W. O. Burnett, the second-in-command, set a magnificent example. The infantry had just come up in the safety of their armoured troop carriers and appeared reluctant to leave them; dismounting from his tank amid the bursting shells, Burnett went on foot from Kangaroo to Kangaroo, encouraging the troops to dismount. He then guided them to their positions. While he was engaged in this fine act of leadership he was killed by a shell. By dark the Canadians were firmly established in the village, and also on the ridge to the north which, until then, Right Flank had been holding alone.

On the northern flank S Squadron, advancing with the Regina Rifles along the edge of the Moyland woods, met very heavy resistance and were even counter-attacked. By nightfall the tanks had managed to reach their primary objective, but their infantry, who had suffered heavily, had made little progress.

The Commanding Officer thought it "one of the hardest battles we have ever had"; the Squadrons, which rallied back behind their objectives, spent an equally nasty night under almost constant shellfire. The opposition had come mainly from German airborne troops who could be as tough opponents as the SS, but the Battalion had been able to kill a great many of them during the day, for the loss of four officers and five other ranks wounded. The Adjutant, Captain Balfour, was severely wounded by a bullet when dismounting from his tank to speak to the Commanding Officer; Lieutenant C. J. O. Clarke, a Troop leader in Right Flank, was hit in the head; and Captain I. S. R. Bruce, the Battalion Technical Adjutant, and Captain Bankes of Left Flank were both slightly wounded but were not evacuated. Captain A. J. C. Seymour succeeded Captain Balfour as Adjutant.

On the following morning S Squadron shot the Regina Rifles into the large wood south of Moyland, but the attack was not a success. In the afternoon an attack by the Canadian Scottish supported by Right Flank on the original S Squadron objective south of Rosskamp was this time successful, despite five hours' heavy shelling; about a hundred

Feb. 16

and fifty parachutists were taken. Lieutenant Scott-Barrett's tank broke down on the objective and was later found to have an 88-mm. shell firmly embedded in its works; otherwise the Battalion suffered neither damage nor casualties this day.[1]

Feb. 17
Feb. 18–20

Casualties or no, the Battalion was glad to be released from the battle, and, less Left Flank, moved back for much needed rest and maintenance on the following afternoon. Left Flank returned during the night, and the whole Battalion spent the next three days in the ruins of Cleve, attempting, despite the shells, to catch up on many hours of lost sleep. During this rest one shell went straight through the building which the Battalion was using as an Officers' Mess, but again everyone escaped unscathed.

Feb. 21

Early in the morning of the 21st, the Battalion, again less Left Flank, moved out of Cleve and along the main road towards Goch, carrying on their tanks companies of the 9th Cameronians, for they had now once again reverted to the command of the 15th Division.

Goch is about eight miles south of Cleve and had been first assaulted on February 18th by 44th Lowland Brigade with the Grenadier tanks in support; after two days' hard fighting they had driven the enemy from the half of the town north of the River Niers. The town bore every sign of the struggle which had raged amongst its buildings, and as the Battalion ground its way through the battered ruins, there was still fighting going on in the suburbs over the river to the south-west. The Brigades to the east of the town were still fighting hard against stiff resistance in the area of Schloss Calbeck, a large castle once used as a shooting lodge, situated on the east bank of the River Niers north of the Goch to Wesel railway. The Battalion was directed into this area, and for the next ten days they were to be engaged in a slow but persistent advance over the eight miles of country to the south-east.

S Squadron moved up through the grounds of Schloss Calbeck under heavy shellfire; two Troops supported the Cameronians, and the other two with the Seaforth successfully crossed the railway line and established the required penetration to the woods beyond. Two Troops of Right Flank with the Glasgow Highlanders then completed the task by clearing the enemy from some houses between S Squadron and the river bank. The shelling, particularly airbursts in the trees, had been most unpleasant, but the Battalion had had no casualties, had taken about a hundred prisoners, and destroyed an ammunition dump which had been set on fire by the tanks of Lieutenant Runcie's Troop of Right Flank. Left Flank, who were detached during the day in support of the 227th Brigade, had been guarding the left rear in the area of the Goch to Calcar road, and their trials had consisted only of shelling.

[1] For his handling of the Battalion in support of the Canadians, Lieutenant-Colonel Dunbar was awarded the D.S.O.

For most of the next day the Battalion remained in a counter-attack role in support of the 46th Highland Brigade, except for one Troop of Left Flank, which moved down to assist the Gordons in their successful attack on Schloss Calbeck village. In the evening the Battalion returned to the ruins of Goch where they were joined by Left Flank the next morning, and where they all remained until February 27th. *Feb. 22* *Feb. 23*

The next task given to the Battalion was to support the 9th Infantry Brigade of the 3rd Division in a continuation of the south-eastward advance. In preparation for this operation, Captain Pember and an Engineer Officer carried out an extremely hazardous night patrol. It was necessary to know whether a small bridge some way into the woods on the line of advance was intact and strong enough to carry Churchills. They managed to secure the information, which was favourable, but to do so they had twice to thread their way through a Schu minefield in which five lives were subsequently lost. On the same night, before midnight, Right Flank moved out from Goch and harboured in a V-shaped bight in the woods north of Schloss Calbeck, in the ruins of which Battalion Headquarters were to establish themselves on the following day. *Feb. 26* *Feb. 27*

The 2nd Lincolns were to lead this new attack supported by Right Flank, and they were required to secure a crossing over a stream near the farm of Krusbechshof which was situated almost on the railway. Then the 1st K.O.S.B. on the right and the 3rd Royal Ulster Rifles on the left, each supported by two Troops of Right Flank and preceded by a barrage, were to continue the advance beyond the bridgehead and press on to cut the Weeze to Udem road, about a mile further on.

Lord Cathcart sent Right Flank forward in darkness at a quarter to five, but for an hour they could make little progress for the track was blocked by Engineer tanks of the 11th Armoured Division who, contrary to orders, were coming along it from the opposite direction. To make matters worse, despite the work of the Sappers throughout the night, the prepared tank track was found to be impassable owing to mines and the wrecks of mined vehicles; instead an unreconnoitred road through the woods had to be taken. This proved to be clear, and after an exasperating journey Right Flank arrived in position to deliver effective covering fire for the Lincolns. Their troubles were still not over, for the stream at Krusbechshof, which had to be crossed before the start of the second phase, was an obstacle to tanks and could only be crossed by a precarious causeway and bridge. With their usual ingenuity the crews eventually got the tanks across, and they formed up with their infantry for the advance to the road. This went well, the main opposition, from some houses in a big clearing, being silenced by the tanks. About three hundred prisoners, including a number of officers, were taken and many enemy killed. By one o'clock the road had been cut and the infantry dug in all round it.

So well had this part of the battle gone that it was immediately decided to exploit the success by sending on one company of the K.O.S.B. to seize another bridgehead over the Muhlen Fleuth, a tributary of the River Niers, half a mile beyond the road at a place called Wettermans Hof. Two Troops of Right Flank were to support this advance but, owing to the speed with which the operation was mounted the artillery plan was necessarily scanty. The ten-minute concentration layed on by the supporting Gunners came down as the attack was forming up, and unfortunately most of the shells landed short among

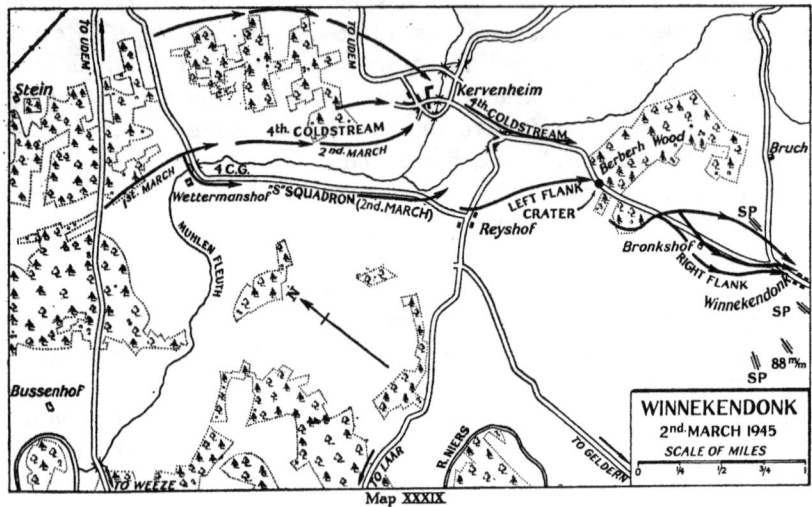

Map XXXIX

the infantry. But the advance got under way, and as the force emerged from the cover of the woods quite close to their objective, they were met by strong fire from Spandaus and S.P. guns sited in and around the houses at Wettermans Hof. Two tanks were immediately knocked out and three others (which were later recovered) became bogged in full view of the enemy while trying to take avoiding action. At the same time the infantry were receiving heavy casualties, and a withdrawal was ordered as the attempt had obviously failed. The gunners now handsomely redeemed themselves; swiftly they brought down an efficient smoke-screen, which was organised by the F.O.O., who, having been forced to "bale out" of his own tank, had immediately jumped on to the outside of another and, fully exposed to the fire of the enemy, continued calmly to direct his guns. It had been an action which might well have succeeded but, as it turned out, too much had been attempted with too little. War is full of such actions, which are hailed as strokes of genius when they are brought off, and are too harshly criticised when they fail.

(c) *Winnekendonk Stormed*

Battalion Headquarters now moved up to the village of Stein beside the railway line; Left Flank joined the other Squadrons in a clearing by the main road, and for two days there they remained. Feb. 28–Mar. 1

Now, on March 2nd, the 9th Infantry Brigade was to make a further advance, which was designed to break through the strong enemy position on the Muhlen Fleuth between Weeze and Kervenheim, seize the Berberh Wood and, if possible, to capture the town of Winnekendonk. S Squadron was to start in support of the K.O.S.B. by breaking out of a bridgehead which the 4th Coldstream had secured over the stream at Wettermans Hof the day before. They were then to advance behind a barrage for almost two miles, to capture what was expected to be a strongly-held position around the cross-roads of Reyshof. Once they were secure in this area, Left Flank and the Royal Ulster Rifles were to pass through and assault the Berberh Wood, also expected to be strongly held. By this time it was hoped that the infantry attack which was being supported by the Coldstream on the left would have sufficiently loosened the enemy's grip on Kervenheim to allow Right Flank and the Lincolns to advance to capture the town of Winnekendonk before dark. This was a bold plan, requiring bold action, and much care was taken to ensure adequate artillery support for all phases. Mar. 1

The day opened inauspiciously when every tank in S Squadron became bogged before they even reached the bridgehead, but the situation was restored, for the Coldstream bridge laid across the Muhlen Fleuth at Wettermans Hof, previously reported as unusable, was in fact sound; the Squadron arrived on the start line muddy, but on time. By nine o'clock the cross-roads at Reyshof had been reached with little trouble, for the enemy had withdrawn, the K.O.S.B. taking about ten prisoners. Mar. 2

The time had now come for Left Flank to pass through, but the Kangaroos intended for their infantry had also got stuck at Wettermans Hof, and, after some delay, the Ulsters decided not to wait for them, but to advance on foot; the advance on Berberh Wood started a little late at half-past twelve.

From Reyshof the wood had appeared clear of enemy, and the Ulsters had wished to cancel the rocket-firing Typhoons who were to have attacked the area before the assault. But there was a misunderstanding, and as a result the aircraft came in over the wood from the east just as the assault was going in, several "overs" falling amongst the leading tanks and infantry, luckily causing no serious damage. By two o'clock the west end of the wood was firmly held and S Squadron and the K.O.S.B. moved across from Reyshof to clear the remainder.

This they managed to do, but further progress to the hamlet of Bruch was prevented by a vast crater which spanned the end of the only possible ride through the wood.

Opposition grew steadily the nearer they came to Winnekendonk itself, and it was obvious that all was not over. Captain Pember was now ordered to move two of his patrols down the east and west edges of the Berberh Wood to discover what the enemy had up his sleeve in Winnekendonk. The westerly patrol became bogged trying to circumnavigate a large crater in the track, but the other, under Captain Pember himself, was able to advance as far as the southern tip of the wood. Here they could observe the northern end of Winnekendonk and the hamlet of Bruch, and were in the act of passing back information to the effect that the latter place was held, when an S.P. gun firing from the area of the town knocked out the Honey tank commanded by Sergeant Brown. The crew got out unhurt, but their position was extremely exposed. Captain Pember, who had quickly backed into cover, realised their plight and called for smoke; this was admirably placed with great speed by Lieutenant J. M. Fearfield's Troop and the Headquarters tanks of Left Flank. Captain Pember drove out behind this screen and was able to rescue the crew, and retire back into the wood.

It was now four o'clock, and the decision was taken to make the final attack on Winnekendonk before dark. The Lincolns, who had just been released by the 185th Brigade after the capture of Kervenheim, were hastily "married up" with Right Flank at the northwest corner of Berberh Wood. After quick reconnaissance it was decided to attack at a quarter to six astride the main road with one Troop and one Company on either side, and the remainder of the Squadron behind them in support; artillery was available as previously arranged.

The going up to the start line was terrible, and the leading Troops only reached it with fifteen seconds to spare. For the first quarter of a mile all went well, but as soon as the leading tanks emerged in the open south of Bronkshof they met armour-piercing shot and high explosive from both the front and flanks. All three Churchills of Lieutenant D. A. S. Gordon's Troop on the right and two of Lieutenant J. Macdonald-Buchanan's on the left were hit, one tank no less than five times; the F.O.O.'s close behind blew up, killing the F.O.O., Pipe-Major Smith, and two Guardsmen; Pipe-Major Smith had been Pipe-Major of the Battalion since its formation. Despite this alarming reception and the extremely heavy going, the remaining tanks continued steadily on. Lord Cathcart immediately ordered up the supporting Troop on the right flank to engage the S.P. guns firing from the west. Lieutenant Runcie advanced his Troop right into the open, the only place from where he could see, and proceeded to engage the enemy to such effect that his tanks knocked out two S.P. guns and an 88-mm. anti-tank gun in a few moments. He also dealt with a number of Spandau posts which were holding up the infantry and enabled them to advance into the town. On the left also, despite trouble from Bruch and from very heavy mortaring and shellfire the tanks and infantry managed to force their way into the town, overrunning another 88 and several 50-mm. anti-tank guns in the process.

It was now quite dark, but in the light of burning buildings fierce hand to hand fighting took place between the Lincolns and the German parachutists, who were holding the town in force. Lieutenant Macdonald-Buchanan's Troop, although several times attacked by bazookas and grenades, supported the infantry through the streets right up to the far end of the town, and remained with them there until recalled. Lieutenant Macdonald-Buchanan's tank fell into a bomb crater and had to be abandoned, and the crew eventually got out on the back of another, fighting off several attacks at close range in the narrow streets on the way. On arrival at "forward rally" Lieutenant Macdonald-Buchanan discovered with dismay that the Slidex card, recording a secret code of much value to the enemy, had been left in the abandoned tank. Accompanied by Guardsman Hunt he immediately made his way back to the crater through the enemy-infested town and returned unscathed through the thick of the fighting with the precious codes.

Fighting went on until nine o'clock when, after a fanatical resistance, the enemy suddenly gave up. Right Flank concentrated for the night round the Lincolns' Headquarters in the houses to the north of the town.

All through the night and the next morning prisoners continued to come in, the final count being 250; forty-three dead were counted, all from the Para Lehr Regiment, a unit of some distinction, composed in the main of young Nazi fanatics whose ages ranged from sixteen to twenty. Only then was it possible for the strength of Winnekendonk to be properly assessed. The town had been held by one battalion of the Para Lehr Regiment with a Fortress Battery in support, and it had obviously been regarded as a nodal point in the German defensive scheme. In addition to the four anti-tank or S.P. guns knocked out during the fighting, two more 88s and six dug-in 50-mm. guns were captured in the town; the tracks of at least one more S.P. gun were found heading away to the south. Taking into account the strength of this anti-tank defence which covered so open an approach, and also the quality of the defending infantry, it was indeed remarkable that the town should have fallen to the assault of one infantry battalion with a single squadron of tanks in support. The speed with which the attack was launched, the forethought given to the prearranged barrage and, above all, the outstanding courage and determination of

Mar. 3

both tank crews and infantry, all combined to achieve a fine feat of arms. For his handling of Right Flank in the capture of Winnekendonk Lord Cathcart was awarded the D.S.O.

While Right Flank were clearing their battlefield, Left Flank and the Ulster Rifles attacked and captured a big wood south of Winnekendonk against negligible opposition, and the Squadrons' tasks in *Veritable* were at an end.

The Reconnaissance Troop had one more task. At half past eleven in the morning the Corps Commander urgently requested a report on the strength of the bridges over the Niers at Kevelaer and Wetten, six miles to the south. A patrol of Honeys commanded by Sergeant Fraser went out, and by a quarter to one the information was in the Corps Commander's hands; such quick service was in the best tradition of this well-trained and excellently led Troop.

That, for the Third Battalion, ended Operation *Veritable*. It had entailed twenty-four days in the line, during which fifteen actions by a squadron or more had been fought. Fourteen officers and men had been killed and twenty-one wounded, and during this period no less than 1,500 of the enemy had been captured by the Squadrons or their infantry. For the crews the weather and physical conditions had been trying in the extreme, and no less so for those who had to keep them supplied. They had advanced nearly twenty-five miles, and had given invaluable support to their infantry. In their final fight at Winnekendonk they had helped to punch an important gap in the enemy's main defences. It was just the gap that was needed for the launching of the faster armour towards the Rhine, but so conjested were the formations on the roads to the rear and so waterlogged was the countryside off those roads, that a memorable traffic jam resulted, which dashed all hopes of swift exploitation. When it had been unravelled, it was the turn of other Scots Guardsmen to head the attack.[1]

(d) *Holding the Ring*

Feb. 8
MAP XXX

The early stages of *Veritable* made little call on the Guards Armoured Division, which at the beginning of the offensive on 8th February was in Corps reserve. On that day the move from Hougaerde began, and that evening, after many detours owing to damaged roads by way of Tirlemont, St. Trond, Herck la Ville, Hasselt, Beeringen, Diest, Gheel, and Turnhout, the Second Battalion crossed the Dutch frontier and entered Tilburg, where everyone except Left Flank, who remained in the town, was billeted in a large Trappist monastery. This, a gaunt and dank building, was to be the battalion's home for eleven days while *Veritable* was slowed down in and around the

---

[1] The Third Battalion continued on p. 422.

Reichswald Forest by the German parachute battalions, heavily reinforced by mud. It was an unsatisfactory life, for little of either training or recreation can be done when notice to move fluctuates continually between one hour and eight. V.1's passed over the Monastery on their way to Antwerp, and the sky-trail of a V.2 on its way to London could occasionally be seen, and it soon became clear that there was no likelihood of employment until the road to and through Cleve became passable. It was possible to ease the strain on the Battalion's overladen transport by getting a few more vehicles, and to enjoy the amenities of Tilburg, principally oysters. On the 10th the Commanding Officer and a selection of other officers left for attachment to the 1st Welsh Guards to see combined armour and infantry in action, but returned on the 12th having seen nothing, as the ground was too wet for the armour to move. Feb. 10
Feb. 12

X Company, which had been billeted in a nunnery south-east of Nijmegen, was the first to enter the line. On the 14th they went with the 1st Welsh on loan to the 51st Highland Division, into the area of Gennep, twelve miles to the south-east. There had been very heavy fighting in this area and as they passed through Gennep on their way to an assembly area beyond, the sight of so many dead Germans was reminiscent of Hechtel. Their immediate task was a relatively easy advance through thick pine woods on the southern fringe of the Reichswald. The Company remained dug-in in these newly won positions until the afternoon of February 16th when the Battalion was ordered to mount a night attack on the large village of Hassum, half-way down the railway line to Goch. For this they were given a weighty barrage, bombing from the air and the "artificial moonlight" of searchlights, under the cover of which they attacked at three o'clock in the morning from positions in front of the Irish Guards at Hommersum. The Company, which was the right forward company in the attack, reached the remains of Hassum without difficulty, finding only a few prisoners and a number of dazed civilians in an area of complete devastation. As they consolidated in the dawn the enemy put down a heavy concentration of shells on to the village, one of which fell into a slit trench occupied by Lieutenant R. J. S. Howard and his servant, Guardsman Walker; they were both badly wounded, and Lieutenant Howard later had both his legs amputated. Feb. 14
MAP XLI

Feb. 16

Feb. 17

During this fighting the "Spectator Group" of the Second Battalion had again come up, but failed to see much armoured action. Their infantry hosts "bore with them admirably, but at times it must have been disquieting to have a pack of eager faces breathing down their necks". They had, on the whole, an exciting trip, "for the new members useful and instructive, but for the old an unpleasant reminder", but suffered no worse damage than a piece of shell through the petrol tank of the Commanding Officer's scout car and numerous shrapnel holes in his valise.

The 32nd Guards Brigade now remained in the line in a holding role for nearly a fortnight. The country was flat and agricultural, and the wary patrols found the farms well stocked with useful supplements to the rations. X Company remained around Hassum, and here they were glad to welcome the Second Battalion into the line for the first time. On the 20th the Battalion had moved out of Tilburg and, after spending the night in dilapidated houses by the roadside outside Gennep, occupied the billets of the 3rd Battalion Irish Guards at Hommersum, with most of the Battalion in Germany and Battalion Headquarters still about twenty-five yards inside Holland. An attack by the Irish Guards soon after midday was at first successful, but they later ran into strong opposition and had to withdraw, making their way back to Hommersum by the light of F Company Headquarters, "conveniently set on fire by a carrier section brewing up in a barn", and the night was spent by the Battalion dispensing what hospitality it could to the exhausted Irishmen. The next day the Battalion took over from the 5th Coldstream south-west of Hassum.

A steady drizzle set in next day and the Battalion suffered the discomforts of war in largely roofless billets, but with little of its dangers, for their position formed as it were an inverted salient, with the 1st Welsh Guards forward on the left and the 6th H.L.I. of the 52nd Division forward on the right. But it was something to know that Battalion Headquarters was occupying part of the Siegfried Line, and the position entailed much useful practice in patrolling. It was on the 23rd that a patrol from Left Flank under Lieutenant J. Swinton called on X Company to pay respects, a social call which was quickly cut short by a routine "hate" on Hassum. The shelling was not all one way, for X Company made full use of the artillery behind them, and Guardsman Harley, only really happy when he was manning the Company's O.P., used to amuse himself by calling down concentrations of shells on solitary Germans who used to come out of the farm buildings opposite the Company position to relieve themselves. Also Lieutenant P. J. H. Leng took out a patrol to escort a Gunner officer, who was armed with a telephone on the end of a prodigious length of cable; together they roamed the woods in front of the enemy positions calling down fire on anything they could see and making life hideous for the Germans.

Attacks by the 51st Division on the nights of the 25th and 26th, and by H.L.I. in particular on the morning of the 27th, completely pinched out the Brigade from the front line, and on the 28th it became non-operational. The fog of war immediately descended: in four days the Second Battalion was under four different notices to move, ranging from forty-eight hours to one hour, and twice an advance party went to reconnoitre a reputedly vacant area south of Goch only to find it impossibly crowded with troops. But as the break-through south of Goch proceeded and the head of the column reached Kapellen the fog thinned, and by the evening of 5th March, creeping nose to tail in a solid mass of traffic, the Battalion had passed Goch and Weeze and reached Kevelaer. There, at 2100 hours, orders were received to attack and occupy the eastern end of the Bonninghardt woods next day in conjunction with the 1st Welsh Guards and, of course, X Company. An Order Group was hurriedly assembled and Lieutenant-Colonel Dunbar and a party of officers from the Third Battalion, fresh from their brilliant crowning action at Winnekendonk, were hurriedly ushered away from dinner. There was no time to spare; the Battalion was going into its first attack in Germany, and X Company into their last.

Mar. 5

(e) *Bonninghardt*

At six in the morning of the 6th March the Battalion embussed and, passing through the Siegfried Line, dismounted at Kapellen and moved forward to its first attack on German soil. The situation was of a kind so frequent as to be normal: an attack from the map over ground which no-one had seen, and with insufficient time for junior officers fully to brief their men. The task of the Battalion was to clear the northern, Haagscher Wood, part of the great wooded area of slightly rising ground known as the Bonninghardt feature. All that was known of the Haagscher Wood was that it was held by the Germans and had some farmed clearings among the trees. The northern boundary ran approximately east and west, and conveniently placed rides gave the start line and inter-company and battalion boundaries. The Battalion was to clear the northern sector, with the 1st Welsh Guards, with X Company, on the right. Right Flank (Major W. D. M. Raeburn, M.B.E.) was to attack on the right with Left Flank (Major N. M. Romer) in support. G Company (Major A. E. Cameron) was to attack on the left. F Company (Major D. H. A. Kemble, M.C.) would follow G and pass through them on their objective and occupy an isolated wood a little farther to the east. A tank squadron of the 2nd Welsh Guards would be in support, and the 5th Coldstream in reserve.

Mar. 6

At eleven there was "a roaring of guns firing behind us, a whistling overhead, the reverberating crump of shells in front, and 2 SG was off again"; it was the anniversary of Medenine. The shortage of time was such that Right Flank was unable to form up at the correct place but "had to shake out and swing right through it over the start line. However, we soon caught up with the barrage and things went with a swing". The wood was very thick, and this combined with suspected mines and fallen trees made it impossible for the supporting tanks to make much headway. But they were not needed, for the leading platoons went into it with a dash that nearly carried them into the barrage, and the Germans, who belonged to the 1062nd Grenadier Regiment and were not of the highest quality, mostly made the mistake of coming out of their holes when the barrage had passed instead of remaining hidden in the thick undergrowth whence they could have done a lot of damage. G Company on the left met with the stiffest opposition. Their part of the wood was thicker, one platoon got out of touch with the rest of the Company, and they were heavily fired on both from a position to the left outside their line of advance and from behind by a party of the enemy whom they had unwittingly by-passed. They were skilfully extricated by Major Cameron and CSM J. H. Foulstone, and F Company, following behind, cleared up the remainder of the difficulty and then passed on through the first objective to attack and occupy their isolated wood.

The ground on the objectives was very soft, and the Battalion was able to get well dug in before the counter-shelling started. This was heavy, "up to the old Italian style", for the German artillery had been forced back into the rapidly closing Wesel pocket. F Company in particular, "had an extremely sticky time—the Grenadier Company Commander who relieved us told me it was the worst shelling he had ever seen". Support Company, too, came in for a share of the shelling and a mortar detachment was knocked out by a direct hit. But "all the old Anti-Tank Sweats . . . were splendid—a great inspiration to the younger men—wandering about under shell-fire saying, 'This is nothing to what we got at Medenine' (not quite true, but still!)".

The shelling and machine-gun fire was so heavy that F Company could not be brought out until after dark on the 7th. In the circumstances the casualties were numerically very light. But they included one particularly bitter blow, for CSM W. Lumsden, D.C.M., M.M. and bar, of F Company, was killed by a 25-pounder falling short during the final advance. A very great soldier and personality, his experience and leadership had been invaluable to the Battalion in good times and in bad. He had won his first Military Medal exactly two years before at Medenine. In all, eight other ranks were killed, and Lieutenant F. R. Taylor of G Company and twenty-five other ranks were wounded. About a hundred and fifty prisoners were taken by the Battalion, Right Flank collecting about a hundred including a complete platoon which came into the area and surrendered to the reserve platoon after being "flushed" from Welsh Guards territory. In addition, "a reasonable number of Boche" were killed, three of them falling to an ex-R.A.F. Guardsman firing a Bren from the hip at about eighty yards.

X Company's part in the battle, which was to be its last as a company, had been less strenuous. The Welsh Guards attack had begun a bit late, and for the most part they had been slightly behind the

Second Battalion. Shelling had been the Company's main worry, and once the woods were in our hands they were ordered to take part in the capture of the village of Bonninghardt, which lay on the farther edge of the woods. For this attack, which went in with strong artillery support shortly after five o'clock in the afternoon, X Company was placed as left forward company. There was a certain amount of open ground to cover between the shelter of the woods and that of the houses and here the Company suffered casualties from small arms and mortar fire, which came at them from their open left flank until this was smoked off and effectively silenced by the guns of the supporting tanks. Captain Ritchie (who was commanding the Company during the absence on leave of Major Hope) was one of the nine wounded, and the Company was taken over by Lieutenant Vernon. There was some brisk fighting in Bonninghardt itself, but by the time darkness fell the enemy had been driven from the village and all Companies were digging in among its houses. As was now becoming normal the bag of prisoners was considerable and amongst them was the Commanding Officer of the defending battalion who expressed himself greatly honoured to have been captured by "the Guards Panzers".

In the afternoon of the 7th the Battalion, less F Company which followed after dark, was moved up to an area between the Welsh Guards in Bonninghardt and the forward elements of the 52nd Division south of Alpon. Immediately to the north-east of the Battalion the ground sloped steeply to the little River Romer which formed the western side of a rough parallelogram, of which the north-eastern apex was formed by the crossing of two railway embankments. A bridge was marked on the map, and it was the task of the Battalion to get across the Romer by this bridge—if it still existed—form a bridgehead, and then advance and occupy the apex, while the 5th Coldstream followed and passed through to attack to the north-east.

Mar. 7
MAP XL

Immediately on getting into position Captain N. H. Barne, M.C., took a patrol to examine the approaches to the stream, and was sniped from houses to the west of the bridge, which was thenceforward known as "Nigel" after him. The task of capturing the Romer bridge was naturally given to Left Flank (Major Romer), and Lieutenant C. M. Campbell's platoon, with Captain Barne as guide, was sent forward as soon as it was dark. To their surprise they found not only that the sniper had gone, but that "Nigel" was intact and capable of bearing tanks. A considerable amount of mortar fire followed the occupation, in the course of which Lieutenant Campbell was wounded and his servant killed, but he remained with his platoon until evacuated next morning.

Mar. 8

Possession of "Nigel" considerably simplified the crossing of the Romer, but the operation was still one of some complexity, for the Battalion was about a mile ahead of the forward troops of the 52nd

Division and was therefore advancing with its right flank exposed to the enemy in and around Alpon. It was, in fact, in a salient, and it had to deepen that salient to the north with a single bridge as its only line of advance and communication. The only approach to the bridge itself was down a narrow gully with steep banks debouching on to dead flat ground at the river bank.

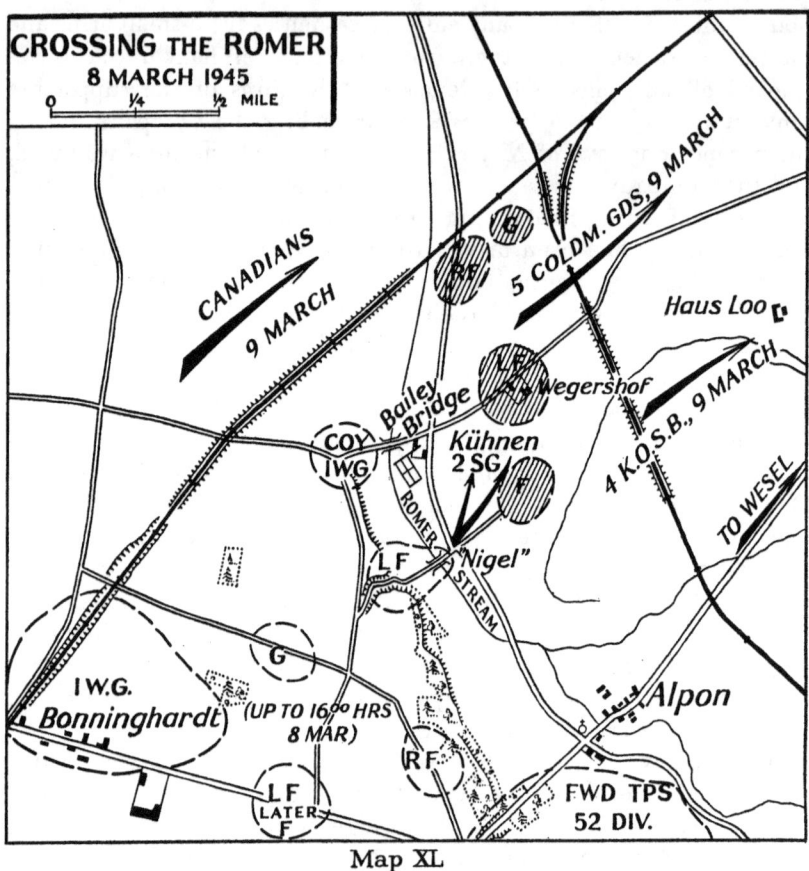

Map XL

At half-past four in the afternoon, Left Flank, supported by heavy covering fire from tanks and artillery, doubled across "Nigel" and formed a tight bridgehead. Right Flank, which had had five casualties while waiting to start, followed and was caught by shelling in the gully and lost several more including Lieutenant W. A. Elliott, M.C., wounded. After crossing the bridge under small arms fire Right Flank swung left through the farm buildings of Kühnen, where Lieutenant I. G. Gow was killed by a shell, and pushed on in the smoke and dust and twilight to the railway a little to the east of where it crossed the Romer. Sergeant A. McPhee, who had taken over Lieutenant Gow's platoon, displayed the utmost gallantry, and by his leadership and organisation of supporting fire from the tanks saved the Company from heavy casualties; Right Flank took over forty prisoners. G Company, which had Lieutenant N. T. Torrance wounded, followed and, keeping farther to the east, passed through the farm buildings of Wegershof, where more prisoners were taken, and went on to the apex where the railway embankments met, consolidating under heavy fire from both embankments about a hundred yards away. F Company was the last to cross, and formed a flank guard north-east of the bridge, while Left Flank followed G Company to Wegershof; on their way they suffered some twenty casualties, including the two remaining Platoon Commanders, Lieutenants Swinton and M. S. MacDonald, wounded. They received heavy fire from the embankments, and from an S.P. gun in Alpon, but killed a handful of Germans and took twenty prisoners. The tanks of the 2nd Welsh Guards followed the Battalion and did invaluable work in support, in spite of the fact that only three Troops had managed to cross before the laconic message "Nigel is crumbling" brought the news that the bridge was no longer usable.

The fact that the attack had started late prevented the clearing of the railway embankment before dark, but the darkness enabled the Battalion to get deeply dug in during the night, and thus protect themselves against the Germans who attempted to engage them from the railways when day came again. Right Flank managed to get a Bren under Sergeant McPhee on to the bank nearest them, and thus forstalled a group with a Spandau, bent on a similar mission. Major Cameron of G Company made good practice with a sniper's rifle, firing from a cow-byre, for any German who raised his head on the embankments was clearly silhouetted against the sky. The companies remained under close observation and heavy fire particularly from the direction of Alpon throughout that night and the next day, and most of the night of the 9th/10th as well. By day, they were able to give the 1st Coldstream the exact locations of the enemy and watch their tanks blow the posts to pieces. But in the meantime the Battalion was holding a front of about a mile with two exposed flanks, and the situation was "most interesting, but very noisy"—noisy even without the darkness round Right Flank being "made hideous with a dispute as to who had managed to get a sniper between the eyes". However, no counter-attack developed, and during the night a Bailey bridge was put across the Romer, and at four in the afternoon the 5th Coldstream passed through and "did an excellent attack, and we felt a lot safer when we had them in front of us. It was magnificently done; just like something out of the drill book". It was the beginning of the end of the Wesel pocket, and as the Germans fell back and the shelling diminished, more and more troops poured into the Battalion area,

Mar. 9

"all with the intention of advancing in various directions and chasing non-existent Germans". For, though they did not then realise it, *Veritable* was ended, and the enemy was retreating across the Rhine. In the meantime "every one of our Company positions had at least two other Battalion Headquarters with it. It made one realise what the Battalion had done in getting this bridgehead when one saw all the mass of stuff that came through." In addition to the bridgehead, another 110 prisoners from the 22nd and 24th Parachute Regiments had fallen to the Battalion, as well as "bags of loot"; the eggs and bacon found in the captured positions were particularly good. The Battalion's losses, in addition to those already mentioned, had been seven other ranks killed, and one missing, and thirty-three other ranks wounded.

Mar. 10   In the next afternoon the Battalion began slowly to move out of the chaos which had taken possession of its battlefield, and that night, after passing through Issum, Geldern, Kevelaer, Asperden, and Ottersum, it moved into comfortable billets in Heumen, about six miles south of Nijmegen, to prepare for the next and final phase. But the most important part of that preparation had already been achieved. It was a battalion that "had been blooded and had grown up" in those few crowded days. It was conscious of having done "extremely well" in difficult circumstances. The typical reaction of an experienced infantry officer was that "both attacks were nearly a prime bog, through no fault of the Battalion's, but both were made successes by the performances of everyone".[1]

(f) *X Company Disbanded*

Mar. 13   On the 13th it was learned that the 1st Battalion Welsh Guards, then billeted in Malden, a mile and a half away, was being sent— "poor things"—to Stobs, and that the Second Battalion was at last going to take its place fully in the Welsh Guards Battle Group.

X Company, which had come out of battle commanded by Lieutenant Leng, then but nineteen years old, were met at Malden by Major Hope, who broke to them the news of their impending disbandment. "I don't think any Commanding Officer has ever had a better Company than them under his command" wrote Lieutenant-Colonel C. H. R. Heber-Percy, who commanded the 1st Welsh Guards. The comradeship[2] between the Company and the Welsh men was an excellent augury for the future of the Scots/Welsh Group; it had been as successful a liaison as that between S Company and the 2nd

---

[1] The Second Battalion continued on p. 430.

[2] A comradeship which had been suitably emphasised by a tactful presentation on St. David's Day. The Company Runner had found leeks in an abandoned German garden, and at a little ceremony outside his Headquarters Captain Ritchie had presented these to the Welshmen attached to the Company.

Coldstream in Italy, and those who had served in the Company were proud to have carried the spirit of the Fourth Battalion into battle and on to victory. The Company paraded for the last time in front of the village school of Malden. Both General Adair, commanding the Division, and Brigadier Johnson, commanding the 32nd Guards Brigade, were present, and each addressed the Company in most complimentary terms. That evening there was a grand farewell dance given by the Welsh Guards and on the following morning two parties left Malden, one for absorption into the Second Battalion at Heumen, and the other, *via* Bourg Leopold, for leave and rest. X Company was at an end.

Mar. 17

Mar. 18

Later in the year there was a brief revival and reminder of this fine fighting unit. On the 28th July the survivors paraded in Brussels under the command of Major Steuart-Fothringham, who now wore the ribbon of a well-earned D.S.O.; with the Welsh Guards they took part in the parade at which the grateful city presented standards to the Division which had liberated them. A special plaque was presented to the Company, and the Welsh Guards accorded them the signal honour of providing the escort to the Standard presented to their Group. This escort was Sergeant Dannfald and Lance-Sergeant Forbes.

On the 21st Army Group's front all Germans had now withdrawn across the Rhine; preparations for the crossing went on apace. Both the Second and Third Battalions of the Regiment were to be involved in the next and final stage of the advance through Germany. The end was near, but there was to be bitter fighting before the "cease fire" sounded.

V. FROM THE RHINE TO THE BALTIC

The final break-out across the Rhine and the advance across the north German plain involved both the Second and Third Battalions. Paradoxically, in the early stage of the offensive the heavy Churchill tanks of the 6th Brigade had a role which would normally have been given to an Armoured Division, while the Guards Armoured Division found itself engaged in country badly cut up by water courses, and hardly suitable to that type of formation.

The planning of the offensive, which was christened *Plunder*, had been going on for many months. With the elimination of the German bridgehead round Wesel the enormous task of assembling the assault and follow-up formations began, and with them the guns which were to cover the assault and the supplies which were to sustain the subsequent advance. Bridges, ammunition, petrol, rations, and stores of all descriptions had to be brought up. The traffic on the roads was such that a strict discipline had to be maintained over unauthorised travellers. Right Flank of the Second Battalion was detailed for traffic-control duties under the XXX Corps over a large area south of Goch, and returned with many good stories and one unsolicited testimonial: "One sentry is convinced that he stopped the Field Marshal and told him to switch his light off, and Lance-Sergeant Graham had the pleasure of being told by an officer whom he stopped, 'I knew the Military Police were ——s, but you Guards are worse ——s'."

In the midst of these preparations the officers of the two Battalions found time to meet. The Third Battalion had moved into Kevelaer to join the rest of the 6th Brigade, and here in the Kölnerhof Hotel on March 20th they entertained the officers of the Second Battalion to dinner—"a tremendous success. We sat down sixty-four to dine and a good time was had by all. Twelve Pipers played round the table." All at that table were aware that great events were impending; obviously the Rhine was to be crossed, but as yet, save for Colonel Dunbar and his Squadron Leaders, they could only speculate. Four days later the assault went in.

(a) *The Bridgehead*

Mar. 15 On the 15th March Colonel Dunbar and the Squadron Leaders had left the Third Battalion under the thin disguise of "a visit to France
Mar. 18 to buy champagne"; on their return without so much as a cork, and with lips as tightly sealed as Mr. Baldwin's, the suspense was hardly
Mar. 22 to be borne. On the 22nd the period of Asquithian "wait and see" was ended; all officers were briefed in the details of the Battalion's plans. The Churchill tanks of the newly re-named 6th Guards Armoured Brigade were to be among the first British armour to cross the river.

Colonel Dunbar's party had in fact been to England and there had consorted with the 6th Airborne Division in the arrangements for *Varsity–Plunder*; *Varsity* being the landing of the airborne troops, and *Plunder* the subsequent breakout. As a prelude to *Varsity* the 15th Scottish and 51st Highland Divisions and the Commandos were
MAP XLI to make assault crossings of the river on the night of Friday the 23rd in the area of Xanten, Rees and Wesel respectively. When these bridgeheads had been established and the airborne troops had landed the Churchills would cross; they were to make sure that the Airborne Divisions were speedily relieved. For the lesson of Arnhem had been learnt, and this time the paratroops were to drop within easy range of the ground forces. This vital task, allotted in the planning stage six months before to the Guards Armoured Division, was now entrusted to the 6th Guards Armoured Brigade. The Battalion had long considered that its Churchills would prove a match for the Shermans of the Guards Armoured Division, not only in armour but

also in speed, and now they were to prove that this had been no braggart's boast.

On the morning of the 24th March all eyes watched the cloudless blue sky west of the Rhine fill with the vast armada of aircraft and gliders, which passed over to drop their loads beyond the great white smoke-screen which for the past weeks had obscured the left bank from prying German eyes. During the night the Commandos had captured Wesel, and the Scottish Divisions had gained their bridgeheads on the eastern bank. Impatiently the Battalion followed the progress of the airborne force, whose Divisional Headquarters was picked up on the wireless soon after they had landed; no hint came of the heavy casualties they were suffering. Mar. 24

During Sunday, the tanks moved down to the river bank near the village of Wardt, where they crossed that night on rafts in inky darkness; the wheeled vehicles following in the early hours of the morning over a bridge at Xanten, built with remarkable speed by the Sappers. As soon as they were ashore on the far bank, Left Flank (Major Mann) at once pushed on to the east for four miles and linked up with 6th Airborne Division in a clearing in the Dierfordter Wald. They were immediately placed in support of 6th Air Landing Brigade for an attack on a ridge north of Brünen, five miles farther on, but this came to nothing, as the tanks were hindered by a stream near Hamminkeln, and, unsupported, the infantry captured their objective. Mar. 25
Mar. 26

Battalion Headquarters had already moved with the Airborne Division's Headquarters to Köpenhof, and Right Flank (Lord Cathcart) and S Squadron (Major Farrell) were in the area of Hermannschot, one mile to the east. Before nightfall they were on the move once more across the stream below Hamminkeln, and morning found them formed up in a large field near Shöpping for a break out to the east, in support of the 3rd Parachute Brigade. This advance began, but no sooner had the leading tanks crossed the Issel south of Brünen than the whole plan was changed and the Squadrons halted where they were. A more daring stroke was to be their lot. Mar. 27

(b) *To Münster*

The fighting of the past four days had revealed that the enemy had no firm line or organised defensive system behind the Rhine, and it appeared that a bold and speedy thrust might well make a deep penetration into the heart of the country. The 6th Guards Armoured Brigade was therefore hastily reformed for a rapid advance to capture the city of Münster—fifty miles away along the main road from Wesel. It was ironic that this Brigade, which had once been considered so slow that it was not worth moving up to the front, was now to be asked to undertake a task more suited to an armoured division.

Brigadier Greenacre was to command this thrust to Münster and his force was raised to the status of a Brigade Group. The Battalion and the 4th Coldstream, the 515th Parachute Regiment of the 17th United States Airborne Division, the Reconnaissance Regiment of the British 3rd Infantry Division, the 6th Field Regiment R.A., and the 61st Medium Regiment R.A. made up the Brigade Group; the Grenadiers remained with the British airborne troops. The Brigade Group congregated on the Wesel–Münster road at Peddenburg during

Mar. 27 March 27th, where the Battalion joined them and picked up their infantry, the 2nd Battalion of the American Parachute Regiment, commanded by Lieutenant-Colonel A. C. Miller.

The advance began at three o'clock in the afternoon when the Reconnaissance Regiment led off down the main road to the east, followed by this powerful column, with Americans riding on every vehicle; it was, in reality, a small armoured division armed with heavy tanks.

Soon opposition was found at the village of Damm, and the Battalion passed through with S Squadron in the lead, leaving the Reconnaissance Regiment to clear up the trouble. Almost at once S.P. guns opened up on the leading Troop and knocked out the tank commanded by Sergeant Irwen, but for fear of getting entangled in the advance of a neighbouring American formation a halt was ordered for the whole Brigade. During this wait, which came as an unwelcome anti-climax

MAP XLIV after the flying start, the Battalion received orders to advance to Dorsten, a small but important communications centre some eight miles away on the northern fringe of the Ruhr. Their objectives were the bridges over the River Lippe. The Commanding Officer decided to advance by night, a somewhat daring venture, for it was to be the

Mar. 28 first night operation undertaken by the Brigade. At a quarter-to-one, in pitch darkness and a light fog, the column set off.

Right Flank led, preceded by a patrol of Honeys under Sergeant Fraser, to whom was entrusted the tricky task of finding the way. American paratroops were carried on each tank as a protection against bazooka parties, and hundreds of pairs of eyes peered into the murk as the column rumbled slowly through the blackness. All went well for about three miles until, in the village of Schermbeck, the Honeys encountered a road block which Captain Pember declared immovable. Sergeant Fraser was therefore sent off to find a way round it to the south and, with much assistance from Captain Pember and despite the thick mist, a route was eventually discovered. But this detour was over very soft ground; several tanks became bogged and had to be towed out. It was therefore not until three o'clock that the advance could be resumed. No more obstacles hindered progress and at six o'clock, as it was getting light, the column reached Dorsten and entered its northern outskirts. It was disappointed, for the bridges had been blown, and

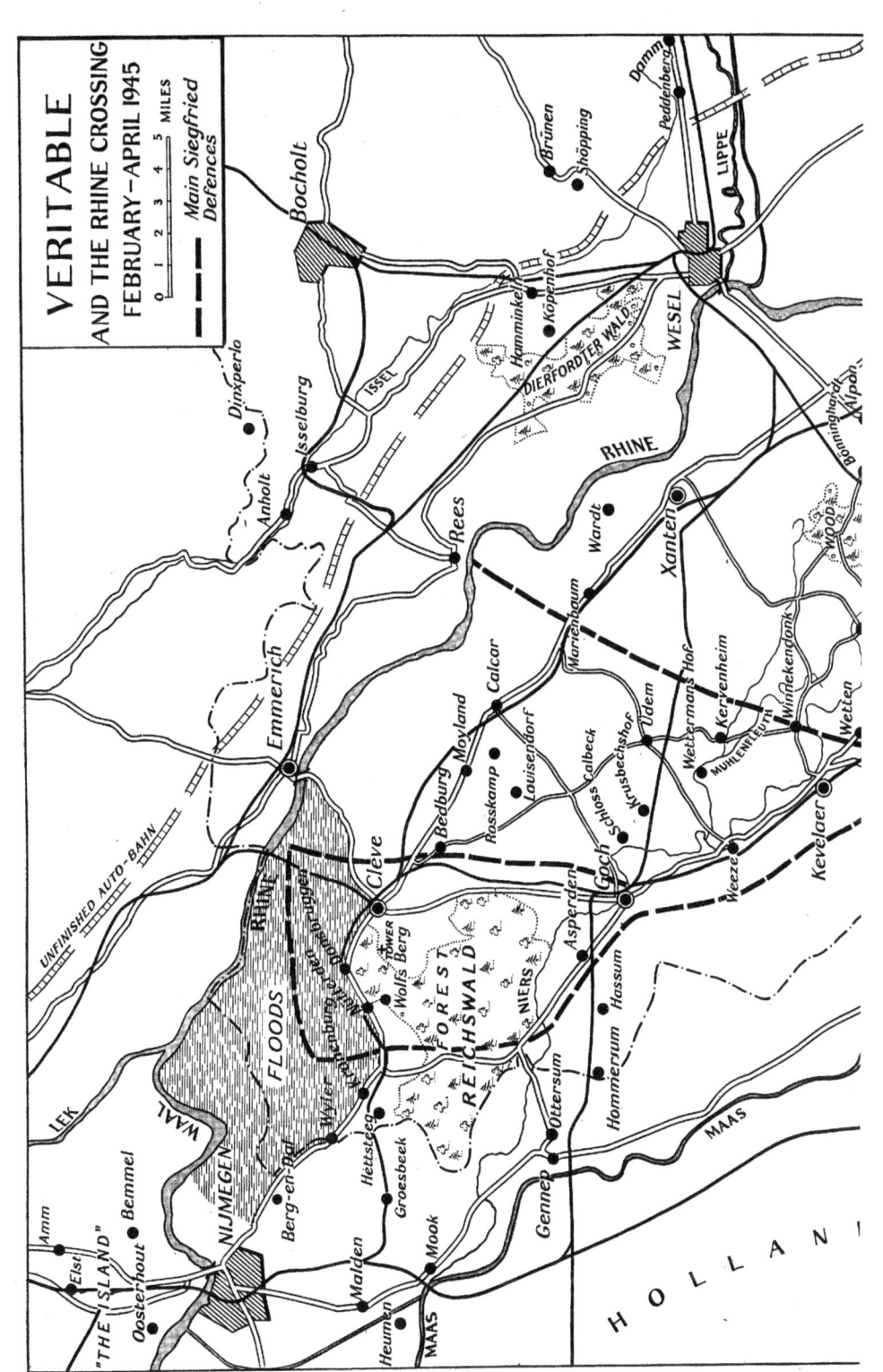

the enemy, who were more alert than had been hoped, put up a certain amount of resistance until dealt with by the Americans. Bazooka parties claimed one tank of Lieutenant A. K. McC. Elliott's Troop of Left Flank and killed its Commander, Sergeant Gordon; and a sniper dealt the Battalion one of its most grievous blows by killing Captain Pember while he was placing his Honeys on the outskirts of the town. An outstanding leader and commander of the Reconnaissance Troop, he had distinguished himself in almost every battle in which the Battalion had been engaged; it was he who had been mainly responsible for the success of the previous night's advance. Such an officer is not easy to replace.

Thanks to brisk work by the Americans, resistance in Dorsten ended at seven o'clock, and when a little later the American Corps Commander, Major-General Matthew B. Ridgeway,[1] arrived in the town, he sat on Colonel Dunbar's tank and wrote out a short despatch announcing that "the Scots Guards of the 6th Guards Armoured Brigade, commanded by Brigadier Greenacre, had captured the town of Dorsten". This message, duly encoded, was passed back to Second Army Headquarters; to the Battalion's surprise and delight it was broadcast by the B.B.C's one o'clock news from London only a few hours later. This was the first time that the security veil on the Brigade's activities had been lifted, and from then on gratifying publicity was frequent.

Now that Dorsten was secure, an attempt was made at about ten o'clock to find out if the bridge was still intact over the Lippe Canal at Hervest, some three miles to the east. Lieutenant Fearfield's Troop, and later the whole of Left Flank, went out to assist a company of parachutists in this mission, but there was so much opposition from enemy infantry with bazookas in the woods surrounding the village that it was found impossible to get up to the bridge, and at one o'clock the attack was called off.

Meanwhile the Coldstream Group had been passed through along the main road to the north and, while they fought their way towards Haltern, the Battalion remained in Dorsten, spending an uncomfortable night under airburst shelling at close range from across the river.

Next day, in response to a report that the Coldstream had met trouble from S.P. guns in the area of Lippramsdorf, five miles along the main road, an attack was organised to destroy them. S Squadron were to have carried out a supporting shoot, but the Americans did so well on their own, collecting 500 prisoners, that no fire was needed and the Battalion came up later in the morning to pick them up. The

Mar. 29

---

[1] Later to become United Nations Commander in Korea in 1951, Supreme Commander Allied Powers in Europe in 1952 and Chief of Staff, United States Army, in 1953.

whole column then pushed on at speed in the wake of the Coldstream, covering nearly twenty miles until they halted for the night just short of the ruins of Dülmen.

Mar. 30 Early next morning, as the Battalion was preparing to move on, a lone Messerschmitt flew low over the column, a rare event now, and a reminder of how free the advance had been from enemy air attack. By contrast, as the Battalion drove through Dülmen, they saw for the first time the effects of strategic bombing. The town had almost ceased to exist and the main road along which they drove was no more than a track across a desert of rubble.

Three miles beyond Dülmen the Battalion turned off to the left along a side road in order to by-pass the Coldstream, who were heavily engaged around the village of Buldern. After a further three miles, S Squadron in the lead bumped a fairly strong enemy position in open country, and were able to identify a tank and several well-sited S.P. guns. The Americans quickly dismounted and stalked the position on their feet; Right Flank worked round to the left, and in the face of this double threat the enemy were induced to withdraw, but their resistance had cost S Squadron one Honey and Right Flank two Churchills. Save for the glare of blazing corn ricks and nearby farm buildings set on fire in this action, it was now quite dark; the column harboured for the night. During the night the Americans patrolled into Nottuln, and found it clear of troops. Nottuln was the first undamaged inhabited place that the Battalion had met so far in Germany,

Mar. 31 and at dawn the column moved into the town and started to make themselves comfortable. But there was little time to enjoy the new billets, for the Coldstream had by now captured Appelhausen on the

SEE INSET main road, and soon after midday the Battalion was ordered on to
ON MAP Roxel, some nine miles away, and on the outskirts of Münster itself.
XLIV The simplest and most direct route to Roxel lay across the high ground of the Bauberge but this was clearly held by the enemy. Therefore the artillery distracted the attention of these Germans, and the tanks set off to make a detour to the south. By dusk Left Flank had brushed aside light opposition and the column found itself in the area of Boesensell with four miles still to go. The country was wooded and cut up by streams, and the patrols which had been sent out to test the route to Roxel were unable to send back their reports until a very late hour. A night march had been considered, but a halt was ordered from above in view of the uncertainty about the country ahead and to prevent any possible confusion with other American formations to the south.

April 1 Most of Easter Sunday was spent in Boesensell where tank crews and infantry were able to catch up on a little of the sleep they had lost during the last five days and nights of exhausting and almost continuous operations. By five in the evening they were on the move once more to the farm of Ahlebrandt, half a mile south of Roxel; from here it was planned to capture the village, push across the River Aa and then to seize the large Hermann Goering Barracks on the outskirts of Münster, less than a mile beyond. The attack was arranged for nine o'clock, when infantry, with S Squadron to support them, would seize Roxel cross-roads, secure the near bank of the Aa, and then cross to form a bridgehead. Right Flank and S were to cover the last phase; if the bridge was intact Left Flank were to pass through them and to join the Americans in their bridgehead on the east side. The capture of this bridge was essential, as the Battalion's bridgelayer had broken down, and one which was to be borrowed from the Coldstream had not yet arrived. Lieutenant H. L. C. Greig, who was hunting for it, became involved in a remarkable incident when he was fired upon quite close to his own Headquarters by a man who claimed, rather unconvincingly, to be a Canadian engineer erecting a road block.

The cross-roads were taken with ease, but when the tanks were moving up to cover the river crossing very accurate airburst shells caused some casualties to the infantry. But, still undaunted, the Americans pressed on over the Aa and, after a stiff fight in the dark, gained their bridgehead. But the bridge was blown, and since the ground was most unsuitable for a bridgelayer tank, Left Flank were reduced to supporting the bridgehead from the home side of the river. This was unsatisfactory, and, in order that the infantry should not be left on their own, S Squadron were ordered to move round the left flank and to cross the river by another bridge about two miles upstream. They would then link up with the bridgehead from the north.

Piloted by Lieutenant J. C. J. Shearer in a Honey, this column moved off at dawn and reached the bridge without incident. It was intact, and the tanks crossed the Aa, and began to double back towards the Americans at the destroyed bridge.

April 2

Lieutenant Shearer chose a route along the high ground above the river and led the way past Degener farm into a narrow lane bounded on the north by a small wood and on the south by an exceptionally deep ditch. This lane was pointing rather north of east, and so to regain the proper direction the column turned off it after only two hundred yards and, crossing the ditch, made for the woods round Nunning Hospital, over the fields to the south.

The rear Troop, commanded by Lieutenant T. E. P. Gilpin, which consisted of only two tanks together with some M.10 S.P. guns, was just turning right to cross this ditch when they were heavily shelled. Lieutenant Gilpin's tank was hit with A.P. shot as it sought to climb out of the ditch and would move no farther. Sergeant Robertson's tank behind burst into flames, and another hit killed its driver, Guardsman McBride. Both crews at once "baled out" and, with the American infantry whom they had been carrying, sought what cover they could. Lieutenant Gilpin now surveyed a tricky situation. The enemy, with what appeared to be several S.P. guns, were only just round the corner; his M.10's were useless to him because of the little wood; the Americans now turned out to be fresh and unorganised reinforcements going into battle for the first time; the Squadron had gone on; and, finally, he had no map. It was clearly foolhardy to follow the Squadron, and so, placing his seven remaining Guardsmen with the Americans to hold the small wood, Lieutenant Gilpin addressed himself to the task of turning the rest of the column round for withdrawal to the Aa. While this was going on, Lieutenant Shearer arrived on the scene with a map, and for the first time it was possible to send an accurate situation report over the air. Meanwhile Guardsmen Candlish and Gray, with an American, entirely on their own initiative and at great hazard, wormed their way up to the abandoned tanks and, getting inside without being observed, managed to retrieve all the Slidex codes and other documents of value. Some German signallers with a telephone, who had no doubt been responsible for the whole situation, were now found cowering in a ditch and, upon being questioned, declared that there were four S.P. guns up the road. This turned out to be a gross understatement, but it made little difference, as in the circumstances the M.10s could hardly take on even four S.P's, and so, under cover of Lieutenant Shearer's Besa fire, the column made its way back across the river to Battalion Headquarters.

At first the remainder of S Squadron had been sitting in the woods round Nunning Hospital, bewildered by what was happening to its tail; but, after Lieutenant Shearer had passed his wireless messages, they had continued on their way and had joined up with the American bridgehead at about ten o'clock.

The "four S.P. guns" which Lieutenant Gilpin had encountered were later found to be a German anti-aircraft site containing no less than nine 88's, three tanks, many smaller anti-aircraft guns and at least two hundred infantry. Why they had allowed the major part of S Squadron to pass them at less than three hundred yards range before shooting at the tail, is a mystery that was never solved.

During the early afternoon the original plan for the capture of the Goering Barracks was considerably modified. S Squadron, not Left Flank, were now to consolidate this area; the remainder of the Battalion were to undertake a wide left flanking movement through Nienberge, three miles to the north, where they were to join up with a new American Parachute Regiment, the 194th, and then to rush Münster from that side. The Coldstream were to enter the city from the south. The speed with which the attack had to be laid on left little time to worry over the dangers of assaulting such a large city with so little preparation. As it was the Battalion hardly had time to reach

Nienberge before the attack was due to start. Two things only were known, and neither was pleasant. First, the assault would have on its right flank the strong-point already encountered near Degener, and secondly the attack would be opposed, for so the German commander of Münster had assured a Coldstream officer who had visited him that morning with proposals for a surrender.

Pushing on to Nienberge the Flank Squadrons arrived to meet their new infantry with seven minutes in hand, and formed up astride the main road with Right Flank placed on the right—a diplomatic concession to troops unfamiliar with Scots Guards organisation! Despite the impossibility of making any kind of concerted plan, the attack went like clockwork. There was plenty of opposition from infantry and from anti-aircraft guns, and Right Flank used up its entire supply of smoke in an effort to screen off the known danger to their right. Before dark both Squadrons and their infantry were firmly established in the very heart of the city, and by the evening of the next day the occupation was complete.

April 3

S Squadron, followed by A and B Echelons, came up that morning, while the Americans, without tank support, cleared up the strongpoint near Degener. All major resistance in the area of Münster was at an end.

Münster was the largest German town that had fallen to British troops so far, and to reach it from the Rhine, a distance of over fifty miles, in eight days of constant fighting against a tenacious enemy defending his own soil, was, by any standards, remarkable. For Churchill tanks it was quite outstanding. The cost to the Battalion throughout this advance had also been gratifyingly low; it amounted to four killed, fifteen wounded and thirteen tanks destroyed; a small price indeed to pay for what they had achieved.

"The liaison with the Americans," wrote Colonel Dunbar, "has been quite splendid. They are some of the finest fighters I have ever met and we got on together like a house on fire." It was with real regret that the Battalion said goodbye to Colonel Miller and his Battalion of born soldiers on April 4th. Between them there had been complete mutual confidence and understanding. Their battle-cry, "Come on boys, let's go", remained a pleasant memory for those Scots Guardsmen who fought with them on the way to Münster.

The Battalion remained in Münster until April 6th. It was in an indescribable state from bombing and shelling, but a considerable portion of its 141,000 inhabitants seemed to have stayed behind and to have lived through its ordeal, and were now busily engaged in looting each other's houses. Prisoners flocked in by the thousand and rumour had it that villages and towns for miles ahead were putting out white flags. The Allies were penetrating deeper into Germany, and the Grenadiers with the 6th British Airborne Division were reported at Osnabrück, nearly thirty miles to the north-west.

April 6

Although many stragglers surrendered easily, formed bodies of the enemy were in no mood to give in—particularly where the allied force was small or militarily impotent. For on the day after the capture, while exploring some garages in the Battalion area, Lieutenants Fletcher and Runcie discovered to their joy a magnificent Delage staff-car, still flying the flag of a German Army Commander. Their ownership of this prize was, alas, short-lived, for news of their find reached Brigade Headquarters, and by evening they had been induced to present it to the Brigadier. The three of them took the car out to try its paces; after driving for a while in low gear around the battered streets, it was decided that they should go on a road really worthy of such a prize. Seeing a signpost pointing to Greven, a place which they knew to have been captured by the Grenadiers several days before, they turned the wheel in that direction and sped along behind an American jeep. Quite suddenly, shots rang out and the jeep in front went up in flames. Four bullets went through the Delage, slightly wounding Brigadier Greenacre, and in the next second the whole party was in the ditch and crawling at their best speed for home. More shots followed, and a burst of Spandau. Pausing to look back Lieutenant Fletcher observed a German on the roof of the Delage taking aim. However, the ending was a happy one, and after crawling nearly a quarter of a mile, the party broke into a run which soon subsided into a walk, and they eventually arrived at Brigade Headquarters a trifle late for dinner. The car was recovered little worse for its adventure on the following day.

At Münster the Third Battalion rested. Since the date of the 6th Brigade's crossing the Guards Armoured Division had also crossed the Rhine and, away to the north, the Second Battalion had been engaged in another armoured drive.[1]

(c) *The Celtic Group across the Rhine*

The Guards Armoured Division, which was included in the XXX Corps, did not cross the Rhine until five days after the initial assault. At Heumen, on the 24th, Lieutenant-Colonel Clowes had briefed all officers, warrant officers and sergeants of the Second Battalion in the details of Operation *Plunder*, and the Battalion had been placed at six hours' notice to move. In the excitement of the news from near at hand a letter from A. A. Beeshin, Military Contractor, Haifa, offering to deal with the Battalion's haircutting and laundry, was like a message from another world!

At midnight on the 28th the Battalion crossed the Brigade start-line south of Heumen, and before dawn, moving slowly by Ottersum, Goch, and Weeze, bivouaced at Udem. There it was placed at three

[1] The Third Battalion continued on p. 438.

hours' notice to move, and that afternoon the companies "married up" successfully with the squadrons of the 2nd Welsh Guards, "a bit surprising as we had never done it before". The Scots/Welsh Battle-Group, commanded by Lieutenant-Colonel J. C. Windsor Lewis, D.S.O., M.C., Welsh Guards, was in being. At half-past four, moving very slowly, it set off along the narrow road past Marienbaum. Night had fallen long before the river was reached. It lay there broad and dark, its ripples silver in the searchlights, and across it a pontoon bridge, which had taken the place of the peacetime ferry, led to the shattered houses of Rees on the far bank. By "London Bridge" the Battalion crossed the Rhine.

An hour later, after passing through the ruins of Rees, the Battalion harboured in a field about a mile south-east of Anholt. With the morning came the capture of Isselburg by the 5th Brigade, and soon afterwards the news that the Household Cavalry Regiment were three miles north of that town. At 1130 the Scots/Welsh Group moved off following the Coldstream on a centre line to the left of the 5th Brigade. Progress was very slow owing to the badness of the roads, but Dinxperlo on the Dutch frontier was reached by one o'clock and "*Plunder* in its wider sense had to be temporarily forgotten". After two-and-a-half hours the Brigade moved on again and, by-passing Borculo, leaguered for the night just north of Beltrum. But "why weren't we in front with our fast Cromwells instead of the Coldstream and their lumbering Shermans, speed was the point . . . it was maddening". The "lumbering Shermans" still led in the dawn start next day, but the route was through villages lined with rejoicing Dutchmen and "we tasted some of the joys of liberation which our fellows had experienced last summer". During the morning the Coldstream captured the approaches to Enschede and passed one squadron through the town, and in the afternoon the Scots/Welsh Group passed through them and received a great welcome in the crowded streets, losing its way in the process and suffering a certain amount of anxiety, for German tanks were still in and about the town. But nothing untoward occurred, though one Company Commander had some difficulty in explaining that it was not the Germans but his own tanks that he was trying to find, and, after Lieutenant H. Brooking Clark had liberated his mother-in-law, the Group found its way on to the road to Oldenzaal. Right Flank and its Squadron were diverted up the Hengelo road to the north-west, where it had a successful skirmish and captured a number of Germans. Almost immediately two leading tanks of the main body were knocked out by an anti-tank gun as they were trying to pass an aerodrome, and as the failing daylight made it impossible to locate the enemy, it was decided to leaguer by the road-side and attack next morning.

This was done, but the Germans who had been present in some

Mar. 29

MAP XLIV

Mar. 30

April 2

strength but not in good heart, had withdrawn leaving three anti-tank guns and much other equipment behind them, and by half-past ten the advance continued. A squadron of the Household Cavalry Regiment led the way and the Group was soon passing through Oldenzaal where the inhabitants "were almost crazy with joy and gave us their precious tea and tied strips of orange bunting to the vehicles. They looked like their countryside, neat and clean, but hungry." Eight miles ahead lay the German frontier. Just under three miles beyond it was the little town of Nordhorn, with narrow, tortuous streets and canals cutting across the line of advance. Nordhorn had to be taken before nightfall.

At the frontier the Household Cavalry were held up by a blown bridge and an S.P. gun. Another bridge was found and hurriedly strengthened, and Right Flank riding on a Squadron of tanks raced on to Nordhorn and successfully rushed the first bridge. The second bridge was blown but repairable. The third was not only effectively demolished as they arrived but was covered both by small arms and S.P. gunfire. The opposition was duly overcome, and a bridgehead formed, but the situation remained unattractive, for orders were to push on with all possible speed to Lingen twelve miles away and try to get a bridge over the Ems. Unless a means of getting the tanks and vehicles across the canal could be found, the Battalion was faced with an unsupported night march against an enemy whose strength and dispositions were wholly unbroken. But, "as always, the Household Cavalry turned up trumps", and another bridge was found, and the "Mad Night Dash" to the Ems was on.

It began half an hour before midnight in heavy rain. Right Flank led, riding on No. 2 Squadron's tanks, which clattered through the town with headlights blazing, and then roared out into the unknown dark. Left Flank and No. 3 Squadron followed, and then two platoons of F and half of No. 1 Squadron, before the bridge collapsed, leaving the rest of the Group and the two Commanding Officers on the wrong side of the canal. They sent the column on and sat back in some disgruntlement to listen to the result.

April 3

The column "got off to a fair start after a stray German had thrown a phosphorous grenade at one of the tanks, and then the Welshmen fairly went to town." The procedure was simple enough. The infantry defended the tanks against bazooka-men. The tanks blazed off with everything they had at point-blank range at any object that loomed up in the pitchy darkness. They found a lot of targets; groups of German soldiers walking or driving down the road towards Nordhorn; motor-cycles, carts, lorries laden with equipment; two S.P. guns being towed by a captured Sherman. "It must have been most terribly exciting," one of the officers wrote who had been stranded the wrong side of the bridge, "and also very nerve-racking for both tanks and infantry, but it was completely successful." How successful was seen next day: "As we neared Lingen the road was lined with charred bodies (like burnt wood) at the side of gutted vehicles. Horses and limbers littered the roadside in ghastly confusion. There were some knocked out 88s on trailers and I thought it must be the work of rocket-firing Typhoons, till I saw the fresh blood of the horses and that the trucks were still smouldering, showing it to be the work of the previous night."

Such an advance, with infantry and tanks working in the closest co-operation in the dark, could be claimed, fairly enough, as an innovation, and the Germans were taken completely by surprise: so much so that they failed to blow a bridge over an anti-tank ditch about halfway, and when the column reached the Ems the great river bridge was still intact. Lieutenant A. N. Mannock immediately led two sections of his Platoon across it, and the leading tanks were just about to follow when the enemy realised the position and blew the bridge. Lieutenant Mannock, whose left arm had been rendered useless by falling debris, then withdrew his two sections across the girders of the wrecked bridge under heavy Spandau fire, saving one of his men from drowning in the process, and rejoined his company which, with Left Flank behind it, took up positions along the bank.

It was a disappointing ending to a daring attempt but, although it had failed in its primary purpose, there was gratification in the knowledge that the advance had split the Divisions of the Parachute Corps by cutting their lines of retreat. And as to the liaison between Scots and Welsh there could no longer be any possibility of doubt. Major Raeburn, whose handling of Right Flank at Nordhorn, during the night dash, and under heavy shelling in the positions near the bridge throughout the 3rd, had been outstanding, was awarded the D.S.O.

At Lingen the Battalion welcomed back one of its veteran platoon commanders. Lieutenant W. A. Elliott, M.C., who had been wounded in March on the other side of the Rhine, had refused his sick leave. The staff and patients of the Convalescent Depot had thought him mad to do so, since leave at home was his for the asking. Two other officers had already been reprimanded by a Sub-Area Commander for "deserting" back to the Battalion.

By the evening of the 3rd the Group had reassembled, and that night the Coldstream in a brilliant action (in which Captain I. O. Liddell won the Victoria Cross) had seized intact another bridge farther to the north which the Household Cavalry had discovered. The 3rd Division attacked through this bridgehead, and the Coldstream then worked down between the river and the canal and had cleared down to the wrecked bridge by the evening. The Scots/Welsh Group suddenly found itself non-operational. But one more task remained, and a platoon of G Company under Lieutenant the Hon. A. R. H.

April 3

April 4

28—S.H.G.

Erskine, M.C., spent the night in the more than normally athletic employment of carrying rations and ammunition over the girders of the wrecked bridge.

April 5 The 5th was chiefly notable for an ineffective low-flying attack by fighters on the Group's rest positions along the Nordhorn–Lingen road at a moment when the Brens were being cleaned—a Company Commander with a razor in one hand and a pistol in the other was seen trying to deal with the situation—and by the 3rd Division clearing enough of the Lingen area to make a further advance possible. In the

April 6 morning of the 6th the Group set off once more, crossed the Coldstream bridge, and moved out along the axis road by the Forest of Lingen towards Furstenau, with the object of seizing a crossing over the Hase. F Company in the lead almost immediately ran into considerable opposition from mined road blocks, S.P. guns, and infantry in the woods, and in trying to clear it the Company Commander, Major Kemble, was killed by a burst of Spandau fire, and Lieutenant H. R. Tempest wounded. The impracticability of further advance along narrow roads through thickly wooded country was at once apparent. The two-day battle in and around Lingen had given the enemy, whose courageous resistance led to their being described as fanatical, ample time to prepare their defences, and the nature of the ground made the tanks an easy mark to concealed guns at close range. Colonel Windsor-Lewis therefore switched the line of advance to a more northerly axis in an attempt to reach Lengerich, and F Company was with some difficulty extricated.

The loss of Major Kemble was a particularly heavy blow; he had been wounded and awarded the Military Cross when seconded to the King's African Rifles in the East African campaign, and had again been wounded, losing the sight of one eye, while serving with the Battalion in North Africa. A great personality and leader of men, he was leading the Company in the attack when he was killed; he was succeeded in command by Captain J. S. Burn-Clerk-Rattray.

The new route was little better, and further opposition, during which the Group lost a tank and a carrier on mines, Lieutenant Mannock was wounded, and four enemy 88-mm. guns were knocked out by the Welsh tanks, led to the Group still being short of Lengerich at nightfall. The day had been typical of many there were to follow: a fighting withdrawal forcing frequent deployments and infantry assaults, in circumstances which allowed just enough mobility to warrant the use of tanks, over eighty of which were to be lost before the close of the campaign.

April 7 On the next day the Group, with infantry riding on all except the leading tanks, "set off down the road at 30 m.p.h. in the frozen sunshine of the early morning," firing into any likely cover as it went.

The procedure was very necessary, since the flanks were found to be exposed, and each hedge or clump of bushes might contain a bazooka. But it had the disadvantage of giving full warning of approach. About six miles were passed without incident, and then the advance was held up by a strong log road block outside Lengerich. A platoon of Right Flank under Lieutenant Elliott pushed forward, and was in the middle of removing it when our own guns, who apparently thought it still held by the Germans, began to put down a prolonged and accurate concentration. Some time elapsed before this could be stopped and a number of casualties were suffered, the killed including Lance-Sergeant W. Wilson who had been an outstanding character in the Battalion from the Libyan and Italian campaigns. With perfect timing the German parachutists waited until work was restarted on the great logs of the block, and then, having worked themselves into a favourable position, poured in heavy and accurate fire from close range, causing further casualties and reducing one section to two men. Another platoon of Right Flank under Lieutenant V. E. de S. C. de Soissons was then sent forward to attack the position from a flank while the first platoon gave covering fire, but with the exception of one section under another veteran of Africa and Italy, Lance-Sergeant G. White, was itself quickly held up by Spandau fire. In the meantime a Troop of tanks that had moved round into a supporting position was knocked out one by one by an S.P. gun firing from behind. Lance-Sergeant White, however, dashed on ahead of his section and charged the first post single-handed and killed the whole crew. He then, followed by his section which had never stopped moving, pressed on to attack a machine-gun post in some trees the other side of the road, but was himself killed before reaching it. He had killed two more Germans after leaving the first gun post, the second of them after he had been hit. As a result of his heroic action his platoon was able to continue its advance and occupy the position, where the Germans mostly surrendered.

The village of Lengerich still remained, and the opposition was such that a full-scale infantry attack had to be put in, preceded by an artillery and mortar bombardment and two doses of "lime juice" from Typhoons. Perhaps this was enough, or perhaps they had learned that the Coldstream group was pressing up from the south. At any rate there was no further opposition, and except for the collection of a few more prisoners and a little ineffective shelling, the village was occupied without further incident, and the Group leaguered with the knowledge that the Coldstream were about five miles to the east along the road to Berge. This action at Lengerich was typical of much of the later fighting and illustrates the difficulties with which the Group had to contend in close country against a skilled and determined enemy who made the best possible use of the ground.

April 8   The next day the Coldstream took the lead, and while they drove on and cleared Berge, the Group rested among its vehicles in the sunshine of a perfect spring day. All about it, unheard in the clangour of the previous day, was the incessant song of birds. But about it, too, were the shattered ruins of farmhouses, and in the byres the charred remains of animals tethered when the incendiaries had done their work. The automatic "brewing-up" of farmhouses on the line of advance by firing incendiaries into their thatch-lined roofs was regrettable, but necessary; any one of them might have concealed an ambush.

In the evening the Group moved off behind Brigade Headquarters. Tragedy immediately followed, for the two seconds-in-command, Major H. D. Tweedie of the Regiment and Major R. B. Hodgkinson, Welsh Guards, who had gone on ahead to reconnoitre positions for the night, took a wrong turning in Ohrte and ran into an ambush. Major Tweedie and a Belgian who had attached himself as an interpreter in the Brigade on the liberation of Brussels were killed outright by a bazooka, and Major Hodgkinson wounded. The Group leaguered that night in Ohrte and Berge and in the woods beside the road between them. Major Raeburn assumed the appointment of second-in-command of the Battalion.

April 9   At seven next morning the Group moved out along the Menslage road, passed through the Coldstream, and followed a squadron of Household Cavalry in the lead. After about three-and-a-half miles Left Flank was held up by a bazooka party. This was quickly dealt with, but a little farther on road blocks and blown bridges over a small stream and a canal covered by heavy machine-gun fire made further progress impossible. Another bridge over the canal, however, was found intact to the north, and this was seized and held by G Company and a squadron of the tanks. Lieutenant J. F. Cory-Wright of G Company was killed at this crossing—it was his first attack—as was Lieutenant R. A. Berridge of F Company, when out on a patrol the same night.

April 10   Next morning there was a sharp frost, and a fog, which reduced visibility to twenty yards, delayed the start. Opposition was very soon met in the lingering haze and continued throughout the day in the bright spring sunlight. "Road blocks were taken and by-passed, bridgeheads held, T.C.L.s left, tanks climbed on, tanks jumped from. The unromantic and relentless routine of an armoured column in a country thick with wood and waterways. It was an odd life. The Company/Squadron Groups that were not committed in a skirmish stayed on the road, smoked, sat in the sun, 'brewed up', and visited each other. Always they could hear the battle in front, sometimes could watch it. It was strange to be the spectator of your friends' imminent danger, perhaps their death, while you yourself were eating a fried egg." Casualties on the whole were light, though Lieutenant de Soissons was killed by a bazooka while standing beside a tank, and in the afternoon the outskirts of Menslage were reached. The Left Flank Group passed through G Company and, to the accompaniment of considerable shelling by both sides, quickly cleared the village, the greater part of which was burned down in the process. The Group leaguered that night among the smouldering houses, one platoon being somewhat disturbed by the sound of rifle shots from a burning cottage, but on investigation next morning it was found that the noise had been caused by the explosion of vast quantities of bottled peas. During the previous day heavy casualties had been inflicted on the enemy, and over a hundred and fifty prisoners taken.

The Coldstream passed through at dawn next day and attacked northwards and crossed the River Hase, and the Group settled down to two days' rest. The 5th Brigade passed through the Coldstream next day, and on the afternoon of the 13th the Group followed, moving very slowly behind Brigade Headquarters, to Lüsche, only to find that "the Coldstream Group had had a party with their rockets". The statement attributed to a German officer that the use of rockets was "not cricket" found some support among those who had hoped for comfortable billets, but in the end everyone managed to squeeze into the few surviving barns. That afternoon the Group moved into Cappeln and prepared for three or four days' complete rest. *April 11* *April 12* *April 13*

The rest, however, as usual, was to be interrupted and curtailed. The first thing was a joyful welcome from a large number of liberated Frenchmen, on whose information Captain Sir John Worsley-Taylor and Lieutenant the Master of Erskine arrested the local SS *Ortsgruppenführer* who, having burned all his papers and uniform, was hiding in civilian clothes. Next morning the Master of Erskine had to go off again, with a Troop of tanks, to make contact with 43rd Division in Cloppenburg as the Battalion had to be ready to counter-attack Cloppenburg if the enemy recaptured it. And then in the middle of the following afternoon came the news that the Brigade was to leave the XXX Corps and to move at first light to join the XII Corps, which in better country to the south had made faster progress and was now across the Weser. The remaining hours were spent in preparation, and the Battalion settled down to as much sleep as it could get. But such as it was, the rest was perfect enough, as the bright spring sunlight streamed down from a lark-filled sky. The countryside was unravaged by war. The surrounding beechwoods, lightly touched with green, seemed to isolate the pink-washed, timbered houses, with their green-painted woodwork, among the cowslip-studded meadows, from the world and from the war outside.[1] *April 14–15* *April 16* *April 17*

[1] The Second Battalion continued on p. 449.

(d) *The Churchills fight from Celle to Uelzen*

During the Second Battalion's advance to Cappeln the Third had rested, moved up, and entered into its final week of battle.

April 6
April 7
On April 6th the Battalion left Münster and moved to Hagen, six miles south of Osnabrück; next day they moved on again, in glorious spring weather, over the lovely Wiehen Gebirge, meeting on the way thousands of released Allied prisoners and escaped or liberated slave workers, all trudging westwards with their scanty belongings piled high on handcarts, prams and bicycles, or carried on their backs. A march of fifty-four miles brought the tanks to the village of Sapelloh, a few miles from the River Weser and on the northern fringe of the Forest of Minden. Here they rested until April 10th.

April 8–10

The Ruhr was now encircled, Hanover was in American hands, and the Russians were beginning their final advance on Berlin; the British Second Army was now directed north-eastward in a drive to defeat the German forces in Schleswig-Holstein, and to reach the Baltic. Far-seeing statesmen noted that this would also prevent any Russian penetration into Denmark. For this blow, which was to be struck across the broad Elbe and beyond to the very shores of the Baltic Sea, the 6th Guards Armoured Brigade reverted to the command of the Second Army, and the Third Battalion were able to end their fighting as they had begun it at Caumont, driving into battle with "Jocks" of the 15th Scottish Division riding on their tanks. No sooner had the Battalion joined the Division than orders were received to continue the advance towards the Baltic, passing on through the 6th Airborne Division to capture the towns of Celle and Uelzen.

In preparation for this long advance, for Uelzen was almost 120 miles from the Weser, the Battalion moved up with the 227th Brigade on the afternoon of 10th April to Wunstorf, a small town thirteen miles to the west of Hanover. Colonel Dunbar and his Squadron Leaders had gone on ahead to plan the advance, and that evening the orders were given out. The Brigade Group was to capture Celle. Left Flank was to lead, with S Squadron carrying the Gordons immediately behind them; Right Flank with the Argylls and the H.L.I. brought up the rear.

April 10

April 11
Wunstorf was left shortly after seven next morning, and by midday the column had covered twenty-five miles with only one blown bridge to impede it. An hour later, when the leading tanks had reached a point on a roundabout about eleven miles from Celle, they came up against another demolished bridge, which, this time, was defended. Lieutenant Fearfield's tank was hit by a bazooka which wounded two of his crew, and shells from an enemy S.P. gun fell on the cross-roads farther back and slightly wounded Lieutenant A. G. Laing, who

commanded the Reconnaissance Troop since Captain Pember's death, and Sergeant Jackson, who commanded the Churchill bridgelayer; Guardsman Copland, Lieutenant Laing's driver, was killed. Quickly Lieutenant Duffin's Troop moved up to the bridge and supported the Gordons across the river, after which a bridge was successfully laid, the enemy were dispersed, and the advance continued. Almost exactly the same thing occurred three miles farther on, but for the tanks the affair was bloodless; once again Lieutenant Duffin was able to cover the infantry across and then continue on himself.

The column was now only three miles from the outskirts of Celle, but since the light was fading a halt was called for replenishment. According to the prisoners picked up along the way—a motley collection mostly recruited with great haste from various schools and convalescent centres nearby—the town of Celle was full of hospitals containing, among others, a number of Allied prisoners of war, and for this reason the enemy had no intention of defending the place. This intelligence was so persistently repeated that it was decided to advance at midnight, in the hope that it might prove accurate. It was a very dark night, but this did not prevent Lieutenant Duffin, with the Gunner's O.P. tank, and two companies of Gordons clinging to his Churchills, from going off down the road at a spanking pace. Such good progress did he make that his Troop had reached the centre of the town before Right Flank and the H.L.I. (who should have passed through to take the lead before a town was entered) had time to catch up. The prisoners' stories had been correct and Celle was unoccupied, but all the main bridges over the River Aller had been expertly demolished, and the H.L.I. had to use assault boats to get themselves across into the eastern half of the town.

April 12
MAP XLII

The map showed two other bridges over the river and canal at Altencelle, two miles to the south, and the Reconnaissance Troop with a platoon of the Gordons raced off to see if they were all right. They were, and, charging across at top speed, the Honeys and their infantry captured both intact, killing a few very startled Germans on the way. This splendid *coup* called for a swift alteration in plan, and soon the whole column was redirected through Altencelle, though not without some anxiety, as the bridges were only rather inadequate wooden affairs, certainly not designed to carry a large column of Churchill tanks. The westerly one in particular swayed alarmingly every time a tank went over it, but in the end it proved to be the stronger of the two, for the other collapsed and fell into the canal while the leading Squadron, Right Flank, was in the process of going across. Luckily no tank went down with it, but the resulting traffic jam was appalling and could not be sorted out until the Engineers were able to bridge the canal with a Bailey. Those tanks of Right Flank which had got across now drove on northwards towards Lachtehausen, but here they found a bridge over a tributary of the Aller which clearly was not up to the weight of a Churchill and, since the bridgelayer tank was still behind the canal in Celle, there was nothing that they could do but

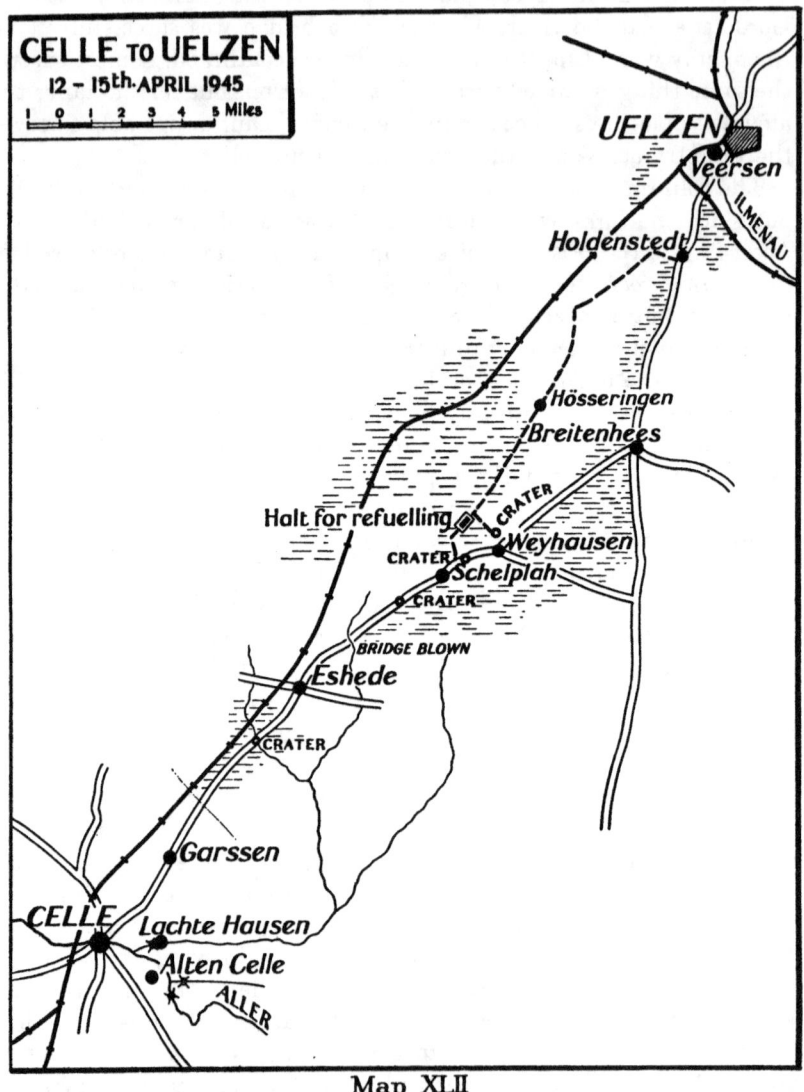

Map XLII

wait. Meanwhile their infantry went on alone and without opposition seized their objective, two miles on, the high ground at Garssen.

While Right Flank's tanks sat by their bridge unable to move either forward or back, the Sappers had been working like beavers, and by four o'clock had erected a Bailey bridge over the canal. The bridgelayer tank was sent up to span the gap at Lachtehausen. Now the whole route was open, and by eight o'clock Right Flank had joined the H.L.I. in the northern half of Celle, S Squadron joined the Argylls at Garssen, and the rest of the Battalion were safely over a second Bailey bridge in the centre of the town, and leaguered for the night in the eastern outskirts.

Celle had fallen to the Battalion without much of a fight, but the Coldstream advancing on it from the south had been held up at the village of Ramlingen, six miles away, by a party of some fifty German officer cadets, whose resistance was described as fanatical. In the fierce fight which ensued Lieutenant J. L. R. Currie, Scots Guards, commanding a Troop of the leading Coldstream Squadron, was killed by a sniper after his tank had been set on fire by a bazooka and the crew forced to bale out. He and Lieutenant Sir Thomas Buxton, Bt., had been lent to the Coldstream to help them out in their shortage of Troop Leaders.

April 13th, 1945, was a Friday, an inauspicious date on which to start the fifty-mile advance to Uelzen; and for once the superstitious were confirmed in their fears. The Brigade Group moved off from Celle at a quarter-to-nine with Right Flank and the H.L.I. in the lead, and since their route lay through thick forest in which the Germans would find it easy to delay them, a Coldstream Squadron moved on either flank. Seven miles along the road they met the first of many obstructions, but this was only a minor crater and was by-passed with comparative ease. Then a bridge beyond Eshede was found to be partially blown but passable; while the tanks were negotiating it, several youthful prisoners from disorganised Luftwaffe units were collected.

Ominous explosions were now heard from the north-east, clearly the work of demolition parties not far ahead, and the rate of advance was increased in an effort to overtake them. This was not to be, for after only a couple more miles a further crater was found in the road with small holes all round it, obviously intended for Teller mines, and the advance was halted while a bridgelayer came up to allow the tanks to cross. If the enemy was so pressed that he had not time to lay mines in holes that he had already dug, it seemed that there was hope of catching him yet, so Right Flank pushed on, brushing aside some bazooka and small arms opposition, only to be brought to a complete halt by another even larger crater, most cleverly sited with boggy ground on either side of the road where diversion was impossible. Expert Sapper advice confirmed that only a 40-foot Bailey bridge would answer here, and a party came forward to look at the place before bringing up their stores. As they were inspecting the hole, a time bomb, of which there were later discovered to be eight, exploded, destroying their vehicle, and wounding eleven of them as well as Lieutenant D. A. S. Gordon, Sergeant Aitken and Guardsman Walley

April 13

of Right Flank. Another route had to be found, and at six o'clock the column set off on a detour through the forest to the north, skilfully led by Lieutenant Macdonald-Buchanan. Map-reading his way along the narrow forest rides, after about a mile he came to the cross tracks where the column would have to turn right to rejoin the main road. As he arrived at the intersection he caught sight of a German busily engaged in blowing down trees across the track. This man was promptly shot, but unfortunately he had done his work well before he died, and there was more delay while the tanks negotiated these new obstructions. The light was now failing rapidly and, as dusk came on, the leading Troop plunged on towards the main road, only to find the way barred not far from their goal by a gigantic crater, quite the biggest yet encountered, and carefully sited to preclude any chance of a simple diversion.

It was now dark, Uelzen was still twenty miles ahead and more explosions warned of still bigger and better craters to come. Brigadier Colville, who commanded the 227th Brigade, therefore made a bold decision. The main axis up the road was to be abandoned, and instead the Brigade Group would advance by night through the unknown forest tracks on its left. This was something of a gamble, for although it might gain surprise and by-pass the enemy's obstructions, it was certain to present to the enemy a most vulnerable target, a narrow column moving in thick country in the dark. But the risk was taken, as it seemed likely that the enemy were in no state to make a concerted plan to interfere.

Meanwhile the tanks required fuel and the troops food, and a place was found in the ride where the eight hundred or so vehicles could treble-bank and still allow the supplies to come up; the advance was due to begin at one in the morning. There was excitement enough during the halt, for a large number of Germans in all types of transport came crashing down the track only to be captured on arrival. One, a despatch rider, was more determined than the rest; approaching from the rear he failed to stop when challenged and was pursued up the length of the column by a hail of revolver bullets until finally killed by the leading Troop.

April 14   An hour after midnight the column set off on its daring journey, led once again by Lieutenant Macdonald-Buchanan, who was slightly assisted in his unenviable task by some newly arrived searchlights which produced a little of "Monty's Moonlight" to illuminate the route. The pace was terrific. In order to keep up with the leading tanks those behind had to go flat out, with the branches whipping the faces of the tank commanders as they peered ahead into the dust and darkness, and brushing the infantry, who clung on for dear life, with their toes roasting on the hot engine covers. It was a wild drive, and the Germans who witnessed it from their hamlets on the way were far too astonished to take any action. Several enemy vehicles were encountered with their headlights blazing and a number were destroyed while the final score of prisoners after the night's advance amounted to about eight hundred. The Third Battalion had emulated the Second in their dash from Nordhorn to Lingen; a Scots Guards Group at night would indeed have been a formidable weapon.

Shortly after dawn Right Flank and the H.L.I. reached the original axis road at Holdenstedt, and as they did so red flares and Verey lights began to go up from the direction of Uelzen, now only four miles away. The element of surprise had evidently been lost. However, that was not the only disadvantage for, as at Estry the previous August, Uelzen was to be held by better troops than had recently been met by the Battalion; some Panzer Grenadiers had just come down from Denmark, and were fresh to the fight. Unaware of this reinforcement, the leading Troop dashed on up the main road, shooting up many enemy vehicles parked on the verges. Unfortunately, as they neared a level crossing only a mile from the town Sergeant Shearer despatched a hail of tracer at one lorry which was loaded with ammunition. The resulting barrier of flames and exploding shells was impenetrable, even to a Churchill, and Right Flank was forced to halt.

The enemy now reacted viciously and attacked the column from all sides at once. Infantry swarmed from the woods on the right; self-propelled multi-barrelled anti-aircraft guns appeared in the open country on the left, and, with rapid fire, destroyed at a blow all the H.L.I.'s carriers and many of their unarmoured vehicles. Some very confused fighting now followed, during which Right Flank managed to deploy off the road and overcome the guns without loss to themselves. While this battle raged on the outskirts of Uelzen, the remainder of the column was halted about Holdenstedt, for, so long as the ammunition lorry blazed, there was no hope of pushing on. A detour was obviously required, and at seven-fifteen Brigadier Colville despatched a company of the H.L.I. to clear a wood on the left of the road to the south-west of the suburb of Veersen. Right Flank, less Lieutenant Macdonald-Buchanan's Troop, which remained by the level crossing, supported this attack, but although prisoners soon began to come in, it was not a success and the infantry were eventually forced to withdraw. Soon afterwards the position was made worse by a German counter-attack by infantry and armoured cars which came in from the woods on the right and cut the main road behind the level crossing. This tricky situation continued for about an hour, until at half-past nine S Squadron was ordered forward to open the road, while at the same time the Argylls chased the enemy from out of the woods.

In the rear the situation was not clear, and considerable trouble was experienced from enemy troops who, having been over-run during the night, were now trying to get back to Uelzen. The Battalion

Headquarters tanks actually fired their guns during the morning for the first time, "Pepperpot" excluded, since leaving Normandy! Farther back still at B Echelon, the Quartermaster, Captain F. Morley, M.B.E., with RQMS Duff and Lance-Sergeant Todd, decided to drive forward in a jeep to visit the Battalion. Knowing nothing of the diversion through the forest, they motored up the main road, only to run straight into an enemy position which promptly took them prisoner, an incident which was witnessed from afar by the Argyll's carrier platoon, who were powerless to act for fear of shooting the wrong people. This was a major blow to the administration of the Battalion, for RSM Brown also was still away in hospital. Fortunately, Lieutenant J. M. Gow had just rejoined from hospital in England, and he assumed the Quartermaster's duties at this critical stage of the operation.

Left Flank relieved Right Flank in the level crossing area in the early afternoon, but enemy resistance showed no signs of weakening. If anything it was more determined, and it was decided that the infantry should hold firm in their positions astride the road until nightfall, when a full-scale attack would be mounted on Uelzen with artillery support. This was to begin about midnight, when the H.L.I. were to attack and seize the suburb of Veersen; Left Flank and the Gordons were to push down the main road beyond the level crossing into Uelzen itself, to clear the town and to capture the bridge over the River Ilmenau. Finally, if this bridge was gained intact, S Squadron, who in the early stages were to fire a "Pepperpot" into the woods to the north-west, were to pass through and across the river to link up with the Argylls, who should by then have captured the wooded high ground to the south of the town. As it turned out the attack on the right was the only part of this plan which met with success, for here the opposition was negligible; elsewhere it was savage.

April 15 The enemy held his ground with many Spandaus and S.P. guns, and these he sited skilfully to cover every approach, filling in the gaps with squads of determined Panzer Grenadiers. This defence soon held up Left Flank on the outskirts of Uelzen where they lost their leading tank to a bazooka, and Lieutenant J. M. Barne, M.C., was seriously wounded by small arms fire when "baling out". On the left, despite heavy casualties, the H.L.I. battled their way once again into the wood south of Veersen and before dawn had pushed their leading Companies into the edge of the village. Lieutenant H. Laing's Troop of Right Flank supported these forward Companies throughout the night, and the rest of the Squadron gave fire support from the south. Veersen was strongly held by infantry who, with half a dozen S.P. guns to support them, showed not the slightest disposition to withdraw. The fighting became extremely confused, the leading platoons of the H.L.I. and their supporting Churchills were cut off for some time, and in the midst of the confusion a German infantryman came up to Lieutenant Laing's tank and asked if he could be of any help. As it became light the remainder of Right Flank went forward, but their advance was quickly spotted by the enemy guns who knocked out Lieutenant Macdonald-Buchanan's tank—he was badly burned—and forced the others to proceed with considerable caution. Captain the Hon. W. H. C. J. R. Watson-Armstrong also received a severe wound at this juncture, and he and other casualties from both tanks and infantry received magnificent care and assistance from the Battalion Chaplain, the Rev. G. T. H. Reid, who, on this hectic morning in particular, seemed to be everywhere at once, always appearing where required most, and usually in the places of the greatest danger. He had done so in all the Battalion's previous battles.[1] Unable to get on very far in their tanks, Right Flank spent most of the morning in dismounted action, stalking the enemy S.P. guns with P.I.A.T.'s, and in this way they accounted for one, but the enemy quickly evened the score by knocking out an M.10 which Right Flank had with them in support.

In Uelzen, the fight was no less severe, nor progress any better. Lieutenant Duffin's Troop with the leading Gordons was forced to lie very low by rifle and Spandau fire directed at them from the shortest range. However, they achieved a slight measure of revenge about midday when a German staff car full of officers came dashing down the street towards them, having obviously taken the wrong road; it was blown to bits as it drew level with the leading tank.

The whole Brigade Group was now extremely tired, for this was the second day's fighting after the great night dash, and there had been little sleep before that. Plans were therefore made for the 46th Brigade to come forward to relieve them, and this was effected during the night, most of Left Flank getting out at ten o'clock, but Right Flank and Lieutenant Duffin's Troop of Left Flank were not relieved until five o'clock on the following morning, by which time they had been advancing and fighting without sleep for seventy-two hours on end which, in the noise, heat and buffeting of a tank, could reasonably be thought to exceed the permissible limit. The weary squadrons returned to the area behind Holdenstedt where they joined S Squadron, which, after firing its "Pepperpot", had been pulled back to defend this area from a possible German counter-attack which had been delivered with considerable force during the night against the Coldstream and Glasgow Highlanders at Stradensen, four miles to the south-east. Here for the next three days the Battalion rested while the 46th Brigade and the Coldstream fought on into Uelzen and eventually forced the enemy out of the town.

April 16

April 16–18

[1] The subsequent award of the Military Cross to Padre Reid gave the greatest pleasure to the whole Battalion.

April 19	On the 19th the Brigade Group moved on once more, in high spirits, heading for the River Elbe, with S Squadron and the Argylls in the lead. It turned out to be a long and tedious march, for although it was evident that the fighting could hardly last much longer, there were still bazooka parties in the woods and craters in the roads to cause apprehension and delay. By dark the column had reached the area of Scharmbeck, only five miles from the Elbe, having crossed the open Lüneberg Heath and passed through the town of Vastorf. On the
April 20	following day plans were made for an attack on Artlenburg, a village on the river bank almost opposite the town of Lauenburg but this did
April 21	not go in until one o'clock on the morning of the 21st, and in the very small engagement which resulted, Lieutenant H. Laing's Troop supported the H.L.I.; the remainder of Left Flank fired a "Pepperpot", but the policemen who formed the garrison soon decided to surrender, and the place was taken after little resistance. Two hundred prisoners went back to swell the already bursting cages in the rear.

The whole of 15th Scottish Division was now up to the Elbe, and the tanks were able to withdraw. The Battalion retraced its steps for about twenty miles to join the Grenadiers, who they had not seen for weeks, at Bevensen. Here they were released from the 227th Highland Brigade for the last time and an association which had begun in the Yorkshire moors, which had flourished at Caumont, and in the Bocage, which had grown stronger throughout the battles in the Low Countries and in Germany, now ended on the banks of the Elbe. This happy comradeship is commemorated by a fine set of silver-mounted pipes which the 227th Highland Brigade later presented to the Regiment.

(e) *To the Baltic*

April 22–30	At Bevensen the Third Battalion spent a week, during which a few officers took the opportunity of visiting the notorious Belsen Concentration Camp not far away and of witnessing its unspeakable horrors. They took with them a jeep full of chocolate and sweets for the unfortunate children there, and returned with the universal impression that "such horror, beyond description . . . must never be forgotten."
May 1	By now it was clear that the end was near at hand, and that there could be little further serious fighting. On 1st May the Brigade, now consisting of no more than the Scots Guards and Brigade Headquarters, received sudden orders to move on with 5th Division to effect a junction with the Russians on the Baltic. "We shall soon be in the caviar," wrote Colonel Dunbar, somewhat hopefully. The Battalion
May 2	crossed its last start line at the inconvenient hour of two o'clock in the morning and headed north. By eight they were in Lüneberg, stuck fast in an apparently hopeless traffic jam. While halted in the streets

of this ancient town the news came over the wireless of Hitler's death in Berlin, and this was joyfully communicated by the tank crews in "dog German" to the very glum inhabitants. This news, however, was the only bright spot in an otherwise miserable day, spent in edging forward from one jam to the next on the road down to the Elbe. Eventually, in the middle of the afternoon the Battalion reached the crossing at Artlenburg and once across the river was able to move at a better speed. But their troubles were not all over, for after about five miles a small bridge collapsed under the weight of the leading Squadron and a further delay was caused while a detour was found. At long last, after seventeen hours on the road, the column reached the village of Siebeneichen and stopped for the night. There they received the news of the other momentous events of the day; the 6th Airborne Division had reached the Baltic; the 11th Armoured Division had captured Lübeck, the Brigade's original objective; and whole enemy formations were "in the bag".

Early next morning Colonel Dunbar went off to Brigade Headquarters and returned with the news that, for the Third Battalion, the war in Europe was practically over, and that there was a reliable rumour to the effect that the enemy were already suing for an armistice. The larger proportion of the German Army facing the Western Allies had anticipated the surrender. A "swanner" who visited Lübeck observed that "all the way there and back the eye could see practically nothing but streams of grey-clad German soldiers flooding back in countless thousands to the cages, with every now and then a cheering Briton, liberated from a large camp which had been overrun by the Grenadiers". One "cheering Briton" was particularly enterprising; RQMS Duff succeeded at this time in getting out of a camp at Schwerin further to the east. His liberators refused him permission to go in search of the Battalion, but, nothing daunted, he "acquired" a motor-bicycle and driving day and night contrived to join the Battalion in time to be with them at the moment of victory.[1]

May 3

Eventually at nine o'clock on the evening of 4th May the long awaited official news of the surrender came over the air, and within ten minutes the noise in Siebeneichen was as loud as any battle. Besas, smoke-bombs, Sten guns and Verey pistols, all were loosed off at angles less than safe, until eventually the celebrations gravitated towards a hollow in the village green where an enormous bonfire appeared to start as if from spontaneous combustion, furniture, farm carts and even an old German lorry quickly feeding the flames.

May 4

After the spontaneous celebrations the official rejoicings were bound to fall a trifle flat, though one or two incidents rescued them from complete anti-climax. A notable horse race was held with "liberated" German mounts at which the firm of "Bruce and Stephenson, Turf

May 8

[1] RQMS Duff was unfortunately killed in a traffic accident in July 1945.

Accountants" lost a considerable sum of money, and on another occasion the second-in-command, Major Whitelaw, M.C., was compelled by the terms of a wager publicly to smoke his first cigar. On May 9th the Battalion went back to work, and moved to the Lütjenburg area near the sea coast where "the problems were legion". The war in Europe was over and occupation duties had begun.

One of the first duties undertaken was a somewhat unexpected one for a tank battalion. A boarding party from Right Flank captured a U-boat. Lieutenant Runcie had seen it lying at anchor about three-quarters of a mile off shore. There were no reinforcements immediately available, so he returned to the Squadron. Captain Graham quickly organised a boarding-party, consisting of Lieutenant Fletcher, Sergeant Shearer, Guardsmen Bogle and Pearson as bodyguards, and a German ex-naval cook, named Leo, who was at that time the Squadron's interpreter.

After a hair-raising drive, with Captain Graham at the wheel of the squadron's *Volkswagen*, the party arrived at a little fishing village. Two ancient fishermen were ordered to launch their craft and row out to the U-boat, which was evidently by this time aware that an attempt was to be made on her. Some of her crew could be discerned on deck, pointing and gesticulating. Spurred on by Leo, the two elderly oarsmen succeeded at last in getting alongside, and the party found itself faced with its first real problem—that of getting on board without falling into the water. The sides of the submarine stood up fairly high, they were rounded and slippery, and there was no ladder available. The difficulty was solved by the crew, who leant over and dragged the party to the comparative safety of the U-boat's deck. Here they were met by the Captain. He was inclined to be truculent, but nevertheless saluted and asked in intelligible English what was wanted. He was told that he and his crew were prisoners and would remain on board until the submarine could sail to Kiel; any member of the crew found ashore would be put in close arrest and probably shot. These terms appeared to relieve him, for he now dropped his arrogance and, after arranging for a supply of fresh water, offered a conducted tour of the ship. During this investigation one of the crew asked Guardsman Bogle where he had been born, and, on being told by Bogle that he came from a village near the coast of Ireland, smiled broadly and said that he knew the place quite well and that the crew had many friends there!

Finally, after a repeated warning to the Captain, the party once again negotiated the slippery plates and rowed back without further incident to the shore. The U-boat remained at anchor for some days and then slipped off to Kiel on the first stage, no doubt, of her last voyage—to Rockall Deep in the Atlantic.

The advance from the Rhine to the Baltic had been a hard fought

32. WITH THE UNITED STATES 17TH AIRBORNE DIVISION   A tank of S Squadron Headquarters in a Münster street; note that it mounts a 95-mm. close-support howitzer. The crew of the tank are, from left to right, SSM J. Todd, Captain W. P. Bull, Guardsmen A. Crawford, J. Wilkie and C. Albutt

ACROSS THE RHINE

33.   THROUGH THE WOODS TO UELZEN   A Third Battalion tank carrying infantry of the 227th Highland Brigade across a bridge laid between two craters in the ride. Leaning against the car on the right are Lieutenant-Colonel Dunbar and Brigadier Colville

34. ON THE WAY TO CUXHAVEN   Men of the Second Battalion, riding on a Cromwell tank of the 2nd (Armoured Reconnaissance) Battalion Welsh Guards, arrive at the German naval base, 7th May 1945. The German guides on the tanks appear apprehensive. On the left is Lieutenant C. M. Campbell

THE SURRENDER

35. LANDING ON HELIGOLAND   Men of Right Flank disembarking from a German minesweeper to the music of Corporal Crabbe, 11th May 1945. For the somewhat artificial circumstances in which this photograph was taken, see p. 461

one; it had cost fourteen tanks, and the sad, though light, loss of one officer and seven other ranks killed, and four officers and thirty wounded. In their final thrust the Second Battalion had had as stiff a time.¹

(f) *The Second Battalion's Fierce Finale*

The cause of the transfer of the Guards Armoured Division from the XXX Corps to the XII was that the operations in which they had been engaged had confined the 1st Parachute Army to the coastal area between Emden and Bremen and there was no longer a role for an armoured division in the XXX Corps. Instead, the intention was for the armour to threaten Bremen from the right flank while the infantry divisions of the XXX Corps attacked frontally. The XII Corps had already crossed the Weser and the Aller, and the 7th Armoured Division had broken through towards Soltau and was making for Hamburg.

Early on 17th April the Scots/Welsh Group moved off at the head of the Brigade. The drive was long and tedious, though under peace-time conditions. The route was by Emstek, then south-west on to the main road and down through Vechta to Diepholz and east through Sulingen to Nienburg, where the Weser was crossed; then north-east to Rethem and the crossing of the Aller, and on to Walsrode late in the evening. April 17

The stay at Walsrode was brief but restless. The 11th Hussars produced a convincing rumour that an SS Battalion was approaching from the north, and F Company, guarding the northern approaches, as the story grew in strength felt a sense of increasing nakedness. G Company in consequence was sent up in support, but no counter-attack developed to justify G Company being turned out of their billets, and their remarks about a wasted night's rest were commensurate with the occasion. But "that there had been enemy in the vicinity was proved when a Sergeant in F Company cleared his Sten gun at first light, which produced two bedraggled Marines from a neighbouring bush". It was to be found that there were in fact almost too many enemy north of Walsrode. April 18

At seven in the morning, the Group moved northwards out of Walsrode. F Company led and after about six miles came up against strong opposition from infantry with bazookas at the road junction at the southern end of the village of Kettenburg. An attempt was made to by-pass this and approach Visselhövede from the south-east, and the Left Flank Group met with stiff opposition in and around Ottingen, but successfully cleared it and pressed on to the railway about a mile to the north. In this attack Lieutenant Leng showed outstanding MAP XLIII

---

¹ The Third Battalion's history continues on p. 464. For its Order of Battle on May 18th, see p. 555.

29—S.G.H.

determination and skill, during which he commanded for a period two platoons and took sixty-three prisoners. Both the other Platoon commanders were wounded; Lieutenants P. W. P. Comyns, and J. Swinton who had rejoined after refusing sick leave only a few days previously. The latter lost his left leg below the knee, a wound exactly similar to that of his father, Brigadier (then Captain) A. H. C. Swinton, M.C., when serving with the same company of the same Battalion a week before the end of the Great War. To complete the parallel

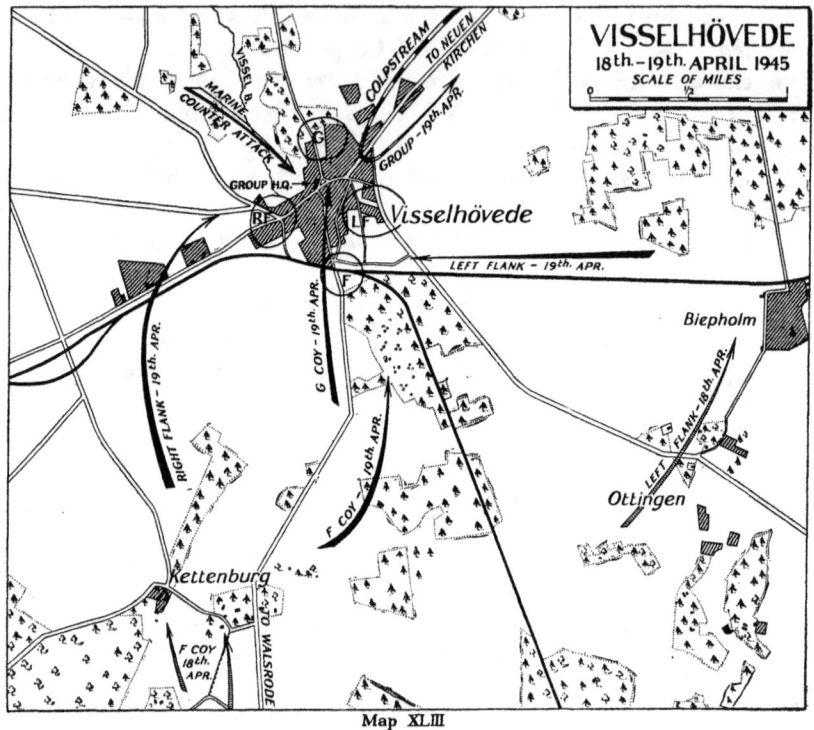

Map XLIII

Swinton *père* arrived home on Armistice Day 1918; Swinton *fils* on V.E. Day 1945!

In the meantime the Coldstream had captured Neuenkirchen and appeared to threaten Visselhovede from the north-east. But the remains of the 2nd Marine Division "had got plenty of fight left in them and a set piece attack on Kettenburg had to be staged." This attack, which took place during the afternoon, developed into a considerable battle, but eventually Kettenburg was cleared and the Group was able to push on towards Visselhövede. Two hundred and fifty prisoners had been taken, and a number of enemy killed. A platoon of F Company, engaged in a private battle on the left flank, took no prisoners. The resistance in front of them was to the death.

When it was overcome they rejoined the column already moving on towards Visselhövede. Right Flank and G Company Group led, and on approaching the outskirts of the town came under heavy fire from the woods on the right, and, owing to the rapidly approaching darkness and wireless communication difficulties, permission was received to postpone the attack. The events of the following day were to show the soundness of this decision. Left Flank was still engaged at the railway north of Ottingen. The men were tired after the fight for Kettenburg. The two forward companies, Right Flank and G, were down to about fifty men each, and F Company had suffered heavily in the attack on Kettenburg. In addition to those already mentioned, the Battalion's casualties during the advance on Visselhövede had been Lieutenants P. A. Winter of F Company and F. A. L. Waldron of Right Flank wounded, the latter seriously, and seven other ranks killed and twenty-six wounded. The capabilities of the tanks were doubtful as a support weapon in a strange town in the dark. Intelligence reports were that there were five Marine companies in and around the town. The Group withdrew and rested in a tight defensive position round Kettenburg, F Company first removing a party of Marines found sleeping in the position chosen for its Company Headquarters.

The attack on Visselhövede went in next morning, Right Flank Group on the left and G Company Group on the right. It was believed that the approach of the Coldstream from the north-east would cause the enemy to withdraw, but either they did not know of it or, as Marines, considered themselves part of the undefeated German Navy and as such so superior to the German Army that they preferred to stay. At any rate, the Coldstream, with whom Left Flank, advancing down the railway, made contact, moved into the northern end of the town, found nothing, and, as ordered, moved out again to continue the advance. *April 19*

In the meantime Right Flank (Captain H. L. St. V. Rose), advancing up the road on the tanks, came under heavy fire again from the woods on the right. Several casualties were suffered, including an outstanding soldier, Lance-Sergeant M. Ross, killed. By skilled use of tanks this opposition was by-passed, and the Group was able to push on and turn east along the railway and start clearing the suburbs; in this work Lance-Sergeant J. H. Foster greatly distinguished himself in command of a platoon which he had taken over that morning; he was awarded the D.C.M. G Company Group worked its way through to the north, and F Company, who had no tanks, cleared the woods on the right. This last entailed a considerable battle before they could get to grips, and when they "at last got in among them, they were pretty wild and taking no prisoners". In this fight, Lance-Sergeant T. Hogg, a stalwart of the former X Company, was mortally wounded.

Up to this point, though stiff opposition had to be overcome in places, all had gone according to plan and the two Battalion Headquarters were quickly installed in a hotel in the middle of the town. An Order Group had just been summoned when the 1st Battalion of the 7th Marine Grenadiers put in a sudden counter-attack from the woods to the west. A platoon of G Company was surrounded in the main street and had about a dozen casualties, who were tended by two German nurses in a cellar, and some tanks parked in the street were temporarily unable to move or fire for fear of hitting the infantry. Two mortar carriers went up in flames; the Headquarters hotel was surrounded, and its occupants were reduced to firing revolvers from the windows: the Commanding Officer's tank driver had a successful shoot from the scullery. But the few revolvers and rifles available could not have held out indefinitely, and "it was most unpleasant for some hours and really quite critical, but eventually law and order were restored". Wireless messages had been got through to the two Company/Squadron Groups in the town—"this caused a lot of amusement, as we thought Battalion H.Q. were just flapping because there were a few bullets flying around for once"—and Lieutenant the Hon. A. R. H. Erskine, M.C., of G Company from the north, and Lieutenant W. A. Elliott, M.C., of Right Flank from the west, started to work their way towards the hotel: these two were the only officers from the Italian campaign still in command of platoons. Lieutenant Elliott with the Welsh tanks eventually succeeded in forcing a way through. The leading tank had been hit by a bazooka which fortunately failed to explode, and Lieutenant Elliott's platoon had been reduced to fourteen men by the time they arrived and found the joint headquarters looking "like Gordon of Khartoum waiting for the natives, who were definitely hostile, to come in on them". They were barely in time. Another rush might have done it.

The G Company Platoon had been less fortunate; a burst of Spandau fire from a projecting window, when they were in a position of comparative safety between a tank and a wall, hit Lieutenant Erskine and every member of his Platoon Headquarters; Lieutenant Erskine died while being taken to the rear in an ambulance later in the day. He had earned the reputation of being "the best soldier in the Battalion", and "soldiering came naturally to him . . . he could concern himself therefore with the embellishments while we were struggling with the fundamentals".

The skill, suddenness and completeness of the Marines' infiltration and counter-attack were such that not only did none of the Company Commanders get through to the Order Group, but neither they nor anyone else knew that the enemy were back in the town at all. Captain Rose on his way from Right Flank had a particularly narrow escape, but got away with his driver, Guardsman W. L. Chadwick, D.C.M.; Corporal R. Perks, M.M., and Guardsman A. Connell, who were with them in the carrier, were killed. But Chadwick got his revenge later in the day when "a stray German" shot at him when he went back to look at his carrier: "You got pretty savage after all you had been through when someone tried to bump you off at that stage of the war."

The situation remained confused for some time, as "it was impossible to see any distance, difficult to move from house to house, and bullets seemed to come from the most unexpected directions". The tanks, too, had a busy time in the course of their zealous co-operation, and "about half their Besas ceased to function through having fired too much ammunition, and tanks could be seen shooting at individual Germans with their 17-pounder guns at about forty yards range". But once ascendancy had been gained the end came quickly, and the Germans "came pouring out of all the cellars". Four hundred prisoners were taken that day, a hundred of them within a hundred yards of Headquarters, and among them, only two houses away, Colonel Jordan and most of the Staff of the 5th Marine Panzer Grenadiers. "The fighting in and around Visselhövede was about the toughest we ever had", and in addition to those already mentioned the Battalion lost eight other ranks killed, and twenty-eight wounded.[1] Visselhövede had been a main defensive position covering the important road and rail junction of Rotenburg. The next stage could now begin. But the battle of Visselhövede, in so far as that was possible, had also drawn closer the bonds between the Scots and the Welsh: "the Welsh Guards are quite beyond praise, and we could not be better friends or work more closely together".

The next morning a battalion of the 71st Brigade took over in Visselhövede and it was possible to continue the advance on Rotenburg: doubtless much to the relief of the Coldstream, who had shown extreme impatience the day before over what, to them, had seemed an inexplicable delay. At any rate they immediately pushed on and captured Scheessel on the main road to the north-east of Rotenburg. The Scots/Welsh Group was less fortunate, and was held up by a blown bridge and cratered road and nebelwerfers near Hemslingen. A three-inch mortar detachment under Sergeant White claimed one of the nebelwerfers, but by that time dark was approaching, and the Group settled down to a night of pouring rain reminiscent, to the older hands, of Italy. However, "we had a laugh next morning when two Germans were produced out of an adjoining trench. They had been there all night, too terrified to move since Left Flank had captured the positions and the tanks had knocked out their 88-mms. the evening before". *April 20*

The losses the Battalion had suffered were partially made up by replacements; the most welcome of these was undoubtedly Major

[1] The wounded included Lieutenant A. R. C. Arbuthnot.

Steuart-Fothringham who had commanded the Battalion in Italy and X Company in this campaign; he assumed the appointment of second-in-command, and Major Raeburn went back to command Right Flank.

April 21   The Coldstream had little difficulty next day in reaching their start line for their attack on Rotenburg from the north-east, but the Scots/Welsh Group had another day of delays, this time caused by having to clear several small villages and deal with about seven hundred prisoners, two hundred and fifty of whom were rounded up by a platoon of G Company under Sergeant Graham working with a troop of tanks. "It was the sort of thing one had been reading about in the papers for the last fortnight as taking place everywhere, but this was our only experience". This was the ordinary Wehrmacht: it was plain that Visselhövede and the Marines had been the main defence of Rotenburg. F Company added to the bag that night when an absent-minded party of six Germans with a handcart under a disgruntled and booted and spurred artillery officer (he had been turned into an infantryman that morning) walked into their position.

April 22   Next morning the attack on Rotenburg went in. G Company led, followed by Left Flank, and after little more than an appearance of resistance "the prisoners came pouring out in every stage of undress and dejection". Soon F Company had passed through Left Flank, and Right Flank through F and on to the final objective. To the north the Coldstream were equally successful, and the whole town had fallen. Six hundred prisoners were taken that day, and G Company had the pleasure of finding in a military hospital one of its men who had been wounded and captured a fortnight before. The Battalion had two men wounded, both in Right Flank, when its leading section bumped a German platoon position from behind on the final objective. But an enthusiastic section of Wasps (flame-throwing carriers) who were anxious to try their new weapons, joined in, and there was no further trouble. Reconnaissance parties from a battalion of the 71st Brigade arrived in Rotenburg shortly afterwards and enabled the Group to move out "just as the nebelwerfers from the N.W. were getting a bit close". That night, having passed through Hemslingen and Scheessel, the Group leaguered with Battalion Headquarters at Sittensen, F Company and Left Flank in Kleine Meckelsen, and G Company and

April 23–24   Right Flank in Hamersem, and settled down to two days' rest and reorganisation. But the carrier and anti-tank platoons had to be sent out to occupy the bridge over the autobahn west of Sittensen so as to be able to give a good warning of any counter-attack from the south-west. For Corps Ems, with the 6th and 7th Parachute and the 15th Panzer Grenadiers Divisions compressed into the Cuxhaven peninsula, maintained an unbroken front. It seems to have had the idea of continuing the war in Norway, and two days before the Irish Guards had had to deal with a tank-supported counter-attack on the autobahn at

Elsdorf, about seven miles to the south-west. But there were no further developments, and Bremen fell to the 52nd, 53rd and 49th Divisions.

But no chances could be taken with Corps Ems, and the Group was ordered to advance westward from Zeven in order to cut off the 15th Panzer Grenadiers from the Parachutists, and also to liberate several large prisoner of war camps in the vicinity. The relief of these might well become an urgent humanitarian task should the organisation for feeding them collapse. Therefore at five in the morning of the 26th the Group moved out to the west, passing through the Coldstream at Zeven an hour later. Almost at once strong opposition was met at a road block covered by infantry and guns in the woods. An infantry gun was knocked out, but casualties were caused by an S.P. gun and Lieutenant W. H. Struthers was killed; it was his first battle. Farther to the south the G Company Group met with lighter opposition at Oldendorf, where it took thirty prisoners. Lieutenant G. C. W. Radcliffe was wounded in this stage of the advance. Eventually, the woods were cleared, but the Group came under heavy artillery fire at Badenstedt and had several more casualties. The advance was further held up by mines and blown bridges, but Ostertimke was reached and cleared by nightfall. During the day the Battalion had had thirty-six casualties, most of them from shellfire, four Guardsmen being killed. Three miles to the south-west, at Westertimke, about eight thousand prisoners of war, mostly Merchant Navy, were awaiting liberation, and that afternoon the Camp Commandant and a Naval Lieutenant brought a letter from General Rodht, commanding the 15th Panzer Grenadier Division, suggesting a ten-hour truce in which to evacuate them through our lines. The emissaries were passed back to Brigade, and the suggestion was not accepted: the Geneva Convention laid down that prisoners should not be moved, and the truce would have given General Rodht time to withdraw his disorganised troops.

April 25

April 26

Fortunately there has come down to us an account of the fighting written by General Rodht's staff; the Germans described the events of the 26th as follows:

> After strong preparation the enemy attacks Zeven with the main thrust to the south-west. As our fighting strength has decreased considerably we have to give up the wood near Zeven after only a few hours' fighting. A new defence line is built between Badenstedt and Badenmuhlen, but Badenstedt falls into enemy hands [*Right Flank*] after little resistance. Some of our tanks succeed in holding out east of Ostertimke.
>
> We learn constantly from wireless intercept about positions of enemy spearheads, successes of our artillery, and planning and preparations for coming attacks. . . . To-day brings a crisis for the Division. It is only due to the superb work of our wireless intercept

that we are able to prevent a break-through at several points and to build up again and again new centres of resistance wherever the enemy tries to break through our lines.

The Division sends envoys to arrange for the hand-over of Westertimke P.W. Camp. We follow, by wireless intercept, their way, as all enemy units report the arrival of these officers. We get to know by this means that the GOC of the Guards Armoured Division decided to retain these two officers as prisoners and that he ordered an attack by all available tanks for 1800 hrs. to break through to Westertimke. As the Bailey bridge north of Badenstedt was finished by 1700 hrs. the order to attack was already given at 1730 hrs. Immediately after we knew about this attack, all available units, especially anti-tank units, were regrouped accordingly. The Division considers it a matter of honour that this attack on Westertimke should not be allowed to succeed and the Camp should not be reached to-day by the enemy, as we wanted to hand over the Camp through our envoys. The Guards Armoured Division may have considered the sending of two officers to parley as a sign of our weakness. Divisional H.Q. moves into the area west of Kirchtimke to be able to prepare everything necessary for the defence of the spot.

After concentrated artillery fire the enemy attacks with tanks and armoured cars and infantry towards Ostertimke, but this attack is broken up by our own well-directed artillery fire and the enemy suffers heavy losses. [*An exaggeration*: F Company took Ostertimke by nightfall.] The enemy withdraws to Badenstedt. [*Not so: probably the impression given by the tanks "rallying back" at last light.*] This was the decisive success of the day. Our tank troops and artillery deserve the highest praise; they knew what was at stake.

The Germans' satisfaction that things were not worse seems to have distorted their view of the last few hours of fighting.

April 27 There remained one more obstacle before Westertimke, and at nine in the morning the Group moved forward to clear Kirchtimke. Left Flank was on the right and F Company on the left, and the attack was made through the fields on either side of the road. Strong supporting fire was given by the 4·2-inch mortars and artillery, but the German shelling and mortaring was exceptionally heavy and Lieutenant R. G. Mutter, Left Flank, who had brought back valuable information about enemy positions after a patrol the previous night, was killed by a shell in the village. Owing to the wetness of the ground the tanks and carriers followed down the road, but their progress was soon stopped by mines. Only two tanks got through before the road was blocked, and Lieutenant C. M. Campbell, Left Flank, who had been wounded by shell splinters early in the advance, found himself senior officer in

the village, for by this time there was only one other officer, Lieutenant
A. J. Sinclair, F Company; Lieutenant D. Mycock, also of F Company,
had been wounded. Campbell immediately took command of both
Companies, co-ordinated their attack, and took control of the two
tanks which was his only form of direct support, and when the two
Company Commanders arrived they found the companies consolidated, the village clear of snipers, and three S.P. guns destroyed, one
of them by a P.I.A.T. under Lieutenant Campbell's personal direction.
In the meantime further difficulties developed on the mined road.
After some time it was announced as clear, but after going about a
hundred yards the leading tank went up on a mine. Further investigation by the Engineers led to the disconcerting discovery that the
detectors were made ineffective by the magnetic quality of the cobble
stones, and that the mines were laid so deep that the leading tanks
could easily go over one, "packing down the earth on top of it so that
a later tank touched it off". Both Commanding Officers went over
mines unscathed and the vehicle following in their tracks went up.
However, it was necessary to press on, and "vehicles continued to get
blown up as we took the risk of continuing". The Welsh Guards lost
nine tanks that day, but by "about 6.30 p.m. we had pretty well
blown up all the mines and were able to push a squadron and G Company through to liberate the camp. They had a bit of a battle and some
terrific shelling, no casualties, and got 35 prisoners before they reached
the camp and finally liberated it, just as it got dark".[1]

Again we get a picture drawn from "the other side of the hill";
the staff of the enemy division described the day's events as follows:

> We leave only rearguards behind in Ostertimke.... The Divi-
> sion's task is to slow down the enemy's advance and to make a slow
> fighting withdrawal [*northwards*] and also to preserve our own
> strength. The enemy [*Left Flank and F*] starts a new attack and
> penetrates through Ostertimke into Kirchtimke, which he reaches
> at 1100 hrs. From Kirchtimke he advances to the North and NW.
> ... At 1800 hrs. a new enemy concentration is reported at Kirch-
> timke, and we direct all our artillery on to it.[2] At 1830 hrs. the
> enemy [*G Company*] attacks from Kirchtimke to the west. In the
> evening he succeeds in penetrating into the northern part of
> Westertimke after a stubborn battle.

The shelling that day was the heaviest experienced by the Battalion
in Germany and was continuous from dawn to dusk, and in the circumstances the casualties were amazingly light. In addition to those
already mentioned, sixteen other ranks were wounded and Guardsmen
Y. McKinney and G. McKeand were killed. The death of the latter on

---
[1] For his leadership that day Lieutenant-Colonel Clowes was awarded the D.S.O.
[2] A pencilled comment in the margin of the original document: "Too true!"

the mined road was particularly tragic. He had been with the Battalion continuously since 1940, in the Desert, in North Africa, and in Italy, and this was the last day the Battalion was in action.

April 28   The next day as many as could visited the prisoners' camp. "It was worth while enduring the shelling yesterday to see the joy of these liberated men. They were all in terrific form and had been treated very well indeed, especially just lately. They were absolutely amazed that we had been able to free them without any "overs" hitting them. There were about 8,000 of all sorts, a lot of Merchant Navy, and a few Guardsmen who were captured recently, but none of ours." Nearby, in another camp, were a large number of Polish and Russian slaves, who "had been most interested spectators of the previous day's battle, and were loud in their praise of our care to see that no shells landed in their camp". That afternoon Major-General Adair visited the Battalion and expressed high appreciation of the work it had done. In the evening the leading Troops of the 51st Division, coming up from the

April 29   south, reached the Brigade, and the next day the Group entered upon the last stages of its advance through Germany. It was a "peace-time" move, for both the Coldstream and Brigade Headquarters were in front of the Group, and that night, after moving by Zeven, Heeslingen and Wangersen, it was billeted in and around Ahrenswohlde and Bokel. The Group formed an impressive convoy, for each Company/Squadron Group was at least twice its normal length owing to the number of German vehicles that had been acquired. "Particularly useful additions were mobile field cookers which were towed behind cooking trucks of each company. These were a tremendous boon to companies engaged in a long advance with tanks who were, of course, practically self-contained. Cookers used to come steaming up the road whenever the column halted and feed as many vehicles as possible before it moved on again. In this way we got many hot meals on days when we should certainly have had none relying on our own equipment."

Since crossing the Rhine but a month before the Battalion had suffered very heavy casualties in the Rifle Companies. No less than seventeen subaltern officers commanding the twelve platoons had been hit, six of them being killed. There had been two hundred and twenty other rank casualties of which forty-five were fatal; Right

April 30   Flank alone had suffered ninety-five. On the 30th F Company was temporarily disbanded, its platoons being distributed among the other companies, and the Group moved on to Harsefeld, and the G Company Group, after the blown bridge over the Aue had been repaired, went on to billets in Issendorf. By that time the Household Cavalry, closely followed by the Coldstream, were well on their way to Stade, where the little River Schwinge sinks to the flat banks of the Elbe.

May 1   On 1st May the Group moved forward again, passed through the

Coldstream, and occupied Wiepenkathen and Haddorf and the high ground in front of them preparatory to attacking the water-ringed town of Stade from the west. But the Household Cavalry did all that was necessary, and that evening the Group moved in without firing a shot and found the town completely undamaged and full of comfortable billets.

May 2–3 The most important incident of the next two days was the gift of nine hundred bottles of excellent claret by a "kind Swiss lady", who preferred that they should not go to the Russians. The Gunners had a successful shoot at a ship anchored at extreme range in the Elbe, and through field-glasses the crew could be seen jumping overboard. With the help of the medium machine-guns they also shot up a village whence the Hitler Youth had fired on a Household Cavalry patrol.

May 4 The 4th began to be notable from the number of German soldiers who gave themselves up in the town and were lodged in the gaol under the Regimental Police. In the afternoon the rumours of negotiations between the German Army in the north and Field Marshal Montgomery began to circulate, and just before nine the B.B.C.

May 5 announced that the unconditional surrender would take place at eight next morning. Celebrations immediately broke out in each Mess and were nicely under way when a civilian brought in two German officers representing the Artillery between the Elbe and the Oste who asked for a three days' truce so that they could find out from the higher command whether they could surrender with honour. In the meantime, it seemed, they were prepared to resist for about a week. They were sent back to Division: "We couldn't have cared less."

Just before eight o'clock on the 5th "when most of us were going to bed" the 25-pounder battery attached to the Group fired a *Feu de Joie*. It lasted for one minute, during which one gun got off seventeen rounds, and included every kind of coloured smoke: "It looked like the fireworks on Coronation Day, only it felt better." Two hours later the Battalion was on Drill Parade, the last to be attended by Captain M. J. Fitzherbert-Brockholes as Adjutant before handing over to Captain A. N. B. Ritchie. He had been Adjutant since before the crossing of the Garigliano.

May 6 On the 6th the Group held a joint Church Parade and Thanksgiving Service in the old Lutheran church in Stade. The Battalion's Chaplain, the Reverend D. H. Whiteford, took part and the names of all those who had lost their lives since the crossing of the Rhine were read out by the two Commanding Officers. Then the Last Post was sounded from outside the great west door, and, as its last echoes ceased, from beside the altar Pipe-Major Bain began "The Flowers of the Forest", and, while he marched slowly down the church and out into the bright spring sunshine and the notes faded into the distance and were hushed, thoughts turned to the long line of graves that marked where the

Scots Guards—and, in particular, the Second Battalion—had been: "The flowers of the forest, that fought aye the foremost. . . ."

VI. THE OCCUPATION

The fighting was at an end, but there were problems in plenty to occupy the victors. Germany was devastated, both materially and morally. There were the German armed forces to be disbanded. The Russians' westward advance had driven before it hordes of Germans who had no desire to return to their homes to brave the rigours of an occupation from the east. In Germany were millions of slaves, voluntary workers and prisoners of war from all over Europe, and of these, also, there were many who showed little eagerness to return to the eastern countries. These "Displaced Persons" had little or no work to occupy them, and the baser elements soon began to take a violent revenge on the population, terrorising them with murder and predatory raids. The sole effective authority was the Allied Control Commission, supported by the victorious army—an army which, its tasks fulfilled, was soon to melt away as the vast majority of its soldiers returned to their homes and peaceful pursuits.

The Second Battalion

The Second Battalion's first task was to take part in *Eclipse*, the code name given to the measures for the disbandment of the German forces. To this end, with the Welsh Guards tanks they moved up to the naval base of Cuxhaven on the afternoon of the 7th May. Strict instructions were given to the German commanders to ensure that all mines on the roads were lifted, but, to make assurance doubly sure, the German Naval officer in command of Cuxhaven was placed in the leading tank; after a few miles he was replaced by one more junior in rank, though more for the relief of his nerves than from respect of his dignity.

"Just outside Cuxhaven Left Flank mounted on the tanks of No. 3 Squadron, and then, with the help of guides, made straight for the docks and took up position covering the harbour, where several German submarines, destroyers, "E-boats" and tankers were berthed. All of us were impressed by the efficiency of the local Germans in carrying out our orders. The streets were empty, guides were ready, and the German Admiral, General and Chief Policeman were waiting outside Dolles Hotel for the arrival of the Commanding Officer and Captain Lawford, R.N. A long conference followed, at which the Chief Policeman was the star turn. He was everyone's caricature of a German official. He had a shaved, square head, he clicked his heels and gave his answers with the utmost efficiency. He was incredible. It was a pity that he tripped over the carpet and fell flat on his face when he left!

SECOND BATTALION

"VE Day was an anti-climax. The outward and visible signs of victory were none; there was no rejoicing. Rather we were concerned with the galling sight of surly submariners leaning over the dockyard wall talking to their attractive girl-friends, the prevention of massacre by the recently liberated slave workers, and the thought that to-morrow we would return to the normal routine of soldiering in the Marine Barracks."

May 8

From these excellent barracks were mounted the first of a multitude of guards and escorts, the tedious features of which were common to the whole army. Apart from the satisfaction of escorting the officers of the 7th German Parachute Division to the Westertimke prisoner of war camp, so recently freed by the Battalion, and the interest aroused by visits to U-boats in the harbour, the main event of the stay at Cuxhaven was a unique expedition by Right Flank.

Until 1890 the island of Heligoland had been the sole relic of the Hanoverian patrimony enjoyed by the British Crown; in that year it had been ceded to Germany in exchange for Zanzibar. For the next thirty years, the island, now heavily fortified, stood sentry over the German North Sea ports. In 1920, in accordance with the terms of the Treaty of Versailles, the Kaiser's fortifications were totally destroyed[1] —only to be reconstructed, more formidable than ever, with the advent of German rearmament and the Nazis. During the war massive bomb-proof shelters for small submarines and coastal craft had been added. In the latter part of the conflict the island had frequently been attacked by Bomber Command, and in the last months it had suffered a thousand-bomber raid.

On the 11th May Right Flank, accompanied by Colonel Clowes and other officers, sailed from Cuxhaven in four enemy minesweepers, manned by their German crews, to accept the surrender of Heligoland. Off the mouth of the Elbe the little flotilla was met by a German motor gunboat, carrying Rear-Admiral Muirhead-Gould, R.N., Flag-Officer, Germany. On arrival off the island the garrison could be seen already embarked in the ships which were to take them to the mainland.

> The Naval party, together with our more important military representatives, disembarked immediately to conduct the formalities of surrender, whilst Right Flank moved more slowly. Blankets, compo boxes, cookers and all the paraphernalia of a Company on the move had to be carried up and down gangways and on to the bombed remains of the quay. It was a very warm day and very warm work, and in the opinion of an official photographer who appeared in the middle of the operation this was not the right way

[1] See *A Sailor's Odyssey*, Admiral of the Fleet Viscount Cunningham of Hyndhope, K.T., who supervised the demolitions.

for the Guards to arrive in Heligoland. CSM Lindsay was drawn aside, the stage arrangements planned, and, as soon as the last of the kit was ashore, five chosen Guardsmen returned to the ship. Then with caps straight, heads held high, and Piper Crabbe in the lead, the landing of the Scots Guards was recorded for posterity.[1]

The Company was quartered in the naval barracks, which, for all its air-raid damage, provided greater amenities than those which British troops are accustomed to find in corresponding quarters at home. The task of supervising the evacuation of all save some two hundred essential workmen was quickly put in hand, but there was ample time for exploration.

The damage done by the bombing was stupendous:

> There were craters every 50 yards, guns flung from their mountings, all houses were heaps of rubble, red powdery dust everywhere, and when one looked into the shallow waters of the sea from the edge of the cliffs the sea bottom was seen to be cratered like the surface of the Moon. There was one particular battery of 12-inch guns which became a showpiece to be pointed out to all our visitors, where monstrous weapons weighing many tons, solidly mounted in steel and concrete, had been lifted bodily from their mountings and turned upside down.

The submarine shelter also had been heavily bombed, and its roof hit in more than a dozen places, but no bomb had been of sufficient weight to penetrate the great thickness of concrete to the workshops and submarines below.

But the explorers found better things: the vast subterranean galleries proved to be veritable "Aladdin's Caves":

> Torpedo rooms, ration stores, wine stores, offices, power stations, hospitals, all are contained there. We were seized by the spirit of exploration, though perhaps we resembled gold prospectors more than explorers; at any rate we could certainly be said to have struck it rich. A room containing five thousand bottles of beer was the first strike, and as the news spread the gold rush was on. Throughout the next week, at all hours of the day, one saw Guardsmen stumbling along the cratered road and disappearing into the cliff like rabbits into a warren, or returning heavy-laden with an astonishing assortment of trophies. One met them in remote passages beneath the farthest batteries; one stumbled into them in the dark on the numerous occasions when the lighting failed. Cameras were discovered, then bottles of Benedictine, then a cache of peaches and hams; shot-guns and soap, field-glasses and frozen beef, tinned

[1] See photograph No. 35.

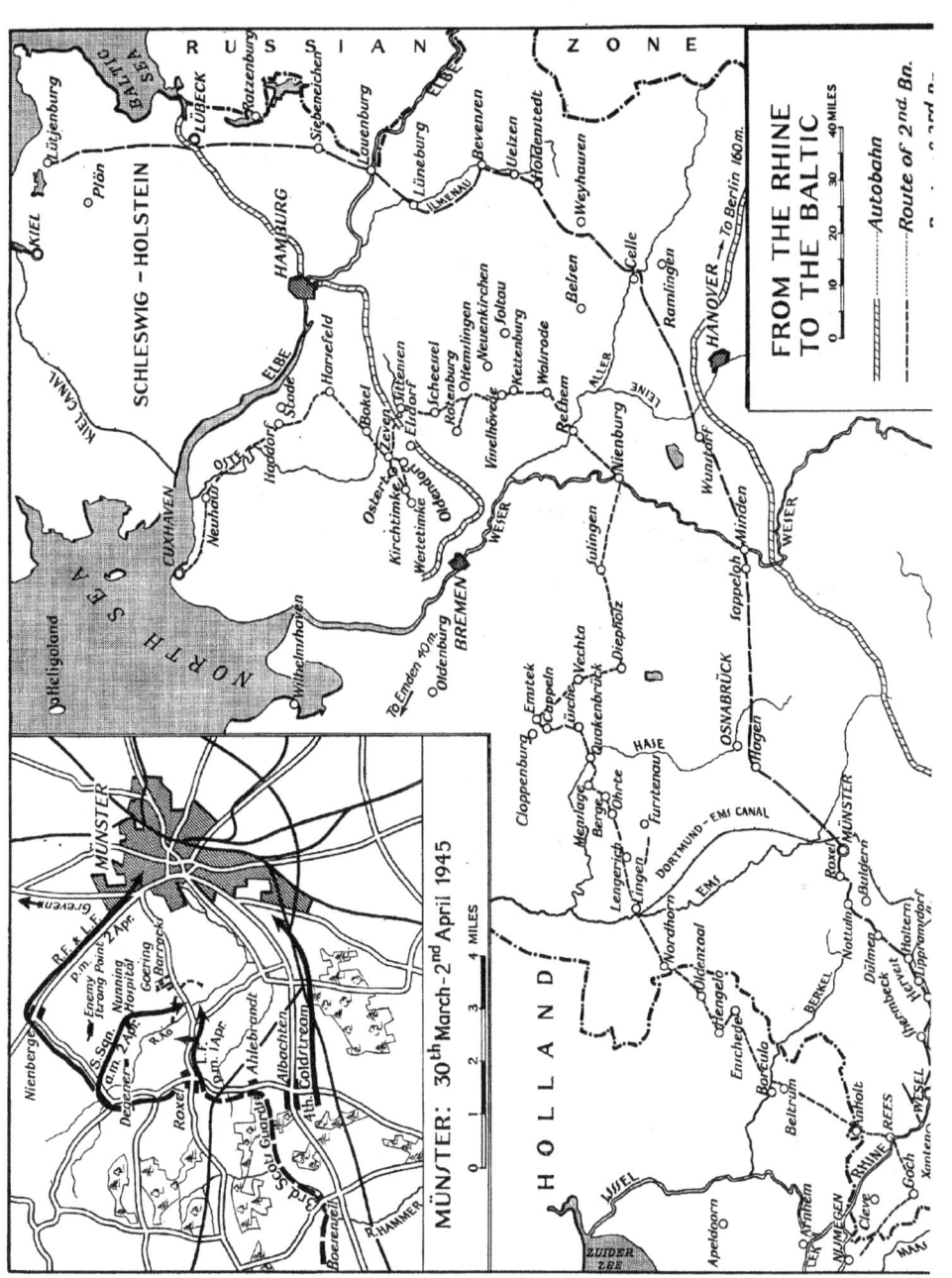

asparagus and toy trains, all were carried out into the hot May sunshine and displayed to spur the treasure-seekers to further efforts. The fame of our gold-mine spread until it reached the Battalion at Cuxhaven, and the morning R-boat which brought our mail and rations also brought visitors from other Companies, and in the evening few of them returned empty-handed.

The Battalion's Doctor, Captain A. J. Briggs, acquired some magnificent equipment for his Aid Post, while the Quartermaster, Captain Greenwood, made a methodical search for things likely to be of use to the Battalion. It was fitting that he should be there, for he had given sterling service to the Battalion throughout the war, both as a Warrant Officer and as Quartermaster. It was indeed his just deserts that he should be at "the Battalion's Ultima Thule, its farthest point in the advance; and it was not unfitting that the road which had started from Cairo, through the desert where a jerrycan of water found by a brewed-up truck was untold riches, through Italy where a discarded Luger [pistol] was a major discovery, should end in such a place."

On the 17th May Right Flank returned to the mainland, and two days later the Battalion moved south to Rotenburg to take over the supervision of a camp containing eight thousand Russian prisoners of war, with Poles and Czechs besides; during the next month these began to depart to their respective countries. The Battalion sent a detachment to take part in the "Farewell to Armour" parade on the nearby aerodrome, and then, on the 17th June, moved away to the south-west and back to the Rhine, to take up billets in the pleasant little country town of Wipperfürth, twenty miles north-east of Cologne.

At Wipperfürth began the humdrum tasks of occupation and the dissolution consequent on demobilisation. Guards on ammunition trains, searches for Black Marketeers, hunts for marauding Russians, war-crimes trials, road-blocks and escorts constituted the staple activities of the Battalion. Left Flank had the most interesting task when they went to Berlin for the period of the Potsdam conference between the heads of the Allied Governments, and at which they found the guards on the residence of the successive Prime Ministers, Mr. Churchill and Mr. Attlee. Variety was provided for F and G Companies in September when they went on long company "marches" (in their transport!) to Lake Constance on the Swiss frontier. In November the Colours were brought out from home. A large draft from the Third Battalion early in the New Year heralded that Battalion's impending disbandment, and the winter ended with a move to another province of Germany.

1946

In March the Guards Division, now commanded by Major-General J. C. O. Marriott, formerly of the Regiment, moved back to Schleswig-Holstein; the Second Battalion went to excellent barracks at Wandsbek, six miles north-east of Hamburg. Here they found that many of the problems of prisoners of war and displaced persons had been solved since they were last in the neighbourhood, but nevertheless on arrival there were heavy daily guards, to provide which were required no less than twenty-five Sergeants, twenty-five Lance-Corporals and 150 Guardsmen. Hamburg had its compensations, for it was one of the chief centres of the Army of Occupation, and welfare services and entertainments were on a lavish scale. At the end of May Colonel Clowes gave up command of the Battalion which he had led through its final campaign, and was succeeded by Lieutenant-Colonel the Viscount Dalrymple, M.B.E., who came from the Training Battalion on its disbandment. In June the Colour Party went to London to take part in the Victory March; it consisted of Lieutenants A. J. Sinclair and D. G. Thomas carrying the King's and Regimental Colours respectively, and CQMS R. Balcombe, M.M., as escort. The autumn marked the end of the Battalion's service in Germany, and on December 4th it arrived at Victoria Barracks, Windsor, to begin its first tour of peacetime duty at home since 1938.

The Third Battalion

The postwar duties of the Third Battalion were very similar to those of the Second; the prisoners of war, the displaced persons and the problems of military government were theirs as well. The area round Kiel contained many hundreds of thousands of persons who had fled from East Prussia by sea in the largest "combined operation" ever carried out by the German Navy. May was spent sorting out these refugees, and in despatching to their homes those who had homes to go to. In the middle of the month the Battalion moved south to the neighbourhood of Plön, where "the Plöner See gave much scope for sailing and for gathering gulls' eggs, and, in general, our stay in Schleswig was one of the pleasantest periods of our time overseas."

June saw the end of the Battalion's armoured life. On the 2nd a Troop of highly burnished Churchills took part in a parade through Kiel in honour of His Majesty's Birthday; within a week, in operation *Swan-Song*, the Honey and Churchill tanks had rumbled away for the last time to an ignoble tank-park on the autobahn near Hamburg, where they were left to rust—before being beaten, it must be supposed, into tractors. In consequence it was a dismounted detachment which took part in the memorable "Farewell to Armour" Parade on Rotenburg airfield, at which Field Marshal Sir Bernard Montgomery gave sound reasons for the return of the Foot Guards to their traditional role. "We need you in the infantry; we need your high standards, your great efficiency in all matters, and your old traditions of duty and service. All these are needed to help weld the infantry arm into a firm and solid basis on which to build." The Regimental

36. HIS ROYAL HIGHNESS HENRY, DUKE OF GLOUCESTER

25th Colonel of the Regiment

On 23rd March 1943 at Sutton Veny, the Duke of Gloucester presented pennants to all Squadron Troop and Tank Commanders of the Third Battalion. He is seen handing a pennant to Lieutenan C. R. T. Cunningham, of S Squadron. Others in the photograph are, from left to right, Sergean C. Greig, Lieutenant-Colonel Kindersley, Commanding Officer; Major Dunbar, Second-in Command; Captain P. E. G. Balfour; and Captain Whigham, Adjutant

37. THE SECOND BATTALION AT POTSDAM Mr. Churchill leads President Truma down the ranks of a Guard of Honour mounted by Left Flank, 18th May 1945

38. GENERAL EISENHOWER WITH THE THIRD BATTALION   At Helmond on 30th November 1944 the Supreme Commander is seen inspecting the crew of a Churchill bridge-layer attached to Headquarter Squadron. Also in the photograph are, from left to right, Major Sir Charles Maclean, Lieutenant-Colonel Dunbar, Lieutenant C. J. O. Clarke, and SSM Pickard

39. GENERAL ALEXANDER WITH THE SCOTS GUARDS   On the 3rd June 1944 a Guard of Honour was mounted in Naples by the Scots Guards Company of the Reinforcement Depot when General Sir Harold Alexander opened a new rest camp. He is seen inspecting the Guard accompanied by Captain J. V. Rob

Band, with that of the Welsh Guards, provided the music for the parade. Later the Field Marshal paid a special visit to the 6th Brigade, and presented to many officers and men the ribbons of the decorations they had won. The same night the officers entertained to dinner ten of their opposite numbers of the 227th (Highland) Brigade, in support of which most of their triumphs had been achieved. On the 16th the Battalion set out for the Rhineland to join the Guards Division; while on the way the designation "Tank" was dropped from the Battalion's title, and it was as infantry that General Sir Miles Dempsey, commanding the 2nd Army, inspected them at Euskirchen. In his address the General said that the 6th Brigade had been rewarded for its hard and unobtrusive work west of the Rhine by the success of its rapid and spectacular advance into the heart of Germany. Yet he would always think of it first and foremost as the tank brigade which broke through at Caumont, for after that battle he considered that victory was only a question of time.

The Battalion now settled down in an area fifteen miles west of Cologne; at first Battalion Headquarters were at Horrem, and later at Gymnich, with the Companies dispersed in the nearby villages. But on the 1st November the Battalion concentrated at Weiden, a northern suburb of Cologne, where it was quartered in comfortable villas, with the Officers' Mess in the sumptuous residence of a coal magnate. In the Rhineland there was still the dreary round of guards and escorts, though these gradually lessened as the Control Commission built up its own police force. The veterans began to leave on demobilisation, to be replaced by many fresh young faces from home. A fourth company, T, was formed, and the Battalion finally assumed the correct appearance of an infantry unit when an edict went forth on the 15th October putting an end to the wearing of the tankman's black beret, a practice some nostalgic individualists were vainly trying to perpetuate. At the same time Colonel Dunbar left to take command of the First Battalion in Italy; he had commanded the Third Battalion for nearly two and a half years, and had led them with distinction in all their battles. Since the death of Major Cuthbert at Caumont, Colonel Dunbar had been the only pre-war Regular officer in the Battalion. His going marked the beginning of the Battalion's dissolution. Lieutenant-Colonel P. Steuart-Fothringham, D.S.O., succeeded to the command, and it was under him that a parade was held early in November to receive the Colours from home; these Colours,[1] the oldest pair in use in the Brigade of Guards, were trooped down the ranks of the Companies for all to see and honour.

By the New Year, as the larger demobilisation Groups began to depart, the demands of the two Regular Battalions became more pressing. In dismal weather on the 9th February a farewell parade

1946

[1] See p. 324.

was held in the garden of the Officers' Mess, at which General Marriott addressed the Battalion, recalled its past services, and wished all ranks God-speed. "As to your conduct in battle," said General Marriott, "your Brigade Commander, Brigadier Douglas Greenacre, knows far more than I do . . . but I believe he looked upon you as the best Battalion in his Brigade—a Brigade which never failed the Infantry to whom it was allotted, and especially the 15th Scottish Division who have shown by various presentations their great appreciation of your worth."

The Battalions now dispersed. Eight officers, Regimental Sergeant-Major Brown and 330 other ranks went to Trieste and the First Battalion; to the Second Battalion at Wipperfürth went four officers and 120 rank and file. By the end of the month a bare hundred were left at Weiden, but this hundred included the Battalion's famous football team, captained by Guardsman Girdwood; it had beaten the Second Battalion in an epic final for the championship of the Guards Division, and it penetrated to the semi-finals of the Army Championships. In the scramble between the Regular Battalions for the assets of the Third, none was more coveted than these eleven men! The military duties were all handed over to Belgian troops, and on the 28th February the Third Battalion was formally disbanded.

Let another extract from Field Marshal Montgomery's Rotenburg speech serve as the epitaph of this Battalion—and of all the Battalions which fought in the Guards Armoured Division and in the 6th Guards Tank Brigade.

"I want to say, here and now, that in the sphere of armoured warfare the Guards have set a standard that it will be difficult for those that come after to reach.

"In modern war it is the co-operation of all arms, armoured and unarmoured, that wins the battle, and in this respect you have achieved great results. In fact, the Guards have shown that whatever they are asked to do—whatever they take on—they do well: maintaining always the highest standards and giving a lead to all others. You will long be remembered for your prowess in armoured war."

PART VII

Post-War: 1945–1955

WHEREAS the two regular battalions of the Regiment had returned from Germany to London within six months of the Armistice of 1918, after the Second World War it was, as we have seen, not until December 1946 that the Second Battalion (Lord Dalrymple) arrived at Windsor from Hamburg, and not until October 1947 that the First Battalion (Lieutenant-Colonel Clowes) arrived at Pirbright Camp from Italy. Owing to their absence abroad the battalions had had little part in the Victory celebrations, the Colours of the Second Battalion only being carried in the procession of 1946.

Meanwhile Colonel G. F. Johnson, D.S.O., had been presiding over the demobilisation of the Regiment. At the end of hostilities in Europe there had been some 450 officers and 8,000 men in the uniform of the Scots Guards. Two years later these numbers were reduced to less than half, and by May 1948 the strength had fallen to 116 officers and as few as 1,303 men. The main reason for the weakness in the ranks was the sluggishness of voluntary recruiting in the new conditions of full employment and rapidly rising wages. In the immediate post-war years it was hoped that the Regiment would be able to rely, as before, on volunteers alone; the initial engagement was to be for five years with the Colours and seven with the Reserve. Despite the lowering of the height standard to five feet eight inches the response was less than half that required, and soon young men called up under the National Service Acts were arriving at the Depot to fill the ranks. These conscripts served with the Colours for periods varying between one and two years, after which they were liable for annual training periods of a fortnight for the next five years. Despite the variations in the length of Colour service—variations in which it was sometimes easier to detect the calls of political expediency rather than the demands of military logic—the proportion of National Servicemen has remained fairly constant. Since 1948 between one-sixth and one-quarter of the officers and men serving with the Colours at any given moment joined the Regiment under the compulsion of the National Service Acts.

The weak numbers of 1948 were not required to complete the establishments of two standard infantry battalions. After the withdrawal from India and Burma it was expected that the peace-time need for infantry would be much reduced. In the country's straitened financial circumstances many regular battalions were placed in "suspended animation"; in fact, nearly all regiments of the line were reduced to a single battalion each. In the Brigade of Guards the cuts were less drastic. The ten pre-1939 battalions were retained, but of these three were to become static training units, one at Pirbright, one at Aldershot, and one in Germany. The duties of the Training Battalion at Pirbright were assigned to the First Battalion of the Regiment, and on the 1st April 1948 it assumed its new guise, only Battalion Headquarters, Headquarter Company and Right Flank being composed of Scots Guardsmen. The other companies were found from other regiments of the Brigade, for to Pirbright were to come all the recruits from the Depot to undergo their training in minor tactics before joining the active battalions of their respective regiments. Not until April 1951 was the First Battalion to be reformed on a normal establishment.

Thus the Regiment started on what was hoped would be a new era of tranquillity with one full battalion, the Second, and one of little more than cadre strength. But, of course, behind these two battalions stood a huge reserve of trained veterans who were still liable to recall in an emergency.

Outside the Regiment there had come into being a new unit which attracted many Scots Guardsmen. This was No. 1 Guards Independent Company, the Parachute Regiment. Originally it had been hoped that the Brigade would be able to maintain a full battalion of parachutists, but soon, with the reduction of the Airborne Division to a single brigade, only this "Pathfinder" Company was to be drawn from the Household Brigade. Since its inception the Company has frequently been commanded by an officer of the Regiment.

A steady peace-time routine comparable to that of the 'twenties and 'thirties can hardly be said to have evolved in the turbulent years immediately following 1945. More than half the battalions of the Brigade were stationed abroad in Germany or in the Middle East, there was no Aldershot Tattoo, there were no manœuvres at home. A new feature of life in the London District was the frequent and erratic calls upon the Guardsmen to intervene in unofficial strikes which threatened essential supplies and services. Both battalions became familiar with the Smithfield meat-market and with the vast wilderness of quays, warehouses and cranes which make up the London docks. But portents of stability began to appear. In June 1947 the ceremony on the Horseguards Parade in honour of the King's Birthday was revived: in that year the troops were still dressed in khaki battledress, the parade being commanded by Lord Dalrymple, and the Second Battalion finding the two Guards on the left of the line. Later in the year, still in khaki and envious of the newly returned glory of the Household Cavalry, the same battalion lined the streets for the marriage of the then Princess Elizabeth; on that day the King's Guard found by the Second Battalion was mounted as a Guard of Honour in the Quadrangle of Buckingham Palace.

Sport, too, began to revive, and two former officers of the Regiment gained the highest prizes in their particular spheres. Major R. C. Petre rode *Lovely Cottage* to win the Grand National of 1946, and Major F. G. Mann, D.S.O., M.C., led the winning English cricket team which toured South Africa in the winter of 1948–49. The Regiment's former pre-eminence in Bayonet Fencing was reasserted as Drill-Sergeant J. Rioch and others fought a victorious progress through many team and individual competitions.

An innovation in July 1947 was the visit of the Second Battalion to Scotland. Based upon Eastfield Camp, Dreghorn, Edinburgh, the Battalion made every effort to show itself in as many parts of Scotland as possible. The visit opened in the capital with a Church Parade in St. Giles Cathedral and a march down Princes Street, an event which recalled for many the similar service three years before during the respite between the Battalion's Italian and German campaigns. The next week the whole Battalion moved to Glasgow, home of many of its men. Here another march was made through the streets and here also the hospitality always associated with Scotland's largest city was at its warmest. On the 15th Their Majesties arrived in Edinburgh for a State visit, and the Battalion was busily employed lining Princes Street and mounting, at the Palace of Holyroodhouse, a Guard of Honour with the State Colour. It was the first time this Colour had been taken out since before the war. The companies now dispersed on independent marches. They went into Fife; into Wigtownshire and Dumfries; to Dundee and Aberdeenshire; into the Highlands to Perth and Inverness; to Kilmarnock and to Ayr. The (relatively) old soldiers of Headquarter Company displayed their prowess at drill before the critical eyes of the boys of the Queen Victoria School, Dunblane, for long a nursery for the Regiment. Wherever the Guardsmen went the members of the Scots Guards Association did all they could to make their stay enjoyable, and, taken all in all, the tour was an outstanding social and recreational success. But it must be admitted that in another of its purposes, that of raising urgently needed recruits, it was a failure. However, its long-term effects in this direction have been valuable, for the visit marked the beginning of a period of closer association between the Regiment and its Homeland than at any time since the Union.

Meanwhile great efforts were being made to assemble sufficient articles of full dress uniform to fit out the battalions stationed in London, an account of which will be found on another page.[1] Suffice it to say here that these efforts were successful in scraping together enough clothing and equipment for the Birthday Parade of 1948. On

[1] See p. 594.

this occasion the Second Battalion, then in barracks at Chelsea, was to troop its King's Colour, but before the ceremony had begun the empty threat of a thunderstorm caused it to be abandoned, to the audible regret of participants and spectators alike. It was not until the following year that the regular public duties in London and at Windsor were once again resplendent in scarlet and blue.

However, the Second Battalion was not to be left to preen itself in gaudy plumage. Towards the end of the summer of 1948 came an unexpected call to an unprecedented destination. On 13th August—Black Friday to all concerned—the Battalion was warned for service in Malaya. The smartest of uniforms was to be exchanged for drab jungle-green.

Malaya

1948

On the 17th June 1948 the Government of the Federation of Malaya had declared a State of Emergency. This step had been forced upon it by the growing lawlessness and terrorism of the Communist party in Malaya. During the war against Japan the Communists had been encouraged to take up arms against the occupiers, and British officers had worked in close liaison with the "Malayan Peoples' Anti-Japanese Army". With the declaration of the Emergency, the fighting part of what was now called the "Malayan Peoples' Anti-British Army"[1] retired into the thick jungle which covers nine-tenths of the country and in which they had hidden the arms supplied to them for the war against Japan. Those who went into hiding were mainly Chinese and numbered at most 4,000, but they left behind them many times that number of sympathisers among the Chinese community. To these allies, the most active of whom were known as the Min Yuen, the bandits looked for food, money and intelligence.

At the outset the police and military resources in Malaya were quite inadequate to deal with the situation. The effects of the reductions in the Infantry now became apparent. The War Office ordered the formation of the 2nd Guards Brigade from the battalions in the London District, for they were the only ones approaching full strength anywhere at home. The Brigade was to consist of the 3rd Grenadiers, 2nd Coldstream and the Second Battalion of the Regiment. It was to be commanded by Brigadier M. D. Erskine, D.S.O., who was relieved in command of the Regiment by Lord Dalrymple. Lieutenant-Colonel J. S. Sanderson, O.B.E., was appointed to command the battalion, which he joined after its arrival at Singapore; Captain A. N. B. Ritchie was his Adjutant. To complete the Battalion to its establishment of a headquarter company and four rifle companies, the First Battalion at

[1] Later styled the "Malayan Races Liberation Army", with a grandiose organisation of divisions, brigades and regiments.

Pirbright had to provide a large draft from its slender resources of Scots Guardsmen.

After the briefest of leaves, on the 5th September the Coldstream and Scots Guards (the latter under the second-in-command, Major A. E. Cameron, M.C.) embarked in the *Empire Trooper* at Southampton and sailed for the east the same day, heartened by the cheers and good wishes of their many friends who had come to the docks to see them off. On the 4th October the Battalion disembarked at Singapore and went at once to the tented transit camp at Nee Soon. Here they equipped and acclimatised themselves, experiencing for the first time the regular tropical downpours and quickly discovering the utter inability of canvas to exclude them. A ceremonial march by both battalions through the city of Singapore with Colours uncased marked the end of conventional peace-time soldiering; already the Guardsmen were taking their first steps in jungle training in the swamps behind the camp. On the 26th October, having been preceded by Right Flank, the Battalion travelled by train northwards from the Colony of Singapore into the Federation of Malaya. Active service had begun again.

MAP XLV

Before giving some account of the Battalion's service in Malaya a word must be said of the difficulties, at that time common to all regiments, which resulted from trying to run a far-flung army on short-service men. The majority of the Guardsmen who served in Malaya were National Service men, and at the time in question the period of Colour service was eighteen months. Therefore, by the time he had finished his recruit training at the Depot and his elementary tactical training at Pirbright, by the time he had spent a month in a trooper on the voyage out and had undergone another month of jungle training and acclimatisation, the National Service man had at most ten or eleven months' useful service to give the Battalion. A month before his period of service expired he had to be back on a trooper heading west. As yet large-scale trooping by air, which would have reduced the time spent on passage to a tenth, had not been sufficiently developed. Furthermore, short service was prevalent also in the regular element of the Battalion; for when the Commanding Officer's health was proposed at the Men's Christmas Dinners in 1950, it was proposed by a Guardsman with only six and a half years' service: he was the Guardsman with the longest service in the Battalion.

Nor was it only in the ranks that the turnover was rapid and continuous. Thirty officers went out with the Battalion: by the time it returned a total of eighty had served with it. No less than fifty-three subalterns had commanded platoons. From these junior officers the Battalion was lucky if it got six months' useful service, for part of their eighteen months was consumed away at the Officer Cadet Training Unit. And it was these junior officers who had to bear the main burden

Map XLV

of responsibility on patrol, responsibilities which were greater—if that were possible—in this remote jungle warfare than in European warfare, where lavish medical aid was always readily available. In fact, the only officers to serve with the Battalion throughout the whole two and a half years were the Padre, the Reverend D. H. Whiteford, and the Quartermaster, Captain Greenwood. The advantage derived from the presence of the latter will be fully understood when it is realised that the complicated and responsible appointment of Company Quartermaster Sergeant in the five companies changed hands no less than twenty-three times.

To train the original Battalion to fighting pitch and then to keep it there through all these vexatious changes was a problem which was solved to the satisfaction of both the Battalion and its superiors—and to the confusion of the usual band of dismal critics who, in their perennial manner, had prophesied woe immediately the dispatch to Malaya of the 2nd Guards Brigade had been announced. How this was achieved is described by Major P. F. Fane Gladwin, at first in command of Right Flank, then a missionary to Pirbright to shed light on Malayan problems, and finally second-in-command, in which capacity the main weight of the Battalion's training fell to him.

"Let it be freely admitted that when the Battalion stepped ashore in Malaya the standard of training of the majority was extremely low. This was due to the fact that the Battalion had been heavily involved in London Duties for more than a year, and had been made up hurriedly to strength with a number of men who had not completed even their Basic Training. However, it is possible that this fact helped us in certain ways, as few men were instilled with any form of tactical theory at all, and having no pre-conceived notions they may have found it easier to absorb the rather special techniques required for jungle warfare. . . .

"The first objective was to master the technique of the instant, killing shot with any weapon against a fleeting target, a technique which always leaves room for further improvement.

"The second objective was to learn all about the art of moving through jungle, *belukar*,[1] rubber and swamp silently and alertly. How to lay ambushes of all kinds, to cross rivers, follow tracks, and, let it be said, to burn *bashas*[2] with the greatest efficiency.

"The third objective was to achieve the highest degree of endurance in the jungle so that time was no object on our operations, and so that we should never be troubled by sickness, fatigue or the discomforts of jungle life.

[1] Very dense scrub.
[2] A hut or shelter made from interwoven leaves of the attap palm; highly inflammable, particularly when inhabited by cigarette addicts or mess-tin cooking experts.

"That we managed to progress far towards our first two objectives is proved by the many successful operations which stood out over two and a half years from the usual dreary round of failures. That we achieved our third objective to the fullest extent was borne out by the almost rampaging morale of the Battalion throughout the tour, and by a sickness rate so low as to be considered phenomenal in any climate and under any conditions.

"The first break in operations occurred at the end of 1949 when the Battalion spent a two months' re-training period in Singapore and the opportunity was taken by means of tactical discussions to review our whole state of training in the light of experience. At this time promotion in the Battalion was very rapid, and large numbers of new junior leaders were taking over platoons and sections. It therefore became obvious that standardised tactical manœuvres and drills should be introduced at once throughout the Battalion so that in all likely situations these new leaders should have a proverbial peg on which to hang their equally proverbial hats.

"Accordingly this was the policy adopted, and from January 1950 onwards training in the Battalion entered upon a new and more realistic phase, which lasted up to the time of our departure from Malaya.

"Early in 1950 drafts from home began arriving at steady intervals, and in fourteen successive courses each of three full weeks' duration a carefully selected training staff taught them all that we ourselves knew about operations in Malaya, including standardised techniques for patrolling, acting on contact, the laying of ambushes and other common forms of action.

"As the rifle companies gradually filled up with these carefully trained men during 1950 so the operational efficiency of the Battalion may fairly be said to have improved, an improvement borne out by the ever greater percentage of 'kills' to 'contacts' as compared with the previous year.

"But what of the human material that reacted to all forms of training over two and a half years with a vigour and an enthusiasm that knew no bounds?

"It has sometimes been said that the system of the Brigade of Guards tends to strangle the initiative of young soldiers and junior leaders, and had this been in the slightest degree true one could have expected to see every sign of it in the platoon and section warfare of Malaya. But it was never true and never looked like being true even from the start. On the contrary, the great standards of junior leadership displayed and the initiative, alertness and endurance of our younger Scots Guardsmen should remain an everlasting source of pride and pleasure to all those who took any part in their training either at home or in Malaya."

It is not proposed to describe in exhaustive detail the two and a half years of operations against the bandits.[1] There were literally hundreds of patrols, ambushes, raids, searches, false alarms, road convoys, train guards, mortar and artillery shoots, air strikes and air drops. With each passing month these were conducted with ever-increasing efficiency, and, above all, with ever-closer co-operation with the Police. For it was on the Police, as always "in aid of Civil Power", that the main burden of acquiring information lay, and without information the military could do little more than blunder about in the manner of the blind-folded—the more so since the language of the local population was so completely strange to them. Some were quick to pick up a smattering of simple Malay, but Chinese, with its many dialects, was never mastered. Despite these handicaps liaison with the other branches of the security forces was close. A helping hand and hospitality were frequently exchanged with the rapidly expanding Malay Regiment, with the Brigade of Gurkhas and with the new Home Guards of the estates and *kampongs*.[2] Especially welcome was the hospitality of the Malay Regiment at Port Dickson and that of the 1st Battalion The King's Own Yorkshire Light Infantry at Penang. The K.O.Y.L.I. housed three of the companies for a period of training and recreation, and to mark the Second Battalion's appreciation a suitably inscribed silver bugle was presented to them.

Perhaps the most unusual of the Battalion's allies was the Iban trackers imported from Borneo. Formerly addicted to head-hunting, they now applied their unrivalled knowledge of jungle lore to the elimination of the bandits; they accompanied many patrols and developed a very proper pride in their association with the Scots Guards.

The first year was spent mainly in the state of Selangor, a state in which the Chinese formed the largest racial group. Battalion Headquarters was established at Batu Arang, the site of Malaya's only coal mine, which had been one of the first targets of the Communists. Fifteen miles away, near the flesh-pots of the Federal capital of Kuala Lumpur, was Brigade Headquarters. Usually two or three of the companies were based upon Batu Arang, living in an assortment of tents, old bungalows and a disused plywood factory. Every week this conglomeration took on a better appearance as one and all laboured to make the place fit for Scots Guardsmen to live in. But nothing could be done to eliminate the sulphurous stench, the all-pervading red dust and the rattling din which emanated day and night from the opencast workings. From the outset one company, at first G, was stationed

---

[1] See *The Second Battalion Scots Guards: 1948–1951*, a privately printed and profusely illustrated account of the Battalion's tour in Malaya. A copy is in the Library of the Imperial War Museum.

[2] Villages.

thirty miles away to the north at Kuala Kubu Bahru, an attractive village at the foot of the Fraser's Hill range, and one which was to become very familiar to the Battalion in the months ahead. Soon F Company was detached even farther to the north to the Slim River area: the Battalion was not to concentrate again until a year had gone by.

The first success was scored on the 5th November when Lance-Sergeant J. McCubbin of G Company killed a bandit near Kerling, and this was followed a week later when Lieutenant T. N. Rivett-Carnac's platoon of the same company killed another in the Ulu Yam area. By early in the New Year all the rifle companies had bandits to their credit.

It must be admitted that an incident in December which resulted in the death of twenty-four Chinese could not properly be claimed in the same category. A patrol from G Company under the command of a Sergeant was guarding the men of a *kongsi*[1] near the village of Batang Kali, who were under strong suspicion of having supplied the bandits with food. Thinking their guard was easily to be evaded, the suspects made a dash for the jungle. Needless to say, the Guardsmen were on the alert and twenty-four of the men were shot down as they ran. The local press commented in strong and unfavourable terms on this incident, for the expression "shot while attempting to escape" has come to be looked upon with a certain cynicism. But in this case the expression was applicable, and the action of the Guardsmen legitimate. By their own folly, the suspected bandit helpers paid a far heavier price than they would have done had they been found guilty of the crime. The incident illustrates the sudden emergencies which can confront the most junior leader in this type of operation and the weighty decisions he must make at the shortest notice. It was many months before there was any further trouble around Batang Kali.

On the same day, however, a far more satisfactory incident befell two platoons of Right Flank. They closed in on an old *basha* near an estate called Utan Simpan and killed the leader of the notorious Rawang gang, wounded and captured his second-in-command, and made prisoner another three of his henchmen. The only casualty to Right Flank was Guardsman O'Fee who was knocked out with the butt of a pistol by a bandit who was trying to make a silent escape. These leading bandits had high prices on their heads, sometimes as much as $15,000; but the successful soldiers saw none of it, as rewards were only paid to the Police and civilian informers.

It was inevitable that these operations must result in losses to our own side, and on the 3rd February 1949 Left Flank suffered the first fatality of the campaign. Lance-Sergeant A. Ferguson was mortally

[1] A large native hut used by Chinese, or a Chinese syndicate of rubber tappers.

wounded when fired at by a bandit sentry at close range; the day before he had himself accounted for a bandit. It was also on Left Flank that the next blow fell. After a week in which the Company had claimed five bandits without loss, on the 19th May a less satisfactory enounter took place. Captain O. W. Priaulx set out with a force consisting of a platoon under the command of Second-Lieutenant P. W. B. Graham-Watson, an Iban tracker, a Chinese Liaison Officer, a police officer and ten policemen with the intention of locating and destroying a bandit camp and its occupants. While searching for the camp and examining tracks in the jungle the patrol was ambushed, Graham-Watson, Lance-Sergeant H. Lea and a police constable being killed, and four Guardsmen being wounded, one seriously. On this occasion no compensating loss could be claimed to have been inflicted on the enemy, but some of the gang were almost certainly accounted for a month later when Second-Lieutenant the Hon. P. Lindsay's platoon of F Company killed two bandits who were found to be armed with a Bren gun taken from Left Flank in the previous encounter.

And so patrolling went on. For many men weeks and months might go by without a contact, but no-one could relax his vigilance. Once contact had been made victory nearly always went to the more alert, speedier and better-trained side. The discomforts of jungle life, the darkness, the dankness and the unfamiliar noises had to be mastered to ensure that all a man's faculties could be concentrated on the one fleeting chance an encounter might give.

In May F Company made an excursion to Seremban in the State of Negri Sembilan, and patrolled extensively on the marches of that state with Johore and Malacca. In July Right Flank moved to South Selangor to take over from the 3rd Grenadiers, who were returning home. Here the bandits were thick on the ground; within a month five of the greatly feared Kajang gang had been eliminated, the same number had been wounded, and thirty of its packs had been captured. These, which contained their precious food and equipment, were always specially sought after; the bandits lived on the shortest of commons and their equipment was of the scantiest. Left Flank also came south to the outskirts of Kuala Lumpur to help the 1st Battalion The Suffolk Regiment in its duties while that battalion trained for the jungle.

At the end of August came the first large combined operation in which the Battalion was engaged. This was *Lemon*, which was conducted from a joint Police–Military Operations Room set up in the Chinese School building at Kuala Kubu. From it the Commanding Officer and the Officer Commanding the Police controlled a force of some three or four companies and a large detachment of police, supported by artillery and aircraft. The object was to drive the bandits out of a large area of jungle, to harry them continuously, and to give them no rest. For a change noise was encouraged on some of these operations; bandits who heard the sounds of the pipes and of inter-platoon noise competitions must certainly have been mystified, if not frightened. For nine weeks air supply was employed on a large scale, no less than a hundred and twenty drops being made to the troops in their jungle bases. These drops might be either with the use of parachutes or "free". In the latter method those on the ground had frequently to take smart evasive action to prevent this routine "Q" work assuming the characteristics of a lethal bombing raid. Every kind of store was delivered by air: food—including special ration packs for Iban trackers and Malay police—ammunition, batteries for the wireless sets which were the only means of communication, medical supplies, canteen wares and the mail. *Lemon*, by nature of its purpose, was not notable for the number of bandits directly eliminated; for instance neither of the Flank Companies made contact at all. But on the 25th September a platoon of F Company was involved in a fierce close-range action in which three bandits were killed, but at the exorbitant price of the deaths of Second-Lieutenant J. A. Forbes-Leith, Sergeant W. A. Riach and Guardsman D. Moore. During the engagement Lance-Corporal Morgan kept his Bren in action single-handed, giving effective covering fire to the wounded and later returning to the patrol base to lead a relief party to the scene of the action; he never flagged for eighteen hours. For his courage, endurance and leadership, Morgan was awarded the Military Medal, the first ever to be won by a member of the Regiment in peace-time. A month later G Company also sustained a serious loss when Lieutenant R. A. C. McKenzie was killed after finding a camp in almost impenetrable *belukar*. It was with relief that early in November the Battalion extracted itself from the jungle and from evil-smelling Batu Arang, and travelled south by train to Singapore.

In the final week before its departure another severe blow had been struck at the Brigade. On the 27th October Brigadier Erskine took off in a small Auster aircraft from Mentakab in the state of Pahang to fly to Kuala Lumpur. The route took the aircraft across the central range of mountains at a time when severe tropical rainstorms were in progress. The Auster never reached Kuala Lumpur, and immediately an extensive search was organised by air and on the ground. First reports indicated that the aircraft had never crossed the mountains, so the search was concentrated on the eastern side. No trace of the wreck was seen. The hunt was not finally abandoned until the next February, when the Battalion, then operating in Pahang, took part in a search on the jungle-clad hills, relying on the guidance of a Chinese woman medium living in Malacca. Her directions were passed to the troops by means of an elaborate wireless link, but they proved to be of no greater value than had those provided by another

40. F Company's three-inch mortar detachment in action near Rasa, 24th April, 1950. the extreme left is Captain O. Priaulx

MALAYA

41. No. 10 Platoon of Left Flank with the skin of the tiger shot by Sergeant J. Duff (fou from right). In front is the Company " char wallah "

(*The Scots*)

42. HOLYROODHOUSE. 28th June 1951

On behalf of The King, H.R.H. The Duke of Gloucester presented new Colours to both Battalions of the Regiment. The Colonel has just handed the new King's Colour of the First Battalion to Lieutenant R. Mayfield.

In the foreground is the Second Battalion in battle-dress, and, on its right, the First Battalion in Guard Order. With their backs to the Abbey are the members of the Scots Guards Association

medium at home in November. It was not until July 1954 that a patrol chanced upon the wreckage of the aircraft. It lay in the Ulu Gombok Forest Reserve only a dozen miles north of Kuala Lumpur. Contrary to the original assumptions it appeared that the aircraft had in fact nearly crossed the hills before it crashed, and it was found more than twenty-five miles further west than the mediums had predicted. No trace of either Brigadier Erskine or the pilot was found, but fragments of ribbon in the wreck were believed to have been part of the Brigade Commander's D.S.O. ribbon. He had won the Order while in command of the Second Battalion at the great victory over the German tanks at Medenine. Besides commanding the Regiment, both its regular battalions and the 24th Guards Brigade in Italy, Brigadier Erskine was a well-known amateur rider. His loss was most widely mourned. To succeed him in command of the 2nd Guards Brigade came another officer of the Regiment, Brigadier C. I. H. Dunbar, D.S.O.

The Battalion had moved down to Singapore under the command of Major Fane Gladwin, now second-in-command, for the Commanding Officer and his Adjutant (now Captain J. Swinton) had gone to Hong Kong on a thinly disguised reconnaissance in case the Battalion should be called on to bolster up the defences against the new Communist threat. Fortunately the scare abated, and Colonel Sanderson was able to return in peace with the news that the Regimental Star which the Battalion had laid out on the hill above Fanling in 1928 was still in good order and had recently been refurbished.[1]

On Singapore Island the Battalion was housed in the excellent barracks of Selarang, near to the sea and only a dozen miles from a city which offered all the attractions of civilisation. Here, besides engaging in many sporting and recreational activities, the Battalion found itself in constant demand for ceremonial duties, including finding all the troops for the funeral of the assassinated Governor of Sarawak. The departure for release of over a hundred and thirty National Service men reduced the companies to two platoons each, for the drafts which were arriving were not yet fit to swell the ranks; the third platoons could not be reformed until late the following year. The Corps of Drums and the Pipe Band had a busy time, for, outside their musical duties, not only did they have to find a large share of

[1] It was in Hong Kong that the Canadian regiment allied to the Scots Guards fought its only battle of the 1939–45 war. After a period of service in the West Indies, in November 1941 the Winnipeg Grenadiers were sent to the Colony in the forlorn hope of reinforcing the garrison against the expected Japanese attack. This came in overwhelming strength on the 8th December, and on Christmas Day, after the most gallant resistance in which one of the Grenadiers won a posthumous Victoria Cross, the garrison was forced to lay down its arms. The original Winnipeg Grenadiers languished in captivity for the remainder of the war, but a new battalion of the same name took part in the amphibious operations off Alaska in the summer of 1943. See *Six Years of War: Volume I of the Official History of the Canadian Army*.

31—S.G.H.

the Intelligence staff and stretcher-bearers, but also of the new three-inch mortar teams which were now being trained; these mortar detachments were to fire tens of thousands of rounds in the months ahead. A great programme of musketry and specialist training was put in hand, and, as the new Commander-in-Chief (General Sir John Harding) predicted when he inspected the Battalion on the 23rd December, it returned to the Federation "refreshed, invigorated and better equipped than before." On the 3rd January 1950 the Battalion left Singapore for the north; only the proximity of Hogmanay can explain the arrival at the destination of certain parts of the main body *before* the advance party.

The destination on this occasion was a surprise. The rifle companies went to the State of Pahang on the eastern side of the central range of mountains. Tactical Headquarters and one company were established at Mentakab, with the other companies widely spread among the villages and estates of the Semantan and Triang rivers. Main Battalion Headquarters and the draft training staff had returned to Batu Arang, and from here, a hundred and fifty miles by road across the mountains, the Battalion had to be maintained; it was a period of nightmares for the Quartermaster and the Transport Officer.

Pahang was the most primitive area in which the Battalion operated. The state covers an area of swamps, rivers and flat jungle, with a few isolated hills leading up to the central range of mountains. It is inhabited in the main by aborigines, whose remote dwellings were difficult enough to find, let alone to govern. At this time was instituted the "Briggs Plan", named after the Director of Operations, Lieutenant-General Sir Harold Briggs, which aimed at bringing the whole population of Malaya under effective control. Thereby it was hoped to cut off the bandits from their food supplies, and to break up their intelligence organisation. Huge schemes were put in hand for moving hundreds and thousands of "squatters" living in remote areas to new villages in areas where they could be more easily supervised; their old inhabitations and cultivations were then destroyed, and life was rendered yet more uncomfortable for the Communists. It was while patrolling round one of these new squatter areas that Right Flank scored the Battalion's only certain kill in Pahang when four bandits were shot near Triang at the time of the Chinese New Year. Otherwise the two months spent in the state were chiefly notable for the sudden rises and falls of the flood-waters and for the hunt for Brigadier Erskine by G Company and Left Flank previously mentioned. It was back at Batu Arang that the principal engagement of the period took place. On the 16th January while making a reconnaissance for a jungle training range, a patrol from Headquarter Company was ambushed at the entrance to a Communist camp; Guardsman K. Holland was killed and Local Sergeant G. Reilly was wounded. Despite two wounds Sergeant

Reilly continued single-handed to engage the enemy, and was later awarded the Military Medal.

On the 6th March the Battalion was delighted to leave the wet jungles of Pahang for the more civilised state of Negri Sembilan. After a disorganised move during which the train carrying all the accommodation stores was derailed near Mentakab by a mine sprung by the bandits, Tactical Headquarters and two companies were established in a pleasant camp at Tampin, with the other two companies at Rompin and Bahau. It was another period of enforcing the Briggs Plan, and it included a large-scale operation involving five battalions designed to clear the whole state. Perhaps the most characteristic feature of Negri Sembilan was its narrow and easily ambushed estate roads. Fortunately the Battalion was not caught in any of these traps, and even its new armoured decoy lorry *Frankenstein* (Registered Number B. 1642) failed to provoke one by trailing its coat in some rather thin disguises. Only one certain success could be claimed during the month spent in the State, which was that of Lance-Corporal M. Dunbar of Left Flank, who killed a bandit near Rompin. In mid-April the Battalion, less Right Flank, moved back to its old hunting-grounds of North Selangor, which were to be the scene of its final year's operations. Right Flank remained at Tampin for another month, engaged on the wearisome duties of train guard and in patrols under the command of the 26th Field Regiment, R.A. By mid-May that company also was back in Selangor.

From mid-April until early December the Battalion was responsible for a huge tract of country. This included the whole of the State of Selangor, and small parts of Perak to the north and of Negri Sembilan to the south; its extent was some 4,000 square miles, it was about 110 miles long and it contained nearly a million inhabitants. The whole of Battalion Headquarters was now established at Kuala Kubu, where, during months of hard work by Guardsmen and local inhabitants alike, the camp was transformed from one of tents on ground liable to severe flooding to one of attap huts on concrete bases with a relatively efficient drainage system. As usual, the most magnificent structure proved to be the Sergeants' Mess, which was constructed for nothing by the Sakai aborigines. The growth of this camp was a gradual process, but when completed towards the end of the year it was fully worthy of the name it was given. A plaque was later erected outside the guard-room which read as follows:

Erskine Camp

This camp is named in memory of Brigadier Malcolm David Erskine, C.B.E., D.S.O., Commander 2nd Guards Brigade. Lost on Active Service over Pahang 27th October 1949.

He was a former Adjutant and Commanding Officer of 2nd Bn.

Scots Guards who first occupied this camp and erected this memorial.

To cope with the huge area now entrusted to the Battalion, two conpanies were based upon Kajang under command of Major Fane Gladwin as Detachment Commander, later to be succeeded by Major the Hon. W. E. H. Lawson. This body looked after the southern part of Selangor, while the Commanding Officer, with the remainder of the Battalion and a squadron of the Royal Air Force Regiment, looked after the north.

Space does not permit any detailed account of the operations of the next year. They were continuous and unrelenting, and were conducted with ever-closer liaison with the Police, to which the permanent Joint Army–Police Operations Room at Kuala Kubu made an important contribution. Notable successes against the bandits in 1950 included the shooting on the 30th May by Lance-Corporal Catling (Left Flank) of Win Hong, a desperado with $15,000 on his head; the killing of six bandits by Second-Lieutenant B. A. Stewart-Wilson's platoon of G Company in July; and on 5th November, in an extensive operation near Kajang simultaneously involving no less than eight small patrols of Left Flank, three bandits were killed and another three captured. One of the dead was identified as Wong Yiu Fan, a leader of the Kajang gang and responsible for many murders, including the death of five Grenadiers. The patrol which scored this success was led by Major E. I. Ll. Mostyn and was composed entirely of men from Company Headquarters. Major Mostyn, who threw eight grenades during the engagement and who killed one of the bandits for certain, was later awarded the Military Cross[1] and Lance-Sergeant J. Allan, who used his rifle with great accuracy to kill a bandit who was about to shoot Major Mostyn from a range of five yards, was awarded the Military Medal. This action was gratifying in many ways. Not only had it been fought and won against an extremely aggressive force of about thirty bandits armed with at least two Bren guns, but also it had demonstrated admirably the value of the standard contact and battle drills devised by the training staff; despite the fact that the patrol was composed of men who did not frequently undertake this type of work, yet not one order had to be given by Major Mostyn from the start of the battle until its successful conclusion. The disciplined fire and calm courage of eight men had routed nearly four times their number.

But this period also included a disaster. On the 11th June a jeep driven by Guardsman D. Murray and carrying three officers ran into a party of bandits who were holding up a civilian bus in the Kanching

---

[1] This was the first Military Cross to be won by a member of the Regiment in peace-time.

Pass. Captain M. G. Bax, who had given valuable service as Intelligence Officer earlier in the campaign, and Second-Lieutenant M. J. Morrice, both of G Company, were killed, and Captain M. P. de Klee, the Signal Officer, was wounded. Fortunately the bandits did not allow themselves sufficient time thoroughly to inspect the wreck before they withdrew, and thereby Captain de Klee and Guardsman Murray escaped with their lives. Nevertheless they had struck a bitter blow at the Battalion.

Early in July Lieutenant-Colonel Sanderson, who had received the D.S.O. for his services, left Malaya to take command of the First Battalion at home, and, until the arrival of Lieutenant-Colonel A. E. Cameron, M.C., at the end of August, Major Fane Gladwin commanded the Battalion. Furthermore, on the departure for home of the 2nd Coldstream in early August the 2nd Guards Brigade had ceased to exist and had become the 18th Infantry Brigade. With the change of title came a change of commander, for Brigadier Dunbar gave place to Brigadier R. T. K. Pye. The Brigade sign also was changed, its field of the Brigade colours of blue-red-blue becoming the conventional infantry red, though the device of a crossed bayonet and Gurkha *kukri* remained unaltered.

One of the features of the Battalion's tour in Malaya was the myriad of its official visitors. Not only did the successive Commanders-in-Chief, Generals Sir Neil Ritchie and Sir John Harding, and the various other Generals in Malaya visit the Battalion, but many came from home as well. Early in 1949 the Battalion had been very pleased to see two of its former Commanding Officers, Major-General J. C. O. Marriott, then Major-General Commanding the Brigade of Guards; and Lord Dalrymple, then commanding the Regiment, who contrived a second visit in 1950. Among other visitors were the Secretary for War, Mr. John Strachey; the Chief of the Imperial General Staff, Field-Marshal Sir William Slim; an assortment of Members of Parliament; and a galaxy of press-men, whose subsequent effusions were regarded with mixed feelings. When the Flag Officer, Malaya, visited the Battalion, his Flag Lieutenant expressed a wish to go into the jungle; not long after his disappearance into the *ulu*[1] with F Company, a wireless message was received saying that Lieutenant P. Chambers, R.N., was "listing badly to port owing to incorrect stowage of kit."

In December the Kajang detachment came to an end, and the Battalion could give undivided attention to North Selangor. All the companies were now based on Erskine Camp, though they were never all in camp together. It had been decreed that only one company could be at Battalion Headquarters at any one time, so a routine of six weeks on an outlying base and two weeks at Kuala Kubu was instituted. The

[1] Army slang for jungle; in Malay it means "headwaters of a river".

company bases were either in the outbuildings of rubber estates or in derelict tin-mining bungalows, and varied much in the comforts to be found. At Kerling the troops lived in tents, cheek by jowl with a horde of unsavoury Tamils, and sometimes in feet of mud—yet the compensation was a heated bathing pool. At Kapar Bharu they lived in three derelict bungalows, but there was no electricity and little water and it was reached by appalling roads. Trolak, in southern Perak, was the most comfortable, due largely to the helpfulness of the resident planter; but here the stench of drying rubber was overpowering until familiarity had bred indifference. During the fortnight allowed them at Erskine Camp, the companies could send their platoons in turn for a couple of days by the sea at Port Dickson. Those remaining were taken for duty as emergency platoon and vehicle escorts. Only rarely could RSM D. McG. Fraser (who held the appointment throughout the Battalion's Malayan tour) lay his hands on sufficient men to make a quorum for a respectable drill parade.

In this situation it was inevitable that the final Malayan Christmas had to be celebrated in relays. Not long before the feast the Quartermaster, at this time of year by far the most influential member of any battalion, ran into a bandit party who were burning a bus on the main road, but the expenditure of twelve magazines from the twin Vickers K guns mounted on the top of his scout car and a barrage of blistering invective preserved him from massacre. The site of this memorable outrage was christened "Greenwood's Gulch". Another insolent affront was offered by the bandits soon after the New Year when they burnt down the railway station buildings at Kuala Kubu, destroying a consignment of the Battalion's mail.

1951

The first three months of 1951 saw the Battalion's final operations. The Briggs Plan, which had dispersed the companies so widely, was relaxed and the Kapar Bharu out-station abandoned, whereby a reserve was more readily available to the Commanding Officer to deal with emergencies. The first success was that of Second-Lieutenant the Hon. G. E. D. Elliot's platoon of Right Flank which killed two bandits in a camp near Ulu Yam; one of these was identified as Hither, a notorious Malay enemy of the Grenadiers, priced again at $15,000. Another wounded bandit was taken the next day, but the same afternoon the final casualty of the campaign was suffered when Sergeant D. McMillan of G Company was killed by the first burst of fire in an engagement nearby. In February Major R. A. Carnegie with men of G Company killed two near Rasa, and two days later Major Lawson with F Company acting swiftly "on information received"—as the old police-court saying has it—surrounded a Min Yuen camp near Kuala Kubu at dawn, and by a cunning pincer movement killed all its five occupants. This was a highly satisfactory performance since one of the dead was identified as Mock Meng, the head of all the local bandit suppliers; the ambushing of Captain Greenwood had been appropriately revenged. Two days later Right Flank again scored, when a force under Captain S. C. M. Bland killed two on the edge of a rubber estate near Tanjong Malim. Left Flank, in Perak State, could find no bandits, but Sergeant J. Duff made the unique kill of the campaign. In the Behrang Forest Reserve with a light No. 5 rifle he shot dead a large tigress, the range being fifty yards, the beast being hit between the eyes as it made to attack the patrol in defence of its two cubs. From head to tail it measured nine feet six inches.

On the 21st March Major-General Hedley, who commanded the South Malaya District, reminded the Battalion that it had one more week of operations ahead of it, and that its score stood at ninety-six bandits eliminated. Plainly a century must be scored. On Easter Day this goal was attained when Left Flank killed four and captured a printing press, being welcomed back to camp by the Pipe Band and an enthusiastic crowd. But the bare hundred did not satisfy the Battalion. At dawn on Easter Monday Right Flank under Major A. D. G. Llewellyn, M.C., surrounded a camp in the Slim area of Perak and, by skilfully driving the occupants first into a line of stops and then back on to the bayonets of the beaters, killed ten armed men, only two escaping, one of whom was tracked down and killed a few days later, the other surrendering to the Police. Thus a complete gang was eliminated, a most satisfactory finale to the long months of hard work. In all, the Second Battalion Scots Guards killed one hundred, captured eleven and wounded twenty-four Communist bandits.

Before leaving the country there were many farewells to be taken. The most notable was the assembly at Erskine Camp of many of the officers of the Malayan Police who had worked with the Battalion all over the Federation. The Chief Police Officer, Mr. O'Flynn, presented to the officers a silver cigarette box, and to the Battalion as a whole a magnificent engraved silver shield; in return Colonel Cameron presented a silver shield to the Selangor Police Contingent to mark the two and a half years of happy co-operation.

By the end of March the duties in Selangor had been handed over to the 1st Battalion The Royal West Kent Regiment, and, for the final time delayed by a derailment, the Battalion went by train to Singapore, being greeted at all the intermediate stations by hosts of well-wishers. By the 1st April the whole Battalion was back in Selarang Barracks, concentrated for the first time in fifteen months. Here on the 5th General Harding addressed the Guardsmen, and on the 10th, after the conventional Malayan postponement of twenty-four hours, they embarked in the transport *Empire Halladale*, the authentic and tangible "boat wi' the tartan funnel", disembarking at Liverpool on the 12th May. The Battalion went on well-earned leave, after which it reassembled at Glencorse Barracks, Edinburgh, on the 13th June.

The words which General Harding wrote in the foreword of the Battalion's own account of its operations may well be used to sum up its Malayan achievements.

"In all their operations all ranks have displayed courage and endurance of the highest order. In addition they have shown a fine spirit of co-operation and good comradeship with all those with whom they have worked. They have confounded the critics and proved again, if further proof were needed, that there is nothing Guardsmen cannot achieve when they put their minds and hearts to it."

* * *

The Second Battalion had arrived home in time to participate in the most outstanding domestic occasion in the Regiment's post-war history. For the First Battalion, as will shortly be related, had now reassumed a normal infantry organisation, and it was possible to assemble both Battalions in Scotland.

On the morning of the 28th June 1951 in the Gardens of the Palace of Holyroodhouse, King George VI was to present new Colours to both Battalions. Not since the year 1709 had the whole Regiment been together in its native land, and now, by the special wish of His Majesty, this long period of exile was to be ended. There was to be one disappointment only; already the King's fatal illness was upon him, and he was forced to delegate the presentation to His Royal Highness the Colonel.

For the ceremony the Scots Guards, under the command of the Lieutenant-Colonel, Lord Dalrymple, was drawn up in three sides of a square. On the long side facing the saluting base stood the two battalions; the First under Lieutenant-Colonel Sanderson, 350 strong and clothed in bearskins and tunics, and the Second under Lieutenant-Colonel Cameron, 600 strong and clothed in khaki battledress, for there had been no opportinuty of fitting it out in full dress since its return from Malaya. Facing inwards from the outer flanks of the Battalions were two totally different bodies of men, the one old and the other new. On the left of the Second Battalion stood a hundred young recruits from the Depot, dressed in scarlet and blue; on the right of the First Battalion stood seven hundred be-medalled members of the Scots Guards Association—and what these veterans lacked in uniformity of dress they made up for in the smartness of their bearing. The Regimental Band with the Corps of Drums and the Pipe Bands of both battalions, all in full dress, provided the music for the parade.

After the Colonel had been received with a Royal Salute, the ceremony followed the usual form. First the Troop by the band and the pipes, the former in slow and the latter in quick time; then the marching off of the old Colours to the tune of Auld Lang Syne; the uncasing and laying on the piled drums of the new Colours, and their blessing; and then the presentation to the kneeling Ensigns. After being received with a General Salute the Colours were marched to the centres of their battalions to the strains of the National Anthem.

The Duke of Gloucester then addressed the Regiment. First he read a message from His Majesty:

"Please tell all ranks of the Scots Guards how deeply disappointed I am to be unable to present their new Colours to them to-day. I am sure that their parade will be worthy of the finest traditions of the Regiment and I send my best wishes to all who are present on this great occasion. GEORGE R. Colonel-in-Chief."

The Colonel then drew attention to the very special link which His Majesty had with the Regiment, for the Scots Guards was the first regiment which the Duke of York, by profession a sailor, had joined; the Colonel said that he had regarded it as a personal honour to have succeeded his brother in that capacity. After recalling the campaigns in Norway, Africa, Italy, Western Europe and Malaya, His Royal Highness concluded: "As Colonel of the Scots Guards I am proud of your record, as indeed you must be yourselves, and it is with the greatest confidence that I now, on behalf of the King, entrust these new Colours to your keeping."

Lord Dalrymple replied on behalf of the Regiment, requesting the Colonel to convey to the King the great regret of all present at his absence. Lord Dalrymple pointed out that there was assembled at Holyrood that day the largest number of past members of the Regiment ever to be gathered together, and he concluded: "It is in the presence of so many who have added to the reputation of the Regiment in the past that we pledge ourselves to you, our Colonel, that we will maintain the safety and honour of our new Colours, and with deep and constant loyalty to our King and Country will uphold the good name of His Majesty's Scots Guards wherever we may be called upon to serve."

The parade in the garden concluded with a Royal Salute and three rousing cheers. Until then the ceremony had in the main been confined to the Regiment and its invited guests: now all Edinburgh was to enjoy the sight of the Scots Guards and its Association marching through the city. The Colonel, accompanied by the Lord Provost, Mr. James Miller, took up his position at a saluting base at the Mound in Princes Street. The huge crowd which had turned out to watch was in no way disappointed in its expectations.

The next day the Second Battalion held the third of its recent services in St. Giles' Cathedral. This time the service was dedicated to the memory of those who had fallen in Malaya.

Entertainments and spectacles during the visit were almost continuous. The Lord Provost entertained the officers to lunch and a large party of other ranks to tea. The Regiment was At Home to the

Association at Glencorse, where an exhibition of trophies and relics was to be seen. The Third Guards Club and the Warrant Officers and Sergeants (Past and Present) Association held their annual dinners: the Subalterns celebrated at a less formal meal, relenting sufficiently for one evening to invite as their only guests the two Battalion Adjutants. Daily the Holyrood and Castle Guards were found by the First Battalion or by K Company, and on four evenings Retreat was beaten on the Esplanade.

All in all, the visit was memorable both for its ceremonies and its friendliness. Its concluding note was admirably expressed by the Lord Provost in his speech to the officers: "Haste ye back."

The two new Regimental Colours displayed the badges of Nos. 1 and 2 Companies, and, for the first time, the name SALAMANCA appeared among the Battle Honours. This honour, commemorating the First Battalion's presence at Wellington's victory over Marmont on the 22nd July 1812, had been awarded, somewhat belatedly, by Army Order 136 of 1951. Both sets of old Colours were laid up in Scotland. On the 9th August 1952 that of the Second Battalion was placed in St. Machar's Cathedral, Aberdeen; and on the 14th April 1956 that of the First Battalion was placed in St. Mungo's Cathedral, Glasgow, on which occasion His Royal Highness the Colonel unveiled a stained glass memorial window dedicated to all Scots Guardsmen who had given their lives for their country.

The depositing of another set of old Colours deserves mention here. On the 30th September 1950 the pair carried by the Second Battalion between the years 1886 and 1891 was laid up in Falkland Palace, Fife. These Colours had been given back to the Regiment by the late Sir Arthur du Cros, into whose possession they had come by purchase. Falkland was a most suitable resting place for them, for it was there on the 22nd July 1650 that King Charles II, on his way to receive the Honours of Scotland at Scone, had presented colours to the companies of his Life Guard of Foot, from which corps the Regiment is descended. Equally appropriate was the fact that the Hereditary Keeper of Falkland was a former officer of the Regiment, Major M. D. D. Crichton-Stuart, M.C.

The revival of the First Battalion had come about as part of the rearmament programme set on foot after the outbreak of the war in Korea. With the intention of creating a strategic reserve at home, several Regiments of the Line revived their moribund second battalions, while in the Brigade of Guards those battalions which had been relegated to training duties were brought forward to an active establishment. On 1st April 1951 the new Guards Training Battalion took the place of the First Battalion at Pirbright.

Under the command of Lieutenant-Colonel Sanderson the Battalion moved to Colchester to take its place in the 32nd Guards Brigade of the 3rd Division. There it began steadily to grow in strength as men joined it direct from the Depot, and as the restrictions on the release of time-expired Regulars and the prolongation of the National Service man's Colour service began to take effect. Save for the visit to Edinburgh previously described, the Battalion devoted the whole summer and autumn to intensive training, and to refreshing the military minds of hordes of Reservists. Not only did the Battalion receive five hundred Scots Guards Reservists, but it also ministered to some two thousand five hundred from the other regiments of the Brigade. It also gave administrative assistance for the test mobilisation of many Territorial units. Late in August, now under the command of Lieutenant-Colonel P. F. Fane Gladwin, M.B.E., the Battalion moved to a field training area in Norfolk, where it took part in a series of exercises of an ever-increasing complexity, which in October culminated in the first Army manœuvres at home since before the war. By mid-October the Battalion was back at Colchester, where its stay proved all too brief, for the new strategic reserve was to be called upon almost before it had assembled. In November, leaving the Second Battalion in barracks at Chelsea and a new L Company at Pirbright to train young soldiers from the Depot, the First Battalion moved by air and sea to Cyprus to begin what was to prove the longest peace-time foreign tour yet undertaken by the Regiment.

On the 6th February 1952 His Majesty King George VI died at Sandringham. There is no need to recall the King's very special connection with the Regiment, which played a fitting part in his last progress through London. The Second Battalion mounted a Guard of Honour at Westminster Hall to receive the coffin from Sandringham, the officers kept vigil round the catafalque during the lying-in-state, a detachment with the Band and pipers marched in the procession through London, and a final Guard of Honour was mounted at Paddington Station. No King has been more sincerely mourned throughout the Empire, and not the least of the mourners were his Scots Guards.

A year later the same battalion, then stationed at Windsor, had the sad duty of escorting the coffin of Queen Mary, the late King's mother, from Marlborough House to Westminster Hall. Queen Mary had always taken the keenest interest in all the Brigade's activities, especially during its two greatest wars.

Just as in 1901 the Regiment had been on guard in London at the time of the death of the last Queen to reign over the United Kingdom, so in 1952 it was on guard at the Accession of the next. Far away in Cyprus the First Battalion found a full Guard of Honour in Nicosia when the Governor proclaimed Queen Elizabeth II. Her Majesty immediately assumed the Colonelcy-in-Chief of the Regiment, which was greatly honoured when the Second Battalion was ordered to find the Escort to the Colour for the first Birthday Parade of the new reign; on that occasion the Queen appeared in the uniform of the Regiment.[1]

On Coronation Day, 2nd June 1953, the Second Battalion found the Army detachment of the Combined Services Guard of Honour outside the West Door of Westminster Abbey. The State Colour was taken out, and the Combined Guard was the responsibility of Colonel C. I. H. Dunbar, C.B.E., D.S.O., then Lieutenant-Colonel commanding the Regiment. In the procession marched representative detachments from both battalions, each of five officers and ninety-six men, the detachment from the First Battalion having flown home from Egypt to take part. The remainder of the Second Battalion was engaged in street-lining round the Victoria Memorial and in The Mall. Beyond the seas in Egypt the First Battalion at Port Said marked the day by firing a ceremonial *feu-de-joi* and by treating its men to a special dinner. Later in June a detachment of the Second Battalion went to Edinburgh to attend upon the Queen during her State Visit to Scotland. It mounted Guards of Honour in the capital and in Glasgow, it provvided a detachment to march in the procession from Holyrood to St. Giles', and it found the Castle Guard on the day Her Majesty formally received the keys from the Governor. At Port Said the First Battalion gave a party at which the film of Her Majesty's Coronation was shown; the whole British community was invited, as were also many Egyptian officials, including the Egyptian Governor of the Canal Zone.

Germany

After its arduous but pleasurable duties the Second Battalion was off on its travels again. On the 6th July 1953, under the command of Lieutenant-Colonel W. D. M. Raeburn, D.S.O., M.B.E., it left Windsor for Germany to join the 4th Guards Brigade in the 2nd Division.

In Germany the Battalion was stationed in excellent barracks to the east of Düsseldorf, and very soon it was heavily involved in the intensive training which was the predominant feature of life in the British Army of the Rhine. In all sorts of weather it became well acquainted with the heaths and ranges of Sennelage and Borkenberge; it took part in the great international manœuvres organised by the Northern Army Group of the North Atlantic Treaty Organisation; and it was deeply preoccupied with the new problems of organisation and tactics posed by the introduction of atomic weapons. Nevertheless it found time to triumph in a new sphere of sport: twice the Battalion team won the Army Ski Championship.

It must be admitted that to predict the future in military history is to border on the foolhardy, but, should there prove to be any permanence in the pledge given in 1954 by Sir Anthony Eden that, for the

[1] See Frontispiece.

next fifty years, Britain would maintain on the Continent a force equivalent to four divisions, it seems likely that a future historian of the Scots Guards will have to record further periods of service in Germany.

Cyprus and Egypt

If at the time of writing it seemed that in the future the Regiment would see much of Germany, it seemed equally likely that, for the time being, at least, it had seen the last of Egypt.[1] The reason for the despatch of the First Battalion to the Middle East in the autumn of 1951 was the denunciation by the Egyptian Government of the Treaty of 1936, by the terms of which Britain had been granted the right to station troops in the Canal Zone. The growing unrest in Egypt constituted a serious threat not only to the lives of British subjects but also to the safety of the huge military installations and dumps of stores which had been assembled in the Zone during the previous fifteen years. During the Battalion's tour in Egypt, sporadic negotiations between the two governments were to drag on, until in October 1954 an agreement was signed whereby Britain agreed to withdraw her troops in return for the right to maintain some of the installations in the charge of civilian contractors and to re-occupy the base in certain strictly limited circumstances.

Thus the Regiment was involved in every stage of the era of British predominance in Egypt. It had landed with Abercromby at Aboukir Bay in 1801; in 1882 it had marched with Wolseley to Tel-el-Kebir, a victory which marked the beginning of the occupation; it had been stationed in Kasr-el-Nil Barracks in peace-time, when Gezira and Shepheard's were in their heyday; and it had fought in the immortal battles in the Western Desert from 1941 to 1942. Now it was to be present as the era came to a close. The final phase was one of wearisome guard duties and few comforts.

In great haste, the main body of the Battalion was flown to Cyprus; it was the first time that a battalion of the Regiment had been transported by air. By the 1st December it was assembled in a tented camp at Zyggi, where it was joined by its transport which had made the journey in H.M. Aircraft Carrier *Illustrious* and the transport *Empire Doric*. The strength of the Battalion was 27 Officers and 632 Other Ranks, organised into three rifle companies and a support company. Within a fortnight of its arrival it had moved to a camp at Nicosia where it experienced a most violent storm, in the course of which the s.s. *Porlock Hill* ran aground off Famagusta and broke in two; the hold where the ship parted contained all the battalion's possessions and heavy baggage, very little of which was recovered from the sea.

In Cyprus the Battalion was given an internal security role, but as

[1] Written July, 1956.

yet the movement for union with Greece was quiescent. Its main task was to hold itself ready to move to Egypt to protect the lives of European residents should they be in danger. In January 1952 violent riots raged in Cairo and it looked as if the Battalion would be called upon. In fact it had already embarked for its task when the disorders abated, and in consequence no landing took place. A month later the situation again looked grave, and this time the Battalion was hurried across the Mediterranean in three corvettes and the *Empire Doric* to Port Said.

At Port Said the Battalion was quartered in the Golf Course Camp, with a company detached to Port Fuad on the other side of the Canal. The Golf Course Camp was to be its home for nearly two and a half years, and its immediate surroundings were said to "combine the disadvantages of East and West: the dirt of both and the charm of neither". The camp lay "a mile from the domed building of the Canal Company, across seven railway lines emerging from the station, through the Garrison Engineer's Yard and immediately adjacent to the prison. Each evening the westerly breeze bears with it the delicious scent of Lake Manzala, which serves as a sewage farm for the Arab quarter . . . ." From this depressing base the Battalion plunged immediately into a period of extremely heavy duties, all the while standing by at the shortest notice to undertake any action deemed necessary to protect lives and property from violence. By early April the tension had greatly eased, and the guard duties, which at the outset had taken 170 Non-Commissioned Officers and Guardsmen for duty every night, were reduced to more manageable proportions. The Port Fuad detachment came to an end, and, punctuated by periodic scares, the routine life of the Canal Zone could begin.

1952–54   That life had the makings of being tedious in the extreme, for there was little entertainment outside camp, little spare time and an unfriendly atmosphere; nor, in the early stages, could the married men be joined by their families. Nevertheless morale, health and turn-out were of the highest order throughout, for which a large measure of the credit must go to Colonel Fane Gladwin and his two Adjutants, at first Captain J. B. Denham and after July 1952 Captain N. G. Ramsay. Just as the Second Battalion had transformed the appearance of its camps in Malaya, so also the First Battalion at Port Said did all it could to make its camp a more comfortable habitation; the Pioneers performed wonders, and the less skilled indulged in orgies of self-help.

There would be no point in describing chronologically the changes in the duties of the Battalion, or in cataloguing the many exercises in which it took part; and to list its sporting and musketry victories would require a separate Appendix. At various times it guarded the great Ordnance Depot of Abu Sultan and the El Firdan bridge over the

Canal, and it did duty at Ismalia and Moascar. Its main enemies were the cable cutter, whose intentions were more predatory than political, and the familiar Egyptian thief, who was now elevated by nationalistic propaganda to the dignity of a hero. Few of these fleet and slippery customers were caught, but many were deterred.

By great good fortune the Battalion suffered only one fatal casualty at the hands of the thugs. This was Guardsman K. Wallace, who was fatally wounded in Port Said during April 1954 while on vehicle escort, a task which occupied many weary hours. In the same month the Battalion was also greatly grieved by the death after a short illness of Second-Lieutenant G. Paynter, whose father, the late Brigadier-General Sir George Paynter, had commanded the Regiment from 1923 to 1927.

As in Malaya, air travel enabled the Lieutenant-Colonels to visit the Battalion in Egypt, both Lord Dalrymple and Colonel Dunbar making the journey. In March 1954 an especially welcome visitor was Major-General G. F. Johnson, C.B., C.B.E., D.S.O., formerly of the Regiment, who had recently assumed command of the Household Brigade.

By July 1954, when the Battalion moved down the Canal from Port Said to Moascar, exchanging what was now a well-found camp for one far inferior, King Farouk had abdicated, General Neguib had been supplanted, and Colonel Nasser was in power. In that month the heads of agreement were initialled, and in October the new Treaty was signed. The evacuation, which was not concluded until June 1956, began at once, but before the Battalion left it was able to send to Cairo the first leave parties to go there since the British had withdrawn into the Canal Zone in 1947. The main body of the Battalion, which since August had been under the command of Lieutenant-Colonel T. F. R. Bulkeley, M.B.E., embarked at Port Said in the *Georgic* on the 11th December, arriving at Liverpool on the 19th, in time to spend Christmas and Hogmanay at home for the first time in four years.

* * *

The First Battalion reassembled at Wellington Barracks in January 1955, for its first tour of duty in the West End since marching off to Euston Station in April 1940 on its way to Norway. It suffered a severe disappointment when the Queen's Birthday Parade, at which it was to have found the Escort, was cancelled owing to the railway strike. Instead it found itself ministering to the needs of Servicemen in transit: over 15,000 passed through the Battalion's hands in the two weeks the strike lasted.

The Regimental Band, under the direction of Lieutenant-Colonel S. Rhodes, M.B.E., now Senior Director of Music of the Brigade of Guards, has continued to provide music of outstanding excellence throughout the length and breadth of the land. Certainly the most notable event since the war has been its tour of Canada and the United States in the winter of 1955. It went under the auspices of a well-known impresario, Mr. Hurok, and was accompanied by Major A. N. B. Ritchie. To add to the spectacle there went also the massed pipes and drums of both battalions, which could provide from their ranks several talented Highland dancers. After a tour lasting ten weeks the party could lay claim to a set of statistics impressive even by American standards. It had covered 15,000 miles by bus, it had visited two Provinces of the Dominion and thirty-six States of the Union, it had given sixty-three performances in fifty-two different cities, and it had played to close on half a million people. Specially notable had been the opening march through Washington, the generous good wishes and hospitality extended by many Americans of Scottish descent and by the Household Brigade Association of America, and finally there was the triumph of playing on four separate occasions to full houses at Madison Square Garden, New York. After one of these concerts a correspondent of *The Times* was inspired to write that there was "an indescribable feeling in the air that was probably international good will bursting out all over".

The standard of the Pipers in the Regiment has continued to reflect the greatest credit on the Pipe Majors. Since 1954 a Piping School has been established at Pirbright, to which aspiring Pipers are sent after leaving the Guards Depot. Later they join the battalions as trained Pipers, instead of being trained by the battalions as was previously the case. The publication in 1954 of *Scots Guards Standard Settings of Pipe Music*,[1] prepared under the direction of Major D. S. Robertson, has done much to fulfil the need for an up-to-date pipe manual, both inside and outside the Regiment.

In addition to the alliance concluded before the war with the Winnipeg Grenadiers, in 1951 a new one was formed with the 3rd Battalion The Royal Australian Regiment. Prior to 1939 the Australian Permanent Military Forces contained no regular infantry battalions, but after the war, mainly for the task of occupying Japan, a regular Brigade was formed, and the 67th Battalion of Australian Infantry became the 3rd Battalion The Australian Regiment, the distinction "Royal" being conferred in 1950. The 3rd Battalion greatly distinguished itself in the war in Korea, and at the date of publication of this history it was stationed in Australia. As yet the Scots Guards has had no opportunity of meeting its new Australian ally as a body, and has had to content itself with entertaining any of its members who may find themselves in Britain.

* * *

[1] Patterson's Publications Ltd., 36 Wigmore St., W.1. The Manual includes chapters on the history, dress and duties of the Pipers.

43. CAPTAIN THE LORD LYELL, V.C.
First Battalion, Scots Guards

Killed in Action in Tunisia on Gebel Bou Aoukaz,
27th April 1943

Reproduced by kind permission of Lady Lyell

From left to right

44. ORDERS OF DRESS, 1956

Back Row: (1) QUARTERMASTER, FULL DRESS (Captain (QM) D. McG. Fraser, M.B.E.); (2) No. 1 DRESS, CEREMONIAL (Captain O. B. Varney).
Centre Row: DRILL ORDER (Guardsman G. Laut); (2) DRILL ORDER, TROPICAL (Sergeant F. Gourlay); (5) DRILL ORDER (RSM D. McN. Whyte); BATTLE ORDER (Guardsman J. Knox).

To conclude this History it seems proper to record the state of the Regiment at the time of going to press in July 1956.

Her Majesty was Colonel-in-Chief of the Regiment, and her uncle, His Royal Highness the Duke of Gloucester, who had been promoted Field Marshal on the 31st March 1955, was Colonel. Colonel H. N. Clowes, D.S.O., O.B.E., held the appointment of Lieutenant-Colonel, with Major G. P. M. Ramsay as his Adjutant. The First Battalion, commanded by Lieutenant-Colonel T. F. R. Bulkeley, M.B.E., was stationed at Lee-Mitford Camp, Lydd, and the Second Battalion, commanded by Lieutenant-Colonel the Hon. Michael Fitzalan Howard, M.V.O., M.B.E., M.C., was stationed at Llanelly Barracks, Hubbelrath, near Düsseldorf, Germany. K Company was instilling drill and discipline into the recruits at the Guards Depot, Caterham, and L Company was attending to their tactics as part of the Guards Training Battalion at Pirbright. On the 1st May the strength of the Regiment was 109 officers and 1,892 other ranks, of whom 28 officers and 472 men were serving under the provisions of the National Service Acts.

APPENDICES

APPENDICES

A ROLL OF HONOUR

I	Officers 1939–1945.	503
II	Other Ranks 1939–1945.	506
III	All Ranks, Malaya, 1948–1951.	524
IV	Statistics of Casualties 1939–1945.	526

B HONOURS AND AWARDS

I	Victoria Cross.	528
II	British Decorations for Gallantry 1939–1945.	530
III	Other Honours and Awards 1939–1945:	
	(*a*) British;	534
	(*b*) Foreign.	535
IV	Statistics of Decorations 1939–1945.	536
V	Malaya 1948–1951.	537

C OFFICERS AND WARRANT OFFICERS WHO HELD THE PRINCIPAL APPOINTMENTS 1934–1955

I	Colonels-in-Chief.	538
II	Colonels.	538
III	Lieutenant-Colonels Commanding the Regiment.	538
IV	Commanding Officers.	538
V	Regimental Adjutants.	539
VI	Battalion Adjutants.	539
VII	Quartermasters.	540
VIII	Directors of Music.	541
IX	Regimental Sergeant Majors.	541
X	Superintending Clerks.	541

D ORDERS OF BATTLE 1939–1945   542

E **NOMINAL ROLL OF OFFICERS,** in continuation of that in Vol. II of *The History of the Scots Guards*.   559

F **THE DRESS OF THE REGIMENT**   589
by Major John Swinton, Scots Guards.

APPENDIX A

Roll of Honour

I. OFFICERS WHO WERE KILLED IN ACTION, WHO DIED OF WOUNDS OR WHO DIED ON ACTIVE SERVICE

1939–1945

Rank, Name and Decorations	Unit	Country	Date of Death
Captain Sir F. H. R. Astley-Corbett, Baronet	2nd Bn.	Italy	10.9.43
Captain P. G. Atkinson-Clark	2nd Bn.	Italy	26.1.44
Lieutenant D. M. H. Bailie	1st Bn.	Italy	30.1.44
Captain A. M. Balfour, M.C.	1st Bn.	Italy	9.2.44
Lieutenant R. A. E. Balfour	2nd Bn.	Italy	17.9.43
Major T. L. Ballantine-Dykes	2nd Bn.	Cyrenaica	13.6.42
Lieutenant J. E. Baxter	1st Bn.	Italy	16.10.44
Lieutenant W. Beckett	2nd Bn.	Italy	11.9.43
2nd Lieutenant M. F. Beeson	2nd Bn.	Egypt	19.7.42
Captain N. W. Beeson	3rd Bn.	France	30.7.44
Lieutenant R. A. Berridge	2nd Bn.	Germany	9.4.45
Lieutenant D. J. N. Bland	2nd Bn.	Tunisia	27.4.43
2nd Lieutenant The Lord Blythswood	Trg. Bn.	U.K.	14.9.40
Lieutenant The Hon. J. P. Bowes-Lyon (Master of Glamis)	2nd Bn.	Egypt	19.9.41
Lieutenant H. R. Bridgeman	S Coy.	Italy	28.5.44
Major R. H. Bull, M.C.	1st Bn.	Italy	30.1.44
Captain J. W. Burden	HQ. Gds. Armd. Div.	France	21.7.44
Captain R. W. O. Burnett	3rd Bn.	Germany	16.2.45
Lieutenant The Hon. P. H. S. D. Butler	1st Bn.	Italy	28.2.44
Lieutenant C. Campbell	3rd Bn.	Germany	17.2.45
Lieutenant J. P. Carpenter-Garnier	2nd Bn.	Italy	22.9.43
Lieutenant Sir N. J. Cayzer, Baronet	2nd Bn.	Italy	11.9.43
Captain The Earl of Chichester	HQ. 6th Gds. Tank Bde.	U.K.	21.2.44
Major J. M. Cobbold	War Office	Guards Chapel	18.6.44
Lieutenant D. A. Colquhoun	1st Bn.	Italy	5.4.45
Lieutenant J. F. Cory-Wright	2nd Bn.	Germany	9.4.45
2nd Lieutenant J. G. Critchley	2nd Bn.	Cyrenaica	27.12.41
Lieutenant J. S. Cuninghame	2nd Bn.	Italy	22.10.43
Lieutenant J. L. R. Currie	att. 4th Bn. Coldm. Gds.	Germany	11.4.45
Major S. J. Cuthbert	3rd Bn.	France	30.7.44
Lieutenant V. E. de S-C. De Soissons	2nd Bn.	Germany	10.4.45
Lieutenant H. W. Dods	W. Grsn. Bn.	Guards Chapel	18.6.44
Captain (QM.) W. J. Dorman, M.B.E.	3rd Bn.	France	2.9.44
2nd Lieutenant J. A. G. Duberly	W. Grsn. Bn.	Guards Chapel	18.6.44

APPENDIX A

Rank, Name and Decorations	Unit	Country	Date of Death
Lieutenant W. M. C. Duberly	2nd Bn.	Italy	8.12.43
Major J. H. Elwes, M.C.	2nd Bn.	Tunisia	18.3.43
Lieutenant The Hon. A. R. H. Erskine, M.C.	2nd Bn.	Germany	19.4.45
Lieutenant H. J. H. Eves	2nd Bn.	Tunisia	18.3.43
Major C. A. Fletcher	1st Bn.	Italy	27.1.44
Lieutenant D. I. Fyfe-Jamieson, M.C.	2nd Bn.	Italy	12.11.43
Captain M. J. A. Gordon	2nd Bn.	Italy	8.10.43
Lieutenant V. M. Gordon-Ives	2nd Bn.	Italy	22.1.44
Lieutenant I. G. Gow	2nd Bn.	Germany	8.3.45
Captain R. de M. Grant Watson	Special Boat Service	Cyrenaica	27.3.42
Captain R. D. M. Gurowski	Hldg. Bn.	Dunkirk	2.6.40
Captain M. D. C. Hanbury-Tracy	HQ. 9th Inf. Bde.	U.K. (of wounds received at Dunkirk)	22.8.40
Lt.-Colonel F. H. H. B. Harris	2nd Bn.	Italy	27.2.44
Lieutenant N. de P. Henderson-Scott	2nd Bn.	Tunisia	20.4.43
Lieutenant R. Humble	3rd Bn.	France	30.7.44
Captain R. T. Hunter	1st Bn.	Italy	1.10.44
Major D. H. A. Kemble, M.C.	2nd Bn.	Germany	6.4.45
Captain H. Knight	2nd Bn.	Egypt	17.6.41
Lieutenant C. Lewis	1st Bn.	Tunisia	23.4.43
Captain T. C. Lindsay-Peto, M.C.	1st Bn.	Italy	24.4.45
Lieutenant D. E. Loder	2nd Bn.	Italy	23.10.43
Lieutenant T. M. F. E. Lowinsky	1st Bn.	Italy	16.2.44
Captain The Lord Lyell, V.C.	1st Bn.	Tunisia	27.4.43
Lieutenant K. B. Mackenzie	2nd Bn.	Italy	22.12.43
Major J. D. C. S. Macrae, D.S.O.	2nd Bn.	Egypt	19.7.42
Major W. B. Malone	2nd Bn.	Italy	7.12.43
Lieutenant H. W. S. Marshall	3rd Bn.	Holland	26.11.44
Captain T. Marsham-Townsend	HQ. 201 Gds. Bde.	Italy	24.1.44
Captain I. K. Matheson	G.H.Q., B.E.F.	France	23.5.40
Captain D. G. Mathieson	3rd Bn.	France	6.8.44
Major D. V. C. McBarnet	1st Bn.	Italy	28.2.44
Lieutenant R. C. McLeod	2nd Bn.	Italy	11.9.43
Lieutenant D. G. S. McMurtrie	1st Bn.	Italy	4.2.44
Lieutenant K. A. P. Monfries	1st Bn.	Italy	18.11.44
Lieutenant G. F. Mundy	1st Bn.	Italy	26.5.44
Lieutenant R. G. Mutter	2nd Bn.	Germany	27.4.45
Captain A. S. Neilson, D.S.O.	S Coy.	Italy	16.7.44
Lieutenant M. G. R. Nevill	1st Bn.	Tunisia	28.4.43
Captain R. C. G. Pember, M.C.	3rd Bn.	Germany	29.3.45
Captain A. H. R. M. Ramsay	2nd Bn.	South Africa	19.8.43
Lieutenant J. S. M. Ramsay	3rd Bn.	Holland	26.10.44
Major H. S. N. Rathbone	2nd Bn.	Italy	9.11.43
Captain T. C. D. Russell, M.C.	G.H.Q., M.E.F.	Roumania	4.9.43
Lieutenant E. M. Sharp	S Coy.	Italy	8.5.44
Lieutenant P. H. Shaw Stewart	1st Bn.	Italy	31.1.44
Captain J. H. L. Sinclair	1st Bn.	Italy	8.2.44
Lieutenant H. A. W. Smith	1st Bn.	Italy	4.8.44
Lieutenant H. M. Snell	1st Bn.	Italy	4.8.44
Lieutenant R. O. Stewart	1st Bn.	Italy	26.1.44
Lieutenant H. J. Stirling	2nd Bn.	Egypt	24.4.41

APPENDIX A

Rank, Name and Decorations	Unit	Country	Date of Death
Captain J. S. Stockton	1st Bn.	Tunisia	27.4.43
Lieutenant W. H. Struthers	2nd Bn.	Germany	26.4.45
Lieutenant I. McC. Tait	2nd Bn.	Italy	28.12.43
Lt.-Colonel G. A. D. Taylor, M.C.	1st Bn.	Italy	26.6.44
Lieutenant T. C. H. Thomson	2nd Bn.	Italy	10.10.43
Lieutenant N. Thorpe, M.C.	X Coy.	Belgium	9.9.44
Major H. D. Tweedie	2nd Bn.	Germany	8.4.45
Major J. E. Tyldesley Jones	1st Bn.	Italy	27.1.44
Captain The Hon. W. H. Vestey	1st Bn.	Italy	26.6.44
Lt.-Colonel D. S. Wedderburn, D.S.O.	1st Bn.	Italy	1.3.44
Major A. J. A. Weir, M.C.	1st Bn.	Italy	28.2.44
Lieutenant L. E. Widderson	1st Bn.	Italy	28.2.44
Lieutenant J. Wilson	3rd Bn.	Holland	20.11.44
Lieutenant E. F. Winter	1st Bn.	Italy	24.4.45

II. WARRANT OFFICERS, NON-COMMISSIONED OFFICERS AND GUARDSMEN WHO WERE KILLED IN ACTION, WHO DIED OF WOUNDS OR WHO DIED ON ACTIVE SERVICE
1939–1945

Note: The following abbreviations are used in this Roll.

Cdo.	Commando	Hld.	Holding Battalion
G.A.T.W.	Guards Armoured Training Wing	PW.	Prisoner of War
		Trg.	Training Battalion
Gds. Dep.	Guards Depot	W. Grsn.	Westminster Garrison Battalion
S.A.S.	Special Air Service		

Number, Rank, Name and Decorations	Battalion or Company	Country	Date of Death
2703125 L/Cpl. Abbot, G. W.	2nd	Germany	6.4.45
2697882 Gdsm. Abbot, R.	2nd	Italy	23.9.43
2699398 L/Cpl. Abercromby, R.	1st	Italy	26.1.44
2698470 Gdsm. Ackerley, R.	3rd	France	6.8.44
2697069 Gdsm. Adam, J.	1st	Tunisia	29.4.43
2696263 L/Sgt. Adam, R. C.	1st	Italy	29.1.44
2696360 Gdsm. Adams, T.	1st	Norway	17.5.40
2698373 Gdsm. Adams, V. J.	1st	Italy	9.2.44
2699669 Gdsm. Agnew, W. E.	1st	Italy	1.10.44
2699175 Gdsm. Aiton, A.	X	Belgium	9.9.44
2696561 Gdsm. Allan, D. G.	2nd	At sea: PW.	14.11.42
2701796 L/Cpl. Allan, J. E.	S	Italy	9.6.44
2701873 Gdsm. Allan, J. M.	S	Italy	21.6.44
2697637 Gdsm. Allardyce, A.	3rd	Holland	4.10.44
2699224 Gdsm. Allen, S. E. G.	X	France	11.8.44
7685099 Gdsm. Anderson, A. C.	1st	Tunisia	1.5.43
2695866 Gdsm. Anderson, D.	2nd	Italy; PW.	25.11.42
2702982 Gdsm. Anderson, J. D. McR.	2nd	Germany	8.3.45
2696384 Gdsm. Anderson, N.	2nd	Italy	17.9.43
2693499 Gdsm. Andow, S. R.	1st	Italy	30.1.44
2697063 L/Cpl. Armstrong, A. E.	2nd	Italy	10.10.43
2700720 L/Cpl. Atkinson, S. P.	1st	Italy	30.1.44
2693687 Gdsm. Autherson, W.	1st	Italy	26.6.44
6204831 L/Sgt. Bagge, G. J.	2nd	Germany	6.3.45
2696371 Gdsm. Baines, A.	1st	Tunisia	27.4.43
2700313 Gdsm. Balfour, J. N.	X	France	19.7.44
2695835 Gdsm. Balfour, J. R.	2nd	Italy	31.4.43
2700582 Gdsm. Ball, R. E.	2nd	Italy	30.9.43
2698355 Gdsm. Banford, H. McK.	3rd	Holland	11.10.44
2700608 Gdsm. Banks, G.	1st	Tunisia	27.4.43
2694324 L/Cpl. Banks, W.	1st	Italy	22.2.44
2699280 L/Cpl. Barber, R.	X	France	1.8.44
2695340 L/Sgt. Barclay, G. W.	2nd	Italy	11.10.43
2696058 L/Cpl. Barclay, H.	1st	Italy	17.2.44
2695896 L/Sgt. Barlow, H.	2nd	Egypt	7.8.42

APPENDIX A

Number, Rank, Name and Decorations	Battalion or Company	Country	Date of Death
2700314 Gdsm. Barnetson, A.	2nd	Italy	12.11.43
2696582 L/Cpl. Barr, J. A.	1st	Tunisia	26.4.43
2698832 Gdsm. Barrett, D. A.	1st	Tunisia	29.4.43
2697253 Gdsm. Barron, J. J.	1st	Italy	17.4.45
2699885 Gdsm. Batchelor, C. G.	1st	Tunisia	29.4.43
2693491 Gdsm. Bateman, O. J.	Trg. Bn.	U.K.	14.12.40
2700711 Gdsm. Bateson, J.	2nd	Tunisia	18.4.43
2696077 Gdsm. Baxter, A.	2nd	Italy	16.9.43
2695247 Gdsm. Bayliss, F.	1st	Italy	1.10.44
2699357 L/Cpl. Beaton, R. McL.	Hld.	U.K.	1.7.42
2699957 L/Cpl. Beattie, J.	2nd	Italy	9.11.43
2695097 Sgt. Beevers, F.	1st	Tunisia	24.4.43
37321 CSM. Begg, J. C.	1st	Italy	30.1.44
2696797 Sgt. Bell, C. M.	2nd	Italy	11.9.43
2699440 Gdsm. Bennett, G. W. H.	1st	Tunisia	25.4.43
2701671 Gdsm. Bennett, J.	1st	Italy	4.12.44
2693553 Gdsm. Bennett, W. G.	1st	Tunisia	30.4.43
2696420 Gdsm. Bennett, W. H.	2nd	At sea; PW.	14.11.42
2700672 Gdsm. Berry, W.	1st	Italy	29.8.44
2697109 Gdsm. Best, G.	1st	Tunisia	23.4.43
2701932 Gdsm. Bettinson, A.	1st	Italy	30.10.44
2698400 Gdsm. Beveridge, A.	2nd	Italy	22.10.43
2701978 Gdsm. Bilsby, D. E. W.	2nd	Germany	8.3.45
2693289 Gdsm. Birrell, A.	1st	U.K.	21.10.42
2696468 Sgt. Birss, J.	3rd	France	6.8.44
2696695 L/Cpl. Bisset, D. C.	2nd	Egypt	16.6.41
2697567 Gdsm. Black, J.	1st	Italy	17.4.45
2695136 Cpl. Blackford, D. C.	1st	Italy	8.2.44
2703132 Gdsm. Blyton, J.	2nd	Germany	6.3.45
7347286 L/Cpl. Boath, W.	1st	Italy	10.2.44
2696934 Gdsm. Bolland, S.	8th Cdo.	Middle East	20.11.41
2700663 Gdsm. Borthwick, D. W.	2nd	Italy	20.2.44
2694384 L/Cpl. Boulton, J.	1st	U.K.	7.7.40
4341128 Gdsm. Bowman, J. W.	2nd	Italy	12.2.44
2696552 Gdsm. Bowman, W. C.	1st	Tunisia	30.4.43
2698037 Gdsm. Boyd, N.	1st	Italy	22.8.44
2701876 Gdsm. Boyd, W.	X	Holland	1.10.44
2697421 Gdsm. Boyes, J.	1st	Tunisia	24.4.43
2693141 L/Sgt. Bradford, H.	2nd	Cyrenaica	13.6.42
2695880 Gdsm. Bradley, E. W.	2nd	Italy	11.9.43
2700604 Gdsm. Brady, T. S.	1st	Italy	17.4.45
2698234 Gdsm. Brand, W. McD.	3rd	France	11.8.44
2698632 Gdsm. Brazier, F.	3rd	Germany	8.2.45
2702899 Gdsm. Brett, A. L.	2nd	U.K. (From wounds received in Germany.)	23.10.45
2700233 Gdsm. Britton, T.	2nd	Italy	8.10.43
2699212 Gdsm. Brogan, J.	1st	Italy	26.6.44
2699980 L/Cpl. Broom, G. M.	2nd	Tunisia	6.3.43
2692609 L/Sgt. Brown, A. V.	2nd	North Africa	20.7.43
2695933 Gdsm. Brown, A. W.	2nd	Cyrenaica	9.12.41
2702083 Gdsm. Brown, C.	2nd	Germany	19.4.45
2701342 Gdsm. Brown, F. B.	1st	Italy	29.9.44
2695625 Gdsm. Brown, J. McC.	2nd	Cyrenaica	11.12.41
2697330 Gdsm. Brown, M. C.	1st	Italy	31.1.44
2693555 L/Cpl. Brown, S.	2nd	Italy	21.9.43

APPENDIX A

Number, Rank, Name and Decorations	Battalion or Company	Country	Date of Death
2753247 CSM. Brown, T. W., **D.C.M.**	S	Italy	15.7.44
2696377 L/Cpl. Browne, H. C.	1st	Tunisia	29.4.43
2698452 L/Cpl. Bruce, A. W.	1st	Italy	30.1.44
2700701 Gdsm. Bruce, R.	1st	Italy	10.2.44
2701177 Gdsm. Bruce, W.	3rd	Germany	16.2.45
2696882 L/Cpl. Bruin, A. C.	2nd	Cyrenaica	26.2.42
2696646 Gdsm. Bryce, J.	2nd	Cyrenaica	23.11.41
2695855 L/Cpl. Bryden, J. A.	2nd	Egypt	19.9.41
2697375 Gdsm. Brydon, J.	1st	Tunisia	28.4.43
2694706 L/Cpl. Bryson, J. H., **D.C.M.**	2nd	Italy	26.2.44
2697200 Gdsm. Buchanan, T.	1st	Tunisia	29.4.43
2701110 Gdsm. Budge, W.	2nd	Italy	13.11.43
2702952 Gdsm. Burden, W. R.	2nd	Germany	19.4.45
2699454 Gdsm. Burnett, J.	X	Germany	6.12.44
2696586 L/Sgt. Burton, E. G.	1st	Italy	20.10.44
2701675 Gdsm. Burton, J.	2nd	Germany	7.3.45
2694198 Gdsm. Busby, J.	1st	U.K.	29.1.40
2695806 Gdsm. Butcher, W. C.	2nd	Cyrenaica	8.1.42
2696329 L/Cpl. Butterwood, R. E.	1st	Italy	21.4.45
2700683 Gdsm. Buxton, R. H.	1st	Italy	30.1.44
2697302 Gdsm. Cairns, J. M.	1st	Tunisia	26.4.43
2696619 L/Sgt. Caider, J. W.	2nd	Italy	17.9.43
2698326 Gdsm. Caider, R. G.	3rd	France	9.8.44
2700768 Gdsm. Caldwell, R.	2nd	U.K. (From wounds received in Italy.)	3.5.44
2702953 Gdsm. Callaghan, H.	2nd	Germany	2.4.45
2700321 Gdsm. Cameron, T.	1st	Italy	1.10.44
2698406 Gdsm. Campbell, A. K.	3rd	Holland	1.10.44
2699183 Gdsm. Campbell, D. J.	1st	Italy	30.1.44
2696525 L/Sgt. Campbell, D. R.	S	Italy	28.5.44
2699167 Gdsm. Campbell, F.	1st	Italy	30.1.44
2697058 Gdsm. Campbell, H. R.	2nd	Italy	11.9.43
3852732 L/Sgt. Campbell, J.	Trg.	U.K.	12.6.41
2697985 Gdsm. Campbell, J.	1st	Tunisia	24.4.43
2698627 Gdsm. Campbell, J.	3rd	Germany	2.3.45
2697390 Gdsm. Campbell, L.	3rd Cdo.	France	6.6.44
2700811 L/Cpl. Campbell, R. C.	X	Belgium	7.9.44
2696247 Gdsm. Campbell, R. F.	1st	Norway	22.5.40
3697886 Gdsm. Capperauid, D. H.	Hld.	U.K.	15.3.41
2700397 Gdsm. Carnell, E. H. N.	1st	Italy	22.11.44
2697570 L/Sgt. Carney, M.	2nd	Tunisia	28.3.43
2700713 L/Cpl. Carroll, J.	2nd	Italy	11.9.43
2698237 L/Sgt. Carson, J.	3rd	U.K.	1.11.41
2696953 Gdsm. Carter, R. A.	1st	Italy	20.7.44
2696123 L/Cpl. Cartwright, J.	2nd	Cyrenaica	13.6.42
2700326 Gdsm. Cartwright, J. E.	1st	Tunisia	10.5.43
2696023 L/Sgt. Cashmore, G. A., **M.M.**	1st	Italy	30.1.44
2698105 Gdsm. Cassidy, G.	1st	Italy	30.1.44
2695931 Gdsm. Caukwell, J. W.	2nd	Egypt	30.9.39
2703061 Gdsm. Causton, L.	2nd	Germany	9.4.45
2695749 Gdsm. Charles, W. A.	2nd	Italy; PW.	22.11.43
2696458 L/Sgt. Cheyne, P.	1st	Italy	10.2.44
2696465 Gdsm. Cheyne, R.	1st	Italy	20.10.44
2696168 Gdsm. Chopping, F.	1st	U.K.	19.5.41
2701930 Gdsm. Churchyard, E. J.	1st	Italy	11.2.44

APPENDIX A

Number, Rank, Name and Decorations	Battalion or Company	Country	Date of Death
2698639 Gdsm. Clark, A. D.	2nd	Italy	7.10.43
2697845 Gdsm. Clark, C. J.	2nd	Italy	3.10.43
2696166 Gdsm. Clark, J.	2nd	Egypt	17.6.41
2699127 Gdsm. Clark, J.	1st	Italy	23.6.44
2689049 Gdsm. Clark, J. J.	2nd	Egypt	24.10.40
2694773 Gdsm. Clark J. Y.	1st	Norway	23.5.40
2700244 Gdsm. Clark, T.	1st	Italy	9.2.44
2699101 Gdsm. Clarke, G.	2nd	Italy	15.2.44
2692964 Gdsm. Clarke, G. H.	1st	U.K.	18.10.40
2696560 L/Cpl. Clarke, J.	2nd	Cyrenaica	27.5.42
2696773 Gdsm. Clarke, J.	2nd	Italy; PW.	29.12.41
2694147 Gdsm. Clarke, S.	1st	U.K.	17.3.41
2700400 Gdsm. Clarkson, J. E.	1st	Italy	26.5.44
2695143 Sgt. Clement, J., M.M.	1st	Italy	19.10.44
2694813 Gdsm. Cleworth, E.	2nd	Egypt	22.6.41
2696978 L/Sgt. Cockburn, J. F.	1st	Italy	4.2.44
2696991 Gdsm. Cockburn, R. L.	1st	Tunisia	29.4.43
2696889 L/Cpl. Collie, E.	2nd	Italy	11.9.43
2695007 Gdsm. Colligan, G.	1st	Italy	1.2.44
2695231 Gdsm. Collin, R.	1st	Italy	9.2.44
2696764 L/Sgt. Colston, L. G.	1st	Italy	30.1.44
2701401 Gdsm. Combes, D. W.	Gds. Dep.	U.K.	25.3.43
2701883 Gdsm. Connell, A.	2nd	Germany	19.4.45
2696267 Sgt. Connelly, R.	2nd	North Africa	6.9.43
2695363 Gdsm. Conner, J.	2nd	Egypt	16.6.41
2697757 Gdsm. Connolly, W. H.	1st	Italy	23.6.44
2698846 Gdsm. Cook, A. B.	1st	Italy	10.2.44
2693012 CQMS. Coonie, A.	1st	Italy	1.10.44
2700366 Gdsm. Copland, D. McK.	1st	Tunisia	4.5.43
2701229 Gdsm. Copland, P. J. S.	3rd	Germany	11.4.45
2692855 Gdsm. Corby, J. A.	1st	Italy	6.7.44
2699330 Gdsm. Corris, J.	2nd	Italy	21.1.44
2701615 L/Cpl. Coull, A. J. C.	1st	Italy	17.4.45
2698604 L/Cpl. Coulton, G.	2nd	Italy	14.10.43
2693117 Gdsm. Cowans, R.	Trg.	U.K.	22.3.41
2696538 Gdsm. Crabtree, J.	1st	Italy	10.2.44
2694140 Sgt. Craib, W. McP.	1st	Italy	17.9.44
2697688 Gdsm. Craig, A.	2nd	Egypt.	27.8.41
2700909 Gdsm. Craig, J.	1st	Italy	30.1.44
2694827 Gdsm. Craven, J. J.	1st	Italy	25.7.44
2697381 Gdsm. Crellin, E. S.	1st	Italy	2.3.44
2699455 Gdsm. Crerar, E.	1st	Italy	1.10.44
2697412 L/Cpl. Crichton, D. S.	2nd	Egypt	19.9.41
2694224 Sgt. Croydon, E. V.	1st	Tunisia	29.4.43
2699536 L/Cpl. Cruickshanks, A.	2nd	Italy	25.9.43
2703085 Gdsm. Culling, H.	2nd	Germany	6.4.45
2698376 Gdsm. Currie, A. T.	1st	Italy	12.2.44
2702044 L/Sgt. Cuthbertson, I. C.	2nd	Germany	6.3.45
2697873 Gdsm. Dalglish, D.	1st	Italy	14.7.44
2695166 Sgt. Dalton, P. J.	1st	Italy	30.1.44
2702113 Gdsm. Daly, J. A.	2nd	Germany	25.4.45
2693874 Sgt. Daniels, G. H.	1st	Italy	9.2.44
2696447 Gdsm. Dann, I. E.	1st	Italy	4.9.44
2702316 Gdsm. Darlington, T.	2nd	Germany	18.4.45
2696300 Gdsm. Davidson, A.	2nd	Italy; PW.	12.2.43

APPENDIX A

Number, Rank, Name and Decorations	Battalion or Company	Country	Date of Death
2698027 Gdsm. Davidson, A. J. M.	2nd	Italy	22.10.43
2698024 L/Cpl. Davidson, A. McM.	2nd	Italy	11.9.43
2699040 Gdsm. Davidson, G.	1st	Italy	28.7.44
2694597 L/Sgt. Davidson, J.	S	Italy	28.5.44
2702547 Gdsm. Davidson, P. B.	2nd	Germany	10.4.45
2697670 Gdsm. Davidson, W. H.	1st	Italy	27.1.44
2694120 Gdsm. Davies, F.	1st	Norway	17.5.40
2696616 L/Sgt. Davies, T., M.M.	2nd	Tunisia	25.4.43
2694287 Gdsm. Davis, A. G.	1st	U.K.	8.3.41
2981539 Gdsm. Davis, L. C.	2nd	Cyrenaica	10.12.41
2695933 Gdsm. Dawson, G.	2nd	Italy; PW.	28.10.42
2702892 Gdsm. Dempster, W.	2nd	Germany	18.4.45
2698076 Gdsm. Dennison, J.	1st	Italy	11.2.44
2698869 L/Cpl. Dewar, D. W.	1st	Italy	30.1.44
2701465 Gdsm. Dews, A. H.	1st	Italy	10.2.44
2698551 L/Cpl. Dixon, T.	2nd	Italy	21.1.44
2701082 L/Cpl. Dixon, W.	2nd	Italy	20.9.43
2697157 Gdsm. Dochard, J.	1st	U.K.	23.6.41
2697002 Gdsm. Docherty, F.	2nd	Italy	11.9.43
2693522 Sgt. Dodd, A. J.	2nd	Germany	18.4.45
2700306 Gdsm. Doherty, M. H.	1st	Tunisia	28.4.43
2695647 L/Sgt. Doig, R.	1st	Italy	30.1.44
2699373 Gdsm. Donald, E.	3rd	France	11.8.44
2974474 Gdsm. Donald, J.	1st	Tunisia	29.4.43
2695577 Dmr. Donaldson, D. B.	2nd	Cyrenaica	31.5.42
2695780 L/Sgt. Doran, J.	2nd	Egypt	19.7.42
2696224 Gdsm. Dorsie, T.	2nd	Italy; PW.	5.11.42
2697310 L/Sgt. Dougall, R. S., M.M.	1st	Italy	19.10.44
2693514 L/Cpl. Douglas, A.	1st	Italy	30.1.44
2695423 Sgt. Douglas, D. J.	2nd	Cyrenaica	29.12.41
2698303 Gdsm. Douglas, N. G.	2nd	Italy	11.9.43
2697714 L/Cpl. Drew, N.	4th	U.K.	4.10.42
2695218 Cpl. Drongin, A.	2nd	Middle East	16.9.42
2697332 Gdsm. Drummond, W. R.	1st	Italy	22.2.44
2698182 L/Cpl. Drury, A.	1st	Italy	25.7.44
2698953 Gdsm. Dunbar, W. J. H.	2nd	Italy	10.11.43
2696884 Gdsm. Duncan, A.	4th	U.K.	15.6.43
2696155 Gdsm. Duncan, A.	1st	Italy	10.2.44
2697700 Gdsm. Duncan, J. R.	2nd	Germany	24.4.45
2701302 L/Sgt. Duncan, T. J.	2nd	Germany	4.4.45
2698413 Gdsm. Dunlop, J. A.	3rd	France	1.8.44
2697701 Gdsm. Dunn, D. McG.	1st	Italy	27.11.44
2698496 Gdsm. Dunn, J. K.	3rd	U.K.	31.1.45
2695025 Dmr. Dunn, R. F.	2nd	Egypt	22.4.41
2702707 Gdsm. Dunstone, C. W.	2nd	Germany	19.4.45
2700881 L/Sgt. Dyson, A.	S	Italy	4.12.44
2696824 L/Cpl. Easton, A.	2nd	Italy	12.10.43
3054349 Gdsm. Easton, J.	2nd	Egypt	12.2.41
2697877 L/Cpl. Eastwood, R.	1st	Italy	24.4.45
2702288 Gdsm. Eaves, T.	2nd	Germany	19.4.45
4124450 L/Cpl. Edmondson, F.	2nd	Egypt	3.11.42
2695825 Gdsm. Edwards, R. H.	2nd	Cyrenaica	30.5.42
2698194 Sgt. Elcock, E. B.	3rd	U.K. (From wounds received in France.)	18.8.44
2696730 Gdsm. Elsender, J. M.	1st	Italy	4.2.44

APPENDIX A 511

Number, Rank, Name and Decorations	Battalion or Company	Country	Date of Death
2695864 L/Sgt. Elwell, F.	2nd	Italy (From wounds received in Egypt/PW.)	13.10.42
2701659 L/Cpl. England, J. M. H.	S	Italy	28.5.44
14325604 Gdsm. Espley, J. L.	X	Belgium	9.9.44
2702108 Gdsm. Evans, F.	2nd	Germany	21.3.45
2695500 L/Cpl. Evitts, H.	2nd	Cyrenaica	10.1.42
2698331 Gdsm. Fairbairn, P.	2nd	Italy	17.9.43
2696634 Gdsm. Fairley, C. B.	Trg.	U.K.	9.3.44
2698162 L/Cpl. Falls, J. W.	S	Italy	14.5.44
2697336 L/Cpl. Farquhar, R.	1st	Italy	22.2.45
2699446 Gdsm. Farquhar, R. G.	2nd	Italy	24.10.43
2703049 Gdsm. Farrar, L.	2nd	Germany	8.3.45
2696921 Sgt. Faulkner, R. M.	No. 1 Wing, Glider Pilot Regt.	U.K.	25.3.45
2697313 L/Cpl. Featherstone, E.	1st	U.K. (From wounds received in Italy.)	24.3.44
2702202 Gdsm. Ferguson, D.	Gds. Dep.	U.K.	12.5.44
2694165 Sgt. Ferguson, P. C.	1st	Italy	28.7.44
2698511 Gdsm. Ferguson, R.	2nd	Italy	9.11.43
2699226 Gdsm. Finch, C. A.	3rd	France	6.8.44
2699011 L/Cpl. Finlayson, J. F.	2nd	Tunisia	6.3.43
2696592 Gdsm. Flannigan, R.	2nd	Italy	13.2.44
2702003 Gdsm. Fletcher, J. M.	2nd	Germany	4.4.45
2700519 Gdsm. Fletcher, W. M.	1st	Italy	30.9.44
2700611 Gdsm. Flynn, J.	2nd	Italy	15.10.43
2690454 Gdsm. Ford, J.	Trg.	U.K.	6.8.44
2697128 L/Sgt. Fordice, D. V.	1st	Italy	28.7.44
2697851 Gdsm. Forrest, D. L.	2nd	Italy	20.2.44
2693388 CSM. Forster, J.	2nd	Egypt	23.8.41
2697517 Sgt. Forsyth, A. D.	2nd	Italy	15.2.44
2699229 Gdsm. Forsyth, R.	2nd	Italy	30.10.43
2700469 L/Cpl. Foster, J.	X	Belgium	9.9.44
2694634 Gdsm. Fowler, A.	Trg.	U.K.	20.12.39
2697013 Gdsm. Fowler, T. J.	2nd	Italy	15.10.43
2700500 Gdsm. Fraser, A.	2nd	Italy	9.11.43
2696697 Gdsm. Fraser, A. H.	2nd	Italy	15.2.44
2698134 Gdsm. Fraser, J.	1st	Italy	10.2.44
2700249 Gdsm. Fraser, J.	1st	Tunisia	2.5.43
2702510 Gdsm. Fraser, W.	2nd	Germany	18.4.45
2700449 Gdsm. Fraser, W. G. D.	2nd	Italy	14.11.43
2700765 L/Cpl. Frazer, S.	1st	Italy	1.10.44
2703293 Gdsm. Freel, W.	2nd	Germany	18.4.45
2697857 Gdsm. Freeman, F.	3rd	U.K.	25.8.41
2693831 Gdsm. Freeman, F. E.	1st	Tunisia	29.4.43
14259595 Gdsm. French, S.	3rd	Holland	19.11.44
2694416 L/Cpl. French, W. H.	1st	U.K.	31.12.42
2693464 Gdsm. Frost, J.	1st	U.K.	18.10.40
2702825 Gdsm. Fullarton, W.	2nd	Germany	9.4.45
2697047 Gdsm. Fuller, H. M.	1st	Tunisia	25.4.43
2698450 L/Sgt. Galbraith, B.	1st	Italy	25.6.44
2692800 L/Cpl. Gale, J. E. S., **M.M.**	1st	Italy	28.1.44
2701819 Gdsm. Gardner, A. P. C.	S	Italy	28.5.44
2701923 Gdsm. Geddes, W. H.	1st	Italy	1.10.44
2696770 L/Sgt. Gedrin, J. M.	3rd	France	6.8.44

APPENDIX A

Number, Rank, Name and Decorations	Battalion or Company	Country	Date of Death
2702618 Gdsm. Giannotti, P.	2nd	Germany	6.3.45
2700986 Gdsm. Gibb, A. J.	1st	Italy	17.11.44
2693699 L/Cpl. Gibbs, G.	1st	Tunisia	23.4.43
2697887 Gdsm. Gibson, A.	3rd	U.K.	22.8.44
14764346 L/Cpl. Giles, W. S.	2nd	Germany	11.3.45
2696160 L/Sgt. Gill, G. H.	1st	Italy	17.4.45
11006460 Gdsm. Gill, H.	X	Belgium	7.9.44
2700978 L/Sgt. Gilles, D. M.	3rd	France	30.7.44
2700831 L/Cpl. Gillespie, H. McA.	2nd	Italy	8.10.43
2699910 L/Cpl. Gillespie, R.	1st	Italy	22.11.44
2695592 L/Sgt. Glaister, H.	2nd	Germany	6.3.45
3128231 L/Cpl. Gold, T.	1st	Italy	27.1.44
5382067 Gdsm. Goodchild, F. A.	2nd	Italy; PW.	27.10.42
2873917 Sgt. Gordon, A. E.	3rd	Germany	28.3.45
2700183 Gdsm. Gordon, D. W.	1st	Italy	10.2.44
2695770 Gdsm. Gordon, G. McQ.	2nd	Tunisia	11.4.43
2694820 CSM. Gore, W.	2nd	Tunisia	24.7.43
2697419 Gdsm. Gorman, J. McN.	2nd	Italy	11.9.43
2696232 Gdsm. Gowans, D.	3rd Cdo.	France	7.6.44
2699748 Gdsm. Grady, R.	1st	Tunisia	2.5.43
2695569 Gdsm. Graham, A.	2nd	Egypt	17.12.40
2688107 Gdsm. Graham, W.	Trg.	U.K.	22.12.42
2692461 Gdsm. Grainger, W. C.	Trg.	U.K.	13.5.41
2820463 Gdsm. Grant, J.	2nd	Cyrenaica	23.11.41
2695051 Gdsm. Gray, H.	2nd	Italy; PW.	18.1.43
2698307 Gdsm. Gray, W.	1st	Tunisia	23.4.43
2702893 L/Cpl. Gray, W.	2nd	Germany	6.4.45
2693126 Gdsm. Green, A. McK.	1st	Tunisia	29.4.43
2702146 L/Sgt. Green, F. C.	2nd	Germany	19.4.45
2698165 Gdsm. Green, W.	3rd	France	30.7.44
2700987 Gdsm. Greig, T. P. A.	1st	Italy	1.10.44
2700988 Gdsm. Grieve, A. N. S.	3rd	Holland	20.11.44
2696181 L/Cpl. Grimley, A.	1st	Italy	15.7.44
2701945 Gdsm. Grix, F.	S	Italy	26.11.44
2698722 Gdsm. Grubb, W. C.	2nd	Italy	11.9.43
2691766 Gdsm. Grubb, W. S.	1st	Italy	4.2.44
2701048 Gdsm. Guy, A. S.	S	Italy	15.7.44
2701756 Gdsm. Halbert, J.	1st	Italy	11.2.44
2700188 Gdsm. Haldaine, A.	1st	Italy	28.7.44
2699849 Gdsm. Hallett, W. J. D.	1st	Tunisia	4.7.43
2699719 Gdsm Halley, J. T.	1st	Italy	8.2.44
2697822 L/Cpl. Halliwell, S. D.	3rd	Germany	8.2.45
2697459 Gdsm. Hamilton, A.	X	U.K. (From wounds received in France.)	21.7.44
2696747 Gdsm. Hamilton, J. S.	1st	Italy	30.1.44
2692612 Gdsm. Handley, F.	1st	Tunisia	24.4.43
2693194 Sgt. Hannah, J. W.	1st	Italy	10.2.44
2693720 Gdsm. Hannah, W.	1st	Tunisia	5.5.43
2701924 Gdsm. Hannay, R. M.	S	Italy	14.5.44
2701236 Gdsm. Hanson, E.	1st	Italy	1.2.44
2697272 Gdsm Hardie, G.	2nd	Italy	19.10.43
2695691 Gdsm. Hardy, P. M.	2nd	North Africa; PW.	13.11.42
2694398 Sgt. Hargadon, J.	1st	Italy	30.1.44
2695798 Gdsm. Harris, J. G.	2nd	Egypt	16.6.41

APPENDIX A

Number, Rank, Name and Decorations	Battalion or Company	Country	Date of Death
2692441 L/Sgt. Harrison, A.	2nd	Italy	8.10.43
2695905 L/Sgt. Harrison, R.	2nd	Egypt	21.1.41
2697094 Gdsm. Harrold, A. J.	2nd	Italy	11.9.43
2700615 Gdsm. Harvey, J. W.	3rd	France	30.7.44
2696494 L/Cpl. Harvie, W. D.	1st	Italy	29.9.44
2698812 Sgt. Hay, A.	3rd	France	30.7.44
2701050 Gdsm. Hay, H. G.	3rd	France	6.8.44
2698215 Gdsm. Hay, J. H. G.	2nd	Cyrenaica	1.3.42
2702942 Gdsm. Heald, E. E.	2nd	Germany	10.3.45
2701419 L/Cpl. Heap, J., **M.M.**	1st	Italy	24.4.45
2875855 Sgt. Heatherwick, A.	1st	Italy	19.2.44
2703075 Gdsm. Helm, T. H.	2nd	Germany	9.3.45
2697324 Gdsm. Helsby, T. E.	1st	Tunisia	24.4.43
2697764 Gdsm. Henderson, A. D.	2nd	Italy	26.10.43
2706046 Gdsm. Henderson, J.	1st	Tunisia	24.4.43
2695776 L/Sgt. Henderson, J. B.	2nd	Italy	5.10.43
2699520 Gdsm. Henderson, J. H.	1st	Tunisia	25.4.43
2694698 L/Sgt. Henderson, R. J.	2nd	Egypt	26.9.40
2699050 Gdsm. Henderson, W. J.	1st	North Africa	20.9.43
2696508 Gdsm. Hendry, A. L.	1st	Italy	28.6.44
2700414 Gdsm. Hendry, G. N.	2nd	Italy	20.11.43
2692689 Gdsm. Henshell, H. J.	2nd	Tunisia	6.3.43
2701152 Gdsm. Heron, S. P.	3rd	France	30.7.44
2691415 CSM. Higham, F.	1st	Norway	17.5.40
2696648 Gdsm. Hill, H.	2nd	Cyrenaica	11.12.41
2697505 Gdsm. Hill, J.	3rd	France	21.7.44
2697220 Sgt. Hill, J. J. C., **M.M.**	1st	Italy	20.7.44
983333 L/Sgt. Hodgson, H.	X	Holland	4.10.44
2700416 Gdsm. Hogarth, A.	2nd	Italy	9.11.43
2701118 L/Sgt. Hogg, T. C.	2nd	Germany	20.4.45
5042987 Gdsm. Holden, F. H.	1st	Tunisia	24.4.43
2698194 S/Sgt. Holdren, C. R.	No. 2 Wing, Glider Pilot Regt.	Holland	25.9.44
2697938 Gdsm. Holmes, D. C.	2nd	Tunisia	6.3.43
2700474 L/Sgt. Hopkins, A. M.	1st	Italy	31.7.44
1611958 L/Sgt. Horner, W. J.	1st	Italy	20.10.44
2697374 Gdsm. Hornsby, R.	2nd	Germany	19.4.45
14241849 Gdsm. Houghton, W. R.	2nd	Tunisia	18.7.43
2695180 Gdsm. Houston, J.	1st	Italy	6.11.44
2703101 Gdsm. Houston, W.	2nd	Germany	6.4.45
2695907 Gdsm. Howie, C.	2nd	Egypt	31.1.41
2703020 Gdsm. Huck, F. H.	1st	Italy	17.4.45
2697620 Gdsm. Hudson, J. T.	2nd	Tunisia	17.3.43
2698022 Gdsm. Huggins, R.	1st	Italy	26.1.44
2696902 Gdsm. Hughes, G. H.	2nd	Germany	7.3.45
2692976 Sgt. Hughes, J.	Trg.	U.K.	19.9.43
2698456 L/Cpl. Hughes, J. F.	1st	Italy	30.1.44
2698261 Gdsm. Hughes, W. N.	4th	U.K.	4.10.42
2697338 Gdsm. Hughey, M. B.	4th	U.K.	26.6.42
2698766 Gdsm. Hunt, A.	1st	Italy	17.4.45
2697348 Gdsm. Hunt, W.	1st	Tunisia	20.9.43
2693656 Sgt. Hunt, W. H. E.	2nd	Germany	19.4.45
2699411 Gdsm. Hutchison, J. F.	3rd	U.K.	22.2.42

33—S.G.H.

514   APPENDIX A

Number, Rank, Name and Decorations	Battalion or Company	Country	Date of Death
2698573 L/Cpl. Hyde, H.	W. Grsn.	Gds. Chapel	18.6.44
2695545 Gdsm. Iddon, J.	2nd	Italy; PW.	31.10.42
2697469 L/Cpl. Imrie, J. H.	S	Italy	4.12.44
2694682 L/Sgt. Innes, H.	3rd	France	30.7.44
2702907 Gdsm. Ireson, T. W.	2nd	Germany	6.3.45
2694614 Sgt. Irvine, A. T.	1st	Italy	30.1.44
2693243 Gdsm. Irvine, J.	3rd	Holland	26.11.44
2693363 Gdsm. Jardine, J.	1st	Tunisia	21.4.43
2699338 L/Cpl. Jardine, J. J.	X	France	20.7.44
2698328 Gdsm. Jardine, R.	X	France	4.7.44
2699109 Gdsm. Jarvie, W.	2nd	Italy	10.9.43
2695826 Gdsm. Jeffrey, C. G.	2nd	North Africa	7.12.42
(From wounds received in Egypt/PW.)			
2693446 Sgt. Jennings, L.	2nd	Italy	2.2.44
2699472 Gdsm. Johnson, K.	1st	Italy	1.10.44
2700336 L/Cpl. Johnston, D.	3rd	France	1.8.44
2701221 Gdsm. Johnston, M.	G.A.T.W.	U.K.	14.9.44
2696478 Gdsm. Johnstone, G. S.	1st	Norway	15.4.40
2696759 Gdsm. Jones, A.	2nd	Egypt	21.9.40
2701366 Gdsm. Jones, A.	1st	Italy	16.2.44
2694876 L/Sgt. Jones, P., M.M.	S	Italy	15.7.44
2695564 Gdsm. Jones, W.	2nd	South Africa	6.4.41
2697499 Gdsm. Kaulback, K. C.	2nd	Italy	17.9.43
2698352 Gdsm. Keeton, H. R.	1st	Italy	8.2.44
2697956 L/Cpl. Kelly, J.	2nd	Italy	17.10.43
2698991 Gdsm. Kelly, M.	2nd	Italy	22.10.43
2699091 L/Cpl. Kelly, P.	2nd	Italy	20.10.43
14226213 Gdsm. Kennan. R. W.	1st	Italy	17.4.45
2696678 L/Sgt. Kennedy, G.	2nd	Italy	26.9.43
2695404 L/Cpl. Kennedy, S. C.	1st	Tunisia	28.4.43
2697311 Gdsm. Kennedy, T. C.	2nd	Italy	20.9.43
2692758 L/Sgt. Kercher, H.	1st	Tunisia	27.4.43
14315028 L/Sgt. Kerr, D. R.	3rd	Germany	31.3.45
2702012 Gdsm. Kerr, J.	S	Italy	15.7.44
2695509 Piper Kettles, R. S.	2nd	Egypt	17.12.40
2700471 Gdsm. Kidd, R. W.	X	France	11.8.44
2697056 L/Sgt. Kilmarnock, W.	1st	Italy	14.2.44
2691879 CQMS. King, D. J.	2nd	Cyrenaica	23.11.41
2695783 L/Sgt. Kinrade, G.	2nd	Italy	16.9.43
2694252 Gdsm. Laird, D.	1st	Italy	21.8.44
2700697 L/Cpl. Laird, R.	2nd	Italy	11.9.43
2764252 Gdsm. Laird, S.	2nd	Tunisia	6.4.43
2695717 Gdsm. Lamb, A. J.	2nd	Cyrenaica	27.5.42
2696787 CSM. Lambie, D.	S.A.S.	at Sea; PW.	18.1.43
2693819 L/Sgt. Lamming, J. W.	Trg.	U.K.	18.10.41
2695834 L/Sgt. Lamonby, D.	2nd	Italy	17.9.43
2699810 L/Sgt. Lancashire, C.	1st	Tunisia	29.4.43
2697306 Gdsm. Landles, P.	1st	Italy	17.4.45
2697892 L/Cpl. Lauder, D.	1st	Italy	23.6.44
2696615 L/Cpl. Laurie, J. M.	2nd	Cyrenaica	27.12.41
2693634 CSM. Law, A.	X	Belgium	12.9.44
2693280 Gdsm. Law, D.	2nd	Germany	8.3.45
2698642 Gdsm. Lawless, S. G.	1st	Italy	30.1.44
2695356 Gdsm. Lawrie, G.	Gds. Dep.	U.K.	7.6.40
2697131 L/Cpl. Lawrie, W.	3rd	France	30.7.44

APPENDIX A

Number, Rank, Name and Decorations	Battalion or Company	Country	Date of Death
2698629 Gdsm. Lees, F.	3rd	Germany	2.3.45
2701824 Gdsm. Lees, H.	1st	Italy	30.1.44
2690815 RSM. Leiper, F. G.	2nd	Egypt	17.6.41
2820788 Sgt. Leitch, S.	2nd	Italy	11.9.43
2699340 Gdsm. Lewis, R.	3rd	Holland	26.10.44
2696784 L/Sgt. Lindsay, J. S.	3rd	France	11.8.44
2701323 Gdsm. Lingwood, J., M.M.	S	Italy	5.10.44
2699303 Gdsm. Linn, W.	1st	Italy	6.7.44
2695471 L/Sgt. Liptrot, T.	2nd	Egypt	10.12.41
2695982 CSM. Little, R. H., M.M.	2nd	Italy	12.11.43
2701631 Gdsm. Little, W. J.	1st	Italy	10.2.44
2696009 L/Cpl. Littlefair, J.	1st	Tunisia	29.4.43
2700196 Gdsm. Littlejohn, J. W.	1st	Italy	10.2.44
2699574 Gdsm. Loch, R.	X	France	4.8.44
1035186 Muscn. Loney, A. W.	Band	U.K.	7.11.43
2694778 Sgt. Longworth, T. M.	2nd	Cyrenaica	30.5.42
2697939 L/Sgt. Louden, J. M.	3rd	France	30.7.44
2691355 L/Cpl. Loveland, R.	1st	Tunisia	24.4.43
2700925 Gdsm. Lowe, J. D.	2nd	Italy	11.9.43
2694174 CSM. Lumsden, W., D.C.M., M.M. and Bar	2nd	Germany	6.3.45
2698854 Gdsm. Lynch, F.	3rd	France	30.7.44
2699159 Gdsm. Maguire, J. A.	1st	Italy	10.2.44
2698188 L/Sgt. Malcolm, A.	3rd	Holland	14.12.44
2698227 L/Cpl. Malcolm, J. M.	3rd	France	30.7.44
2698588 L/Sgt. Mallen, R. J.	1st	Italy	24.4.45
2698353 L/Sgt. Marsden, D.	3rd	Holland	25.10.44
2696184 Gdsm. Marsden, S.	2nd	Cyrenaica	13.6.42
2698915 Gdsm. Marsden, T.	2nd	Italy	11.9.43
2697524 L/Cpl. Marshall, H. L.	1st	Italy	9.2.44
2698873 Gdsm. Martin, J.	2nd	North Africa	15.7.43
2657365 Gdsm. Mason, F. A. B.	2nd	Italy	22.10.43
2702112 L/Cpl. Massey, C.	2nd	Germany	8.3.45
2701579 Gdsm. Masterson, T.	1st	Italy	19.4.45
2699641 Gdsm. Matthews, H.	1st	Tunisia	5.5.43
2695837 Gdsm. Maxwell, T. T.	2nd	Tunisia	5.4.43
2703116 Gdsm. Mayes, F. P.	2nd	Germany	26.4.45
2702915 L/Cpl. Meeks, R.	2nd	Germany	6.3.45
2698245 L/Sgt. Meikle, R. N.	2nd	Germany	19.4.45
2699963 Gdsm. Melrose, A. G. A.	Trg.	U.K.	10.12.41
2699964 L/Sgt. Melville, G. S.	2nd	Germany	6.4.45
2701062 Gdsm. Melville, H. M.	3rd Cdo.	France	18.8.44
2701581 Gdsm. Menzies, H. J.	1st	Italy	26.10.44
2701841 Gdsm. Messer, G.	S	Italy	26.11.44
2701501 Gdsm. Millar, G.	1st	Italy	11.7.44
3054492 L/Cpl. Millar, W. M., M.M.	2nd	Italy	22.10.43
2701844 Gdsm. Miller, A.	S	Italy	20.4.44
2697828 L/Sgt. Miller, H. S.	2nd	Germany	18.4.45
2701371 Gdsm. Miller, J.	2nd	Italy	20.12.43
2697173 L/Sgt. Miller, R. N., M.M.	1st	Italy	30.1.44
2700200 Gdsm. Milne, H.	Trg.	U.K.	3.6.42
2697342 L/Cpl. Milne, J. D.	2nd	Italy	22.9.43
2701845 Gdsm. Milne, W. I.	S	Italy	28.5.44
2696359 Gdsm. Milroy, R.	2nd	Egypt	13.12.41
2697248 Gdsm. Milton, C.	1st	Italy	5.2.44

APPENDIX A

Number, Rank, Name and Decorations	Battalion or Company	Country	Date of Death
2821512 Gdsm. Minty, J. C.	2nd	Italy	27.10.43
2700896 L/Sgt. Monaghan, J.	2nd	Germany	2.4.45
2695594 Gdsm. Moody, R.	S	Italy	28.5.44
2703112 Gdsm. Moon, J. W.	2nd	Germany	6.4.45
3307335 L/Sgt. Moore, W. N.	Trg.	U.K.	20.5.41
4688962 Sgt. Moorhouse, S. H.	1st	Tunisia	24.4.43
2701910 L/Cpl. Morgan, J. Mc.	1st	Italy	25.7.44
2700515 Gdsm. Morrison, D.	1st	Italy	1.10.44
2693633 Gdsm. Morrison, J.	2nd	Egypt	13.8.41
2692830 CQMS. Morrison, J. E.	2nd	Italy	10.2.44
2929762 Gdsm. Morrison, M.	Trg.	U.K.	17.4.41
2700423 Gdsm. Morrison, R. N.	1st	Italy	17.4.45
2701462 Gdsm. Moscrop, J.	1st	Italy	13.2.44
2699776 Gdsm. Moseley, H. W.	1st	Italy	1.10.44
2698435 Gdsm. Muir, J.	2nd	Italy	25.9.43
2697746 Gdsm. Munro, D.	1st	Italy	1.2.44
2699793 Gdsm. Munro, J.	1st	Italy	11.3.44
2697068 L/Cpl. Munro, K.	1st	Tunisia	29.4.43
2697001 Gdsm. Murphy, M.	1st	Tunisia	30.4.43
2697501 L/Sgt. Murray, G. M.	3rd	France	30.7.44
2700657 Gdsm. Murray, J. B.	2nd	Italy	22.9.43
2698436 L/Sgt. Murray, K. B.	3rd	Holland	30.11.44
2698837 Gdsm. Murray, L.	1st	Tunisia	29.4.43
2697222 L/Cpl. Murray, M.	1st	Italy	28.6.44
2695795 Sgt. Murray, O.	2nd	Cyrenaica	13.6.42
2698061 Gdsm. Murray, W.	4th	U.K.	23.7.43
2692600 L/Sgt. Musgrave, G. S.	2nd	Italy	23.1.44
2698517 Gdsm. MacCallum, G.	1st	Tunisia	23.4.43
403286 Gdsm. MacDonald, A.	1st	Tunisia	27.4.43
2697463 Gdsm. McDonald, A. B.	1st	Tunisia	29.4.43
2700378 Gdsm. MacDonald, G.	1st	Italy	28.7.44
2700429 Gdsm. MacDonald, H.	2nd	Italy	17.10.43
2695689 Gdsm. MacDonald, J.	2nd	Tunisia	29.5.43
2695675 Gdsm. MacDougall, J.	2nd	Cyrenaica	13.6.42
2694429 Gdsm. MacDougall, W. L.	2nd	Italy	21.9.43
401941 Sgt. MacFarlane, J.	1st	Italy	13.2.44
2698476 Sgt. MacFarlane, P. W.	3rd	France	11.8.44
2696643 L/Cpl. McKay, R.	2nd	Cyrenaica	7.1.42
2701904 L/Cpl. Mackenzie, W. J.	S	Italy	28.5.44
2692485 Gdsm. MacLeod, D. A.	2nd	Cyrenaica	27.12.41
2701907 Gdsm. MacLeod, W. S.	X	Belgium	9.9.44
2697868 Gdsm. MacMasters, W.	X	Holland	4.10.44
2695296 Gdsm. MacMillan, A.	Trg.	U.K.	13.9.43
2697296 Gdsm. MacNeil, J. A.	1st	Tunisia	29.4.43
2694154 Gdsm. MacRae, J.	2nd	Italy	22.10.43
2695171 Gdsm. MacAllister, S.	1st	Tunisia	5.5.43
2698545 Gdsm. McAndrew, H. A.	1st	Italy	30.1.44
4340893 Gdsm. McAndrews, R. P.	1st	Italy	21.10.44
2698729 Gdsm. McArthur, R. W.	1st	Italy	6.7.44
2700583 Gdsm. McBride, W.	3rd	Germany	2.4.45
2699555 Gdsm. McCall, G. M.	Gds. Dep.	U.K.	27.9.40
2695616 L/Sgt. McCall, J.	2nd	Cyrenaica	28.12.41
2701213 Gdsm. McCallum, C. F.	1st	Italy	25.4.44
2700544 Gdsm. McCammick, R. V.	1st	Tunisia	30.4.43
2697475 L/Cpl. McConnell, W.	2nd	Italy	26.9.43

APPENDIX A

Number, Rank, Name and Decorations	Battalion or Company	Country	Date of Death
2693629 Sgt. McCracken, D.	2nd	Italy	17.10.43
2696267 Gdsm. McCrorie, J. P.	1st	Italy	30.7.44
2695306 L/Cpl. McCurdy, J.	1st	Italy	20.10.44
2694574 Sgt. McCurdy, J.	1st	Italy	30.1.44
2693742 CQMS. McDade, A.	S	Italy	10.6.44
2696459 Gdsm. McDonald, A.	3rd Cdo.	France	7.6.44
68078 Gdsm. McDonald, D.	2nd	Tunisia	20.4.43
2700428 Gdsm. McDonald, D.	2nd	Italy	25.9.43
2697556 Gdsm. McDonald, J.	1st	Italy	28.7.44
2698239 Gdsm. McDonald, R.	4th	U.K.	20.5.42
2697934 Gdsm. McDowall, J. A.	1st	Italy	6.7.44
2697464 Cpl. McEachan, R.	1st	Tunisia	29.4.43
2694136 Gdsm. McElnea, D.	1st	Italy	28.2.44
2700619 Gdsm. McEwen, I. D. W.	Gds. Dep.	U.K.	5.6.41
2696693 Gdsm. McFadyen, C., M.M.	2nd	Italy	5.12.43
2701698 Gdsm. McFadyen, D.	1st	Italy	24.4.45
2698768 Gdsm. McGee, J.	1st	U.K. (From illness contracted in Italy.)	18.4.44
2699138 Gdsm. McGhee, J. T.	1st	Italy	28.12.43
2697345 Gdsm. McGilvray, A. R.	2nd	Italy	14.10.43
2700772 Gdsm. McGonnigle, J.	3rd Cdo.	Germany	11.4.45
2697482 Gdsm. McGoochan, J.	2nd	Italy	23.10.43
2701123 Gdsm. McGrath, J.	2nd	Italy	9.10.43
2697187 Gdsm. McGregor, J.	2nd	Italy	10.11.43
7340490 Gdsm. McGuigan, W.	2nd	Italy	24.10.43
2724091 L/Cpl. McHattie, W. H.	2nd	Germany	8.3.45
2697261 Gdsm. McHugh, A.	1st	Italy	9.2.44
2699254 L/Cpl. McIntosh, A. McA.	2nd	Italy	6.12.43
2698689 Gdsm. McIntosh, C. W.	2nd	Germany	8.3.45
2693760 Gdsm. McIntosh, H.	2nd	Italy	11.9.43
2699761 Gdsm. McIntosh, T.	4th	U.K.	1.1.43
2698814 Gdsm. McIntyre, T. G.	3rd	France	6.8.44
2699162 Gdsm. McKay, J. W.	1st	Italy	11.1.45
2694989 L/Sgt. McKay, T. A.	1st	Italy	24.4.45
2697562 Gdsm. McKeand, G.	2nd	Germany	27.4.45
2696536 Gdsm. McKee, J.	Hld.	U.K.	23.9.40
2872135 Gdsm. McKen, L. J.	1st	Italy	1.3.44
2696563 Gdsm. McKenzie, D.	2nd	Cyrenaica	14.6.42
2697830 Gdsm. McKenzie, D.	1st	Tunisia	29.4.43
2701058 Gdsm. McKenzie, D. J.	1st	Italy	30.1.44
2697193 Gdsm. McKerron, J. B.	2nd	Italy	9.11.43
2701381 Gdsm. McKie, A. A. S.	1st	Italy	1.10.44
2693676 L/Sgt. McKie, R.	2nd	Italy	14.11.43
2698229 Gdsm. McKillop, D.	2nd	Tunisia	17.3.43
2702518 Gdsm. McKinney, T.	2nd	Germany	27.4.45
2694246 CQMS. McLay, G. J.	S	Italy	6.8.44
2696516 Gdsm. McLean, A.	2nd	North Africa	9.9.43
2696511 L/Sgt. McLean, C. G.	1st	Italy	30.1.44
2694040 Gdsm. McLean, H.	1st	Norway	18.5.40
2700268 Gdsm. McLellan, W.	2nd	Middle East	12.6.43
2702474 Gdsm. McLelland, J.	2nd	Germany	9.4.45
2697100 L/Cpl. McLelland, J. B.	1st	Italy	30.1.44
2699969 L/Sgt. McLure, A.	1st	Tunisia	29.4.43
2698562 Gdsm. McManiman, T.	1st	Italy	30.1.44
2695487 Gdsm. McMurdo, T.	2nd	Cyrenaica	30.5.42

APPENDIX A

Number, Rank, Name and Decorations	Battalion or Company	Country	Date of Death
2688242 L/Sgt. McNab, J. G.	Trg.	U.K.	29.7.42
2701840 Gdsm. McNinch, W.	S	Italy	21.6.44
14226218 Gdsm. McPheat, A.	1st	Italy	30.1.44
2697959 Gdsm. McPhee, J. M.	X	France	4.8.44
2697642 Gdsm. McQuaker, A.	1st	Tunisia	24.4.43
2697496 L/Cpl. McQueen, N. S.	1st	Italy	28.7.44
2697953 Gdsm. McSorley, K. C.	2nd	Cyrenaica	6.6.42
6848500 Gdsm. McSorley, R.	2nd	Cyrenaica	1.1.42
2694378 Gdsm. Napier, A. R.	1st	U.K.	27.9.39
2689847 L/Cpl. Nealey, J. A.	1st	Italy	27.1.44
2695694 L/Sgt. Ness, A.	2nd	Cyrenaica	13.6.42
2694474 L/Sgt. Nichol, T.	1st	Tunisia	29.4.43
2701912 Gdsm. Nicholson, J.	2nd	Germany	9.3.45
2698690 Gdsm. Nicholson, J.	2nd	Italy	12.11.43
2699936 Gdsm. Nicholson, J.	1st	Italy	24.4.45
2697594 Gdsm. Nicholson, L. D.	3rd	France	30.7.44
2700545 L/Cpl. Nicholl, W.	1st	Italy	23.1.44
2695346 Gdsm. Nimmo, P.	2nd	Cyrenaica	23.11.41
2694939 Gdsm. Nisbet, F. J. D.	2nd	Cyrenaica	23.11.41
2696966 Gdsm. Nisbet, J. G.	2nd	Cyrenaica	13.6.42
2698500 L/Sgt. Nisbet, S.	1st	Italy	5.4.45
2696868 Gdsm. Nisbet, T. H.	2nd	Cyrenaica	28.12.41
2695640 L/Cpl. Norman, E.	2nd	Egypt	21.1.41
2695231 Sgt. Oldershaw, E.	2nd	Italy	1.1.44
2700726 Gdsm. Oliver, J. E. W.	2nd	Italy	21.1.44
2698003 Gdsm. Oliver, L. G.	2nd	Italy	24.10.43
2695369 L/Sgt. O'Neill, E.	2nd	Cyrenaica	23.11.41
2699184 Gdsm. O'Neill, H. H.	3rd	France	30.7.44
3769016 Gdsm. Orme, H.	1st	Italy	27.2.45
2695287 L/Sgt. Orr, J. A.	4th	U.K.	21.6.42
2703067 Gdsm. Owen, J.	2nd	Germany	6.4.45
2698774 Gdsm. Pallett, B. E.	X	Belgium	9.9.44
2697085 L/Cpl. Park, D. K.	2nd	Italy; PW.	1.11.42
2697526 Gdsm. Park, W. M.	1st	Tunisia	5.5.43
2698669 L/Cpl. Parkin, L.	3rd	France	30.7.44
2985909 L/Cpl. Paterson, J. A.	1st	Italy	30.1.44
2693974 Gdsm. Patience, G.	1st	Italy	30.1.44
2696547 Gdsm. Paton, A. D.	2nd	Cyrenaica	10.12.41
2695195 Gdsm. Peacock, N.	2nd	Cyrenaica	10.12.41
2693480 CQMS. Pearson, J.	Trg.	U.K.	18.11.42
2699435 L/Cpl. Peddie, C. McL.	2nd	Italy	10.9.43
2214074 Gdsm. Peebles, J.	2nd	Tunisia	28.3.43
2696292 L/Cpl. Perkins, H.	1st	Italy	4.2.44
2700554 L/Cpl. Perks, R., M.M.	2nd	Germany	19.4.45
2700509 Gdsm. Perry, R.	2nd	Italy	23.9.43
2697672 Gdsm. Petty, R. C.	3rd	Holland	26.11.44
2698176 Gdsm. Philbin, M.	1st	Italy	20.10.44
2694092 L/Cpl. Phillips, G.	3rd	Holland	11.10.44
2702997 Gdsm. Phillips, J.	2nd	Germany	9.3.45
1507306 Gdsm. Picknell, E. F.	X	Belgium	9.9.44
2698775 L/Cpl. Plimmer, H. S.	1st	Italy	7.7.44
2696519 Gdsm. Pool. J.	2nd	Cyrenaica	31.12.41
2699558 Gdsm. Pool, N. R.	1st	Italy	19.2.44
2695673 Gdsm. Porteous, W.	2nd	Tunisia	6.3.43
2697078 L/Sgt. Porter, J.	4th	U.K.	25.6.42

APPENDIX A 519

Number, Rank, Name and Decorations	Battalion or Company	Country	Date of Death
2701003 Gdsm. Porter, J.	1st	Tunisia	29.4.43
2697572 Gdsm. Porter, W.	1st	Tunisia	28.4.43
2700551 Gdsm. Poutney, A.	2nd	Tunisia	6.3.43
2700759 L/Cpl. Powell, E. W.	2nd	Italy	7.12.43
2699711 Gdsm. Pratt, W.	1st	Italy	30.1.44
2697126 Gdsm. Prentice, J. P.	3rd	France	30.7.44
2703119 Gdsm. Price, W. A.	2nd	Germany	9.3.45
2697406 Gdsm. Proudfoot, A.	3rd	Germany	8.2.45
2700355 Gdsm. Proudfoot, H.	1st	Italy	10.2.44
2697478 Gdsm. Prytherick, J.	1st	Italy	25.3.44
2696604 Gdsm. Quinn, T.	1st	Italy	11.7.44
2701505 Gdsm. Rae, A.	S	Italy	15.7.44
2977259 Pipe-Major Raeburn, J. W.	2nd	Italy	21.9.43
2699661 Gdsm. Ralston, G.	3rd	U.K.	1.9.41
2697124 Sgt. Ramsay, F. J.	3rd	Germany	10.2.45
2702117 Gdsm. Ramsay, G. W.	2nd	Germany	19.4.45
2698672 Gdsm. Randall, A. D.	X	Holland	29.11.44
2701508 Gdsm. Rankin, J. D.	1st	Italy	5.10.44
2696901 Gdsm. Rawlins, W. M. Mc.	1st	Italy	11.2.44
2694015 Gdsm. Read, J. F.	2nd	Tunisia	17.5.43
2698224 Gdsm. Reed, W.	2nd	Italy	17.9.43
2698361 Gdsm. Reeder, J. J.	3rd	Germany	16.2.45
2697238 Gdsm. Reeve, K.	Hld.	U.K.	8.12.40
4605929 CSM. Regan, C.	Hld.	U.K.	10.8.42
2696613 Gdsm. Reid, A. H.	2nd	Cyrenaica	15.3.42
2693992 Gdsm. Reid, B.	1st	Italy	11.2.44
2696955 Gdsm. Reid, C. J.	1st	Italy	19.4.45
2699232 Gdsm. Reid, R.	2nd	Italy	23.9.43
2697273 Gdsm. Reidy, J. F.	1st	Italy	28.12.43
755665 Gdsm. Rennie, J. F.	2nd	Italy	22.10.43
2697989 Gdsm. Reynolds, J.	1st	Italy	22.10.44
7885741 Gdsm. Riach, W. A. C.	2nd	Italy; PW.	13.12.42
2695762 Gdsm. Ribeiro, L.	2nd	Italy; PW.	25.12.42
2698648 L/Cpl. Richardson, B.	3rd	Germany	16.2.45
2698141 Gdsm. Richardson, W. J.	4th	U.K.	1.1.43
2692726 D/Sgt. Richmond, J., **D.C.M.**	2nd	Tunisia	6.3.43
2701287 Gdsm. Riley, F.	2nd	Italy	20.2.44
2698136 Gdsm. Rintoul, A.	1st	Italy	30.1.44
2697444 Gdsm. Rintoul, W.	1st	Tunisia	30.4.43
2700560 Gdsm. Ritson, J.	1st	Tunisia	24.4.43
2703121 Gdsm. Roberts, G. J.	2nd	Germany	7.3.45
2698792 Gdsm. Robertson, A.	1st	Tunisia	24.4.43
3312857 Cpl. Robertson, C. S.	2nd	Italy	17.9.43
2693592 Gdsm. Robertson, D.	Trg.	U.K.	21.5.40
2696523 Gdsm. Robertson, D.	2nd	Italy; PW.	15.6.44
14688133 Gdsm. Robertson, D. G.	2nd	Germany	6.4.45
2693453 L/Sgt. Robertson, G.	1st	Italy	30.1.44
2698583 L/Sgt. Robertson, J.	1st	Tunisia	27.4.43
2694562 Gdsm. Robertson, J.	1st	Italy	23.1.44
2698861 L/Cpl. Robertson, J.	1st	Tunisia	24.4.43
2978978 Gdsm. Robertson, L. M. P.	Gds. Dep.	U.K.	19.4.42
2701131 Gdsm. Robertson, W. S.	S	Italy	15.7.44
2701433 Gdsm. Robinson, I. P.	1st	Italy	1.10.44
2696167 Gdsm. Robinson, J.	1st	Tunisia	13.4.43
2701394 Gdsm. Robinson, M.	1st	Italy	1.10.44

APPENDIX A

Number, Rank, Name and Decorations	Battalion or Company	Country	Date of Death
2697530 Sgt. Robson, R. G.	1st	Tunisia	28.4.43
2700664 Gdsm. Roche, J. F.	2nd	Egypt	16.6.41
2695921 Gdsm. Rolfe, R. G. A.	2nd	Egypt	16.6.41
2696041 Gdsm. Rosie, J.	2nd	Italy	21.9.43
2818431 Gdsm. Ross, D.	2nd	Egypt	16.6.41
2700736 Gdsm. Ross, J. D.	Trg.	U.K.	30.6.42
2699668 Gdsm. Ross, J. F.	Trg.	U.K.	19.2.41
2699123 Gdsm. Ross, K.	2nd	Tunisia	30.4.43
2702321 L/Sgt. Ross, M. B.	2nd	Germany	19.4.45
2693789 Gdsm. Ross, T. A.	2nd	Egypt	16.6.41
2723132 Gdsm. Rowley, S.	1st	Italy	17.4.45
2692834 Gdsm. Rumbutis, Y.	2nd	Italy	9.11.43
2702794 Gdsm. Russell, H. R.	2nd	Germany	26.4.45
2699391 Gdsm. Russell, T.	1st	Italy	20.10.44
2702068 Gdsm. Ryan, G. K.	3rd	Germany	7.5.45
2695974 Gdsm. Rymer, F. W.	2nd	Italy; PW.	12.11.44
2696471 L/Cpl. Sandbach, R.	1st	Tunisia	29.4.43
2695163 L/Cpl. Sanders, E. C.	1st	Tunisia	26.4.43
2702367 Gdsm. Sanderson, C.	2nd	Germany	26.4.45
2691967 L/Cpl. Sanderson, G.	2nd	Cyrenaica	23.1.42
2698012 L/Sgt. Sandilands, D.	1st	Italy	10.2.44
4609714 L/Sgt. Savage, F.	3rd	Germany	16.2.45
2693525 Gdsm. Scott, E. F.	1st	Tunisia	27.4.43
2698025 Gdsm. Scott, G. R.	2nd	Italy	11.9.43
2698826 L/Cpl. Scott, J.	3rd	U.K.	17.7.43
820304 Gdsm. Scott, J.	1st	Italy	1.10.44
2695083 Gdsm. Scott, J. D.	1st	Italy	17.4.45
829113 Gdsm. Scott, K.	1st	Tunisia	29.4.43
2694890 L/Cpl. Scott, T. W.	2nd	Italy	29.3.44
2698442 L/Cpl. Scott, W.	3rd	France	30.7.44
7880990 L/Sgt. Scott, W.	G.A.T.W.	U.K.	8.5.45
2699227 Gdsm. Scougall, J.	Hld.	U.K.	30.12.40
1659264 Gdsm. Scragg, G.	2nd	Germany	26.4.45
2696509 Gdsm. Screen, J. C.	1st	Tunisia	16.4.43
2698092 Gdsm. Seaton, J.	2nd	Italy	13.11.43
2696965 L/Sgt. Senior, F.	2nd	Middle East	15.1.43
2693193 Cpl. Shand, A. E.	1st	Norway	25.4.40
2701027 Gdsm. Shanks, A.	2nd	Italy	22.10.43
2696560 L/Cpl. Sharp, J. C.	2nd	Cyrenaica	27.5.42
2694884 Gdsm. Shepherd, T. C.	1st	U.K.	19.10.40
2702739 Gdsm. Sheppard, W.	2nd	Germany	9.3.45
2696153 Sgt. Sheridan, J.	1st	U.K.	17.2.43
2701084 Gdsm. Shiells, J.	3rd	Holland	21.11.44
2873719 Gdsm. Sim, A. H.	2nd	Italy	9.11.43
2696570 Gdsm. Simpson, J. S.	2nd	Italy	17.9.43
2697455 Gdsm. Skelly, J.	2nd	Tunisia	6.3.43
2696136 Gdsm. Skidmore, E. R.	1st	U.K. (From wounds received in Norway.)	18.6.40
2693225 Gdsm. Skinner, J.	2nd	Italy	21.1.44
2700700 Gdsm. Skinner, R. L.	2nd	Italy	12.11.43
11053091 Gdsm. Slinn, C.	1st	Italy	16.10.44
2700714 Gdsm. Small, A. G.	2nd	Tunisia	28.4.43
2699115 Gdsm. Small, H.	3rd	France	6.8.44
2697711 Gdsm. Smith, A.	2nd	Cyrenaica	26.5.42
2694881 L/Cpl. Smith, A.	2nd	Middle East	22.9.42

APPENDIX A 521

Number, Rank, Name and Decorations	Battalion or Company	Country	Date of Death
2697708 Gdsm. Smith, A.	2nd	Tunisia	26.6.43
2694741 L/Sgt. Smith, A. S.	2nd	Egypt	3.7.42
2692992 L/Sgt. Smith, B.	1st	Tunisia	4.5.43
14705656 Gdsm. Smith, C. A.	X	Holland	23.9.44
2697039 Gdsm. Smith, D. W.	1st	Tunisia	30.4.43
2699699 Gdsm. Smith, E.	1st	Italy	17.4.45
4104622 L/Sgt. Smith, F. W.	2nd	Italy	28.12.43
2700488 Gdsm. Smith, G.	2nd	Italy	14.9.43
2698686 Gdsm. Smith, H.	1st	Italy	1.10.44
2701298 Gdsm. Smith, J.	1st	Italy	10.2.44
2694423 Gdsm. Smith, J. H.	2nd	Italy	22.10.43
2693202 Sgt. Smith, J. K.	1st	Norway	18.5.40
2699879 Gdsm. Smith, M.	2nd	Italy	11.9.43
2698281 L/Sgt. Smith, R.	1st	Italy	17.4.45
2693155 Pipe-Major Smith, W.	3rd	Germany	2.3.45
2702024 Gdsm. Smout, J.	X	France	11.8.44
2701273 Gdsm. Somers, W. H.	2nd	Italy	10.11.43
2693829 Gdsm. Sorlie, J. Mc.	1st	Tunisia	27.4.43
2698506 Gdsm. Speris, A.	1st	Italy	30.1.44
2696682 Gdsm. Squire, A. P.	2nd	Italy	9.11.43
801799 Gdsm. Stabler, W. W.	1st	Tunisia	21.4.43
2699139 Gdsm. Stark, A.	1st	U.K. (From wounds received in North Africa.)	15.3.44
2699133 Gdsm. Steane, S. T.	1st	Italy	22.6.44
2696649 Gdsm. Stenhouse, A.	2nd	Egypt	22.7.40
2692609 Gdsm. Stephen, G. R.	2nd	Egypt	10.5.41
2697387 L/Sgt. Stewart, A.	2nd	Italy; PW.	7.1.43
2700495 L/Sgt. Stewart, A. W.	1st	Tunisia	4.5.43
2702250 Gdsm. Stewart, C.	3rd	Germany	14.4.45
2696970 Cpl. Stewart, G. L.	3rd	France	6.8.44
2699637 Gdsm. Stewart, G. P.	X	Belgium	9.9.44
2698458 Gdsm. Stewart, G. R.	1st	Italy	28.7.44
2696624 L/Sgt. Stewart, R.	2nd	Cyrenaica	27.12.41
2692673 Sgt. Stone, S. J.	2nd	Cyrenaica	5.12.41
2695190 L/Sgt. Storey, G.	1st	Tunisia	24.4.43
2699951 Gdsm. Stothard, L.	1st	Italy	10.2.44
2697154 Cpl. Stuart, C. E.	1st	Italy	23.6.44
2696118 L/Cpl. Sturrock, D. R.	1st	Italy	10.2.44
2690313 Musn. Sullivan, H. G.	Band	U.K.	7.11.43
2697719 L/Cpl. Sutherland, D.	3rd	France	7.8.44
2695481 L/Sgt. Syme, D.	2nd	At Sea; PW.	14.11.42
2697584 Gdsm. Tavendale, D. H.	1st	Italy	8.2.44
2697820 Gdsm. Taylor, A. H. K.	1st	Italy	1.10.44
2697738 Gdsm. Taylor, R. C.	2nd	Italy	28.10.43
2700757 L/Cpl. Telfer, A.	2nd	Italy	12.11.43
2700648 Gdsm. Telfer, W.	2nd	Italy	17.9.43
2696038 Gdsm. Terrell, C. E. J.	1st	Tunisia	29.4.43
2698387 L/Sgt. Tessier, F.	X	France	4.8.44
2700521 Gdsm. Thomas, L.	2nd	North Africa	5.7.43
2692782 Sgt. Thomas, R.	2nd	Italy	31.1.44
2691338 Gdsm. Thompson, A. E.	Gds. Dep.	U.K.	27.9.40
2697876 Gdsm. Thompson, H. W.	3rd	France	25.8.44
2695722 Gdsm. Thompson, J.	2nd	Cyrenaica	21.1.42
2696396 Gdsm. Thomson, R.	2nd	Italy; PW.	7.2.43
2699112 L/Cpl. Thomson, R.	3rd	France	30.7.44

Number, Rank, Name and Decorations	Battalion or Company	Country	Date of Death
2692633 Gdsm. Thomson, T.	1st	Italy	29.1.44
2699612 Gdsm. Thomson, W.	1st	Italy	6.6.44
2699987 L/Cpl. Thomson, W.	3rd	France	11.8.44
2697497 Gdsm. Thomson, W.	2nd	Cyrenaica	27.5.42
2694375 Gdsm. Thomson, W.	1st	Norway	23.5.40
2696837 Gdsm. Thomson, W. J. C.	2nd	Cyrenaica	5.2.42
2692032 Sgt. Thorn, E.	3rd	France	30.7.44
2695944 Sgt. Thorne, C. V.	2nd	Italy; PW.	12.1.43
2699783 Gdsm. Tierney, M. F.	3rd	France	1.8.44
2693919 Gdsm. Tilley, P.	3rd	U.K.	2.9.41
2692756 L/Sgt. Todd, W.	2nd	Egypt	14.9.41
2694399 CSM. Tulloch, J. A.	2nd	Italy	17.9.43
2697522 Gdsm. Torrance, S.	1st	U.K. (From wounds received in Tunisia.)	2.7.44
2700616 Gdsm. Towers, C. E.	3rd	France	16.8.44
2701656 Gdsm. Tracey, J.	1st	Italy	8.2.44
2695860 Gdsm. Tranter, G.	W. Grsn.	Gds. Chapel	18.6.44
2702368 Gdsm. Trotter, R.	2nd	Germany	3.4.45
409820 Gdsm. Turnbull, J.	2nd	Tunisia	6.3.43
2699568 Gdsm. Tweedie, D. F.	2nd	Italy	21.10.43
2695392 Gdsm. Tweedie, J. B.	2nd	Egypt	24.9.41
2697096 Gdsm. Umphray, R.	1st	Tunisia	26.4.43
2692276 Sgt. Urquhart, E. R.	Trg.	U.K.	2.3.42
2693711 Gdsm. Uzzell, W. A. E.	1st	Tunisia	21.4.43
2695800 Gdsm. Verechia, P.	2nd	Egypt	15.5.41
2701974 Gdsm. Waddell, D.	S	Italy	30.5.44
2695682 L/Cpl. Waight, R. F.	2nd	Cyrenaica	13.6.42
2700292 Gdsm. Walker, A. Mc.	1st	Italy	16.2.44
2700550 L/Sgt. Walker, J. S., **M.M.**	1st	Italy; PW.	28.10.44
2696271 Gdsm. Walker, R.	1st	Italy	30.1.44
2691643 L/Cpl. Wall, F. G.	1st	Tunisia	29.4.43
2697931 Gdsm. Wallace, C. D.	1st	Tunisia	29.3.43
3188308 Sgt. Wallace, G.	2nd	Germany; PW.	21.1.45
2701138 Gdsm. Wallace, I. R.	3rd	France	6.8.44
2701315 Gdsm. Walton, G.	1st	Italy	1.10.44
2694995 L/Sgt. Ward, T. A.	2nd	Cyrenaica	28.12.41
2699629 Gdsm. Wardrope, A.	3rd	Germany	11.2.45
2700677 Gdsm. Warner, S. W.	1st	Italy	2.2.44
2697255 Gdsm. Waterston, A.	1st	Tunisia	24.4.43
2698494 L/Cpl. Watkins, H.	2nd	North Africa	2.9.43
2695799 Gdsm. Watson, A. G.	2nd	Cyrenaica	7.1.42
2701519 L/Cpl. Watson, D. R.	1st	Italy	24.4.45
2696836 L/Cpl. Watson, J.	1st	Tunisia	16.4.43
3188696 Sgt. Watson, J.	2nd	Italy; PW.	31.12.42
2700293 Gdsm. Watson, K. S.	1st	Italy	6.7.44
2698026 Gdsm. Watson, R. C.	1st	Tunisia	24.4.43
2700879 Gdsm. Watts, D.	3rd	France	30.7.44
2701652 Gdsm. Weir, J.	S	Italy	28.5.44
844178 Gdsm. Wells, A. B.	1st	Tunisia	29.4.43
2699032 Gdsm. Welsh, R. S.	1st	Italy	2.3.44
2699811 Gdsm. Welton, H. C.	Hld.	U.K.	24.7.42
2698721 Gdsm. Wharrie, N.	2nd	Tunisia	11.4.43
2696894 Gdsm. Whellan, W.	1st	Tunisia	24.4.43
2700674 Gdsm. Whetton, J. A.	2nd	Tunisia	6.3.43
2700747 L/Sgt. White, G.	2nd	Germany	7.4.45

APPENDIX A

Number, Rank, Name and Decorations	Battalion or Company	Country	Date of Death
2698602 Gdsm. White, H.	1st	Italy	28.1.44
2697699 Gdsm. Whitehead, J.	1st	Italy	11.2.44
2698841 Gdsm. Whyte, H. B. D.	1st	Italy	5.4.45
2696339 Gdsm. Wignall, H.	1st	Italy	30.1.44
2699824 Gdsm. Wilkinson, H. J.	1st	Tunisia	28.4.43
2693449 L/Cpl. Wilkinson, J.	1st	Italy	17.2.44
2694754 L/Cpl. Williams, N. C.	1st	Italy	30.1.44
2040988 Gdsm. Williamson, W.	2nd	Italy	12.9.43
2702692 Gdsm. Wilson, A. Mc.	2nd	Germany	9.3.45
14226229 Gdsm. Wilson, D.	1st	Italy	30.1.44
2700903 Gdsm. Wilson, F.	3rd	France	30.7.44
2698232 Gdsm. Wilson, F.	1st	Italy	1.10.44
2700446 Gdsm. Wilson, G.	1st	Italy	11.2.44
2695997 Gdsm. Wilson, H.	1st	Italy	9.2.44
2700447 Gdsm. Wilson, J.	2nd	Italy	10.9.43
2701012 L/Cpl. Wilson, P.	2nd	Italy	12.11.43
2701785 Gdsm. Wilson, R.	W. Grsn.	U.K.	5.4.45
2697397 L/Sgt. Wilson, W.	2nd	Germany	7.4.45
2694808 Gdsm. Wilson, W.	1st	Italy	17.4.45
2694493 Gdsm. Windsor, F.	1st	Norway	18.5.40
2701522 Gdsm. Winstanley, A. E.	1st	Italy	17.2.44
2701316 Gdsm. Winton, J. D.	1st	Italy	24.4.45
2699569 Gdsm. Wisley, W. J.	2nd	Italy	11.11.43
2696503 Gdsm. Withers, R. F.	1st	Italy	24.6.44
2697859 L/Cpl. Withnell, W.	1st	Italy	31.1.44
14003067 Gdsm. Wittcombe, R. J.	S	Italy	28.5.44
2695267 L/Cpl. Wood, W.	1st	Italy	28.2.44
2698464 L/Cpl. Woodward, J.	2nd	Italy	17.10.43
2695548 Sgt. Workman, J.	2nd	Egypt	18.9.41
2701265 Gdsm. Worthington, S.	1st	Italy	16.2.44
2694825 Gdsm. Wright, A.	2nd	Tunisia	6.3.43
2696621 L/Cpl. Wrisberg, F. G.	2nd	Egypt	15.6.41
2689058 CQMS. Wyness, J. A.	G.A.T.W.	U.K.	10.5.42
2702726 Gdsm. Wyper, M. P.	2nd	Germany	18.4.45
2700650 L/Cpl. Yarwood, E.	1st	Italy	8.2.44
2697761 Gdsm. Yates, R. S.	3rd	U.K.	28.6.42
2695366 L/Sgt. Young, D.	2nd	Middle East	18.11.42
2693074 Sgt. Young, L.	1st	Tunisia	28.4.43
2695842 Gdsm. Young, W. A.	1st	Italy	9.7.44
2695087 L/Sgt. Yule, J. Mc.	2nd	Italy	16.9.43

III. OFFICERS AND OTHER RANKS OF THE SCOTS GUARDS WHO WERE KILLED OR WHO DIED ON ACTIVE SERVICE IN MALAYA

1948–1951

Brigadier M. D. Erskine, C.B.E., D.S.O.　　27th October, 1949.
(Commanding 2nd Guards Brigade)

	Captain M. G. Bax	11th June, 1950.
	Lieutenant R. A. C. McKenzie	21st October, 1949.
	2nd Lieutenant M. J. Morrice	11th June, 1950.
	2nd Lieutenant P. W. B. Graham-Watson	19th May, 1949.
	2nd Lieutenant J. A. Forbes-Leith	25th September, 1949.
2818374	Sergeant W. A. Riach	25th September, 1949.
1439050	Sergeant D. McMillan	25th January, 1951.
2695480	Lance-Sergeant A. Ferguson	4th February, 1949.
2704864	Lance-Sergeant H. D. Lea	19th May, 1949.
22022534	Guardsman D. Moore	25th September, 1949.
22215040	Guardsman K. Holland	16th January, 1950.
2705401	Guardsman W. Clucas	19th July, 1950.
22215373	Guardsman E. Duffell	29th December, 1950.

IV. STATISTICS OF

TABLE I. ANALYSIS BY BATTALIONS, ETC.

Unit	Theatre	Killed[1]		Wounded[2]		Prisoners of War		Totals	
		Off.	O.R.	Off.	O.R.	Off.	O.R.	Off.	O.R.
FIRST BATTALION	Norway	—	13	2	38	—	36	2	87
	Tunisia	4	98	12	250*	—	—	16	348
	Italy	26	243	29	645	4	268	59	1,156
	Total	30	354	43	933	4	304	77	1,591
SECOND BATTALION	Middle East	8	99	17	275*	13	314	38	688
	Tunisia	4	57	13	60*	—	6	17	103
	Italy	20	141	25	286	3	84	48	511
	Germany	9	76	17	248	—	5	26	329
	In Captivity[3]	—	24	—	—	—	—	—	24
	Total	41	377	72	869	16	409	129	1,655
THIRD BATTALION	North-West Europe	12	74	19	105	1	8	32	187
S Company	Italy	3	29	5	80*	—	5	8	114
X Company	N-W Europe	1	27	5	88	1	7	7	122
Commandos, Special Forces and Staffs, etc., Abroad		6	8	6	1	5	17	17	26
All Bns. and Units At Home		5	74	—	23	—	—	5	97
Whole Regiment, 1939–1945		98	943	150	2,099	27	750	275	3,792
compared with		Combined Total:						4,067	
1914–1918		111	2,730	216	4,002	Not Available.			

* See note 2 on p. 527

CASUALTIES: 1939–1945

TABLE II. ANALYSIS BY THEATRES OF WAR

Theatre	Killed[1]		Wounded[2]		Prisoners of War		Totals	
	Off.	O.R.	Off.	O.R.	Off.	O.R.	Off.	O.R.
Norway	—	13	2	38	—	36	2	87
France and Belgium, 1940	3	—	—	—	1	—	4	—
Middle East	9	100	18	275	16	331	43	706
Tunisia	8	135	25	310	—	6	33	451
Italy	49	413	59	1,011	8	357	116	1,781
North-West Europe	23	184	45	441	2	20	70	645
In Captivity[3]	—	24	—	—	—	—	—	24
Other Theatres	1	—	1	1	—	—	2	1
At Home	5	74	—	23	—	—	5	97
Totals	98	943	150	2,099	27	750	275	3,792

Notes

[1] Includes Killed in Action, Died of Wounds, Accidentally Killed and Died on Active Service.

[2] The total of 2,099 wounded was calculated immediately after the war, but the basis of that calculation has been lost. The figures marked with an asterisk are, therefore, approximations, but they are believed to be very nearly correct. According to information from the War Office Records Centre, the total number of men wounded was 1,615. In the main the discrepancy between the two totals is accounted for by the fact that the War Office figures for the African (Middle East and Tunisian combined) and Italian campaigns are respectively 250 and 200 *less* than those given in Table II. Probably the Regiment's figures include many who were only slightly wounded, and therefore not evacuated by the Medical Services.

[3] Includes those killed while attempting to escape or while at liberty, those drowned at sea when an Italian transport was sunk, and those who died in the camps.

APPENDIX B

Honours and Awards

I. THE VICTORIA CROSS

Extract from The London Gazette No. 36129 dated 12th August, 1943.

The King has been graciously pleased to approve the posthumous award of the Victoria Cross to:

Lieutenant (temporary Captain) THE LORD LYELL (57781) SCOTS GUARDS (Kirriemuir, Angus).

From the 22nd April, 1943, to 27th April,[1] 1943, Captain The Lord Lyell commanded his Company, which had been placed under the orders of a Battalion of the Grenadier Guards, with great gallantry, ability and cheerfulness. He led it down a slope under heavy mortar fire to repel a German counter-attack on 22nd April,[2] led it again under heavy fire through the Battalion's first objective on 23rd April in order to capture and consolidate a high point, and held this point through a very trying period of shelling, heat and shortage of water. During this period, through his energy and cheerfulness, he not only kept up the fighting spirit of his Company but also managed through Radio Telephony, which he worked himself from an exposed position, to bring most effective artillery fire to bear on enemy tanks, vehicles and infantry positions.

At about 1800 hours on 27th April, 1943, this Officer's Company was taking part in the Battalion's attack on Djebel Bou Arara.[3] The Company was held up in the foothills by heavy fire from an enemy post on the left: this post consisted of an 88 millimetre gun and a heavy machine gun in separate pits. Realizing that until this post was destroyed the advance could not proceed, Lord Lyell collected the only available men not pinned down by fire—a sergeant, a lance-corporal and two guardsmen[4]—and led them to attack it. He was a long way in advance of the others and lobbed a hand grenade into the machine gun pit destroying the crew. At this point his sergeant was killed and both the guardsmen were wounded. The lance-corporal got down to give covering fire to Lord Lyell who had run straight on towards the 88 millimetre gun pit and was working his way round to the left of it. So quickly had this officer acted that he was in among the crew with the bayonet before they had time to fire more than one shot. He killed a number of them before being overwhelmed and killed himself. The few survivors of the gun crew then left the pit, some of them being

APPENDIX B

killed while they were retiring, and both the heavy machine gun and 88 millimetre gun were silenced.

The Company was then able to advance and take its objective.

There is no doubt that Lord Lyell's outstanding leadership, gallantry and self-sacrifice enabled his Company to carry out its task which had an important bearing on the success of the Battalion and of the Brigade.

[1] These dates should be 19th and 20th April.

[2] Should be 20th April.

[3] It was on Djebel Bou *Aoukaz*, not on Bou *Arara*, that Lord Lyell won his Victoria Cross; it is interesting to note that several officers describing the battle in contemporary letters wrongly refer to the hill as Bou Arara, which is one of the "Hills Ridiculous" from which the attack was launched.

[4] They were 2698583 Lance-Sergeant J. Robertson (killed), 2699878 Lance-Corporal J. R. Lawrie, 2698033 Guardsman J. Chisholm and 2697572 Guardsman W. Porter: Lawrie and Chisholm both received the Military Medal: Porter died the next day.

II. BRITISH DECORATIONS FOR GALLANTRY, 1939–1945

(a) FIRST BATTALION

NORWAY
Military Cross — Major J. H. Elwes
Distinguished Conduct Medal — Gdsm. J. Bryson
Military Medal — PSM. W. Washington
Gdsm. J. Howard

TUNISIA
Victoria Cross — Captain The Lord Lyell
Military Cross — Captain R. H. Bull
Captain F. G. Mann
Lieut. The Hon. D. A. Bethell

Military Medal —
CSM. J. Lunn
CSM. H. Tomlinson
Sgt. J. J. C. Hill
L/Sgt. J. E. Raine
L/Cpl. W. A. Barber
L/Cpl. G. A. Cashmore
L/Cpl. J. R. K. Lawrie
L/Cpl. R. N. Miller
Gdsm. E. G. Cross
Gdsm. J. Chisholm

ITALY

(a) ANZIO

Distinguished Service Order — Lieut.-Col. D. S. Wedderburn
Military Cross —
Captain G. R. E. Blois
Lieut. J. Graham
Lieut. T. C. Lindsay-Peto

Distinguished Conduct Medal —
L/Cpl. R. R. Bates
Sgt. F. Bennett

Military Medal —
Sgt. J. H. Kelly
Sgt. J. Pirie
Sgt. T. Rimmer
L/Sgt. R. Ashcroft
L/Sgt. D. C. MacKay
Gdsm. H. W. Caulfield
Gdsm. R. S. Dougall
Gdsm. J. A. Duff
Gdsm. J. H. Hopgood

(b) FROM MARCH 1944

Distinguished Service Order —
Major T. C. Harvey
Major F. G. Mann, M.C.

Military Cross —
Lieut. P. H. Batholomew
Lieut. T. R. Bland
Lieut. A. O. Worthington-Wilmer
Lieut. I. J. Fraser
Lieut. Sir David Moncrieffe, Bt.

Bar to the Military Cross — Captain J. D. K. Hague, M.C.

Distinguished Conduct Medal —
CSM. W. M. Robertson
CSM. R. H. Thomson
Sgt. W. A. Hill
L/Sgt. G. S. Dudgeon

Military Medal —
Sgt. J. Allardyce
Sgt. J. Clement
Sgt. H. Cockburn
Sgt. T. Taylor
L/Sgt. A. Black
L/Sgt. A. Bremner
L/Sgt. J. Moir
Gdsm. W. G. Cocker
Gdsm. J. Hastings
Gdsm. J. Wade
L/Sgt. C. Ogg
L/Sgt. C. H. Starkey
L/Sgt. J. S. Walker
Cpl. P. G. Cox
L/Cpl. W. McCallum
L/Cpl. D. McLaren
Gdsm. D. Clarkson
Gdsm. J. McInnes
Gdsm. C. Ogilvy

APPENDIX B

(b) SECOND BATTALION

EGYPT AND CYRENAICA
Distinguished Service Order	Capt. J. D. C. S. MacRae	
Military Cross	Capt. A. B. C. Maxwell	Lieut. The Hon. B. Bruce*
	Capt. J. A. L. Timpson*	Lieut. D. H. Butter
	Lieut. N. H. Barne	Lieut. I. M. Calvocoressi
	Lieut. J. R. S. Clarke	
Distinguished Conduct Medal	CSM. J. Richmond	
	L/Sgt. J. M. Cooper*	
Military Medal	Sgt. J. Hope	L/Cpl. J. Stephenson
	Sgt. F. P. Riley	L/Cpl. W. W. Sutherland*
	Sgt. A. Turner	
	L/Sgt. W. G. Brough*	Gdsm. A. Brown
	L/Sgt. G. Johnstone	Gdsm. R. Duncalf*
	L/Cpl. R. H. Little	Gdsm. C. McFadyen
	L/Cpl. T. C. McAllister	Gdsm. W. M. Millar
		Gdsm. A. Watson
	L/Cpl. S. R. McCormick	Gdsm. M. A. Welsh*
	L/Cpl. A. Milroy*	Gdsm. A. Wingham

* *Denotes Long Range Desert Group*

TUNISIA
Distinguished Service Order	Lieut.-Col. M. D. Erskine	
Military Cross	Maj. R. G. Lewthwaite	Capt. M. D. D. Crichton-Stuart
	Maj. G. A. D. Taylor	
	Lieut. A. J. A. Weir	Lieut. W. J. Brown
Military Medal	Sgt. W. Lumsden	L/Cpl. T. Howe
	Sgt. V. N. Mutch	L/Cpl. J. H. Jenkins
	L/Cpl. T. Davies	L/Cpl. J. McComb

ITALY
Military Cross	Capt. A. M. Balfour	Lieut. W. A. Elliott
	Capt. R. L. Coke	Lieut. the Hon. A. R. H. Erskine
	Capt. R. S. Dollard	
		Lieut. D. I. Fyfe-Jamieson
Distinguished Conduct Medal	Sgt. W. Lumsden, M.M.	
	Gdsm. W. L. Chadwick	
Military Medal	L/Sgt. R. Balcombe	Gdsm. J. Hutchinson
	L/Sgt. C. H. Riches	Gdsm. B. J. McSorley†
	L/Cpl. J. McIlhargey	Gdsm. J. Mitchell†
	Gdsm. G. H. Connor	Gdsm. R. Perks
	Gdsm. H. J. Spraggon	

† *As escaped Prisoners of War*

Bar to the Military Medal	CSM. W. Lumsden, D.C.M., M.M.

GERMANY
Distinguished Service Order	Lieut.-Col. H. N. Clowes	
	Maj. W. D. M. Raeburn, M.B.E.	
Military Cross	Maj. A. E. Cameron	Lieut. P. J. H. Leng
	Lieut. C. M. Campbell	Lieut. A. N. Mannock
Distinguished Conduct Medal	Sgt. J. H. Foster	
Military Medal	CSM. J. H. Foulstone	Sgt. E. F. McGoun
	Sgt. A. McPhee	L/Sgt. J. D. French
	L/Sgt. J. W. Townsend	

APPENDIX B

(c) THIRD BATTALION

NORTH-WEST EUROPE

Distinguished Service Order
Lieut.-Col. C. I. H. Dunbar
Maj. The Earl Cathcart, M.C.

Military Cross
Maj. W. S. I. Whitelaw
Maj. The Earl Cathcart
Maj. The Hon. M. Fitzalan Howard
Maj. J. P. Mann
Maj. C. O'M. Farrell
Capt. V. F. Erskine Crum
Capt. R. C. G. Pember
Capt. D. W. Scott-Barrett
Capt. G. Cameron
Capt. H. W. L. Smith
Capt. I. S. R. Bruce
Lieut. J. M. Barne
Lieut. A. R. G. Stevenson
Lieut. R. A. K. Runcie
Lieut. J. MacDonald-Buchanan
Lieut. A. G. Laing
Lieut. E. P. Hickling
SSM. A. Price

Military Medal
Sgt. L. Aitkin
Sgt. J. Brown
Sgt. T. Coleman
Sgt. T. Irwen
Sgt. H. R. Jackson‡
Sgt. T. Shearer
Sgt. R. Thomson
L/Sgt. J. T. Hackling
L/Cpl. T. Ollerton
Gdsm. D. Crawford
Gdsm. R. Drummond
Gdsm. J. Thomson

‡ *Headquarters 6th Guards Tank Brigade*

(d) S COMPANY

(Attached to 2nd Battalion Coldstream Guards)

ITALY

Distinguished Service Order
Maj. R. L. Coke, M.C.
Capt. A. S. Neilson

Military Cross
Lieut. H. F. G. Charteris

Distinguished Conduct Medal
CSM. T. W. Brown
Sgt. W. G. Young

Military Medal
L/Sgt. P. Jones
L/Sgt. A. MacPhail
L/Cpl. W. G. Downie
L/Cpl. J. Heap
L/Cpl. A. McMinn
L/Cpl. T. G. Smythe
Gdsm. G. Lingwood
Gdsm. F. G. Munday
Gdsm. G. H. Rush
Gdsm. R. J. Tinlin

(e) X COMPANY

(Attached to 3rd Battalion Irish Guards and 1st Battalion Welsh Guards)

NORTH-WEST EUROPE

Distinguished Service Order
Maj. P. Steuart-Fothringham

Military Cross
Capt. E. J. Hope
Lieut. A. Drewe
Lieut. A. D. G. Llewellyn
Lieut. N. Thorpe

Military Medal
Sgt. M. Dannfald
Sgt. M. Dunderdale
Sgt. C. McClelland
L/Sgt. J. Mitchell
L/Cpl. R. Floyd
Gdsm. E. Gibson
Gdsm. A. B. Harley

(f) HOLDING BATTALION

KENLEY AERODROME

Military Cross
2nd Lieut. J. D. K. Hague

Military Medal
L/Cpl. J. E. S. Gale
L/Cpl. J. Miller

APPENDIX B

(g) EXTRA-REGIMENTALLY EMPLOYED

Distinguished Service Order	Brig. J. K. Edwards, M.C.	Brig. G. F. Johnson
	Brig. I. D. Erskine	Lieut.-Col. A. D. Stirling
Bar to the Distinguished Service Order	Brig. J. C. O. Marriott, C.V.O., D.S.O., M.C.	
Military Cross	Maj. S. L. E. Hastings	Maj. J. C. A. Roper
	Maj. D. H. A. Kemble	Capt. T. C. D. Russell
	Maj. R. W. B. Purvis	
Military Medal	Sgt. J. Wilson	L/Cpl. C. Dalziel
	L/Sgt. W. Nicol	L/Cpl. G. Downes
	L/Cpl. M. B. P. Fraser	Gdsm. L. A. Gibson
George Medal	L/Sgt. W. Carruthers	

III. OTHER HONOURS AND AWARDS, 1939–1945

(a) BRITISH

(i) OFFICERS

Order of the Thistle — Lieut.-Col. The Earl of Airlie, G.C.V.O., M.C.

Order of the Bath
Companions — Colonel F. H. Ballantine-Dykes, D.S.O., O.B.E., A.D.C.
Maj.-Gen. W. P. A. Bradshaw, D.S.O.
Maj.-Gen. J. C. O. Marriott, C.V.O., D.S.O., M.C.

Royal Victorian Order
Commanders — Brig. E. W. S. Balfour, D.S.O., O.B.E., M.C.
Maj. The Hon. J. S. Coke

Member — Col. J. F. Gault, M.B.E.

Order of the British Empire
Commanders — Brig. The Hon. H. K. M. Kindersley, M.B.E., M.C.
Brig. T. B. Trappes-Lomax

Officers
- Lt.-Col. C. A. R. Coghill
- Lt.-Col. E. B. W. Cardiff
- Lt.-Col. J. E. M. Bland
- Lt.-Col. A. D. B. Crabbe
- Lt.-Col. J. W. H. Gow
- Lt.-Col. G. M. Kinmont
- Lt.-Col. J. S. Sanderson
- Col. A. D. Stirling, D.S.O.
- Lt.-Col. F. Ward, M.C.

Members
- Capt. E. R. M. Alston
- Capt. C. P. R. Bowen-Colthurst
- Maj. T. F. R. Bulkeley
- Capt. I. M. Calvocoressi, M.C.
- Lt.-Col. The Viscount Dalrymple
- Capt. (QM) W. J. Dorman
- Maj. T. D. Dundas
- Lt.-Col. J. F. Gault, M.V.O.
- Capt. (QM) W. Hanson
- Maj. J. L. Harvey
- Lt.-Col. The Hon. H. K. M. Kindersley, M.C.
- Lt.-Col. R. N. Macdonald-Buchanan, M.C.
- Maj. A. B. C. Maxwell, M.C.
- Maj. W. M. M. Milligan
- Capt. (QM) F. Morley
- Maj. (QM) J. H. Holden
- Maj. W. D. M. Raeburn
- Maj. C. A. A. Robertson
- Capt. (QM) A. Ross
- Maj. D. Traill
- Maj. R. C. Whigham
- Capt. (Q.M.) J. Quinn

(ii) OTHER RANKS

Order of the British Empire
Members
- RSM. L. C. Archer, M.M.
- RSM. F. Foley
- RSM. S. M. Hamilton
- RSM. R. A. Kelly
- RSM. S. Kilpatrick
- RSM. J. Lunn, M.M.
- RSM. R. L. McNally
- RSM. J. B. Robertson
- Suptg. Clerk H. Smith
- RSM. A. Wilford
- QMS. W. Woodford

British Empire Medal
- Sgt. W. T. Craig
- C/Sgt. J. Davidson
- Sgt. C. Greig
- Pipe-Maj. A. MacDonald
- Sgt. W. Ross-Gower

APPENDIX B

(iii) MENTIONS IN DESPATCHES

One hundred and twelve Officers and one hundred and thirty-five Warrant Officers, Non-Commissioned Officers, and Guardsmen were Mentioned in Despatches for their services in the War of 1939–1945.

(b) FOREIGN
(i) OFFICERS

Croix de Guerre 1940, *with Palm* Brig. G. F. Johnson, D.S.O.
  (Belgian) Lt.-Col. P. Steuart-Fothringham, D.S.O.
  Lt.-Col. E. B. W. Cardiff, O.B.E.
  Lt.-Col. J. W. H. Gow, O.B.E.
Croix de Guerre, with Palm Lt.-Col. C. I. H. Dunbar, D.S.O.
  (French) Lt.-Col. R. G. Lewthwaite, M.C.
Croix de Guerre (French) Capt. N. G. R. Davidson
  with Gilt and Vermilian Stars Capt. P. E. G. Balfour
  with Silver Star Capt. C. S. S. Burt
Chevalier of the Order of Leopold II, with Palm (Belgian)
  Lt.-Col. P. Steuart-Fothringham, D.S.O.
Commander of the Order of Leopold II, with Palm (Belgian)
  Brig. G. F. Johnson, D.S.O.
Chevalier of the Legion of Honour (French)
  Capt. G. R. E. Blois, M.C.
Officer of the Legion of Merit (U.S.A.)
  Col. J. F. Gault, M.V.O., M.B.E.
Silver Star Medal (U.S.A.) Lt.-Col. C. I. H. Dunbar, D.S.O.
Bronze Star Medal (U.S.A.) Lieut. H. Laing Maj. D. R. B. Mynors
  Maj. G. C. Lampson Lt.-Col. F. Ward, O.B.E.
  Maj. R. N. Macdonald-Buchanan, M.B.E., M.C.
Order of the Bronze Lion (Dutch) Maj. J. P. Mann, M.C.
Order of the Bronze Cross (Dutch) Maj. A. J. C. Seymour
Order of the White Lion, 4th Class (Czechoslovack)
  Maj. C. V. R. Blundell-Hollinshead-Blundell
Meritorious Service Medal, Class I (Czechoslovack)
  Capt. I. Weston Smith

(ii) OTHER RANKS

Distinguished Service Cross (U.S.A.)
  CSM. J. W. Threadingham
Croix de Guerre, with Silver Star (French)
  RSM. A. K. Madden
  SSM. J. Todd
Croix de Guerre, with Palm (Belgian)
  Gdsm. A. Garland Gdsm. H. Sanderson
  Gdsm. J. Pettigrew
Silver Star (U.S.A.) L/Cpl. T. Morrison
Bronze Star (U.S.A.) Sgt. W. Hill Gdsm. R. Rose
  L/Cpl. D. Lawson

IV. STATISTICS OF DECORATIONS 1939–1945

Officers		Other Ranks	
V.C.	1	M.B.E.	11
K.T.	1	M.C.	1
C.B.	3	D.C.M.	14
C.V.O.	2	M.M.	116
M.V.O.	1	Bar to M.M.	1
C.B.E.	2	G.M.	1
O.B.E.	9	B.E.M.	5
M.B.E.	22		
D.S.O.	16		
Bar to D.S.O.	1		
M.C.	62		
Bar to M.C.	1		
Mentions in Despatches	112	Mentions in Despatches	135
Foreign Awards	23	Foreign Awards	10

Note—In the War of 1914–1918, 5 V.C.s, 26 D.S.O.s, 85 M.C.s, 95 D.C.M.s and 338 M.M.s were awarded to Officers and Men of the Regiment.

V. MALAYA 1948–1951

Order of the British Empire	
Commanders	Brig. M. D. Erskine, D.S.O.
	Brig. C. I. H. Dunbar, D.S.O.
Members	Maj. P. F. Fane Gladwyn
	Maj. the Hon. M. Fitzalan Howard, M.C.
Distinguished Service Order	Lt.-Col. J. S. Sanderson, O.B.E.
Military Cross	Maj. E. I. Ll. Mostyn
Military Medal	L/Cpl. W. Morgan Loc./Sgt. G. Riley
	Loc./Sgt. J. M. Allan
British Empire Medal	Loc./Sgt. F. Howarth Sgt. P. L. Pointon
	Loc./Sgt. T. Hughes
Mentions in Despatches	Fifteen Officers and fourteen Other Ranks were Mentioned in Despatches for services in Malaya 1948–1951.

APPENDIX C

Officers and Warrant Officers who held the Principal Appointments 1934–1956

Note: Such of these lists as are in continuation of those in the General Appendices II, IV and V of Volume II of *The History of the Scots Guards*, start with the last name therein. The others start from 1920.

I. COLONELS-IN-CHIEF

2.	His Majesty King George V	1910
3.	His Majesty King Edward VIII	1936
4.	His Majesty King George VI	1936
5.	Her Majesty Queen Elizabeth II	1952

II. COLONELS

24th Colonel Major-General H.R.H. Albert Frederick George, Duke of York, Earl of Inverness, K.G., K.T., G.C.M.G., G.C.V.O. (*H.M. King George VI d.* 1952)	1932
25th Colonel Field-Marshal H.R.H. Henry William Frederick Albert, Duke of Gloucester, Earl of Ulster, K.G., K.T., K.P., G.C.B., G.C.M.G., G.C.V.O.	1937

III. LIEUTENANT-COLONELS COMMANDING THE REGIMENT

Colonel Sir Edward Courtenay Thomas Warner, Bt., D.S.O., M.C.	1931
Colonel Edward William Sturgis Balfour, D.S.O., O.B.E., M.C.	1934
Colonel William Patrick Arthur Bradshaw, D.S.O.	1938
Colonel Edward William Sturgis Balfour, D.S.O., O.B.E., M.C.	1939
Colonel Edward Dighton Mackenzie, C.M.G., C.V.O., D.S.O.	1943
Colonel William Heneage Wynne-Finch, M.C.	1944
Colonel George Frederick Johnson, D.S.O.	1945
Colonel Malcolm David Erskine, D.S.O.	1947
Colonel John Aylmer, Viscount Dalrymple, M.B.E.	1948
Colonel Claude Ian Hurley Dunbar, C.B.E., D.S.O.	1952
Colonel Henry Nelson Clowes, D.S.O., O.B.E.	1954

IV. COMMANDING OFFICERS

(*All holding rank of Lieutenant-Colonel*)

1st Battalion			2nd Battalion	
A. H. C. Swinton, M.C.	1933		The Viscount Dalrymple	1944
G. L. Tyringham	1937		G. A. D. Taylor, M.C. (*Killed in action*)	1944
T. B. Trappes-Lomax	1939		R. D. Cardiff	1944
M. D. Erskine	1941		R. G. Lewthwaite, M.C.	1945
The Viscount Dalrymple	1942		C. I. H. Dunbar, D.S.O.	1945
M. E. St. J. Barne	1943		H. N. Clowes, D.S.O.	1947
C. I. H. Dunbar	1943		J. S. Sanderson, D.S.O., O.B.E.	1950
M. E. St. J. Barne	1943		P. F. Fane Gladwin, O.B.E.	1951
D. S. Wedderburn, D.S.O. (*Killed in action*)	1944		T. F. R. Bulkeley, M.B.E.	1954

APPENDIX C

2ND BATTALION

W. H. Wynne-Finch, M.C.	1931
W. P. A. Bradshaw	1935
J. C. O. Marriott, D.S.O., M.C.	1938
I. D. Erskine, D.S.O.	1940
B. Mayfield	1941
P. C. H. Grant	1942
M. D. Erskine, D.S.O.	1942
G. A. D. Taylor, M.C.	*1943
F. H. H. B. Harris (*Killed in action*)	*1943
H. N. Clowes, D.S.O.	*1944
The Viscount Dalrymple, M.B.E.	1946
J. S. Sanderson, D.S.O., O.B.E.	1948
A. E. Cameron, M.C.	1950
W. D. M. Raeburn, D.S.O., M.B.E.	1953
The Hon. M. Fitzalan Howard, M.V.O., M.B.E., M.C.	1956

* Between November 1943 and May 1944 the 2nd Battalion was for several periods under the command of Major P. Steuart-Fothringham.

3RD BATTALION

G. F. Johnson	1940
The Hon. H. K. M. Kindersley, M.B.E.	1941

C. I. H. Dunbar, D.S.O.	1943
P. Steuart-Fothringham, D.S.O.	1945

4TH BATTALION

A. V. C. Douglas	1941
F. H. H. B. Harris	1943

5TH BATTALION

J. S. Coats, M.C., *Coldstream Guards*	1940

TRAINING BATTALION

A. H. C. Swinton, M.C.	1939
A. V. C. Douglas	1943
M. E. St. J. Barne	1945
The Viscount Dalrymple, M.B.E.	1945
M. E. St. J. Barne	1946

HOLDING BATTALION

E. D. Mackenzie, C.V.O., C.M.G., D.S.O.	1940
J. E. M. Bland	1940
E. D. Mackenzie, C.V.O., C.M.G., D.S.O.	1941
J. E. M. Bland	1942

V. REGIMENTAL ADJUTANTS

Captain J. E. M. Bland	1932
Captain The Viscount Dalrymple	1935
Captain A. V. C. Douglas	1938
Major the Hon. P. C. Kinnaird, M.C.	1939
Major A. D. B. Pearson	1943
Major A. D. Murray	1945

Major V. F. Erskine Crum, C.I.E., M.C.	1948
Major The Earl Cathcart, D.S.O., M.C.	1951
Major P. E. G. Balfour	1953
Major G. P. M. Ramsay	1954

VI. BATTALION ADJUTANTS

1ST BATTALION

E. D. Mackenzie, D.S.O.	1919
W. P. A. Bradshaw	1920
I. D. Erskine	1923
W. G. Horton	1926
G. F. Johnson	1929
The Viscount Dalrymple	1932
C. I. H. Dunbar	1935
H. N. Clowes	1938
T. F. R. Bulkeley	1940
A. H. M. Thavenot	1941
J. E. Tyldesley-Jones	1942
D. Traill	1943
A. L. Logue	1944
E. I. Ll. Mostyn	1945

A. L. Logue	1945
P. E. G. Balfour	1946
A. D. G. Llewellyn, M.C.	1948
A. J. C. Seymour	1948
J. Macdonald-Buchanan, M.C.	1950
J. B. Denham	1951
N. G. Ramsay	1952
The Lord Napier and Ettrick	1955

2ND BATTALION

H. C. E. Ross	1919
C. H. L. F. M. T. Chamberlayne	1920
H. L. Graham, M.C.	1923
B. Mayfield	1924

540   APPENDIX C

J. E. M. Bland	1927	P. E. G. Balfour	1944
C. A. R. Coghill	1930	A. J. C. Seymour	1945
M. D. Erskine	1933	The Hon. J. F. H. Erskine	1945
The Hon. T. H. Fermor-Hesketh	1936		
J. D. C. S. MacRae	1937	4TH BATTALION	
T. L. Ballantine-Dykes	1940		
A. E. Cameron, M.C.	1942	O. Priaulx	1941
J. R. S. Clarke, M.C.	1942	R. C. Whigham	1941
The Hon. G. C. Lampson	1943	T. C. Harvey	1942
W. J. Brown, M.C.	1943	A. N. B. Ritchie	1942
Sir Henry Astley-Corbett, Bt.		P. G. Atkinson-Clark	1943
(*Killed in action*)	1943	M. H. Fitzherbert-Brockholes	1943
A. J. A. Weir, M.C.	1943		
M. J. Fitzherbert-Brockholes	1944	5TH BATTALION	
A. N. B. Ritchie	1945		
A. I. D. Fletcher	1946	W. D. M. Raeburn	1940
P. E. G. Balfour	1948		
A. N. B. Ritchie	1948	HOLDING BATTALION	
J. Swinton	1949	Lord Robert Crichton-Stuart	1940
M. P. J. de Klee	1952	A. P. Bristowe	1941
B. A. Stewart-Wilson	1955		
		TRAINING BATTALION	
3RD BATTALION		I. K. Matheson	1939
J. L. Harvey	1940	A. D. B. Pearson	1939
R. C. Whigham	1942	K. N. Fisher	1943
V. F. Erskine Crum, M.C.	1943	I. M. Tennant	1946

VII. QUARTERMASTERS

1ST BATTALION		Captain F. Morley, M.B.E.	1944
Major J. S. Tate, M.B.E., M.C.	1919	Captain H. H. Spalding	1945
Captain J. Cook	1933	Captain C. Robertson	1945
Lieutenant J. Turner	1934		
Captain A. Ross, M.B.E.	1939	4TH BATTALION	
Captain J. Quinn, M.B.E.	1944		
Major A. Ross, M.B.E.	1946	Captain J. Quinn	1941
Captain H. Smith, M.B.E.	1949		
Captain D. McG. Fraser, M.B.E.	1952	5TH BATTALION	
		Lieutenant J. Quinn	1940
2ND BATTALION			
Captain E. T. Cutler, M.C.	1919	HOLDING BATTALION	
Lieutenant-Colonel J. H. Holden, M.B.E.	1933	Lieutenant J. Quinn	1940
Captain W. Hanson, M.B.E.	1941	Captain H. Spalding	1941
Major A. O'C. Greenwood, M.B.E.	1942	Captain C. Robertson	1943
Lieutenant S. R. Watts	1955		
Lieutenant R. H. Thomson, D.C.M.	1956	TRAINING BATTALION	
		Lieutenant A. Ross, M.B.E.	1939
		Captain F. Morley, M.B.E.	1939
3RD BATTALION		Lieutenant L. C. Archer, M.B.E. M.M.	1942
Captain W. J. Dorman, M.B.E. (*Killed on Active Service*)	1940	Major A. Ross, M.B.E.	1944

APPENDIX C

VIII. DIRECTORS OF MUSIC

Captain F. W. Wood, M.V.O.	1919	Lieut-Colonel S. Rhodes, M.B.E., Mus.Bac., A.R.C.M.	1938
Captain H. E. Dowell, L.R.A.M.	1929		

IX. REGIMENTAL SERGEANT-MAJORS

1st Battalion

J. Barwick, M.C.	1916
J. McDonald, D.C.M.	1924
W. A. Blakeley	1931
W. J. Dorman, M.B.E.	1939
F. A. Foley, M.B.E.	1940
S. M. Hamilton, M.B.E.	1944
H. A. Garner	1945
G. F. Brown	1945
H. Tomlinson, M.M.	1948
F. Hall	1951
R. Thomson, D.C.M.	1952
D. McN. Whyte	1956

2nd Battalion

A. E. Pettit, M.C.	1917
W. Murray, M.B.E., D.C.M.	1923
J. H. Holden, M.B.E.	1930
A. Ross, M.B.E.	1933
F. Leiper (*Killed in action*)	1939
A. O'C. Greenwood	1941
R. C. Douglas	1942
R. A. Wessel	1943
A. Barnstaple	1944
A. K. Madden	1945
J. Chapman	1946
D. McG. Fraser, M.B.E.	1948
D. C. Gibson	1952
J. Braid	1954

3rd Battalion

E. C. Gray	1940
C. Robertson	1940
G. F. Brown	1943
W. Washington, M.M.	1944
D. McG. Fraser	1945

4th Battalion

A. Wilford	1941

5th Battalion

A. K. Madden	1940

Training Battalion

L. C. Archer, M.B.E., M.M.	1939
G. F. Brown	1942
A. Wilford, M.B.E.	1943
J. Chapman	1945
P. Standing	1946

Holding Battalion

C. Robertson	1940
A. Wilford	1941
A. K. Madden	1941
F. Curtis	1942

X. SUPERINTENDING CLERKS AT REGIMENTAL HEADQUARTERS

C. Spivey	1909	H. Smith, M.B.E.	1939
J. Cook	1917	H. Marchant	1947
R. Adams	1924	N. Saxon	1951
J. Turner	1932	R. Tillotson	1954
F. Morley	1934	W. Wilbur	1956

APPENDIX D

Orders of Battle 1939—1945

Note: While every effort has been made to ensure the accuracy of these Orders of Battle, it is regretted that there may still be one or two minor errors in the earlier ones.

First Battalion   543
- (1) On Embarkation for Norway: 7th April 1940.
- (2) On Embarkation for North Africa: 26th February, 1943.
- (3) On Embarkation for Anzio: 22nd January 1944.
- (4) On joining 6th South African Armoured Division: 19th May 1944.
- (5) On joining 56th (London) Division: 18th March 1945.

Second Battalion   548
- (6) On first entering the Desert: 7th April 1941.
- (7) At the opening of the Battle of Gazala: 27th May 1942.
- (8) At the Battle of Medenine: 6th March 1943.
- (9) On Embarkation for Salerno: 4th September 1943.
- (10) On joining the Guards Armoured Division: 8th February 1945.

Third Battalion   553
- (11) On formation: 15th October 1940.
- (12) At the Battle of Caumont: 30th July 1944.
- (13) At the end of the War in Europe: 8th May 1945.

Fourth Battalion   556
- (14) On formation: 11th October 1941.

Fifth Battalion   557
- (15) On Embarkation for France: 29th February 1940.

S Company   558
- (16) On formation; at Monte Piccolo; at Monte Penzola.

X Company   558
- (17) On Embarkation for France; at Hechtel; on Disbandment.

APPENDIX D 543

(1) FIRST BATTALION

7TH APRIL, 1940

On Embarkation for Norway

Commanding Officer: Lieutenant-Colonel T. B. Trappes-Lomax
Second-in-Command: Major H. L. Graham, M.C.
Adjutant: Captain H. N. Clowes
Intelligence Officer: Captain G. A. D. Taylor

Quartermaster: Lieutenant A. Ross
Medical Officer: Lieutenant W. M. Burgess, R.A.M.C.
Chaplain: The Rev. J. Hamilton, R.A.Ch.D.
Interpreter: Lieutenant O. B. W. Aarvold

Regimental Sergeant-Major: W. J. Dorman
Regimental Quartermaster Sergeant: H. Spalding
Drill Sergeants: F. Foley
 R. McNally
Pipe Major: A. MacDonald (*also commanding A.A. section*)

	Headquarter Company	*Right Flank*	*B Company*	*C Company*	*Left Flank*
Coy. Comds.	Capt. F. H. H. B. Harris	Capt. A. D. B. Crabbe	Major J. H. Elwes	Capt. P. Steuart-Fothringham	Major The Viscount Garnock
2nds i/c	Capt. J. S. Sanderson	Capt. C. A. Fletcher	Capt. J. Godman	Capt. D. V. C. McBarnet	Capt. J. F. Milburne
	(*Signal*)	Lieut. D. S. Wedderburn	Lieut. The Lord John Hope	Lieut. D. R. Forwood	Lieut. A. H. R. M. Ramsay
	Lieut. R. D. Cardiff				
	(*M.T.O.*)				
	Lieut. A. D. Murray				
	(*Carriers*)				
CSMs.	W. Curtis (*Acting*)	F. Higham	A. Barnstaple	A. Clark	F. Bradley
	H. McMillan	H. Dey	H. Martin	?	J. Aitken
PSMs.	C. Regan	H. Tomlinson	D. Tolmie		M. Morrison
	D. Forret				

First Reinforcements: Lieut. R. C. Petre
 2nd Lieuts. H. L. St. V. Rose
  T. C. Harvey
  A. M. Balfour
 CSM. S. Hamilton
 PSM. W. Washington

Brigade Transport Officer: Capt. D. R. Daly

APPENDIX D

(2) FIRST BATTALION

26TH FEBRUARY, 1943

On Embarkation for North Africa

Commanding Officer: Lieutenant-Colonel The Viscount Dalrymple
Second-in-Command: Major M. E. St. J. Barne
Adjutant: Captain J. E. Tyldesley Jones
Intelligence Officer: Lieutenant C. Lewis

Quartermaster: Captain A. Ross
Medical Officer: Captain G. C. Hodge, R.A.M.C.
Chaplain: The Rev. J. Hamilton, R.A.Ch.D.

Regimental Sergeant-Major: F. Foley
Regimental Quartermaster Sergeant: S. R. Watts
Drill Sergeants: A. Barnstaple
S. Hamilton
Pipe-Major: A. MacDonald

	Headquarter Company	*Right Flank*	*B Company*	*C Company*	*Left Flank*
Coy. Comds.	Major C. A. Fletcher	Capt. T. F. R. Bulkeley	Major D. V. C. McBarnet	Capt. G. C. Rush	Capt. R. H. Bull
2nds i/c		Capt. F. G. Mann	Capt. M. W. Rowe	Capt. The Lord Lyell	Capt. J. S. Stockton
Pl. Comds.	Capt. A. H. Piper *(Carriers)*	Lieut. M. R. G. Nevill	Lieut. J. D. Forrester	Lieut. The Hon. P. H. S. D. Butler	Lieut. R. T. Hunter
	Lieut. H. S. Keith *(A/Carriers)*	Lieut. J. L. Sinclair	Lieut. D. M. H. Bailie	Lieut. T. M. F. E. Lowinsky	Lieut. R. O. Stewart
	Lieut. E. A. G. Balfour *(M.T.O.)*	Lieut. H. A. W. Smith	Lieut. A. B. Brown	Lieut. J. Graham	Lieut. The Hon. D. A. Bethell
	Lieut. J. Cumming *(Pioneers)*				
	Lieut. D. J. Forbes *(Signal)*				
	Lieut. A. F. Tuke *(Anti-Tank)*				
	Lieut. M. J. Jardine *(Mortars)*				
CSMs.	R. Russel	D. Fraser	D. C. Gibson	H. Tomlinson	J. Lunn

First Reinforcements: Captain D. P. M. Malcolm
Lieutenants D. Traill, T. C. Lindsay-Peto, L. E. Widderson, and P. H. Shaw Stewart
CSM. J. C. Begg

APPENDIX D

(3) FIRST BATTALION

22ND JANUARY, 1944
On Embarkation for Anzio

Commanding Officer: Lieutenant-Colonel D. S. Wedderburn
Second-in-Command: Major D. V. C. McBarnet
Adjutant: Captain D. Traill
A/Adjutant: Lieutenant C. P. Whitehead
Intelligence Officer: Lieutenant H. S. Keith

Quartermaster: Captain A. Ross
Medical Officer: Captain G. C. Hodge, M.C., R.A.M.C.
Chaplain: The Rev. J. Hamilton, R.A.Ch.D.

Regimental Sergeant-Major: F. Foley
Regimental Quartermaster Sergeant: S. R. Watts
Drill Sergeants: P. Standing
S. Hamilton
Pipe-Major: A. MacDonald

	Headquarter Company	*Support Company*	*Right Flank*	*B Company*	*C Company*	*Left Flank*
Coy. Comds.	Capt. G. R. E. Blois	Major C. A. Fletcher	Major A. J. A. Weir, M.C.	Major J. E. Tyldesley Jones	[Major F. C. Usher, *sick*]	Major R. H. Bull, M.C.
2nds i/c			Capt. M. J. Jardine	Capt. E. A. G. Balfour	Capt. D. P. M. Malcolm	Capt. H. D. Cuthbert
Pl. Comds.	Lieut. D. J. Forbes (*Signal*)	Capt. A. H. Piper (*Carriers*)	Lieut. J. H. L. Sinclair	Lieut. J. D. Forrester	Lieut. D. M. H. Bailie	Lieut. R. O. Stewart
	Lieut. H. A. W. Smith (*Pioneers*)	Lieut. The Hon. P. H. S. D. Butler (*A/Carrier*)	Lieut. H. M. Snell	Lieut. P. H. Shaw Stewart	Lieut. J. W. Stuart-Menteth	Lieut. P. G. Henderson
	Lieut. F. McL. Hayward (*M.T.O.*)	Capt. A. F. Tuke (*Anti-Tank*)	Lieut. T. C. Lindsay-Peto	Lieut. D. G. S. McMurtie	Lieut. J. Graham	Lieut The Hon. D. A. Bethell
		Lieut. L. E. Widderson (*A/Anti-Tank*)				
		Lieut. T. M. F. E. Lowinsky (*Mortars*)				
CSMs.	R. Russel	T. Wilkinson	J. C. Begg	F. Hall	H. Tomlinson (*later* G. Ward, of 1st Reinforcement Coy.)	D. C. Gibson

546   APPENDIX D

(4) FIRST BATTALION

19TH MAY, 1944

On joining the 6th South African Armoured Division

Commanding Officer: Lieutenant-Colonel G. A. D. Taylor, M.C.
Second-in-Command: Major R. D. Cardiff
Adjutant: Captain D. Traill
A/Adjutant: Lieutenant D. J. Forbes
Intelligence Officer: Lieutenant H. S. Keith

Quartermaster: Captain J. Quinn
Medical Officer: Captain H. N. Mansfield, R.A.M.C.
Chaplain: The Rev. D. W. Hay, R.A.Ch.D.
(*after 15th June*: The Rev. A. A. McArthur, R.A.Ch.D.)

Regimental Sergeant-Major: S. Hamilton
Regimental Quartermaster Sergeant: S. R. Watts
Drill Sergeants: H. Garner
                 J. Mackenzie
Pipe-Major: A. MacDonald

	Headquarter Company	Support Company	Right Flank	B Company	C Company	Left Flank
Coy. Comds.	Major R. C. Petre	Capt. A. H. Piper	Major F. G. Mann, M.C.	Capt. J. C. Blackett-Ord	Major The Hon. F. Fermor-Hesketh	Major T. C. Harvey
2nds i/c			Capt. M. J. Jardine	Capt. E. A. G. Balfour	Capt. D. P. M. Malcolm	Capt. The Hon. W. H. Vestey
Pl. Comds.	Lieut. G. P. M. Ramsay (*Signal*)	Capt. R. A. Readman (*Carriers*)	Lieut. The Hon. D. A. Bethell, M.C.	Lieut. D. E. C. Price	Lieut. D. H. Deane	Lieut. T. Bland
	Lieut. M. D. Asprey (*A/Signal*)	Lieut. E. R. Yates (*A/Carrier*)	Lieut. H. M. Snell	Lieut. E. Crutchley	Lieut. E. F. Winter	Lieut. E. I. Ll. Mostyn
	Lieut. H. A. W. Smith (*Pioneers*)	Capt. A. F. Tuke (*Anti-Tank*)	Lieut. Sir David Moncreiffe	Lieut. M. E. V. Baillie	Lieut. G. F. Mundy	Lieut. R. A. Carnegie
	Lieut. F. McL. Hayward (*M.T.O.*)	Lieut. D. Tylden-Wright (*A/Anti-Tank*)				
		Lieut. R. S. Jenkinson (*Mortars*)				
CSMs.	F. Hall	T. Wilkinson	W. Robertson	D. Gidman	G. Ward	A. Coonie

APPENDIX D 547

(5) FIRST BATTALION

18TH MARCH, 1945

On joining 56th (London) Division

Commanding Officer: Lieutenant-Colonel R. G. Lewthwaite, M.C.
Second-in-Command: Major T. F. R. Bulkeley
Adjutant: Captain A. L. Logue
Intelligence Officer: Lieutenant H. S. Keith
Sniping and Patrol Officer: Lieutenant Sir David Moncreiffe, M.C.

Quartermaster: Captain J. Quinn, M.B.E.
Medical Officer: Captain H. N. Mansfield, R.A.M.C.
Chaplain: The Rev. A. A. McArthur, R.A.Ch.D.

Regimental Sergeant-Major: S. Hamilton
Regimental Quartermaster-Sergeant: S. Watts
Drill Sergeants: J. Mackenzie
H. Garner
Pipe-Major: A. MacDonald, B.E.M.

	Headquarter Company	*Support Company*	*Right Flank*	*B Company*	*C Company*	*Left Flank*
Coy. Comds.	Capt. M. J. Jardine		Major F. G. Mann, M.C.	Major R. L. Coke, D.S.O, M.C.	Major D. P. M. Malcolm	Major A. F. Tuke
2nds i/c		Major A. H. Piper	Capt. The Hon. W. E. H. Lawson	Capt. The Hon. C. J. Dalrymple	Capt. T. C. Lindsay-Peto, M.C.	Captain E. I. Ll. Mostyn
Pl. Comds.	Captain D. J. Forbes *(Signal)*	Capt. R. S. Jenkinson *(Mortars)*	Lieut. A. W. Goodinge	Lieut. J. S. Wilson	Lieut. P. J. Blandy	Lieut. M. Garratt
	Lieut. M. D. Asprey *(A/Signal)*	Capt. E. R. Yates *(Carriers)*	Lieut. The Hon. D. H. Erskine	Lieut. P. W. Bartholomew	Lieut. A. O. Worthington-Wilmer	Lieut. D. A. Colquhoun
	Lieut. R. M. C. Nunneley *(Pioneers)*	Lieut. D. H. Deane *(A/Carrier)*	Lieut. E. H. L. Wallace	Lieut. I. J. Fraser	Lieut. J. Warnock	Lieut. S. C. M. Bland
	Lieut. F. McL. Hayward *(M.T.O.)*	Lieut. T. N. Douglas *(Flame)*				
CSMs.	J. Mitchell	T. Wilkinson	W. Robertson	T. Taylor, M.M.	D. Gidman	R. Thomson

APPENDIX D

(6) SECOND BATTALION

7TH APRIL, 1941

On first entry into the Desert

Commanding Officer: Lieutenant-Colonel B. Mayfield
Second-in-Command: Major P. C. H. Grant
Adjutant: Captain T. L. Ballantine-Dykes
Intelligence Officer: Lieutenant T. Marsham-Townsend

Quartermaster: Captain J. E. Holden
Medical Officer: Captain A. H. Dickie, R.A.M.C.
Chaplain: The Rev. V. C. Clarke, R.A.Ch.D.

Regimental Sergeant-Major: F. Leiper
Regimental Quartermaster Sergeant: W. Hanson
Drill Sergeants: R. C. Douglas
                  A. Greenwood
Pipe-Major: W. Speedy

	Headquarter Company	Right Flank	F Company	G Company	Left Flank
Coy. Comds.	Major G. M. Kinmont	Capt. J. D. C. S. MacRae	Capt. G. C. Rush	Major C. A. R. Coghill	Capt. The Hon. T. W. E. Coke, M.V.O.
	Capt. P. F. Fane Gladwin (*M.T.O.*)	Lieut. A. H. R. M. Ramsay	Lieut. H. J. Stirling	Lieut. M. N. Romer	Capt. R. A. Orr-Ewing
	Capt. R. A. H. Rivers-Bulkeley (*Carriers*)	2nd Lieut. I. M. Tennant	2nd Lieut. N. G. R. Davidson	2nd Lieut. The Hon B. Bruce	2nd Lieut. The Hon. P. J. Boyle
	Capt. H. S. Knight (*Signal*)			2nd Lieut. A. J. Coats	
	Lieut. D. S. Robertson (*Mortars*)				
CSMs.	F. W. Lindley	J. Bromhead	J. F. Chapman	J. Richmond	F. Nelson

First Reinforcements: 2nd Lieutenants G. C. Lampson
                                        H. H. Houldsworth
                                        P. Dawson
                                        J. G. Critchley

At Headquarters 22nd Guards Brigade: Brigadier I. D. Erskine
                                       Capt. R. de M. Grant-Watson (*Brigade I.O.*)
                                       Capt. W. D. M. Raeburn (*L.O.*)
                                       2nd Lieut. H. J. H. Eves (*Camp Commandant*)

(7) SECOND BATTALION (Motor Battalion)

27th MAY, 1942

At the opening of the Battle of Gazala

Commanding Officer: Lieutenant-Colonel P. C. H. Grant
Second-in-Command: Major J. H. Elwes, M.C.
Adjutant: Captain A. E. Cameron
Intelligence Officer: Lieutenant J. R. S. Clarke, M.C.

Quartermaster: Lieutenant A. Greenwood
Medical Officer: Captain R. I. Mitchell, R.A.M.C.
Chaplain: The Rev. V. C. Clarke, R.A.Ch.D.

Regimental Sergeant-Major: R. C. Douglas
Regimental Quartermaster Sergeant: A. Wigham
Drill Sergeants: J. Richmond, D.C.M.
J. F. Chapman
Pipe-Major: W. Speedy

	Headquarter Company	Right Flank	F Company	G Company	Left Flank (Anti-Tank Coy.)
Coy. Comds.	Capt. P. F. Fane Gladwin	Capt. I. D. C. S. MacRae, D.S.O.	Major T. L. Ballantine-Dykes	Capt. R. A. Orr-Ewing	Major J. D. B. Drury-Lowe
	Capt. M. N. Romer (*M.T.O.*)	Capt. R. A. H. Rivers-Bulkeley	Lieut. A. B. C. Maxwell	Lieut. D. S. Robertson	Lieut. C. S. S. Burt
	Lieut. G. C. Lampson (*Signal*)	Lieut. R. N. Brooke	Lieut. T. Marsham-Townshend	Lieut. R. W. Ferguson-Cunninghame	Lieut. Sir Henry Astley-Corbett
	Lieut. M. J. A. Gordon (*B Echelon*)	Lieut. B. D. Carris	Lieut. H. L. St. V. Rose	2nd Lieut. A. M. Archdale	Lieut. I. M. Calvocoressi
		Lieut. R. A. Willis	Lieut. H. H. Houldsworth	2nd Lieut. M. F. Beeson	Lieut. D. H. Butter
			2nd Lieut. G. P. Burnett		
CSMs.	A. Rattray	E. T. Bromfield	W. K. Eden	W. Gore	F. Nelson

Note: Before the action on Rigel Ridge, 13th June, the following officers joined the Battalion: Lieutenants A. J. O. Maxtone-Graham (*Left Flank*); J. N. Cochrane-Barnett (*F Company*), and 2nd Lieutenant P. Dawson (*G Company*).

APPENDIX D

(8) SECOND BATTALION (Motor Battalion)

6TH MARCH, 1943

The Battle of Medenine

Commanding Officer: Lieutenant-Colonel M. D. Erskine
Second-in-Command: Major J. H. Elwes, M.C.
Adjutant: Captain J. R. S. Clarke, M.C.
Intelligence Officer: Lieutenant N. H. Barne, M.C.
Quartermaster: Lieutenant A. Greenwood
Medical Officer: Captain J. D. Finnegan, R.A.M.C.
Chaplain: The Rev. J. M. Gow, M.C., R.A.Ch.D.
Regimental Sergeant-Major: R. C. Douglas
Regimental Quartermaster Sergeant: A. Wigham
Drill Sergeants: J. Richmond, D.C.M.
J. F. Chapman

	Headquarter Company	Right Flank	F Company	G Company	Left Flank (Anti-Tank Coy.)
Coy. Comds.	Capt. D. H. A. Kemble, M.C.	Major A. E. Cameron	Capt. M. D. D. Crichton-Stuart	Major R. G. Lewthwaite	Major G. A. D. Taylor
	Lieut. R. L. Stuart (M.T.O.)	Capt. Sir Henry Astley-Corbett	Capt. H. L. St. V. Rose	Capt. J. A. L. Timpson, M.C.	Capt. M. J. A. Gordon
	Lieut. A. H. M. Thavenot (Technical Officer)	Lieut. R. A. Willis	Lieut. A. J. A. Weir	Lieut. D. J. N. Bland	Lieut. F. A. L. Waldron
	Lieut. The Hon. G. G. C. Lampson (Signal)	Lieut. D. I. Fyfe-Jamieson	Lieut. A. T. Philipson	Lieut. W. J. Gunther	Lieut. J. D. A. Stainton
	Lieut. L. D. Cambridge (A/Signal)	Lieut. D. G. Morphett	Lieut. R. C. McLeod	Lieut. A. Drew	Lieut. G. D. Shrubshall
			Lieut. H. J. H. Eves	Lieut. J. S. Cuninghame	Lieut. A. N. J. Gordon
			Lieut. P. H. Gibbs		
Ms.	S. Hughes	E. T. Bromfield	R. Tillotson	W. Gore	A. Turner, M.M.

At Headquarters 201st Guards Motor Brigade: Capt. J. D. Henderson (*Brigade Transport Officer*); Lieut. P. H. Tunnard (*Liaison Officer*)

APPENDIX D

(9) SECOND BATTALION

14TH SEPTEMBER, 1943

On Embarkation for Salerno

Commanding Officer: Lieutenant-Colonel G. A. D. Taylor, M.C.
Second-in-Command: Major P. Steuart-Fothringham
Adjutant: Captain Sir Henry Astley-Corbett
A/Adjutant: Captain A. H. M. Thavenot
Intelligence Officer: Lieutenant T. R. Bland

Quartermaster: Lieutenant A. Greenwood
Medical Officer: Captain J. R. Dow, R.A.M.C.
Chaplain: The Rev. J. M. Gow, M.C., R.A.Ch.D.

Regimental Sergeant-Major: R. Wessell
Regimental Quartermaster Sergeant: A. Mutch
Drill-Sergeants: J. Lunn, M.M.
R. Tillotson
Pipe-Major: J. W. Raeburn

Headquarter Company
Capt. R. S. P. Home

Capt. Hon. G. C. Lampson
(*Signal*)
Lieut. L. D. Cambridge
(*A/Signal*)
Lieut. The Lord Cross
(*M.T.O.*)

Support Company
Major J. F. Milburne

Capt. F. A. L. Waldron
(*Anti-Tank*)
Lieut. J. D. A. Stainton
(*A/Anti-Tank*)
Capt. A. J. A. Weir, M.C.
(*Carriers*)
Lieut. H. Brooking-Clark
(*A/Carriers*)
Lieut. D. G. Morphett
(*Mortars*)
Lieut. C. R. S. Buckle
(*Pioneers*)

Right Flank
Major R. A. H. Rivers-Bulkeley

Capt. R. A. Willis

Lieut. W. A. Elliott

Lieut. R. T. S. Clarke

Lieut. I. J. Fraser

Lieut. C. P. R. Bowen-Colthurst

F Company
Major M. D. D. Crichton-Stuart

Capt. M. N. Romer

Lieut. A. T. Philipson

Lieut. W. Beckett

Lieut. R. C. McLeod

G Company
Major I. A. L. Timpson, M.C.

Capt. I. Weston-Smith

Lieut. Sir Nigel Cayzer

Lieut. The Hon. A. R. H. Erskine

Lieut. R. S. Dollard

Lieut. N. T. Torrance

Left Flank
Major H. H. Houldsworth

Capt. M. J. A. Gordon

Lieut. D. I. Fyfe-Jamieson

Lieut. K. B. Mackenzie

Lieut. J. D. Henderson

CSMs.: G. McKirdy   H. Watson   L. Parkes   J. Tulloch   R. Little, M.M.   J. Hope, M.M.

First Reinforcements: Captains: N. H. Barne, M.C.
W. J. Brown, M.C.

Lieutenants: R. A. E. Balfour
T. N. Douglas
P. C. Carter
P. R. Methuen
J. Carpenter-Garnier

CSM.:   L. Gray

(10) SECOND BATTALION

8TH FEBRUARY, 1945

On joining the Guards Armoured Division

Commanding Officer: Lieutenant-Colonel H. N. Clowes
Second-in-Command: Major H. D. Tweedie
Adjutant: Captain M. J. Fitzherbert-Brockholes
Intelligence Officer: Lieutenant The Hon. J. F. H. Erskine

Quartermaster: Captain A. Greenwood
Medical Officer: Captain A. S. Fairbairn, R.A.M.C. (*later* Capt. A. J. Briggs, R.A.M.C.)
Chaplain: The Rev. D. H. Whiteford, R.A.Ch.D.

Regimental Sergeant-Major: A. Barnstaple
Regimental Quartermaster Sergeant: D. Tolmie
Drill Sergeants: D. Fraser, G. McKirdy
Pipe-Major: P. Bain

Headquarter Company	*Support Company*	*Right Flank*	*F Company*	*G Company*	*Left Flank*
Capt. G. L. S. Pike	Capt. The Lord Robert Crichton-Stuart (*later* Capt. E. J. Hope, M.C.)	Major W. D. M. Raeburn, M.B.E.	Major D. H. A. Kemble, M.C.	Major A. E. Cameron	Major M. N. Romer
Capt. R. L. Stuart (*M.T.O.*)	Capt. Sir John Worsley-Taylor (*Carriers*)	Capt. H. L. St. V. Rose	Capt. J. S. B. Clerk-Rattray	Capt. R. A. Willis	Capt. N. H. Barne, M.C.
Lieut. L. D. Cambridge (*Signal*)	Lieut. H. Brooking-Clark (*A/Carriers*)	Lieut. I. G. Gow	Lieut. K. E. Seel	Lieut. The Hon. A. R. H. Erskine, M.C.	Lieut. M. S. Macdonald
Lieut. S. R. Douglas (*A/Signal*)	Capt. F. A. L. Waldron (*Anti-Tank*)	Lieut. W. A. Elliott, M.C.	Lieut. R. A. Berridge	Lieut. N. T. Torrance	Lieut. C. M. Campbell
	Capt. G. D. Morphett (*Mortars*)	Lieut. V. E. de S. C. de Soissons	Lieut. H. R. Tempest	Lieut. F. H. Taylor	Lieut. J. Swinton
	Lieut. A. N. J. Gordon (*Pioneers*) (*later* Lieut. D. G. Thomas)				
CSMs.: T. Liddle	P. Lyall	J. Lindsay	W. Lumsden, D.C.M., M.M.	J. Foulstone	J. Kerr

APPENDIX D

(11) THIRD BATTALION

15TH OCTOBER, 1940

On Formation

Commanding Officer: Lieutenant-Colonel G. F. Johnson
Second-in-Command: Major J. A. Burns
Adjutant: Captain J. L. Harvey
Intelligence Officer: 2nd Lieutenant J. R. S. Clarke

Quartermaster: Lieutenant W. J. Dorman
Medical Officer: Captain R. C. Droop, R.A.M.C.
Chaplain: The Rev. G. T. H. Reid, R.A.Ch.D.

Regimental Sergeant-Major: E. C. Gray
(later C. Robertson)

Right Flank	*S Company*	*T Company*	*Left Flank*
Capt. A. D. B. Crabbe	Major G. A. D. Taylor	Major P. Steuart-Fothringham	Capt. D. S. Wedderburn
Capt. The Hon. M. Fitzalan Howard	Capt. W. M. M. Milligan	Capt. Sir Charles Maclean	Capt. R. H. Gubbins-Mounsey-Heysham
2nd Lieut. J. A. L. Timpson	2nd Lieut. The Earl Cathcart	2nd Lieut. R. W. O. Burnett	2nd Lieut. A. J. C. Seymour
2nd Lieut. C. R. S. Graham	2nd Lieut. N. W. Beeson	2nd Lieut. V. F. Erskine Crum	2nd Lieut. J. H. Taylor

Headquarter Company
Capt. A. D. Murray
2nd Lieut. W. S. I. Whitelaw (*M.T.O.*)
2nd Lieut. R. L. Coke (*Signal*)
2nd Lieut. W. P. Bull (*Carriers*)
2nd Lieut. C. O'M. Farrell (*Carriers*)

(12) THIRD (TANK) BATTALION

30TH JULY, 1944

At the Battle of Caumont

Commanding Officer: Lieutenant-Colonel C. I. H. Dunbar
Second-in-Command: Major S. J. Cuthbert
Adjutant: Captain V. F. Erskine Crum
Intelligence Officer: Lieutenant P. B. Fraser
i/c Bn. H.Q. Tanks: Lieutenant D. L. Bankes

Quartermaster: Captain W. J. Dorman, M.B.E.
Medical Officer: Captain A. T. MacKnight, R.A.M.C.
Chaplain: The Rev. G. T. H. Reid, R.A.Ch.D.
Electrical and Mechanical Engineer Officer:
　Captain C. E. Pring, R.E.M.E.

Regimental Sergeant-Major: G. Brown
Regimental Quartermaster Sergeant: D. Duff
Drill Sergeants: J. Smith
　　　　　　　　　I. Moore
Technical Quartermaster Sergeant: A. Arber
Mechanical Quartermaster Sergeant: J. McGowan
Pipe-Major: W. Smith

	Headquarter Squadron	*Right Flank*	*S Squadron*	*Left Flank*
Sqn. Leaders	Major Sir Charles Maclean	Major The Earl Cathcart	Major W. S. I. Whitelaw	Major The Hon. M. Fitzalan Howard
2nd i/c	Capt. A. J. C. Seymour	Capt. J. P. Mann	Capt. W. P. Bull	Capt. C. O'M. Farrell
Recce Offrs.		Capt. D. G. Mathieson	Capt. N. W. Beeson	Capt. P. E. G. Balfour
Troop Leaders	Capt. I. S. R. Bruce (*Technical Adjutant*)	Lieut. D. W. Scott-Barrett	Lieut. R. Humble	Lieut. J. M. Barne
	Capt. R. W. O. Burnett (*Liaison Officer*)	Lieut. R. A. K. Runcie	Lieut. E. P. Hickling	Lieut. H. W. S. Marshall
	Lieut. R. C. G. Pember (*Recce Troop*)	Lieut. H. Laing	Lieut. C. R. T. Cunningham	Lieut. The Lord Bruce
	Lieut. H. Llewellyn Smith (*Signal*)	Lieut. A. I. D. Fletcher	Lieut. A. R. G. Stevenson	Lieut. C. J. R. Duffin
	Lieut. E. C. H. Warner (*A/A. Troop*)	Lieut. I. L. Thorpe	Sgt. E. Thorne	Lieut. G. Cameron
SSMs.	R. Pickard	C. Craggs	J. Todd	A. Price

Detached at Forward Delivery Squadron: Lieut. J. W. O. Elliot
　　　　　　　　　　　　　　　　　　Lieut. H. N. Nevile
　　　　　　　　　　　　　　　　　　Lieut. The Hon. J. S. P. Dormer

APPENDIX D 555

(13) THIRD (TANK) BATTALION

8TH MAY, 1945

At the end of the War

Commanding Officer: Lieutenant-Colonel C. I. H. Dunbar, D.S.O.
Second-in-Command: Major W. S. I. Whitelaw, M.C.
Adjutant: Captain A. J. C. Seymour
Intelligence Officer: Lieutenant H. L. C. Greig
i/c Bn. HQ. Tanks: Captain G. Cameron, M.C.

Quartermaster: Captain F. Morley (Temp. P.W.)
Medical Officer: Captain A. T. MacKnight, R.A.M.C.
Chaplain: The Rev. G. H. T. Reid, R.A.Ch.D.
Electrical and Mechanical Engineer Officer: Captain R. Owen, R.E.M.E.

Regimental Sergeant-Major: G. Brown
Regimental Quartermaster Sergeant: D. Duff (*Temp. P.W.*)
Drill Sergeants: A. Mathieson
                I. Moore
Technical Quartermaster Sergeant: A. Arber
Mechanical Quartermaster Sergeant: J. McGowan
Pipe-Major: C. Craig

	Headquarter Squadron	*Right Flank*	*S Squadron*	*Left Flank*
Sqn. Leaders	Major Sir Charles Maclean	Major The Earl Cathcart, D.S.O., M.C.	Major C. O'M. Farrell, M.C.	Major J. P. Mann, M.C.
2nds i/c	Capt. R. H. Gubbins-Mounsey-Heysham	Capt. C. R. S. Graham	Capt. H. N. Nevile	Capt. D. L. Bankes
Recce Offrs.	Capt. I. S. R. Bruce, M.C. (*Technical Adjutant*)	Capt. D. W. Scott-Barrett, M.C.		Capt. C. J. R. Duffin
		Capt. R. A. K. Runcie, M.C.		
Troop Leaders	Capt. H. Llewellyn Smith (*Signal*)	Lieut. H. Laing	Lieut. E. P. Hickling, M.C.	Lieut. M. Fearfield
	Lieut. J. M. Gow (*Acting Quartermaster*)	Lieut. A. I. D. Fletcher	Lieut. A. R. G. Stevenson, M.C.	Lieut. A. K. McC. Elliott
	Lieut. A. G. Laing, M.C.	Lieut. F. J. N. Curzon	Lieut. M. Law	Lieut. J. L. M. Crick
	Lieut. J. C. J. Shearer	Lieut. D. P. M. S. Cape	Lieut. P. M. Ward	Lieut. A. B. Purvis
	Lieut. E. G. Paterson		Lieut. T. E. P. Gilpin	
SSMs.	R. Pickard	C. Craggs	J. Todd	A. Price, M.C.

Detached at Forward Delivery Squadron: Captain W. P. Bull

APPENDIX D

(14) FOURTH BATTALION

11TH OCTOBER, 1941

On Formation

Commanding Officer: Lieutenant-Colonel J. E. M. Bland (*On 29th October succeeded by* Lieut.-Col. A. V. C. Douglas)
Second-in-Command: Major F. H. H. B. Harris
Adjutant: Captain O. Priaulx (*On 29th November succeeded by* Captain R. C. Whigham)
Intelligence Officer: 2nd Lieutenant J. V. Rob

Quartermaster: Lieutenant J. Quinn
Medical Officer: Captain A. B. D. Hunter, R.A.M.C.
Chaplain: The Rev. D. W. Hay, R.A.Ch.D.

Regimental Sergeant-Major: A. Wilford
Regimental Quartermaster Sergeant: E. Gray
Drill Sergeants: A. K. Madden
P. Standing
Pipe-Major: P. Bain

Company Commanders
Major C. V. R. Blundell-Hollinshead-Blundell (*Headquarter*)
Major D. S. Wedderburn (*Right Flank*)
Captain R. D. Cardiff (*X Company*)
Captain The Lord Robert Crichton-Stuart (*W Company*)
Captain J. S. Scott (*Left Flank*)

Captains:
R. W. B. Purvis
R. C. Petre
T. C. Dundas
H. W. Blyth
F. A. Hopkinson

Lieutenants:
R. N. Brooke
J. C. Blackett-Ord (*M.T.O.*)
J. S. Burn Clerk-Rattray
P. G. Atkinson-Clarke

2nd Lieutenants:
T. R. Bland
M. H. Cardiff (*Anti-Tank*)
R. A. Carnegie
T. R. Edwards-Moss
M. J. Fitzherbert-Brockholes
R. S. Jenkinson
E. I. Ll. Mostyn
J. C. A. Roper (*Signal*)
A. N. B. Ritchie
J. D. A. Stainton
I. McC. Tait
Sir John Worsley-Taylor

*Other Officers**

Company Sergeant-Majors
J. Kerr (*Headquarter*)
H. Garner (*Right Flank*)
W. Kirby (*W Company*)
J. Morrison (*X Company*)
K. Howitt (*Left Flank*)

* Insufficient information is available to allot Officers to their Companies.

APPENDIX D 557

(15) FIFTH BATTALION (SKI)

29TH FEBRUARY, 1940

On Embarkation for France

Commanding Officer: Lieutenant-Colonel J. S. Coats, M.C., *Coldstream Guards*
Second-in-Command: Major B. Mayfield*
Adjutant: Captain W. D. M. Raeburn*
A/Adjutant and i/c Ski equipment: Captain M. Lindsay, *Royal Scots*
Liaison Officer: Major A. F. Purvis, M.C.*

Quartermaster: Lieutenant J. Quinn*
Medical Officer: Lieutenant E. H. L. Wigram, R.A.M.C.
Pay Adviser: Captain C. B. V. Rooker, M.M., R.A.P.C.

Regimental Sergeant-Major: A. K. Madden*
Regimental Quartermaster Sergeant: A. Wilford*
Orderly Room Quartermaster Sergeant: L. Parsons*

W Company	*X Company*	*Y Company*	*Left Flank*
Captain J. L. M. Gavin, *Royal Engineers*	Major L. C. D. Ryder, *Norfolk Regiment*	Captain R. D. M. Gurowski*	Captain C. J. Stone, *East Surrey Regiment*
Lieutenant J. P. Hall, *Middlesex Regiment*	Lieutenant V. A. P. Budge, *Grenadier Guards*	Lieutenant G. W. E. Potter, *Grenadier Guards*	Lieutenant J. R. G. Bird, *Sherwood Foresters*
Lieutenant C. W. Suter, *London Rifle Brigade*	Lieutenant R. N. Charrington, *Suffolk Regiment*	Lieutenant P. S. Chaplin, *King's Royal Rifle Corps*	Lieutenant A. G. Dickson, *Cameron Highlanders*
Lieutenant F. G. Gough, *London Rifle Brigade*	Lieutenant D. C. Baynes, *Queen's Regiment*	Lieutenant M. R. G. Howard, *King's Royal Rifle Corps*	Lieutenant M. R. E. Kealy, *Devonshire Regiment*
J. Royle	–. Russell	J. R. Fraser	J. A. Lindsay

Right Flank
Major A. D. B. Crabbe*
Lieutenant K. R. Ashburner, *Royal Fusiliers*
Lieutenant N. E. MacMullen, *10th Royal Hussars*
Lieutenant P. M. G. Anley, *Royal Fusiliers*
CSMs.: D. H. Stacey

* Denotes Scots Guards Officer or Warrant Officer

558   APPENDIX D

(16) S COMPANY
(Attached to 2nd Battalion Coldstream Guards)

(a)
On Formation
28th March, 1944

Major H. D. Cuthbert
Captain A. S. Neilson

Lieutenant J. S. Wilson
Lieutenant H. R. Bridgeman
Lieutenant J. W. F. Lloyd-Johnes
CSM. T. Brown

(b)
At Monte Piccolo
27th–28th May, 1944

[Major H. D. Cuthbert, *sick*]
Captain A. S. Neilson

[Lieutenant J. S. Wilson, *on leave*]
Lieutenant H. R. Bridgeman
Lieutenant H. F. G. Charteris
CSM. T. Brown

(c)
At Monte Penzola
4th–5th December, 1944

Major R. L. Coke, M.C.
[Captain The Hon. C. J. Dalrymple, *sick*]
Lieutenant J. S. Wilson
Lieutenant I. J. Fraser
Lieutenant J. H. Inskip
CSM. W. Young, D.C.M.

Note: For the Order of Battle on 1st March, 1945, on transfer to the First Battalion, see B Company on p. 547.

(17) X COMPANY
(Attached to 3rd Battalion Irish Guards and 1st Battalion Welsh Guards)

(a)
On Embarkation for France
20th June, 1944

Major P. Steuart-Fothringham
Captain E. J. Hope
Lieutenant A. Drewe
Lieutenant N. Thorpe
Lieutenant A. D. G. Llewellyn
CSM. A. Law

(b)
At Hechtel
8th–12th September, 1944

Major P. Steuart-Fothringham
Captain E. J. Hope, M.C.
Lieutenant N. Thorpe, M.C.
Lieutenant A. D. G. Llewellyn
Lieutenant The Hon. J. L. Vernon
CSM. A. Law

(c)
On Disbandment
18th March, 1945

Major E. J. Hope, M.C.
Captain A. N. B. Ritchie
Lieutenant P. J. H. Leng
Lieutenant J. B. Denham
Lieutenant G. C. W. Radcliffe
CSM. C. McClelland, M.M.

APPENDIX E

Nominal Roll of Officers

Note—Volume II of *The History of the Scots Guards* contains a Nominal Roll of all Officers who served in the Regiment from 1642 to 1934. The following Roll brings the former one up to date to the end of 1955.

The third column, "Highest rank reached in the Regiment", shows the highest rank, irrespective of type—e.g. substantive, acting or temporary—held by each Officer whilst borne on the active establishment of the Regiment. Higher ranks reached in extra-regimental employment are, therefore, not shown.

In the fourth column, "War Service", the various theatres are named for the 1939–1945 War. These correspond with the Campaign Stars gained by individuals. Mention is also made of the Palestine campaigns before and after the 1939–1945 War, and of the Malayan campaign 1948–1951.

(W) stands for wounded and (PW) for Prisoner of War. Officers who died of wounds have been shown as killed in action.

Name	Period of Service in the Regiment	Highest rank reached in the Regiment	War Service
ABERCROMBY, Robert Alexander	1914–1933 1939–1945	Major	First Great War (W) North Africa Italy
ACLAND, John Hugh Bevil	1948 to date	Captain	Malaya
ADAIR, John Eric	1953–1955	2nd Lieut.	
AIRLIE, David Lyulph Gore Wolseley, 11th Earl of	1940–1943	Major	First Great War in the 10th Royal Hussars
ALSTON, Edward Rowland Milles	1921–1926 1939–1946	Major	
ALSTON, Francis George	1900–1925 1927–1931	Colonel	South Africa (W) First Great War
ALSTON, Paul Francis	1940–1945	Captain	
ARBUTHNOT, Andrew Robert Coghill	1944–1947	Lieutenant	North-West Europe (W)
ARCHDALE, Audley Montgomery	1940–1946	Captain	Middle East (PW)
ARCHER, Leonard Castella	In the ranks 1914–1937 In the ranks 1939–1942 1942–1945	Lieutenant (QM)	First Great War (W) Italy
ARTHUR, John Reginald	1955 to date	2nd Lieut.	

APPENDIX E

Name	Period of Service in the Regiment	Highest rank reached in the Regiment	War Service
ASHLEY-CARTER, Philip Charles	1940–1948	Captain	Middle East North Africa Italy
ASPREY, Edward Algernon	1941–1946	Captain	
ASPREY, Maurice Desmond	1942–1946	Captain	North Africa Italy
ASTLEY-CORBETT, Sir Francis Henry Rivers, 5th Bt.	1940–1943	Captain	Middle East (W) North Africa Italy Killed in action
ATKINSON-CLARK, Peter George	1940–1944	Captain	Italy Killed in action
AYERS, Mowbray	1945–1947	Lieutenant	
BAILIE, Douglas Michael Hugh	1941–1944	Lieutenant	North Africa (W) Italy Killed in action
BAILLIE, Michael Evan Victor	1943–1947	Lieutenant	Italy
BALFOUR, Anthony Melville	1939–1944	Captain	Norway Middle East North Africa Italy Killed in action
BALFOUR, Eustace Arthur Goschen	1940–1946	Captain	Middle East North Africa Italy (W)
BALFOUR, Edward William Sturgis	1921–1933 1934–1938 1939–1943	Colonel	First Great War in 5th Dragoon Guards
BALFOUR, Peter Edward Gerald	1940–1954	Major	North-West Europe (W)
BALFOUR, Roy Angus Emmanuel	1941–1943	Lieutenant	Middle East North Africa Italy Killed in action
BALLANTINE-DYKES, Thomas Lamplugh	1933–1942	Major	Middle East Killed in action
BANKES, David Lindsay	1940–1946	Captain	North-West Europe (W)
BARCLAY, James David Innes	1955 to date	2nd Lieut.	
BARNE, John Michael	1942–1947	Lieutenant	North-West Europe (W)
BARNE, Michael Ernest St. John	1925–1935 1939–1946	Lt.-Colonel	North Africa Italy
BARNE, Nigel Hugh	1940–1946	Captain	Middle East North Africa Italy (W) North-West Europe Palestine
BARTHOLOMEW, Peter Hugh	1944–1947	Lieutenant	Italy
BASSET, Bryan Ronald	1952 to date	Lieutenant	
BAX, Melbourne Goodson	1945–1950	Captain	Malaya Killed in action
BAXTER, John Edward	1943–1944	Lieutenant	Italy (W) Killed in action
BAYNE, Peter William Gordon	1944–1945	2nd Lieut.	.

APPENDIX E

Name	Period of Service in the Regiment	Highest rank reached in the Regiment	War Service
BECKETT, William	1941–1943	Lieutenant	Middle East North Africa Italy Killed in action
BEESON, Christopher William Restarick	1945–1948	Lieutenant	
BEESON, Maurice Fisher	1941–1942	2nd Lieut.	Middle East Killed in action
BEESON, Nigel Wendover	1940–1944	Captain	North-West Europe Killed in action
BELL, Bruce Alec Jeffrey	1949 to date	Captain	Malaya
BENITZ, Brian Macintosh	1953 to date	Lieutenant	
BENN, Timothy John	1956 to date	2nd Lieut.	
BENTHALL, James Holme	1953–1954	2nd Lieut.	
BENTHALL, Richard Pringle	1953–1954	2nd Lieut.	
BERESFORD-PEIRSE, Henry Grant de la Poer	1952–1953	2nd Lieut.	
BERRIDGE, Richard Anthony	1944–1945	Lieutenant	North-West Europe Killed in action
BERTIE, Andrew Willoughby Ninian	1949–1950	2nd Lieut.	
BERTIE, Charles Peregrine Albemarle	1950–1954	Lieutenant	
BETHELL, Hon. David Alan	1941–1949	Captain	North Africa (W) Italy (W)
BEVAN, Humphrey John Mackenzie	1945–1947	Lieutenant	
BEVAN, Hugo Peter Charles	1955–1956	2nd Lieut.	
BEVAN, Lawrence Emlyn Douglas	1940–1943	2nd Lieut.	
BEVAN, Morier Geoffrey Bosanquet	1942–1945	Captain	
BEWICKE, Calverly	1905–1907 1915–1920 1940–1945	Major	First Great War
BLACK, Charles Archibald Adam	1956 to date	2nd Lieut.	
BLACKETT-ORD, Andrew James	1941–1946	Lieutenant	Italy (W) (PW)
BLACKETT-ORD, John Christopher	1939–1946	Major	Italy (W)
BLAIR, John Woodman	1956 to date	2nd Lieut.	
BLAND, David John Nevile	1941–1943	Lieutenant	Middle East North Africa Killed in action
BLAND, John Edward Michael	1918–1947	Lt.-Colonel	Italy
BLAND, Simon Claud Michael	1943 to date	Major	Italy Malaya
BLAND, Thomas Riviere	1941–1946	Captain	North Africa Italy (W)
BLANDY, Peter Bernard John	1944–1946	Lieutenant	Italy (W)
BLOIS, Gervase Ralph Edmund, afterwards 10th Bt.	1921–1929 1939–1946	Captain	North Africa Italy North-West Europe
BLUNDELL-HOLLINSHEAD-BLUNDELL, Christian Victor Richard	1924–1939 1939–1945	Major	Italy

APPENDIX E

Name	Period of Service in the Regiment	Highest rank reached in the Regiment	War Service
BLYTH, Hugh William	1939–1946	Captain	Middle East (PW)
BLYTHSWOOD, Philip Archibald, 7th Baron	1939–1940	2nd Lieut.	Killed in an accident
BOAM, Thomas Anthony	1952 to date	Lieutenant	
BORRETT, Percy Rygate	1916–1920 1940–1945	Captain	First Great War (W)
BOSVILLE MACDONALD, Nigel Donald Peter	1946 to date	Major	Malaya
BOURCIER, Maurice Edmond	1944–1948	Lieutenant	North-West Europe
BOWATER, Euan David Vansittart	1954–1955	2nd Lieut.	
BOWATER, Michael Ian Vansittart	1955 to date	2nd Lieut.	
BOWEN-COLTHURST, Charles Patrick Russell	1942–1946	Lieutenant	North Africa Italy (W)
BOWES-LYON, Fergus Michael Claude	1949 to date	Captain	Malaya
BOWES-LYON, Hon. John Patrick (Master of Glamis)	1929–1941	Lieutenant	Middle East Killed in action
BOWSER, David Stewart	1945–1947	Captain	
BOYD, Ian Walter	1955–1956	2nd Lieut.	
BOYD, Walter Alastair	1914–1922 1940–1948	Major	First Great War (W)
BOYD-CARPENTER, John Archibald	1940–1945	Major	Italy
BOYD WILSON, Timothy Lawrie	1952–1953	Lieutenant	
BOYLE, Hon. Patrick James	1940–1946	Captain	Middle East (PW)
BRADSHAW, William Pat Arthur	1914–1939	Colonel	First Great War Palestine, 1936
BRECKNOCK, David George Edward Henry, Earl of	1949–1950	2nd Lieut.	Malaya
BRIDGEMAN, Humphrey Reginald	1943–1944	Lieutenant	Italy Killed in action
BRIDGEMAN, Peter Orlando Ronald	1952–1954	2nd Lieut.	
BRISTOWE, Alan Percy	1940–1945	Captain	
BROOKE, Richard Neville	1940–1946	Lieutenant	Middle East (W) (PW)
BROUGHTON-ADDERLEY, Arthur Ralph	1917–1919 1941	Lieutenant	First Great War
BROWN, Alan Brock	1940–1946	Captain	North Africa (W) Italy
BROWN, Alexander Bruce Hargreaves	1940–1941	2nd Lieut.	Transferred to Reconnaissance Corps, and killed in action in North-West Europe
BROWN, Harold Ellett	1941–1945	Captain	North-West Europe
BROWN, William John	1942–1946	Major	North Africa (W) Italy
BRUCE, Andrew Douglas Alexander Thomas, Lord	1943–1946	Lieutenant	North-West Europe (W)
BRUCE, Hon. Bernard	1939–1946	Major	Middle East North Africa Italy
BRUCE, Ian Stuart Rae	1940–1945	Captain	N.-W. Europe (W)

APPENDIX E 563

Name	Period of Service in the Regiment	Highest rank reached in the Regiment	War Service
BRUCE, Hon. James Michael Edward	1946–1948	Lieutenant	
BUCHANAN, George	1918–1919 1941–1945	Captain	First Great War Middle East Italy
BUCKLE, Christopher Richard Sandford	1940–1946	Major	Italy
BULKELEY, Thomas Foster Rivers	1936 to date	Lt.-Colonel	Palestine, 1936 North Africa Italy
BULL, Richard Henry	1940–1944	Major	France North Africa (W) Italy Killed in action
BULL, William Perkins	1940–1945	Captain	North-West Europe
BULMER, James Edmond	1954 to date	2nd Lieut.	
BURDEN, Joseph Warren	1940–1944	Captain	North-West Europe Killed in action
BURGE, Stephen Franck Milward	1918 1940–1945	Captain	
BURNETT, George Parry	1941 to date	Major	Middle East (PW) Malaya
BURNETT, Roger William Odo	1939–1945	Captain	North-West Europe (W) Killed in action
BURNS, John Alan	1927–1949	Major	North-West Europe Palestine
BURT, Clive Stuart Saxon	1940–1945	Captain	Middle East (W) North Africa Italy North-West Europe
BUTLER, Hon. Patrick Henry Stanley Danvers	1941–1944	Lieutenant	North Africa Italy Killed in action
BUTTER, David Henry	1940–1948	Major	Middle East (W) North Africa Italy
BUXTON, Sir Thomas Fowell Victor, 6th Bt.	1944–1948	Lieutenant	North-West Europe
CALVOCORESSI, Ian Melville	1940–1946	Major	Middle East (W) North Africa Italy South-East Asia
CAMBRIDGE, Leslie Duncan	1940–1945	Captain	Middle East North Africa Italy North-West Europe
CAMDEN, John Charles Henry Pratt, 5th Marquess	1918–1927 1941–1945	Captain	
CAMERON, Angus Ewen	1936–1956	Lt.-Colonel	Palestine, 1936 Middle East North-West Europe Malaya
CAMERON, Geoffrey	1942–1946	Captain	North-West Europe

APPENDIX E

Name	Period of Service in the Regiment	Highest rank reached in the Regiment	War Service
CAMPBELL, Colin	1944–1945	Lieutenant	North-West Europe Killed in action
CAMPBELL, Colin Moffat	1944–1947	Captain	North-West Europe (W)
CAMPBELL, George Herbert Lorne	1954 to date	Lieutenant	
CAMPBELL, John Alastair	1945–1947	Lieutenant	
CAMPBELL, Robin Dudley	1941–1946	Lieutenant	Middle East North Africa (W)
CANTLIE, Hugh	1952 to date	Lieutenant	
CANTLIE, Paul	1954–1955	2nd Lieut.	
CAPE, Donald Paul Stewart	1944–1945	Lieutenant	North-West Europe
CARDIFF, Ereld Boteler Wingfield	1928–1950	Lt.-Colonel	Palestine, 1936 Middle East North Africa Italy North-West Europe
CARDIFF, Maurice Henry	1940–1946	Captain	Middle East Italy
CARDIFF, Richard Derek	1930–1950	Lt.-Colonel	Norway Italy
CAREY, Simon Henry Dundas Tupper	1948–1949	2nd Lieut.	Malaya
CARMICHAEL, Keith Macfarlane	1953–1954	2nd Lieut.	
CARNEGIE, Raymond Alexander	1940–1952	Major	Italy (W) Malaya
CARPENTER-GARNIER, John Prideaux	1942–1943	Lieutenant	North Africa Italy Killed in action
CARRIS, Bertram Dudley	1940–1945	Lieutenant	Middle East (W)(PW)
CATHCART, Alan, 6th Earl	1939 to date	Major	North-West Europe
CATT, Philip Herbert	1918–1949	Major	Palestine, 1936 Middle East North-West Europe Italy Palestine
CAYZER, Sir Nigel John, 4th Bt.	1941–1943	Lieutenant	Middle East North Africa Italy Killed in action
CHAMBERLAYNE, Crinus Henry Leopold Francis Mary Tankerville	1916–1930 1939–1946	Captain	First Great War (W) France Middle East
CHANCE, Andrew Frederick Seton	1946–1947	Lieutenant	
CHARTERIS, Hugo Francis Guy	1942–1946	Lieutenant	Italy (W) Netherlands East Indies
CHICHESTER, John Buxton, 8th Earl of	1940–1944	Lieutenant	Killed in an accident
CHUBB, John Oliver	1940–1946	Captain	
CLARK, Hugh Brooking	1942–1946	Captain	North Africa Italy (W) North-West Europe

APPENDIX E 565

Name	Period of Service in the Regiment	Highest rank reached in the Regiment	War Service
CLARKE, Christopher John Officer	1944–1946	Captain	North-West Europe (W)
CLARKE, John Robertson Stephenson	1939 to date	Lt.-Colonel	Middle East North Africa (W) Italy
CLARKE, Richard Thomas Stephenson	1942–1947	Captain	Italy (PW)
CLENDENIN, James Gordon Angus Storm	1944–1947	Lieutenant	
CLOWES, Henry Nelson	1931 to date	Colonel	Norway North-West Europe
COATS, Archibald James	1940–1946	Captain	Middle East (W) Italy
COBBOLD, John Murray	1915–1919 1939–1944	Captain	First Great War (W) Killed by enemy action
COBBOLD, Patrick Mark	1953 to date	Lieutenant	
COCHRANE-BARNETT, John Norman	1940–1945	Lieutenant	Middle East (PW)
COGHILL, Charles Archibald Richard	1922–1948	Major	Middle East North Africa Italy North-West Europe
COKE, Gerald Edward	1939–1945	2nd Lieut.	
COKE, Richard Lovel	1939–1946	Major	Italy
COKE, Thomas William Edward, Viscount, afterwards 5th Earl of Leicester	1928–1948	Major	Middle East North-West Europe
COLQUHOUN, Donald	1940–1946	Captain	France (in the Black Watch) North Africa North-West Europe
COLQUHOUN, David Angus	1944–1945	Lieutenant	Italy Killed in action
COLQUHOUN, Ernest Patrick	1956 to date	2nd Lieut.	
COLQUHOUN, Sir Iain, 14th Bt.	1908–1920 1940–1941	Lt.-Colonel	First Great War (W)
COLQUHOUN, William Reginald	1918–1919 1940–1943	Captain	First Great War (W)
COMRIE, Nigel John Martin	1945–1947	Lieutenant	
COMYNS, Peter William Patrick	1944–1947	Captain	North-West Europe (W)
CONNELL, Charles Raymond	1951–1952	2nd Lieut.	
COPELAND, Paul John Norman	1954–1955	2nd Lieut.	
CORY-WRIGHT, David Arthur	1944–1947	Captain	
CORY-WRIGHT, Jonathan Francis	1944–1945	Lieutenant	North-West Europe Killed in action
CRABBE, Archibald Douglas Brodie	1922–1936 1939–1945	Major	France Norway North-West Europe
CRABBE, Peter Gordon	1941	2nd Lieut.	Later died of wounds serving in H.L.I.
CRICHTON-STUART, Lord James Charles	1954 to date	2nd Lieut.	

APPENDIX E

Name	Period of Service in the Regiment	Highest rank reached in the Regiment	War Service
CRICHTON-STUART, Michael Duncan David	1937–1947	Major	Middle East North Africa Italy (W)
CRICHTON-STUART, Lord Robert	1939–1945	Major	North-West Europe
CRICK, John Louis Mingaye	1944–1947	Lieutenant	North-West Europe
CRITCHLEY, John Galt	1940–1941	2nd Lieut.	Middle East Killed in action
CROSS, Assheton Henry, 3rd Viscount	1940–1946	Lieutenant	North Africa Italy
CROSSMAN, Anthony David	1955 to date	2nd Lieut.	
CRUTCHLEY, Edward	1941–1946	Lieutenant	Italy (W)
CRUTCHLEY, Gerald Edward Victor	1914–1919 1940–1943	Lieutenant	First Great War
CUMMING, Ewan Lewis Thornewill	1940–1952	Major	Italy (PW) Malaya
CUMMING, James	1940–1944	Captain	North Africa (W)
CUNINGHAME, John Smith	1941–1943	Lieutenant	Middle East North Africa (W) Italy Killed in action
CUNNINGHAM, Cyril Robert Tucker	1941–1946	Captain	North-West Europe (W)
CUNNINGHAM, Samuel Knox	1940–1943	Lieutenant	
CURRIE, Bertram Frances George	1918–1922 1939–1944	Captain	
CURRIE, John Lawrence Rowland	1944–1945	Lieutenant	North-West Europe Killed in action
CURZON, Francis John Nathaniel	1943–1947	Captain	North-West Europe
CUTHBERT, Harold David	1940–1945	Major	North Africa Italy
CUTHBERT, John Aidan	1953–1954	2nd Lieut.	
CUTHBERT, Sidney John	1936–1944	Major	Palestine, 1936 North-West Europe Killed in action
DALGLISH, Alec Charles	1950–1952	2nd Lieut.	
DALRYMPLE, Hon. Colin James	1940–1956	Major	Italy
DALRYMPLE, John Aymer, Viscount	1926–1952	Colonel	Middle East North Africa Italy
DALRYMPLE-HAMILTON, North Victor Cecil	1902–1908 1914–1921 1940–1945	Lt.-Colonel	First Great War France
DALTON, John William	1921–1926 1939–1948	Major	Served in Essex Regiment and Irish Gds. in First Great War (W)
DALY, Dermot Ralph	1930–1949	Major	Palestine, 1936 Norway Middle East (PW) Italy
DAVIDSON, Nigel George Rupert	1940–1946	2nd Lieut.	Middle East Italy
DAWSON, Hugh Halliday Trevor	1952 to date	Lieutenant	
DAWSON, Peter	1939–1946	Lieutenant	Middle East (PW)
DAY, Julian Curtis	1939–1945	Captain	Italy

APPENDIX E 567

Name	Period of Service in the Regiment	Highest rank reached in the Regiment	War Service
DAY, Michael George	1945–1950	Captain	Malaya
DEANE, Donald Humphry	1943–1947	Captain	Italy
DE KLEE, Murray Peter John	1946 to date	Captain	Malaya (W)
DELMAR-MORGAN, Michael Walter	1955 to date	2nd Lieut.	
DENHAM, John Bovill	1944 to date	Major	North-West Europe Malaya
DENT, Joseph Alan Guthrie	1917–1919 1939–1946	Captain	First Great War North-West Europe
DE SALIS, Count Anthony Denis Rudolph	1921–1927 1939–1944	Captain	Served in Irish Guards in First Great War (W) France (W) (PW)
DE SALIS, Count Charles John	1948 to date	Captain	Malaya
DE SALIS, Francis Michael	1951–1953	2nd Lieut.	
DE SOISSONS, Guy Maurice de Savoie-Carignan	1946–1948	Lieutenant	
DE SOISSONS, Victor Eugene de Savoie-Carignan	1943–1945	Lieutenant	North-West Europe Killed in action
DODD, Peter	1945–1947	Lieutenant	
DODS, Harold William	1941–1944	Lieutenant	Killed by enemy action
DOLLARD, Ralph Seaver	1942–1946	Lieutenant	North Africa Italy (W) North-West Europe
DORMAN, William James	In the ranks 1919–1940 1940–1944	Captain (QM)	Palestine, 1936 Norway North-West Europe Killed in an accident
DORMER, Hon. Joseph Spencer Philip	1944–1946	Captain	North-West Europe
DOUGLAS, Archibald Vivian Campbell	1925–1950	Lt.-Colonel	
DOUGLAS, Henry James Sholto	1930–1938 1939–1945	Major	Palestine, 1936
DOUGLAS, Robert Charles Deboice	In the ranks 1924–1943 1943–1950	Major (QM)	Middle East Italy
DOUGLAS, Robert Duncan	1944–1947	Lieutenant	
DOUGLAS, Stuart Robert	1944–1946	Captain	North-West Europe Killed in an accident
DOUGLAS, Thomas Neil	1942–1954	Major	Italy (W) Malaya
DOWELL, Horace Edwin	1929–1938	Captain and Director of Music	
DREW, Alexander	1941–1946	Lieutenant	Middle East North Africa (W)
DREWE, Anthony	1940–1946	Major	North-West Europe (W)
DRURY-LOWE, Patrick John Boteler	1950 to date	Captain	
DRYSDALE, John Duncan	1955 to date	2nd Lieut.	
DUBERLY, James Arthur Grey	1944	2nd Lieut.	Killed by enemy action
DUBERLY, William Michael Cunliffe	1943	Lieutenant	Italy Killed in action

APPENDIX E

Name	Period of Service in the Regiment	Highest rank reached in the Regiment	War Service
DUFFIN, Charles John Riddel	1942 to date	Major	North-West Europe (W) Malaya
DUMFRIES, John, Earl of	1951–1953	2nd Lieut.	
DUNBAR, Claude Ian Hurley	1929–1954	Colonel	North Africa North-West Europe Malaya
DUNBAR-NASMITH, James Duncan	1945–1948	Lieutenant	
DUNCAN, James Alexander Lawson	1918–1920 1940–1945	Lieutenant	First Great War
DUNDAS, Robert David Ross	1956 to date	2nd Lieut.	
DUNDAS, Thomas Calderwood	1940–1945	Captain	North-West Europe
DUNKELD, Stuart Bruce	1944–1947	Lieutenant	
DUNSMURE, Henry John Alexander	1940–1945	2nd Lieut.	Middle East
DUNSMURE, James Alexander	1955 to date	2nd Lieut.	
EDWARDS, John Keith	1917–1939	Lt.-Colonel	First Great War (W) Middle East East Africa North-West Europe
EDWARDS-MOSS, Thomas Richard	1941–1948	Captain	North-West Europe
ELLIOT, Hon. George Esmond Dominic	1950–1951	2nd Lieut.	Malaya
ELLIOT, John William Owen	1940–1946	Captain	North-West Europe (W)
ELLIOT-BAXTER, Normile Edward Alexander George Wyndham	1949–1956	Captain	Malaya
ELLIOTT, Andrew Kirkwood McCosh	1944–1947	Captain	North-West Europe
ELLIOTT, Walter Archibald	1942–1946	Captain	North Africa Italy (PW) North-West Europe (W)
ELMHIRST, Roger Thomas	1954 to date	2nd Lieut.	
ELWES, Henry William George	1954–1956	2nd Lieut.	
ELWES, John Hargreaves	1926–1943	Major	Norway Middle East North Africa Killed in action
ENCOMBE, John, Viscount	1956 to date	2nd Lieut.	
ERSKINE, Hon. Alistair Robert Hervey	1942–1945	Lieutenant	North Africa Italy North-West Europe Killed in action
ERSKINE, Hon. David Hervey	1943–1947	Captain	Italy Palestine
ERSKINE, Hon. Francis Walter	1917–1924 1939–1947	Captain	First Great War
ERSKINE, Ian David	1917–1941	Lt.-Colonel	First Great War (W) Palestine, 1936 Middle East

APPENDIX E 569

Name	Period of Service in the Regiment	Highest rank reached in the Regiment	War Service
ERSKINE, John Francis Ashley, Lord	1915–1920 1941–1945	Major	First Great War
ERSKINE, John Francis Hervey, (Master of Erskine), afterwards Lord Erskine, later Earl of Mar and Kellie.	1941–1954	Major	Middle East North Africa Italy (W) North-West Europe
ERSKINE, Malcolm David	1924–1949	Colonel	Palestine, 1936 France, 1940 Middle East North Africa Italy Malaya Killed on Active Service
ERSKINE, Philip Neil	1953 to date	Lieutenant	
ERSKINE, Hon. Robert William Hervey	1949–1950	2nd Lieut.	Malaya
ERSKINE CRUM, Vernon Forbes	1940 to date	Major	North-West Europe
EVANS, John Palmer	1944–1947	Lieutenant	Italy (W)
EVES, Hubert John Heath	1940–1943	Lieutenant	Middle East North Africa Killed in action
EYRES, Philip Henry Townsend	1945–1947	Lieutenant	
FANE GLADWIN, Peter Francis	1935 to date	Lt.-Colonel	Palestine, 1936 Middle East (W) Malaya
FARNHAM, Ronald Godfrey	1950–1953	Lieutenant	Malaya
FARQUHARSON, Peter William Mackay	1945–1947	Lieutenant	
FARRELL, Charles O'Meara	1939–1946	Major	North-West Europe
FEARFIELD, Joseph Mark	1944–1948	Lieutenant	North-West Europe
FELLOWES, Charles	1917–1919 1939–1945	Major	First Great War (W)
FELLOWES, William Albemarle	1940–1945	Captain	
FERGUSON, Ian Alexander	1952 to date	Lieutenant	
FERGUSSON-CUNINGHAME, Robert Wallace	1939–1949	Captain	Middle East Italy
FERMOR-HESKETH, Hon. Thomas Sharon	1930–1937	Lieutenant	Palestine, 1936 Killed in an accident
FISHER, Kenneth Neill	1940–1946	Captain	
FITZALAN HOWARD, Hon. Michael	1938 to date	Lt.-Colonel	North-West Europe Palestine Malaya
FITZHERBERT-BROCKHOLES, Michael John	1940–1946	Major	Italy North-West Europe
FITZHERBERT-BROCKHOLES, Ernest Joseph Fulks	1953–1954	2nd Lieut.	
FLEMING, Michael Edward Willis	1946–1948	Lieutenant	
FLETCHER, Archibald Ian Douglas	1943 to date	Major	North-West Europe Palestine Malaya

APPENDIX E

Name	Period of Service in the Regiment	Highest rank reached in the Regiment	War Service
FLETCHER, Christopher Andrew	1929–1944	Major	Palestine, 1936 Norway North Africa Italy Killed in action
FORBES, Donald James	1941–1946	Captain	North Africa Italy (W)
FORBES LEITH, John Alexander	1949	2nd Lieut.	Malaya Killed in action
FORRESTER, John Digby	1941–1946	Captain	North Africa Italy
FORRESTER, Peter Moncrieff	1943–1946	Lieutenant	Italy
FORWOOD, Dudley Richard	1939–1945	Major	Norway Middle East
FRASER, Donald McGregor	In the ranks 1931–1952 1952 to date	Captain (QM)	North Africa North-West Europe Malaya
FRASER, Ian James	1942–1946	Captain	North Africa Italy (W)
FRASER, Peter Basil	1942–1947	Lieutenant	North-West Europe
FRASER, Roderick Andrew	1945–1948	Lieutenant	
FULLERTON-CARNEGIE, George Travers	1942–1946	Lieutenant	Middle East North Africa Italy
FYFE-JAMIESON, Colin John	1945–1947	Lieutenant	
FYFE-JAMIESON, David Ian	1941–1943	Lieutenant	Italy Killed in action
GADSBY, Henry Martin	1944–1947	Lieutenant	North-West Europe
GARDINER-HILL, Michael Anthony	1948–1949	2nd Lieut.	Malaya
GARDINER-HILL, Peter Farquhar	1945–1948	Lieutenant	
GARDINER-HILL, Richard Temple	1951–1952	2nd Lieut.	
GARDNER, Ralph Rowland Gray	1953–1955	2nd Lieut.	
GARNOCK, Viscount; See LINDSAY			
GARRATT, Michael Murray	1944–1947	Captain	Italy
GAULT, Sir James Frederick	1939–1945	Major	Middle East North Africa Italy North-West Europe
GEORGE, Timothy David	1952–1953	2nd Lieut.	
GIBB, John Philip Ogilvy	1955 to date	2nd Lieut.	
GIBBS, Peter Houldsworth	1941–1947	Captain	Middle East North Africa (W) Italy
GILLETT, Raymond; See LORT-PHILLIPS			
GILPIN, Timothy Ernle Purcell	1944–1947	Captain	North-West Europe
GLOUCESTER, H.R.H. Henry William Frederick Albert, Duke of	1937 to date	Field Marshal, 25th Colonel of the Regiment	France Middle East Pacific
GODFREY-ISAACS, Godfrey	1943–1946	Captain	Italy
GODMAN, James Frederic	1945–1948	Lieutenant	

APPENDIX E

Name	Period of Service in the Regiment	Highest rank reached in the Regiment	War Service
GODMAN, Joseph	1925–1938 1939–1945	Major	Palestine, 1936 Norway
GODSAL, Alan Anthony Colleton	1945–1947	Lieutenant	
GOFF, Robert Lionel Archibald	1945–1948	Lieutenant	
GOFF, Thomas Robert Charles	1916–1919 1939–1945	Lieutenant	First Great War (W)
GOODINGE, Anthony Wallinger	1944–1948	Captain	Italy
GORDON, Alastair Ninian John	1942–1946	Captain	Middle East North Africa Italy North-West Europe (W)
GORDON, Donald Alasdair Seton	1944–1947	Captain	North-West Europe (W)
GORDON, Michael James Andrew	1939–1943	Captain	Middle East (W) North Africa Italy Killed in action
GORDON-IVES, Victor Matthew	1941–1944	Lieutenant	North Africa Italy Killed in action
GORDON LENNOX, Reginald Arthur Charles	1940–1945	Captain	North-West Europe
GOSSELIN, Timothy Patrick Arnold	1955 to date	2nd Lieut.	
Gow, Ian Graham	1941–1945	Lieutenant	Middle East North Africa Italy North-West Europe Killed in action
Gow, Donald John Harper	1951–1954	2nd Lieut.	
Gow, John Alexander Harper	1945–1947	Lieutenant	
Gow, John Donald	1947–1948	2nd Lieut.	
Gow, James Michael	1943 to date	Major	North-West Europe Malaya
Gow, John Wesley Harper	1917–1921 1940–1945	Lieutenant Lt.-Colonel	First Great War (W)
GOWANS, James	1917–1922 1941–1942	Lieutenant (QM)	
GRAHAM, Charles Spencer Richard	1940–1950	Major	North-West Europe Malaya
GRAHAM, Herbert Leslie	1917–1919 1921–1941	Lt.-Colonel	First Great War (also served 1914–1917 with South Staffordshire Regiment) (W) Norway
GRAHAM, John	1941 to date	Major	North Africa (W) Italy (PW) Malaya
GRAHAM-WATSON, Paul William Bruce	1948–1949	2nd Lieut.	Malaya Killed in action
GRANT, Alasdair Edward	1948–1953	Lieutenant	Malaya
GRANT, Patrick Charles Henry	1919–1949	Lt.-Colonel	Middle East

APPENDIX E

Name	Period of Service in the Regiment	Highest rank reached in the Regiment	War Service
GRANT WATSON, Robert de Merve	1934–1942	Captain	Palestine, 1936 Middle East (W) Killed in action
GREEN, Anthony Arthur Ramsay	1945–1947	Captain	
GREENWOOD, Alexander O'Conner	In the ranks 1926–1942 1942 to date	Major (QM)	Middle East North Africa Italy North-West Europe Malaya
GREIG, Henry Louis Carron	1944–1947	Lieutenant	North-West Europe
GRIGG, Wilfred Bernard Francis	1940–1943	Lieutenant	Middle East
GRIMSTON, Robert Walter Sigismund	1944–1947	Lieutenant	North-West Europe
GROTRIAN, John Appelbe Brent	1942	2nd Lieut.	
GUBBINS-MOUNSEY-HEYSHAM, Richard Heysham	1926–1928 1939–1945	Major	North-West Europe
GULL, Michael Swinnerton Cameron	1939–1940	2nd Lieut.	
GUNNERY, Cedric	1953–1954	2nd Lieut.	
GUNTHER, William John	1940–1946	Captain	Middle East North Africa Italy
GURNEY, David Hugh	1941–1946	Captain	
GUROWSKI, Richard Dudley Melchior	1930–1940	Captain	Palestine, 1936 France Killed in action
HAGUE, James Derek Kenyon	1940–1946	Major	North Africa Italy (W)
HAMILTON, Arthur Digby	1933–1954	Major	Middle East North-West Europe
HAMILTON-DALRYMPLE, John David	1947–1948	2nd Lieut.	
HANBURY-TRACY, Michael David Charles	1929–1940	Captain	France Killed in action
HANBURY-TRACY, Ninian John Frederick	1940–1941	2nd Lieut.	
HANKINSON, Michael Ernle Sykes	1945–1956	Major	Malaya
HANSON, Walter	In the ranks 1920–1941	Lieutenant (QM)	Middle East Italy
HARRIS, Francis Henry Herbert Bolton	1928–1944	Lt.-Colonel	Norway Italy Killed in action
HARRISON, Antony James Robinson	1949 to date	Captain	Malaya
HARVEY, John Leslie	1939–1945	Captain	North-West Europe
HARVEY, Roger Edward Lennox	1935–1946	Captain	Middle East (W) (PW)
HARVEY, Thomas Cockayne	1939–1946	Major	Norway Italy (W)
HASTINGS, Stephen Lewis Edmonstone	1939–1952	Major	Middle East North Africa Italy

APPENDIX E

Name	Period of Service in the Regiment	Highest rank reached in the Regiment	War Service
HAWKINS, Anthony Louis Rowland	1945–1948	Captain	
HAYWARD, Fred McLean	1942–1947	Captain	North Africa Italy
HAYWOOD-FARMER, Robin Edward	1943–1947	Lieutenant	North-West Europe (W)
HEATON-ARMSTRONG, Thomas Michael Robert	1944–1949	Captain	Italy
HENDERSON, John Desmond	1939–1949	Major	Middle East North Africa Italy
HENDERSON, James Stewart Barry	1955 to date	2nd Lieut.	
HENDERSON, Peter Gordon	1942–1944	Lieutenant	Italy (W)
HENDERSON-SCOTT, Nigel de Paiva	1941–1943	Lieutenant	Middle East North Africa Killed in action
HEPBURN, William Bruce	1945–1947	Lieutenant	
HESKETH, Frederick, 2nd Baron	1939–1946	Major	Middle East Italy (W)
HICKLING, Edmund Peter	1942–1946	Captain	North-West Europe
HILL, Barrington Julian Warren	1940–1946	Lieutenant	North-West Europe
HILLEARY, Ruaraidh Edward MacLeod Robertson	1945–1947	Lieutenant	
HOBSON, Anthony Robert Alwyn	1941–1946	Lieutenant	Italy
HODSON, Michael Robin Adderley	1953 to date	Lieutenant	
HOLDEN, John Henry	In the ranks 1908–1933 1933–1941	Captain	First Great War (in the ranks) Palestine, 1936 Middle East
HOME, Robert Swinton Patrick	1934–1937 1939–1945	Major	Italy (W)
HOPE, Arthur Clement	1914–1920 1940–1947	Captain	First Great War (W) Middle East Italy
HOPE, Edward James	1940–1945	Major	North-West Europe
HOPE, Hon. Henry John	1917–1919 1939–1945	Lieutenant	First Great War (W)
HOPE, Lord John Adrian	1939–1945	Major	Norway Italy
HOPKINSON, Anthony Erik	1953 to date	Lieutenant	
HOPKINSON, Francis Archibald	1941–1945	Major	Italy
HORTON, William Gray	1917–1932 1939–1945	Major	First Great War (W) France North-West Europe
HORTON, William Robin Gray	1951–1953	2nd Lieut.	
HOUISON-CRAUFURD, John Peter	1949–1950	2nd Lieut.	
HOULDSWORTH, Henry Hamilton	1939–1949	Major	Middle East North Africa Italy (W) North-West Europe

APPENDIX E

Name	Period of Service in the Regiment	Highest rank reached in the Regiment	War Service
HOWARD, Alexander	1950–1951	2nd Lieut.	
HOWARD, Robin Jared Stanley	1943–1946	Lieutenant	North-West Europe (W)
HOYER MILLAR, Alastair James Harold	1956 to date	2nd Lieut.	
HOYER MILLAR, Robert Charles Renake	1954–1955	2nd Lieut.	
HUGHES-HALLETT, Michael Wyndham Norton	1945–1948	Lieutenant	
HULSE, Edward Jeremy Westrow	1953 to date	Lieutenant	
HULSE, Richard Arthur Samuel	1955–1956	2nd Lieut.	
HUMBLE, Richard	1943–1944	Lieutenant	North-West Europe Killed in action
HUNTER, Richard Tod	1941–1944	Captain	North Africa (W) Italy Killed in action
HUNTER BLAIR, James	1945–1948	Lieutenant	
HUTTON, Rupert Edward Kilpatrick	1954–1955	2nd Lieut.	
IND, Harold Hugh Brodie	1934–1935	2nd Lieut.	
INGILBY, Joslan William Vivian (afterwards 5th Bt.)	1928–1948	Major	Palestine, 1936 Middle East
INGLIS, James Craufuird Roger	1944–1947	Lieutenant	North-West Europe
INNES, William Anthony Wolsely	1955 to date	2nd Lieut.	
INSKIP, John Hampden	1943–1946	Lieutenant	Italy (W)
INVERCLYDE, John Alan, 4th Baron	1916–1922 1940–1941	Captain	First Great War (W) France
IRVINE, Andrew Comyn	1951–1953	2nd Lieut.	
JARDINE, Michael James	1940–1946	Captain	North Africa Italy (W)
JENKINSON, Ronald Stewart	1941–1946	Captain	Italy
JOHNSON, George Frederick	1925–1947	Colonel	Palestine, 1936 Middle East (PW) North-West Europe Palestine
JOHNSTON, Robert Gordon Scott	1956 to date	2nd Lieut.	
JOHNSTONE, Andrew James	1952–1953	2nd Lieut.	
KEELING, Michael Edward Allis	1945–1947	Lieutenant	
KEITH, Henry Shanks	1941–1945	Captain	North Africa Italy
KEITH, James David Agar	1944–1947	Lieutenant	North-West Europe
KEMBLE, David Horace Abercromby	1935–1945	Major	East Africa (W) Middle East North Africa (W) Italy North-West Europe Killed in action
KENNEDY, Archibald David	1944–1947	Lieutenant	North-West Europe
KERR, Lord John Andrew Christopher	1945–1948	Lieutenant	
KINDERSLEY, Hon. Hugh Kenyon Molesworth (afterwards 2nd Baron Kindersley)	1917–1919 1939–1943	Lt.-Colonel	First Great War North-West Europe (W)

APPENDIX E

Name	Period of Service in the Regiment	Highest rank reached in the Regiment	War Service
KINDERSLEY, Robert Hugh Molesworth	1948–1949	2nd Lieut.	Malaya
KINMONT, George Milne	1918–1919 1921–1944	Lt.-Colonel	Palestine, 1936 Middle East
KINNAIRD, Hon. Patrick Charles	1917–1920 1939–1943	Major	First Great War (W)
KNIGHT, Harold	1936–1941	Captain	Middle East Killed in action
KNOLLYS, Hon. David Francis Dudley	1950–1951	2nd Lieut.	Malaya
KOCH DE GOOREYND, Timothy	1949–1950	2nd Lieut.	Malaya
KUNG, Lingchieh	1942–1945	Lieutenant	South-East Asia
LAING, Alexander Grant	1943–1947	Captain	North-West Europe (W)
LAING, Hector	1943–1947	Captain	North-West Europe
LAING, Hugh Charles Desmond	1952 to date	Captain	
LAING, Robert Douglas Grant	1949–1950	2nd Lieut.	
LAMB, Michael Francis Rutherford	1951–1953	Lieutenant	
LAMPSON, Hon. Graham Curtis	1940–1947	Captain	Middle East North Africa Italy
LAW, Michael	1943 to date	Major	North-West Europe Malaya
LAWSON, Hon. Hugh John Frederick	1950–1951	2nd Lieut.	
LAWSON, Hon. William Edward Harry	1941 to date	Major	France (in the Buckinghamshire Yeomanry) Middle East North Africa Italy Malaya
LEA, Michael John MacLeod	1945–1947	Lieutenant	
LEAF, Charles Henry Gordon	1948–1949	2nd Lieut.	Malaya
LENG, Peter John Hall	1944 to date	Major	North-West Europe (W)
LENNARD, Sir Stephen Arthur Hallam Farnaby, 3rd Bt.	1918–1925 1940–1945	Lieutenant	France Middle East
LENNOX-BOYD, Donald Breay Hague	1928–1937	Lieutenant	Palestine, 1936
LEWIS, Clive	1940–1943	Lieutenant	North Africa Killed in action
LEWTHWAITE, Rainald Gilfrid	1934 to date	Lt.-Colonel	Palestine, 1936 Middle East North Africa (W) Italy North-West Europe
LINDESAY-BETHUNE, Hon. John Martin	1949–1950	2nd Lieut.	Malaya
LINDSAY, Hon. Patrick	1948–1949	2nd Lieut.	Malaya
LINDSAY, William Tucker, 14th Earl of	1924–1947	Major	Palestine, 1936 France Norway (W) Italy

APPENDIX E

Name	Period of Service in the Regiment	Highest rank reached in the Regiment	War Service
LINDSAY-PETO, Timothy Clement	1941–1945	Captain	North Africa (W) Italy (W) Killed in action
LINKLATER, Peter Stronach	1945–1947	Lieutenant	
LLEWELLYN, Arthur David George	1941–1954	Major	North-West Europe (W) (PW) Malaya
LLOYD-JOHNES, John Walter Ferlex	1943–1945	Lieutenant	Italy (W)
LODER, David Eustace	1941–1943	Lieutenant	Italy Killed in action
LOFTUS, Maurice Pierse Murrough	1940–1944	Lieutenant	North Africa Italy
LOGUE, Antony Lionel	1941–1946	Captain	North Africa Italy
LORT-PHILLIPS, Raymond, formerly GILLETT	1924–1929 1939–1943	Lieutenant	
LOTHIAN, Peter Francis Walter, 12th Marquess of	1942–1946	Lieutenant	
LOVAT, Simon Christopher Joseph, 17th Baron	1932–1939	Lieutenant	
LOWINSKY, Justin Mark Esmond	1948–1949	2nd Lieut.	Malaya
LOWINSKY, Thomas Martin Frances Esmond	1941–1944	Lieutenant	North Africa Italy Killed in action
LUCAS-TOOTH, Hugh John	1952–1953	2nd Lieut.	
LUDFORD-ASTLEY, Benjamin Alexander	1935–1937	2nd Lieut.	Palestine, 1936 Killed in an accident
LUMSDEN, David Malcolm	1950–1955	Captain	Malaya
LYELL, Alastair Hew Roderick	1944–1947	Lieutenant	
LYELL, Charles Antony, 2nd Baron, V.C.	1939–1943	Captain	North Africa Killed in action
MCBARNET, Donald Victor Charles	1922–1932 1939–1944	Major	North Africa Italy Killed in action
MCBARNET, Peter David	1947–1949	2nd Lieut.	Malaya
MCCONNEL, James Cecil Irving	1916–1919 1939–1941	Lieutenant	First Great War
MACDONALD, Murray Somerled	1943–1945	Lieutenant	North-West Europe (W)
MACDONALD-BUCHANAN, Alexander James	1950–1951	2nd Lieut.	
MACDONALD-BUCHANAN, John	1944–1952	Captain	North-West Europe (W) Malaya
MACDONALD-BUCHANAN, Reginald Narcissus	1916–1926 1939–1945	Major	First Great War (W) France North-West Europe
MACDOUGAL, Ernest Trevor Murray	1915–1919 1939–1946	Captain	First Great War
MACGREGOR OF MACGREGOR, Gregor	1944 to date	Captain	North-West Europe Palestine Malaya
MACINDOE, James Douglas	1909–1928 1939–1945	Major	First Great War

APPENDIX E

Name	Period of Service in the Regiment	Highest rank reached in the Regiment	War Service
McInDOE, Alastair Ros	1946–1947	Lieutenant	
Mackay, Angus Bourne Sutherland	1947–1948	2nd Lieut.	
Mackay, Peter John Sutherland	1945–1948	Lieutenant	
Mackenzie, Eric Dighton	1911–1926 1939–1944	Colonel	First Great War (W) France
Mackenzie, Ian David Mountain	1944–1947	Lieutenant	
Mackenzie, Kenneth Bruce	1941–1943	Lieutenant	North Africa Italy Killed in action
McKenzie, Roderick Alexander Clyde	1945–1949	Lieutenant	Malaya Killed in action
Mackintosh, Christopher Douglas	1949–1950	2nd Lieut.	Malaya
Mackintosh, Charlack Rob Douglas	1954 to date	2nd Lieut.	
Mackworth-Praed, Cyril Winthrop	1915–1919 1939–1945	Captain	First Great War
McLaren, Ian	1943–1946 1951–1954	Lieutenant	North-West Europe
Maclean, Sir Charles Hector Fitzroy, 11th Bt.	1939–1949	Major	North-West Europe
McLeod, Roderick Campbell	1941–1943	Lieutenant	Middle East North Africa (W) Italy Killed in action
McMurtrie, Duncan Gilbert Scott	1942–1944	Lieutenant	North Africa Italy Killed in action
Macpherson, William Alan	1945–1947	Lieutenant	
MacRae, John Donald Christopher Stuart	1934–1942	Major	Palestine, 1936 Middle East Killed in action
Malcolm, David Peter Michael	1939–1946	Major	North Africa Italy
Malcolm, Sir Michael Albert James, 10th Bt.	1916–1923 1939–1945	Captain	First Great War (W)
Malone, William Bernard	1941–1943	Major	Italy Killed in action
Mann, Francis George	1940–1946	Major	North Africa Italy (W)
Mann, John Pelham	1940–1946	Major	North-West Europe
Mannock, Anthony Nigel	1944–1947	Lieutenant	North-West Europe (W)
Marchant, Herbert Henry John	In the ranks 1926–1951 1951–1953	Lieutenant (QM)	
Marr, Donald Alexander Cameron	1953–1954	2nd Lieut.	
Marriott, Sir John Charles Oakes	1920–1941	Lt.-Colonel	First Great War in Northamptonshire Regiment (W) Middle East

APPENDIX E

Name	Period of Service in the Regiment	Highest rank reached in the Regiment	War Service
MARSHALL, Henry William Somerville	1943–1944	Lieutenant	North-West Europe Killed in action
MARSHAM-TOWNSHEND, John	1940–1945	Captain	Italy
MARSHAM-TOWNSHEND, Thomas	1938–1944	Captain	Middle East Italy Killed in action
MARTIN, Edward Alexander	1945–1947	Lieutenant	
MARTIN. Mervyn Harold Acquin	1941–1943	Lieutenant	
MARWICZ, Frederick Alfred de	1941–1945	Lieutenant	North-West Europe
MASSEY, David John Orgill	1944–1947	Lieutenant	Italy
MASSEY, Daniel Raymond	1952–1953	2nd Lieut.	
MATHESON, Ian Keith	1931–1940	Captain	France Killed in action
MATHIESON, Douglas Graham	1940–1944	Captain	North-West Europe Killed in action
MAXTONE GRAHAM, Anthony James Oliphant	1940–1946	Captain	Middle East (PW)
MAXTONE GRAHAM, James Anstruther	1943–1947	Captain	Italy
MAXTONE GRAHAM, Robert Mungo	1950–1951	2nd Lieut.	Malaya
MAXWELL, Andrew Bernard Constable	1939–1945	Captain	Middle East (W) (PW) Italy
MAXWELL, Sir Aymer, 8th Bt.	1939–1945	Captain	
MAXWELL-HYSLOP, Hugh Mark	1954 to date	2nd Lieut.	
MAXWELL, Gavin	1939–1945	Major	
MAXWELL SCOTT, Michael Fergus	1944–1947	Lieutenant	North-West Europe
MAYFIELD, Bryan	1918–1937 1939–1945	Lt.-Colonel	Palestine, 1936 Middle East (W) North Africa
MAYFIELD, Richard	1949 to date	Captain	Malaya
MCCOWEN, Donald William Henry	1956 to date	2nd Lieut.	
MELGUND, Gilbert Edward George Lariston, Viscount	1948–1956	Captain	Malaya
METHUEN, Paul Ayshford, 4th Baron	1914–1920 1940–1945	Lieutenant	First Great War North-West Europe
METHUEN, Paul Rodney	1942–1948	Lieutenant	Italy (W)
MEYER, Sir Anthony John Charles, 3rd Bt.	1941–1945	Lieutenant	North-West Europe (W)
MILBURNE, Jack Frank	1925–1936 1939–1945	Major	Norway Middle East North Africa Italy
MILLAIS, Hesketh Raoul le Jarderay	1940–1945	Captain	
MILLAR, Keith Malcolm Hedley	1952–1953	2nd Lieut.	
MILLER, Alexander Alfred	1920–1949	Major	North-West Europe
MILLER, David Clunie	1944–1947	Captain	North-West Europe
MILLER-THOMAS, Brian Alexander	1953–1956	Lieutenant	
MILLIGAN, Wyndham Macbeth Moir	1940–1945	Captain	North-West Europe

APPENDIX E

Name	Period of Service in the Regiment	Highest rank reached in the Regiment	War Service
MOFFAT, Peter Ian	1949–1955	Captain	Malaya
MONCREIFFE, Sir David Gerald, 10th Bt.	1942–1946 1952–1954	Captain	Italy (W)
MONCREIFFE, Rupert Iain Kay	1940–1946	Captain	Middle East Italy (W)
MONCRIEFF, Charles St. John Graham	1951 to date	Captain	
MONEY, John Douglas	1946–1948	Lieutenant	
MONFRIES, Kennett Alexander	1944	Lieutenant	Italy Killed in action
MOORE, Maurice	1931–1935	Lieutenant	Transferred to Army Air Corps and killed in action in North Africa
MORISON, Harold Thomas Brash	1940–1945	Major	Middle East
MORISON, John Kenneth	1945–1947	Lieutenant	
MORISON, Ronald Peter	1940–1944	2nd Lieut.	North-West Europe
MORLEY, Frank	In the ranks 1915–1939 1939–1945	Captain (QM)	North-West Europe (PW)
MORPHETT, Derek George	1941–1946	Captain	Middle East North Africa Italy (W) North-West Europe
MORRICE, Michael James	1949–1950	2nd Lieut.	Malaya Killed in action
MORRISON-LOW, Sir Walter John, 2nd Bt.	1918–1919 1940–1945	Captain	First Great War
MORSE, Arthur David	1950–1951	2nd Lieut.	Malaya
MOSTYN, Edwyn Inigo Lloyd	1941–1955	Major	Italy Malaya
MORSOVSKY, Nicholas	1953–1955	2nd Lieut.	
MUNDY, Giles Firbank	1942–1944	Lieutenant	Italy (W) Killed on Active Service
MURRAY, Alexander Douglas	1934–1949	Major	Norway
MUTTER, Ronald Graham	1944–1945	Lieutenant	North-West Europe Killed in action
MYCOCK, David	1944–1947	Lieutenant	North-West Europe (W)
MYNORS, David Rickards Baskerville	1940–1946	Lieutenant	Middle East North Africa Italy
NAINBY-LUXMOORE, Bertie Chave	1945–1947	Lieutenant	
NAINBY-LUXMOORE, Chave Charles	1917–1928 1939–1945	Captain	First Great War (W)
NAPIER AND ETTRICK, Francis Nigel, Baron (14th and 5th)	1950 to date	Captain	Malaya
NASON, Michael Carey	1955 to date	2nd Lieut.	
NAYLOR, Richard Christopher	1955 to date	2nd Lieut.	
NEILSON, Andrew Shennan	1941–1944	Captain	Italy (W) Killed in action
NEVILE, Henry Nicholas	1940–1946	Captain	North-West Europe

APPENDIX E

Name	Period of Service in the Regiment	Highest rank reached in the Regiment	War Service
NEVILL, Michael George Ralph	1940–1943	Lieutenant	North Africa Killed in action
NICHOLSON, John Ward Randolph	1943–1944	Lieutenant	Italy
NICKERSON, George Stewart	1944–1948 1952 to date	Major	North-West Europe
NOBLE, Horace Westmacott	1918–1919 1939–1945	2nd Lieut.	
NUNNELEY, Robin Michael Charles	1943–1945	Captain	Italy
NUNNELEY, Charles Kenneth Roylance	1955 to date	2nd Lieut.	
OGILVIE, Walter Milne	1945–1948	Lieutenant	
OGILVIE-GRANT, Charles Randolph Mark	1940–1946	Lieutenant	Middle East (PW)
OGILVY, Hon. Angus James Bruce	1947–1948	2nd Lieut.	
OGILVY, David George Patrick Coke, Lord	1945–1950	Captain	Malaya
OGILVY, Hon. James Donald Diarmid	1953–1954	2nd Lieut.	
OLIVER, Guy Marriott	1915–1919 1940–1945	Lieutenant	
ORMROD, Peter Charles	1942–1948	Captain	North-West Europe
ORR, Andrew Ian Dundas	1942–1944	Lieutenant	Italy
ORR EWING, Ronald Archibald	1932–1953	Major	Middle East (PW)
PACKE-DRURY-LOWE, John Drury Boteler	1927–1949	Major	Middle East Italy
PARRY, Donald Morris	1942–1946	Captain	Italy
de la PASTURE, Peter Anthony Gerard	1941–1943	Lieutenant	Middle East
PATERSON, Edward Gordon	1944–1947	Lieutenant	North-West Europe
PAYNTER, George	1954	2nd Lieut.	Died on service in Egypt
PEARSON, Archibald David Barclay	1918–1919 1939–1945	Major	
PEASE, Hon. Christopher Henry Beaumont (afterwards 2nd Baron Wardington)	1943–1947	Captain	Italy (W)
PEMBER, Rawdon Cecil George	1940–1945	Captain	North-West Europe (W) Killed in action
PERCIVAL, Thomas William Douglas	1940–1945	Captain	
PETRE, Robert Charles	1932–1934 1939–1945	Major	Norway Italy
PHILIPSON, Anthony Thirlwall	1940–1946 1952 to date	Major	Middle East North Africa Italy (PW)
PIKE, George Livesey Stenhouse	1938–1947	Major	Middle East Italy (W) North-West Europe
PILKINGTON, Alan Roger Douglas	1944–1947	Captain	North-West Europe
PIM, George Cecil	1918–1935	Captain	
PIPER, Arthur Harry	1940–1946	Major	North Africa Italy

APPENDIX E

Name	Period of Service in the Regiment	Highest rank reached in the Regiment	War Service
Polson, Keith David	1951–1952	2nd Lieut.	
Ponsonby, Robert Noel	1945–1948	Lieutenant	
Porter, Nigel David Sykes	1954 to date	Lieutenant	
Porter, William Dudley MacNish	1918–1919 1939–1943	Major	First Great War
Prain, David Eustace Gurney	1956 to date	2nd Lieut.	
Priaulx, Osmond	1918–1923 1940–1946	Captain	
Priaulx, Osmond William	1945 to date	Major	Malaya
Price, David Ernest Campbell	1943–1946	Lieutenant	Italy
Prior, Douglas Christopher	1949 to date	Captain	Malaya
Prior, Ian Redvers	1944–1946	Lieutenant	North-West Europe
Purvis, Arthur Blaikie	1944–1946	Lieutenant	North-West Europe
Purvis, Arthur Frederic	1915–1936 1939–1945	Major	First Great War (W) France North-West Europe (W)
Purvis, Robert William Berry	1939–1946	Captain	Middle East Italy North-West Europe
Quinn, James	In the ranks 1919–1940 1940–1947	Captain (QM)	Italy
Radcliffe, Edmund Lyons Willoughby	1945–1946	Lieutenant	Transferred to Oxfordshire and Buckinghamshire Light Infantry and killed in action in Korea
Radcliffe, Gilbert Courtney Willoughby	1944–1946	Captain	North-West Europe (W)
Raeburn, William Digby Manifold	1936 to date	Lt.-Colonel	Middle East Italy North-West Europe
Ramsay, Alexander Henry Richard Maule	1939–1943	Captain	Norway (W) Middle East Died on Active Service
Ramsay, George Patrick Maule	1942 to date	Major	Italy (W) Malaya
Ramsay, John Charles Maule	1945–1955	Major	Malaya
Ramsay, James Surtees Maule	1943–1944	Lieutenant	North-West Europe Killed in action
Ramsay, Michael Graham	1952–1954	2nd Lieut.	
Ramsay, Neil Gordon	1948 to date	Captain	Malaya
Rankin, Alick Michael	1954–1955	2nd Lieut.	
Rankin, Arthur Niall Talbot	1939–1945	Major	Burma
Rankin, Ian Niall	1952–1953	2nd Lieut.	
Rathbone, Henry Stephen Nicholas	1933–1943	Major	North Africa Italy Killed in action
Rattray, James Silvester Clerk	1941–1946	Captain	Middle East North Africa Italy North-West Europe
Raw, George Rupert	1939–1946	2nd Lieut.	Middle East Italy

Name	Period of Service in the Regiment	Highest rank reached in the Regiment	War Service
READMAN, Robert Anthony	1940 to date	Major	Middle East Italy South-East Asia Palestine Malaya
REES, Peter Wynford Innes	1945–1948	Lieutenant	
REYNTIENS, Nicholas Patrick	1944–1947	Lieutenant	
REYNTIENS, Robert Alfred Michael	1943–1947	Lieutenant	Italy (W)
RHODES, Sam	1938 to date	Lt.-Colonel Director of Music	North-West Europe
RITCHIE, Alastair Newton Bethune	1940 to date	Major	North-West Europe Malaya [(W)
RIVERS-BULKELEY, Robert Arthur Henry	1935–1949	Major	Palestine, 1936 Middle East Italy
RIVETT-CARNAC, Thomas Nicholas	1945–1955	Captain	Palestine Malaya
ROB, John Vernon	1941–1945	Captain	Italy (W)
ROBERTS, Owen George Endicott	1932–1934	Lieutenant	
ROBERTSON, Alastair Barry	1956 to date	2nd Lieut.	
ROBERTSON, Anthony Neil	1955 to date	2nd Lieut.	
ROBERTSON, Charles	In the ranks 1923–1943 1943–1947	Captain (QM)	
ROBERTSON, Charles Albert Amherst	1917–1938 1939–1945	Major	First Great War (W) France, 1940
ROBERTSON, Donald Struan	1939–1955	Major	Middle East (W) Italy Malaya
ROMER, Malcolm Nigel	1936 to date	Major	Middle East Italy (W) North-West Europe Malaya
ROPER, John Charles Abercromby	1940–1946	Captain	Middle East North Africa Italy North-West Europe
ROPER-CURZON, Hon. Ralph Henry	1920 1940–1947	Captain	Served in First Great War in Royal East Kent Regiment (W)
ROSE, Hugh Lancelot St. Vincent	1939–1953	Major	Norway Middle East North Africa Italy North-West Europe
ROSE, Roderick Angus Campbell	1954 to date	Lieutenant	
Ross, Alexander	In the ranks 1919–1939 1939–1949	Major (QM)	Served in Queen's Own Cameron Highlanders in First Great War (W) Palestine, 1936 Norway North Africa Italy (W)

APPENDIX E

Name	Period of Service in the Regiment	Highest rank reached in the Regiment	War Service
Ross, Donald John	1943–1946	Lieutenant	North-West Europe
Ross-Thompson, Ian Angell	1945–1947	Lieutenant	
Rowe, John Vincent	1942–1946	Lieutenant	Italy (W)
Rowe, Michael William	1940–1944	Captain	North Africa (W)
Rowe, Ronald George	1940–1946	Major	Middle East Italy (W)
Runcie, Robert Alexander Kennedy	1942–1946	Captain	North-West Europe
Rush, George Campion	1932–1946	Major	Middle East North Africa Italy
Russell, Albert Muir Galloway	1944–1947	Lieutenant	North-West Europe
Russell, Thomas Charles David	1940–1943	Lieutenant	Middle East Killed in action
Sanderson, John Christopher	1955 to date	2nd Lieut.	
Sanderson, John Stratford	1930–1954	Lt.-Colonel	Norway Italy Palestine Malaya
Scott, Alexander Malcolm	1915–1922 1939–1945	Lieutenant	First Great War (W)
Scott, Donald Dundas	1945–1947	Captain	
Scott, John Swire	1939–1946	Captain	North-West Europe
Scott, Michael Balfour	1953 to date	Lieutenant	
Scott, Mason Charles	1951–1956	Captain	
Scott-Barrett, David William	1942 to date	Major	North-West Europe Malaya
Scrimgeour, Robin Neville Carron	1945	2nd Lieut.	
Scriven, Richard Gordon	1947–1948	2nd Lieut.	
Seel, Kenneth Edward	1944–1946	Lieutenant	North-West Europe
Seymour, Adrian John Conway	1940 to date	Major	North-West Europe
Seymour, William Napier	1936–1949	Major	Palestine, 1936 Middle East Burma Palestine Malaya
Sharp, Edmund Michael	1942–1944	Lieutenant	Italy (W) Killed in action
Shaw-Kennedy, David Verner	1939–1945	Major	Middle East Italy
Shaw Stewart, Michael	1945–1947	Lieutenant	
Shaw Stewart, Patrick Hugh	1942–1944	Lieutenant	North Africa Italy Killed in action
Shearer, John Charles Johnston	1944–1949	Captain	North-West Europe (W)
Sheller, Charles Simon Comac	1955–1956	2nd Lieut.	
Sherwood, John Cresswell	1945–1947	Lieutenant	
Shrubsall, Graham Douglas	1941–1945	Lieutenant	Middle East North Africa
Shutes, Robert Arthur David	1946–1948	Lieutenant	
Shuttleworth, Noel Charles	1953 to date	Lieutenant	
Sinclair, Angus John	1944–1947	Lieutenant	North-West Europe

APPENDIX E

Name	Period of Service in the Regiment	Highest rank reached in the Regiment	War Service
SINCLAIR, John Henry Lund	1941–1944	Captain	North Africa (W) Italy Killed in action
SLADE, Sir Alfred Fotheringham, 5th Bt.	1916–1922 1940–1945	Lieutenant	First Great War
SMAIL, Timothy John	1951–1953	2nd Lieut.	
SMITH, Harold Anthony Warrington	1941–1944	Lieutenant	North Africa (W) Italy (W) Killed in action
SMITH, Harold Wyatt Llewellyn	1942–1946	Lieutenant	North-West Europe
SMITH, Harry John Kevin	1944–1947	Lieutenant	North-West Europe
SMITH, Herbert	In the ranks 1920–1947 1947 to date	Major (QM)	
SNELL, Hugh Mortain	1942–1944	Lieutenant	Italy Killed in action
SOUTHESK, Charles Alexander, 11th Earl of	1913–1925 1939–1944	Major	First Great War France
SPALDING, Herbert	In the ranks 1919–1941 1941–1945	Captain (QM)	Palestine, 1936 Norway North-West Europe
SPENCER, Victor George, Hon.	1953–1955	Lieutenant	
SPENCER-NAIRN, Robert Arnold	1952–1954	2nd Lieut.	
STACEY, Thomas Charles Gerrard	1949–1950	2nd Lieut.	Malaya
STAFFORD, Basil Francis Nicholas, 14th Baron	1945–1948	Lieutenant	
STAINTON, Andrew Thomas	1944–1947	Lieutenant	
STAINTON, John David Adam	1940–1946	Captain	Middle East North Africa Italy North-West Europe
STARKEY, Edmund Arthur	1917–1920 1940–1943	Lieutenant	First Great War
STEUART-FOTHRINGHAM, Patrick	1929–1948	Lt.-Colonel	Norway Italy North-West Europe
STEUART-MENZIES, David Ronald	1954 to date	2nd Lieut.	
STEVENSON, Anthony Ronald Guy	1942–1948	Captain	North-West Europe (W)
STEWART, Hugh	1940–1941	2nd Lieut.	
STEWART, Ian Douglas Battersby	1944–1945	Lieutenant	
STEWART, Robert Christie	1945–1947	Lieutenant	
STEWART, Russell Oldfield	1942–1944	Lieutenant	North Africa (W) Italy Killed in action
STEWART-WILSON, Blair Aubyn	1949 to date	Captain	Malaya
STIRLING, Archibald David	1939–1946	Major	Middle East (W)(PW)
STIRLING, Hugh Joseph	1938–1941	Lieutenant	Middle East Killed in action
STIRLING, William Joseph	1932–1945	Major	Middle East North Africa North-West Europe

APPENDIX E

Name	Period of Service in the Regiment	Highest rank reached in the Regiment	War Service
STIRLING, Roderick William Kenneth	1951–1952	2nd Lieut.	
STIRLING-HOME-DRUMMOND-MORAY, Andrew Charles	1926–1930 1939–1945	Major	North-West Europe
STIRLING-HOME-DRUMMOND-MORAY, James William	1921–1938 1939–1945	Major	Palestine, 1936
STOBART, Timothy Robin	1945–1947	Lieutenant	
STOCKTON, John Samuel	1940–1943	Captain	North Africa Killed in action
STORMONT, William David Mungo James, Viscount	1949–1950	2nd Lieut.	Malaya
STRACHAN, Duncan Neilson	1942–1946	Captain	
STRUTHERS, William Hutchison	1944–1945	Lieutenant	North-West Europe Killed in action
STRUTT, Hon. Hedley Vicars	1940–1946	Captain	North-West Europe
STUART, Arthur Patrick Avondale, Viscount	1947–1948	2nd Lieut.	
STUART, Robert Livingstone	1941–1946	Captain	Middle East North Africa Italy North-West Europe
STUART, Hon. Simon Walter Erskine	1949–1950	2nd Lieut.	Malaya
STUART-MENTETH, Charles Granville	1947–1949	2nd Lieut.	
STUART-MENTETH, James Wallace, afterwards 6th Bt.	1942–1944	Lieutenant	Italy (W)
STUDHOLME, Henry Gray later 1st Bt.	1917–1919 1940–1944	Captain	First Great War (W)
SWINTON, Alan Henry Campbell	1914–1938 1939–1944	Lt.-Colonel	First Great War (W)
SWINTON, John	1944 to date	Major	North-West Europe (W) Malaya
SYMINGTON, Courtenay William	1940–1945	Captain	Middle East Italy
TAIT, Ian McCall	1941–1943	Lieutenant	Italy Killed in action
TALBOT, Thomas George	1940–1944	Lieutenant	
TAYLOR, Frank Roy	1944–1947	Lieutenant	North-West Europe
TAYLOR, Guy Aime Dubosc	1930–1944	Lt.-Colonel	Norway [(W) Middle East North Africa (W) Italy Killed in action
TAYLOR, James Houston	1940–1941	2nd Lieut.	
TEMPEST, Henry Roger	1944–1947	Lieutenant	North-West Europe
TEMPEST, Stephen	1939–1945	Captain	[(W)
TENNANT, Andrew Duff	1946–1948	Lieutenant	
TENNANT, Anthony John	1949–1950	2nd Lieut.	Malaya
TENNANT, Archibald	1941–1946	Captain	North-West Europe
TENNANT, Hugh Rinnes Duff	1951–1952	2nd Lieut.	
TENNANT, Iain Mark	1939–1946	Captain	Middle East (PW)
TENNANT, Michael Francis	1916–1919 1939–1945	Captain	First Great War

APPENDIX E

Name	Period of Service in the Regiment	Highest rank reached in the Regiment	War Service
THAVENOT, Alexander Henry Moncaster	1940–1946	Captain	Middle East North Africa Italy
THOMAS, David Graeme	1944–1947	Captain	North-West Europe
THOMPSON, James Douglas	1942–1946	Lieutenant	North-West Europe
THOMSON, Ian Vert	1945–1947	Lieutenant	
THOMSON, Trevor Charles Heudeborck	1941–1943	Lieutenant	Italy Killed in action
THOMSON, William Bennett	1952 to date	Lieutenant	
THORPE, Ivor Lawrence	1943–1947	Lieutenant	North-West Europe (W)
THORPE, Ninian	1941–1944	Lieutenant	North-West Europe Killed in action
TIMPSON, John Alastair Livingston	1940–1946	Major	Middle East North Africa (W) Italy (W)
TORRANCE, Neil Teulon	1942–1947	Lieutenant	Italy (W) North-West Europe
TOWNSHEND, George John Patrick Dominic, 7th Marquess	1940–1945	Captain	[(W)
TRAFFORD, Edward Bernard	1905–1922 1939–1941	Major	First Great War (PW)
TRAFFORD, Edward Willoughby	1943–1948	Lieutenant	Italy
TRAFFORD, John Edward	1953–1955	2nd Lieut.	
TRAFFORD, Peter Hugh	1945–1948	Lieutenant	
TRAILL, David	1942–1946	Captain	North Africa Italy
TRAPPES-LOMAX, David Edward	1950 to date	Captain	Malaya
TRAPPES-LOMAX, Michael Roger	1940–1946	Captain	Middle East Italy
TRAPPES-LOMAX, Thomas Byrnand	1917–1948	Lt.-Colonel	First Great War (W) Norway
TREADWELL, John William Ferguson	1925–1947	Major	France
TREFUSIS, Robert John Rodolph	1940–1946	2nd Lieut.	North-West Europe
TUCK, Bruce Adolph Reginald	1944–1947	Lieutenant	
TUFNELL, Carleton John Richard	1943–1945	Lieutenant	
TUKE, Anthony Favill	1940–1946	Major	North Africa Italy
TUNNARD, Peter Humfrey	1940–1946	Captain	Middle East North Africa Italy (W)
TURNBULL-KEMP, Peter	1945–1947	Lieutenant	
TURNER, Alexander Frederick Charles	1926–1930 1939–1945	Lieutenant	
TURNER, John	In the ranks 1914–1934 1934–1939	Captain (QM)	First Great War
TURNER, Simon John Edward	1955 to date	2nd Lieut.	
TWEEDIE, Hugo Douglas	1931–1945	Major	Middle East North-West Europe Killed in action

APPENDIX E

Name	Period of Service in the Regiment	Highest rank reached in the Regiment	War Service
TYLDEN-WRIGHT, David	1942–1946	Lieutenant	Italy (W)
TYLDESLEY JONES, John Everard	1940–1944	Major	North Africa Italy Killed in action
TYRINGHAM, Giffard Loftus	1914–1945	Lt.-Colonel	First Great War (W)
URQUHART, Kenneth Leslie	1939–1941	Lieutenant	
USHER, Francis Simeon Caverhill	1925–1930 1939–1945	Major	Middle East Italy
VARNEY, Owen Buckingham	1951 to date	Captain	
VERNON, Hon. John Lawrance	1942–1946	Lieutenant	North-West Europe (W)
VESTEY, Hon. William Howarth	1940–1944	Captain	Italy Killed in action
WAKE-BOWELL, Hereward Robert	1940–1946	Captain	Middle East (PW)
WALDRON, Frank Arthur Lovegrove	1940–1948	Captain	Middle East North Africa (W) Italy North-West Europe (W)
WALLACE, Edward Hamish Lachlan	1943–1947	Captain	Italy
WALTER, David Finlayson Wylie-Hill	1954 to date	2nd Lieut.	
WALTON, John Allan	1945–1947	Lieutenant	
WARD, Francis	1915–1920 1939–1947	Captain	First Great War (W)
WARD, Peter Michaeljohn	1943–1947	Lieutenant	North-West Europe
WARNER, Edward Courtenay Henry, afterwards 3rd Bt.	1942–1945	Lieutenant	North-West Europe (W)
WARNER, Sir Edward Courtenay Thomas, 2nd Bt.	1905–1934 1939–1942	Colonel	First Great War France
WARNER, Thomas Seymour	1922–1928 1943–1948	Captain	
WARNOCK, James	1943–1947	Captain	Italy
WARRE CORNISH, Francis Hubert	1943–1946	Lieutenant	
WATERS, Philip Duncan Joseph	1918–1919 1939–1945	Major	Served in first Great War in Yorkshire Regiment (W) Middle East Burma
WATTS, Samuel Roy	In the ranks 1937–1953 1953 to date	Lieutenant	North Africa Italy
WATSON-ARMSTRONG, Hon. William Henry Cecil John Robin	1941–1946	Captain	North-West Europe (W)
WEBB, Michael Hinton	1952 to date	Major	Served in the Transvaal Scottish 1940–1946 Middle East
WEDDERBURN, David Scrymgeour	1932–1944	Lt.-Colonel	Palestine, 1936 Norway Italy Killed in action

APPENDIX E

Name	Period of Service in the Regiment	Highest rank reached in the Regiment	War Service
WEIR, Adrian John Anthony	1941–1944	Major	Middle East North Africa (W) Italy Killed in action
WEMYSS, Andrew Michael John	1945–1947	Lieutenant	
WESTON SMITH, Ian	1940–1947	Captain	Middle East (W) North Africa Italy (PW)
WHIGHAM, Robin Campbell	1939–1946	Captain	North-West Europe Killed in an accident
WHITEHEAD, Charles Parkin	1940–1945	Captain	Italy
WHITELAW, William Stephen Ian	1939–1947	Major	North-West Europe Palestine
WHITELEY, Frank Geoffrey Lee	1940–1945	Lieutenant	Middle East
WHITNEY, William Dwight	1940	2nd Lieut.	
WIDDERSON, Leslie Edward	1942–1944	Lieutenant	North Africa Italy Killed in action
WILLIS, Raymond Allan	1940–1946	Major	Middle East (W) North Africa Italy North-West Europe
WILLS, Ernest Edward de Winton	1926–1931 1939–1940	Lieutenant	
WILSON, Harold William Curjel	1945–1947	Lieutenant	
WILSON, James Samuel	1943–1948	Captain	Italy
WILSON, Jonathan	1943–1944	Lieutenant	North-West Europe Killed in action
WINCH, Henry Herman Evelyn Montagu	1931–1932 1940–1945	Captain	
WINGFIELD-STRATFORD, Mervyn Verner	1928–1937	Lieutenant	Palestine, 1936
WINTER, Ernest Fitzgerald	1943–1945	Lieutenant	Italy Killed in action
WINTER, Patrick Antony	1944–1950	Captain	North-West Europe (W) Malaya
WOOLLAN, Dudley Frank	1917–1932 1939–1945	Major	First Great War
WORSLEY-TAYLOR, Sir John Godfrey, 3rd Bt.	1940–1948	Captain	North-West Europe
WORTHINGTON WILMER, Andrew Ogilvie	1943–1947	Captain	Italy (W)
WYNNE FINCH, William Heneage	1912–1938 1939–1945	Colonel	First Great War (W)
YATES, Edward Robert	1942–1945	Captain	Italy
YORK, H.R.H. Albert Frederick Arthur George, Duke of (*H.M. King George VI*)	1932–1936	Maj.-Gen. 24th Col. of the Regiment	
YOUNG, John McIntosh	1940–1945	Lieutenant	North-West Europe
YOUNGER, Gavin William	1945–1947	Lieutenant	
YOUNGER, Simon Gerard	1950–1951	2nd Lieut.	

APPENDIX F

The Dress of the Regiment

By Major J. Swinton, Scots Guards

IN his History of the Regiment from its origin until the eve of the First World War, Sir Frederick Maurice includes a very full account of the evolution of Scots Guards dress which was written for him by Mr. Percival Reynolds. It would seem, therefore, that this volume, covering as it does a period during which the changes in uniform throughout the Army have been, to say the least, considerable, would be incomplete if it did not bring up to date the story of this most important part of Regimental life.

For simplification, and also to bring out more clearly the similarity in economies which came into force after each world war, this Appendix is divided into three parts: the period between the wars, the Second World War, and the present day.

I. BETWEEN THE WARS, 1919–1939

As soon as war was declared in 1914 all forms of dress, other than Service Dress, were packed away and the Regiment spent "the duration" in unrelieved khaki. Either long trousers or "knicker-bocker" trousers with puttees were worn with the Service Dress and it was the custom, although quite contrary to orders, to cut the trousers below the knee when wearing the latter so that they looked smarter.

Even when the Guards Division returned from France in 1919 there was no immediate return to Full Dress and in fact the only hint of pre-war dress conditions to be seen during that first year of peace was in April when officers were directed to wear "Blue" (serge undress blue jacket or "jumper" over Full Dress trousers) during the evenings in barracks, "if in possession". When the wearing of Full Dress was finally authorised in the following year, the Regiment were the first in the Brigade of Guards to wear it, a Scots Guards Guard-of-Honour appearing in tunics and bearskin caps for the first time since 1914 in Edinburgh during July 1920. King's Guard in London did not follow suit until the Second Battalion of the Regiment mounted the first post-war guard in Full Dress in October 1922. Pre-war officers' mess kit also began to reappear at about this time.

In the name of economy the War Office took the opportunity, whilst authorising the re-introduction of Full Dress, to reduce much of its pre-war splendour and although several of their reforms did not last very long, Army Order 293 of 1920 which set out their intentions, can still be regarded as a milestone in the evolution of the dress of the Brigade of Guards. This

Order abolished the white jacket for other ranks, the red serge tunic for Warrant Officers and Staff-Sergeants and the black anklets or leggings previously worn by all ranks in "marching order". It also directed that in future the gold embroidery on the collar, cuffs and skirt of officers' tunics would be reduced and become the same for all ranks, an innovation known as "skeleton lace" which was so universally unpopular that in August 1925 it was cancelled. Few such tunics, half a dozen at the most, were ever made, officers preferring to buy second-hand tunics of pre-war type rather than wear the modern and less imposing article. However, "skeleton lace" was still to be seen in wear up to, and possibly even later than, May 1931, and a good example of this kind of tunic exists today in the Scottish United Services Museum in Edinburgh Castle.

Another economy was for dismounted officers to wear the same type of ankle boots as issued to the Gentlemen Cadets at Sandhurst instead of the usual calf-length wellingtons. Since, however, most officers already had wellingtons to wear with "Blue" in the evenings and had to have them in due course should they become Field officers, this part of the order also proved unpopular and was rescinded in 1923, few ankle boots ever having been worn. The blue frock coat was another casualty in the name of economy, but this most useful and hard-wearing garment reappeared again for wear by all officers in 1923.

To sugar the pill of these 1920 economies, and also to cancel them out as far as the officers' pockets were concerned, came the pleasing introduction of new Regimental badges of rank for officers. Hitherto, Scots Guards officers had worn the same rank stars as the rest of the army—the Star of the Order of the Bath—but this was now altered to the Star of the Order of the Thistle, to be worn in polished brass on Service Dress, in silver embroidery on tunics and in gold embroidery on blue jumpers and on frock coats. Up to 1919 all buttons and rank badges on officers' Service Dress had been bronze and this was only changed to polished metal shortly before Army Order 293 altered the design.

As soon as Full Dress was reintroduced recruits at the Guards Depot were issued with one of each of the articles of Full Dress clothing during their last weeks of training, but by the time they had undergone twelve months' service they were expected to be in possession of at least two tunics and two pairs of blue trousers, facilities being provided for them to buy the additional items off "time expired" men at regular "kit sales". The best of this clothing was then directed to be worn on the following occasions only: State occasions, Guards-of-Honour, Public Duties, Reviews, Inspections, on Sundays and when especially ordered. Members of the Regimental Band were expected to have at least three sets.

In December 1926 the Army Council ordered the Brigade of Guards to wear khaki greatcoats on all parades except Full Dress occasions, but after a short period of compliance this was soon modified to provide for the wearing of blue-grey coats on all drill and ceremonial parades whenever Service Dress and white buff equipment was worn.

A word must here be said on head-dress and particularly about that of the officers. Before 1914 khaki covers were worn over officers' forage caps on training and no doubt many of these covered caps went to Flanders.

Quite early in the war, however, forage caps began to be made with khaki tops above the dice band, the remainder of the cap being as it is today. These were worn until abolished in 1920. The modern type of forage cap took their place and were worn with all orders of dress except Full Dress. By custom, officers of the Regiment have never worn forage caps with tunics although it is standard practice for other ranks.

Khaki Service Dress caps of various designs had been worn by both officers and men before 1914 and they have been worn ever since, although at the time of writing their continued existence is threatened by the ubiquitous beret. During the First War years other ranks had worn small blue numbers on the sleeves of their Service Dress jackets to show to which battalion they belonged. This practice was not, however, adopted by the officers and in 1916, in order to provide a differentiation between battalions, the First Battalion officers began to wear a small patch of Royal Stuart tartan on each side of their Service Dress caps. Not to be outdone, the officers of the Second Battalion countered this by wearing a full circle of forage cap diceing right round their Service Dress caps; an expensive addition which, in 1917, was altered to two patches of diceing of nine squares each. At the end of the war, the First Battalion kept their tartan patches but the Second Battalion discarded theirs altogether.

When the First Battalion went to Egypt in 1935 it was rightly considered that tartan riband would not stand the sun, and so the same twelve squares of diceing as the Second Battalion had worn in China in 1928 were adopted for wear with the sun helmets. Precedent for this was found from the South African war when both Battalions of the Regiment had worn diceing, but the large helmet stars worn during that war did not appear again after 1918.

In February 1928 King George V presented feather bonnets to the Pipers of the Regiment for wear with Full Dress on occasions when the Drummers would be wearing bearskin caps. The hackle which he chose for these bonnets was blue and red, the colours of the Royal Household. This was the last innovation to be made in the dress of the Regiment until 1936, when, during his brief reign, King Edward VIII made some considerable changes in the clothing and equipment of his Household Troops.

For many years "mounted" officers of the Foot Guards had worn butcher boots and pantaloons when actually in the saddle, but this order of dress was now abolished and in its place mounted officers were to wear overalls with wellington boots and box spurs. Strappings, hitherto permitted for officers riding in overalls, were forbidden and in due course King Edward VIII approved the adoption of a brass slide of Regimental pattern which was to be worn at the bottom of the stirrup leather when officers were mounted in Full Dress or Un-Dress uniform.

Up to 1936 "Guard Order" for other ranks had consisted of a folded greatcoat worn on the back above a rolled cape, with much buff equipment, including two pouches, to keep these articles in place, but in October all this was changed. Folded capes, fourteen inches by six-and-a-half, with three folds, and a valise star worn in the centre, replaced the greatcoat altogether; the top of the cape now being worn in line with the piping on the top of the collar of the tunic. The cape was worn in a similar fashion

592   APPENDIX F

when greatcoats were in wear and the new order of dress applied equally to drummers who had previously escaped without wearing a folded greatcoat at all. As a result of these changes considerable alteration was made in the following year to the buff equipment and during the next two years there was much juggling with pouches and shoulder straps.

II. WORLD WAR, 1939–1945

The declaration of war in 1939 found the Second Battalion of the Regiment in Egypt dressed equally well for peace or war in khaki drill. At home, as in 1914, all forms of Full Dress clothing were handed into store and the Regiment prepared for active service in Service Dress, which was almost immediately replaced by the new Battledress. Throughout the war, Officers, Warrant Officers, the Regimental Band, Pipers, Drummers and individual other ranks continued to wear Service Dress on appropriate occasions.

Cloth shoulder titles, which had been worn during the First World War and which had been authorised for wear with Service Dress in 1936 but never used, gradually made their appearance in 1939. On mobilisation, however, these blue and gold shoulder titles were scarce and for some time the white metal thistles and brass "SG" which had been worn between the wars on other ranks Service Dress were used on Battledress. At one time pieces of khaki cloth designed to slip over the shoulder straps, embroidered with the letters "SG" in black, were also issued but were most unpopular and seldom worn. Polished buttons and badges of rank continued to be worn on Service Dress, but officers were ordered to wear bronze badges of rank on Battledress. Battalions did not adopt the First War practice of wearing numerals on their sleeves and after a Regimental Order dated 11th November 1940 had said "All Officers of the Regiment will now wear a patch of Royal Stuart Tartan on the side of the S.D. Cap", there was no way of telling to which battalion an officer or other rank belonged unless he was in Battledress and wearing a formation sign.

Throughout the war individual Scots Guardsmen wore on their sleeves almost every formation sign in the British army. Signs worn by battalions or by Independent Companies of the Regiment were, however, few, and the list is as follows:

	Formation	*Sign*
1st Battalion	24th Guards Brigade	An heraldic pinion in red on a dark blue background.
	1st Division	Small white triangle.
	6th South African Armoured Division	A yellow triangle within a larger green triangle.
	56th (London) Division	A black cat on a red background.
2nd Battalion	Never wore a sign until they joined the Guards Armoured Division in February 1945.	The ever open eye.

APPENDIX F

	Formation	Sign
3RD BATTALION	Guards Armoured Division	The ever open eye.
	15th Scottish Division	Scottish lion rampant, set in a yellow circle with a white border, on a black square.
	2nd Army	A blue cross on a white shield with a crusader's sword on the upright of the cross, hilt uppermost.
	6th Guards Tank Brigade	A gold sword, point uppermost, set in the centre of a white shield and superimposed on a bend of Household Brigade colours.
4TH BATTALION	32nd Guards Brigade	Eight-pointed star of eight diamonds, four red, four blue alternatively.
	Guards Armoured Division	The ever open eye.
S COMPANY	6th Armoured Division	A clenched mailed fist in white on a square black background. *N.B.* This Company also wore the red numerals II of the 2nd Bn. Coldstream Guards of which Bn. it formed a part.
X COMPANY	Guards Armoured Division	The ever open eye.

Since there was little scope for Regimental difference on the universal Battledress, what innovations in dress the Regiment did make were mainly with head-dress. The standard head-dress for all ranks during World War II was the khaki Service Dress cap and as has already been noted the First Battalion custom of wearing a Royal Stuart tartan patch on officers' caps soon spread to the whole Regiment. Other ranks were issued with a stiff S.D. cap but many of the old pre-war soft variety, or privately bought copies with rings of soft stitching on the soft peak, survived until the last month of the war.

For a fatigue cap, the Regiment was first issued with a universally unpopular khaki "fore-and-aft", designed for wear on the side of the head and therefore very liable to fall off during drill. The Fifth Battalion found them particularly unsuitable for skiing. In due course these were replaced by khaki or black berets or by an ungainly beret-like headgear made of several pieces of rough cloth stitched together, called a Cap G.S. The Third Battalion wore black berets throughout the time that they were armoured, the officers even wearing them with Service Dress.

In Italy berets were more an item of dress than of uniform.[1] At first black was the only colour procurable, and the officers and many other ranks of the Second Battalion wore these, but later on all ranks of the First Battalion and of S Company did their best to acquire khaki ones, which were on issue to Motor Battalions in Armoured Divisions. Nevertheless, some black ones were still to be seen as late as 1945. The stocking cap was often worn in the line, particularly before the advent of the beret, which was eventually replaced for other ranks by the hideous Cap G.S.

When the Second Battalion reformed in Scotland in 1944 they were issued with Caps G.S. for all other ranks, and in order that the officers should be able to appear on parade dressed similarly to their men, special Caps G.S. of a fine khaki cloth were made for them. These hats, which became known as Killwhillies, had a patch of Royal Stuart tartan as a backing to the cap-star but they were not worn for very long and were soon replaced by khaki berets. This practice of wearing a patch of tartan-backing on officers' berets found favour in all battalions except the Third, and in many cases the metal cap-star was replaced by an embroidered star taken from the shoulder strap of a then unwanted blue "jumper".

The Guardsman's cap-star remained the same throughout the war. In 1943 an attempt was made by Ordnance, no doubt with the laudable intention of saving metal, to foist on all regiments a plastic substitute for the usual brass. The plastic star was very ugly and extremely unpopular, and it was worn only at the last resort when no brass ones were available.

Transfers of forage cap diceing, three red and two white squares, were worn on each side of the steel helmet by all battalions throughout the war; after any time in the line these distinctions became few and far between.

III. 1945 TO DATE

After the First World War eighteen months elapsed before Full Dress was restored: after the Second World War it took exactly twice as long. To make

[1] On 3rd February 1944 the following variations in head-dress were noted by an officer of the Second Battalion:

(1) *"Tin Hats"*—with or without diceing, and with or without camouflage nets.
(2) *Service Dress Caps*—usually threadbare and dirty. Some officers had lost their silver stars, and had Cairo imitations in base metal which did not shine.
(3) *Berets.*
    (a) Small black, with tartan flash.
    (b) Large black, Chasseur-type.
    (c) Small brown, with or without tartan flash; some with proper silver stars, some with embroidered stars. "X—— has a brass shoulder star on top of a flash, which is terrible!"
    (d) One man, who had been in the Commandos, wore a green beret.
(4) *Stocking Caps*—worn by some with a silver star.
(5) *Blue Fatigue Caps.*
(6) *"Fore-and-Afts"*—the khaki Cap F.S.
(7) *Service Dress Caps—Other Ranks*—some still of the old soft variety.
(8) *American Stocking Caps*—made of wool with a little peak.
(9) *Balaclava Helmets.*
(10) *Glengarrys*—among the Pipers, very ragged.
(11) *Balmoral Bonnet*—"just creeping in" among the Pipers.

matters worse, whereas in 1920, there had been a gap of six years without tunics, in 1948 this gap had widened to nine years, which, in a matter of such complicated detail, is more than the average memory can easily span.

Once again the wearing of "Blue" in the evenings by officers and by a few senior warrant officers who happened to own it heralded the return to peacetime uniform. History was also allowed to repeat itself when it fell to the Second Battalion of the Regiment to be the first to wear Full Dress. This Battalion had mounted the first King's Guard to wear Full Dress after the 1914–1918 War and now they were intended to be the first of the Brigade of Guards to Troop their Colour on the Horse Guards Parade in Full Dress since 1939. There had been a King's Birthday Parade in 1947, but that had been in Battledress for all except the mounted officers, who had worn Service Dress. Now, in 1948, the bearskin caps, tunics and buff equipment of pre-war days were brought out of store, some not in the best of condition, and the Regiment was hard put to it to find tailors to fit the clothing to the men chosen to wear it.

The greatest difficulty of all was the fitting out of the officers and since none were expected, and indeed none could have afforded, to buy Full Dress, appeals were made to ex-officers of the Regiment to give, loan or sell any items of Full Dress or equipment that they had. Such second-hand articles as resulted from this appeal were placed in a pool and distributed as Public Clothing to those officers who were selected to wear it. Those who could not be fitted had to be left off parade and in 1948 no-one worried too much if an Ensign appeared in a Field officer's tunic or if he carried a light sword instead of a heavy one. Other ranks Full Dress also became public property and there was so little of it at first that only men required for an actual parade were issued with it. It was for these reasons that the mere threat of rain was sufficient to cancel the 1948 King's Birthday Parade after the crowds had gathered and the troops were about to leave their barracks.

The "Guard Order" worn by other ranks on the rehearsals for this ill-fated parade was identical to 1939 as regards dress and only slightly dissimilar in equipment. The rifle and the short-blade bayonet were new, whilst the only equipment carried was a belt and bayonet frog; capes were not worn at all but kept in transport on the edge of the parade ground in case of rain. This "Guard Order" has not been altered in any way since, but because of its greatly enhanced value and also because there are no longer "second tunics" for everyone, "walking out" in Full Dress has had to be stopped, at great loss to the London scene, and "swagger canes" have disappeared as a result.

The officers for this 1948 parade were also dressed exactly as they had been in 1939 and they still are, although their new tunics are now made of material very inferior to that which was used before the war. After this false start, Full Dress did not return for the Public Duties in London until 1949, by which time there were so few Foot Guards battalions in the country that most of the guards were being mounted by Regiments of the Line.

Although no comprehensive Army Order appeared after the Second World War to limit the dress of the Brigade of Guards as it had in 1920, there were just as many economies and some were very similar to those of

1920. The main losers in 1948 were the musicians of the Regimental Band who were entirely shorn of their former splendour and now have to wear ordinary rank and file tunics in place of their pre-war gold-braided and winged Musicians' tunics. At the time of writing there is no sign that this unfortunate economy, which so greatly diminishes the splendour of the Massed Bands on the Queen's Birthday Parade, is anything else but permanent. Musicians' forage caps with gold gimping on the peak—one row for a Musician, two for a Corporal and three for a Sergeant—have also been abandoned as have the distinctive Musicians' swords. Drum-Majors, who for a time also wore rank and file tunics, have, since the 1953 Coronation, worn tunics proper to their appointment; they have also continued to wear their State Dress on appropriate occasions.

That distinguished garment, the officer's blue frock coat, also a casualty in 1920, was not immediately re-introduced, although, as before, it was not long in being rescued from oblivion. It can now be worn only by the Officers Commanding the Regiment and Battalions, by their Adjutants and by the Director of Music, and to date they have had to rely on the stocks of old frock coats which exist in the Regimental Store. Officers' Mess kit has taken ten years to emerge from the aftermath of wartime economy and it has now been authorised by the Army Council; it will be the same as that worn before 1939. Ankle boots for officers, now known as "George Boots" have again made their appearance as an economy from wellingtons but, as in the 1920's, the latter are generally preferred and a number were even issued by Ordnance at the time of the 1953 Coronation.

In Malaya, from 1948 to 1951, the Second Battalion wore jungle green clothing for the first time. Apart from the colour, the floppy jungle hats and the high laced jungle boots, there was little difference from the khaki drill that they had worn during the war. On special occasions their Pipers and Drummers, and those of the First Battalion in Egypt from 1951 to 1954, wore a white cotton jacket over kilts and blue trousers respectively, the former wearing Glengarry caps with Blackcocks feathers, and the latter forage caps.

As before the war, officers have continued to turn to the blue "Fatigue" cap edged with gold lace, which opens out to form a complete Balaclava helmet, whenever they have gone on board ship. These useful caps are also worn in camp or with "Blue" or with tropical Mess kit in the evenings.

In 1951 details of the new Number One Dress—the new pattern "walking out" and ceremonial dress for the British army—were announced. For officers this consists of the pre-war "Blue" with the jacket cut slightly differently from the old Blue "jumper"; the new version having vents in the skirts and detachable shoulder straps. On "non-ceremonial" occasions this order of dress is worn with a Sam Browne belt and sword, but when "ceremonial" is ordered the plain blue shoulder straps are replaced by "boards" similar to the shoulder straps of a tunic, a gold "Guard-of-Honour" sash is worn in place of the Sam Browne and the sword is worn with gold slings and gold sword knot. Mounted officers wear overalls and spurs with Number One Dress and the forage cap is the only permissible head-dress. Officers who have joined the Regiment since 1951 possess this dress and wear it when others wear "Blue", but to date only individual

APPENDIX F

officers (e.g. Staff-Officers and the Adjutant at Sandhurst) have worn "Number One Dress, ceremonial" and none has yet worn either form on parade with the Regiment.

Other ranks' Number One Dress is very similar to that worn by the officers and consists of the same type of blue jacket without vents or interchangeable shoulder straps, but with the same Regimental button spacing. Blue serge trousers and a forage cap complete this dress which is worn with a buff belt on parade and a cloth belt at other times. So far this dress has only been issued in the Regiment to non-commissioned officers, although the Regimental Band and the Pipers and Drummers were provided with it as a special case for their historic tour of Canada and the United States in the autumn of 1955.

Number Three Dress, a tropical version of Number One, has also been authorised, but, so far, has only been worn by one officer in the Regiment. It is a white drill uniform cut in exactly the same fashion as Number One Dress and worn with the same accoutrements. At the time of writing nothing is known of Number Two Dress.

At home and abroad Service Dress still survives, although declared to be obsolete immediately after the war. Officers are no longer allowed to buy it new, but a great number who still have it in their possession wear this useful form of dress off parade, whilst for mounted officers, a Service Dress jacket, field boots and breeches still remains the only possible order of dress to wear on a horse when parading with troops dressed in Battledress. In hot climates the gaberdine form of Service Dress remain the officers' smartest khaki uniform. The Regimental Band also continues to wear Service Dress and it is still worn on occasions by the Pipers and Drummers, though this will presumably cease when—and if—Number One Dress becomes a universal issue.

In 1950 the forage cap was allowed to be worn with Battledress by Warrant Officers, Staff-Sergeants, Drummers and a few special persons such as orderlies and in succeeding years as these caps became more plentiful, they were worn with Battledress by all other ranks. They are now an authorised issue. Occasionally, mainly in Germany, officers are ordered to do likewise, but this order of dress, which includes a Sam Browne belt, is most unpopular. Warrant Officers and Staff-Sergeants have been wearing their swords on white buff belts when on parade since 1948, and when off parade Regimental Sergeant-Majors and Drill Sergeants wear Sam Browne belts. For "walking out" in Battledress all other ranks may now wear a forage cap with a buff belt *or* a Service Dress cap with a web belt, but not a combination of these.

The beret now issued to the Regiment is a dark blue woollen one.

In conclusion, mention must be made of the uniform worn by the Colonel-in-Chief, Her Majesty the Queen, when she attends her Birthday Parade on the years when a battalion of the Scots Guards is furnishing the Colour and its Escort; this occurred in the first year of Her Majesty's reign, 1952, when the Second Battalion trooped its Queen's Colour, and would have occurred in 1955 when the parade at which the First Battalion was to have trooped its Colour was cancelled owing to the rail strike. Her Majesty wears a Scots Guards Field Officer's tunic with "Guard-of-Honour" sash over a blue riding habit. Her Majesty's cap has been a blue tricorn trimmed with black fur with a backing to the cap-star similar to the blackcock feathers worn by Pipers; the cap-star which Her Majesty has worn has been that presented to her by the members of the Third Guards Club in 1952.

Index

Note: No entry is made in this Index for names in the Roll of Honour (Appendix A) or for those in the Nominal Roll of Officers (Appendix E), since both these Appendices are arranged in alphabetical order.

Index

Aa, river: Holland, 380; Germany, 427
Aamsche Bridge, 378
Aarvold, Lt. O. B. W., 543
Abercromby, Maj. R. A., xx, 59
Aberdeen, 490
Achnacarry, 56, 335
Acland, Capt. J. H. B., xx
Acroma Box, 97
Acuto, 239
Adair, Maj.-Gen. Sir A., 325, 329, 368, 421, 458
Adams, S/Clerk R., 541
Adjutants: Battalion, 539; Regimental, 539
African campaign, 73–161
Africa Star, 190
Agedabia, attack on, 91–3; 94, 120
Agheila, 93–4
Ahlebrandt, 426
Airlie, Maj. Earl of, 543
Aitken, PSM J., 543
Aitken, Sgt. L., 441, 532
Alamein Line, defence of, 108–14
Albert Canal, 369
Aleppo, 119
Alexander, F.-M. Earl, 115, 173, 196, 201, 224, 231, 263, 287, 296, 316, 319, 328
Alexander, Gdsm. (1st Bn.), 147
Alexandria, 10, 12
Alexandria, H.M. Queen, 12
Algeria, 131–4
Algiers, 133
Allan, Sgt. J. M., 484, 537
Allardyce, Sgt. J., 306, 530
Aller, river, 439, 449
Allied Regiments, *see* Royal Australian Regt. and Winnipeg Grenadiers
Alpon, 417–19
Alston, Maj. E. R. M., 64, 534
Alston, Col. F. G., 6
Altencelle, 439
American Army, *see* United States
Amerika, 389
Amiriya, 108, 114
Ancona, 298
Anderson, Lt.-Gen. Sir K., 131
Andfjellneset, 43
Andio canal, 311–14
Anholt, 431

Antelat, 94
Antwerp, 369, 379, 413
Anzio, 58, 196–227
Appelhausen, 426
Appendices, responsibility for, xx, 501–98
Aprilia (*see also* "Factory"), 203
Arber, TQMS A., 554, 555
Arbuthnot, Lt. A. R. C., 453 n
Arce, 236
Archer, Capt. (QM) L. C., 60, 287, 534, 540, 541
Ardennes offensive, 391–3
Arezzo Line, 247, 259–61, 282–3; city taken, 261
Argenta, 269; Battle of, 302–9
Arms:
    Anti-tank guns, 2-pdr, 96, 98–100; 6-pdr, 99–100, 108, 113; *see* Medenine; 137, 149–50, 201, 204, 220, 222
    Anti-tank rifle, 7, 95
    "Bazooka" (German), tactics described, 345
    Bren, 7, 23, 43–4, 61 *et passim*
    Grenades, Hawkins, 123, 207
    Lewis gun, 7, 67
    Mortars, 2-inch, 7, 29, 50 *et passim*; 3-inch, 29, 482 *et passim*
    P.I.A.T. (Anti-tank bomb launcher), 149, 167, 260, 313–14, 352, 357, 371–6
    Rifle (Lee-Enfield ·303), No. 4, 23; No. 5 in Malaya, 487
    Sten, 371
    Vickers medium M.G., 7, 96, 112, 217–19, 272
    "Wasp" flame-thrower, 296, 302, 454
Armies (British):
    First, 118, 122; Tunisia 131–55; 157
    Second, 332; N.-W. Europe, 337–95, 384, 421–60
    Eighth, Desert, 85–115; Tunisia, 121–31, 157; Italy, 172, 231–62, 296–318
    of the Rhine, 463–6, 492
Army Groups:
    15th (and A.A.I.), Italy, 168–316
    21st, N.-W. Europe, 337–460
Arnhem, 377–8
Arno, river, 255, 264; crossing of, 265
Arras, 368

Arromanches, 338, 340
Artillery system described, 207, 213–14
Artlenburg, 446
Ashburner, Lt. K. A. R. (5th Bn.), 557
Ashcroft, L/Sgt. R., 530
Ashley-Carter, Lt. P. C., 551
Asprey, Lt. M. D., 546
Asten, 384
Astley-Corbett, Capt. Sir F., 67, 98, 156, 170, 540, 549–51
Astrone, river, 243–5
Atkinson-Clark, Capt. P. G., 64, 192, 540, 556
Atrocities, 266, 446
Auchinleck, F.-M. Sir C., 41, 42, 48, 83
Au Cornu, 354
Australian Army:
gunners, 85; 9th Div., 78
Authorship, xvii
Avellino, 174

Baalbeck, 118
Badenstedt, 455
Badges, plastic, 594
Bagnoregio, 241
Bailey, Sgt. D., 237
Bailie, Lt. D. M. H., 152, 210, 544, 545
Baillie, Lt. M. E. V., 220, 546
Bain, Pipe-Maj. P., 335, 397, 459, 552, 556
Balcombe, L/Sgt. R., 464, 531
Balfour, Capt. A. M., 178, 221, 531, 543
Balfour, Capt. E. A. G., 209, 210, 221, 232, 544–6
Balfour, Col. E. W. S., 24, 26, 27, 49, 55–8, 328, 534, 538
Balfour, Maj. P. E. G., 328, 355, 362, 386, 394, 405, 535, 439, 540, 554
Balfour, Lt. R. A. E., 173, 551
Balfour, Gdsm. (2nd Bn.), 96
Ballantine-Dykes, Col. F. H., 534
Ballantine-Dykes, Maj. T. L., 76, 104, 115, 120, 540, 548, 549
Baltic, advance to, 438, 446–9
Banana Ridge, 136–8
Band, Regimental, 13, 59, 333, 465, 488; American Tour, 495
Bando, 305–9
Bankes, Capt. D. L., xx, 348, 357, 387, 405, 554, 555
Bank of England, 14
Baqqush Box, 83
Barber, Sgt. W. A., 141, 307, 530
Bardia, 78
"Bare Arse" ridge, 180
Barletta, 196
Barne, Lt. J. M., 356, 362, 444, 532, 554
Barne, Lt.-Col. M. E. St. J., 136, 140, 144, 145, 149, 160, 197, 538, 539, 544

Barne, Capt. N. H., 112, 130, 184, 417, 531, 550–2
Barnstaple, RSM A., 396, 541, 543, 544, 552
Bartholomew, Lt. P. H., 313, 530, 547
Barttelot, Brig. Sir W., 351, 365
Barwick, RSM J., 541
Bastia, 264
Batang Kali, 478
Bates, Cpl. R., 204, 216, 530
Battleaxe, 80–3
Battle drill, 55, 62, 157
Battle honours, 13, 490
Battipaglia, 168–73
Batu Arang, 477–83
Bax, Capt. M. G., 485
Baxter, Lt. J. E., 252, 278
Bayeux, 338
Baynes, Lt. D. C. (5th Bn.), 557
Bazooka, see Arms
Beauvais, 368
Beckett, Lt. W., 171, 551
Beda Fomm, 90, 94
Bedburg, 405
Beedie, L/Cpl. (1st Bn.), 141
Beeringen, 369–72
Beeson, 2/Lt. M. F., 112, 120, 549
Beeson, Capt. N. W., 348, 553, 554
Begg, CSM J., 212, 544, 545
Beja, 134
Belgium, 368–77, 391–3, 398–9, 412
Bell, L/Sgt. (1st Bn.), 310
Bella and Bertha, 3
Bellizzi, 170n
Bellona, 177
Belsen, 446
Beltrum, 431
Ben Gardane, 121
Benghazi, 93
Bennett, Sgt. F., 135, 530
Bentley, 340
Benvignante canal, 308
Benzadrine tablets, 179
Berberh Wood, 409
Berge, 436
Berg-en-Dal, 401
Beringen, 387, 389
Berridge, Lt. R. A., 436, 552
Bethell, Lt. Hon. D. A., 139, 140, 143, 144, 157, 263, 530, 544–6
Bevensen, 446
Bir Belefaa, 97, 101
Bir Hakeim, 90, 97, 100, 101
Bir Weir, 78
Bird, Lt. J. R. G. (5th Bn.), 557
Birgden, 391
Bizerta, 153, 154, 161, 196
Black, L/Sgt. A., 314, 530
Blackcock (exercise), 332
Blackett-Ord, Lt. A. J., 222

INDEX

Blackett-Ord, Capt. J. C., 242, 245, 546, 556
Blakeley, RSM W., 541
Bland, Lt. D. J. N., 131, 550
Bland, Lt.-Col. J. E. M., 68, 69, 334, 534, 539, 540, 556
Bland, Maj. S. C. M., 312, 487, 547
Bland, Capt. T. R., 252, 530, 546, 551, 556
Blandy, Lt. P. B. J., 285, 301, 547
Blitterswijk, 390
"Blitz, The", 67, 68
Blois, Capt. Sir G. R. E., 211, 530, 535, 545
Blue-coat (Caumont), 332, 342–50
Blundell, Maj. C. V. R. B.-H.-, 535, 556
Blyth, Capt. H. W., 556
Blythswood, 2/Lt. Lord, 503
Bocage, 333; described, 343, 345, 350; 352
Bodo, 31, 33; retreat to, 41–6; 47–8
Boesensell, 426
Bogle, Gdsm. (3rd Bn.), 448
Bois du Homme, 342–50
Bokel, 458
Bologna, 263, 267–8; captured, 309
Bone, 133
Bonninghardt, 415–17
Bootle-Wilbraham, Brig. L., 334
Borculo, 431
Bordon, 19, 21–4, 25
Borgo San Lorenzo, 286
Borj Frendj, 153
Borkenes, 48
"Bou, The", *see* Djebel Bou Aoukaz
Bou Ficha, 130
Bourdjine, 129
Bovington, 327
Bowen-Colthurst, Lt. C. P. R., 170, 534, 551
Bowes-Lyon, Lt. the Hon. J. P., 84
Boyle, Gdsm. J., 104
Boyle, Capt. Hon. P. J., 86, 548
Bracken, Sgt. W. R., 25
Bradley, CSM F., 543
Bradshaw, Maj.-Gen. W. P. A., 11, 13, 55, 56, 534, 538, 539
Braid, RSM J., 541
Brand, Gdsm. W., 362
Bree, 393
Breistrand, 31
Bremen, 449, 455
Bremner, L/Sgt. A., 279, 330
Brevity, attack at Halfaya, 78–9
Bridgeman, Lt. H. R., 237, 558
Brigades (British), *see also* Guards:
  Airlanding
    6th, 422

  Armoured
    2nd, 102
    4th, 80, 82–3, 86–7, 102, 113
    7th, 78, 80–3
    8th, 122
    22nd, 86, 122
    26th, 258, 259
  Commando
    2nd, 299, 300
  Infantry
    1st, 8
    2nd, 138, 197–201, 215
    3rd, 142, 150, 209, 212–15
    9th, at Winnekendonk, 407–12
    13th, 10
    18th, 226
    29th, 54
    36th, 134
    44th, 388, 400, 406
    46th, 380; *see* Tilburg; 400, 406, 445
    61st, 258, 291
    69th, 114
    71st, 453–4
    131st, 122, 124, 125
    139th, 174
    150th, 99
    167th, 168, 179, 186, 300–1, 308–309
    168th, 179
    169th, 168, 175, 179, 186–7, 308–10
    185th, 410
    227th: supported by 3rd Bn., *see* Caumont, Estry, Peel, Siegfried Line; 406; Celle, Uelzen; presents pipes to 3rd Bn., 449; 465
  Parachute
    2nd, 303
Briggs, Capt. A. J. (RAMC), 463, 552
Briggs Plan, 482, 486
Brignano, 174
Bristowe, Capt. A. P., 540
Broekenhuizen, 390
Bromfield, CSM E., 549, 550
Bromhead, CSM J., 548
Brooke, Lt. R. N., 105, 549
Brough, L/Sgt. W. G., 531
Brown, Gdsm. A., 106, 530
Brown, Capt. A. B., 137, 544
Brown, 2/Lt. A. B. K., 562
Brown, RSM G., 390, 444, 466, 541, 544, 555
Brown, Sgt. J., 532
Brown, CSM T., 238, 260–1, 532, 558
Brown, Maj. W. J., 130, 155, 531, 540, 558
Brown, Gdsm. W., 375
Brown, Sgt. (3rd Bn.), 410
Browning, Lt.-Gen. Sir F., 54
Brownlees, Gdsm. (2nd Bn.), 119

INDEX

Bruce, Maj. Hon. B., 74, 229, 531, 548
Bruce, Capt. I. S. R., 405, 447, 532, 554, 555
Bruce, Lt. Lord, 356, 362, 554
Bruch, 410
Brunen, 423
Brussels, 368, 391, 393, 421
Bryson, L/Cpl. J., 39, 195, 530
Buckle, Capt. C. R. S., 67, 185, 194–5, 297, 551
Budge, Lt. V. A. P. (5th Bn.), 557
"Buffalos", *see* "Fantails"
Buldern, 426
Bulkeley, Lt.-Col. T. F. R., xx, 148, 257, 297, 318, 495, 497, 534, 538, 539, 544, 547
Bull, Maj. R. H., 66, 139, 140, 201, 206, 212, 530, 544, 545
Bull, Capt. W. P., 361, 553–5
Buonriposo ridge, 204, 213, 222
Buq Buq, 83, 84
Burden, Capt. J. W., 340n
Burgess, Lt. W. M. (R.A.M.C.), 45, 543
Burnett, Maj. G. P., 105, 549
Burnett, Gdsm. J., 373
Burnett, Capt. R. W. O., 359, 405, 553, 554
Burns, Maj. J. A., 325, 553
Burt, Capt. C. S. S., 105, 535, 549
Butler, Lt. Hon. P. H. S. D., 141, 147, 217, 219, 226, 544, 545
Butter, Maj. D. H., 106, 115, 117, 229, 531, 549
Buxton, Lt. Sir T., 441

Caen, 338–40, 342
Cagny, 339
Cairo, 10, 76, 495
Calabritto, 181
Calcar, 404
Callow, Sgt. (Coldm. Gds.), 63
Calvocoressi, Maj. I. M., 87, 103, 113, 229, 531, 534, 549
Cambrai, 379
Cambridge, Capt. L. D., 191, 550, 551, 552
Cameron, Lt.-Col. A. E., 120, 122, 415, 416, 419, 473, 485, 488, 531, 539, 540, 549, 550, 552
Cameron, Capt. G., 382, 385, 532, 554, 555
Camino Griff, newspaper, 185
Campbell, Lt. C., 402
Campbell, Capt. C. M., 417, 456–7, 531, 552
Campbell, Maj-Gen. J., v.c., 85
Campbell, Lt. R. D., 130
Campi, 246
Campoleone, 202, 209, 213, *see also* Gold Flake

Canadian Army:
 First Can. Army, 393, 399
 I Can. Corps, 296
 7th Can. Inf. Bde., 404–6
 Can. Scottish, 405
 Regina Rifles, 404–5
 Royal Canadian Regt., 256
 Winnipeg Rifles, 404–5
Canal de Deurne, 387
Canal Zone, Suez, 77, 115, 494
Canale Bianco, 311–14
Candlish, Gdsm. (3rd Bn)., 428
Canosa di Puglia, 196
Canteloup, 354, 355, 357
Canterbury, Depot at, 13; service at, 333
Canton, 9
Cape, Lt. D. P. S., 555
Cape Bon, 153
Capelln, 437
Capri, 228
Capua, 175–7
Capuzzo, 78
Cardiff, Lt.-Col. E. B. W., 534, 535
Cardiff, Capt. M. H., 556
Cardiff, Lt.-Col. R. D., 30, 245–90 *passim, esp.* 255, 268; 538, 543, 546 556
Carnegie, Maj. R. A., 194, 248–9, 253, 288, 486, 546, 556
Carpenter-Garnier, Lt. J. P., 174, 551
Carpiquet Airfield, 338
Carris, Lt. B. D., 99, 549
Carroceto, 215–24
Carruthers, L/Sgt. W., 533
Carso Hills, 318
Casa Borgazzetto, 308
Casa Budriolo, 291
Casa Valla, 289
Caserta, 175, 197, 315
Cashmore, L/Cpl. G. A., 212, 530
Castel del Rio, 283, 285, 291, 294
Castel di Brolio, 246, 249
Castel di Sangro, 231–2
Castellammare di Stabia, 229
Castelnuovo Berardenga, 246
Castiglione dei Pepoli, 268, 269, 271, 276, 290
Caterham, *see* Guards Depot
Cathcart, Maj. Earl, 345, 357, 359, 385, 393, 407, 410–12, 423, 532, 539, 553–5
Catling, L/Cpl. (2nd Bn.), 484
Cator, Maj.-Gen. A. B. E., 6
Catt, Maj. P. H., 76
"Cauldron, The", 100–1
Caulfield, Gdsm. H., 530
Caumont, Battle of, 342–50; Gen. Dempsey's views on, 465
Cayzer, Lt. Sir N., 171, 551
Celle, 438–41
"Celtic Group", 399

INDEX 605

Ceprano, 238
Cerreto Guidi, 265
Cetona, 242
Chadwick, Gdsm. W., 172, 179, 452, 453, 531
Chamberlayne, Maj. C. H. L. F. M. T., 539
Chamonix, 24–5, 324
Chaplin, Lt. P. S. (5th Bn.), 557
Chapman, RSM J., 541, 548–50
Charrington, Lt. R. N. (5th Bn.), 557
Charruba, 95
Charteris, Lt. H. F. G., 238, 259–60, 532, 558
Chebba, nautical exploit at, 129
Chelsea Barracks: Depot at, 59; Holding Bn. at, 68
Chênedollé, 358–63
Cherua, 95
Chianti Mts., 249–53
Chichester, Capt. Earl of, 332
Chigwell, 324–8
China, 2nd Bn. in, 8–10
Chisholm, Gdsm. J., 145–6, 528–30
Chislehurst, 55
Churchill, Sir Winston, 67, 158, 328, 332
Churchill tank, 329–31, 333, 349; life in, 350–1, 386; tank names, 381
Cigar: see also "Fly-over", 202, 203, 224
Cisterna, 203, 213
Civita Castellana, 241
Clark, CSM A., 543
Clark, Capt. H. B., 177, 185, 341, 551, 552
Clark, Gen. Mark (U.S.A.), 167, 173, 296
Clarke, Capt. C. J. O., 405
Clarke, Lt.-Col. J. R. S., 87, 92, 110, 112, 131, 531, 540, 549, 550, 553
Clarke, Capt. R. T. S., 172, 551
Clarke, Rev. V. C., 115, 548, 549
Clarkson, Gdsm. D., 530
Clement, Sgt. J., 279, 530
Cleve, 400–6, 413
Clive, Brig. A. F. L., commands 24th Gds. Bde., 225–88 *passim*
"Clo", house at Anzio, 208
Cloppenburg 437
Clowes, Col. H. N., xx, 47, 49, 320, 396, 430, 457n, 460, 461, 464, 469, 497, 531, 538, 539, 543, 552
Club, Third Guards, 490, 598
Coatbridge, 49
Coates, Lt.-Col. R. E. J. C. M. (Coldm. Gds.), 258, 260, 285, 292, 295
Coats, Capt. A. J., 80, 105, 548
Coats, Lt.-Col. J. S. (Coldm. Gds.), 21–6, 324, 539, 557
Cobbold, Lt.-Col. J. M., 58
Coccanile, 311
Cochrane-Barnett, Lt. J. N., 105, 549
Cockburn, Sgt. H., 530

Cocker, Gdsm. W. G., 275, 530
Codford, 328
Coghill, Maj. C. A. R., 78, 82, 83, 87, 96, 534, 540, 548
Coghill, 2/Lt. H. F. D., 6
Coke, Maj. Hon. J. S., 534
Coke, Maj. R. L., 182, 184, 261, 282, 292–4, 300, 310, 531, 532, 547, 553, 558
Coke, Maj. Viscount, 79, 548
Colchester, 491
Coldstream Guards:
　1st Bn., 351, 419
　2nd Bn., 8, 134, 228; see S Company; 297, 299–314 *passim*
　3rd Bn., 11; Africa, 76–84, 90, 93; Knightsbridge, 97–102, 106–7; Composite Bn. with 2 S.G., 108–14; Medenine, 122–3; "The Horseshoe", 127; 158; Italy, 172–3, 177, 181, 184, 187, 189, 191, 193; transferred to 24th Gds. Bde., *which see, esp.* 252–3, 271, 275, 280; return home, 297
　4th Bn., 325, 344, 347, 354–5, 393, 409, 424–8, 441, 445
　5th Bn., 334, 360, 362, 415, 419, 450, 455
Coleman, Sgt. T., 536
Cologne, 463, 465–6
Colombelles, 351
Colonels-in-Chief and Colonels, 538
Colours, 13, 319; 3rd Bn's., 324; 464, 465, 469, 471, 475, 488–90, 492
Colquhoun, Lt..D. A., 290, 301, 547
Column warfare, 83–5, 87–90, 95–6
Colville, Brig. E. C., 442
Colvin, Brig. R. R. B., 132, 137, 185, 187, 190
Commanding Officers of Bns., 538–9
Commandos, 331
　Household Brigade, 75
　9th, 190, 303
　42nd, 300
　43rd, 302
Compo Rations, 173, 206
Comyns, Lt. P. W., 450
Connaught, H.R.H. Duke of, 10
Connell, Gdsm. A., 452
Connor, Gdsm. G. H., 183, 531
Connor, Gdsm., J., 81
Conscripts, 57, 60, 469, 473, 497
Consuma, 281
Cook, Capt (QM) J., 540, 541
Coonie, CSM A., 276, 546
Copland, Gdsm. (1st Bn.), 267
Copland, Gdsm. P., 439
Copparo, 311
Cork and Orrery, Adm. Earl of, 29, 48
Cornezzano, 283–5

INDEX

Corps, British:
  V, 138, 152, 302, 309, 315
  VIII, 332, 342
  IX, 138, 152
  X, 128, 167, 168, 191, 257, 282
  XII, 380, 437, 449
  XIII, 85, 87, 90, 241, 257, 259, 264, 281, 317–18
  XXX, 85, 126, 333, 343, 399, 400, 422, 430, 437, 449
Coronations, 1936, 12; 1953, 492
Cortona, 259
Cory-Wright, Lt. J. F., 436
Courteil, 352
Covenanter tank, 328
Cows, regimental, 3
Cox, L/Cpl. P. G., 530
Crabbe, Maj. A. D. B., 28, 35, 39, 40, 534, 543, 553, 557
Crabbe, 2/Lt. P. G., 565
Crabbe, P/Maj., 462
Craggs, SSM C., 554
Craig, P/Maj. C., 555
Craig, Sgt. W., 534
Crawford, Gdsm. D., 532
Crichton-Stuart, Maj. M. D. D., 74, 86, 95, 117, 118, 122, 127, 129, 154, 169, 170, 490, 531, 550, 551
Crichton-Stuart, Maj. Lord R., 65, 540, 552, 556
Crick, Lt. J. L. M., 555
Critchley, 2/Lt. J. G., 92, 548
Crittenberger, Lt.-Gen. W. (U.S.A.), 264, 276
Cromwell tank, 365, 399, 431
Cross, Lt. Viscount, 551
Cross, Gdsm. E. G., 530
Crozier, Lt. (R.E.M.E.), 121
Crusader offensive (1941), 85–93
Crutchley, Lt. E., 245, 546
Cumming, Maj. E. L. T., 227
Cumming, Capt. J., 152, 544
Cuninghame, Lt. J. S., 130, 178, 550
Cunningham, Lt.-Gen. Sir A., 85, 87
Cunningham, Capt. C. R. T., 347, 348, 553
Currie, Lt. J. L. R., 441
Curtis, RSM F., 541, 543
Curzon, Capt. F. J. N., 555
Cuthbert, Maj. H. D., 230, 233, 237, 545, 558
Cuthbert, Maj. S. J., 330, 348, 349, 554
Cutler, Capt. (QM) E. T., 540
Cuxhaven, 454, 460–1
Cyprus, 491, 493–4

Daba, 83, 85, 106, 120
Dalrymple, Maj. Hon. C. J., 259, 294, 547, 558
Dalrymple, Col. Viscount, 56, 65, 132, 136, 227, 328, 464, 469, 470, 472, 483, 488–9, 495, 534, 538, 539, 544
Dalsklubben, 35–40
Daly, Maj. D. R., 543
Dalziel, L/Cpl. C., 533
Damascus, 117
Damm, 424
Dannfald, Sgt. M., 372–7, 421, 532
Davidson, L/Sgt. J., 234
Davidson, C/Sgt. J., 534
Davidson, 2/Lt. N. G. R., 535, 548
Davies, L/Sgt. T., 124, 130, 531
Dawnay, Maj. R. (Coldm. Gds.), 106
Dawson, Lt. P., 105, 549
Deane, Capt. D. H., 546, 547
Decorations, Appx. B, 528 ff
Degener, 427, 429
De Klee, Capt. M. P. J., 485, 540
Dempsey, Gen. Sir M., 390, 465
Denham, Maj. J. B., 494, 539, 558
Deserters, 277
Desert, life, 89; sores, 84, 89
De Soissons, Lt. V. E. S.-C., 435, 437, 552
Dey, PSM H., 39, 543
Dickie, Capt. A. H. (R.A.M.C.), 548
Dickson, Lt. A. G. (5th Bn.), 557
Dier ez Zor, 119
Dicomano, 282
Dierfordter Wald, 423
Diest, 369
Dinxperlo, 431
Directors of Music, 541
Divisions (British), *see also* Guards:
  Airborne
    6th, 331, 339, 378, 392, 423, 447
  Armoured
    1st, 94, 96–106, 136, 138
    2nd, 78, 122
    6th, Tunisia, 131, 136, 138, 153, 156; Italy, *see* S Company, 302, 309, 311
    7th, Africa, 78, 85, 90, 121, 126, 152–4; N.-W. Europe, 339, 351, 449
    11th, 339, 343, 369, 391, 407, 447
  Infantry
    1st, 1st Bn. in, *see* Tunisia *and* Anzio
    2nd, 492
    3rd, 366, 407–12, 433–4, 491
    4th, 132, 138, 153, 187, 234, 252, 254–5
    5th, 191, 296, 446
    6th, 77
    15th, 3rd Bn. in, 329–32; 3rd Bn. in support of, *see* Caumont, Estry, Tilburg, Peel, Siegfried Line, 406–407, Celle, Uelzen
    43rd, 343, 347–8, 393–5, 403, 437
    46th, 131, 138, 150, 168, 172, 175, 191

Divisions (British)—*cont.*
  Infantry—cont.
    49th, 455
    50th, 107, 128
    51st, 122, 128, 332, 340, 413–14, 458
    52nd, 26, 414, 417, 455
    53rd, 455
    56th, 131; 2nd Bn. in, 167–94; 215; 1st Bn. in, 296–319
    78th, 131, 135, 144, 156, 259, 302, 305, 309
Djebel Bou Aoukaz, 138; 1st attack on, 144–6; 2nd attack on, 147–8; taken, 150
Djebel Hoka, 137
Djebiniana, 129
Dodds, Lt. J. C. (Irish Gds.), 219
Dods, Lt. H. W., 58
Dollard, Lt. R. S., 170, 171, 531, 551
Donald, Gdsm. E., 363
Donsbruggen, 403–4
Doran, Sgt. J., 112, 120
Doria-Pamphili, villa, 297
Dorman, Capt. (QM) W. J., 325, 365, 534, 540, 541, 543, 553, 554
Dormer, Capt. Hon. J. S. P., 554
Dorsten, 424, 425
Douai, 368
Dougall, Gdsm. R. S., 279, 530
Douglas, Lt.-Col. A. V. C., 56, 62, 65, 334–7, 339, 556
Douglas, Sgt. D., 92
Douglas, Maj. (QM) R. C. D., 541, 548, 549, 550
Douglas, Capt. S. R., 552, 567
Douglas, Maj. T. N., 184, 302, 551, 547
Dow, Capt. J. R. (R.A.M.C.), 551
Dowell, Capt. and Dir. of Mus., H. E., 541
Downes, L/Cpl. G., 533
Downie, L/Cpl. W. G., 532
'Dragon Boat", 10
Dress; generally Appx. F, 589 ff; xx, 4, 14, 27, 157, 195, 286, 465, 470–2
Drew, Lt. A., 127, 550
Drewe, Maj. A., 364, 532, 558
Drill, 7, 12
Droop, Capt. R. C. (R.A.M.C.), 553
Drummond, Gdsm. R., 358, 532
Drummond, Capt. D. (Irish Gds.), 216, 218, 219
Drummond-Hay, Lt. A. (Coldm. Gds.), 110
Duberly, 2/Lt. J. A. G., 58
Duberly, Lt. W. M. C., 187
Dudgeon, L/Sgt. G. S., 307, 530
Duff, RQMS D., 444, 447 and n, 554, 555
Duff, Sgt. J., 487
Duff, Gdsm. J. A., 211, 530

Duffin, Maj. C. J. R., 355–6, 439, 445, 554, 555
Dulmen, 426
Dunbar, Brig. C. I. H., xx, 160, 319, 328, 331, 346n, 347, 362, 366. 404 406n, 422, 425, 429, 438, 446, 447, 465, 481, 485, 532, 535, 537–9, 554, 555
Dunbar, L/Cpl. M., 483
Duncalf, Gdsm. R., 531
Dundas, Maj. T. C., 534, 556
Dunderdale, Sgt. M., 375–7, 532
"Dung Farm" at Anzio, 205–13
Dunkirk, 66
Dyle, river, 369
Dyson, L/Sgt. A., 293

Eames, Gdsm. I., his poem, 116
Eastcote, 336
Easton, Gdsm. J., 74
Eastwell Park, 332
Eclipse (disbandment of German Army), 460, 464
Eden, Sir A., 54, 493
Eden, CSM W., 549
Edinburgh, 3, 4, 12, 397, 471, 487–90, 492
Edinburgh, H.R.H. Duke of, 63
Edward VIII, H.M. King, 5, 13
Edwards, Maj-Gen. J. K., 533
Edwards-Moss, Capt. T. R., 556
Egginton House, RHQ at, 59
Egypt, 10, 11, 12, 58, 75–85, 96, 106–16, 119–20, 492–5
Eiklenbosch, 389
Eindhoven, 380, 384
Eisenhower, Gen. D. W., 131, 158; visits 3rd Bn., 390
El Adem, 87, 101
Elbe, river, 446, 459
El Djem, 129
Elizabeth II, H.M. Queen, 470, 497, 597
Elizabeth, H.M. Queen (Queen Mother), 84
Ellinger, Capt. T., 35, 37, 43, 44, 47, 63
Elliot, Lt. Hon. G. E. D., 486
Elliot, Capt. J. W. O., 403, 554
Elliott, Capt. A. K. McC., 425, 555
Elliott, Capt. W. A., 170, 172, 174, 418, 433, 435, 452, 531, 551, 552
Elwes, Maj. J. H., 28, 36, 37, 40, 42, 124, 530, 543, 549, 550
"Embankment, The", 202; *see also* State Express
Ems, river, 432
Enfidaville, 129–31, 158
England, L/Cpl., J., 237
Enschede, 431
Equile Lippizzano, 319
Equipment, *see* Dress *and* Arms

Erskine, Lt. Hon. A. R. H., 185, 434, 452–3, 531, 551, 552
Erskine, Capt. Hon. D. H., vii, 329, 547
Erskine, Maj.-Gen. G. W. E. J., 126
Erskine, Maj.-Gen. I. D., 76, 77, 533, 539, 548
Erskine, Maj. Lord (J. F. H.), 187, 437, 540, 552
Erskine, Brig. M. D., 54, 56, 115, 117, 126, 154, 159, 224, 226, 288, 301–5, 318, 472, 480, 483, 531, 537–40, 550
Erskine Camp, Malaya, 483
Erskine Crum, Maj. V. F., xx, 332, 380, 386, 532, 539, 540, 553, 554
Escaut Canal, 377
Eshede, 441
Esquay, 340
Estry, 353–8
Eves, Lt. H. J. H., 124, 125, 548, 550
Ewart, Mr. Wilfred, 14
Eynatten, 393

"Factory, The", 203; *see also* Aprilia
Fairbairn, Capt. A. S. (R.A.M.C.), 552
Falaise, 339, 366
Falkland Palace, 490
Famagusta, 493
Fane Gladwyn, Lt.-Col. P. F., 79, 475, 481, 484, 485, 491, 494, 537, 538, 548, 549
Fanling, 8
Fano, 298
"Fantails", 299–300, 303
"Farewell to Armour" Parade, 463, 466
Farouk, King, 11, 495
Fauske, 47
Farrell, Maj. C. O'M., 22n, 333, 351, 359, 361, 402, 423, 532, 553–5
Faulkner, Lt.-Col. W. D. (Irish Gds.), 32, 37
F Company on M. Camino, 181–4
Fearfield, Lt. J. M., 410, 425, 438, 555
Feminamorta, 267, 268
Fenton, L/Sgt. A., 389
Ferguson, Sgt. (1st Bn.), 312
Ferguson, L/Sgt. A., 478
Fergusson-Cuninghame, Capt. R. W., 549
Fermor-Hesketh, Lt. Hon. T. S., 6, 540
Fernana, 134
Fiesole, villa Medici at, 281
Finale de Rero, 310–11
Finch, Gdsm. C., 356
Fingland, Gdsm. (2nd Bn.), 99
Finland, 21–6
Finnegan, Capt. J. D. (R.A.M.C.), 550
Finneid, 35–7
Firenzuola, 283
Fisciano, 175
Fisher, Capt. K. N., 540
Fitzalan Howard, Lt.-Col. Hon. M., 347, 356, 359, 362, 365, 497, 532, 537, 539, 553, 554

Fitzherbert-Brockholes, Maj. M. J., 191, 459, 540, 552, 556
Fitz-Wygram, Maj. Sir F., 6
Fiuggi, 239
"Five Year Men", 63, 190, 228
Fletcher, Maj. A. I. D., 354, 357, 381, 385, 430, 448, 540, 554, 555
Fletcher, Maj. C. A., 140, 201, 543–5
Florence, advance to, 241–56; seen, 252; entered, 255
Floyd, L/Cpl. R., 375, 532
"Fly-Over, The", 202; *see also Cigar*
Foley, RSM F., 534, 541, 543–5
Forbes, Capt. D. J., 198, 201, 205–6, 21f 244, 302, 544–7
Forbes, Patrick, xviii
Forbes, L/Sgt. (X Coy.), 421
Forbes Leith, 2/Lt J. A., 480
Forlí, 282, 298–9
Forrester, Capt. J. D., 146, 147, 544, 545
Forret, PSM D., 543
Forster, CSM J., 84
Forster, L/Cpl. J., 377
Forsyth, Sgt. A., 194
Forwood, Maj. D. R., 543
Fossa Benvignante, 308–9
Fossa Marina, 302–7
Foster, Sgt. J. A., 451
Fouchana, 153
Foulstone, CSM J. H., 416, 531, 552
France, *see* Normandy
Frankenstein (armd. car), 483
Fraser, Capt. (QM) D. McG., 145, 396, 486, 540, 541, 544, 552
Fraser, Capt. I. J., 172, 174, 282, 313, 530, 547, 551, 558
Fraser, Capt. J. A. (R.A.), 214
Fraser, L/Sgt. J. N., 130
Fraser, CSM J. R., 557
Fraser, L/Cpl. M. B. P., 533
Fraser, Lt. P. B., 554
Fraser, Sgt. (3rd Bn.), 412, 424
Fraser, Brig. Hon. W., 26–32
French, L/Sgt. J. D., 531
French Army:
  XIX Corps, 131–2
  Chasseurs Alpins, 21, 24, 31
  Free French, 74, 101, 157
  Goums, 188
Frenouville, 339
Freyberg, Lt.-Gen. Sir B., v.c., 317
Frossinone, 239
Fuad, King, 11
Fudella, 288
Funeral ceremonies, 5, 11; George V, 12; George VI, 491
Furstenau, 434
Futa Pass, 267, 283
Fyfe-Jamieson, Lt. D. I., 170, 182, 183, 531, 551

INDEX 609

Gabes, 121
Gab-Gab Gap, 149
Gale, L/Cpl. J. E. S., 67, 207, 530
Gangelt, 394
Gardelletta, 289–90
Garigliano river, 179, 187, 189–95
Garland, Gdsm. A., 535
Garner, RSM H. A., 541, 546, 547, 556
Garnock, Maj. Lord, 31, 35, 39, 543
Garratt, Capt. M.M., 547
Garrdimaou, 133, 134
Garssen, 440–1
Gascoigne, Brig. J. A., 118, 167, 170, 185
Gatehouse, Brig. A., 87
Gault, Brig. Sir J., 390, 534, 535
Gavin, Capt. J. L. M. (5th Bn.), 557
Gazala, 90; Line, 95–7; battle of, 97–106
Gebel Kalakh, 114
Gebel Saikra, 128
Geilenkirchen, 394–5
Geldrop, 379–84
Gemert, 380
Gennep, 413
George V, H.M. King, 3, 12, 13
George VI, H.M. King, as D. of York appointed Colonel, 5; 13, 26, 53, 60, 158, 261, 327, 332, 334, 336, 488–9, 491
Germany, operations in, 391, 394–5, 399–460; occupation, 460–6; 492–3
German Army:
 Armies
  1st Para, 449
  10th, 296
  14th, 296
 Corps
  Afrika Korps, 78–114 *passim*, 121–128, 155, 197
  LXXVI Pz., 315
 Divisions
  1st Para., 236
  2nd Marine, 450
  2nd Mountain, 34–48
  2nd Pz., 345
  4th Para., 220, 223, 242, 276, 289, 290
  5th Light Pz., 83
  6th Para., 454
  7th Para., 454, 461
  8th Mountain, 290
  9th SS Pz., 355
  10th Pz., 125; SS, 137, 352
  15th Pz., 78, 83, 85, 125
  15th Pz. Gr., 181, 259, 324, 454–7
  16th Pz., 173; SS Pz. Gr. 267, 271–276, 277, 278, 280, 288
  21st Pz., 85; at Rigel Ridge, 102–5; at Medenine, 123–5; 155
  29th Pz. Gr., 173, 300, 303, 306
  42nd Jaeger, 300, 303

39—S.G.H.

German Army—*cont.*
 Divisions—cont.
  65th Inf., 220, 268, 271,
  90th Light, 85, 128, 155; Pz. Gr., 192
  94th Inf., 192, 278, 280
  98th Inf., 312
  162nd (Turkoman), 300
  356th Inf., 249, 254
  361st Inf., 345
  715th Inf., 249
  Hermann Goering, 137, 153, 175 242, 373
Gerusalemme Ridge, 177
Gezira, 11, 115, 493
Ghent, 398
Gibbs, Capt. P. H., 123, 550
Gibson, RSM D. C., 137, 541, 544, 545
Gibson, Gdsm. E., 371–7, 532
Gibson, Gdsm. L. A., 553
Gibson, CQMS (2nd Bn), 86
Gibraltar, 132, 133
Gidman, CSM D., 546, 547
Gill, L/Sgt. G. H., 307
Gilpin, Capt. T. E. P., 427–8, 555
Giogo Pass, 267
Girdwood, Gdsm. (3rd Bn.), 466
Glasgow, 3, 25, 27, 471, 490, 492
Gloucester, H.R.H. Duke of, vii; appointed Col., 6; 96, 325, 328, 330, 396–7, 488 ff; promoted F.-M., 497
Goch, 406–7, 413, 415
Godfrey-Isaacs, Capt. G., 307
Godman, Maj. J., 47, 543
Gold Flake, 202–5, 209, 212, 213; *see also* Campoleone
Goodinge, Capt. A. W., 547
Goodwood (Caen), 338–40
Gordon, Sgt. A., 425
Gordon, Capt. A. N. J., 398, 550, 552
Gordon, Capt. D. A. S., 410, 441
Gordon, Capt. M. J. A., 90, 117, 124, 175, 550, 551
Gordon-Ives, Lt. V. M., 191
Gordon-Lennox, Capt. R. A. C., 397
Gore, CSM W., 105, 127, 549, 550
Gorizia, 316, 320
Gosport, 340
Gothic Line, 240, 241n, 255, 263, 264, 266, 268, 281–2
Gott, Lt.-Gen. W., 78, 86
Gough, Lt. F. C. (5th Bn.), 557
Goubellat, 153
Gourock, 132
Gow, Lt. I. G., 418, 552
Gow, Maj. J. M., 444, 555
Gow, Brig. J. W. H., 534, 535
Gow, Rev. J. M., 170, 550, 551
Graham, Maj. C. S. R., 387, 448, 553, 555

610 INDEX

Graham, Brig. H. L., xx, 9, 10, 28, 29, 31, 32, 37, 41, 43–6, 54, 538, 539, 543
Graham, Maj. J., 152, 222, 232, 530, 544, 545
Graham, Sgt. (2nd Bn.), 454
Graham, L/Sgt. (2nd Bn.), 422
Graham-Watson, 2/Lt. P. W. B., 479
Grant, Lt.-Col. P. C. H., 77, 96–115 passim, 539, 548, 549
Grant-Watson, Capt. R. de M., 75, 548
Grave, 378
Gray, RSM E. C., 325, 541, 553, 556
Gray, CSM L., 551
Gray, Gdsm. (3rd Bn.), 428
Green, Gdsn. A. McK., 148
Greenacre, Brig. W. D. C., 365, 424, 430, 466
Greenock, 27
Greenwood, Maj. (QM) A. O'C., 190, 195, 463, 475, 482, 486, 540, 541, 548–52
Greig, Sgt. C. (1st Bn.), 534
Greig, Sgt. C. (3rd Bn.), illustration 36
Greig, Lt. H. L. C., 427, 555
Grenadier Guards:
  1st Bn., 416
  3rd Bn., 10, 11, 228; M. Grande, 236–237; Farfa, 257; Lignano, 260; Gothic Line, 282; 297
  4th Bn., 325; Normandy, 344–5, 354–355; Germany, 400, 402, 404, 406, 446, 447
  5th Bn., 132; see also Tunisia, esp. 137–138, 144–8: Anzio, 201–6, 208, 215–18, 222–3; Italy, 228, 239, 241–255 passim; 268, 275–7, 280, 297
  6th Bn., 118, 122; The Horseshoe, 127; Italy, 169, 172, 174, 175, 177, 178; on M. Camino, 181–4, 186; 187–9; 193; 228–9
Grenadier Hill, 136–7
Grenadier Wood, 180–4
Gresham, Lt.-Col. J. F. (Welsh Gds.), 364
Greve, 253
Grich-el-Oued, 136, 138
Grieve, Gdsm. A. N. S., 388
Griffin, Capt. (R.A.S.C.), 367
Grizzana Station, 277
Groesbeek, 401
Gromballa, 154
Guards Armoured Division, 228; formed, 326–9; at home, see 4th Bn.; N.-W. Europe, see X Company and 2nd Bn.; "Farewell to Armour", 463–6
Guards Armoured Training Wing, 62, 326
Guards Brigades:
  1st, 134, 154, 155, 228; see S Company; 297
  2nd (in Malaya), 472–85

Guards Brigades—cont.
  4th, 320, 492
  5th Armoured, 328, 329, 431, 437
  6th Armoured/Tank, xviii, 228; at home, 327–33; Normandy, 340–51, 353–63, 365–7; Holland, 379–91; Ardennes offensive, 393–5; Germany, 400–12, 422–30, 438–49, 464–6
  22nd, 77–85, 90–4 (renumbered 200th)
  24th, Norway, 26–50; at home, 53–6; Tunisia, 132–52, 157, 158, 160–1; Italy, 196–320 passim, esp. reorganisation, 228; Castel di Sangro, 231; joins 6th S. African Armd. Div.; Staff, 257; 2nd reorganisation, 297; joins 56th Div., 298
  30th, 325
  32nd, 329; 4th Bn. in, 334–7; N.-W. Europe, see X Company and 2nd Bn.; post-war, 490, 493–5
  200th, see 22nd above; 94–7 (renumbered 201st)
  201st, see 22nd and 200th above; Desert, 97–108; Rommel's views on, 107; Syria, 117–19; Tunisia, 120–31, 152–60; Italy, 167–95, 227–9; at home, 395–7
Guards Chapel, 58, 261n, 290
Guards Depot (K Coy.), 13, 59–60, 469, 488, 497
Guardsman, title introduced, 3
Guards Parachute Company, 470
Gubbins, Maj.-Gen. Sir C., 34, 41, 42, 54
Gubbins-Mounsey-Heysham, Maj. R. H., 553, 555
Gunther, Capt. W. J., 550
Gurowski, Capt. R. D. M., 23, 66, 557
Gustav Line, 179

Haagscher Wood, 415
Hackling, L/Sgt. J. T., 532
Hadsel Fiord, 28
Hagen, 438
Hague, Maj. J. D. K., 66, 246, 254–5, 266, 272, 275, 279, 530, 532
Haldane, Maj.-Gen. Sir V. A., 14
Halfaya Pass, 78–9, 80, 83
Halfway House Pass, 83
Hall, RSM F., 276, 541, 545–7
Hall, Lt. J. P. (5th Bn.), 557
Halle, 368
Hallabet et Ezba, 90
Haltern, 425
Hamadet, 130
Hamburg, 449, 464
Hamilton, Rev. J., 142, 213, 221, 287, 543–545
Hamilton, RSM S., 277, 534, 541, 543–7
Hammamet, 154, 155, 158, 160
Hammam Lif, 154

INDEX

Hammelkeln, 423
Hanbury-Tracy, Capt. M. D. C., 66n
Hanmer, Capt. N. B. (R. Sussex Regt.), describes position on Rigel Ridge, 107
Hannah, Gdsm. R., 391
Hanson, Lt. (QM) W., 534, 540, 548
Harding, F.-M., Sir J., 317, 327, 482, 485, 487–8
Harley, Gdsm. A. B., 371, 372, 376, 377, 414, 532
Harris, Lt.-Col. F. H. H. B., 31, 41, 188, 195, 334, 337, 539, 543, 556
Harrold, Gdsm. A., 171
Harstad, 29, 31, 37, 43, 45, 48
Harvey, Capt. J. L., 325, 328, 534, 540, 553
Harvey, Capt. R. E. L., 87, 92, 93
Harvey, Maj. T. C., 193, 228, 242, 244, 251, 269, 272–6, 336, 530, 540, 543, 546
Hase river, 437
Hassum, 413–14
Hastenrath, 394
Hastings, Gdsm. J., 530
Hastings, Maj. S. L. E., 533
Hawick, 596–8
Hay, Rev. D. W., 546, 556
Haydon, Brig. J. C., 230
Haysenhof, 404
Hayward, Capt. F. McL., 211, 224, 301, 545–7
Haywood-Farmer, Lt. R. E., 351n
Head-dress, *see* Dress; esp. 594n
Heap, L/Cpl. J., 294, 314, 532
Heber-Percy, Lt.-Col. C. H. R. (Welsh Gds.), 420
Hechtel, 349–77, 379
Heinsburg, 394
Helchteren, 371
Heligoland, 461–3
Helmond, 384, 386, 390, 393
Helwan, 12
Hemnes, 34–5, 38
Hemslingen, 453
Henderson, Maj. J. D., 183, 185, 550, 551
Henderson, Lt. P. G., 212, 545
Henderson, Sgt. J., 374
Henderson-Scott, Lt. N. de P., 130
Hermannschot, 423
Hesketh, Maj. Lord, 224, 242, 248, 251, 272–3, 546
Hess, Rudolf, 64–5, 68
Hettsteeg, 402
Heumen, 420–1, 430
Heusden, 385, 389
Hickling, Capt. E. P., 361, 385, 532, 554, 555
Higham, CSM F., 40, 543
Hill, L/Sgt. J. J. C., 252, 530
Hill, Sgt. W. A., 311, 530
Hinnoy, 29

Hislop, Sgt. T., 357
Histories of the Regiment, xvii, 14
Hobson, Capt. A. R. A., xviii, 241, 257
Hodge, Capt. G. C. (R.A.M.C.), 141, 148, 213, 221, 287, 544, 545
Hogg, L/Sgt. T., 373, 451
Holden, Lt.-Col. (QM) J. H., 534, 540, 541, 548
Holdenstedt, 443–5
Holding Bn., 65–9
Holland, 378–95, 400–1, 412–14, 420–1, 430–2
Holland, Gdsm. K., 482
Holyrood, 471, 488 ff., 492
Home, Maj. R. S. P., 183, 184, 551
Hommersum, 413–14
Hong Kong, 8, 9, 481
Honours and Awards, Appx. B; 1939–1945, 528–36; Malaya, 537
Hopen, 46–8
Hope, Maj. E. J., 352–3, 378, 417, 420, 532, 552, 558
Hope, Sgt. J., 105n., 531
Hope, Maj. Lord J., 27, 543
Hopgood, Gdsm. J., 530
Hopkinson, Maj. F. A., 556
Hornby, Maj. (R.E.), 222
Horseshoe, Battle of the, 127
Horst, 389
Horton, Maj. W. G., 539
Hougaerde, 391–3, 398, 412
Houldsworth, Maj. H. H., 87, 169, 178, 393, 548, 549, 551
Household Brigade Magazine, xviii
Houssemagne, 360
Houston, Gdsm. (3rd Bn.), 355
Howard, Gdsm. J., 39, 530
Howard, Lt. M. G. R. (5th Bn.), 557
Howard, Lt. R. J. S., 413
Howard, Capt. R. M. C. (Gren. Gds.), 182
Howarth, Sgt. F., 537
Howe, L/Cpl. T., 131, 531
Howitt, CSM K., 556
Hughes, CSM S., 550
Hughes, L/Sgt. T., 537
Hughes, CSM J., 86
Hughey, Gdsm. M., 335
Humble, Lt. R., 347, 348, 554
Hunstanton, 336
Hunt, Gdsm. (3rd Bn.), 411
Hunter, Capt. A. D. B. (R.A.M.C.), 556
Hunter, Capt. R. T., 139, 152, 274, 276, 544
Hutchinson, Gdsm. J., 531

Ikingi, 108
Illustrations, xiii, xx
Ilmenau, river, 444
Impruneta, 254–5
Imrie, L/Cpl. J., 293

INDEX

Independent Companies in Norway, 34–39, 44–5, 48
Independent Companies, Scots Guards, xix; *see also* S and X Companies
Indian Army:
  4th Div., 78, 80, 85, 128, 152
  8th Div., 234, 302
  10th Div., 282
  10th Bde., 101
  11th Bde., 80
  4/13th Frontier Force Rifles, 271, 290
Infantry Reinforcement and Training Depot (I.R.T.D.) in Italy; at Rotondi, 230; at Fano, 298
Inskip, Lt. J. H., 293, 558
Irish Guards:
  1st Bn., Norway, 28, 33, 35, 37, 46–9; Tunisia, 132–51 *passim, esp.* 135, 141, 143, 147, 151; Anzio, 201–22 *passim, esp.* No. 4 Coy., 216–22; 228–9
  2nd Bn., 340, 362
  3rd Bn., 337; Normandy, *see* X Company; 413–14, 454
Irvine, Gdsm. J., 390
Irwen, Sgt. T., 424, 532
"Island, The" (Arnhem), 378
Ismalia, 115, 495
Isselburg, 431
Issel river, 423
Issendorf, 458
Italy, 165–320

Jackson, Sgt. H. R., 439, 532
Jardine, Capt. M. J., 211, 544–7
J Company, 59–60
Jeeps, 1st Bn.'s surplus, 299, 315
Jenkins, L/Cpl. J. H., 124, 531
Jenkinson, Capt. R. S., 546, 547, 556
Jerusalem, 11
Johnson, Maj.-Gen. G. F., 14, 59, 106, 320, 324, 328, 337, 359, 363, 421, 469, 495, 533, 535, 538, 539, 553
Johnson, Maj. (Australian), 83–4
Johnstone, Lt.-Col. A. H. (Pretoria Regt.), 235
Johnstone, L/Sgt. G., 98, 531
Jones, L/Sgt. P., 238, 260, 532
Jugoslavs or "Jugs", 316–20

Kabrit, 77
Kairouan, 152
Kajang, 484–5
Kanching, 484
"Kangaroos" (armd. troop carriers), 296, 298, 382–3, 405, 409
Kapellen, 415, 423
Kasr-el-Nil, 10, 11, 12, 75, 493
Kassasin, 77
Kasteel, 390
Kealy, Lt. M. R. E. (5th Bn.), 557

Keith, Capt. H. S., 198, 202, 210, 211, 212n, 216, 248, 271–2, 314, 544–7
Kelly, Sgt. J. H., 530
Kelly, RSM R. A., 534
Kemble, Maj. D. H. A., 122, 127, 415, 434, 535, 552
Kenley Aerodrome, 55, 66–7
Kent, 3rd Bn. in, 332–3
Kerr, CSM J., 552, 556
Kervenheim, 409–10
Kesselring, F.-M. Albert, 235, 240, 266, 268
Kettenburg, 449–51
Kevelaer, 412, 415; dinner at, 422
Keys, Ceremony of the, 68
Kiddle, CQMS S., 286
Kiel, 448, 464
Kilpatrick, RSM S., 534
Kindersley, Lt.-Col. Lord, 328–31, 534, 539
King, CQMS D., 86
Kingsmill, Lt.-Col. W. H. (Gren. Gds.), 185, 187
Kinmont, Lt.-Col. G. M., 534, 548
Kinnaird, Maj. Hon. P. C., 56, 58, 539
Kirby, CSM W., 556
Kirchtimke, 456–7
Kirkman, Lt.-Gen. Sir S., 241
Klioua Farm, 145
Knight, Capt. H. S., 80, 548
"Knightsbridge", 96–100, 104, 106, 107
Korean War, 490
Kowloon, 8, 9
Kranenburg, 400–2, 404
Krokstranden, 41–3
Krusbechshof, 407
Kuala Kubu Bharu, 478–80, 482–7
Kuala Lumpur, 477, 479–80
Kufra Oasis, 74
Kuhnen, 418–19
Kung, Lt. L., 63, 329

La Bayeud, 338
La Caverie, 354, 357
Lachtehausen, 439
La Foce, 244, 245
L'Aigle, 368
Laing, Capt. A. G., 357, 438, 532, 555
Laing, Capt. H., 390, 444–6, 535, 554, 555
La Mancellière, 353
La Motte, 353
La Mougeraye, 346
Lampson, Capt. Hon. G. C., 105, 131, 535, 540, 548–51
Lampson, Sir M., 9, 11
La Prieurie, 339
La Quercia, 288–9
Lassy, 354
Latakia, 118

INDEX

Lauenburg, 446
Law, CSM A., 376–7, 558
Law, Maj. M., 361, 555
Lawrie, L/Cpl. J. R. K., 145, 529, 530
Lawson, L/Cpl. D., 535
Lawson, Maj. Hon. W. E. H., 484, 486, 547
L Company, 59–60, 491, 497
Lea, L/Sgt. H., 479
Leave home, from Italy, 288, 318; from N.-W. Europe, 394
Le Bas Perrier, 359–63
Le Bourg, 344–5
Le Busq, 364
Leese, Gen. Sir O., 126, 229, 234, 328
Le Mans, 77
Lemon (Malaya), 479–80
Leng, Maj. P. J. H., 414, 420, 449, 531, 558
Lengerich, 434–5
Les Andelys, 367, 379
Les Loges, 345–9
Leuze, 368
Lewenhaupt, Capt. Count E., 42n.
Lewis, Lt. C., 139, 544
Lewis, Sgt. (2nd Bn.), 194
Lewthwaite, Lt.-Col. R. G., 122, 126, 297–319 *passim*, 531, 535, 538, 547, 550
Liddle, CSM T., 552
Lillico, Gdsm. (1st Bn.), 301
Lindley, CSM F. W., 548
Lindsay, Earl of, *see* Garnock
Lindsay, L/Sgt. J., 363
Lindsay, CSM J., 462, 552
Lindsay, CSM J. A. (5th Bn.), 557
Lindsay, Capt. M. (5th Bn.), 23, 557
Lindsay, 2/Lt. Hon. P., 479
Lindsay-Peto, Capt. T. C., 152, 209, 222, 227, 311, 313, 530, 544, 545, 547
Lingen, 432–4
Lingwood, Gdsm. G., 238, 283, 532
Lippe, river, 424–5
Lippramsdorf, 425
Liri Valley, 231
Little, CSM R. H., 88, 185, 531, 551
Llandwrog battle camp, 62
Llewellyn, Maj. A. D. G., 371–7, 487, 532, 539, 558
Lloyd-Johnes, Lt. J. W. F., 262, 558
Loder, Lt. D. E., 178
Loder, Lt.-Col. G. H., 15
Logue, Capt. A. L., 257, 272, 539, 547
Longbridge Deverill, 335
Long Range Desert Group, 74, 95, 531
"Longstop Hill", 134, 138
Longworth, Sgt. T., 98
Loraine Petre, Mr. F., 14
Louisendorf, 404–5
Louvain, 369, 393
Lovat, Brig. Lord, 331
Lower Maas, *see* Tilburg

Lowinski, Lt. T. M. F. E., 135, 220, 225, 544, 545
Lowther, Maj.-Gen. Sir C., 14
Lo-Wu, 8
Loyd, Lt.-Gen. Sir Charles, 276
Luard, Maj. B. E. (Coldm. Gds.), 109
Lubeck, 447
Lucas, Lt.-Gen. J. P. (U.S.A.), 197
Ludford-Astley, 2/Lt. B. A., 6
Lumsden, Maj.-Gen. H; letter to Lt.-Col. Grant, 107
Lumsden, CSM W., 124, 170–1, 188, 416, 531, 552
Lundenget, 39–40
Luneberg, 446
Lunn, RSM J., 140, 530, 534, 544, 551
Lusche, 437
Lusciano, 190
Lutain wood, 345
Lutjenburg, 448
Lyall, CSM P., 552
Lydd, 497
Lyell, Lady, xix, 161
Lyell, Capt. Lord, 137, 140; wins V.C., 145–6; 161; citation, 528; 530, 544
Lynn, Miss Vera, 283
Lynton, 335

M 25 (Anzio), 205, 208, 213–16, 220
Maas River, 380; advance to, 384–90; 391, 399
Maastricht Appendix, 393–5
McAllister, L/Cpl. T., 92, 531
MacArthur, Rev. A. A., 287, 546, 547
McBarnet, Maj. D. V. C., 196, 226, 543–5
McBride, Gdsm. W., 427
McCall, L/Sgt. J., 92
McCallum, L/Cpl. W., 530
McClelland, CSM C., 373, 374, 377, 532, 558
McComb, L/Cpl. J., 124, 531
McConnel, L/Sgt. (2nd Bn.), 88
McCormick, L/Cpl. S., 112, 531
McCreery, Lt.-Gen. Sir R., 173, 185, 188, 296, 298, 311
McCubbin, Sgt. J., 478
McDade, CQMS A., 258
MacDonald, P/Maj. A., 55, 318n, 534, 543–7
McDonald, RSM J., 541
Macdonald, Lt. M. S., 419, 552
Macdonald-Buchanan, Capt. J., 410–11, 442–5, 532, 539
Macdonald-Buchanan, Maj. R. N., 61, 534, 535
McFadyen, Gdsm. C., 106, 531
MacFarlane, Sgt. P., 361
McGoun, Sgt. E., 531
McGowan, MQMS J., 554, 555
McIlhargey, L/Cpl. J., 178, 531

614 INDEX

McInnes, Gdsm. J., 530
MacKay, L/Sgt. D., 430
McKeand, Gdsm, G., 457
McKee, Gdsm. J., 67
Mackenzie, Col. E. D., 58, 65–7, 69, 193, 215, 538, 539
Mackenzie, D/Sgt. J., 546, 547
Mackenzie, Lt. K. B., 187
Mackenzie, Lt. R. A. C., 480
Mackenzie, Lt.-Col. Sir V., 3, 8, 9, 58
Mackesy, Maj-Gen. P. J., 29
McKinny, Gdsm. Y., 457
McKirdy, D/Sgt. G., 396, 551, 552
MacKnight, Capt. A. T. (R.A.M.C.), 358, 554, 555
McLaren, Cpl. D., 530
McLay, CQMS J., 258, 262
Maclean, Maj. Sir C., 349, 380, 404, 553–555
MacLennan, P/Sgt. A., 113
McLeod, L/Sgt. A., 103
McLeod, Lt. R. C., 128, 171
McMillan, Sgt. D., 486
McMillan, Lt.-Gen. Sir G., 342, 347
McMillan, PSM H., 543
McMinn, L/Cpl. A., 293–4, 532
MacMullen, Lt. N. E. (5th Bn.), 557
McMurtrie, Lt. D. G. S., 215, 545
McNally, RSM R., 534, 540, 543
MacPhail, L/Sgt. A., 260–1, 532
McPhee, Sgt. A., 418–19, 531
MacRae, Maj. J. D. C. S., 78, 81, 87, 88, 92, 95, 97, 109, 112, 113, 115, 120, 531, 540, 548, 549
McSorley, Gdsm. B., 531
Madden, RSM A. K., 535, 541, 556, 557
"Maidan Serenade", 116
Maisoncelles, 352
Malaya (2nd Bn. in), 472–88
Malcolm, Maj. D. P. M., 148, 206, 208, 301, 306, 544–7
Malden, 420–1
Malone, Maj. W. B., 64, 187, 336
Malton, 337
Mann, Maj. F. G., 53, 139–41, 146, 232, 242, 265, 267, 279–80, 301, 306–8, 314, 471, 530, 544, 546, 547
Mann, Maj. J. P., 358, 360, 365, 382, 388, 390, 403, 423, 532, 535, 554, 555
Mannock, Capt. A. N., 433–4, 531
Manouba, 156
Manpower, 56–8, 227–8, 297, 326
Mansfield, Capt. H. N. (R.A.M.C.), 287, 305, 546, 547
Maps, xv, xx
"Marble Arch", 120
Marchant, S/Clerk H., 541
Mareth Line, 74, 121, 123, 126–8
Marienbaum, 431

Marriott, Maj.-Gen. Sir J., xx, 11, 19, 75, 76, 85, 94, 106, 335, 463, 466, 485, 533, 534, 539
Marsden, L/Sgt. D., 382
Marshall, Gen. G. C. (U.S.A.), 328
Marshall, Lt. H. W. S., 355–6, 390, 554
Marshall, Gdsm. (1st Bn.), 141
Marsham-Townshend, Capt. T., 192, 548, 549
Marston Bigot, 335
Martin, PSM H., 543
Mary, H.M. Queen, 328, 491
Matheson, Capt. I. K., 60, 540
Mathieson, Capt. D. G., 355, 554
Matmata Hills, 121
Maugham, Sgt. (1st Bn.), 207
Maurice, Maj.-Gen. Sir F., xvii, 14
Maxtone Graham, Capt. A. J. O., 105, 549
Maxwell, Capt. A. B. C., 22n, 98, 101, 104, 105, 109, 111, 531, 534, 549
Mayfield, Lt.-Col. B., 21, 77–96 *passim*, 539, 557
Mayfield, Capt. R., illustration 42
Mechanisation, 10
Medenine, Battle of, 121–6; 415, 416
Medjerda river, 138
Medjez-el-Bab, 128, 134–8; battle of Medjez Plain, 135–43
Meijel, 384, 387
Mellor, Gdsm. W., 284
Memorials, 12; to S Company, 295; 483, 490
Mena, 114–15
Menate, 303
Menslage, 436–7
Mentions in Despatches, 535–7
Mersa Matruh, 10, 12, 19, 76, 78, 120
Methuen, Lt. P. R., 227, 551
Methuen, F.-M. Lord, 5, 10, 13
Meyer, Lt. Sir A., 340n
Michie, Gdsm. (X Coy.), 375
Mieli, 185
Mignano, 179, 188
Milburne, Maj. J. F., 39, 543, 551
Millar, Gdsm. N., 357
Millar, Gdsm. W. M., 82 and n, 178, 531
Miller, Lt.-Col. A. C. (U.S.A.), 424–9
Miller, L/Cpl. J., 67, 532
Miller, L/Cpl. R. N., 212, 530
Milligan, Capt. W. MacB. M., 534, 553
Mills, Maj. F. (R.A.), 207
Milroy, L/Cpl. A., 105, 531
Minden, 238
Minturno, 58, 191–5
Mitchell, CSM J., 547
Mitchell, L/Sgt. J., 532
Mitchell, Gdsm. J., 531
Mitchell, Capt. R. I. (R.A.M.C.), 549
Mo, 32
Moergestel, 380

INDEX

Moir, L/Sgt. J., 314, 530
Monastery Hill, see M. Camino
Moncrieffe, Capt. Sir D. G., 189, 256, 265, 267, 271, 530, 546, 547
Monfries, Lt. K. A. P., 288
Mondragone, 189–90
Monsumano, 266
Mont'Abelle, 288
Montchamp, 352–3
Montcharivel, 353, 358
Montevarchi, 261
Monte Alcino, 278–9
Monte Battaglia, 283–5
Monte Bersano, 267
Monte Camino, 179; 1st Battle of, 180–6; 2nd Battle of, 186–9
Monte Caprara, 288
Monte Catarelto, 269–76, 280n
Montecatini, 266
Monte Castellaro, 319
Montecchio canal, 311–14
Monte Cetona, 242
Monte Cocusso, 319
Monte Collegalle, 253
Monte dell'Acqua Salata, 291
Monte Domine, 252–3
Montefollonico, 245
Monte Grande, 236–7
Monte Lignano, 259–61
Monte Majone, 249
Monte Natale, 191–4
Monte Ornito, 230
Monte Pacciano, 258–9
Monte Pagano, 232
Monte Penna, 282
Monte Penzola, 286; attack on, 291–4
Monte Petrella, 191
Montepiano, 268
Monte Piccolo, 236–8, 261
Monte Providero, 236
Montepulciano, 245
Monte Querciabella, 251
Monte Rosso, 241
Monte Salvaro, 271, 277–80
Monte San Michele, 249–52
Monte Scalari, 254–5
Monte Sole, 277–80, 286, 288–90; captured, 309
Monte Sorrate, 241 and n
Monte Stanco, 277
Monte Termine, 279–80
Monte Verro, 291, 294
Montgomery, F.-M. Viscount, 109, 121, 123, 126, 327, 338, 369, 459
Monti Albano, 266
Monti Sabini, 257
Mont Pincon, 342; Battle of, see Caumont
Montrose (tank), 381 and n
Moore, Gdsm. D., 480
Moore, D/Sgt. I., 554, 555

Moore, Lt. M., 579
Moorehouse, Sgt. S., 44, 142
Morella, 169
Morgan Line, 318–19
Morgan, L/Cpl. W., 480, 537
Morley, Capt. (QM) F., 60, 365, 444, 534, 540, 541, 555
Morphett, Capt. D. G., 550, 551
Morrice, 2/Lt. M. J., 485
Morris, Gdsm. (1st Bn.), 314
Morrison, CSM J., 556
Morrison, PSM M., 543
Morrison, L/Cpl. T., 535
Morthoe, 334
Mostyn, Maj. E. I. Ll., 306, 308, 312, 484, 537, 539, 546–8
Moyland, 404–5
Msus, 90
Muhlen Fleuth, 408–9
"Mulberry Harbour", 338
Mules, 179, 183, 232, 242, 284, 286, 287
Munday, Gdsm. F., 237, 532
Mundy, Lt. G. F., 177, 546
Munich crisis, 15
Münster, advance to, 423–30; 438
Murray, Maj. A. D., 30, 59, 539, 543, 553
Murray, Brig. A. S. P., 201
Murray, Gdsm. D., 484
Murray, RSM W., 541
Murzuk, 74
Musaid, 78, 79, 81, 82
Musketry, 14
Mutch, RQMS A., 551
Mutch, Sgt. V. N., 118, 124, 531
Mutter, Lt. R. G., 456
Mychett Place, 64–5
Mycock, Lt. D., 457
Mynors, Lt. D. R. B., 131, 535

Nabeul, 156
Naevernes, 42
Namsos, 38, 34
Namur, 391
Napier and Ettrick, Capt. Lord, 539
Naples, 168, 175, 196, 198, 229
Naqb el Khadhim, 111–14
Narni, 258
Narvik, 20, 26–32
Nasser, Col., 495
National Service, see Conscripts
Negri Sembilan, 479, 483
Neguib, Gen., 495
Neilson, Capt. A. S., 62, 230, 237–8, 259–61, 336, 532, 558
Nelson, CSM F., 548, 549
Nesbit, L/Sgt. S., 301
Netley Common, 338
Neuenkirchen, 450
Nevile, Capt. H. N., 554, 555
Nevill, Lt. M. G. R., 148, 544

616 INDEX

Newman, Maj. (S. African), 101–4
New Zealand Army:
  2nd Div., 85, 108, 122, 123, 128, 131, 155, 259, 315, 317
  5th Bde., 125
Nicol, Lt. T. A., 107
Nicol, L/Sgt. W., 533
Nicosia, 493
Nielson, Col. R. (Norwegian), 37
Nienberge, 428–9
Nienburg, 449
Niers, river, 406, 412
"Nigel", bridge, 417
Night Week, 4th Bn., 335
Nijmegen, 378, 380, 391, 395, 399–401, 404, 413, 420
Nisbet, Gdsm. J., 108
Nocelleto, 193
Nockles, Gdsm. D., 107
Nordhorn, 432–3
Norman, Lt.-Col. H. R. (Coldm. Gds.), 230, 258
Normandy, 337–67
North-East London Sub-District, 57
North-West Europe campaign, 337–459; *see also* Normandy, Belgium, Holland, Germany
Norton, Lt. Hon. J. R. B. (Gren. Gds.), 223
Norway, 20, 25, 26–50
Nottuln, 426
Nunneley, Capt. R. M. C., 287, 301, 547
Nunning, 427
Nutcracker, 387, 390
Nutterden, 400, 402, 403

Oboe, 198
O'Fee, Gdsm., 478
Officers Commanding Battalions, 538
Officers, Nominal Roll of: 1934–1956; Appx. E, 559 ff
Ogg, L/Sgt. C., 312, 530
Ogilvy, Gdsm. C., 530
Ohrte, 436
Oirschott, 380, 382, 383
Oisterwijk, 382–4
Oldendorf, 455
Oldenzaal, 431–2
Oliver, Lt.-Col. G. E. F. (Buffs), 303
Ollerton, L/Cpl. T., 532
Orders of Battle, 542
Orne, river, 339
Orr-Ewing, Maj. R. A., 83, 99, 104, 105, 319, 548, 549
Orvieto, 241, 242
Ostend, 398
Ostertimke, 455–8
Overloon, 380
Overpelt, 377–8
Owen, Capt. R. (R.E.M.E.), 394, 555

Packe-Drury-Lowe, Maj. J. D. B., 86, 87, 96, 549
Padua, 315
Pahang, 482–3
Palermo, 168
Palestine, 11, 12
Pallazzo, 269, 272
Palmanova, 320
Palmyra, 119
Paris, 13
Parkes, D/Sgt. L., 195, 551
Parsons, RQMS L., 557
Partisans, Italian, 240, 245n, 266, 281, 284, 315; Russian, 266; Jugoslav, 316–18
Paterson, Lt. E. G., 555
Patience, Gdsm. G., 212
Paula Line, 253–4
Paynter, 2/Lt. G., 495
Paynter, Brig. Sir G., 6, 495
Pearson, Maj. A. D. B., 58–60, 539, 540
Pearson, Gdsm. (3rd Bn.), 448
Pease, Capt. Hon. C. H. B., 221
Peddenburg, 424
Peel, The, 384–90
"Pegasus Bridge", 339
Pelago, 282–3
Pember, Capt. R. C. G., 381–2, 387, 403, 407, 410, 424–5, 532, 554
Penang, 477
Penny, Maj.-Gen. E. W. S., 205
Pepper-Pot, 294–5, 444, 446
Perak, 483
Perks, L/Cpl. R., 192, 252, 531
Periera, Maj. G. C. (Coldm. Gds.), 109
Perugia, 258–9
Pettigrew, Gdsm. J., 372, 535
Petre, Maj. R. C., 41, 45, 471, 543, 546, 556
Pettit, RSM A. E., 541
Petty, Gdsm. R., 390
Pheasant, 380
Philippeville, 158, 159
Philipson, Maj. A. T., 170, 171, 550, 551
P.I.A.T., *see* Arms
Pickard, SSM R., 552, 555
Pike, Maj. G. L. S., 177, 187
Piper, Maj. A. H., 157, 218, 221, 301, 544–7
Piping:
  Pipe Manual, 496
  Pipers, 14, 150, 257, 317, 334, 393, 496, 596
  Pipes presented by 227th Bde., 446
  Piping School at Pirbright, 495
Pirbright, 60–5, 320, 337, 469, 470, 475, 490, 496, 497
Pistoia, 266
Platoon Sergeant Major—PSM, 7
Plön, 464
Plunder, 421, 422–3, 431

INDEX 617

Po, river, chase to, 309–14; crossing of, 315
Po di Volano, 310–11
Poggio, 278
Poggio Mirteto, 258
Points (all in metres above sea-level):
  206, *see* Battleaxe
  130, 134, 145, 151, 156, 168, 187, *see* Medjez Plain
  106, 117, 154, 157, 171, 181, 212, 214; 226, (The Bou); *see* Djebel Bou Aoukaz
  520, 860, *see* Rocchetta
  615, 727, 819, 963, *see* Monte Camino
  141, *see* Monte Natale
  105, *see* Dung Farm
  550, 685, 846, *see* Sarteano
  707, 751, 761, 885, 893, *see* Monte San Michele
  302, *see* Strada in Chianti
  501, 575, 565, *see* Monte Lignano
  678, 707, *see* Monte Catarelto
  527, 546, 580, *see* Monte Termine
  476, 501, 512, *see* Monte Sole
  411, *see* Monte Penzola
  309, *see* Caumont
  208, *see* Estry
  242, *see* Chênedollé
Pointon, Sgt. P. L., 537
Pola, 316, 319–20
Police, 5, 61, 142
Polish Army:
  II Corps, 234, 296, 309
  3rd Carpathian Div., 231, 234
  Carpathian Bde., 33
  12th Podolski Lancers, 234
Pompeii, 197, 229
Pontasieve, 261, 281
Pontelandolfo, 229
Poole, Maj.-Gen. W. H. E. (S. African), 235, 247, 276
Porter, L/Sgt. J., 335
Porter, Gdsm. W., 145–6, 529
Porto Garibaldi, 300–1
Portomaggiore, 309–10
Port Said, 494–5
Poseggio, 283
Pothus, 46
Potsdam, 463
Potter, Lt. G. W. E. (5th Bn.), 557
Pozzuoli, 199, 227
Prato, 268, 281, 287–9
Prato Magno, 261, 281–2
Pre-O.C.T.U. at Pirbright, 64
Prepotto, 318
Presles, 359–63
Priaulx, Capt. O., 479
Priaulx, Maj. O. W., 540, 556
Price, SSM A., 383, 532, 554, 555
Price, Capt. D. E. C., 546
Pring, Capt. C. E. (R.E.M.E.), 365, 554

Prisoners of War, 196; camp liberated, 455–8; statistics, 526
Pump House at Bando, 305–6
Puntafiume, 189–90
Purfleet, 398
Purvis, Lt. A. B., 555
Purvis, Maj. A. F., 25
Purvis, Capt. R. W. B., 533, 556, 557
Putt, 394

Qatana, 117, 119
Qatatba, 115
Quaret el Himeimat, 119
Quartermasters, 540
Quarry Hill, *see* Caumont
Quinn, Capt. (QM) J., 286, 334, 534, 540, 546, 547, 556, 557

Radcliffe, Lt. E. L. W., 581
Radcliffe, Lt. G. C. W., 455, 558
Raeburn, P/Maj. J., 174, 546
Raeburn, Lt.-Col. W. D. M., 21, 189, 415, 433, 454, 492, 531, 534, 539, 540, 548, 552, 557
Raine, L/Sgt. J., 530
Ramlingen, 441
Raml Ridge, 99, 101
Ramsay, Capt. A. H. R. M., 39, 543, 548
Ramsay, Sgt. F., 403
Ramsay, Maj. G. P. M., 281, 497, 539, 546
Ramsay, Lt. J. S. M., 383
Ramsay, Capt. N. G., 494, 539
Rana river, 40
Randalsvolden, 43
Ran fjord, 34
Rathbone, Maj. H. N. S., 181, 182
Rattray, CSM A., 549
Rattray, Capt. J. S. C., 183, 434, 552, 556
Raufjellet, 43
Ravenna, 299
Rawang gang, 478
Razor Back, *see* M. Camino
Readman, Maj. R. A., 279, 546
Recruiting, 4, 57, 59–60, 469
Rees, 431
Reeve, Gdsm. K., 67
Regan, PSM C., 543
Regimental Exhibition (1934), 14
Regimental Headquarters, 6, 56–9
Regimental Sergeant Majors, 541
Regiments (British), *see also under* Coldstream, Grenadier, Irish and Welsh Guards and Royal Artillery:
  Armoured troops
    Household Cavalry, 368, 431–3, 436, 458–9
    Greys, 170, 172
    10th Hussars, 306–7
    11th Hussars, 94, 119, 449

Regiments (British)—*cont.*
  Armoured Troops—*cont.*
    12th Lancers, 232
    16th/5th Lancers, 261
    17th/21st Lancers, 236, 257, 327
    27th Lancers, 311–15
    2nd Lothian and Border Horse, 262, 291
    Derbyshire Yeomanry, 262
    North Irish Horse, 144
    Westminster Dragoons, 389
    4th R. Tank Regt., 78
    12th R. Tank Regt., 310
    3rd Reconnaissance Regt., 424
  Infantry
    Argyll and Sutherland Highlanders, 2nd Bn., *see* 227th Bde. *passim*
    Black Watch, 234
    Buffs, 80, 82, 226, 297–315
    Cameronians, 344, 383, 406
    Cheshire, 185
    Duke of Cornwall's L.I., 395
    Duke of Wellington's, 136–7, 223
    Durham L.I., 77–80
    Glasgow H., 353, 380, 383, 406
    Gordons, 213, 214, 225; 2nd Bn., *see* 227th Bde. *passim*
    Green Howards, 128
    Hampshire, 172
    Highland L.I., 76; 10th Bn., *see* 227th Bde. *passim*; 414
    K.O.S.B., 8, 380, 407–9
    K.O.Y.L.I., 193–4, 477
    K.R.R.C. (60th), 85
    K.S.L.I., 212, 226
    Lincolnshire, 187–8, 407, 410–11
    London Irish, 179, 216
    London Scottish, 214
    Loyals, 140, 141, 148, 149, 225–6
    Middlesex, 209
    Northamptonshire, 194
    North Staffordshire, 215
    Oxfordshire and Buckinghamshire L.I., 184
    Queen's, 131, 190
    Rifle Brigade, 78, 79, 85, 86, 128, 281
    R. Fusiliers, 185
    R. Inniskilling Fusiliers, 134
    R. Ulster Rifles, 407, 409, 412
    R. West Kent, 134
    Seaforth H., 345, 347, 382–4, 406
    Sherwood Foresters, 213
    South Wales Borderers, 28, 31, 33, 37, 46–8
    Suffolk, 479
    Welch, 297
    York and Lancaster; Hallamshire Bn., 27; 191, 194
Reichswald Forest, 400 404, 413

Reid, Rev. G. H. T., 333, 445, 553, 555
Reilly, Sgt. G., 482–3, 537
Reno river, 299
Rethem, 449
Reyntiens, Lt. R. A. M., 177
Reyshoff, 409
Rhine, river, 369, 378, 399, 420; crossing of, 422–3; 431
Rhineland: Battle of the, 399–420; occupation of, 465
Rhodes, proposed attack on, 77–8
Rhodes, Lt.-Col. and Director of Music S., 59, 495, 541
Riach, Sgt. W., 480
Ricasoli, Barone, 246–9
Richardson, Cpl. E. W. A. (5th Bn.), 25
Riches, L/Sgt. C., 531
Richmond, D/Sgt. J., 82, 87, 126, 531, 548–50
Ridgeway, Gen. M. B. (U.S.A.), 425
Rigel Ridge, 99–108, 120
Rignano, 262
Riley, Sgt. F., 79, 531
Riley, Q.T.P.M. (5th Bn.), 23
Rimmer, Sgt. T., 530
Rioch, D/Sgt. J., 471
Ritchie, Maj. A. N. B., 368, 378, 417, 420n, 459, 472, 485, 496, 540, 556, 558
Rivers-Bulkeley, Maj. R. A. H., 169, 172, 548–50
Rivett-Carnac, Capt. T. N., 478
Road watch (L.R.D.G.), 75
Rob, Capt. J. V., 254, 556
Robbie, Sgt. E., 307
Robertson, Capt. (QM) C., 540, 541, 553
Robertson, Maj. C. A. A., 9, 534
Robertson, Maj. D. S., 105, 496, 548, 549
Robertson, L/Sgt. J., 145, 529
Robertson, P/Maj. J. B., 11
Robertson, RSM J. B., 534
Robertson, CSM W., 276, 530, 546, 547
Robertson, Sgt. (3rd Bn.), 427
Rocca d'Evandro, 187–8
Roccasecca, 238
Rocchetta e Croce, 178–9
Rodht, Gen. (German), 255
Roe, L/Cpl. J., 257
Roer, river, 395, 399
Roermond, 395
Rognan, 34, 46
Roll of Honour, 1939–1945; Officers, 503; Other Ranks, 506; Malaya, 524
Rome, 202, 234–9, 241
Romer, Maj. M. N., 170, 415, 417, 548, 549, 551
Romer, Mrs. M. N., xix
Romer, river, 417–19
Rommel, F.-M. E., 78; raid into Egypt, 87; opinion of 201st Gds. Bde., 107; 369

INDEX

Rooker, Capt. C. E. V. (R.A.P.C.), 23, 557
Roper, Capt. J. C. A., 533, 556
Rose, Maj. H. L. St. V., 37, 96, 104, 105, 130, 187, 189, 451–2, 543, 549, 550, 552
Rose, Gdsm. R., 535
Ross, Maj. (QM) A., 19, 60, 150, 208, 225, 226, 534, 540, 541, 543–5
Ross, Capt. H. C. E., 539
Ross, L/Sgt. M., 451
Ross, L/Cpl. (2nd Bn.), 195
Ross-Gower, Sgt. W., 534
Rosvoll, 41
Rotenburg, 453–4, 463, 466
Rotondi, 230, 298
Roullours, 366–7
Rowe, Lt. J. V., 189
Rowe, Capt. M. W., 135, 544
Rowe, Maj. R. G., 66, 178, 231
Roxel, 426–7
Royal Air Force Regiment, men transferred to 2nd Bn., 396–397, 416
Royal Army Service Corps:
  229 Coy., 367
  550 Coy., 235
Royal Artillery (Regiments):
  2nd R.H.A., 99
  3rd R.H.A., 109, 111
  4th R.H.A., 88
  6th Field, 424
  19th Field, 142, 214, 225
  21st A/Tk., 252, 262
  23rd Field, 235, 271
  61st Medium, 424
  65th Field, 171, 173
  80th Medium (Scottish Horse), 214
  81st A/Tk., 149, 209
  166th (Newfoundland) Field, 271, 274, 275
Royal Australian Regiment, alliance with 3rd Bn., 496
Royal Engineers:
  23rd Field Coy., 220, 222
  42nd Field Coy., 235
Royle, CSM J. (5th Bn.), 557
Ruhr, The, 424, 438
Runcie, Capt. R. A. K., 385, 406, 410, 430, 448, 532, 554, 555
Rush, Maj. G. C., 79, 81, 83, 140, 141, 157, 544, 548
Rush, Gdsm. G. H., 293–4, 532
Russel, CSM R., 544, 545
Russell, Lt. T. C. D., 75, 533
Russell, CSM (5th Bn.), 557
Ruwalla, Emir of the, 117
Ruweisat ridge, 109, 115
Ryder, Maj. L. C. D. (5th Bn.), 557

Sabkha, 119
St. Charles-le-Percy, 352
St. Denis-Maisoncelles, 352
St. Giles' Cathedral, 397, 471, 489
Sainthill, Lt.-Col. H. M. (Coldm. Gds.), 11, 106, 109
Ste. Honorine-le-Ducy, 342–3
St. Martin des Besaces, 344
Salamanca, battle honour awarded, 490
Salangen, 29, 31
Salerno, 168–74, 197, 198
Salisbury Plain, 328–30
Salvetti, Bruno (partisan), 284
Samson, Gdsm. (X Coy.), 375
Sanderson, Gdsm. H., 535
Sanderson, Lt.-Col. J. S., 62, 245, 472, 481, 485, 488, 490, 534, 537, 538, 543
Sandheien, 41
San Godenzo, 282
Sangro, river, 232
San Martino, 280
San Miniato, 265
San Nicola, 188
San Pietro Avellana, 232
San Potito, 230, 234
San Prisco, 175
San Rocco, 271
San Secondino, 177
San Severino Rota, 174
Santa Agata, 262
Santa Maria di Capaa, 175
Santerno, river, 283, 291
Sarteano, 242, 243
Saxon, S/Clerk N., 541
Scafati, 197
Scandinavia, 19–50
Scapa Flow, 28
Scauri, 191
Sceleidima, 90
Scharmbeck, 446
Scheessel, 453
Schermbeck, 424
Schleswig-Holstein, 438, 463–4
Schloss Calbeck, 406
Schwerin, Lt.-Gen. Graf von, 315
Scolo Parato, 303, 307
Scolo Val d'Albero, 306–8
S Company (*att. 2nd Bn. Coldm. Gds.*), formed, 230; Cassino, 233–4; M. Piccolo, 236–7; Farfa, 257–8; Perugia, 258; M. Lignano, 258–61; Arno, 261–2; Gothic Line, 281–3; M. Battaglia, 283–6; M. Penzola, 291–4; joins 1st Bn., 295, 297; Decorations, 532; Casualties, 526; Orders of Battle, 558
Scotland, The Regiment in, 3, 4; 5th Bn., 25; 1st Bn., 27, 56, 132; 2nd Bn., Stobs, 396–7, 471; whole Regiment, 488–90; 492
Scots Guards:
  Association, 12, 471, 488

620 INDEX

Scots Guards—*cont.*
  Battalions
    N.B.—For services 1939–1945 *see* List of Contents
    1st, Egypt (1935–1936), 10–11; becomes Training Bn., 470; revived, 490; Cyprus and Egypt (1951–1954), 493–5; Decorations, 530; Orders of Battle, 543–7
    2nd, China (1927–1929), 8–10; Palestine (1936), 11; Egypt (1938), 11; tour of Scotland (1947), 471; Malaya (1948–1951), 472–88; Germany (1953), 492; Decorations, 531; Order of Battle, 548–552
    3rd, Decorations, 532; Orders of Battle, 553–5
    4th, 333–7; Order of Battle, 556
    5th, 21–6; Order of Battle, 557
    See also under Band; Colours; Guards Depot; Holding Battalion; L Company; Regimental Headquarters; S Company; Statistics; Training Battalion; X Company
Scots/Welsh Group (Gds. Armd. Div.), 398–9, 430–7, 449–60
Scott, Brig. C. A. M. D., 204, 205, 226, 262, 285
Scott, J. M. (5th Bn.), 23
Scott, Capt. J. S., 556
Scott-Barrett, Maj. D. W., 357–8, 367, 402, 406, 532, 554, 555
Searchlights, 287, 301, 304, 442
Seel, Lt. K. E., 552
Seine, river, 367, 368, 379
Selangor, operations in, 447–80, 483–7
Senio, river, 285, 302
Sept Vents, 344
Sergison-Brooke, Maj.-Gen. Sir B., 8, 24 26, 27
Sesana, 320
Setta, river, 277, 287–90
Sevenum, 387, 389
Seymour, Maj. A. J. C., 405, 535, 539, 540, 553–5
Seymour, Maj. C. H. 6
Sfax, 128
Sham-Shui-Po, 8
Shanghai, 8, 9
Sharp, Lt., E. M., 234
Shaw-Stewart, Lt. P. H., 210, 544, 545
Shearer, Capt. J. C. J., 427–8, 555
Shearer, Sgt. T., 443, 448, 532
's Hertogenbosch, 383
Shingle (Anzio), 197
Ships:
  Acasta, H.M.S., 49
  Ardent, H.M.S., 31, 49
  Ark Royal, H.M.S., 33

Aurora, H.M.S., 27, 32, 33
Batory, 27, 29
Cape Town Castle, 229, 395
Chobry, 27, 28, 37
City of Marseilles, 8, 9
Delhi, H.M.S., 8
Delight, H.M.S., 48, 49
Derbyshire, 198–9
Dorsetshire, 11
Echo, H.M.S., 48
Effingham, H.M.S., 37, 44
Empire Doric, 493, 494
Empire Halladale, 487
Empire Trooper, 473
Empress of Russia, 9
Enterprise, H.M.S., 33–5
Fleetwood, H.M.S., 34
Franconia, 49
Georgic, 495
Glorious, H.M.S., 49
Gneisenau, 49
Hesperus, H.M.S., 34
Illustrious, H.M.S., 493
Laurentic, 11
Llangibby Castle, 161, 196, 338
Longford, 398
LST 413, H.M., 340
Margot, 34–5
Porlock Hill wrecked, 493
Protector, H.M.S., 31
Royal Scotsman, H.M.S., 133
Samaria, 132, 133
Scharnhorst, 49
Shropshire, 76
Somersetshire, 10
Southampton, H.M.S., 28–9
Valiant, H.M.S., 49, 174
Vandyck, 11
Vindictive, H.M.S., 49
Wallace, H.M.S., 63
Warspite, H.M.S., 27, 29, 174
Yuang Sang, 9
Zafaran, 10
Shöpping, 423
Shrubshall, Lt. G. D., 550
Sidi Azeiz, 78, 87
Sidi Barrani. 78–80, 83, 84, 89
Sidi Bishr, 10
Sidi Rezegh, 85–7
Sidi Suleiman, 80–3
Siebeneichen, 447
Siegfried Line, attack on, 400–2, 414–15
Siena, 256
Sinclair, Lt. A. J., 457, 464, 552
Sinclair, Capt. J. H. L., 135, 208, 217, 544, 545
Singapore, 473, 480–2, 487
Sittard, 391, 393, 394
Sittensen, 454
Sizzle (exercise in Kent), 333

INDEX 621

Slim, F.-M. Sir W., 485
Small, Gdsm. H., 357
Smith, Lt.-Gen. Sir A., 160
Smith, L/Sgt. A. S., 111
Smith, Maj. (QM) H., 57, 534, 540, 541
Smith, Lt. H. A. W., 152, 207, 256, 544–6
Smith, Capt. H. W. Llewellyn, xviii, 532, 554, 555
Smith, D/Sgt. J., 554
Smith, P/Maj. W., 410, 554
Smythe, L/Cpl. T. G., 237, 532
Snell, Lt. H. M., 256, 545
Sofafi, 78, 80
Sollum, 76, 79; barracks captured, 82; 84
Soloi, Lake, 47
Soltau, 449
Sorbello, 194
Sorrento, 227
Souk Ahras, 159
Souk el Arba, 158
Sources, xviii
Sourdevalle, 363–4
Sousse, 129, 152
South African Army:
  1st Div., 85, 107
  6th Armd. Div., 24th Gds. Bde. service with, 234–90; gift to Gds. Chapel, 290; 298, 315
  5th Bde., 86
  11th Armd. Bde., 241, 246, 268
  12th Motor Bde., 242, 243, 251, 268, 277–8; takes M. Sole, 309
  First City/Cape Town H., 254
  Imp. Light Horse/K.R., 256, 280
  Natal Mounted Rifles, 252, 255, 266, 289
  Pretoria Regt., supports 24th Guards Bde., 234–90 *passim; esp.* 244, 248, 249, 251, 253; farewell parade, 298 and n; 306
  R. Durban L.I., 235, 273
  R. Natal Carbineers, 242, 246, 281
  W. R./de la Rey Regt., 251
  6th Fld. Bty., 101–8
  6th A/Tk. Bty., 101–8
  1/11th A/Tk. Bty., 235, 243
Spalding, Capt. (QM) H., 540, 543
Spartan (exercise), 336
Sparvo, 272–3
Speedy, P/Maj. W., 548, 549
Spencer, Chapman, F. (5th Bn.), 23 and n
"Spit, The", 299–302
Spivey, S/Clerk C., 541
Spoleto, 290, 295, 297–8
Sport, 14, 15, 471
Spraggon, Gdsm. H. J., 185, 531
Spy, shooting of, 68
Stacey, CSM D. H. (5th Bn.), 557
Stade, 458–9
Stahe, 394

Stainton, Capt. J. D. A., 124, 156, 187, 550, 551, 556
Standing, RSM P., 221, 541, 545, 556
Standing Orders, 6
Stanmore, guard on H.Q. Fighter Command, 67
Starkey, Gdsm. C. H., 274, 530
State Express, see also Embankment, 202, 203, 224
Statistics: of casualties, 526; of decorations, 536; of strength, 56, 469, 497
Steele, Lt.-Col. W. L. (Coldm. Gds.), 308
Stephenson, L/Cpl. J., 106, 531
Steuart-Fothringham, Lt.-Col. P., 31, 179, 185, 188, 228, 338–40, 352, 364, 368, 372, 376–8, 396, 421, 454, 465, 532, 535, 539, 543, 551, 553, 558
Stevenson, Capt. A. R. G., 401, 402, 447, 532, 554, 555
Stevenson, Lt. D. J. C. (Welsh Gds.), 377
Stewart, Cpl. A., 357
Stewart, L/Sgt. R., 92
Stewart, Capt. R. O., 152, 204, 544, 545
Stewart-Wilson, Capt. B. A., 484, 540
Stien, *see* Dalsklubben
Stirling, Col. A. D., 22n, 75, 533, 534
Stirling, Lt. H. J., 78, 548
Stirling, Lt.-Col. J. A., 3
Stirling-Home-Drummond-Moray, Maj. A. C., 61
Stobs camp, 396–8, 420
Stockton, Capt. J. S., 145, 544
Stone, Capt. C. J. (5th Bn.), 557
Stoppiace, 260
Storfosshei, 42
Storjord, 45
Storvolden, 41
Strachey, Rt. Hon. John, 485
Strada della Pioppa, 302, 305
Strada in Chianti, 253–5, 287, 294
Stradensen, 445
Straeten, 394–5
Strandjorden, 41
Stratheden, Lt.-Col. Lord (Coldm. Gds.), 64
Strikes; General, 5; 470, 495
Struthers, Lt. W. H., 455
Stuart, Capt. R. L., 397, 550, 552
Stuart-Menteth, Lt. J. W., 226, 545
Stukas, dive-bombers, 89, 98, 135
Subaltern Officers; in Italy, 166; casualties in Germany, 458; shortage of, 7, 58
Superintending Clerks at R.H.Q., 541
Supplementary Reserve, 6
Suter, Lt. C. W. (5th Bn.), 557
Sutherland, L/Cpl. W. W., 106, 531
Swan Song (tanks leave), 464
Swinton, Lt.-Col. A. H. C., 10, 60, 63–65, 450, 538, 539

622 INDEX

Swinton, Maj. J., xvii, xx, 414, 419, 450, 540, 552, 589
Swolgen, 390
Syria, 115–19

Tadjera Khir, 121–5
Tait, Lt. I. McC., 189, 556
Taqa Plateau, attack on, 111–14
Taranto, 161, 196
Tate, Maj. (QM) J. S., 540
Taylor, Lt. F. R., 416, 552
Taylor, Lt.-Col. G. A. D., xx, 37, 38, 46, 119, 122, 123, 126, 127, 158, 167–79, 228–9, 235, 238–44, 245, 531, 538, 539, 543, 546, 550, 551, 553
Taylor, 2/Lt. J. H., 553
Taylor, CSM T., 273, 294, 531
Tebourba, 150
Tel-el-Kebir, 77
Tel Kalak, 118
Tempest, Lt. H. R., 434, 552
Temple, Archbishop, 333
Templer, Gen. Sir G., 190
Tennant, Capt. I. M., 106, 540, 548
Tercentenary (1942), 55 and n, 63, 96, 328, 334
Thavenot, Capt. A. H. M., 121, 539, 550, 551
Thomas, Capt. D. G., 464, 552
Thomson, Gdsm. J., 532
Thomson, Lt. (QM) R., 312, 530, 540, 541, 547
Thomson, Lt. T. C. H., 175
Thoresby Park, 332
Thorn, Sgt. E., 348, 554
Thorpe, Lt. I. L., 388, 554
Thorpe, Lt. N., 339, 353, 371–3, 532, 558
Threadingham, CSM J. W., 535
Tiber river, 239, 257
Tienraij, 387, 389
Tilburg, 380–4, 412–14
Tilbury, 338, 397–8, 404
Tillotson, S/Clerk R., 541, 550, 551
Tilshead Camp, 328
Timpson, Maj. J. A. L., 75, 129, 169, 171, 183, 184, 531, 550, 551, 553
"Tim's Hill" (Point 156), 139–41
Tinlin, Gdsm. R., 293–4, 531
Tirlemont, 391
Tito, Marshal J., 316–20
"Tobacco Factory" (Salerno), 169–73, *esp.* n on p. 170
Tobruk, 78; Battle of, 85–9; 97, loss of, 106
Todd, SSM J., 535, 554, 555
Todd, L/Sgt. R., 444
Todi, 258
Tolmie, RQMS D., 543, 552
Tomlinson, RSM H., 530, 541, 543, 545

Torrance, Capt. N. T., 419, 551, 552
Torritta, 246
Torsoli, 252
Tossignano, 291, 294
Tower of London, H.M., 65–8
Townsend, L/Sgt. J. W., 531
Traill, Maj. D., xviii, 160; account of Anzio, 198n–224; 211, 218, 535, 539, 544–6
"Training Bee" (4th Bn.), 335
Training Battalions:
  Guards, 490, 491
  No. 2 Guards, 65
  Scots Guards, 60–5, 230
  1st Bn. as, 470, 490
Tranter, Sgt. E., 355
Trappes-Lomax, Capt. M. R., xvii
Trappes-Lomax, Brig. T. B., 19, 31, 33. 37, 41–3, 45, 534, 538, 543
Trasimene Line, 235, 242, 258–9
"Triangle, The" (Anzio), 202
Trieste, 316–20
Trimonsuoli, 191–3
Tripoli, 121, 159, 167
Tromso, 30, 49
Truscott, Lt.-Gen. L. (U.S.A.), 296
Tudiano, 278–9
Tufo, 191–3
Tuke, Maj. A. F., 201, 211, 222, 223, 300, 310, 312, 315, 544–7
Tulloch, CSM J., 171, 173, 551
Tunis, 131, 153, 154; victory parade at, 156–7; 160
Tunnard, Capt. P. H., 184, 550
Tura Caves, 76
Turner, CSM A., 112, 531, 550
Turner, Lt. (QM) J., 19, 540, 541
Tusciano river, 169, 172
Tweedie, Maj. H. D., 436, 552
Tylden-Wright, Lt. D., 276, 546
Tyldesley Jones, Maj. J. E., 140, 160, 206, 207, 539, 544, 545
Tyringham, Lt.-Col. G. L., 538

U-boat "captured" (3rd Bn.), 448
Udem, 430
Uelzen, 438, 441–5
Uniform, *see* Dress
United States Army:
  Faulty intelligence from, 202
  Surplus stores, 264
  Armies
    5th, operations with, 167–227, 262–290
    9th, 395, 399
  Corps
    II, 122, 132, 264, 267, 276
    IV, 264
    VI, 168, 197–226 (Anzio)

INDEX

United States Army—*cont.*
  Divisions
    7th Armd., 384
    17th Airborne, 424
    30th Inf., 175
    34th Inf., 268
    85th Inf., 265
    88th Inf., 283, 320
    92nd (Negro), 289
  Regiments
    4th Marine, 9
    194th Para., 428
    504th Para., 214
    515th Para, 424–9
Usher, Maj. F. S. C., 545

Vado, 277
Valetta canal, 300–1
Valkenburg, 393, 395
Vallelata ridge, 213
Valmontone, 239
Vandeleur, Lt.-Col. J. O. E. (Irish Gds.), 337, 339, 340, 364
Varney, Capt. O. B., illustration 44
Varsity, see *Plunder*
Vastorf, 446
Veersen, 443–4
Veggio, 277, 280
Venlo Pocket, 386–90
Venna di Gesso, 291
Verdesca, 169
Veritable, see Rhineland, Battle of
Verney, Brig. G. L., 297, 329, 351
Vernon, 368
Vernon, Lt. Hon. J. L., 371, 417, 558
Vestey, Capt. Hon. W. H., 62, 244, 546
Vesuvius, 175; erupts, 228–9
Veulen, 291
Victoria Cross, 145–6, 528
Vietinghof, Gen. von, 296, 314
Villa Medici (Fiesole), 281
Viterbo, 241
Villore, 282
Vimont, 339
Vinci, 266
Vintelen, 394
Vire, 343, 347
Visciano, 186
Viskiskoia, 43–5
Visselhovede, 449–53
Vitulazio, 177
Volturno river, 175–7
Voorste Stroom, 382

Waal river, 378
Wade, Gdsm. J., 303, 530
Wade, Maj. F. D. (S. African), 235
Wadi Akarit, 128
Wadi Bou Remli, 127
Wadi Chaba, 154

Wadi Hachana, 127
Wake-Bowell, Capt. H. R., 106
Waldenrath, 394
Waldron, Capt. F. A. L., 123, 131, 156, 451, 550–2
Walker, Gdsm. G., 413
Walker, L/Sgt. J. S., 247n, 530
Wallace, Gdsm. C., 135
Wallace, Capt. E. H. L., 289, 308, 547
Wallace, Gdsm. K., 495
Walley, Gdsm. (3rd Bn.), 441
Walsrode, 449
Wandsbeck, 463
Wanstead, 334
Ward, L/Sgt. A., 93
Ward, Lt.-Col. F., 534, 535
Ward, CSM G., 545, 546
Ward, Capt. P. M., 361, 555
Wardt, 423
Warley, 4, 13
Warner, Lt. E. C. H., 358, 554
Warner, Col. Sir E. C. T., 9, 538
Warnock, Capt. J., 547
Warren Camp, see Llandwrog
Washington, RSM W., 40, 530, 541, 543
"Wasp", flame-thrower, see Arms
Waters, Maj. P. D. J., 61
Waterscheide, 395
Watkins, Gino (5th Bn.), 23
Watson, Gdsm. A., 103, 531
Watson, CSM H., 551
Watson-Armstrong, Maj. Hon. W. H. C. J. R., 445
Watts, Lt. (QM) S. R., 208, 226, 540, 544–7
Watts Russell, Capt. D. R. W. R. (Coldm. Gds.), 109
Wavell, F.-M. Earl, 77, 83
W Company, in Italy, 231
Wedderburn, Lt.-Col. D. S., 47n; at Anzio, 197–226 *passim*, 530, 538, 543, 545, 553, 556
"Wedge, The", (Comacchio), 299–302
Weeze, 409, 415
Wegershof, 419
Weiden, 465
Weir, Maj. A. J. A., 127, 128, 130, 206, 224, 226, 531, 540, 545, 550, 551
Welsh, Gdsm. A., 531
Welsh Guards:
  1st Bn., supported by 3rd (Tank) Bn., 359–63; see X Company; return home, 420
  2nd Bn., 323, 364; see X Company; see 2nd Bn. Scots Guards between 421–460 for Scots/Welsh (or "Celtic") Group
  3rd Bn., 228, 236, 237, 258, 261, 283, 285, 292, 294, 297
  Coy. att. to 2nd Bn. Scots Guards, 193

INDEX

Wesel, 406, 419
Weser, river, 437, 438, 449
Wessel, RSM R., 541, 551
Westertimke, 455-7
Westminster Garrison Bn., 69
West Norwood, 49, 53, 55
Weston Smith, Capt. I, 93, 171, 535, 551
Wetten, 412
Wettermans Hof, 408, 409
Weygand, General, 12
Whigham, Capt. R. C., 328, 332, 534, 540, 556
White, L/Sgt. G., 435
White, Sgt. (2nd Bn.), 453
Whiteford, Rev. D. H., 459, 475, 552
Whitehall, defences of, 66
Whitehead, Capt. C. P., 257, 545
Whitelaw, Maj. W. S. I., 345, 349, 351, 380, 448, 532, 553-5
Whiteley, Lt. F. G. L., 94
Whitfield, Maj.-Gen. J. Y., 297, 305
Whyte, RSM D. McN., 541
Whyte, Gdsm. H., 301
Widderson, Lt. L. E., 143, 226, 544, 545
Wigham, RQMS A., 549, 550
Wigram, Lt. E. H. L. (R.A.M.C.), 23, 557
Wilbur, S/Clerk W., 541
Wilford, RSM A., 334, 534, 541, 556, 557
Wilhelmina Canal, 381-3
Wilkinson, CSM T., 545-7
Willis, Maj. R. A., 106, 112, 129, 172, 549-52
Wilson, L/Sgt. A., 284
Wilson, Lt. J., 388
Wilson, Sgt. J., 533
Wilson, Lt. J. S., 238, 260, 547, 558
Wilson, L/Sgt. W., 435
Winch, Capt. H. H. E. M., 64-5
Windsor Lewis, Lt.-Col. J. C. (Welsh Gds.), 431, 434
Wingham, Gdsm. A., 92, 531

Winnekendonk, 409-12, 415
Winnipeg Grenadiers, alliance with, 14, 481n
Winter, Lt. E. F., 313
Winter, Capt. P. A., 451
Wipperfurth, 463, 466
Wolfs Berg, 403
Wood, Capt. & Dir. of Mus. F. W., 541
Wood, L/Cpl. W., 226
Woodford, QMS W., 534
Worsley-Taylor, Capt. Sir J. G., 437, 552, 556
Worthington-Wilmer, Capt. A. O., 307, 530, 547
Wright, Capt. P. A. (R.A.), 414
Wunstorf, 438
Wynne Finch, Col. W. H., 58-99, 254, 397-8, 538, 539
Wyler, 400-1

Xanten, 423
X Company, xix, 323, 337; with 3rd Irish Gds., 337-40, 351-3, 363-5; with 1st Welsh Gds., 364-5, 367-9, at Hechtel, 369-77, 377-80, 391-3, 398-9, 412-417; disbanded, 420-1; Decorations, 532; Casualties, 526; Orders of Battle, 558

Yates, Capt. E. R., 546-7
Y Company (5th Bn.), 23, 25
Yorkshire, 330, 337
York, H.R.H. Duke of, *see* George VI
Young, Lt. J. McI., 64
Young, CSM W., 260-1, 293-4, 532, 558
Ytteren, 36, 37

Zeven, 455, 459
Zon, 380
Zuara, 167
Zuetina, 94
Zuni, 186

www.ingramcontent.com/pod-product-compliance
Lightning Source LLC
Chambersburg PA
CBHW071148230426
43668CB00009B/872